MICHELIN®

Road Atlas of Europe

First published 1988 by
Paul Hamlyn,an imprint of Octopus Illustrated Publishing
Michelin House, 81 Fulham Road, London SW3 6RB
part of Reed International Books

Third edition 1992
First impression 1992

In spite of the care taken in the production of this book, it is possible that a defective copy may have escaped our attention. If this is so, please return it to your bookseller, who will exchange it for you, or contact Octopus Illustrated Publishing.

The representation in this atlas of a road is no evidence of the existence of a right of way.

A catalogue record for this book is available from the British Library.

ISBN Hardback 0 600 57318 4
ISBN Softback 0 600 57319 2

Printed in Great Britain

MICHELIN®

Road Atlas of Europe

MICHELIN®
Touring Services

Michelin

MICHELIN tyres and road maps have a reputation unsurpassed throughout Europe for quality and technical excellence in their respective fields.

It is appropriate that, at a time when the twelve member states of the European Economic Community are preparing for a single European market in 1993, Michelin should provide a new Road Atlas of Europe, compiled from their authoritative cartography, designed to meet the needs of the professional driver and holidaymaker alike.

There are over a hundred pages of mapping in this Atlas, showing the road network from North Cape to Gibraltar and from the Atlantic to the Black Sea. A full range of symbols show road categories and widths, towns and cities and places of interest as well as numerous other details, in keeping with Michelin's reputation for accuracy, legibility and up-to-date information.

Seventy town plans are included to help the driver negotiate built-up areas and the 'Driving in Europe' section provides details of national motoring regulations which are useful to know when crossing national frontiers. The comprehensive index locates about 30 000 towns and features.

The map showing 'Climates in Europe' will assist travellers in deciding which is the best season to visit a particular country.

The indispensable road mapping can be used in conjunction with other Michelin publications which provide complementary information on accommodation and sightseeing. The Red Guides, in particular the 'Europe' volume which contains a selection of hotels and restaurants in major European cities, and the Green Guides to the various countries of Europe are ideal companions for this Atlas.

Michelin are always happy to receive suggestions and comments from readers of their publications; taking these into account when preparing new editions can only improve their service to the public.

Thank you in advance and have a good journey!

MICHELIN maps and guides complement one another: use them together!

Contents

Inside front cover
Key to symbols

IV Michelin
VI **Route Planning**
X **Distances in Europe**
XII **Driving in Europe**

1 **Key to symbols**
2 **Western Europe** at a scale of 1: 1 000 000
78 **Greece** at a scale of 1: 700 000
94 **Scandinavia** at a scale of 1: 1 500 000
110 **Eastern Europe** at a scale of 1: 3 000 000

116 **Index of place names**

Inside back cover
Climates in Europe

Plans of cities and principal towns

118 ● Amsterdam
120 ● Antwerpen
86 ● Athina
122 ● Barcelona
123 ● Basel
124 ● Belfast
125 ● Berlin
126 ● Bern
127 ● Birmingham
126 ● Bologna
128 ● Bonn
129 ● Bordeaux
46 ● Bremen
130 ● Brugge
131 ● Bruxelles-Brussel
130 ● Budapest
136 ● Dijon
137 ● Dublin
137 ● Düsseldorf
138 ● Edinburgh
139 ● Essen
140 ● Firenze
141 ● Frankfurt a. M.
143 ● Genève
143 ● Genova
142 ● Gent
144 ● Glasgow
145 ● Göteborg
146 ● Den Haag
46 ● Hamburg
147 ● Hannover
107 ● Helsinki
149 ● Istanbul
152 ● København
153 ● Köln
155 ● Lausanne
156 ● Liège
157 ● Lille
158 ● Lisboa
159 ● Liverpool
160 ● London
163 ● Luxembourg
162 ● Lyon
164 ● Madrid
165 ● Manchester
33 ● Marseille
166 ● Milano
167 ● Monaco
168 ● München
170 ● Nantes
65 ● Napoli
171 ● Nice
172 ● Nürnberg
174 ● Oslo
69 ● Palermo
176 ● Paris
180 ● Porto
62 ● Roma
184 ● Rotterdam
188 ● Salzburg
190 ● Sevilla
192 ● Stockholm
193 ● Strasbourg
194 ● Stuttgart
196 ● Torino
197 ● Toulouse
199 ● Valencia
200 ● Venezia
203 ● Wien
205 ● Zürich

Route planning

MER DE BARENTS
BARENTS SEA
Nordkapp
Hammerfest
Kirkenes
Murmansk
Kanin Poluostrov
Tromsø
Vesterålen
Lofoten
Inarijärvi
Ivalo
LAPLAND
Kol'skij Poluostrov
ARCTIC CIRCLE
Mezen
Narvik
Kiruna
2111 Kebnekaise
Koùsomen'
MER BLANCHE
WHITE SEA
Bodø
Malmberget
Rovaniemi
Kuusamo
Kem'
Archangel'sk
Severnaja Dvina
Tornionjoki
Torneälven
Kemi
Mo i Rana
Dønna
Luleå
Oulu
Oulujärvi
S
BOTHNIA
BOTNIE
Pielinen
Umeå
SF
Joensuu
Kuopio
Petrozavodsk
Onežkoje Oz.
Trondheim
Vaasa
Östersund
OF
DE
Jyväskylä
Saimaa
Ładozskoje oz.
Sundsvall
GULF
GOLFE
Päijänne
Tampere
Vologda
Lahti
Pori
Čerepovec
Lillehammer
Mora
Turku
HELSINKI
FINLAND
FINLANDE
Leningrad
Rybinsk
Rybinskoje Vdchr.
Glomma
Gävle
Dalalven
GULF OF FINLAND
GOLFE DE FINLANDE
OSLO
Uppsala
Åland
Tallinn
Novgorod
Västerås
Moss
STOCKHOLM
Čudskoje Oz.
Volga
Örebro
Saaremaa
Kalinin
Vänern
Norrköping
BALTIC SEA
Pskov
Zagorsk
Linköping
Rižskij Zaliv
Vättern
Gotland
MOSKVA
SU
Göteborg
Jönköping
Rīga
Frederikshavn
Ålborg
Kattegat
Kalmar
Öland
Daugava
Vitebsk
Århus
Smolensk
KØBENHAVN
Klaipéda
Malmö
MER BALTIQUE
Kaunas
Mogil'ov
Odense
Fyn
Sjælland
Bornholm
Vilnius
Br'ansk
Or'ol
Kaliningrad
Minsk
Kiel
Lolland
Rügen
Gdańsk
Nemunas
Desna
Dnepr
Rostock
Lübeck
Gomel'
Hamburg
Szczecin
Toruń
Prip'at
Černigov
Elbe
Oder
Wisła
WARSZAWA
Brest
BERLIN
Poznań
Magdeburg
Odra
PL
Łódź
Lublin
Kijev
Poltava
D
Dresden
Erfurt
Leipzig
Wrocław
Częstochowa
Žitomir
Kremenčugskoje Vdchr.

A	Austria 1: 1 000 000	CS	Czechoslovakia 1: 3 000 000	GB	Great Britain 1: 1 000 000
AL	Albania 1: 700 000	D	Germany 1: 1 000 000	GR	Greece 1: 700 000
AND	Andorra 1: 1 000 000	DK	Denmark 1: 1 500 000	H	Hungary 1: 3 000 000
B	Belgium 1: 1 000 000	E	Spain 1: 1 000 000	I	Italy 1: 1 000 000
BG	Bulgaria 1: 3 000 000	F	France 1: 1 000 000	IRL	Ireland 1: 1 000 000
CH	Switzerland 1: 1 000 000	FL	Liechtenstein 1: 1 000 000	IS	Iceland 1: 2 400 000

Code	Country	Scale
L	Luxembourg	1: 1 000 000
M	Malta	1: 1 000 000
MC	Monaco	1: 1 000 000
N	Norway	1: 1 500 000
NL	Netherlands	1: 1 000 000
P	Portugal	1: 1 000 000
PL	Poland	1: 3 000 000
R	Rumania	1: 3 000 000
RSM	San Marino	1: 1 000 000
S	Sweden	1: 1 500 000
SF	Finland	1: 1 500 000
SU	Russia	1: 3 000 000
TR	Turkey	1: 3 000 000
V	Vatican City	1: 140 000
YU	Yugoslavia	1: 1 000 000

	Amsterdam	Athina	Barcelona	Bari	Basel	Belfast	Beograd	Bergen	Berlin	Bilbao	Birmingham	Bordeaux	Brest	Brussel/Bruxelles	Bucuresti	Budapest	Clermont-Ferrand	Dublin	Dubrovnik	Edinburgh	Firenze	Frankfurt A. M.	Genève	Göteborg	Hamburg	Hannover	Helsinki	Istambul	Kijev	København	Köln	Leningrad	Lille	Lisboa
Athina	2836																																	
Barcelona	1547	3090																																
Bari	1971	2621	1792																															
Basel	745	2466	1029	1226																														
Belfast	1341	3874	2046	2690	1508																													
Beograd	1718	1118	1972	1503	1348	2756																												
Bergen	1817	4017	3178	3244	2187	3112	2899																											
Berlin	669	2584	1853	1811	862	1906	1466	1463																										
Bilbao	1424	3422	607	2124	1174	1755	2304	3196	1990																									
Birmingham	782	3316	1487	2131	950	535	2198	2554	1348	1196																								
Bordeaux	1081	3240	633	1942	831	1412	2122	2853	1647	334	853																							
Brest	1098	3501	1242	2278	1096	1244	2383	2870	1664	965	686	627																						
Brussel/Bruxelles	204	2792	1365	1777	551	1150	1674	1969	781	1229	591	886	903																					
Bucuresti	2221	1238	2611	2142	1987	3259	639	3200	1711	2943	2701	2761	2886	2177																				
Budapest	1393	1510	1952	1482	1073	2431	392	2372	883	2283	1873	2041	2058	1349	828																			
Clermont-Ferrand	902	2752	648	1485	477	1337	1634	2636	1311	706	779	365	808	706	2273	1614																		
Dublin	1053	3586	1758	2402	1220	165	2468	2824	1618	1467	247	1124	956	862	2971	2143	1049																	
Dubrovnik	2024	1265	2049	1580	1425	2892	525	3204	1771	2381	2333	2199	2480	1970	1164	787	1711	2604																
Edinburgh	1289	3823	1994	2638	1457	251	2705	3061	1855	1703	484	1360	1193	1098	3208	2380	1286	416	2840															
Firenze	1391	2115	1075	720	646	2098	997	2664	1231	1407	1539	1225	1686	1197	1636	976	883	1810	1074	2046														
Frankfurt A. M.	446	2396	1318	1553	327	1549	1278	1864	566	1502	991	1159	1176	402	1781	953	776	1261	1583	1498	973													
Genève	885	2446	770	1203	259	1492	1328	2446	1121	1102	934	682	1081	703	1967	1307	310	1204	1405	1441	611	586												
Göteborg	1005	3205	2366	2432	1375	2300	2087	812	651	2384	1742	2041	2058	1157	2388	1560	1824	2012	2392	2249	1852	1052	1634											
Hamburg	441	2780	1802	2007	811	1736	1662	1384	289	1820	1178	1477	1494	593	2026	1198	1260	1448	1967	1685	1427	488	1070	572										
Hannover	386	2637	1659	1864	668	1623	1519	1527	288	1707	1065	1364	1381	498	2022	1194	1117	1335	1824	1572	1284	345	927	715	151									
Helsinki	1204	2540	2388	2346	1397	2441	1422	1186	505	2525	1883	2182	2199	1316	1858	1030	1846	2153	1893	2390	1766	1101	1656	662	776	823								
Istambul	2665	1171	2919	2450	2295	3703	947	3846	2413	3251	3145	3069	3330	2621	692	1339	2581	3415	1326	3652	1944	2225	2275	3034	2609	2466	2369							
Kijev	2017	2311	3114	2644	2187	3254	1336	2844	1383	3338	2696	2995	3012	2129	1073	1162	2636	2966	1861	3203	2138	1914	2339	2032	1670	1636	1146	489						
København	738	2938	2099	2165	1108	2033	1820	1079	384	2117	1475	1774	1791	890	2121	1293	1557	1745	2125	1982	1585	785	1367	267	305	448	795	2767	1765					
Köln	264	2579	1342	1714	488	1361	1461	1802	575	1440	803	1097	1114	211	1964	1136	802	1073	1766	1310	1134	189	747	990	426	292	1110	2408	1923	723				
Leningrad	1637	2973	2821	2779	1830	2874	1855	1619	938	2958	2316	2615	2632	1749	2625	1463	2279	2586	2326	2823	2199	1534	2089	1095	1209	1256	433	2041	1552	1228	1543			
Lille	283	2910	1308	1836	610	1046	1792	2055	849	1139	487	799	716	116	2295	1467	645	758	2088	994	1256	520	669	1243	679	566	1384	2739	2197	976	329	1817		
Lisboa	2322	4320	1285	3022	2072	2653	3202	4094	2888	907	2094	1232	1863	2127	3841	3181	1604	2365	3279	2601	2305	2400	2000	3282	2718	2605	3423	4149	4236	3015	2338	3856	2037	
Liverpool	971	3504	1676	2320	1138	416	2386	2742	1536	1385	165	1042	874	780	2889	2061	967	167	2522	365	1728	1179	1122	1930	1366	1253	2071	3333	2884	1663	991	2504	676	2283
London	719	3252	1424	2068	886	722	2134	2490	1284	1133	196	790	622	528	2637	1809	715	434	2270	612	1476	927	870	1678	1114	1001	1819	3081	2632	1411	739	2252	424	2031
Luxembourg	391	2637	1148	1560	334	1338	1519	1994	767	1290	779	947	964	218	1993	1165	608	1050	1758	1286	980	248	486	1182	618	484	1302	2466	2115	915	193	1735	334	2188
Lyon	917	2559	630	1292	400	1415	1441	2548	1223	962	857	538	1018	735	2080	1421	172	1127	1518	1364	690	688	151	1736	1172	1029	1758	2388	2548	1469	711	2191	682	1860
Madrid	1812	3760	686	2462	1562	2143	2642	3584	2378	397	1584	722	1353	1617	3281	2622	1094	1855	2719	2091	1745	1890	1440	2772	2208	2095	2913	3589	3726	2505	1828	3346	1527	658
Málaga	2360	4086	1012	2788	2025	2691	2968	4132	2849	945	2132	1270	1901	2165	3607	2948	1644	2403	3045	2639	2071	2314	1766	3320	2756	2643	3384	3915	4110	3053	2376	3817	2075	634
Marseille	1228	2621	493	1323	710	1727	1503	2859	1534	825	1168	648	1218	1046	2142	1483	417	1439	1580	1675	606	999	452	2047	1483	1340	2069	2450	2645	1780	1023	2502	992	1723
Milano	1088	2128	973	878	343	1810	1010	2493	1040	1305	1251	1123	1398	894	1649	989	629	1522	1087	1758	298	670	323	1681	1117	974	1575	1957	2151	1414	831	2008	953	2203
Moskva	2463	3169	3630	3306	2639	3700	2194	2313	1829	3784	3142	3441	3458	2575	1931	1918	3088	3412	2705	3649	2800	2360	2898	1789	2116	2082	1127	1347	858	2211	2369	694	2643	4682
München	837	2063	1370	1224	399	1794	945	2018	585	1615	1236	1272	1421	769	1506	678	918	1506	1184	1743	644	397	599	1206	781	638	1120	1892	1744	939	580	1553	887	2513
Nantes	887	3290	945	1923	847	1168	2172	2659	1453	669	609	325	302	692	2675	1847	465	880	2125	1116	1331	965	726	1847	1283	1170	1988	3119	2801	1580	903	2421	604	1567
Napoli	1878	2602	1562	261	1133	2585	1484	3151	1718	1894	2026	1712	2173	1684	2123	1463	1370	2297	1561	2533	490	1460	1098	2339	1914	1771	2253	2431	2625	2072	1621	2686	1743	2792
Nice	1387	2434	656	1136	658	1886	1316	2808	1355	988	1327	808	1377	1205	1955	1295	577	1598	1393	1834	419	985	478	1996	1432	1289	1890	2263	2457	1729	1146	2323	1152	1886
Nürnberg	666	2171	1427	1391	436	1715	1053	1867	434	1668	1157	1325	1342	622	1556	728	885	1427	1351	1664	811	226	695	1055	610	467	969	2000	1759	788	409	1402	740	2566
Oslo	1321	3521	2682	2748	1691	2616	2403	496	967	2700	2058	2357	2374	1473	2704	1876	2140	2328	2708	2565	2168	1368	1950	316	888	1031	690	3350	2348	583	1306	1123	1559	3598
Palermo	2599	3322	2283	691	1853	3305	2204	3872	2439	2614	2747	2432	2893	2404	2843	2184	2091	3017	2281	3254	1210	2180	1818	3060	2635	2492	2974	3151	3346	2793	2341	3407	2464	3512
Paris	504	2912	1091	1735	553	965	1794	2275	1069	922	407	579	597	308	2297	1469	426	677	1937	914	1143	587	538	1463	899	786	1604	2741	2417	1196	520	2037	221	1820
Porto	2143	4141	1167	2843	1893	2474	3023	3915	2709	728	1915	1053	1684	1948	3662	3002	1425	2186	3100	2422	2126	2221	1821	3103	2539	2426	3244	3970	4057	2836	2159	3677	1858	314
Praha	950	2154	1711	1596	720	1999	1036	1839	350	1952	1441	1609	1626	906	1361	533	1169	1711	1261	1948	1016	510	979	1027	665	603	859	1983	1389	760	693	1292	1024	2850
Roma	1665	2389	1349	449	920	2372	1271	2938	1505	1681	1813	1499	1960	1471	1910	1250	1157	2084	1348	2320	277	1247	885	2126	1701	1558	2040	2218	2412	1859	1408	2473	1530	2579
Rovaniemi	2483	4683	3844	3910	2853	3778	3565	2824	2129	3862	3220	3519	3536	2635	3866	3038	3302	3490	3870	3727	3330	2530	3112	1528	2050	2193	837	4512	2557	1745	3288	1005	2721	4760
Salzburg	980	1932	1539	1172	536	1952	814	2161	728	1772	1393	1429	1578	927	1363	535	1076	1664	1052	1900	660	540	736	1349	924	781	1263	1761	1601	1082	723	1696	1045	2670
Sevilla	2295	4117	1043	2819	2056	2626	2999	4067	2880	880	2067	1205	1836	2100	3638	2979	1577	2338	3076	2574	2102	2345	1797	3255	2691	2578	3415	3946	4141	2988	2311	3848	2010	417
Sofia	2104	818	2358	1889	1734	3142	386	3285	1852	2690	2584	2508	2769	2060	420	778	2020	2854	765	3091	1383	1664	1714	2473	2048	1905	1808	561	1493	2206	1847	2241	2178	3588
Stockholm	1368	3568	2729	2795	1738	2663	2450	1021	1014	2747	2105	2404	2421	1520	2751	1923	2187	2375	2755	2612	2215	1415	1997	497	935	1078	165	3397	2395	630	1353	598	1606	3645
Strasbourg	634	2438	1110	1371	145	1450	1320	2076	751	1264	892	918	1080	439	1881	1053	563	1162	1559	1399	791	216	404	1264	700	557	1286	2267	2076	997	377	1719	549	2162
Stuttgart	622	2302	1258	1404	267	1592	1184	2046	631	1413	1034	1070	1219	558	1745	917	716	1304	1423	1541	824	204	526	1234	670	527	1166	2131	1956	967	365	1599	676	2311
Thessaloníki	2350	511	2604	2135	1980	3388	632	3531	2098	2936	2830	2754	3015	2306	727	1024	2266	3100	779	3337	1629	1910	1960	2719	2294	2151	2054	660	1800	2452	2093	2487	2424	3834
Torino	1154	2263	779	997	409	1699	1145	2596	1157	1110	1140	864	1287	905	1784	1124	492	1411	1222	1647	395	736	252	1784	1220	1077	1692	2092	2286	1517	897	2125	961	2008
Toulouse	1199	2994	388	1696	933	1611	1876	3082	1757	447	1053	244	870	1003	2515	1856	384	1323	1953	1560	979	1222	675	2270	1706	1563	2292	2823	3018	2003	1246	2725	923	1345
Tromsø	3041	5241	4402	4468	3411	4336	4123	1893	2687	4420	3778	4077	4094	3193	4424	3596	3860	4048	4428	4285	3888	3088	3670	2570	2608	2751	1367	5070	3087	2303	3026	1535	3279	5318
Trondheim	1865	4065	3226	3292	2235	3160	2947	717	1511	3244	2602	2901	2918	2017	3248	2420	2684	2872	3252	3109	2712	1912	2494	1394	1432	1575	949	3894	2892	1127	1850	1382	2103	4142
Valencia	1892	3435	361	2137	1374	2391	2317	3523	2198	606	1832	771	1402	1710	2956	2297	993	2103	2394	2339	1420	1663	1115	2711	2147	2004	2733	3264	3459	2444	1687	3166	1653	924
Venezia	1283	1878	1229	760	605	2072	760	2512	1079	1561	1513	1379	1660	1156	1399	739	891	1784	837	2020	254	891	585	1700	1275	1132	1614	1707	1901	1433	1026	2047	1215	2459
Warszawa	1223	2188	2390	2066	1399	2460	1070	2050	589	2544	1902	2201	2218	1335	1506	678	1848	2172	1465	2409	1560	1120	1658	1238	876	842	352	2017	794	971	1129	785	1403	3442
Wien	1150	1862	1833	1341	830	2188	744	2131	642	2141	1630	1798	1815	1106	1071	243	1370	1900	969	2137	835	710	1030	1319	957	951	924	1691	1309	1052	893	1357	1224	3039
Zagreb	1337	1499	1591	1122	967	2375	381	2518	1085	1923	1817	1741	2002	1293	1020	350	1253	2087	618	2324	616	897	947	1706	1281	1138	1287	1328	1512	1439	1080	1720	1411	2821
Zürich	831	2416	1058	1176	86	1594	1298	2267	852	1260	1036	917	1182	637	1816	988	597	1306	1375	1543	596	412	287	1455	891	748	1387	2245	2054	1188	573	1820	696	2158

Distances in Europe

Distances are calculated from centres and along the best roads from a motoring point of view - not necessarily the shortest

Example: **Luxembourg – Warszawa** 1321 km

	Liverpool	London	Luxembourg	Lyon	Madrid	Málaga	Marseille	Milano	Moskva	München	Nantes	Napoli	Nice	Nürnberg	Oslo	Palermo	Paris	Porto	Praha	Roma	Rovaniemi	Salzburg	Sevilla	Sofia	Stockholm	Strasbourg	Stuttgart	Thessaloníki	Torino	Toulouse	Tromsø	Trondheim	Valencia	Venezia	Warszawa	Wien	Zagreb
London	352																																				
Luxembourg	968	716																																			
Lyon	1045	793	518																																		
Madrid	1773	1521	1678	1300																																	
Málaga	2321	2069	2144	1626	548																																
Marseille	1357	1105	829	313	1163	1489																															
Milano	1440	1188	677	436	1643	1969	504																														
Moskva	3330	3078	2561	3000	4172	4626	3311	2817																													
München	1424	1172	557	741	2040	2366	1053	560	2362																												
Nantes	798	546	753	653	1057	1605	973	1043	3247	1210																											
Napoli	2215	1963	1467	1177	2232	2558	1093	785	3287	1131	1818																										
Nice	1516	1264	988	472	1326	1652	187	317	3132	866	1132	906																									
Nürnberg	1345	1093	449	797	2056	2423	1108	614	2211	165	1131	1298	929																								
Oslo	2246	1994	1498	2052	3088	3636	2363	1997	1817	1522	2163	2655	2312	753																							
Palermo	2935	2683	2187	1898	2953	3279	1814	1505	4008	1851	2539	733	1626	2019	3376																						
Paris	595	343	376	462	1310	1858	773	855	2863	832	385	1630	932	753	1779	2350																					
Porto	2104	1852	2009	1681	590	870	1544	2024	4503	2334	1388	2613	1707	2387	3419	3333	1641																				
Praha	1629	1377	733	1081	2340	2707	1392	932	1860	369	1415	1503	1238	296	1343	2223	1037	2671																			
Roma	2002	1750	1254	964	2019	2345	880	572	3074	918	1605	219	693	1085	2442	939	1417	2400	1290																		
Rovaniemi	3408	3156	2660	3214	4250	4798	3525	3159	1699	2684	3325	3817	3474	2533	1560	4538	2941	4581	2505	3604																	
Salzburg	1582	1330	714	877	2209	2535	1070	576	2257	140	1367	1147	882	308	1665	1868	990	2491	353	934	2827																
Sevilla	2256	2004	2175	1657	550	217	1520	2000	4657	2397	1540	2589	1683	2454	3571	3310	1793	653	2738	2376	4733	2566															
Sofia	2772	2520	1905	1827	3028	3354	1889	1396	2351	1331	2558	1870	1702	1439	2789	2590	2180	3409	1422	1657	3951	1200	3385														
Stockholm	2293	2041	1545	2099	3135	3683	2410	2044	1292	1569	2210	2702	2359	1418	525	3423	1826	3466	1390	2489	1170	1712	3618	2836													
Strasbourg	1080	828	222	478	1652	2106	789	488	2528	358	867	1278	948	325	1580	1998	490	1983	609	1065	2742	515	2137	1706	1627												
Stuttgart	1222	970	346	628	1801	2254	939	523	2408	222	1008	1311	838	205	1550	2031	630	2132	489	1098	2712	379	2285	1570	1597	156											
Thessaloníki	3018	2766	2151	2073	3274	3600	2135	1642	2658	1577	2804	2116	1948	1685	3035	2836	2426	3655	1668	1903	4197	1446	3631	307	3082	1952	1816										
Torino	1329	1077	688	299	1449	1775	407	140	2934	620	903	882	220	731	2100	1602	744	1829	980	669	3262	711	1806	1531	2147	554	640	1777									
Toulouse	1241	989	1052	537	835	1384	402	877	3534	1274	568	1466	563	1331	2586	2187	703	1166	1615	1253	3748	1443	1318	2262	2633	1013	1162	2508	683								
Tromsø	3966	3714	3218	3772	4808	5356	4083	3717	2229	3242	3883	4375	4032	3091	1720	5096	3499	5139	3063	4162	597	3385	5291	4509	1719	3300	3270	4755	3820	4306							
Trondheim	2790	2538	2042	2596	3632	4180	2907	2541	2076	2066	2707	3199	2856	1915	544	3920	2323	3963	1887	2986	1119	2209	4115	3333	784	2124	2094	3579	2644	3130	1176						
Valencia	2021	1769	1493	975	351	651	838	1318	3975	1715	1106	1907	1001	1772	3027	2628	1436	941	2056	1694	4189	1884	682	2703	3074	1455	1603	2949	1124	733	4747	3571					
Venezia	1702	1450	939	698	1899	2225	760	267	2563	492	1305	741	573	659	2016	1461	1117	2280	783	528	3178	429	2256	1146	2063	750	672	1392	402	1133	3736	2560	1574				
Warszawa	2090	1838	1321	1760	2932	3386	2071	1577	1240	1122	2007	2047	1892	971	1554	2768	1623	3263	620	1834	1189	1017	3417	1456	1601	1288	1168	1702	1694	2294	3274	2098	2735	1323			
Wien	1818	1566	922	1172	2503	2829	1364	871	1965	435	1604	1322	1177	485	1635	2043	1226	2860	292	1109	2797	292	2860	1130	1682	810	674	1376	1006	1737	3355	2179	2178	598	725		
Zagreb	2005	1753	1138	1062	2261	2587	1122	629	2268	564	1791	1103	935	672	2022	1823	1413	2642	655	890	3184	433	2618	767	2069	939	803	1013	764	1495	3742	2566	1936	379	1028	363	
Zürich	1224	972	420	429	1728	2054	739	293	2629	314	933	1083	608	426	1771	1804	639	1979	675	870	2933	451	2085	1684	1818	231	229	1930	410	962	3491	2315	1403	555	1389	745	917

Driving in Europe

Introduction

The information panels which follow give the principal motoring regulations for all the countries included in this atlas; an explanation of the symbols is given below, together with some additional notes.

- The name, address and telephone number of the national motoring organisation or organisations; the initials FIA and AIT indicate membership of the international touring associations, the Fédération Internationale de l'Automobile and the Alliance Internationale de Tourisme
- Speed restrictions in kilometres per hour applying to:
  - motorways
  - dual carriageways
  - single carriageways
  - urban areas

  Where restrictions for 'trailers' or 'towing' are given, it may be assumed that these apply to both trailers and caravans
- The maximum permitted level of alcohol in the bloodstream. This should not be taken as an acceptable level; it is NEVER sensible to drink and drive
- Whether the wearing of seat belts is compulsory
- Restrictions applying to children
- Whether a warning triangle must be carried
- Whether a first aid kit must be carried
- Whether a spare bulb kit must be carried
- Whether crash helmets are compulsory for motorcyclists
- Whether tolls are payable on motorways and/or other parts of the road network
- Whether petrol concessions or restrictions apply
- The minimum age for drivers
- Documentation required; note that while insurance for driving at home usually provides the legally required minimum third party cover abroad, it will not provide cover against damage, fire, theft or personal accident; for this reason, an International Motoring Certificate (Green Card) is recommended for all countries and essential where 'Green Card required' is given
- ★ In this section are given any other regulations not falling into the categories above

Andorra

Automobil Club d'Andorra, FIA, Babot Camp 13, Andorra-la-Vella Tel: 20-8-90

Motorways	Dual carriageways	Single carriageways	Urban areas
	70	70	40 km/h

- 0.08%
- Children under 10 years of age not allowed in front seats
- Recommended (compulsory if vehicle exceeds 3000 kg)
- Recommended
- Compulsory
- Compulsory for motorcyclists and passengers
- 18
- Valid driving licence; Vehicle registration document or Vehicle on hire certificate; Green Card recommended; National vehicle identification plate

Austria

Österreicher Automobil-, Motorrad- und Touring Club (ÖAMTC), FIA & AIT, Schubertring 1-3, 1010 Wien 1 Tel: (01) 711997

Motorways	Dual carriageways	Single carriageways	Urban areas
100-130		100	50 km/h
If towing trailer over 14.5 cwt:			
100		80	50 km/h
If towing trailer under 14.5 cwt:			
100	100	100	50 km/h

- 0.08%
- Compulsory if fitted for driver and front and rear seat passengers
- Children under 12 years of age not allowed in front seats
- Compulsory
- Compulsory
- Compulsory for motorcyclists and passengers
- Tolls payable on motorways for Brenner (A13), Tauern (part of the A10), and a section of the A9 north of Graz, as well as on certain roads (especially trans-alpine routes) and tunnels
- 18
- Valid driving licence; Vehicle registration document or Vehicle on hire certificate; Green Card recommended; National vehicle identification plate
- ★ Towing is forbidden on certain alpine routes

Belgium

Royal Automobile Club de Belgique (RACB), FIA, 53 rue d'Arlon, 1040 Bruxelles Tel: (02) 2300810

Touring Club Royal de Belgique (TCB), AIT, 44 rue de la Loi, 1040 Bruxelles Tel: (02) 2332211

Vlaamse Automobilistenbond (VTB-VAB), Sint-Jacobs Markt 45, 2000 Antwerpen Tel: (03) 2203211

Motorways	Dual carriageways	Single carriageways	Urban areas
120	90	90	50 km/h

- 0.05%
- Compulsory if fitted for driver and front and rear seat passengers
- Children under 12 years of age not allowed in front seats
- Compulsory
- Recommended
- Compulsory for motorcyclists
- 18
- Valid driving licence; Vehicle registration document or Vehicle on hire certificate; Green Card recommended; National vehicle identification plate

Bulgaria

Union of Bulgarian Motorists (SBA), FIA & AIT, 3 Place Pozitano, Sofia 1090 B.P.257 Tel: (02) 86151

Motorways	Dual carriageways	Single carriageways	Urban areas
100	80	80	60 km/h

- 0.0%
- Compulsory if fitted for driver and front seat passengers
- Children under 10 years of age not allowed in front seats
- Compulsory
- Compulsory
- Compulsory
- Compulsory for motorcyclists
- Foreign motorists must buy fuel with coupons available in unlimited quantities at border posts and within Bulgaria
- 18
- Valid driving licence or International Driving Permit; Vehicle registration document or Vehicle on hire certificate; Green Card required; National vehicle identification plate

Czechoslovakia

Ustředni Automotoklub CSSR, FIA & AIT, Na Strži 4, 14000 Praha 4 Tel: (02) 43 20 41

110 90 90 60 km/h

0.0% any alcohol found in the bloodstream may result in prosecution

Compulsory if fitted for driver and front seat passengers

Children under 12 years of age not allowed in front seats

Compulsory

Compulsory

Crash helmets and goggles compulsory for drivers of motorcycles over 50cc; crash helmets only for passengers

Petrol coupons can be purchased at frontier posts, Tuzex shops and banks; also from Czech Tourist Bureau Cedok (London) Ltd

18

Valid driving licence; Vehicle registration document or Vehicle on hire certificate; Green Card, valid for Czechoslovakia, required; National vehicle identification plate

Finland

Autoliitto (Automobile and Touring Club of Finland) (ATCF), FIA & AIT, Kansakoulukatu 10, 00101 Helsinki 10 Tel: (90) 6940022

120 80-100 50 km/h

Towing if trailer has brakes:

80 80 50 km/h

Towing if trailer unbraked:

60 60 50 km/h

0.05%

Compulsory if fitted for driver and front and rear seat passengers

Compulsory

Recommended

Recommended

Compulsory for motorcyclists and passengers

18

Valid driving licence; Vehicle registration document or Vehicle on hire certificate; Green Card recommended; National vehicle identification plate

★ Compulsory use of headlights at all times outside built-up areas

Germany

ADAC - Allgemeiner Deutscher Automobil-Club, FIA & AIT, Am Westpark 8, 8000 München 70 Tel: (089) 76760

Automobil-Club von Deutschland (AvD), FIA, Lyonerstraße 16, 6000 Frankfurt am Main 71 Tel: (069) 66060

130* 130* 100 50 km/h

If towing:

80 80 80 50 km/h

*recommended

0.08%

Compulsory if fitted for driver and front and rear seat passengers

Children under 12 years of age not allowed in front seats

Compulsory

Compulsory

Compulsory for motorcyclists and passengers

18

Valid driving licence; Vehicle registration document or Vehicle on hire certificate; Green Card recommended; National vehicle identification plate

Denmark

Forenede Danske Motorejere (FDM), AIT, Firskovvej 32, 2800 Lyngby Tel: (45) 93 08 00

100 80 80 50 km/h

If towing:

70 70 70 50 km/h

0.08%

Compulsory in front and in back

Children under 3 need not use seat belt. Between 3 and 7 they may use a child's safety seat or booster cushion and seat belt

Compulsory

Recommended

Compulsory for motorcyclists and passengers

18

Valid driving licence; Vehicle registration document or Vehicle on hire certificate; Green Card recommended; National vehicle identification plate

★ Fire extinguisher recommended

France

Automobile Club de France, FIA, 6-8 Place de la Concorde, 75008 Paris Tel: (01) 42 65 08 26

Association Française des Automobiles-Clubs (AFA), FIA & AIT, 9 rue Anatole de la Forge, 75017 Paris Tel: (01) 42 27 82 00

110-130 110 90 50 km/h

If wet:

100-110 100 80 50 km/h

0.08% or 0.40 mg per litre of air exhaled

Compulsory if fitted for driver and front and rear seat passengers

Children under 10 years of age not allowed in front seats

Compulsory unless hazard warning lights are fitted; triangle and lights compulsory for cars pulling caravans or trailers and for vehicles greater than 3.5 tons

Recommended

Recommended

Compulsory for motorcyclists and passengers

Tolls payable on most motorways although short urban sections of motorway around Paris and some other major cities are free; tolls also payable on some major bridges and in some tunnels

18

Valid driving licence; Vehicle registration document or Vehicle on hire certificate; Green Card recommended; National vehicle identification plate

Great Britain

Automobile Association (AA), FIA & AIT, Fanum House, Basingstoke, Hampshire RG21 2EA Tel: (0256) 20123

Royal Automobile Club (RAC), FIA & AIT, Lansdowne Road, Croydon CR9 2JA Tel: (081) 686 2525

112 112 96 48 km/h

If towing:

96 96 80 48 km/h

0.08%

Compulsory if fitted for driver and front and rear seat passengers

Children under 1 year of age travelling in front seat must be strapped in or placed in a child's safety seat

Recommended

Compulsory for motorcyclists and passengers

Tolls payable on certain major bridges and tunnels

17

Valid driving licence; Vehicle registration document or Vehicle on hire certificate; Green Card recommended; National vehicle identification plate

★ Drive on the left!

Greece

The Automobile and Touring Club of Greece (ELPA), FIA & AIT, 2-4 Messogion, 115 27 Athína Tel: (01) 779 1615

Hellenic Touring Club, AIT, 12 Politehniou, 104 33 Athína Tel: (01) 524 0854

100	80	80	50 km/h

0.05%

Compulsory if fitted for driver and front seat passengers

Children under 10 years of age not allowed in front seats

Compulsory

Compulsory

Compulsory for motorcyclists and passengers

Tolls payable on most 'national' roads

18

Valid driving licence; Vehicle registration document or Vehicle on hire certificate; Green Card required; National vehicle identification plate

★ Fire extinguisher compulsory

Iceland

Felag Islenskra Bifreidaeigenda (FIB), FIA & AIT, Borgatun 33, 105 Reykjavik Tel: (01) 62 99 99

	70	70	50 km/h

0.05%

Compulsory for driver and front seat passengers; rear seat belts recommended

Children in rear seats must be strapped in or placed in a child's safety seat

Recommended

Recommended

Recommended

Compulsory for motorcyclists and passengers

17

Driver's passport; Valid driving licence; Vehicle registration document or Vehicle on hire certificate; Green Card, valid for Iceland, required; Temporary importation permit; National vehicle identification plate

★ Vehicle mud flaps compulsory; headlights compulsory at all times; vehicles with diesel engines are subject to a special charge on entry to Iceland

Italy

Automobile Club d'Italia (ACI), FIA & AIT, Via Marsala 8, 00185 Roma Tel: (06) 49981

Touring Club Italiano (TCI), AIT, Corso Italia 10, 20122 Milano Tel: (02) 85261

110*-130	110*-130	90	50 km/h
If towing:			
110*-130	110*-130	90	50 km/h

* for vehicles up to 1100 cc

Severe penalties for drinking and driving

Compulsory in front (and in back if installed)

Children under 12 not allowed in front unless seat is fitted with child restraint system

Compulsory

Recommended

Compulsory

Compulsory for motorcyclists and passengers

Tolls payable on most motorways

Coupons at a discount available at RAC, AA, and Port Offices and frontier Automobile Clubs to personal callers; must be paid for in foreign currency

18

Valid driving licence (translation in Italian recommended); Vehicle registration document or Vehicle on hire certificate; Green Card recommended; Temporary importation document; National vehicle identification plate

Hungary

Magyar Autóklub (MAK), FIA & AIT, Rómer Flóris utca 4a, Budapest 11 Tel: (01) 152 040

120	100	100	50-60 km/h
If towing:			
80	70	70	50 km/h

0.0% if the alcohol test changes colour, the driver is taken to a hospital for a blood test and his driving licence confiscated

Compulsory if fitted for driver and front seat passengers

Children under 6 years of age not allowed in front seats

Compulsory

Recommended

Compulsory

Compulsory for motorcyclists and passengers

Petrol can only be purchased with coupons obtainable at the border, at IBUSZ offices or in hotels; unused coupons not refundable

18

Valid driving licence; Vehicle registration document or Vehicle on hire certificate; Green Card strongly recommended; National vehicle identification plate

Ireland

Automobile Association (AA), FIA & AIT, 23 Suffolk Street, Dublin 2 Tel: (01) 779481

Royal Automobile Club (RAC), FIA & AIT, 34 Dawson Street, Dublin 2 Tel: (01) 775141

88	88	64-88	48 km/h
If towing:			
56	56	56	48 km/h

0.10%

Compulsory if fitted for driver and front seat passengers

Children under 12 years of age not allowed in front seats unless strapped in or placed in a child's safety seat

Recommended

Recommended

Recommended

Compulsory for motorcyclists and passengers

Toll payable on two bridges over River Liffey in Dublin

17

Valid driving licence; Vehicle registration document or Vehicle on hire certificate; Green Card recommended; National vehicle identification plate

★ Drive on the left!

Luxembourg

Automobile Club du Grand Duché de Luxembourg (ACL), FIA & AIT, 54 route de Longwy, 8007 Bertrange Tel: (012) 45 00 45

120	90	90	60 km/h
If towing:			
90	75	75	60km/h

0.08%

Compulsory if fitted for driver and front and rear seat passengers

Children under 10 years of age allowed in front seats if vehicle is equipped with child's safety seat

Compulsory

Recommended

Compulsory

The purchasing, selling and transporting of petrol in drums or jerrycans is prohibited

18

Valid driving licence; Vehicle registration document or Vehicle on hire certificate; Green Card recommended; National vehicle identification plate

Netherlands

Koninklijke Nederlandsche Automobiel Club (KNAC), FIA, Westvlietweg 118, Leidschendam
Tel: (070) 399 74 51

Koninklijke Nederlandsche Toeristenbond (ANWB), AIT, Wassenaarseweg 220, Den Haag
Tel: (070) 314 71 47

100-120	80	80	50 km/h
If towing:			
80	80	80	50 km/h

0.05%

Compulsory if fitted for driver and front seat passengers

Children under 12 years of age not allowed in front seats unless child is under 4 years of age and using a child's safety seat

Recommended

Compulsory for motorcyclists and passengers

Tolls payable on: Zeeland Brug, Kiltunnel (from Dordrecht to Hoekse Waard) and Prins Willem Alexander Brug

18

Valid driving licence; Vehicle registration document or Vehicle on hire certificate; Green Card recommended; National vehicle identification plate

Poland

Polski Zwiazek Motorowy (PZM), FIA & AIT, Kazimierzowska 66, 02-518 Warszawa
Tel: (022) 499361/499212

Auto Assistance, Krucza 6-14, 00-537 Warszawa Tel: (022) 293541/290467

110	90	90	60 km/h
If towing:			
70	70	70	60 km/h

0.02%

Compulsory, outside built-up areas, if fitted for driver and front seat passenger

Children under 10 years of age not allowed in front seats

Compulsory

Recommended

Recommended

Compulsory for motorcyclists and passengers

In exchange for zlotys (PLZ) in currency

17

Valid driving licence or International Driving Permit; Vehicle registration document or Vehicle on hire certificate; Green Card, valid for Poland, required; National vehicle identification plate

Romania

In the event of breakdown or accident contact **Automobile-Club roumain**, FIA & AIT
Strada Tache Ionescu 27, București
Tel: (400) 155510

70-90*	60-90*	60-90*	60 km/h

*according to cylinder capacity

0.0% any alcohol found in the bloodstream may result in immediate imprisonment

Compulsory if fitted

Children under 12 years of age not allowed in front seats

Compulsory

Compulsory

Recommended

Compulsory for motorcyclists and passengers

Tolls payable on some major routes (Bucharest-Constanta)

Coupons obtainable with convertible currency only at frontier posts, tourist offices, the Automobile Club and some hotels; for use at PECO filling stations

18

Valid driving licence; Vehicle registration document or Vehicle on hire certificate; Green Card, valid for Romania, required; National vehicle identification plate

Norway

Kongelig Norsk Automobilklub (KNA), FIA, Drammensveien 20c, 0255 Oslo 2
Tel: (02) 56 19 00

Norges Automobil-Forbund (NAF), AIT, Storgata 2, 0155 Oslo 1 Tel: (02) 34 15 00

80-90	80-90	80-90	50 km/h
If towing trailer with braking system:			
80	80	80	50 km/h
If towing trailer without braking system:			
60	60	60	50 km/h

0.05%

Compulsory if fitted for driver and front and rear seat passengers

Children are allowed in front if seat is fitted with child restraint system and seat and belt can be adapted to their size

Compulsory

Recommended

Recommended

Compulsory for motorcyclists and passengers

Tolls payable on most new major roads

18 or 20 depending on the type of vehicle

Valid driving licence; Vehicle registration document or Vehicle on hire certificate; Green Card recommended; National vehicle identification plate

★ Dipped headlights compulsory at all times

Portugal

Automóvel Club de Portugal (ACP), FIA & AIT, Rua Rosa Araújo 24, 1200 Lisboa
Tel: (01) 563931

120	90	90	60 km/h
If towing:			
100	70	70	50 km/h

0.05%

Compulsory if fitted for driver and front seat passengers outside built-up areas

Children under 12 years of age not allowed in front seat

Compulsory

Recommended

Compulsory for motorcyclists

Tolls payable on some motorways and bridges

18

Valid driving licence; Vehicle registration document or Vehicle on hire certificate; Green Card required; National vehicle identification plate

★ Vehicle mud flaps are compulsory

Spain

Real Automóvil Club de España (RACE), FIA & AIT, José Abascal 10, 28003 Madrid
Tel: (91) 447 3200

120	100	90-100	60 km/h
If towing:			
80	80	80	60 km/h

these limits are increased by 20 km/h for overtaking

0.08%

Compulsory if fitted for driver and front seat passengers outside built-up areas

Children under 10 years of age not advised in front seats

Two are compulsory for vehicles with 9 or more seats; recommended for other vehicles

Recommended

Compulsory

Compulsory for motorcycles

Tolls payable on most motorways and Cadí tunnel

18

International Driving Permit required if 'pink' EEC licence not held; Vehicle registration document or Vehicle on hire certificate; Green Card required; Bail Bond strongly recommended; National vehicle identification plate

Sweden

Motormännens Riksförbund (M), AIT, Sturegatan 32, Stockholm Tel: (08) 7 82 38 00

110	70-110	70-110	50 km/h
If towing with braking device:			
70	70	70	50 km/h
If towing with no braking device:			
40	40	40	40 km/h

0.02%

Compulsory if fitted for driver and front and rear seat passengers

Compulsory

Recommended

Compulsory

Compulsory for motorcyclists and passengers

18

Valid driving licence; Vehicle registration document or Vehicle on hire certificate; Green Card required; National vehicle identification plate

★ Dipped headlights compulsory at all times

Turkey

Turkiye Turing ve Otomobil Kurumu (TTOK), FIA & AIT, Halaskargasi Cad. 364, 80222 Sisli, Istanbul Tel: (01) 1314631/6

	90	90	50 km/h
If towing:			
	70	70	40 km/h

0.05%

Compulsory if fitted for driver and front seat passengers

Children under 12 years of age not allowed in front seats

Two must be carried – one to place in front of the vehicle, one behind

Compulsory

Compulsory for motorcyclists

Tolls payable on some roads

18

Passport; Valid driving licence; International Driving Permit advised, compulsory if driving Turkish vehicle (obtainable at frontier with 2 photos and 54 000 Turkish Lire); Vehicle registration document or Vehicle on hire certificate; Green Card required – must cover European and Asian regions; National vehicle identification plate

★ Fire extinguisher, chock and towrope compulsory

Yugoslavia

Auto-Moto Savez Jugoslavija (AMSJ), FIA & AIT, Ruzveltova 18, 11001 Beograd Tel: (011) 401699

120	100	80	60 km/h
If towing:			
80	80	80	60 km/h

0.05%

Compulsory if fitted for driver and front and rear seat passengers

Children under 12 years of age not allowed in front seats

Compulsory – two are necessary if towing trailer or caravan

Compulsory

Compulsory

Compulsory for motorcyclists and passengers

Tolls payable on several major roads, Tito Bridge, Krk Island Bridge and Ucka Tunnel

Concessionary petrol coupons available at frontier posts for purchase with convertible currency; unused coupons refundable at place of purchase

18

Valid driving licence; Vehicle registration document or Vehicle on hire certificate; Green Card required; National vehicle identification plate

Switzerland

Automobile Club de Suisse (ACS), FIA, Wasserwerkgasse 39, 3000 Bern 13 Tel: (031) 22 47 22

Touring Club Suisse (TCS), AIT, 9 rue Pierre-Fatio, 1211 Genève 3 Tel: (022) 737 12 12

120	80	80	50 km/h
If towing – up to 20 cwt trailer:			
80	80	80	50 km/h
If towing – over 20 cwt trailer:			
60	60	60	50 km/h

0.08%

Compulsory if fitted for driver and front seat passengers

Children under 7 years of age not allowed in front seats

Compulsory

Compulsory for motorcyclists and passengers

Vignette compulsory: obtainable from frontier posts, post offices or garages; separate vignette required for trailer or caravan

18

Valid driving licence; Vehicle registration document or Vehicle on hire certificate; Green Card; National vehicle identification plate

USSR

In the event of breakdown or accident contact officer of State Automobile Inspection (Militia) or nearest office of Intourist (obliged to give tourists assistance)

90	90	90	60 km/h

0.0%

Compulsory if fitted for driver and front seat passengers

Children under 12 years of age not allowed in front seats

Compulsory

Compulsory

Recommended

Compulsory

Road tax payable on entry to USSR though some foreign cars exempt

Petrol coupons recommended; obtainable at border posts

18

Valid driving licence meeting requirements of International Convention on Road Traffic; Vehicle registration document or Vehicle on hire certificate; Car insurance obtainable on entry to USSR at Ingosstrakh offices or at Intourist offices; Itinerary card, service coupons and motor routes map issued by Intourist; Customs obligation to take the car out of the country on departure; National vehicle identification plate

★ Fire extinguisher compulsory

Signos convencionales

Para más información ver el interior de la cubierta anterior

Importancia de los itinerarios

Autopista con calzadas separadas
con calzada única
Autovía con calzadas separadas
Número de acceso
Accesos: completo – medio acceso
parcial – sin precisión

Carretera de comunicación internacional o nacional asfaltada:
calzadas separadas
4 carriles – 3 carriles
2 carriles anchos – 2 carriles

Carretera de comunicación interregional asfaltada:
calzadas separadas
2 carriles o más – 2 carriles estrechos
Sin asfaltar: transitable, con macadán
Otra carretera asfaltada – sin asfaltar
Autopista, carretera en construcción
(en su caso: fecha de entrada en servicio)

Distancias en kilómetros (totales o parciales)

en autopista:
tramo de peaje
tramo libre
en carretera
GB e IRL: en millas
en kilómetres

Transporte

Línea férrea – Tren-coche
Barcaza – Barcaza (DK, N, S, SF)
Enlace marítimo: permanente – de temporada
Aeropuerto

Segni convenzionali

Vedere la legenda completa all'interno della copertina

Importanza degli itinerari

Autostrada a carreggiate separate
a carreggiata unica
Doppia carreggiata di tipo autostradale
Numero dello svincolo
Svincoli: completo – semi-svincolo
parziale – non precisato

Strada di comunicazione internazionale o nazionale rivestita:
a carreggiate separate
a 4 corsie – a 3 corsie
a 2 corsie larghe – a 2 corsie

Strada di comunicazione interregionale rivestita:
a carreggiate separate
a 2 corsie e più – a 2 corsie strette
Non rivestita: carrozzabile, in macadam
Altre strade con rivestimento – senza rivestimento
Autostrada, strada in costruzione
(se del caso: data di apertura prevista)

Distanze in chilometri (totali e parziali)

su autostrada:
tratto a pedaggio
tratto esente da pedaggio
su strada
GB e IRL: in miglia
in chilometri

Trasporti

Ferrovia – trasporto automobili per ferrovia
Su chiatta – su chiatta (DK, N, S, SF)
Collegamento via-traghetto: tutto l'anno – stagionale
Aeroporto

Zeichenerklärung

Vollständige Zeichenerklärung siehe Umschlaginnenseite

Verkehrsbedeutung der Straßen

Autobahn mit getrennten Fahrbahnen
mit nur einer Fahrbahn
Schnellstraße mit getrennten Fahrbahnen
Nummer der Anschlußstelle
Anschlußstellen: Autobahnein- und/oder
-ausfahrt – ohne Angabe

Internationale bzw. nationale Hauptverkehrsstraße mit Belag:
getrennte Fahrbahnen
4 Fahrspuren – 3 Fahrspuren
2 breite Fahrspuren – 2 Fahrspuren

Überregionale Verbindungsstraße mit Belag:
getrennte Fahrbahnen
2 u. mehr Fahrspuren – 2 schmale Fahrspuren
Ohne Belag: befahrbar, mit Makadam
Sonstige Straßen: mit Belag, ohne Belag
Autobahn, Straße im Bau
(ggf. Datum der Verkehrsfreigabe)

Entfernungsangaben in Kilometern (Gesamt- und Teilentfernungen)

auf der Autobahn:
gebührenpflichtiger Abschnitt
gebührenfreier Abschnitt
auf anderen Straßen
in GB und IRL: in Meilen
in Kilometern

Transport

Bahnlinie – Autoreisezug
Fähre – Fähre (DK, N, S, SF)
Schiffsverbindung: ganzjährig – während der Saison
Flughafen

Verklaring der tekens

Zie voor de volledige verklaring der tekens de binnenzijde van het omslag

Belang van het wegennet

Autosnelweg met gescheiden rijbanen
met één rijbaan
Dubbele rijbaan van het type autosnelweg
Nummer knooppunt/aansluiting
Knooppunten/aansluitingen : volledig – half
gedeeltelijk – niet nader aangegeven

Internationale of nationale verharde verbindingsweg:
gescheiden rijbanen
4 rijstroken – 3 rijstroken
2 brede rijstroken – 2 rijstroken

Regionale verharde verbindingsweg:
gescheiden rijbanen
2 of meer rijstroken – 2 smalle rijstroken
Onverhard: berijdbaar, macadamweg
Andere weg: verhard – onverhard
Autosnelweg, weg in aanleg
(indien van toepassing: datum openstelling)

Afstanden in kilometers (totaal en gedeeltelijk)

op de autosnelweg:
gedeelte met tol
tolvrij gedeelte
op de weg
GB en IRL: in mijlen
in kilometers

Vervoer

Spoorweg – Autotrein
Veerpont – Veerpont (DK, N, S, SF)
Scheepvaartverbinding : permanent – alleen in het seizoen
Luchthaven

Légende

Voir la légende complète à l'intérieure de la couverture

Importance des itinéraires

Autoroute à chaussées séparées
à une seule chaussée
Double chaussée de type autoroutier
Numéro d'échangeur
Echangeurs: complet – demi-échangeur
partiel – sans précision

Route de liaison internationale ou nationale revêtue:
chaussées séparées
4 voies – 3 voies
2 voies larges – 2 voies

Route de liaison interrégionale revêtue:
chaussées séparées
2 voies et plus – 2 voies étroites
Non revêtue: carrossable, en macadam
Autre route revêtue – non revêtue
Autoroute, route en construction
(le cas échéant: date de mise en service)

Distances en kilomètres (totalisées et partielles)

sur autoroute:
section à péage
section libre
sur route
GB et IRL: en miles
en kilomètres

Transport

Voie ferrée – Train-auto
Bac – Bac (DK, N, S, SF)
Liaison maritime: permanente – saisonnière
Aéroport

Key to symbols

A full key to symbols appears inside the front cover

Road classification

Motorway: dual carriageway
single carriageway
Dual carriageway with motorway characteristics
Interchange number
Interchange: complete – half
limited – unspecified

International and national surfaced road network:
dual carriageway
four lanes – three lanes
two wide lanes – two lanes

Interregional surfaced road network:
dual carriageway
two lanes or more – two narrow lanes
Unsurfaced: suitable for vehicles, macadam
Other surfaced road – unsurfaced
Motorway, road under construction
(where available: with scheduled opening date)

Distances in kilometres (total and intermediate)

on motorway:
toll section
free section
on other roads
GB and IRL: in miles
kilometres

Transportation

Railway – Motorail
Ferry – Ferry (DK, N, S, SF)
Car ferry: all the year – seasonal
Airport

A
B
C
1
2
3
4
Flannan I.
LEWIS
Butt of Lewis
Port of Ness
Barvas
Carloway
Stornoway
Garynahine
Broad Bay
Portnaguran
Tiumpan Head
Eye Peninsula
THE MINCH
Hushinish
Clisham
Kebock Head
Tarbert
West Loch Tarbert
WESTERN ISLES
Toe Head
Harris
Leverburgh
Rodel
Renish Point
Sound of Harris
Rubha Réidh
North Uist
Tigharry
Lochmaddy
Sound of Monach
Balivanich
Benbecula
Creagorry
South Uist
Daliburgh
Lochboisdale
The Little Minch
Waternish Point
Dunvegan Head
Loch Snizort
Uig
Staffin
The Storr
Dunvegan
Portree
Bracadale
Idrigill Point
Loch Bracadale
Raasay
Sound of Raasay
Inner Sound
Rona
SEA OF THE HEBRIDES
Sligachan
SKYE
Sconser
Scalpay
The Cuillins
Broadford
Kyle of Lochalsh
Kyleakin
Kylerhea
Glenelg
Elgol
Isleornsay
Ardvasar
Sound of Sleat
Sound of Barra
Barra
Castlebay
Bayhirivagh
Mingulay
Barra Head
Canna
Cuillin Sound
Rhum
Sound of Rhum
Eigg
Muck
Coll
Arinagour
Tiree
Scarinish
Tobermory
Dervaig
Kilchoan
Salen
Strontian
Loch Sunart
Mallaig
Loch Nevis
Loch Morar
Arisaig
Sound of Arisaig
Glenfinnan
Loch Shiel
Corran
Inchree
Onich
Ballachulish
Kentallen
Glen Coe
Bidean nam Bian
Portnacroish
Loch Linnhe
Fort William
Ben Nevis
Loch Eil
Spean Bridge
Loch Lochy
Loch Arkaig
Caledonian Canal
Invergarry
Glen Albyn or Glen More
Fort Augustus
Loch Ness
Foyers
White Bridge
Invermoriston
Loch Quoich
Sgurr na Ciche
A' Chràlaig
Shiel Bridge
Dornie
Eilean Donan Castle
Carn Eige
Cannich
Drumnadrochit
Stromeferry
Lochcarron
Glen Carron
Shieldaig
Torridon
Liathach
Kinlochewe
Achnasheen
Loch Torridon
Wester Ross
Loch Maree
Gairloch
Laide
Gruinard Bay
Dundonnell
Loch Fannich
Sgurr Mór
Beinn Dearg
Garve
Ben Wyvis
Ullapool
Loch Broom
Coigach
Rubha Còigeach
Lochinver
Ledmore
Inchnadamph
Ben More Assynt
Kylestrome
Eddrachillis Bay
Scourie
Laxford Bridge
Kinlochbervie
Foinaven
Cape Wrath
Durness
Whiten Head
Loch Eriboll
Tongue
Ben Hope
Altnaharra
Ben Klibreck
Loch Shin
Lairg
Bonar Bridge
Alness
Dingwall
Contin
Muir of Ord
Tore
Black
Easter
Monadhliath
Carn Ban
Newtonmore
Laggan
Creag Meagaidh
Loch Laggan
Dalwhinnie
Pass of Drumochter
Loch Ericht
Ben Alder
Kinloch Rannoch
Loch Rannoch
Schiehallion
Blackwater Resr.
HIGHLAND
SCOTLAND
GRAMPIAN
HEBRIDES

ORKNEY ISLANDS
SHETLAND ISLANDS
Westray
Pierowall
North Ronaldsay
The North Sound
Westray Firth
Kettletoft
Sanday
Rousay
Eday
Brough Head
Stronsay Firth
Stronsay
Mainland
Shapinsay
Stromness
Stenness
Kirkwall
Skaill
Rora Head
Scapa Flow
Lyness
Hoy
Aberdeen
St. Margaret's Hope
South Ronaldsay
Burwick
Pentland Firth
Dunnet Head
Strathy Point
Scrabster
Dunnet
Duncansby Head
John o' Groats
Thurso
Castletown
Bettyhill
Melvich
Roadside
Reiss
Noss Head
Wick
Kinbrace
Latheron
Morven
Helmsdale
Brora
Golspie
Dornoch
Dornoch Firth
Tarbat Ness
Tain
Invergordon
Moray Firth
Cromarty
Lossiemouth
Buckie
Cullen
Kinnairds Head
Banff
Macduff
Fraserburgh
Nairn
Forres
Elgin
Fochabers
Rattray Head
Rothes
Keith
R. Spey
Deveron
Turriff
Mintlaw
Peterhead
Craigellachie
Dufftown
New Deer
Buchan Ness
Findhorn
Dava
Huntly
Cruden Bay
Grantown-on-Spey
Carrbridge
Dulnain Bridge
Rhynie
Oldmeldrum
Ellon
Newburgh
GRAMPIAN
Tomintoul
Mossat
Aviemore
Glen More Forest Park
Don
Inverurie
Kintore
Stromness
Lerwick
Alford
Craigievar Castle
Cairn Gorm
Colnabaichin
Cairngorm Mountains
Ben Macdui
ABERDEEN
Aboyne
Crathes Castle
Braemar
Balmoral Castle
Ballater
Banchory
Dee
Stonehaven
MOUNTAINS
Glas Maol
Devil's Elbow
Beinn a' Ghlò
N. Esk
Laurencekirk
Inverbervie
Blair Atholl
Marikirk
Pitlochry
TAYSIDE
S. Esk
Isla
Brechin
Kirriemuir
Montrose
Herma Ness
Haroldswick
Unst
Belmont
Gutcher
Fetlar
Isbister
Mid Yell
Yell Sound
Yell
Ulsta
Hillswick
Toft
St. Magnus Bay
Muckle Roe
Laxo
Papa Stour
Whalsay
Sandness
Voe
Mainland
Walls
Whiteness
Foula
Bressay
Scalloway
Lerwick
Tørshavn (Færøerne)
Seydisfjördur
Bergen
Aberdeen
Sumburgh
Sumburgh Head
Fair I.
5

Coll
Tiree
Arinagour
Scarinish
Kilchoan
Salen
Strontian
Corran
Fort William
Ben Nevis
Inchree
Onich
Tobermory
Dervaig
Lochaline
Ulva
Staffa
MULL
Craignure
Ben More
Iona
Fionnphort
Bunessan
Oban
Kerrera
Lismore
Connel
Taynuilt
Kilninver
Seil
Luing
Toberonochy
Scarba
Arduaine
Colonsay
Scalasaig
Crinan
Kilmartin
Lochgilphead
Ardrishaig
JURA
Ardlussa
Rubha a' Mhail
Beinn an Oir
Feolin Ferry
Craighouse
ISLAY
Port Askaig
Bridgend
Port Charlotte
Portnahaven
Rinns Point
Beinn Bheigeir
Ardbeg
Port Ellen
Mull of Oa
Inishtrahull
Gigha I.
Tayinloan
Carradale
Kennacraig
Claonaig
Tarbert
Tighnabruaich
Knapdale
Kintyre
Kilbrannan Sound
Lochranza
Goat Fell
ARRAN
Brodick
Lamlash
Blackwaterfoot
Machrihanish
Campbeltown
Southend
Mull of Kintyre
Glen Coe
Ballachulish
Kentallen
Portnacroish
Bidean nam Bian
Blackwater Resr.
Kinloch Rannoch
Loch Rannoch
Schiehallion
Ben Alder
Pass of Drumochter
Ben Cruachan
Pass of Brander
Dalmally
Tyndrum
Crianlarich
Ben More
Killin
Ben Lawers
Ben Chonzie
Lochearnhead
Ben Vorlich
Crieff
CENTRAL
Callander
The Trossachs
Inveraray
Tarbet
Ben Lomond
Argyll Forest Park
Queen Elizabeth Forest Park
Aberfoyle
Doune
Furnace
Drymen
Stirling
Helensburgh
Kilcreggan
Ardentinny
Otter Ferry
Alexandria
Dumbarton
Kilsyth
Denny
Falkirk
Kirkintilloch
Dunoon
Port Glasgow
Greenock
Gourock
Colintraive
Innellan
Rothesay
Bute
Wemyss Bay
Largs
Millport
Paisley
Erskine Bridge
Clydebank
Johnstone
Barrhead
Coatbridge
Airdrie
Hamilton
Motherwell
Wishaw
GLASGOW
East Kilbride
Kilbirnie
Beith
Dalry
Kilwinning
Stewarton
W. Kilbride
Ardrossan
Saltcoats
Irvine
Kilmarnock
Galston
Strathaven
Lanark
Troon
Prestwick
Ayr
STRATHCLYDE
Mauchline
Muirkirk
Douglas
Cumnock
New Cumnock
Sanquhar
Maybole
Dalmellington
Turnberry
Ailsa Craig
Girvan
Firth of Clyde
Galloway Forest Park
Merrick
Ballantrae
Barrhill
DUMFRIES
New Galloway
Newton Stewart
Castle Douglas
Gatehouse of Fleet
Ringford
Kirkcudbright
Auchencairn
Dalbeattie
Kirkcolm
Cairnryan
Stranraer
Portpatrick
Glenluce
Wigtown
Luce Bay
Wigtown Bay
Port William
Whithorn
Isle of Whithorn
Burrow Head
Drummore
Mull of Galloway
Point of Ayre
Ramsey
Ballaugh
Snaefell
Peel
ISLE OF MAN
Douglas
St. Bees Head
NORTH CHANNEL
Culdaff
Carndonagh
Moville
Inishowen Head
Antrim Coast
Giant's Causeway
Rathlin Island
Fair Head
Portrush
Portstewart
Bushmills
Ballycastle
Castlerock
Coleraine
Cushendun
Cushendall
Trostan
Glenariff or Waterfoot
Red Bay
Eglinton
Limavady
Londonderry
LONDONDERRY
Ballymoney
Antrim Mountains
Garvagh
Kilrea
Dungiven
Claudy
Clogh Mills
Carnlough
Glenarm
Sperrin Mountains
Sawel Mountain
Maghera
Portglenone
Ballymena
Broughshane
Larne
Island Magee
Tobermore
Castledawson
Magherafelt
Randalstown
ANTRIM
Ballyclare
Carrickfergus
Whitehead
Antrim
Moneymore
Cookstown
Lough Neagh
Crumlin
Newtownabbey
Belfast Lough
Bangor
Holywood
BELFAST
Donaghadee
Newtownards
Dungannon
Coalisland
Lisburn
Comber
Greyabbey
Ards Peninsula
Strangford Lough
Portavogie
Portadown
Lurgan
Craigavon
Armagh
Gilford
Dromore
Ballynahinch
Saintfield
Killyleagh
Portaferry
Strangford
Tandragee
Banbridge
ARMAGH
DOWN
Downpatrick
Ardglass
Markethill
Keady
Monaghan
Rathfriland
Castlewellan
Newtownhamilton
Newry
Newcastle
Dundrum Bay
St John's Point
Mourne Mts.
Slieve Donard
Warrenpoint
Rostrevor
Carlingford
Crossmaglen
Castleblayney
Ballybay
Gortin
Aughnacloy
Ballygawley
Work
Whiteha
Liverpool
Douglas (I. of Man)

TAYSIDE
Pitlochry
Blair Atholl
Kirriemuir
Brechin
Laurencekirk
Inverbervie
Montrose
Forfar
Arbroath
Dundee
Perth
Carnoustie
Buddon Ness
Tayport
Newport-on-Tay
Leuchars
St. Andrews
Fife Ness
FIFE
Crail
Anstruther
Pittenweem
St. Monance
Elie
Leven
Methil
Buckhaven
Glenrothes
Kirkcaldy
Dunfermline
Firth of Forth
Burntisland
Inverkeithing
Forth Bridges
S. Queensferry
Grangemouth
Bo-Ness
Hopetoun House
Leith
Prestonpans
Musselburgh
EDINBURGH
Dalkeith
Haddington
North Berwick
Dunbar
East Linton
Aberlady
Tranent
Cockburnspath
St. Abb's Head
Eyemouth
Berwick-upon-Tweed
Holy Island
LOTHIAN
Lammermuir Hills
Pentland Hills
Moorfoot Hills
Penicuik
West Linton
Carnwath
Peebles
Biggar
Innerleithen
Galashiels
Lauder
Earlston
Melrose
Dryburgh
Kelso
Coldstream
Duns
Greenlaw
Newtown St. Boswells
Selkirk
Jedburgh
Hawick
BORDERS
UPLANDS
Broad Law
Moffat
Beattock
Abington
The Cheviot
Cheviot Hills
Carter Bar
Northumberland National Park
NORTHUMBERLAND
Wooler
Belford
Bamburgh
Alnwick
Warkworth
Amble
Felton
Rothbury
Otterburn
The Border Forest Park
Kielder Resr.
North Tyne
Ashington
Newbiggin-by-the-Sea
Morpeth
Blyth
Bedlington
Seaton Delaval
Whitley Bay
Tynemouth
South Shields
NEWCASTLE UPON TYNE
Jarrow
Gateshead
SUNDERLAND
Belsay
Chollerford
Hadrian's Wall
Hexham
Corbridge
Prudhoe
Greenhead
Brampton
Longtown
Canonbie
Langholm
Lockerbie
Lochmaben
GALLOWAY
Annan
Bowness-on-Solway
Carlisle
Wigton
Abbey Town
Thursby
Aspatria
Silloth
Cockermouth
Keswick
Penrith
CUMBRIA
Cross Fell
Alston
Consett
Lanchester
Stanley
Washington
Chester-le-Street
Seaham
Houghton-le-Spring
Durham
Horden
Peterlee
Hartlepool
Wolsingham
Crook
Spennymoor
DURHAM
Sedgefield
Billingham
Redcar
Marske-by-the-Sea
Saltburn-by-the-Sea
Brotton
Loftus
Guisborough
Middlesbrough
Stockton-on-Tees
Middleton-in-Teesdale
W. Auckland
Bishop Auckland
Barnard Castle
Darlington
Eaglescliffe
Appleby
Brough
Kirkby Stephen
Bowes
Scotch Corner
Richmond
Reeth
Leyburn
Bedale
Northallerton
Hawes
Sedbergh
Kendal
Windermere
Ambleside
Grasmere
Patterdale
Ullswater
Shap
Orton
Tebay
Coniston
Bowness
Broughton-in-Furness
Greenodd
Lake District National Park
Cumbrian Mountains
Skiddaw
Scafell Pikes
Buttermere
Rosthwaite
Frizington
Egremont
Gosforth
Whitby
Cleveland Hills
North York Moors National Park
Scalby
Kristiansand
Hirtshals
Oslo
Bergen
Stavanger
Göteborg
Esbjerg

ISLE OF MAN
Point of Ayre
Ramsey
Ballaugh
Snaefell
Peel
Douglas
Port Erin
Port St. Mary
Castletown
Ronaldsway
Belfast
Dublin
Whitehaven
St. Bees Head
Egremont
Lake District National Park
Cumbrian Mountains
Ambleside
Windermere
Coniston
Kendal
Ulverston
Grange-over-Sands
Barrow-in-Furness
Morecambe
Morecambe Bay
Heysham
Lancaster
Carnforth
Fleetwood
Cleveleys
BLACKPOOL
Lytham St. Anne's
Southport
Formby
Ainsdale
LANCASHIRE
Preston
Blackburn
Clitheroe
Burnley
Nelson
Colne
Keighley
BRADFORD
Halifax
Huddersfield
Rochdale
Oldham
Bury
Bolton
Chorley
Leyland
Darwen
Accrington
Wigan
Ormskirk
Skelmersdale
LIVERPOOL
Bootle
Wallasey
Birkenhead
Hoylake
St. Helens
Warrington
Widnes
Runcorn
MANCHESTER
Stockport
Altrincham
Leigh
Ashton-under-Lyne
Glossop
Peak District
SHEFFIELD
Macclesfield
Congleton
Knutsford
Wilmslow
Northwich
Winsford
CHESHIRE
Chester
Crewe
Nantwich
Sandbach
Kidsgrove
Newcastle under Lyme
STOKE-ON-TRENT
Leek
Stafford
Stone
Uttoxeter
Derby
Burton upon Trent
Lichfield
Cannock
Rugeley
STAFFORD
Tamworth
Walsall
Sutton Coldfield
Nuneaton
WOLVERHAMPTON
Dudley
BIRMINGHAM
Stourbridge
Halesowen
Solihull
COVENTRY
Warwick
Royal Leamington Spa
Kenilworth
Kidderminster
Bewdley
Stourport
Bromsgrove
Redditch
Droitwich
Worcester
Stratford-upon-Avon
Evesham
Pershore
Great Malvern
Malvern
Upton
Ledbury
Tewkesbury
Cheltenham
Gloucester
Ross-on-Wye
Hereford
HEREFORD AND WORCESTER
Leominster
Ludlow
Telford
Shrewsbury
SHROPSHIRE
Bridgnorth
Much Wenlock
Newport
Market Drayton
Whitchurch
Wem
Ellesmere
Oswestry
Wrexham
Ruabon
Llangollen
Corwen
Bala
Ruthin
Denbigh
Mold
Flint
Holywell
Prestatyn
Rhyl
Colwyn Bay
Abergele
St. Asaph
Llandudno
Great Ormes Head
Conwy
Bangor
Beaumaris
Menai Bridge
Holyhead
Caergybi
Holy Island
Isle of Anglesey
Amlwch
Llangefni
Caernarfon
Caernarfon Bay
Llanberis
Snowdon
Snowdonia
Betws-y-Coed
Blaenau Ffestiniog
Ffestiniog
Porthmadog
Criccieth
Pwllheli
Abersoch
Aberdaron
Lleyn Peninsula
Harlech
GWYNEDD
Snowdonia National Park
Dolgellau
Barmouth
Cader Idris
Machynlleth
Tywyn
Aberdovey
CLWYD
Welshpool
Newtown
Montgomery
Llanidloes
POWYS
Rhayader
Llandrindod Wells
Builth Wells
Knighton
Presteigne
Kington
Hay-on-Wye
Brecon
Brecon Beacons National Park
Talgarth
Crickhowell
Abergavenny
Black Mountains
Aberystwyth
Cardigan Bay
Aberaeron
New Quay
Tregaron
Lampeter
Llandovery
Llandeilo
Carmarthen
CAMBRIAN MOUNTAINS
WALES
DYFED
Aberporth
Newcastle Emlyn
Llandysul
Whitland
St. Clears
Darlington
Richmond
Leyburn
Hawes
Sedbergh
Kirkby Lonsdale
Kirkby Stephen
Appleby
Barnard Castle
Yorkshire Dales
NORTH YORKSHIRE
Harrogate
Skipton
Settle
Ingleton
Knaresborough
Pateley Bridge
Ripon
Otley
Ilkley
Bingley
Brighouse
Dewsbury
Todmorden
Buxton
Matlock
Ashbourne
Bakewell
Chatsworth House
Chapel-en-le-Frith
High Peak
DERBYSHIRE
Evesham
Banbury
Chipping Norton
Moreton
Broadway
Winchcombe
Shipston-on-Stour
Alcester
Henley
Ettington

D
E
F
5
1
2
3
4
11
Stockton-on-Tees
Middlesbrough
Redcar
Marske-by-the-Sea
Saltburn-by-the-Sea
Guisborough
Whitby
Cleveland Hills
North York Moors National Park
Northallerton
Thirsk
Helmsley
Pickering
Scalby
Scarborough
Filey
YORKSHIRE
Malton
Norton
Flamborough Head
Bridlington
YORK
Wetwang
Gt. Driffield
HUMBERSIDE
Beeford
Hornsea
Leven
Market Weighton
Beverley
KINGSTON-UPON-HULL
Hedon
Withernsea
Patrington
Kilnsea
Selby
Howden
Goole
Humber Bridge
Barton-upon-Humber
River Humber
Scunthorpe
Immingham Dock
Immingham
Great Grimsby
Spurn Head
Cleethorpes
Rotterdam
Zeebrugge
Doncaster
Barnsley
Wakefield
Rotherham
Gainsborough
Market Rasen
Louth
Mablethorpe
Sutton-on-Sea
Lincoln
Horncastle
Alford
Spilsby
Skegness
Chesterfield
Mansfield
Newark-on-Trent
LINCOLN
NOTTINGHAM
Sleaford
Grantham
Boston
The Wash
Hunstanton
Wells-next-the-Sea
Sheringham
Cromer
Sandringham House
Fakenham
King's Lynn
NORFOLK
East Dereham
NORWICH
Great Yarmouth
Gorleston-on-Sea
Lowestoft
Spalding
Stamford
Wisbech
Peterborough
LEICESTER
Loughborough
Melton Mowbray
Oakham
Market Harborough
Kettering
ENGLAND
CAMBRIDGE
March
Ely
Thetford
Swaffham
Downham Market
Huntingdon
St. Ives
St. Neots
Wellingborough
NORTHAMPTON
BEDFORD
Bedford
Cambridge
Newmarket
Bury St. Edmunds
SUFFOLK
IPSWICH
Woodbridge
Aldeburgh
Southwold
Beccles
Haverhill
Sudbury
Saffron Walden
Milton Keynes
Buckingham
Letchworth
Hitchin

Wexford / Loch Garman
Wellington Bridge
Rosslare
Rosslare Harbour / Calafort Ros Láir
Kilmore Quay
Carnsore Point
Saltee Islands
Cherbourg
le Havre
Pembroke
ST. GEORGE'S CHANNEL
Cardigan Bay
Aberdovey
Machynlleth
Aberystwyth
Llanidloes
Llangurig
Devil's Bridge
Llanrhystud
Rhayader / Rhaeadr
Aberaeron
New Quay
Tregaron
Synod Inn
Lampeter
Aberporth
Cardigan / Aberteifi
Newport
Strumble Head
Pembrokeshire Coast National Park
Fishguard / Abergwaun
Newcastle Emlyn
Crymmych
Llandysul
Llanwrtyd-Wells
Llandovery / Llanymddyfri
St. David's Head
St. David's
St. Brides Bay
WALES
DYFED
Carmarthen / Caerfyrddin
Llandeilo
Llangadog
Black Mountain
Brecon Beacons National Park
Brecon / Aberhonddu
Haverfordwest / Hwlffordd
Whitland
Narberth
St. Clears / Sanclêr
Cross Hands
Ammanford
Milford Haven / Aberdaugleddau
Neyland
Pendine
Kidwelly
Saundersfoot
Pembroke Dock / Doc Penfro
Pembroke
Tenby / Dinbych-y-pysgod
Burry Port
Pontarddulais
Pontardawe
Merthyr Tydfil
Hirwaun
Aberdare / Aberdâr
Mountain Ash / Aberpennar
Rosslare
St. Govan's Head
Carmarthen Bay
Llanelli
Swansea / Abertawe
Neath / Castell-nedd
Rhondda
Rhossili
Worms Head
Port-Einon
The Mumbles
Port Talbot
GLAMORGAN
Maesteg
Pontypridd
Porthcawl
Bridgend / Pen-y-bont
Cowbridge
BRISTOL CHANNEL
Lundy
Ilfracombe
Combe Martin
Lynton
Lynmouth
Porlock
Minehead
Dunster
Croyde
Braunton
Exmoor
Simonsbath
Barnstaple
Northam
Exmoor National Park
Hartland Point
Clovelly
Bideford
South Molton
Great Torrington
Bampton
Kilkhampton
Winkleigh
Tiverton
Bude
Stratton
Holsworthy
Hatherleigh
Crediton
Cullompton
DEVON
Okehampton
EXETER
Tintagel
High Willhays
Moretonhampstead
Launceston
Camelford
Dartmoor National Park
Padstow
Bovey Tracey
Wadebridge
Tavistock
Dawlish
Exmouth
CORNWALL
Princetown
Ashburton
Teignmouth
Newquay
Bodmin
Callington
Newton Abbot
Torquay
Torbay
Liskeard
Saltash
Buckfastleigh
Fraddon
Lostwithiel
Plympton
Paignton
Fowey
Torpoint
Looe
Totnes
Truro
St. Austell
Polperro
Plymstock
Modbury
Brixham
Tregony
PLYMOUTH
Dartmouth
Kingswear
St. Ives
Hayle
Redruth
Mevagissey
Newton Ferrers
Camborne
Penryn
Kingsbridge
St. Just
Penzance
St. Michael's Mount
St. Mawes
Santander
Roscoff
Salcombe
Sennen
Land's End
Helston
Falmouth
Start Point
Tresco
St. Martin's
Isles of Scilly
St. Mary's
Mount's Bay
St. Keverne
Lizard
Lizard Point

SHROPSHIRE
LEICESTER
ENGLAND
WOLVERHAMPTON
Walsall
Tamworth
LEICESTER
Oakham
Stamford
Peterborough
Dudley
BIRMINGHAM
Nuneaton
Hinckley
COVENTRY
Rugby
Kidderminster
Ludlow
Kettering
HEREFORD
WARWICK
NORTHAMPTON
Worcester
Wellingborough
NORTHAMPTON
BEDFORD
Stratford-upon-Avon
Hereford
Bedford
WORCESTER
Milton Keynes
Gloucester
Cheltenham
OXFORD
Luton
Stevenage
BUCKINGHAM
HERTFORD
GWENT
GLOUCESTER
Aylesbury
St. Albans
OXFORD
Hatfield
NEWPORT
CASNEWYDD
Swindon
High Wycombe
Watford
CARDIFF
CAERDYDD
BERKSHIRE
Reading
LONDON
BRISTOL
Bath
AVON
Newbury
Windsor
WILTSHIRE
Basingstoke
Guildford
SURREY
Croydon
HAMPSHIRE
Crawley
Salisbury
Winchester
Yeovil
DORSET
W. SUSSEX
SOUTHAMPTON
BRIGHTON
PORTSMOUTH
Worthing
Hove
BOURNEMOUTH
Poole
Weymouth
ISLE OF WIGHT
Bognor Regis
Lyme Bay
Isle of Portland
Bill of Portland
St. Alban's Head
The Needles
St. Catherine's Point
Selsey Bill
Cherbourg
Jersey-Guernsey
Alderney
Guernsey, Jersey
St. Malo
Le Havre
Caen
Dieppe
ENGLISH CHANNEL
LA MANCHE
7
10
18
D
E
F
4

WOLVERHAMPTON
Walsall
Dudley
BIRMINGHAM
Lichfield
Tamworth
Sutton Coldfield
Nuneaton
Hinckley
LEICESTER
Oakham
Stamford
Peterborough
COVENTRY
Rugby
Kidderminster
Stourbridge
Halesowen
Solihull
Bedworth
Kenilworth
Market Harborough
Corby
Kettering
Wellingborough
NORTHAMPTON
Huntingdon
St. Ives
St. Neots
Bedford
Worcester
Redditch
Bromsgrove
Droitwich
Leominster
Stratford-upon-Avon
Royal Leamington Spa
Warwick
Evesham
Banbury
Daventry
Hereford
Great Malvern
Ledbury
Pershore
Tewkesbury
Chipping Campden
Stow-on-the-Wold
Milton Keynes
Buckingham
Bletchley
Luton
Stevenage
Letchworth
Hitchin
Baldock
Royston
Gloucester
Cheltenham
Ross-on-Wye
Monmouth
Bicester
Aylesbury
Dunstable
Hertford
Harlow
Bishop's Stortford
Stroud
Cirencester
Woodstock
Witney
OXFORD
Thame
High Wycombe
Hemel Hempstead
St. Albans
Watford
Chelmsford
Chepstow
NEWPORT
CASNEWYDD
Swindon
Abingdon
Wantage
Marlow
Maidenhead
Slough
LONDON
Brentwood
BRISTOL
Bath
Chippenham
Calne
Devizes
Marlborough
Newbury
Reading
Windsor
Wokingham
Richmond
Kingston
Dartford
Trowbridge
Frome
Wells
Warminster
Andover
Basingstoke
Farnborough
Aldershot
Woking
Guildford
Croydon
Epsom
Reigate
Sevenoaks
Glastonbury
Street
Salisbury
Winchester
Alton
Farnham
Godalming
Haslemere
Crawley
East Grinstead
Royal Tunbridge Wells
Yeovil
Shaftesbury
Romsey
Eastleigh
Petersfield
Horsham
Haywards Heath
Burgess Hill
Blandford Forum
SOUTHAMPTON
Fareham
PORTSMOUTH
Havant
Chichester
Arundel
BRIGHTON
Hove
Lewes
Worthing
Bognor Regis
Dorchester
Poole
BOURNEMOUTH
Christchurch
Lymington
Gosport
Cowes
Ryde
Newport
Sandown
Shanklin
Ventnor
Weymouth
Swanage
Newhaven
Seaford
Beachy Head
Selsey Bill
Isle of Portland
Bill of Portland
St. Alban's Head
The Needles
ISLE OF WIGHT
St. Catherine's Point
Cherbourg
Jersey, Guernsey
Alderney
Guernsey, Jersey
St. Malo
Caen
le Havre
Dieppe
HEREFORD AND WORCESTER
GLOUCESTER
OXFORD
BUCKINGHAM
HERTFORD
BEDFORD
NORTHAMPTON
WARWICK
CAMBRIDGE
BERKSHIRE
WILTSHIRE
HAMPSHIRE
SURREY
W. SUSSEX
E. SUSSEX
AVON
DORSET
ENGLAND
ENGLISH CHANNEL
LA MANCHE
18
9
6

NORFOLK
East Dereham
Swaffham
Stradsett
Watton
Mundford
Brandon
Thetford
NORWICH
Wymondham
Attleborough
Acle
Great Yarmouth
Gorleston-on-Sea
Lowestoft
Bungay
Harleston
Beccles
Diss
Scole
Halesworth
Southwold
Ixworth
Bury St. Edmunds
Newmarket
Stowmarket
Dennington
Yoxford
Saxmundham
Leiston
Aldeburgh
SUFFOLK
Lavenham
Haverhill
IPSWICH
Woodbridge
Clare
Sudbury
Hadleigh
Stour
Finchingfield
Halstead
Felixstowe
Harwich
Zeebrugge
Göteborg
Esbjerg
Hamburg
Hoek van Holland
Braintree
Colchester
The Naze
Walton-on-the-Naze
Frinton-on-Sea
Brightlingsea
Clacton-on-Sea
Witham
W. Mersea
Maldon
Bradwell-on-Sea
Burnham-on-Crouch
Foulness Point
Wickford
Rayleigh
Southend-on-Sea
Benfleet
Canvey Island
R. Thames
Grain
Vlissingen
Sheerness
Queenborough
Isle of Sheppey
Leysdown-on-Sea
Gillingham
Chatham
Whitstable
Herne Bay
Birchington
Margate
North Foreland
Broadstairs
Ramsgate
Sittingbourne
Faversham
Canterbury
Sandwich
Deal
KENT
Ashford
Biddenden
Tenterden
Hawkhurst
South Foreland
Dover
Zeebrugge
Oostende
Hythe
Folkestone
Channel tunnel under construction
New Romney
Lydd
Rye
Winchelsea
Dungeness
Hastings
PAS DE CALAIS
STRAIT OF DOVER
Kingston-upon-Hull
Felixstowe
Dover
Sheerness
Domburg
Walcheren
Middelburg
Vlissingen
Breskens
Knokke-Heist
Zeebrugge
Blankenberge
Heist
Sluis
Oostburg
IJzendijke
De Haan
(BRUGES)
BRUGGE
Oostende
Middelkerke-Bad
Nieuwpoort
Gistel
Jabbeke
Oostkamp
Eeklo
Koksijde-Bad
De Panne
BELGIË
BELGIQUE
Aalter
GENT
(GAND)
Bray-Dunes
Malo-les-Bains
Dunkerque
Veurne
Diksmuide
Torhout
Tielt
Deinze
Gravelines
Hondschoote
Roeselare
(Roulers)
Ingelmunster
Harelbeke
Waregem
Oudenaarde
Calais
Bourbourg
Bergues
Wissant
Cap Gris Nez
Guînes
Ardres
Audruicq
Wormhout
Steenvoorde
Poperinge
Ieper
(Ypres)
Kortrijk
(Courtrai)
Menen
Marquise
Cassel
St Omer
Wimereux
Boulogne
Arques
Hazebrouck
Bailleul
Armentières
Comines
Halluin
Tourcoing
Mouscron
Roubaix
LILLE
Doornik
Tournai
(Renaix)
Ronse
Hardelot
Desvres
Lumbres
Samer
Fauquembergues
Thérouanne
Aire
Merville
Estaires
Hucqueliers
Norrent-Fontes
Lillers
Seclin
Haubourdin
Le Touquet-Paris-Plage
Etaples
Fruges
Heuchin
Béthune
la Bassée
Carvin
Pont-à-Marcq
Orchies
Péruwelz
St Amand-les-Eaux
Condé
Montreuil
Bruay-en-A.
Houdain
Noeux
Lens
Hénin-Beaumont
Douai
Marchiennes
Bruay
Valenciennes
Berck-Plage
Campagne-lès-H.
Hesdin
St Pol-s-T.
Aubigny
Denain
Fort-Mahon
FRANCE
Crécy-en-P.
Frévent
Avesnes-le-Cte
Arras
Vitry-en-A.
Aniche
Bouchain
le Quesnoy
Rue
Nouvion
Auxi-le-Ch.
Beaumetz-lès-L.
Marquion
le Crotoy
Authie
Cambrai
Cayeux
St Valery
St Riquier
Bernaville
Doullens
Pas-en-Artois
Solesmes
Ault
Abbeville
Landrecies
Mers
le Tréport
Aílly-le-H.t Clocher
Canaples
Somme
Bapaume
Acheux
Caudry
le Cateau
Flixecourt
Villers-Bocage
Wassigny

A
B
C
1
2
3
4
Tory I.
Sheep Haven
Bloody Foreland Head
Dunfanaghy
Creeslough
Errigal Mt.
Derryveagh Mountains
Aran Island
Crolly
Dunglow
Letterkenny
Leitir Ceanain
Gweebarra Bay
Fintown
D O N E G A
Glenties
Rossan Point
Glencolumbkille
Ardara
Ballybofey
Blue Stack Mts.
Killybegs
Donegal / Dún na nGall
Lough Derg
Donegal Bay
Bundoran / Bun Dobhráin
Ballyshannon
Pettigoe
Belleek
Lower Lough Erne
Irvinestown
Inishmurray
L. Melvin
F E R M A N
Erris Head
Broad Haven
Belmullet
Glenamoy
Ballycastle
Killala Bay
Easky
Sligo Bay
Rosses Point
Sligo / Sligeach
Strandhill
Manorhamilton
Belcoo
Inishkea
M A Y O
Bangor
Inishcrone
The Ox Mountains
Ballysadare
L. Gill
Dowra
Blacksod Bay
Crossmolina
Ballina / Béal an Átha
S L I G O
Drumkeeran
Swanlinbar
Keel
Achill Island
Ballycroy
Nephin Beg Range
L. Conn
Nephin
Ballymote
Tobercurry
Lough Allen
L. Arrow
Corraun
Mulrany
Pontoon
Foxford
Keadew
Drumshanbo
Ballyconnell
Clare Island
Newport
Clew Bay
Castlebar / Caisleán an Bharraigh
Swinford
Charlestown
Gorteen
Boyle / Mainistir na Búille
L. Key
L E I T R I M
Ballinamore
Carrick-on-Shannon / Cora Droma Rúisc
Killashandra
Connaught
Kiltamagh
L. Gara
Ballaghaderreen
Inishturk
Louisburgh
Croagh Patrick
Westport / Cathair na Mart
Frenchpark
Elphin
Mohill
Inishbofin
Ballintober
R O S C O M M O N
Inishshark
Mweelrea Mts.
Killary Harbour
Ballyhaunis
Claremorris
Castlerea
Strokestown
Tulsk
L O N G F O R
Rinvyle Pt.
Letterfrack
Leenane
Partry Mountains
Lough Mask
Ballinrobe
Ballymoe
Longford / An Longfort
The Twelve Pins
Connemara
Maumturk Mts.
Kilmaine
Dunmore
Lanesborough
Clifden / An Clochán
Clonbur
Cong
Glennamaddy
Roscommon / Ros Comáin
Mostrim (Edgeworthstown)
Slyne Head
Roundstone
Maam Cross
Lough Corrib
Tuam / Tuaim
I R E L A
Headford
Ballymahon
Royal Canal
Gortmore
Oughterard
Mount Bellew
Ballyforan
Lough Ree
Carna
Kilkieran Bay
G A L W A Y
Athlone / Baile Átha Luain
Ballymore
W E S T M E
Lettermullan
Gorumna Island
Galway / Gaillimh
Spiddle
Barna
Oranmore
Athenry
Ballinasloe / Béal Átha na Sluaighe
Moate
Galway Bay
Aran Islands
Inishmore
Kilronan
Black Head
Craughwell
Loughrea
Clonmacnoise
River Shannon
Clara
Tullamore Tulach
Inishmaan
Ardrahan
Clonfert
Ferbane
Grand Canal
Inisheer
Ballyvaughan
Kinvarra
Banagher
Cloghan
O F F
Lisdoonvarna
Gort
Portumna
Kilcormac
Kilfenora
Cliffs of Moher
Lahinch
Ennistimon
Birr
Kinnitty
Slieve Bloom Mts.
Mountmellick
Corrofin
Lough Derg
Spanish Point
Milltown Malbay
C L A R E
Borrisokane
Portlaoise
Scarriff
Mountrath
Nore
Ennis / Inis
Tulla
Roscrea
Creegh
Knappogue Castle
Broadford
Nenagh / An tAonach
Moneygall
Rathdowney
Kilkee
Kilmurry
Killaloe
Newmarket on Fergus
14
Killadysert
Shannon
Bunratty Castle
Dolla
Templemore
Durrow
Kilrush
Killimer
Labasheeda
Newport
T I P P E R A R Y
Loop Head
Kilbaha
River Shannon
Milestone
Freshford
Mouth of
LIMERICK /
Askeaton
Thurles / Durlas
Urlingford

NORTH CHANNEL
IRISH SEA
ISLE OF MAN
NORTHERN IRELAND
LONDONDERRY
ANTRIM
TYRONE
ARMAGH
DOWN
MONAGHAN
CAVAN
LOUTH
MEATH
KILDARE
DUBLIN
WICKLOW
CARLOW
BELFAST
DUBLIN/BAILE ÁTHA CLIATH
Dún Laoghaire
Drogheda/
Droichead Átha
Dundalk/
Dun Dealgan
Londonderry
Coleraine
Ballymena
Larne
Carrickfergus
Bangor
Newtownards
Lisburn
Portadown
Armagh
Newry
Newcastle
Downpatrick
Omagh
Strabane
Dungannon
Monaghan/
Muineachán
Cavan/An Cabhán
Navan/
An Uaimh
Mullingar/
An Muileann gCearr
Naas
Bray
Greystones
Wicklow / Cill Mhantáin
Wicklow Head
Howth
Swords
Balbriggan
Skerries
Rush
Malahide
Portmarnock
Ashbourne
Maynooth
Lucan
Clondalkin
Kildare
Monasterevin
Carlow
Athy
Baltinglass
Kinnegad
Edenderry
Trim
Slane
Ardee
Castleblayney
Carrickmacross
Crossmaglen
Carlingford
Warrenpoint
Rostrevor
Kilkeel
Banbridge
Lurgan
Craigavon
Comber
Saintfield
Ballynahinch
Portaferry
Strangford
Donaghadee
Holywood
Newtownabbey
Whitehead
Antrim
Randalstown
Magherafelt
Cookstown
Limavady
Portrush
Portstewart
Bushmills
Ballycastle
Cushendall
Cushendun
Ballymoney
Giant's Causeway
Rathlin Island
Fair Head
Inishowen
Inishtrahull
Malin Head
Lough Foyle
Lough Swilly
Lough Neagh
Strangford Lough
Belfast Lough
Carlingford Lough
Dundalk Bay
Dundrum Bay
Sperrin Mountains
Mourne Mts
Slieve Donard
Wicklow Mountains
Lugnaquillia Mountain
Mull of Kintyre
Campbeltown
Machrihanish
ARRAN
Brodick
Lamlash
Firth of Clyde
Ailsa Craig
Irvine
Troon
Prestwick
Ayr
Maybole
Turnberry
Girvan
Ballantrae
Galloway Forest Park
Merrick
Newton Stewart
Stranraer
Cairnryan
Portpatrick
Glenluce
Luce Bay
Wigtown Bay
Whithorn
Isle of Whithorn
Mull of Galloway
Burrow Head
Drummore
Port William
Point of Ayre
Ramsey
Peel
Douglas
Port Erin
Castletown
Ronaldsway
Port St. Mary
Holyhead/
Caergybi
Holy Island
Isle of Anglesey
Amlwch
Beaumaris
Bangor
Menai Bridge
Caernarfon
Caernarfon Bay
Llanberis
Snowdon
Beddgelert
Porthmadog
Great Ormes Head

12
A
B
C
1
2
3
4
SLIGO
LEITRIM
ROSCOMMON
LONGFORD
WESTMEATH
OFFALY
GALWAY
IRELAND
CLARE
TIPPERARY
LIMERICK
KERRY
CORK
WATERFORD
Achill Island
Keel
Blacksod Bay
Ballycroy
Bangor
Nephin Beg Range
Crossmolina
L. Conn
Ballina / Béal an Átha
Inishcrone
The Ox Mountains
Sligeach
Ballysadare
Ballymote
Tobercurry
Drumkeeran
Dowra
Lough Allen
Drumshanbo
Carrick-on-Shannon / Cara Droma Rúisc
Mohill
Boyle / Mainistir na Búille
Keadew
Gorteen
Charlestown
Swinford
Foxford
Pontoon
Nephin
Castlebar / Caisleán an Bharraigh
Newport
Mulrany
Corraun
Clare Island
Clew Bay
Westport / Cathair na Mart
Croagh Patrick
Louisburgh
Inishturk
Inishbofin
Inishshark
Mweelrea Mts.
Rinvyle Pt.
Killary Harbour
Letterfrack
The Twelve Pins
Leenane
Partry Mountains
Ballintober
Kiltamagh
Connaught
Ballaghaderreen
Frenchpark
Elphin
Strokestown
Tulsk
Castlerea
Ballyhaunis
Claremorris
Lough Mask
Ballinrobe
Kilmaine
Ballymoe
Dunmore
Glennamaddy
Roscommon / Ros Comáin
Lanesborough
Longford / An Longfort
Clifden / An Clochán
Connemara
Maumturk Mts.
Clonbur
Cong
Lough Corrib
Tuam / Tuaim
Headford
Slyne Head
Roundstone
Maam Cross
Gortmore
Oughterard
Carna
Kilkieran Bay
Lettermullan
Gorumna Island
Mount Bellew
Ballyforan
Athlone / Baile Átha Luain
Lough Ree
Galway / Gaillimh
Spiddle
Barna
Oranmore
Athenry
Ballinasloe / Béal Átha na Sluaighe
Moate
Galway Bay
Aran Islands
Inishmore
Kilronan
Inishmaan
Inisheer
Black Head
Craughwell
Loughrea
Clonmacnoise
Clonfert
Ferbane
Clara
Ardrahan
Kinvarra
Ballyvaughan
Lisdoonvarna
Kilfenora
Cliffs of Moher
Gort
Banagher
Cloghan
Kilcormac
Portumna
Birr
Kinnitty
Slieve Bloom Mts.
Lahinch
Ennistimon
Corrofin
Spanish Point
Milltown Malbay
Ennis / Inis
Tulla
Scarriff
Lough Derg
Borrisokane
Roscrea
Nenagh / An tAonach
Moneygall
Knappogue Castle
Broadford
Killaloe
Creegh
Kilkee
Newmarket on Fergus
Kilmurry
Killadysert
Shannon
Bunratty Castle
Dolla
Templemore
Kilrush
Killimer
Labasheda
Loop Head
Kilbaha
Mouth of the Shannon
River Shannon
LIMERICK / LUIMNEACH
Newport
Milestone
Thurles / Durlas
Holycross Abbey
Urlingford
Tarbert
Askeaton
Adare
Ballybunnion
Ballyduff
Kerry Head
Listowel
Rathkeale
Croom
Ballyheige
Abbeyfeale
Newcastle West
Hospital
Tipperary / Tiobraid Árann
Cashel / Caiseal
Killenaule
Fethard
Brandon Head
Brandon Mountain
Sybil Head
Clogher Head
Dingle
Great Blasket I.
Slea Head
Tralee / Trá Lí
Tralee Bay
Slieve Mish Mts.
Anascaul
Castlemaine
Dingle Bay
Castleisland
Dromcolliher
Rath Luirc (Charleville)
Kilmallock
Galty Mountains
Caher
Clonmel / Cluain Meala
Slievenamon
R. Suir
Killorglin
Glenbeigh
Newmarket
Boherboy
Kanturk
Buttevant
Kildorrery
Mitchelstown
Clogheen
Knockmealdown Mts.
Comeragh Mts.
Killarney / Cill Airne
L. Caragh
Muckross House
L. Leane
Rathmore
Millstreet
Mallow / Mala
Fermoy
Lismore
Cappoquin
Doulus Head
Ring of Kerry
Carrantuohill
Knight's Town
Valencia Island
Cahersiveen
Iveragh
Macgillycuddy's Reeks
Mangerton Mountain
Derrynasaggart Mts.
Tallow
Dungarvan / Dún Garbhán
Dungarvan Harbour
Helvick Head
St. Finan's Bay
Waterville
L. Currane
Sneem
Kilgarvan
Kenmare
Bolus Head
Skellig
Macroom
Coachford
Blarney
CORK / CORCAIGH
Midleton
Youghal / Eochaill
Youghal Bay
Ardmore
Kenmare River
Lauragh
Beara
Caha Mts.
Glengarriff
Pass of Keimaneigh
Cobh / An Cóbh
Ringaskiddy
Crosshaven
Ballycotton
Castletownbere
Dursey Island
Bantry / Beanntraí
Dunmanway
Bandon
Kinsale
Bere I.
Bantry Bay
Sheep's Head
Dunmanus Bay
Timoleague
Clonakilty
Rosscarbery
Skull
Skibbereen
Roaringwater Bay
Mizen Head
Galley Head
Old Head of Kinsale
Toe Head
Roscoff
le Havre

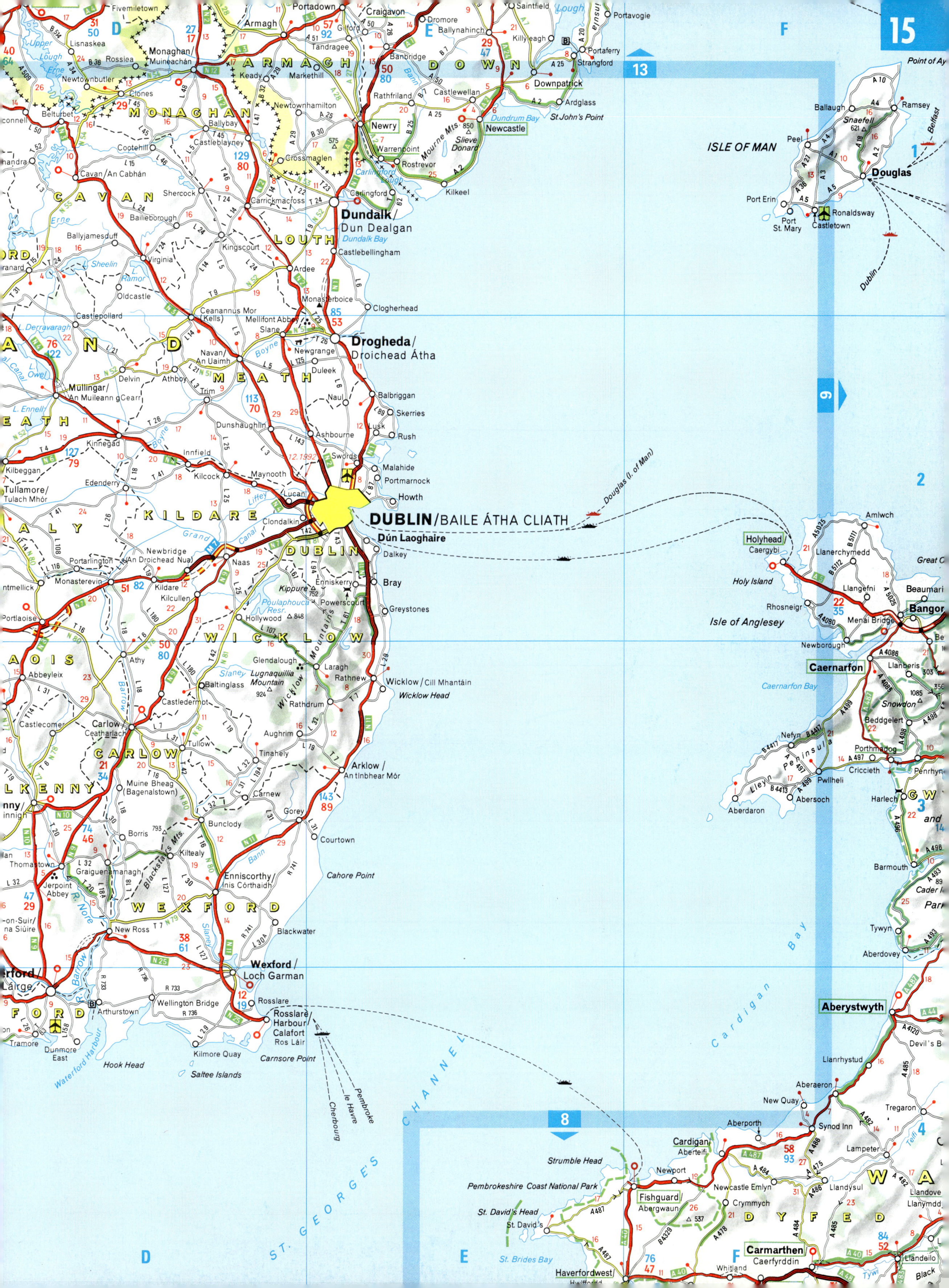

ARMAGH
DOWN
MONAGHAN
CAVAN
LOUTH
MEATH
KILDARE
DUBLIN
WICKLOW
CARLOW
WEXFORD
ISLE OF MAN
Isle of Anglesey
DYFED
Portadown
Craigavon
Armagh
Monaghan/Muineachán
Lisnaskea
Rossiea
Newtownbutler
Clones
Belturbet
Dromore
Ballynahinch
Banbridge
Tandragee
Markethill
Keady
Newtownhamilton
Ballybay
Castleblayney
Cootehill
Crossmaglen
Newry
Warrenpoint
Rostrevor
Rathfriland
Castlewellan
Newcastle
Slieve Donard
Mourne Mts.
Kilkeel
Carlingford
Downpatrick
Ardglass
St. John's Point
Dundrum Bay
Strangford
Portaferry
Killyleagh
Saintfield
Portavogie
Cavan/An Cabhán
Shercock
Carrickmacross
Bailieborough
Dundalk/Dun Dealgan
Dundalk Bay
Castlebellingham
Ballyjamesduff
Kingscourt
Virginia
Ardee
Oldcastle
Monasterboice
Clogherhead
Castlepollard
Ceanannus Mor (Kells)
Mellifont Abbey
Slane
Drogheda/Droichead Átha
Newgrange
Duleek
Navan/An Uaimh
Athboy
Delvin
Mullingar/An Muileann gCearr
Trim
Balbriggan
Naul
Skerries
Dunshaughlin
Ashbourne
Lusk
Rush
Kinnegad
Innfield
Swords
Malahide
Portmarnock
Howth
Kilbeggan
Edenderry
Kilcock
Maynooth
Lucan
Tullamore/Tulach Mhór
DUBLIN/BAILE ÁTHA CLIATH
Clondalkin
Dún Laoghaire
Dalkey
Douglas (I. of Man)
Newbridge/An Droichead Nua
Naas
Portarlington
Monasterevin
Kildare
Kilcullen
Enniskerry
Bray
Powerscourt
Greystones
Kippure
Poulaphouca Resr.
Hollywood
Portlaoise
Athy
Glendalough
Laragh
Rathnew
Wicklow/Cill Mhantáin
Wicklow Head
Lugnaquillia Mountain
Baltinglass
Wicklow Mountains
Abbeyleix
Castledermot
Rathdrum
Castlecomer
Carlow/Ceatharlach
Tullow
Aughrim
Tinahely
Arklow/An tInbhear Mór
Muine Bheag (Bagenalstown)
Carnew
Gorey
Borris
Bunclody
Courtown
Thomastown
Kiltealy
Blackstairs Mts.
Graiguenamanagh
Jerpoint Abbey
Enniscorthy/Inis Córthaidh
Cahore Point
Blackwater
New Ross
Wexford/Loch Garman
Arthurstown
Wellington Bridge
Rosslare
Rosslare Harbour
Calafort Ros Láir
Kilmore Quay
Carnsore Point
Tramore
Dunmore East
Hook Head
Waterford Harbour
Saltee Islands
Cherbourg
le Havre
Pembroke
ST. GEORGE'S CHANNEL
Cardigan Bay
Ramsey
Ballaugh
Snaefell
Peel
Douglas
Port Erin
Port St. Mary
Castletown
Ronaldsway
Point of Ayre
Belfast
Dublin
Amlwch
Holyhead/Caergybi
Holy Island
Llanerchymedd
Llangefni
Rhosneigr
Menai Bridge
Bangor
Beaumaris
Newborough
Caernarfon
Caernarfon Bay
Llanberis
Snowdon
Beddgelert
Nefyn
Lleyn Peninsula
Porthmadog
Criccieth
Pwllheli
Abersoch
Aberdaron
Harlech
Barmouth
Tywyn
Aberdovey
Aberystwyth
Llanrhystud
Aberaeron
New Quay
Synod Inn
Tregaron
Lampeter
Aberporth
Cardigan/Aberteifi
Strumble Head
Newport
Pembrokeshire Coast National Park
Fishguard/Abergwaun
Newcastle Emlyn
Crymmych
Llandysul
St. David's Head
St. David's
St. Brides Bay
Haverfordwest
Carmarthen/Caerfyrddin
Whitland
Llandeilo
Llandovery

A
B
C
1
2
3
4
46
19
50
Waddeneilanden
Terschelling
West-Terschelling
Oosterend
Vlieland
Oost-Vlieland
Texel
De Koog
Den Burg
Den Helder
Den Oever
Afsluitdijk
Harlingen
Leeuwarden
Bolsward
Workum
Sloten
Staveren
Lemmer
IJsselmeer
MER DU NORD
NOORD-HOLLAND
NEDERLAND
Schagen
Medemblik
Enkhuizen
Urk
Emmeloord
Bergen
Bergen aan Zee
Egmond aan Zee
Alkmaar
Hoorn
Markermeer
Purmerend
Edam
Volendam
Monnickendam
Marken
Lelystad
Beverwijk
IJmuiden
Zaandam
AMSTERDAM
Haarlem
Bloemendaal
Zandvoort
FLEVOLAND
Harderwijk
Almere
Heemstede
Amstelveen
Hillegom
Keukenhof
Lisse
Aalsmeer
Bussum
Huizen
Spakenburg
Hilversum
Abcoude
Baarn
Soestdijk
Soest
Amersfoort
Nijkerk
Noordwijk aan Zee
Katwijk aan Zee
Great Yarmouth
Leiden
Wassenaar
UTRECHT
De Bilt
Zeist
Alphen a/d Rijn
Scheveningen
DEN HAAG
('S-GRAVENHAGE)
Voorschoten
Zoetermeer
Boskoop
Bodegraven
Woerden
Driebergen
Doorn
Veenendaal
Amerongen
Rhenen
Gouda
Kingston upon Hull
Harwich
Hoek van Holland
Delft
ZUID-HOLLAND
Europoort
Schiedam
Maassluis
Brielle
Vlaardingen
ROTTERDAM
Schoonhoven
Culemborg
Leerdam
Tiel
Gorinchem
Zaltbommel
WAAL
Haringvlietdam
Goeree
Ouddorp
Spijkenisse
Hellevoetsluis
Oud Beijerland
Zwijndrecht
Sliedrecht
Dordrecht
's-Gravendeel
Biesbosch
Geertruidenberg
MAAS
Oss
's-Hertogenbosch
Middelharnis
Overflakkee
Schouwen Duiveland
Haamstede
Zierikzee
Willemstad
Waalwijk
Kaatsheuvel
Oosterhout
Dongen
Tilburg
Oisterwijk
Boxtel
St.-Oedenrode
Veghel
NOORD-BRABANT
Steenbergen
Stavenisse
Tholen
Oudenbosch
Etten
Breda
Gilze
Goirle
Oirschot
Domburg
Walcheren
Veere
ZEELAND
N^d Beveland
Middelburg
Goes
Z^d Beveland
Vlissingen
Kruiningen
Halsteren
Roosendaal
Bergen op Zoom
Zundert
Baarle Nassau
Hilvarenbeek
Veldhoven
Eindhoven
Sheerness
Felixstowe
Dover
Breskens
Hoedekenskerke
Woensdrecht
Wuustwezel
Hoogstraten
Reusel
Valkenswaard
Terneuzen
Brecht
Turnhout
Arendonk
Knokke-Heist
Zeebrugge
Blankenberge
Heist
Oostburg
Sluis
IJzendijke
Hulst
Brasschaat
Oostmalle
Lommel
De Haan
Oostende
BRUGGE
(BRUGES)
(ANVERS)
ANTWERPEN
ANTWERPEN
Zelzate
Stekene
Beveren-Waas
St-Niklaas
Kasterlee
Herentals
Mol
Geel
Middelkerke-Bad
Nieuwpoort
Koksijde-Bad
De Panne
Bray-Dunes
Jabbeke
Oostkamp
Gistel
Maldegem
Eeklo
Evergem
Lokeren
Temse
Waasmunster
Boom
Kontich
Lier
Heist-o.d.B.
Westerlo
Leopoldsburg
Beringen
Hechtel
Dunkerque
Bergues
Hondschoote
Veurne
Diksmuide
Torhout
Tielt
Aalter
GENT
(GAND)
Zele
Dendermonde
Willebroek
(Malines)
Mechelen
Keerbergen
Aarschot
Herselt
Diest
Genk
Hasselt
WEST-VLAANDEREN
Roeselare
(Roulers)
Kortrijk
(Courtrai)
Ieper
Poperinge
Izegem
Harelbeke
Waregem
Deinze
Ingelmunster
Oudenaarde
OOST-VLAANDEREN
Wetteren
Alost
Aalst
Asse
BELGIË
Vilvoorde
BRUSSEL
Ninove
Tervuren
Leuven (Louvain)
Herk
Zoutleeuw
Tienen
Bilzen
LIMBURG
Scheldt
Demer
Dijle
Albert K.

47
48
51
52
GRONINGEN
Groningen
Emden
Leer
Oldenburg
BREMEN
Delmenhorst
Assen
DRENTHE
Emmen
Meppen
Papenburg
Cloppenburg
Vechta
Diepholz
Coevorden
Lingen
Nordhorn
Zwolle
OVERIJSSEL
Almelo
Hengelo
Enschede
Rheine
Osnabrück
Minden
Bielefeld
Herford
Bad Oeynhausen
Deventer
Apeldoorn
Zutphen
Arnhem
Münster
Gütersloh
Paderborn
Lippstadt
Bocholt
Emmerich
Wesel
Hamm
Recklinghsn
Gelsenkchn
Herne
Bottrop
Oberhsn
ESSEN
Bochum
DORTMUND
DUISBURG
Mülheim
Krefeld
Venlo
Hagen
Iserlohn
Arnsberg
WUPPERTAL
DÜSSELDORF
Mönchengladbach
Neuss
Solingen
Remscheid
Lüdenscheid
Leverkusen
KÖLN
Siegen
Marburg
Dillenburg
AACHEN
Maastricht
Heerlen
Düren
Sittard
Roermond
LIMBURG
NORDRHEIN-WESTFALEN
NIEDE

Yeovil
Sherborne
Honiton
Chard
Crewkerne
Ilminster
Henstridge
Sturminster Newton
Blandford Forum
Fordingbridge
Romsey
Eastleigh
Petersfield
Midhurst
Petworth
Pulborough
Cowfold
W. SUSSEX
DORSET
Beaminster
Axminster
Ottery St. Mary
Sidmouth
Budleigh Salterton
Exmouth
Seaton
Lyme Regis
Bridport
Dorchester
Abbotsbury
Bere Regis
Wareham
Corfe Castle
Swanage
Poole
BOURNEMOUTH
Wimborne Minster
Ringwood
Cranborne
Christchurch
Lymington
Lyndhurst
Beaulieu
Fawley
SOUTHAMPTON
Botley
Fareham
Gosport
PORTSMOUTH
Southsea
Havant
Cosham
Chichester
Arundel
Bognor Regis
Littlehampton
Worthing
Shoreham
BRIGHTON
Selsey
Selsey Bill
Yarmouth
Freshwater
Newport
Cowes
Fishbourne
Ryde
Brading
Sandown
Shanklin
Ventnor
Niton
The Needles
ISLE OF WIGHT
St. Catherine's Point
Foreland
Weymouth
Fortuneswell
Isle of Portland
Bill of Portland
St. Alban's Head
Lyme Bay
Alderney
Jersey-Guernsey
Cherbourg
St. Malo
Caen
Le Havre
Torquay
Rosslare
Poole
Weymouth
Portsmouth
Cap de la Hague
Nez de Jobourg
Cherbourg
Cap Lévy
St. Pierre-Eglise
Pnte de Barfleur
Barfleur
Beaumont
Quettehou
St. Vaast-la-Hougue
les Pieux
Valognes
Montebourg
Bricquebec
Ste. Mère-Eglise
Carteret
Barneville
St. Sauveur-le-V.
Portbail
la Haye-du-Puits
Carentan
Grandcamp-Maisy
St. Laurent
Port-en-Bessin
Arromanches
Courseulles
St. Aubin
Langrune
Luc
Ouistreham
Cabourg
Isigny
Trévières
Bayeux
Lessay
Périers
St. Jean-de-Daye
St. Clair-s-l'E.
St. Lô
Balleroy
Tilly-s-S.
CAEN
Troarn
Caumont-l'Eventé
Villers-Bocage
Evrecy
MANCHE
CALVADOS
St. Sauveur-Lendelin
Marigny
St. Malo-de-la-Lande
Agon-Coutainville
Coutances
Canisy
Torigni
Aunay-s-O.
Thury-Harcourt
Potigny
Montmartin
Cerisy-la-S.
Tessy
le Bény-Bocage
Bréhal
Hambye
Gavray
Percy
Villedieu-les-Poêles
Vire
Vassy
Condé-s-Noireau
Clécy
Falaise
Granville
St. Pair
la Haye-Pesnel
Jullouville
Carolles
Sartilly
Brécey
St. Sever
St. Pois
Pont-d'Ouilly
Tinchebray
Flers
Putanges
Avranches
Sourdeval
Mortain
Messei
Briouze
Juvigny-le-T.
Barenton
Domfront
la Ferté-Macé
Bagnoles-de-l'Orne
Pontaubault
Ducey
St. Hilaire-du-Harcouët
le Teilleul
Pontorson
St. James
Louvigné-du-Désert
Landivy
Passais
Juvigny-s-A.
Couptrain
Lassay
Ambrières-les-Vallées
Gorron
Pré-en-Pail
St. Brice-en-Coglès
Fougères
Antrain
Combourg
Tinténiac
le Mont-St. Michel
le Vivier
Dol-de-B.
Pleine-Fougères
Cancale
Pnte du Grouin
Rothéneuf
Paramé
St. Malo
St. Servan
Châteauneuf
Dinard
St. Lunaire
St. Briac
Dinan
Evran
Caulnes
Plancoët
Plélan-le-Pt.
Jugon
Broons
Lamballe
Moncontour
Collinée
Plouguenast
St. Cast
Matignon
Sables-d'Or
Erquy
Cap Fréhel
le Val-André
Pléneuf
St. Brieuc
St. Quay-Portrieux
Binic
Etables
Plouha
Paimpol
Pnte de l'Arcouest
I. de Bréhat
Lanvollon
Châtelaudren
Plouagat
Quintin
Corlay
Uzel
I. Chausey
Guernsey
St. Peter Port
Sark
Jersey
Gorey
St-Hélier
Alderney
Torquay
Portsmouth
Rosslare
Cork
Mt. des Avaloirs
Villaines-la-Juhel
Carrouges
Ecouché
CÔTES-D'ARMOR
8
22
24
9
10
1
2
3
4
A
B
C

Folkestone
Dunkerque
Calais
Hastings
Eastbourne
E SUSSEX
Hythe
New Romney
Dungeness
Rye
Lydd
Winchelsea
Bexhill
Hailsham
Battle
Lewes
Seaford
Newhaven
Polegate
Beachy Head
Tunnel sous la Manche
(en construction)
Wissant
Cap Gris Nez
Wimereux
Boulogne
PAS DE CALAIS
Dieppe
Gravelines
Bourbourg
Guînes
Ardres
Marquise
Audruicq
S.t Omer
Arques
Cassel
Hazebrouck
Bergues
Hondschoote
Veurne
Poperinge
Ieper (Ypres)
Kortrijk
Roeselare (Roulers)
VLAANDEREN
WEST
Armentières
Bailleul
Tourcoing
LILLE
Desvres
Lumbres
Samer
Hardelot
Fauquembergues
Thérouanne
Aire
Merville
Estaires
Seclin
La Bassée
Béthune
Bruay-en-A.
Carvin
Hénin-Beaumont
Lens
Liévin
Douai
Le Touquet-Paris-Plage
Étaples
Montreuil
Hucqueliers
Fruges
Heuchin
Berck-Plage
Fort-Mahon
Campagne-les-H.
Hesdin
S.t Pol-s-T.
Aubigny
Avesnes-le-C.te
Arras
Frévent
Crécy-en-P.
Le Crotoy
Rue
Cayeux
Nouvion
Auxi-le-Ch.au
Doullens
Pas-en-Artois
Beaumetz-lès-L.
Bapaume
Marquion
S.t Valery
Ault
Mers
le Tréport
Criel
Abbeville
Ailly-le-H.t Clocher
Bernaville
Flixecourt
Albert
Péronne
Villers-Bocage
Corbie
Bray
Amiens
SOMME
Hallencourt
Moyenneville
Gamaches
Oisemont
Airaines
Picquigny
Molliens-Vidame
Boves
Hornoy
Blangy
Aumale
Dieppe
Envermeu
S.t Nicolas-d'A.
Londinières
Varengeville
Veules-les-Roses
S.t Valery-en-Caux
Veulettes
Cany-Barville
Fontaine-le-Dun
Offranville
Arques
Bacqueville
Fécamp
Yport
Etretat
Cap d'Antifer
Criquetot-l'Esneval
Goderville
Valmont
Ourville
Doudeville
Yvetot
Yerville
Longueville-s-S.
Bellencombre
Neufchâtel-en-B.
Tôtes
Clères
Forges-les-Eaux
Formerie
Grandvilliers
Crèvecoeur-le-Gd
Conty
Poix
Ailly-s-N.
Moreuil
Rosières
Chaulnes
Villers-Bretonneux
Montdidier
Roye
Nesle
Ham
Guiscard
Noyon
Lassigny
Ressons
Maignelay
Breteuil
Froissy
Marseille-en-B.
Songeons
Gournay-en-B.
Argueil
Buchy
S.t Romain-de-C.
Bolbec
Montivilliers
Lillebonne
Caudebec
Barentin
Pavilly
Duclair
Jumièges
Villerville
Honfleur
Tancarville
Quillebeuf
ROUEN
Beauvais
Lyons-la-F.t
Boos
Fleury-s-A.
Etrépagny
Gisors
Chaumont-en-V.
Noailles
Mouy
Bresles
Clermont
S.t Just-en-Chaussée
Estrées-S.t Denis
OISE
Compiègne
Pierrefonds
Villers-Cotterêts
Crépy-en-Valois
Verberie
Pont-S.te Maxence
Creil
Neuilly-en-T.
Chantilly
Senlis
Ermenonville
Nanteuil-le-H.
Betz
Pont-Audemer
Bourg-Achard
Bourgtheroulde
Elbeuf
Pont-l'Evêque
Beuzeville
Cormeilles
Blangy-le-Ch.au
Lieurey
Montfort
Le Bec-Hellouin
Brionne
Le Neubourg
Lisieux
Thiberville
Bernay
Orbec
Livarot
Louviers
Val de Reuil
Pont de l'Arche
Les Andelys
Gaillon
Vernon
EURE
Ecos
Magny-en-Vexin
Marines
La Roche-Guyon
Bonnières
Mantes
Pontoise
Meulan
L'Isle-Adam
Beaumont
Luzarches
Montmorency
S.t Denis
S.t Germain
Nanterre
Bobigny
PARIS
Meaux
Dammartin-en-Goële
Claye-Souilly
Lagny
Coulommiers
Crécy-la-Ch.lle
La Rivière-Thibouville
Beaumont-le-Roger
Beaumesnil
Broglie
Conches
Evreux
Pacy
Chaufour
NORMANDIE
Vimoutiers
La Neuve-Lyre
Damville
S.t André-de-l'E.
Ivry-la-Bataille
Anet
Gacé
La Ferté-Frênel
Rugles
Breteuil
L'Aigle
Verneuil
Tillières
Nonancourt
Dreux
Houdan
Pontchartrain
VERSAILLES
Montfort-l'A.
Chevreuse
Orsay
Palaiseau
Créteil
Orly
Evry
Brie-Comte-Robert
Tournan
Fontenay-Trésigny
Rozay-en-Brie
Argentan
Nonant-le-Pin
Le Merlerault
Moulins-la-Marche
Courtomer
Sées
Brezolles
La Ferté-Vidame
Longny
Nogent-le-Roi
Châteauneuf-en-Th.
Senonches
Maintenon
Epernon
Rambouillet
Limours
Arpajon
Corbeil-Essonnes
Melun
Mormant
Nangis
Bazoches-s-H.
Le Mêle
Mortagne-au-Perche
Tourouvre
La Loupe
Courville
Chartres
Gallardon
Auneau
Ablis
Dourdan
Etampes
La Ferté-Alais
Milly
Fontainebleau
Le Châtelet
Montereau
Moret
Alençon
Pervenchères
Rémalard
Bellême
AUTOROUTE DU NORD

BRUSSEL
BRUXELLES
Leuven (Louvain)
Liège
Lille
Roubaix
Tournai
Mons
Charleroi
Namur
Dinant
Valenciennes
Maubeuge
Douai
Arras
Cambrai
St Quentin
Laon
Soissons
Compiègne
Senlis
Meaux
Château-Thierry
Epernay
Reims
Rethel
Charleville-Mézières
Sedan
Verdun
Châlons-s-Marne
Vitry-le-François
St Dizier
Bar-le-Duc
Troyes
Provins
Melun
Fontainebleau
B E L G I Q U E
HAINAUT
NAMUR
LUXEMBOURG
NORD
AISNE
ARDENNES
MARNE
MEUSE
SEINE-ET-MARNE
AUBE
Oudenaarde
Kortrijk (Courtrai)
Ieper (Ypres)
Tourcoing
Mouscron
Halle
Nivelles
Wavre
Waterloo
Tienen
St.-Truiden
Tongeren
Huy
Gembloux
Soignies
Ath
La Louvière
Binche
Philippeville
Givet
Chimay
Couvin
Fumay
Hirson
Vervins
Guise
Avesnes
Le Cateau
Péronne
Noyon
Villers-Cotterêts
Crépy-en-Valois
Bouillon
Bastogne
St Hubert
La Roche
Neufchâteau
Longwy
Stenay
Vouziers
Sézanne
Montmirail
Coulommiers
Nogent-s-S.
Joinville
Ciney
Rochefort
Marche-en-Famenne
Lens
Carvin
Hautmont
Bray
Montereau
Moret
Romilly
Mailly-le-Camp
Ste Menehould

BONN
Bad Godesberg
Koblenz
FRANKFURT
WIESBADEN
MAINZ
Darmstadt
BUNDESREPUBLIK
DEUTSCHLAND
NORDRHEIN
WESTFALEN
RHEINLAND
PFALZ
HESSEN
SAARLAND
LUXEMBOURG
Trier
SAARBRÜCKEN
Kaiserslautern
Ludwigshafen
MANNHEIM
HEIDELBERG
KARLSRUHE
Pforzheim
Baden-Baden
STRASBOURG
Offenburg
METZ
NANCY
MOSELLE
Thionville
Bad Kreuznach
Worms
Speyer
Landau
Pirmasens
Zweibrücken
Sarreguemines
Haguenau
Saverne
Lunéville
Toul
St Dié
Sélestat
Ribeauvillé
Gießen
Bad Homburg
Bad Nauheim
Limburg
Wissembourg
BADEN
WÜRTTEMBERG
Freudenstadt

A
B
C
18
1
2
3
4
24
Guernsey
St. Peter Port
Torquay
Plymouth
Cork
Batz
Roscoff
St Pol-de-Léon
Carantec
Brignogan-Plages
Plouescat
l'Aber-Wrac'h
Ploudalmézeau
Lannilis
le Folgoët
Lesneven
Plouzévédé
Landivisiau
Plabennec
St Thégonnec
Guimiliau
Lampaul
Ile d'Ouessant
Molène
le Conquet
Pnte de St Mathieu
St Renan
BREST
Guipavas
Landerneau
Sizun
Plougastel-Daoulas
Daoulas
Rumengol
Landévennec
le Faou
Camaret
Crozon
Morgat
Pnte de Penhir
Cap de la Chèvre
Ménez-Hom
Châteaulin
Pleyben
Monts d'Arrée
Brennilis
Huelgoat
FINISTERE
Douarnenez
Tréboul
I. de Sein
Pnte du Raz
Pont-Croix
Audierne
Locronan
Briec
Quimper
Plonéour-Lanvern
Pont-l'Abbé
St Guénolé
Pnte de Penmarch
Guilvinec
Loctudy
Bénodet
Fouesnant
Beg-Meil
Concarneau
Iles de Glénan
Rosporden
Pont-Aven
Riec
Moëlan
Port-Manech
Bannalec
Scaër
Coray
Châteauneuf-du-Faou
Montagnes Noires
Gourin
Carhaix-Plouguer
Quimperlé
Arzano
le Pouldu
Lorient
Larmor
Port-Louis
Groix
I. de Groix
Hennebont
Pont-Scorff
Plouay
le Faouët
Kernascléden
Guémené
Primel-Trégastel
Plougasnou
Locquirec
Lanmeur
Morlaix
Taulé
Plouigneau
Plougonven
Plestin
St Michel-en-G.
Tréguier
Trégastel
Ploumanach
Perros-Guirec
Pleumeur-Bodou
Trébeurden
Lannion
Lézardrieux
I. de Bréhat
Pnte de l'Arcouest
Paimpol
la Roche-Derrien
Pontrieux
Plouha
St Quay-Portrieux
Bégard
Lanvollon
Plouaret
Belle-Isle-en-Terre
Guingamp
Châtelaudren
Etables
Binic
Plouagat
St Brieuc
Bourbriac
Callac
CÔTES D'ARMOR
Quintin
St Nicolas-du-Pélem
Maël-Carhaix
Rostrenen
Corlay
Gouarec
Uzel
Mur-de-Bretagne
Loudéac
Plœuc
Moncontour
Collinée
Plouguenast
Lamballe
Jugon
Broons
Sables-d'Or
Erquy
Cap Fréhel
le Val-André
Pléneuf
Matignon
Merdrignac
la Chèze
la Trinité-Porhoët
Mauron
Cléguérec
Pontivy
Rohan
Josselin
Ploërmel
Malestroit
Bubry
Baud
Locminé
St Jean-Brévelay
MORBIHAN
Landes de Lanvaux
Pluvigner
Grd Champ
Ste Anne-d'A.
Elven
Auray
Vannes
Belz
Etel
Carnac
la Trinité
Locmariaquer
Port-Navalo
Sarzeau
St Gildas-de-Rhuys
St Pierre
Quiberon
Sauzon
le Palais
Belle-Ile
Houat
Hœdic
Questembert
Rochefort-en-T.
Muzillac
Damgan
la Roche-Bernard
Pénestin
Herbignac
Piriac
la Turballe
Guérande
le Croisic
Batz
le Pouliguen
la Baule
Pornichet
St NAZAIRE
Pnte de St Gildas
N 12-E 50
N 164
N 165-E 60
N 24
N 166
N 176
D 786
D 787
D 788
D 790
D 768
D 769
D 780
D 781
D 887
D 789
D 765
D 784
D 785
D 783
D 774
D 775
D 92

D
E
F
18
19
25
Cherbourg
Cap de la Hague
Nez de Jobourg
Cap Lévy
Pte de Barfleur
Barfleur
St Vaast-la-Hougue
Valognes
Montebourg
Ste Mère-Eglise
Carentan
Isigny
Grandcamp-Maisy
Port-en-Bessin
Arromanches
Courseulles
Luc
Ouistreham
Cabourg
Houlgate
Villers
Deauville
Trouville
Honfleur
LE HAVRE
Ste Adresse
Montivilliers
Etretat
Cap d'Antifer
Fécamp
Yport
Valmont
Bolbec
Lillebonne
Caudebec
Yvetot
St Valery-en-Caux
Veulettes
Cany Barville
Pont-Audemer
Jumièges
Bourg-Achard
St Helier
Gorey
Carteret
Barneville
Portbail
la Haye-du-Puits
Lessay
Périers
St Lô
MANCHE
Bayeux
CAEN
CALVADOS
Troarn
Dives
Lisieux
Pont-l'Evêque
Orbec
Bernay
Brionne
Coutances
Agon-Coutainville
St Malo-de-la-Lande
Montmartin
Bréhal
Granville
I. Chausey
Villedieu-les-Poêles
Percy
Vire
Condé-s-Noireau
Thury-Harcourt
Falaise
Vimoutiers
Gacé
l'Aigle
Flers
Argentan
Sées
Mortrée
ORNE
Domfront
Bagnoles-de-l'Orne
la Ferté-Macé
Carrouges
Alençon
Mortagne-au-Perche
Bellême
Nogent-le-Rotrou
Mamers
Avranches
le Mont-St Michel
Pontorson
St Hilaire-du-Harcouët
Mortain
St Malo
Dinard
Cancale
Dol-de-B.
Dinan
Combourg
Fougères
ILLE-ET-VILAINE
RENNES
Vitré
Châteaugiron
Janzé
Bain-de-Bretagne
Redon
Châteaubriant
Mayenne
MAYENNE
Laval
Evron
Ernée
Craon
Château-Gontier
Sablé
LE MANS
SARTHE
la Flèche
Château-du-Loir
Montoire
Vendôme
la Ferté-Bernard
Chinon
Saumur
ANGERS
MAINE-ET-LOIRE
Segré
Ancenis
NANTES
LOIRE-ATLANTIQUE
St Nazaire
Savenay
Tours
INDRE-ET-LOIRE
Château-Renault
Langeais
Azay-le-Rideau
Portsmouth
Rosslare
Cork
Poole

18
22
28
RENNES
Fougères
Vitré
Laval
Mayenne
Châteaubriant
Redon
Vannes
Auray
Pontivy
Ploërmel
Josselin
Quiberon
Locmariaquer
la Baule
Guérande
le Croisic
ST NAZAIRE
NANTES
ANGERS
Saumur
Cholet
Château-Gontier
Segré
Sablé
la Flèche
Ancenis
Clisson
Montaigu
Challans
Noirmoutier
Ile de Noirmoutier
Ile d'Yeu
St Jean-de-Monts
St Gilles-Croix-de-Vie
la Roche-s-Yon
les Sables-d'Olonne
Luçon
Fontenay-le-Comte
Bressuire
Parthenay
Thouars
Niort
Ile de Ré
LA ROCHELLE
Rochefort
Ile d'Oléron
Marennes
St Jean-d'Angély
Saintes
ILLE-ET-VILAINE
MAYENNE
MORBIHAN
LOIRE-ATLANTIQUE
MAINE-ET-LOIRE
VENDÉE
DEUX-SÈVRES
CHARENTE-MARITIME
A
B
C
2
3
4

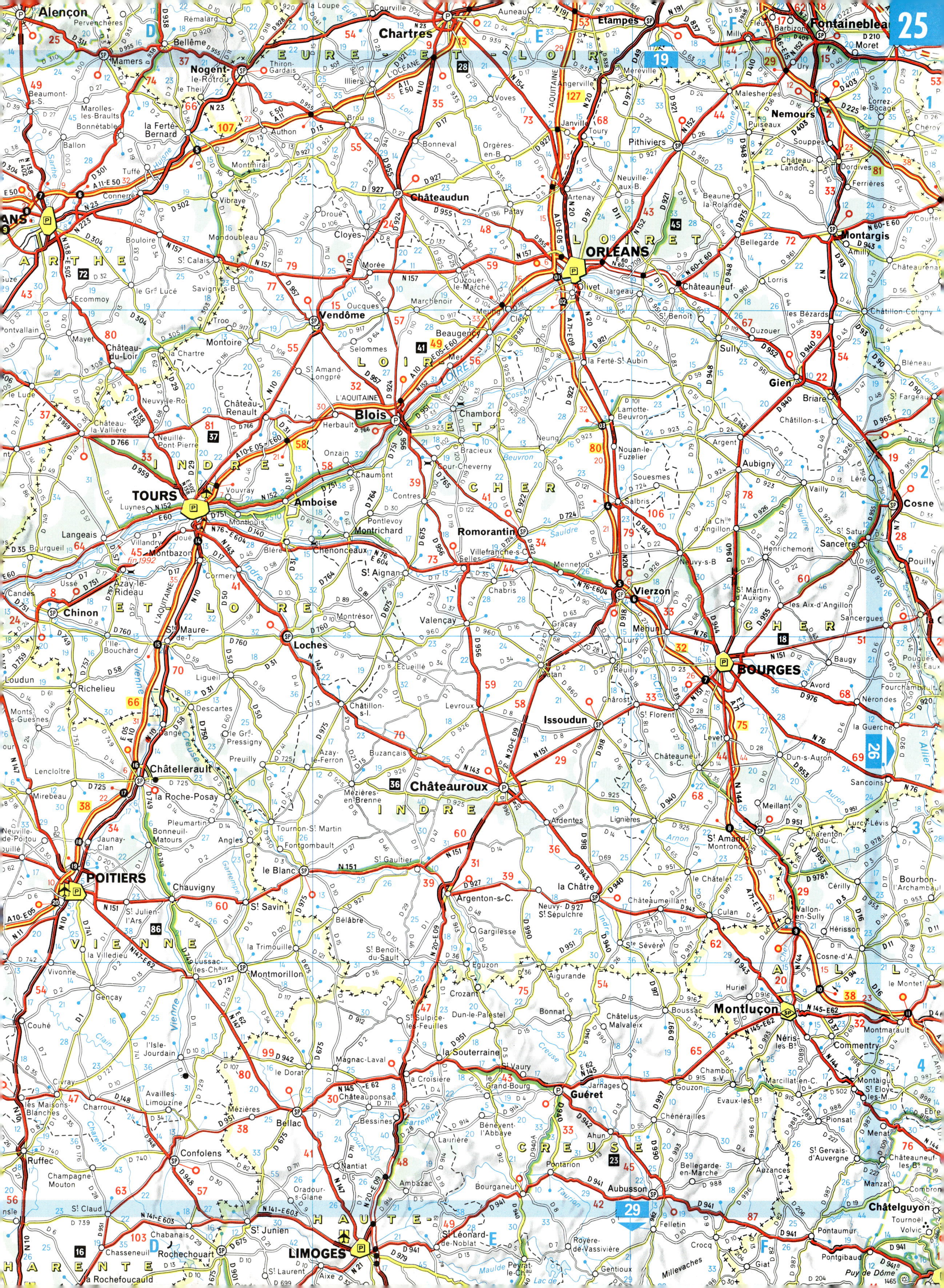

Alençon
Chartres
Étampes
Fontainebleau
Moret
Bellême
Mamers
Nogent-le-Rotrou
Illiers
Beaumont-s-S.
Marolles-les-Braults
Bonnétable
La Ferté-Bernard
Authon
Brou
Bonneval
Voves
Orgères-en-B.
Janville
Toury
Pithiviers
Malesherbes
Nemours
Puiseaux
Château-Landon
Dordives
Ferrières
Montargis
Amilly
Châteaudun
Patay
Artenay
Neuville-aux-B.
Beaune-la-Rolande
Bellegarde
Montmirail
Vibraye
Connerré
Droué
Cloyes
Mondoubleau
Morée
Ouzouer-le-Marché
Bouloire
St Calais
Savigny-s-B.
Le Gd Lucé
Ecommoy
Mayet
Château-du-Loir
La Chartre
Montoire
Troo
Vendôme
Oucques
Marchenoir
Beaugency
Meung
Cléry
Orléans
Olivet
Jargeau
Châteauneuf-s-L.
St Benoît
Sully
Lorris
Ouzouer
Les Bézards
Gien
Briare
Châtillon-Coligny
Bléneau
St Fargeau
Selommes
St Amand-Longpré
Château-Renault
Neuvy-le-Roi
Château-la-Vallière
Blois
Herbault
La Ferté-St Aubin
Chambord
Bracieux
Cour-Cheverny
Lamotte-Beuvron
Nouan-le-Fuzelier
Souesmes
Salbris
Neung
Aubigny
Argent
Châtillon-s-L.
Vailly
Léré
Cosne
Sancerre
St Satur
Henrichemont
Tours
Luynes
Joué
Vouvray
Amboise
Onzain
Chaumont
Pontlevoy
Montrichard
Contres
Romorantin
Villefranche-s-Ch.
Selles
Chabris
Menneto
Vierzon
Mehun
Neuvy-s-B.
La Chle d'Angillon
Les Aix-d'Angillon
Sancergues
St Martin-d'Auxigny
Bourges
Baugy
Avord
Nérondes
La Guerche
Langeais
Bourgueil
Villandry
Montbazon
Azay-le-Rideau
Ussé
Candes
Chinon
Bléré
Chenonceaux
St Aignan
Cormery
Loches
Montrésor
Valençay
Graçay
Lury
Reuilly
Vatan
Charost
Issoudun
St Florent
Levet
Dun-s-Auron
Sancoins
Ile-Bouchard
Richelieu
Loudun
Ste Maure-de-T.
Ligueil
Descartes
Écueillé
Levroux
Châtillon-s-I.
Buzançais
Châteauroux
Ardentes
Lignières
Châteauneuf-s-C.
Meillant
St Amand-Montrond
Charenton-du-C.
Lurcy-Lévis
Bourbon-l'Archambault
Dangé
Le Gd Pressigny
Preuilly
Azay-le-Ferron
Mézières-en-Brenne
Châtellerault
Lencloître
Mirebeau
La Roche-Posay
Pleumartin
Bonneuil-Matours
Tournon-St Martin
Fontgombault
Angles
Jaunay-Clan
Neuville-de-Poitou
Poitiers
Chauvigny
Le Blanc
St Gaultier
Argenton-s-C.
La Châtre
Neuvy-St Sépulchre
Châteaumeillant
Le Châtelet
Culan
Vallon-en-Sully
Cérilly
Hérisson
Cosne-d'A.
Le Montet
St Julien-l'Ars
St Savin
La Trimouille
Bélâbre
Gargilesse
St Benoît-du-Sault
Eguzon
Aigurande
Ste Sévère
Huriel
Montluçon
Néris-les-Bns
Commentry
Montmarault
Vivonne
Lussac-les-Châx
Montmorillon
Gençay
Couhé
L'Isle-Jourdain
Availles-Limouzine
Crozant
Dun-le-Palestel
St Sulpice-les-Feuilles
La Souterraine
Bonnat
Châtelus-Malvaleix
Boussac
Chambon-s-V.
Marcillat-en-C.
Montaigu
St Eloy-les-M.
Evaux-les-Bns
Magnac-Laval
Le Dorat
La Croisière
Grand-Bourg
Guéret
Jarnages
Gouzon
Chénérailles
Pionsat
Civray
Les Maisons-Blanches
Charroux
Mézières
Bellac
Châteauponsac
Bessines
Bénévent-l'Abbaye
Ahun
Bellegarde-en-Marche
Auzances
St Gervais-d'Auvergne
Ruffec
Champagne-Mouton
Confolens
Oradour-s-Glane
Nantiat
Ambazac
Bourganeuf
Pontarion
Aubusson
Menat
Châteauneuf-les-Bns
Manzat
Châtelguyon
Volvic
St Claud
Chabanais
Rochechouart
St Junien
Limoges
St Léonard-de-Noblat
Royère-de-Vassivière
Felletin
Crocq
Pontaumur
Pontgibaud
Chasseneuil
La Rochefoucauld
St Laurent
Aixe
Peyrat-le-Ch.
Gentioux
Millevaches
Giat
Puy de Dôme
EURE-ET-LOIR
LOIRET
LOIR-ET-CHER
INDRE-ET-LOIRE
INDRE
CHER
VIENNE
CREUSE
ALLIER
HAUTE-VIENNE
SARTHE
CHARENTE
L'AQUITAINE
L'OCÉANE

TROYES
Sens
Auxerre
YONNE
Chaumont
HAUTE-MARNE
Langres
Montargis
Joigny
Tonnerre
Châtillon-s-S.
Cosne
Clamecy
Vézelay
Avallon
DIJON
CÔTE-D'OR
Saulieu
Nevers
NIÈVRE
La Charité
Autun
Beaune
Chalon-s-S.
Dole
Le Creusot
Montceau-les-Mines
SAÔNE-ET-LOIRE
Moulins
Tournus
Lons-le-Saunier
Paray-le-Monial
Mâcon
Bourg-en-Bresse
VICHY
Roanne
RHÔNE
Villefranche-s-Saône
Thiers
Riom
CLERMONT-FERRAND
LYON

Vittel
Epinal
VOSGES
Remiremont
Gérardmer
Plombières
Luxeuil
Ribeauvillé
COLMAR
FREIBURG
Emmendingen
Villingen-
Schwenningen
Donaueschingen
Mulhouse
MULHOUSE
Thann
Belfort
Vesoul
HTE SAÔNE
Montbéliard
BASEL
Lörrach
Rheinfelden
Säckingen
Waldshut
Winterthur
ZÜRICH
Baden
Brugg
Aarau
Olten
AARGAU
Delémont
Porrentruy
JURA
Solothurn
Grenchen
Biel/ Bienne
La Chaux-de-Fonds
Le Locle
BESANÇON
DOUBS
Pontarlier
Neuchâtel
BERN
LUZERN
Zug
SCHWEIZ
UNTERWALDEN
Thun
Interlaken
Grindelwald
Fribourg
Yverdon-les-Bains
LAUSANNE
VAUD
SUISSE
Montreux
Vevey
Evian
Thonon
LAC LÉMAN
Gstaad
Sion
Sierre
Martigny
VALAIS
Zermatt
M. CERVINO MATTERHORN
MONTE ROSA
Brig
Simplonpass
Domodossola
GENÈVE
Annemasse
Morzine
Chamonix
Megève
Sallanches
ANNECY
HAUTE-SAVOIE
Aix-les-Bains
Albertville
Courmayeur
Aosta/Aoste
VALLE D'AOSTA
Biella
St. Claude
Champagnole
Arbois
JURA

24
25
36
37
CHARENTE-MARITIME
CHARENTE
GIRONDE
DORDOGNE
LOT-ET-GARONNE
LANDES
GERS
PYRÉNÉES
Royan
Saintes
Cognac
Angoulême
Jarnac
Pons
Barbezieux
La Rochefoucauld
Rochechouart
Marennes
Saujon
Pte de la Coubre
Pte de Grave
le Verdon
Soulac
Meschers
Mortagne
Jonzac
Mirambeau
Montendre
Montlieu
Montguyon
Chalais
Aubeterre
Ribérac
Brantôme
Nontron
Périgueux
Mussidan
Bergerac
Ste-Foy-la-Grande
Lesparre-Médoc
Pauillac
Blaye
St Laurent-Médoc
Hourtin
Carcans
Lacanau
Lacanau-Océan
Castelnau-de-Médoc
St André-de-Cubzac
Libourne
St Emilion
Coutras
Castillon-la-Bataille
Bordeaux
Mérignac
Arcachon
Cap Ferret
Pyla
Pilat-Plage
la Teste
Andernos
Audenge
Créon
Cadillac
Langon
Podensac
la Réole
Marmande
Duras
Tonneins
Villeneuve-s-Lot
Fumel
Aiguillon
Agen
Nérac
Lavardac
Casteljaloux
Bazas
Villandraut
St Symphorien
Belin-Béliet
Sanguinet
Biscarrosse
Biscarrosse-Plage
Parentis-en-Born
Pissos
Sore
Mimizan
Mimizan-Plage
Labouheyre
Sabres
Morcenx
Lit-et-Mixe
St Girons-Plage
Léon
Castets
Vieux-Boucau
Soustons
Hossegor
Capbreton
Dax
Tartas
Mont-de-Marsan
Roquefort
Gabarret
Eauze
Condom
Lectoure
Fleurance
Auch
Vic-Fézensac
Nogaro
Aire-s-l'Adour
St Sever
Grenade
Hagetmau
Orthez
Peyrehorade
Bayonne
Biarritz
Anglet
Bidart
Guéthary
Hendaye
St Jean-Pied-de-Port
Cambo-les-Bains
Ustaritz
Hasparren
Salies-de-Béarn
Sauveterre-de-B.
Mauléon-Licharre
Oloron-Ste Marie
Pau
Lescar
Morlaàs
Tarbes
Rabastens-de-Bigorre
Vic-en-Bigorre
Maubourguet
Mirande
Masseube
Castelnau-Magnoac
Lannemezan
Riscle
Plaisance
Marciac
Miélan
Barbotan
Cazaubon
Villeneuve-de-M.
Mézin
Gironde
Dordogne
Garonne
Charente
Adour
Midouze
Isle
Gers
Lot

LIMOGES
CLERMONT-FERRAND
Riom
Thiers
Royat
le Mont-Dore
la Bourboule
Issoire
Ussel
Tulle
Uzerche
Brive-la-Gaillarde
Brioude
le Puy en-Velay
St Flour
Aurillac
Sarlat-la-Canéda
Rocamadour
Figeac
Cahors
Decazeville
Villefranche-de-Rouergue
Rodez
Espalion
Marvejols
Mende
Florac
Millau
Montauban
Albi
Carmaux
Castres
Mazamet
TOULOUSE
Muret
Castelnaudary
CARCASSONNE
Narbonne
Béziers
Sète
Agde
Lodève
Le Vigan
Ganges
MONTPELLIER
Castelsarrasin
Gaillac
Lacaune
Meyrueis
Ambert
CORRÈZE
PUY-DE-DÔME
CANTAL
LOT
AVEYRON
LOZÈRE
TARN
HÉRAULT
HAUTE-GARONNE
HAUTE-LOIRE

CLERMONT-FERRAND
LYON
Vienne
St ETIENNE
Montbrison
Issoire
Brioude
le Puy en-Velay
Yssingeaux
Annonay
Tournon-s-R.
Romans
Valence
Privas
Aubenas
Montélimar
Mende
Marvejols
Millau
Alès
Orange
Carpentras
AVIGNON
NÎMES
Arles
Salon
Aix-en-Provence
MARSEILLE
MONTPELLIER
Sète
Béziers
Lodève
Le Vigan
Florac
Uzès
Crest
Die
Voiron
Bourgoin-Jallieu
Firminy
Valras-Plage
Narbonne-Plage
Palavas
Aigues-Mortes
Stes Maries-de-la-Mer
Martigues
Cassis
La Ciotat
Aubagne
Bandol
LOIRE
PUY-DE-DÔME
HAUTE-LOIRE
ARDÈCHE
LOZÈRE
GARD
DRÔME
VAUCLUSE
ISÈRE
HÉRAULT
BOUCHES-DU-RHÔNE
Mt Lozère
Mt Ventoux
Mt Aigoual
Mt Mézenc
Monts du Forez
Cévennes
Rhône
A
B
C
1
2
3
4
26
29
32

Aosta/Aoste
Albertville
Chambéry
Bourg-St Maurice
Val d'Isère
Courchevel
Col de l'Iseran
Col du Mt Cenis
Gran Paradiso
Biella
Ivrea
Novara
Vercelli
Chivasso
Vigevano
Casale Monferrato
Susa
Modane
TORINO
Moncalieri
Chieri
Asti
Alessandria
Valenza
L'Alpe-d'Huez
Col du Galibier
Col du Lautaret
Briançon
Sestriere
Pinerolo
Carmagnola
Bra
Alba
Acqui-Terme
Novi Ligure
Saluzzo
Savigliano
Fossano
Mondovì
Cuneo
Ceva
Savona
Varazze
Gap
Embrun
Guillestre
Barcelonnette
Col de Larche
Col de Vars
Sisteron
Digne-les-Bains
Castellane
Grasse
Vence
NICE
Antibes
CANNES
Juan-les-Pins
Menton
Monte-Carlo-Monaco
Beaulieu
Villefranche-s-Mer
Ventimiglia
Bordighera
San Remo
Imperia (Porto-Maurizio)
Alassio
Albenga
Finale Ligure
Col de Tende
Draguignan
Fréjus
St Raphaël
Ste Maxime
St Tropez
Hyères
TOULON
le Lavandou
Cavalaire
Bormes
Brignoles
St Maximin-la-Ste Baume
FRANCE
ALPES DE HTE-PROVENCE
ALPES-MARITIMES
VAR
SAVOIE
PIEMONTE
ALPES
Massif des Maures
Cap Camarat
I. du Levant
Lérins

TOULOUSE
MONTPELLIER
Béziers
CARCASSONNE
Narbonne
PERPIGNAN
Andorra la Vella
BARCELONA
Girona Gerona
Figueres/Figueras
Manresa
Sabadell
Terrassa/Tarrasa
Mataró
Badalona
Sète
Agde
Castres
Mazamet
Lodève
Pamiers
Foix
Limoux
Castelnaudary
Quillan
Prades
Céret
Font-Romeu
Puigcerdà
La Seu d'Urgell
Vich/Vic
Ripoll
Olot
Banyoles
Palafrugell
S. Feliu de Guíxols
Sitges
Vilanova i la Geltrú
Castelldefels
El Prat de Llobregat
Collioure
Port-Vendres
Banyuls
Cerbère
Portbou
Argelès
Canet-Plage
Port-Leucate
Port-Barcarès
Valras-Plage
Narbonne-Plage
Gruissan
Sigean
Port-la-Nouvelle
Palavas
Frontignan
Pézenas
Bédarieux
Lamalou
Revel
Mirepoix
Lavelanet
Tarascon
Ax-les-Thermes
Rivesaltes
Elne
Amélie-les-Bs-Palalda
Prats-de-Mollo
Roses
L'Escala
Palamós
Tossa
Lloret de Mar
Blanes
Calella
Arenys de Mar
Granollers
Igualada
Montserrat
Solsona
Berga
Cardona
Balaguer
Serra del Cadí
CATALUÑA
PYRÉNÉES-OR
AUDE
HÉRAULT
HAUTE-GARONNE
ARIÈGE
TARN
Montagne Noire
Monts de Lacaune
GOLFE
Costa Brava
Genova
Pic Carlit
Pic d'Estats
Pic du Canigou
Col de Puymorens
Golfo de Roses
E. d'Oliana
E. de Boadella
ESTAQUE
AUTRES BASSINS
BASSIN NATIONAL
BASSIN D'ARENC
PORT
MODERNE
BASSIN DE LA GRANDE JOLIETTE
Parc du Pharo
Vallon des Auffes
ST-LAMBERT
ENDOUME
CORNICHE
CHATEAU D'IF
A
B
C
29
37

NÎMES
Arles
Aix-en-Provence
MARSEILLE
TOULON
Hyères
Draguignan
Grasse
Fréjus
St Raphaël
St Tropez
Salon
Istres
Martigues
Aubagne
Cassis
la Ciotat
Bandol
Brignoles
Manosque
BOUCHES-DU-RHÔNE
VAR
LION
Iles d'Hyères
Marseille
CORSE
HAUTE-CORSE
CORSE-DU-SUD
Bastia
Calvi
Corte
Ajaccio
Propriano
Sartène
Porto-Vecchio
Bonifacio
Cap Corse
Bocche di Bonifacio
Arcipelago della Maddalena

A
B
C
Cabo Prior
Ferrol
Cedeira
Ortigueira
Viveiro
Burela
Foz
Ribadeo
Navia
A CORUÑA/
LA CORUÑA
Cabo de S. Adrián
Malpica
Betanzos
Pontedeume
As Pontes de García Rodríguez
Mondoñedo
Villalba
Cabo Vilán
Camariñas
Muxía
Carballo
Ordes
Corcubión
Cabo Fisterra
Lugo
Tambre
Negreira
SANTIAGO DE COMPOSTELA
Melide
Muros
Noia
Padrón
Fonsagrada
A S T
Becerreá
Sarriá
Monterroso
Lalín
Silleda
Vilagarcía de Arosa
Cambados
Caldas de Reis
G A L I C I A
Chantada
Pontevedra
Sanxenxo
Marín
Cangas
Islas Cíes
VIGO
Redondela
Monforte de Lemos
Ponferrada
Villafranca del Bierzo
O Barco
Ourense/
Orense
Ribadavia
Baiona
Cabo Silleiro
Porriño
Tui
Valença do Minho
Celanova
Xinzo de Limia
Verín
Puebla de Sanabria
A Gudiña
Sierra de la
Viana do Castelo
Ponte de Lima
M I N H O
Chaves
Bragança
Braga
Barcelos
Guimarães
Póvoa de Varzim
Vila do Conde
T R A S
O S
M O N T E S
Mirandela
Vila Real
Amarante
Penafiel
Matosinhos
PORTO
Vila Nova de Gaia
Espinho
Peso da Régua
Lamego
D O U R O
RIO DOURO
38
Macedo de Cavaleiros
Mogadouro
Rio Sabor
Torre de Moncorvo

Modifications en cours dans la numérotation des routes
The numbering of roads is subject to modification
Se está cambiando la numeración de las carreteras
D
E
F
Costa Verde
Gijón
Avilés
OVIEDO
Mieres
SANTANDER
Torrelavega
PICOS DE EUROPA
CANTABRIA
LEÓN
Astorga
La Bañeza
Benavente
Zamora
Toro
Tordesillas
VALLADOLID
Palencia
BURGOS
Aranda de Duero
Medina del Campo
Sahagún
Aguilar de Campóo
Reinosa
Llanes
Ribadesella
Cangas de Onís
Covadonga
Cabo de Peñas
Cabo Vidio
Cudillero
Luarca
CASTILLA-LEÓN
Peñafiel
Lerma
Simancas
Villalpando
Valencia de Don Juan
Carrión de los Condes
Osorno
Cervera de Pisuerga
Guardo
Cistierna
Riaño
Embalse del Ebro
Duero
39
40
36

SANTANDER
A
B
C
GOLFO DE
Laredo
Castro Urdiales
Santoña
Bermeo
Algorta
BILBAO
Baracaldo
Gernika-Lumo
Durango
Eibar
Zarautz
DONOSTIA-S. SEBASTIÁN
Hendaye
Irun
St Jean-de-Luz
BIARRITZ
Bayonne
Tolosa
Beasain
Zumárraga
Oñati
VITORIA-GASTEIZ
PAÍS VASCO/EUSKADI
Orduña
Miranda de Ebro
Pancorbo
Briviesca
BURGOS
Haro
Santo Domingo de la Calzada
Nájera
Logroño
Estella
PAMPLONA IRUÑEA
NAVARRA
Tafalla
Olite
Calahorra
LA RIOJA
Arnedo
Alfaro
Tudela
Tarazona
Borja
Agreda
Soria
Numancia
El Burgo de Osma
Aranda de Duero
Lerma
Covarrubias
Santo Domingo de Silos
Almazán
Medinaceli
Sigüenza
Calatayud
Ateca
Daroca
Atienza
Riaza
Ayllón
Sepúlveda
Boceguillas
ESPAÑA
GUADARRAMA
Sierra de la Demanda
Montes de Oca
Peñas de Cervera
Sierra de Urbión
Sierra del Moncayo
Sierra de Ayllón
Río Ebro
Río Duero
Río Arlanza
Río Aragón
Río Jalón
35
40

37
28
29
32
41
TOULOUSE
Auch
PAU
Tarbes
LOURDES
Bagnères-de-B.gorre
Cauterets
S! Gaudens
S! Girons
B.-de-Luchon
Orthez
Oloron-Ste Marie
Mauléon-Licharre
Lannemezan
Mirande
Muret
Vielha
Andorra la Vella
La Seu d'Urgell
Jaca
Sabiñánigo
Huesca
Barbastro
Monzón
Binéfar
Fraga
Lleida Lérida
Balaguer
Tremp
Tàrrega
Valls
Reus
Tarragona
ZARAGOZA
Caspe
Alcañiz
Ejea de los Caballeros
Monte Perdido
Pico de Aneto
MALADETA
Pic d'Estats
Parque Nacional de Ordesa
Puerto de Somport
P Y R É N É E S
A R A G Ó N
C A T A L U N Y A
G E R S
HAUTE-GARONNE
A R I È G E
EBRO
Rio Cinca
Segre

34
42
Espinho
Ovar
Aveiro
Ílhavo
Agueda
Viseu
Mangualde
Lamego
Guarda
Seia
Gouveia
Manteigas
Covilhã
Fundão
Belmonte
Castelo Branco
Mira
Cantanhede
Figueira da Foz
COIMBRA
Lousã
Góis
Pombal
Leiria
Marinha Grande
Batalha
Nazaré
Alcobaça
Fátima
Tomar
Abrantes
Óbidos
Peniche
Caldas da Rainha
Santarém
Torres Vedras
Ericeira
Mafra
Sintra
Cascais
Estoril
LISBOA
Almada
Barreiro
Montijo
Setúbal
Sesimbra
Vila Franca de Xira
Coruche
Montemor-o-Novo
Vendas Novas
Évora
Estremoz
Elvas
Portalegre
Castelo de Vide
Marvão
Ponte de Sor
Alcácer do Sal
Olivenza
Cabo da Roca
Cabo Espichel
Cabo Carvoeiro
Ilha Berlenga
BEIRA ALTA
BEIRA LITORAL
BEIRA BAIXA
ESTREMADURA
RIBATEJO
PORTUGAL
SERRA DA ESTRELA
Rio Douro
Rio Mondego
Rio Tejo
Rio Sorraia
Rio Zêzere
Rio Sado
A
B
C
1
2
3
4

35
40
43
SALAMANCA
Ávila
Plasencia
Cáceres
Mérida
Talavera de la Reina
Navalmoral de la Mata
Trujillo
Guadalupe
Béjar
Ciudad Rodrigo
Medina del Campo
Arévalo
Peñaranda de Bracamonte
Almendralejo
Don Benito
Villanueva de la Serena
Coria
Alcántara
Almadén
Cabeza del Buey
Castuera
Miajadas
Oropesa
Vitigudino
Ledesma
Alba de Tormes
Piedrahita
Arenas de S. Pedro
Jaraíz
Jarandilla de la Vera
Candeleda
Logrosán
Herrera del Duque
Puebla de Alcocer
Siruela
Zalamea de la Serena
Montijo
Lobón
Villafranca de los Barros
Sierra de Gredos
Sierra de Gata
Sierra de Francia
Sierra de Ávila
Sierra de Guadalupe
Montes de Toledo
Peña de Francia
Pico Almanzor
Río Tormes
Río Tiétar
Río Alagón
Río Guadiana
Río Alberche
Embalse de Alcántara
Embalse de Valdecañas
Embalse de Orellana
Embalse de la Serena
Embalse de Gabriel y Galán
Embalse de Cíjara
Embalse de García de Sola
E X T R E M A D U R A

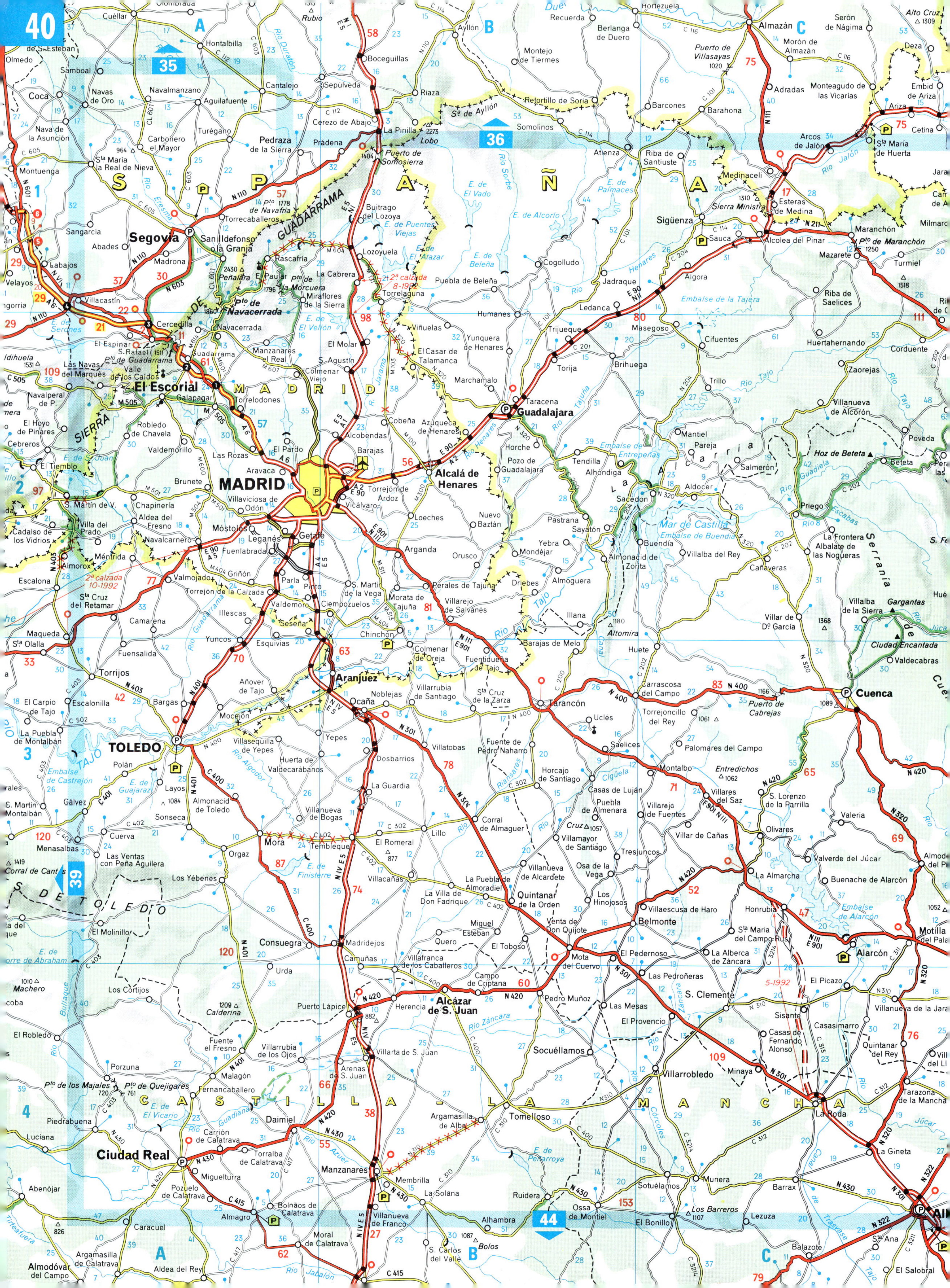
MADRID
Segovia
El Escorial
Guadalajara
Alcalá de Henares
Aranjuez
TOLEDO
Cuenca
Ciudad Real
Alcázar de S. Juan
Tomelloso
Manzanares
Valdepeñas
Consuegra
Madridejos
Ocaña
Tarancón
Belmonte
La Roda
Sigüenza
Almazán
Medinaceli
Arcos de Jalón
Alcolea del Pinar
Sepúlveda
Riaza
Cuéllar
Coca
Villacastín
Cercedilla
Navacerrada
Colmenar Viejo
Torrelaguna
Buitrago del Lozoya
Getafe
Leganés
Móstoles
Fuenlabrada
Torrejón de Ardoz
Arganda
Chinchón
Illescas
Torrijos
Maqueda
Orgaz
Mora
Daimiel
Almagro
Villarrobledo
Socuéllamos
Quintanar de la Orden
Mota del Cuervo
S. Clemente
Alarcón
Motilla del Palancar
Priego
Sacedón
Pastrana
Brihuega
Torija
Cifuentes
Atienza
Ayllón
Boceguillas
Pto de Somosierra
Pto de Navacerrada
Pto de Navafría
Pto de los Leones
Pto Lápice
Pto de Maranchón
Ciudad Encantada
Mar de Castilla
Embalse de Entrepeñas
Embalse de Buendía
Embalse de Alarcón
S I E R R A D E G U A D A R R A M A
M A D R I D
C A S T I L L A - L A M A N C H A
S D E T O L E D O
Rio Tajo
Rio Jarama
Rio Henares
Rio Guadiana
35
36
39
44

Lleida/Lérida
Fraga
Zaidín
Alcarràs
Soses
Seròs
Castelldans
Candasnos
Bujaraloz
Torrente de Cinca
Mequinenza
Embalse de Riba-roja
Embalse de Mequinenza
Maials
Granadella
Flix
La Bisbal de Falset
Fayón
Nonaspe
Caspe
Escatrón
Sástago
Río Ebro
Azaila
Gelsa
Quinto
Pina
Osera de Ebro
Fuentes de Ebro
Belchite
Fuendetodos
Villanueva del Huerva
Cariñena
Longares
Muel
La Muela
La Almunia de Doña Godina
Morata de Jalón
Ricla
Calatorao
Illueca
Brea
Villarroya de la Sierra
Cervera de la Cañada
Calatayud
Ateca
Paracuellos de Jiloca
Maluenda
Codos
Almonacid de la Sierra
Nuévalos
Monasterio de Piedra
Miedes
Mainar
Pto de Paniza
Herrera
Badules
Daroca
Azuara
Moyuela
Lécera
La Puebla de Híjar
Híjar
Samper de Calanda
Albalate del Arzobispo
Muniesa
Oliete
Ariño
Andorra
Alloza
Alcañiz
Alto del Portalet
Maella
Fabara
Batea
La Pobla de Massaluca
Gandesa
Móra d'Ebre
Móra la Nova
Falset
El Pinell de Brai
Rasquera
Tivissa
Vandellòs
Prat de Comte
Calaceite
Valjunquera
Valderrobres
Beceite
Arnes
Xerta
Tivenys
El Perelló
Tortosa
L'Ampolla
L'Aldea
La Cava
Amposta
S. Carles de la Ràpita
Alcanar
Ulldecona
La Sénia
Rosell
Traiguera
Vinaròs
Benicarló
Peñíscola
Càlig
La Jana
S. Mateo
Tirig
Chert
Morella
Pto de Torre Miró
Pto de Las Cabrillas
Forcall
Olocau del Rey
Cinctorres
Ares
Villafranca del Cid
Benasal
Albocácer
Cuevas de Vinromá
Alcalà de Chivert
Sta Magdalena de Pulpis
Torreblanca
Alcocéber
Cabanes
Oropesa
Benicasim
Castelló de la Plana / Castellón de la Plana
El Grau
Almazora
Vila-real
Burriana
Nules
Moncófar
Onda
Borriol
Vall d'Alba
Villafamés
Lucena del Cid
Peñagolosa
Adzaneta
Vistabella del Maestrazgo
Mosqueruela
Linares de Mora
Valdelinares
Peñarroya
Alcalá de la Selva
Mora de Rubielos
Rubielos de Mora
Sarrión
Manzanera
Javalambre
La Puebla de Valverde
Teruel
Cella
Villarquemado
Sta Eulalia
Torre la Cárcel
Monreal del Campo
Caminreal
Calamocha
Bello
Burbáguena
Fonfría
Segura de los Baños
Vivel del Río Martín
Montalbán
Utrillas
Ejulve
Aliaga
Camarillas
Alcorisa
Calanda
Mas de las Matas
Castellote
Aguaviva
Monroyo
Cantavieja
Villarroya de los Pinares
Allepuz
Escorihuela
Aguilar del Alfambra
Perales del Alfambra
Alfambra
Cedrillas
Albarracín
Bronchales
Orea
Noguera
Guadalaviar
Frías de Albarracín
Terriente
Bezas
Villel
Cañigral
Torre Baja
Ademuz
Salvacañete
Huérguina
Cañete
Landete
Sta Cruz de Moya
Talayuelas
Aras de Alpuente
Titaguas
La Yesa
Abejuela
Torrijas
Barracas
Montanejos
Fuentes de Ayódar
Caudiel
Jérica
Viver
Segorbe
Altura
Alcublas
Chelva
Villar del Arzobispo
Casinos
Sinarcas
Aliaguilla
Mira
Camporrobles
Utiel
Requena
Minglanilla
Villargordo de Cabriel
Villalpardo
Chera
Pedralba
Llíria
Benaguasil
Villamarchante
Bétera
Serra
Sagunto
El Puerto de Sagunto
Puçol
Massamagrell
Burjassot
Manises
Cheste
Chiva
Buñol
Torrent
VALENCIA
El Grao
El Saler
La Albufera
El Perelló
Silla
Catarroja
Picassent
Turís
Montserrat
Benifaió
Sollana
Alginet
Carlet
L'Alcudia
Guadassuar
Algemesí
Sueca
Cullera
Alzira
Favareta
Alberique
Carcaixent
La Pobla Llarga
Tabernes de Valldigna
Xeresa
Gandía
Playa de Gandía
Daimuz
Piles
Oliva
Xàtiva
Canals
Enguera
Navarrés
Millares
Cofrentes
Jarafuel
Ayora
Alatoz
Casas de Juan Núñez
Alcalá del Júcar
Alborea
Casas Ibáñez
Villatoya
Mahora
Ledaña
Higueruela
Alpera
Chinchilla de Monte Aragón
Cuerda
Pelado
Cardenete
Enguídanos
GOLFO DE VALENCIA
Costa del Azahar
Islas Baleares
I. Columbretes
VALENCIA

38
A
B
C
1
2
3
4
A L E N T E J O
A L G A R V E
Alcácer do Sal
Grândola
Sines
Cabo de Sines
Santiago do Cacém
Ferreira do Alentejo
Beja
Serpa
Moura
Aljustrel
Castro Verde
Ourique
Odemira
Almodôvar
Mértola
Monchique
Aljezur
Lagos
Portimão
Silves
Albufeira
Loulé
Faro
Olhão
Tavira
Vila Real de Sto António
Ayamonte
Isla Cristina
Lepe
Huelva
Punta Umbría
Moguer
Palos de la Frontera
Valverde del Camino
Aracena
Rosal de la Frontera
Sagres
Vila do Bispo
Cabo de Sta Maria
Reguengos de Monsaraz
Vidigueira
Portel
Odivelas
Rio Guadiana
Golfo de Cádiz
ILHA DE PORTO SANTO
Porto Santo
ARQUIPÉLAGO DA MADEIRA
Porto Moniz
Santana
Pico Ruivo
Funchal
Desertas
ILHA DA MADEIRA
1/2750000
1/2750000
O C E A N O A T L A N T I C O
I S L A S C A N A R I A S
LANZAROTE
Haría
Teguise
Arrecife
Parque Nacional de Timanfaya
Playa Blanca
Corralejo
FUERTEVENTURA
La Oliva
Puerto del Rosario
Betancuria
Pájara
Tuineje
Gran Tarajal
Punta de Jandía
TENERIFE
La Laguna
Sta Cruz de Tenerife
Puerto de la Cruz
Icod de los Vinos
La Orotava
Güimar
Teide
Parque Nacional del Teide
Guía de Isora
Granadilla de Abona
Los Cristianos
LAS PALMAS DE GRAN CANARIA
Gáldar
Arucas
Telde
Cruz de Tejeda
Maspalomas
S. Nicolás de Tolentino
GRAN CANARIA
LA PALMA
Barlovento
Puntagorda
Los Sauces
Parque Nacional de la Caldera de Taburiente
Sta Cruz de la Palma
Los Llanos de Aridane
Fuencaliente
GOMERA
Vallehermoso
Hermigua
Garajonay (Parque Nacional)
S. Sebastián
HIERRO
Valverde
Frontera
Puerto de la Estaca
Cádiz
Cap Juby
Tarfaya
AFRIQUE
A
B
C

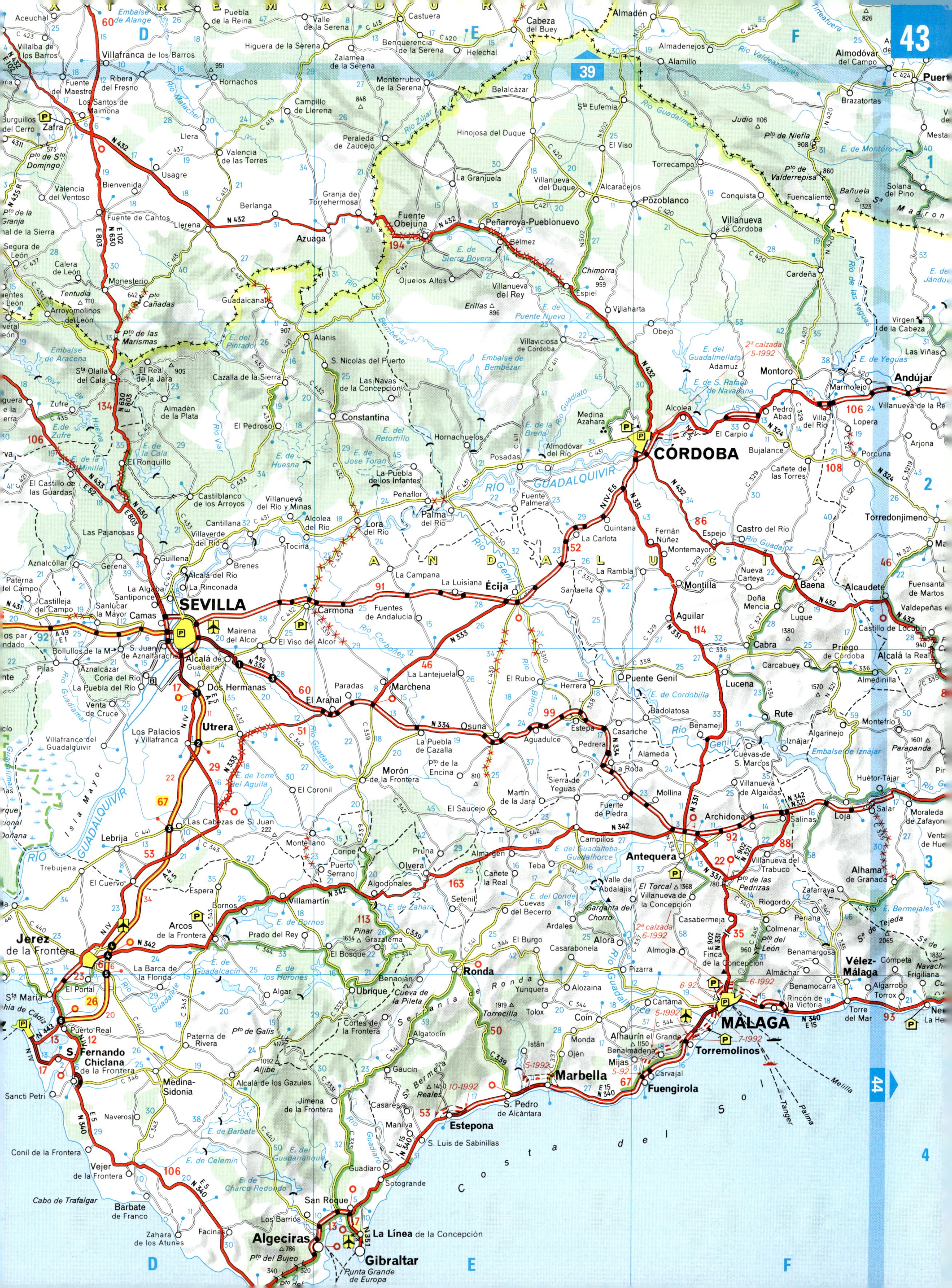
E X T R E M A D U R A
A N D A L U C I A
39
44
D
E
F
1
2
3
4
SEVILLA
CÓRDOBA
MÁLAGA
Jerez de la Frontera
Algeciras
Gibraltar
La Línea de la Concepción
Marbella
Fuengirola
Torremolinos
Estepona
Ronda
Antequera
Écija
Carmona
Utrera
Dos Hermanas
Osuna
Lucena
Puente Genil
Cabra
Baena
Montilla
Aguilar
Andújar
Montoro
Zafra
Llerena
Azuaga
Fuente Obejuna
Peñarroya-Pueblonuevo
Pozoblanco
Villanueva de Córdoba
Almadén
Constantina
Lora del Río
Palma del Río
Marchena
Morón de la Frontera
Lebrija
Arcos de la Frontera
Medina-Sidonia
Chiclana de la Frontera
S. Fernando
Vejer de la Frontera
Barbate de Franco
Tarifa
Vélez-Málaga
Loja
Archidona
Priego de Córdoba
Alcalá la Real
Estepa
Río Guadalquivir
Río Genil
Costa del Sol
Cabo de Trafalgar
Punta Grande de Europa
Melilla
Tánger
Isla Mayor

Puertollano
Valdepeñas
Calzada de Calatrava
Moral de Calatrava
Villanueva de los Infantes
Villahermosa
Montiel
Alcaraz
Robledo
Balazote
Chinchilla de Monte Aragón
Pozo Cañada
Tobarra
Hellín
Sª de Alcaraz
Riópar
Elche de la Sierra
Yeste
Andújar
Bailén
Linares
La Carolina
Desfiladero de Despeñaperros
Baeza
Úbeda
Villacarrillo
Cazorla
Sª de Cazorla
Sª de Segura
Siles
Segura de la Sierra
Santiago de la Espada
Caravaca de la Cruz
Cehegín
Calasparra
Moratalla
Bullas
MURCIA
Jaén
Martos
Alcalá la Real
Huéscar
Puebla de Don Fadrique
Vélez Rubio
Vélez Blanco
Lorca
Puerto Lumbreras
Huércal-Overa
Baza
Guadix
GRANADA
Santa Fe
Loja
Pico Veleta
Mulhacén
SIERRA NEVADA
Alpujarras
Lanjarón
Órjiva
Motril
Salobreña
Almuñécar
Nerja
Berja
Adra
El Ejido
Roquetas de Mar
ALMERÍA
Sierra de Gádor
Sierra de los Filabres
Tabernas
Sorbas
Níjar
Mojácar
Vera
Garrucha
Carboneras
Cabo de Gata
Golfo de Almería
Genova
Palma
Melilla
Costa del Sol

MURCIA
ALICANTE
Elx/Elche
Cartagena
Benidorm
Alcoy
Elda
Novelda
Orihuela
Torrevieja
Gandia
Denia
Jávea
Villena
Yecla
Jumilla
Almansa
Cieza
Archena
Mula
Alcantarilla
Calpe
Altea
Villajoyosa
Cocentaina
Ontinyent
Oliva
Crevillente
Sta Pola
Isla de Tabarca
Guardamar del Segura
S. Pedro del Pinatar
Santiago de la Ribera
Los Alcázares
Mar Menor
la Manga del Mar Menor
Cabo de Palos
La Unión
Portman
Escombreras
Mazarrón
Puerto de Mazarrón
Golfo de Mazarrón
Cabo Tiñoso
Cabo Cope
Cabo de S. Antonio
Cabo de la Nao
Moraira
Pta de Moraira
Peñón de Ifach
Costa Blanca
MENORCA
Ciutadella de Menorca
Mercadal
Fornells
Monte Toro
Ferreries
Alaior
Maó / Mahón
Cabo de Artruix
Cala Sta Galdana
Cala'n Porter
San Luis
Pta Esperó
I. del Aire
MALLORCA
Cabo Formentor
Pollença
Puerto de Pollença
Alcudia
Puerto de Alcudia
Sa Calobra
Puig Major
Puerto de Sóller
Sóller
Deià
Valldemossa
Banyalbufar
Esporles
Inca
Sa Pobla
Sta Margarita
Artà
Cala Ratjada
Cuevas de Artà
Sineu
Petra
Son Servera
Manacor
Porto Cristo
Cuevas del Drac
PALMA
Bellver
Andratx
Paguera
Puerto de Andratx
I. Dragonera
Sta Ponsa
El Arenal
Algaida
Montuiri
Llucmajor
Felanitx
S. Salvador
Campos
Santanyi
Cala d'Or
Porto Petro
Cabo Blanc
Cabo Salinas
I. de Cabrera
Genova
Sète
Málaga (Cádiz, I. Canarias)
Barcelona
Valencia
IBIZA
Cala de Portinatx
S. Juan Bautista
S. Miguel
Furnás
S. Antonio Abad
Sta Eulalia del Rio
S. José
Atalayassa
Eivissa/Ibiza
I. Vedrá
Denia
Alicante
Formentera
S. Francisco Javier
El Caló
Pta Rotja
Cabo de Berbería

Hamburg
0
3 km
KIEL
FLENSBURG KIEL
LÜBECK
LANGENHORN
SCHNELSEN
NIENDORF
FUHLSBÜTTEL
OHLSDORF
WELLINGSBÜTTEL
BRAMFELD
EIDELSTEDT
TIERPARK HAGENBECK
STELLINGEN
LURUP
ALSTERDORF
WINTERHUDE
BARMBEK
EPPENDORF
EIMSBÜTTEL
WANDSBEK
BAHRENFELD
AUSSENALSTER
FLOTTBEK
OTTENSEN
OTHMARSCHEN
ALTONA
ST. PAULI
ST. MICHAELIS
HAFEN
HAMM
HORN
ELBE
Elbtunnel
FINKENWERDER
MICHELIN
BILLBROOK
KÖHLBRANDBRÜCKE
WILHELMSBURG
ALTENWERDER
MOORFLEET
KIRCHDORF
SPADENLAND
OCHSEN-WERDER
MOORWERDER
NEULAND
HARBURG
BREMEN HANNOVER
ROTENBURG SOLTAU
LÜNEBURG
HANNOVER BREMEN
Bremen
0
2 km
BREMERHAVEN
GRÖPELINGEN
HAFEN
WOLTMERSHAUSEN
FINDORFF
SCHWACHHAUSEN
FOCKE MUSEUM
HORN-LEHE
WORPSWEDE, BORGFELD
NEUE VAHR
MARKT PLATZ
HUCHTING
NEUSTADT
HUCKELRIEDE
HABENHAUSEN
HEMELINGEN
MICHELIN
AUTOBAHN (E 22-A 1) OSNABRÜCK
AUTOBAHN (E 22-A 1)
NOORDZEE
NOORD
Waddeneilanden
Terschelling
Oosterend
West-Terschelling
Oost-Vlieland
Vlieland
Leeuwarden
Harlingen
Franeker
Bolsward
Texel
De Koog
Den Burg
Den Helder
Den Oever
Afsluitdijk
Workum
Sloten
Staveren
Lemmer
IJsselmeer
NOORD-HOLLAND
NEDER
Schagen
Medemblik
Enkhuizen
Bergen
Bergen aan Zee
Egmond aan Zee
Alkmaar
Hoorn
Markermeer
Emmeloord
Urk
Lelystad-Haven
Lelystad
Edam
Volendam
Purmerend
Beverwijk
Stavanger
Bergen
Kristiansand
Göteborg
50

108
48
51
NORDSEE
Nordfriesische Inseln
Ostfriesische Inseln
Deutsche Bucht
Sylt
Westerland
List
Kampen
Sylt Ost
Hörnum
Amrum
Föhr
Wyk
Oldsum
Dagebüll
Niebüll
Tønder
Høјer
Klanxbüll
Neukirchen
Klixbüll
Leck
Risum-Lindholm
Nebel
Wittdün
Langeneß
Halligen
Hooge
Pellworm
Nordstrand
Husum
Bredstedt
Friedrichstadt
Garding
Tönning
St-Peter-Ording
Lunden
Heide
Wesselburen
Büsum
Meldorf
Trischen
Friedrichskoog
Marne
Brunsbüttel
Helgoland
Harwich
Scharhörn
Cuxhaven
Otterndorf
Altenwalde
Neuhaus
Cadenberge
Wanna
Dorum
Bederkesa
Langen
Bremerhaven
Mellum
Wangerooge
Spiekeroog
Langeoog
Baltrum
Norderney
Juist
Norddeich
Borkum
Norden
Dornum
Bensersiel
Esens
Harlesiel
Wangerland-Hooksiel
Wittmund
Jever
Schortens
Wilhelmshaven
Sande
Burhave
Nordenham
Blexen
Westerholt
Aurich
Moordorf
Friedeburg
Wiesmoor
Neuenburg
Zetel
Varel
Emden
Hesel
Neermoor
Leer
Westerstede
Apen
Bad Zwischenahn
Edewecht
Rastede
Jaderberg
Hahn
Elsfleth
Brake
Oldenburg
Hude
Delmenhorst
BREMEN
Bremervörde
Beverstedt
Stotel
Hagen
Schwanewede
Osterholz-Scharmbeck
Tarmstedt
Vegesack
Berne
Ottersberg
Oyten
Achim
Stuhr-Brinkum
Ganderkesee
Wardenburg
Friesoythe
Garrel
Cloppenburg
Ahlhorn
Wildeshausen
Harpstedt
Bassum
Twistringen
Syke
Goldenstedt
Vechta
Barnstorf
Sulingen
Lohne
Dinklage
Diepholz
Rehden
Wagenfeld
Steinfeld
Damme
Holdorf
Bersenbrück
Quakenbrück
Essen
Löningen
Lastrup
Sögel
Werlte
Börger
Lathen
Papenburg
Weener
Bunde
Haselünne
Meppen
Haren
Twist
Lingen
Fürstenau
Freren
Nordhorn
Neuenhaus
Lemförde
Rahden
Lavelsloh
Stolzenau
Uchte
Hoya
Espelkamp
Petershagen
Bramsche
Bohmte
Schiermonnikoog
Uithuizen
Eemshaven
Delfzijl
Appingedam
Winsum
Bedum
GRONINGEN
Haren
Eelde
Hoogezand
Veendam
Zuidlaren
Winschoten
Nieuweschans
Oude-Pekela
Vlagtwedde
Stadskanaal
Musselkanaal
Ter Apel
Assen
Borger
Smilde
Beilen
Emmen
Klazienaveen
Hoogeveen
Coevorden
Emlichheim
Hardenberg
Dedemsvaart
Ommen
Zwolle
Hattem
Kampen
Meppel
Steenwijk
Giethoorn
Wolvega
Heerenveen
Gorredijk
Drachten
Roden
Norg
Dokkum
Holwerd
Anjum
Zoutkamp
Bergum
GRONINGEN
DRENTHE
OVERIJSSEL
NIEDERSACHSEN
Oldebroek
IJsselmuiden
Ootmarsum
Papenburg
Küstenkanal
Ems-Jade-Kanal
Weser
Hunte
Ems
Hase
Aue

FALSTER
LOLLAND
Nakskov
Maribo
Rødby Havn
Nykøbing F
Gedser
Gedser Odde
Sønderborg
Augustenborg
Gråsten
Ærø
Ærøskøbing
Marstal
Rudkøbing
Bagenkop
Langelands Bælt
108
Flensburg
Glücksburg
Schleswig
Eckernförde
Kieler Bucht
Oslo-Göteborg
Korsør
Fehmarnbelt
Fehmarn
Puttgarden
Burg
Fehmarnsund
Heiligenhafen
Großenbrode
Hohwachter Bucht
Oldenburg
Mecklenburger Bucht
Rønne
Trelleborg
Helsinki
Lübecker Bucht
SCHLESWIG
HOLSTEIN
KIEL
Friedrichsort
Labøe
Schönberg
Selenter See
Rendsburg
Preetz
Plön
Eutin
Neustadt
Timmendorfer Strand
Travemünde
Neumünster
Bad Segeberg
Bad Oldesloe
LÜBECK
Itzehoe
Glückstadt
Elmshorn
Pinneberg
Wedel
Stade
HAMBURG
Harburg
Buxtehude
Ahrensburg
Norderstedt
Schwarzenbek
Geesthacht
Lauenburg
Ratzeburg
Mölln
Schaalsee
Grevesmühlen
Wismar
Gadebusch
Schwerin
Schweriner See
Kühlungsborn
Bad Doberan
Warnemünde
ROSTOCK
MECKLENBURG
Güstrow
Bützow
Sternberg
Crivitz
Parchim
Ludwigslust
Hagenow
Boizenburg
Zarrentin
Wittenburg
Neustadt-Glewe
Perleberg
Wittenberge
Lenzen
Dömitz
Hitzacker
Dannenberg
Lüchow
Salzwedel
Lüneburg
Winsen
Buchholz
Tostedt
Zeven
Bremervörde
Rotenburg/Wümme
Sittensen
Scheeßel
Schneverdingen
Soltau
Munster
Uelzen
Bad Bevensen
Ebstorf
Verden
Walsrode
Bergen
Celle
Nienburg
Schwarmstedt
Wesendorf
Gifhorn
Wolfsburg
Burgdorf
Lehrte
Peine
HANNOVER
Langenhagen
Neustadt am Rübenberge
Wunstorf
Gardelegen
Klötze
Stendal
Tangermünde
Osterburg
Havelberg
Haldensleben
Wolmirstedt
Burg
NIEDERSACHSEN
SACHSEN-ANHALT
Elbe
47
52

D
E
F
109
112
53
Kap Arkona
Putgarten
Wittow
Dranske
Altenkirchen
Wiek
Stubbenkammer
Jasmund
Sagard
Saßnitz
Witte
Hiddensee
Neuendorf
Schaprode
Gingst
Bergen
Binz
Sellin
Göhren
Thiessow
Kubitzer Bodden
RÜGEN
Putbus
Samtens
Garz
Zudar
Greifswalder Bodden
Stralsund
Lübnitz
Richtenberg
Franzburg
Grimmen
Griebenow
Reinberg
Greifswald
Lubmin
Wolgast
Peenemünde
Zinnowitz
Koserow
Tribsees
Gnoien
Dargun
Demmin
Loitz
Gützkow
Jarmen
Karlsburg
Anklam
Lassan
Usedom
Bansin
Ahlbeck
Heringsdorf
Świnoujście
Zirchow
Warszów
Oderbucht
København
Ystad
Oderhaff
Zalew Szczeciński
Neukalen
Malchin
Reuterstadt Stavenhagen
Altentreptow
Friedland
Ducherow
Ueckermünde
Monkebude
Ferdinandshof
Torgelow
Eggesin
Hintersee
Nowe Warpno
Trzebież
Dobieszczyn
Police
VORPOMMERN
Neubrandenburg
Burg Stargard
Penzlin
Waren
Helpter Berge
Woldegk
Strasburg
Pasewalk
Löcknitz
Linken
Lubieszyn
Brüssow
SZCZECIN
Dąbie
Podjuchy
Pomellen
Kołbaskowo
Kołbacz
Gryfino
Neustrelitz
Feldberg
Fürstenwerder
Prenzlau
Schmölln
Penkun
Mescherin
Gartz
Gramzow
Boitzenburg
Wesenberg
Mirow
Röbel
Müritz See
Lychen
Ravensbrück
Fürstenberg
Templin
Gerswalde
Milmersdorf
Greiffenberg
Vierraden
Schwedt
Angermünde
Chojna
Krajnik Dln
Trzcińsko-Zdrój
Wittstock
Rheinsberg
Zehdenick
Joachimsthal
Werbellinsee
Gransee
Lindow
Alt Ruppin
Neuruppin
Löwenberg
Groß-Schönebeck
Liebenwalde
Finowfurt
Eberswalde
Finow
Oderberg
Cedynia
Moryń
Siekierki
Bad Freienwalde
Kyritz
Wusterhausen
Bückwitz
Fehrbellin
BRANDENBURG
Kremmen
Oranienburg
Wandlitz
Biesenthal
Lanke
Bernau
Wriezen
Tiefensee
Werneuchen
Strausberg
Prötzel
Marxwalde
Buckow
Müncheberg
Friesack
Börnicke
Velten
Hennigsdorf
Birkenwerder
BERLIN
Pankow
Spandau
Falkensee
Nauen
Rathenow
Premnitz
Wachow
Ketzin
Pritzerbe
POTSDAM
Werder
Brandenburg
Plaue
Kirchmöser
Lehnin
Michendorf
Beelitz
Babelsberg
Ludwigsfelde
Teltow
Schönefeld
Tempelhof
Köpenick
Erkner
Blumberg
Altlandsberg
Vogelsdorf
Rüdersdorf
Fürstenwalde
Bad Saarow-Pieskow
Königs Wusterhausen
Friedersdorf
Storkow
Mittenwalde
Rangsdorf
Zossen
Trebbin
Wünsdorf
Teupitz
Halbe
Märkisch Buchholz
Neu Lübbenau
Luckenwalde
Baruth
Beeskow
Golzow
Wollin
Brück
Belzig
Görzke
Ziesar
Frankfurt a.d. Oder
Słubice
Świecko
Lebus
Seelow
Manschnow
Kietz
Kostrzyn
Müllrose
Eisenhüttenstadt
W. Pieck-Stadt Guben
Gubin
Lieberose
Cybinka
Krosno Odrzańskie
Zielona Góra
Świdnica
Kołobrzeg
Ustronie Morskie
Sarbinowo
Mielno
Dźwirzyno
Mrzeżyno
Niechorze
Rewal
Pobierowo
Dziwnów
Trzebiatów
Gościno
Karlino
Białogard
Kamień Pomorski
Wisełka
Wolin
Międzyzdroje
Woliński Park Narodowy
Świerzno
Gryfice
Golczewo
Płoty
Resko
Ryman
Sławoborze
Świdwin
Przybiernów
Nowogard
Dobra
Łobez
Węgorzyno
Stepnica
Goleniów
Maszewo
Chociwel
Ińsko
Dobrzany
Stargard Szcz.
Morzyczyn
Suchań
Recz
Drawno
Choszczno
Pyrzyce
Lipiany
Barlinek
Pełczyce
Dobiegniew
Strzelce Krajeńskie
Myślibórz
Baczyna
Santok
Gorzów Wlkp.
Dębno
Mieszkowice
Boleszkowice
Sarbinowo
Witnica
Bogdaniec
Skwierzyna
WARTA
Krzeszyce
Lubniewice
Ośno Lubuskie
Sulęcin
Pieski
Łagów
Rzepin
Torzym
Świebodzin
ODRA
ODER
Oderbruch

A
B
C
1
2
4
46
20
MER DU NORD
HOLLAND
FLEVOLAND
UTRECHT
ZUID
HOLLAND
ZEELAND
NOORD
BRABANT
ANTWERPEN
LIMBURG
WEST-
VLAANDEREN
OOST-
VLAANDEREN
BELGIË
BELGIQUE
BRABANT
HAINAUT
NAMUR
NORD
PAS-
DE-
CALAIS
Alkmaar
Hoorn
Markermeer
Bergen
Bergen aan Zee
Egmond aan Zee
Beverwijk
IJmuiden
Zaandam
Edam
Volendam
AMSTERDAM
Haarlem
Zandvoort
Lelystad
Almere
Hillegom
Aalsmeer
Bussum
Hilversum
Noordwijk aan Zee
Katwijk aan Zee
Leiden
Wassenaar
Great Yarmouth
Scheveningen
DEN HAAG
('S-GRAVENHAGE)
UTRECHT
Amersfoort
Woerden
Gouda
Delft
Hoek van Holland
Kingston upon Hull
Harwich
Europoort
Schiedam
Maassluis
Vlaardingen
ROTTERDAM
Culemborg
Spijkenisse
Hellevoetsluis
Gorinchem
Dordrecht
Middelharnis
Overflakkee
Schouwen Duiveland
Zierikzee
Willemstad
Waalwijk
's-Hertogenbosch
Oosterhout
Breda
Tilburg
Roosendaal
Steenbergen
Tholen
Domburg
Walcheren
Middelburg
Goes
Vlissingen
Zd Beveland
Bergen op Zoom
Eindhoven
Veldhoven
Breskens
Knokke-Heist
Terneuzen
Hulst
Zeebrugge
Blankenberge
Oostende
De Haan
BRUGGE
(BRUGES)
(ANVERS)
ANTWERPEN
Turnhout
Zelzate
St.-Niklaas
Lokeren
Eeklo
Mol
Lier
Nieuwpoort
Koksijde-Bad
De Panne
Dunkerque
Veurne
Diksmuide
GENT
(GAND)
Dendermonde
Mechelen
(Malines)
Aalst
Aarschot
Diest
Genk
Hasselt
Roeselare
(Roulers)
Kortrijk
(Courtrai)
Waregem
Oudenaarde
BRUSSEL
BRUXELLES
Vilvoorde
Leuven (Louvain)
Tienen
St.-Truiden
Tongeren
Ieper
(Ypres)
Poperinge
Menen
Tourcoing
Mouscron
Roubaix
LILLE
Ronse
(Renaix)
(Doornik)
Tournai
Geraardsbergen
Halle
Enghien
Waterloo
Wavre
Jodoigne
Hannut
Waremme
Hazebrouck
Bailleul
Armentières
Ath
Braine-le-Comte
Soignies
Nivelles
Gembloux
Huy
Béthune
Seclin
Carvin
Lens
Douai
St-Amand-les-Eaux
Mons
(Bergen)
La Louvière
Charleroi
Namur
Andenne
Valenciennes
Maubeuge
Thuin
Dinant
Ciney
Arras
Cambrai
Le Quesnoy
Avesnes
Philippeville
Rochefort
Givet
Le Cateau
Chimay
Couvin
St Hubert
Calais
Kingston upon Hull
Felixstowe
Dover
Sheerness

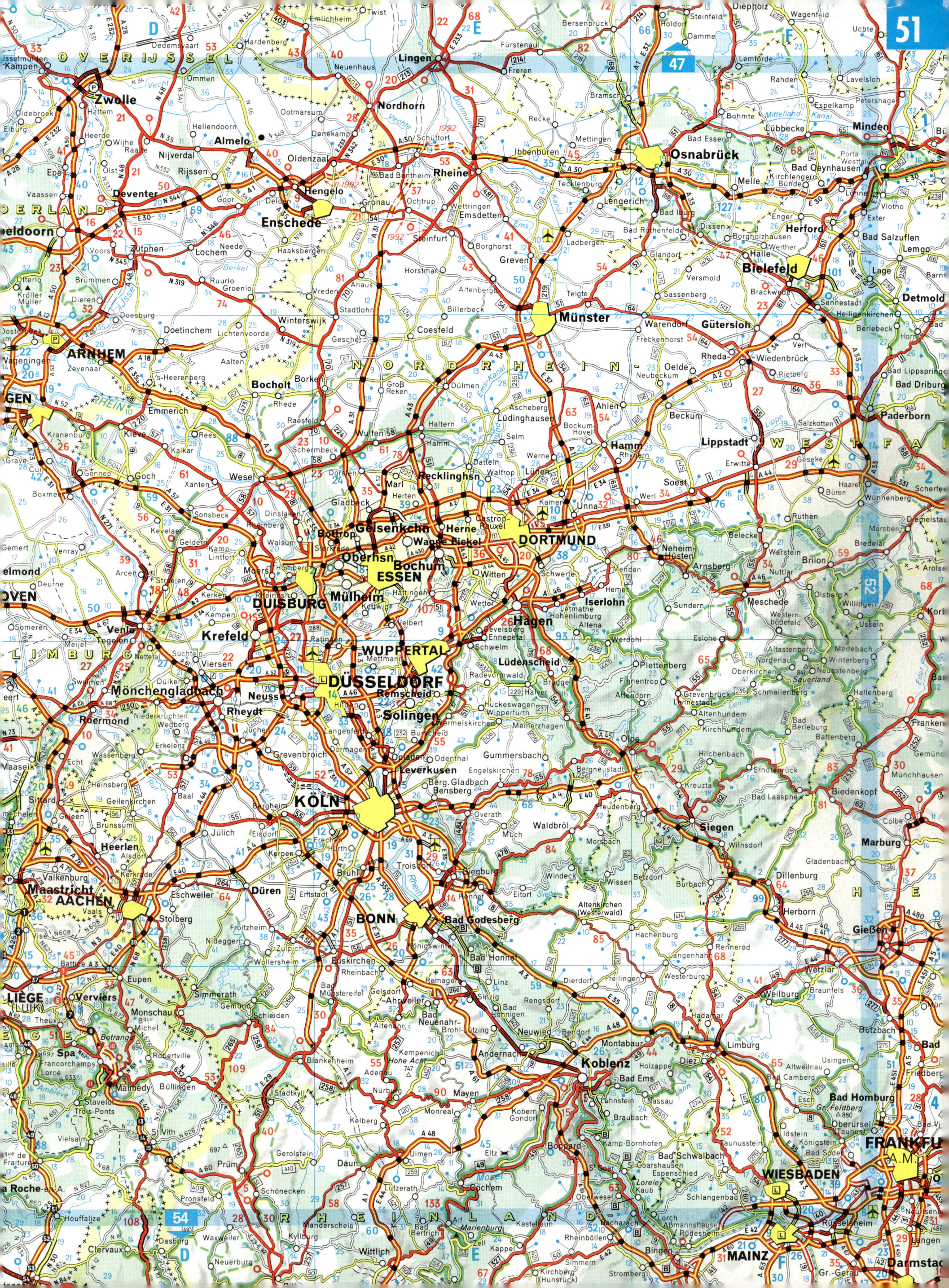
OVERIJSSEL
Zwolle
Deventer
Almelo
Hengelo
Enschede
Lingen
Nordhorn
Rheine
Osnabrück
Bielefeld
Herford
Minden
Detmold
Münster
Gütersloh
Paderborn
Lippstadt
Hamm
Arnhem
Bocholt
Recklinghsn
Gelsenkchn
Herne
Dortmund
Bottrop
Oberhsn
Essen
Bochum
Witten
Mülheim
Duisburg
Krefeld
Venlo
Hagen
Iserlohn
Wuppertal
Lüdenscheid
Düsseldorf
Neuss
Mönchengladbach
Rheydt
Remscheid
Solingen
Leverkusen
Köln
Siegen
Marburg
Gießen
Heerlen
Maastricht
Aachen
Düren
Bonn
Bad Godesberg
Liège
Verviers
Koblenz
Limburg
Bad Homburg
Frankfurt a.M.
Wiesbaden
Mainz
Darmstadt
NORDRHEIN-WESTFALEN
RHEINLAND
LIMBURG
NEDERLAND
47
52
54

HANNOVER
BRAUNSCHWEIG
Wolfsburg
MAGDEBURG
Hildesheim
Salzgitter-Lebenstedt
Wolfenbüttel
Helmstedt
Minden
Bad Oeynhausen
Rinteln
Hameln
Bad Salzuflen
Lemgo
Detmold
Bad Pyrmont
Paderborn
Höxter
Holzminden
Goslar
Bad Harzburg
Wernigerode
Halberstadt
Quedlinburg
Aschersleben
Osterode
Herzberg
Bad Lauterberg
Northeim
Göttingen
Duderstadt
Nordhausen
Sangerhausen
Sondershausen
Mühlhausen
Bad Langensalza
Hann. Münden
KASSEL
Warburg
Korbach
Bad Wildungen
Fritzlar
Melsungen
Eschwege
Bad Sooden-Allendorf
Witzenhausen
Heiligenstadt
Eisenach
Gotha
ERFURT
Weimar
Jena
Bad Hersfeld
Bebra
Rotenburg
Alsfeld
Marburg
Gießen
Fulda
Schlüchtern
Bad Brückenau
Bad Kissingen
Schweinfurt
Meiningen
Suhl
Zella-Mehlis
Ilmenau
Saalfeld
Rudolstadt
Coburg
Kronach
Bamberg
Bayreuth
Lauterbach
Bad Nauheim
Friedberg
Bad Homburg
FRANKFURT A.M.
Offenbach
Hanau
Aschaffenburg
Darmstadt
Würzburg
Gelnhausen
Büdingen
S A C H S E N - A N H A L T
T H Ü R I N G E N
H E S S E N
W E S T F A L E N
H A R Z
Brocken
Vogelsberg
Wasserkuppe 950
48
51
55

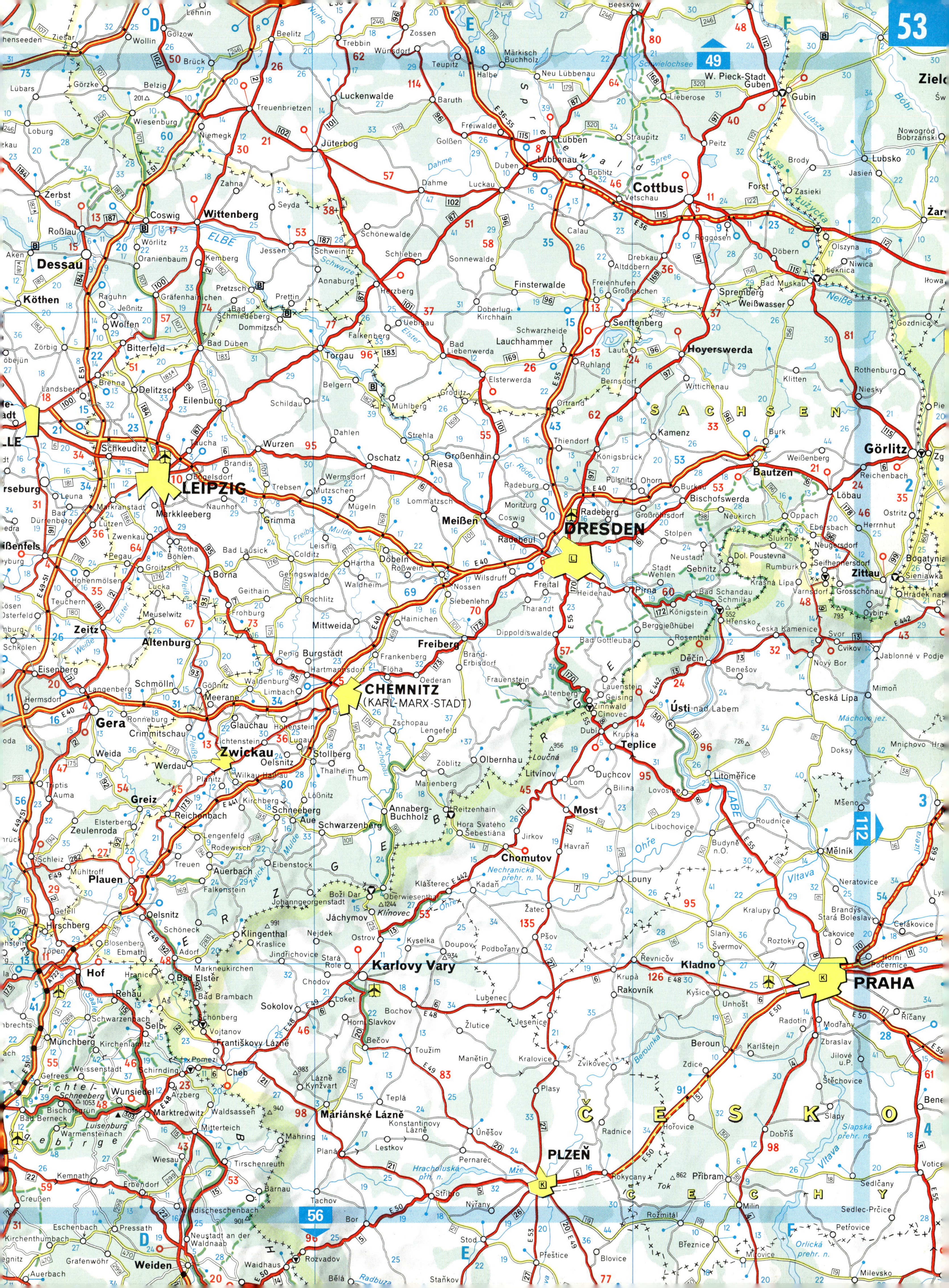
Dessau
Köthen
Bitterfeld
Wittenberg
Jüterbog
Luckenwalde
Lübben
Lübbenau
Cottbus
Guben
Gubin
Forst
Spremberg
Senftenberg
Hoyerswerda
Torgau
LEIPZIG
Grimma
Oschatz
Riesa
Meißen
DRESDEN
Radebeul
Pirna
Bautzen
Görlitz
Zittau
Löbau
Freiberg
CHEMNITZ
(KARL-MARX-STADT)
Zwickau
Gera
Altenburg
Zeitz
Plauen
Greiz
Hof
Cheb
Karlovy Vary
Mariánské Lázně
Chomutov
Most
Teplice
Ústí nad Labem
Děčín
Česká Lípa
Litoměřice
Mělník
Kladno
PRAHA
Beroun
Příbram
PLZEŇ
Rokycany
Weiden
SACHSEN
ČESKO
ELBE
49
56
112

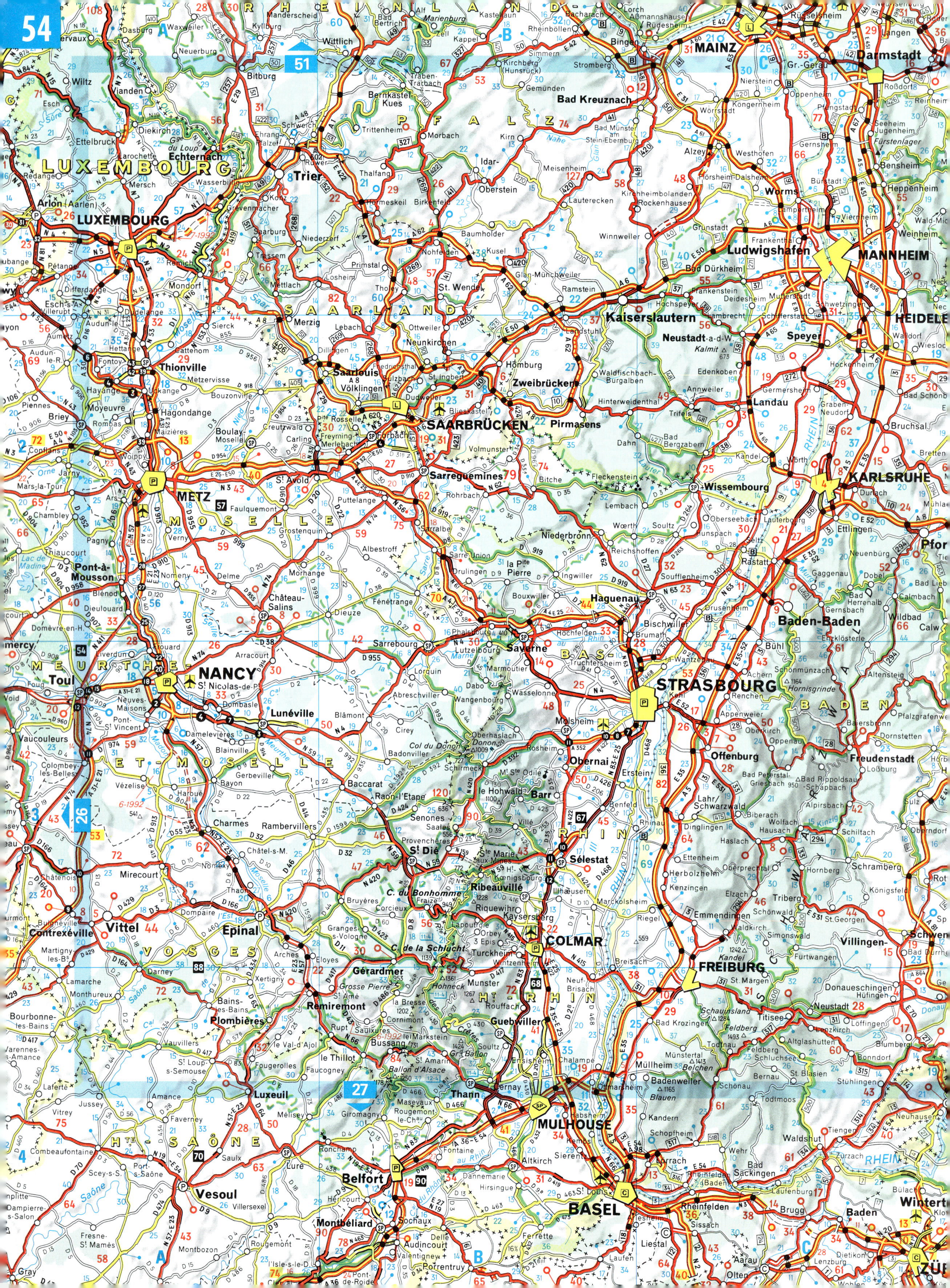
LUXEMBOURG
Luxembourg
Trier
Mainz
Darmstadt
Bad Kreuznach
Worms
Ludwigshafen
Mannheim
Heidelberg
Kaiserslautern
Speyer
Neustadt-a-d-W.
Landau
Pirmasens
Zweibrücken
Saarbrücken
Saarlouis
Völklingen
Merzig
Thionville
Metz
Sarreguemines
Wissembourg
Karlsruhe
Baden-Baden
Rastatt
Haguenau
Saverne
Sarrebourg
Strasbourg
Nancy
Toul
Lunéville
Pont-à-Mousson
Offenburg
Freudenstadt
Sélestat
St Dié
Colmar
Épinal
Vittel
Contrexéville
Gérardmer
Remiremont
Plombières
Luxeuil
Mulhouse
Freiburg
Basel
Belfort
Montbéliard
Vesoul
Rheinfelden
Baden
SAARLAND
PFALZ
MOSELLE
MEURTHE-ET-MOSELLE
VOSGES
BAS-RHIN
HT-RHIN
HTE-SAÔNE
BADEN
51
26
27

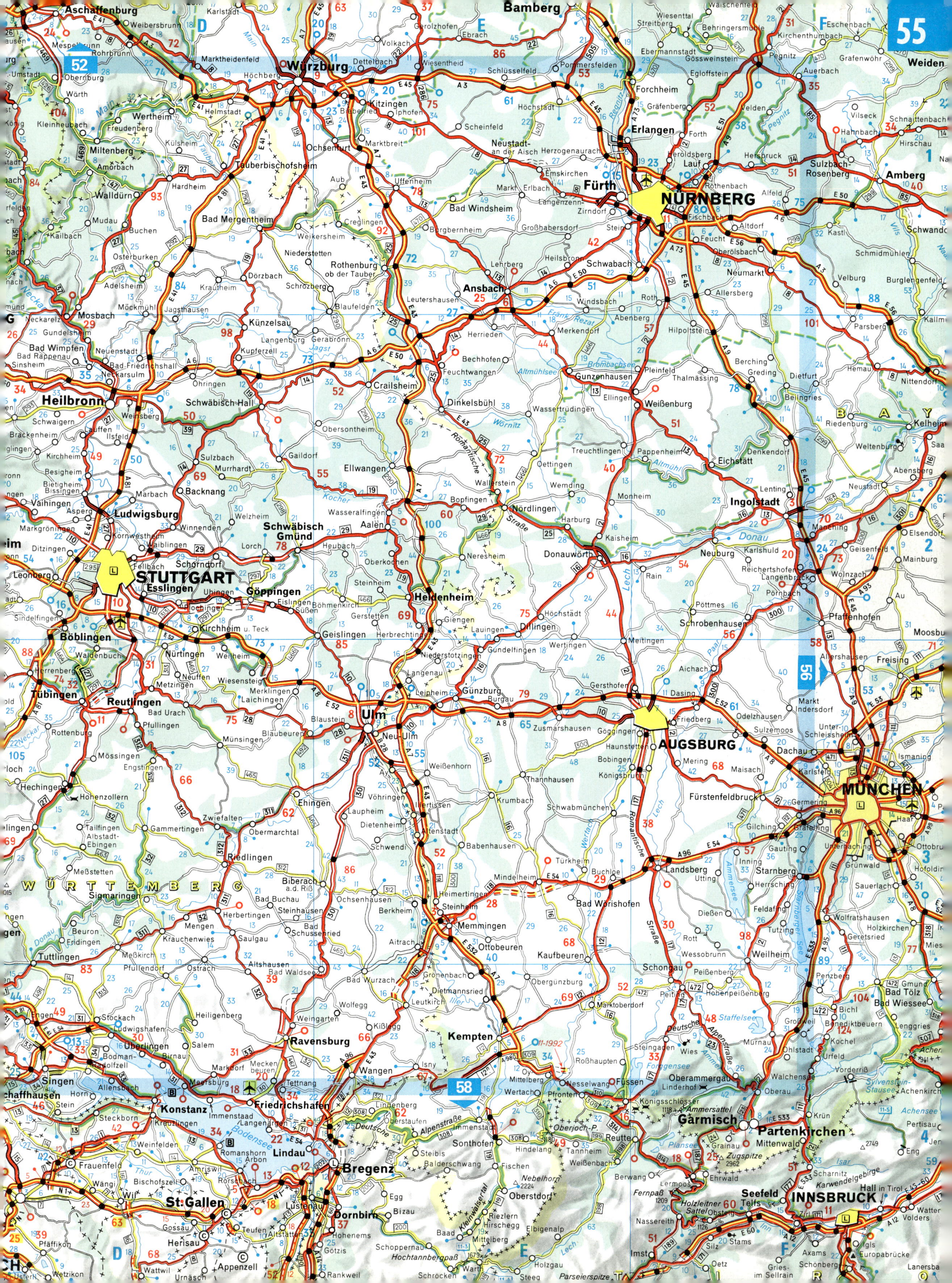
Aschaffenburg
Würzburg
Bamberg
Erlangen
Fürth
NÜRNBERG
Amberg
Weiden
Bad Mergentheim
Rothenburg ob der Tauber
Ansbach
Heilbronn
Schwäbisch Hall
Crailsheim
Dinkelsbühl
Weißenburg
Eichstätt
Ingolstadt
Ludwigsburg
Schwäbisch Gmünd
Aalen
Nördlingen
Donauwörth
STUTTGART
Esslingen
Göppingen
Heidenheim
Böblingen
Tübingen
Reutlingen
Ulm
Neu-Ulm
Günzburg
AUGSBURG
MÜNCHEN
Dachau
Freising
Landsberg
Memmingen
Kaufbeuren
Kempten
Ravensburg
Friedrichshafen
Lindau
Bregenz
Konstanz
Singen
St. Gallen
Dornbirn
Füssen
Garmisch
Partenkirchen
INNSBRUCK
Romantische Straße
WÜRTTEMBERG
52
56
58

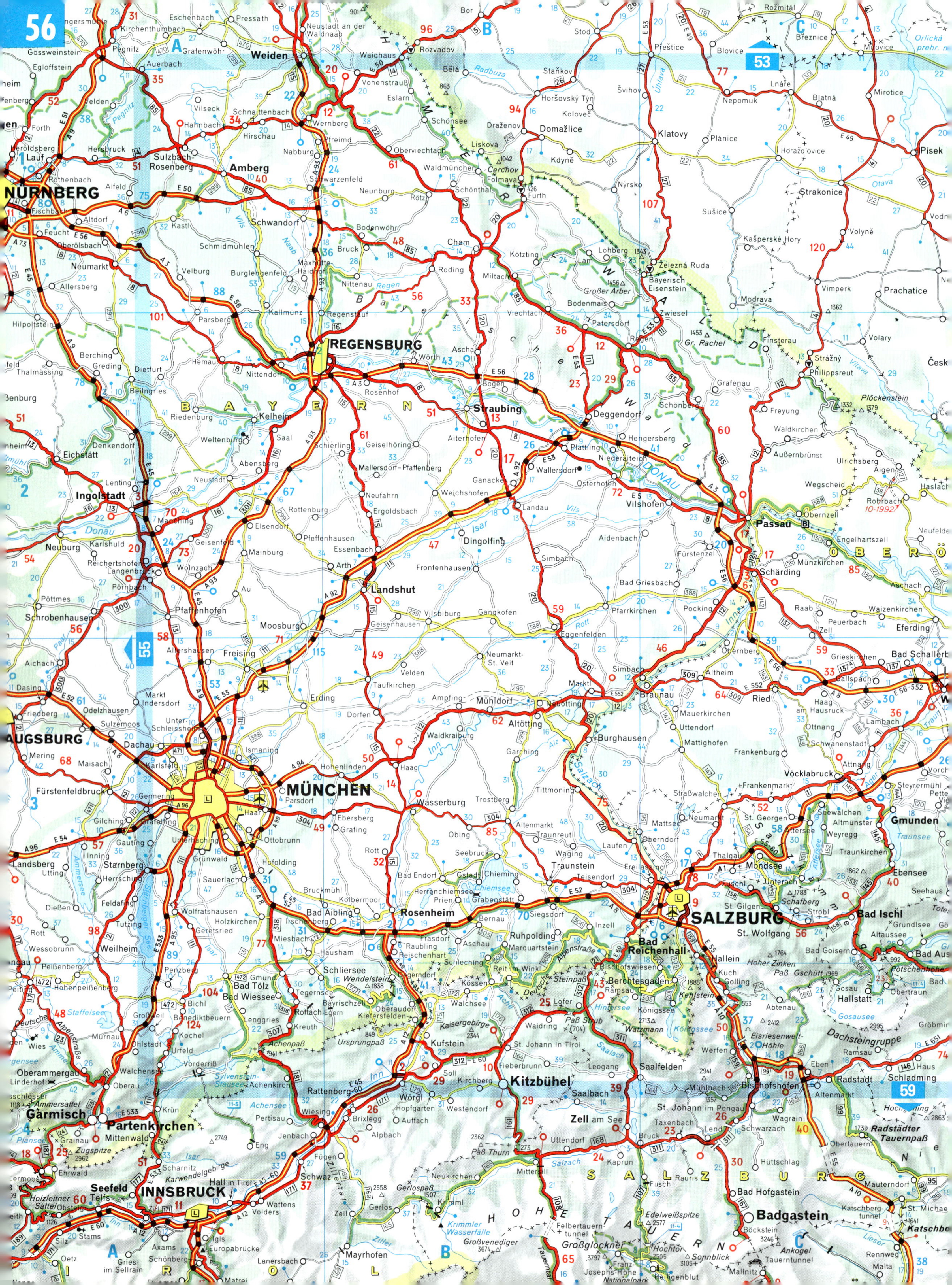

NÜRNBERG
REGENSBURG
MÜNCHEN
SALZBURG
INNSBRUCK
AUGSBURG
Weiden
Amberg
Ingolstadt
Landshut
Straubing
Deggendorf
Passau
Freising
Dachau
Rosenheim
Kitzbühel
Kufstein
Garmisch
Partenkirchen
Badgastein
Bad Ischl
Gmunden
Vöcklabruck
Braunau
Burghausen
Traunstein
Bad Reichenhall
Berchtesgaden
Hallein
Bischofshofen
Zell am See
Saalfelden
Klatovy
Domažlice
Strakonice
Písek
Cham
Schärding
Altötting
Mühldorf
Wasserburg
Erding
Starnberg
Weilheim
Bad Tölz
Schwaz
Wörgl
Seefeld
Telfs
Hall in Tirol
Mayrhofen
Eichstätt
Kelheim
Neumarkt
Pfaffenhofen
Dingolfing
Vilshofen
Ried
Mondsee
St. Wolfgang
Radstadt
Schladming
Großglockner
Hohe Tauern
DONAU
BAYERN
OBERÖ
SALZBURG
53
55
59

BRNO
Jihlava
Tábor
České Budějovice
Znojmo
Břeclav
Hodonín
Mikulov
Gmünd
Horn
Zwettl
Krems
St. Pölten
WIEN
BRATISLAVA
LINZ
Steyr
Amstetten
Melk
Tulln
Stockerau
Korneuburg
Mistelbach
Baden
Wiener Neustadt
Eisenstadt
Neusiedl
Sopron
Mattersburg
Oberwart
Szombathely
Kőszeg
Güssing
Körmend
Fürstenfeld
Hartberg
GRAZ
Leoben
Bruck an der Mur
Mürzzuschlag
Mariazell
Judenburg
Knittelfeld
Liezen
Voitsberg
Köflach
Leibnitz
Deutschlandsberg
Wolfsberg
N I E D E R Ö S T E R R E I C H
Ö S T E R R E I C H
S T E I E R M A R K
B U R G E N L A N D
M O R A V A
DONAU
Neusiedler See
112
70

WÜRTTEMBERG
Sigmaringen
Villingen-Schwenningen
Tuttlingen
Donaueschingen
Memmingen
Ottobeuren
Kaufbeuren
Schongau
Weilheim
Ravensburg
Kempten
Überlingen
Singen
Schaffhausen
Konstanz
Friedrichshafen
Wangen
Füssen
Garmisch
Lindau
Bregenz
Frauenfeld
Winterthur
St. Gallen
Baden
ZÜRICH
Dornbirn
Oberstdorf
Seefeld
Herisau
Appenzell
Säntis
Feldkirch
VORARLBERG
Bludenz
St. Anton
Landeck
Imst
Rapperswil
Zug
LUZERN
Einsiedeln
Vaduz
LIECHTENSTEIN
Glarus
Schwyz
Sargans
Bad Ragaz
Landquart
Klosters
Davos
Chur
Altdorf
Arosa
Engelberg
Andermatt
SVIZZERA
St. Moritz
Pontresina
Bormio
Livigno
Splügen
Thusis
Airolo
Biasca
Bellinzona
Locarno
LUGANO
Chiavenna
Sondrio
Tirano
Domodossola
Como
Lecco
Bergamo
Varese
Stresa
Gallarate
Monza
MILANO
BRESCIA
Treviglio
Chiari
Desenzano
Riva
Malcesine
Edolo
Aprica
Lago di Garda
Lago Maggiore
TICINO
GRAUBÜNDEN
LOMBARDIA
Sirmione
Bellagio
Menaggio

56
57
61
70
SALZBURG
Bad Reichenhall
Berchtesgaden
Bad Ischl
Bad Aussee
Rosenheim
Bad Aibling
Bad Tölz
Kufstein
Kitzbühel
Saalfelden
Zell am See
Bischofshofen
St. Johann im Pongau
Radstadt
Schladming
Badgastein
Großglockner
Lienz
Spittal
Villach
Velden
Millstatt
Tamsweg
INNSBRUCK
Brenner
ÖSTERREICH
OSTTIROL
HOHE TAUERN
Bolzano/Bozen
Bressanone/Brixen
Brunico/Bruneck
Cortina d'Ampezzo
Belluno
Feltre
Trento
Udine
Pordenone
Gorizia
Monfalcone
TRIESTE
Koper
Piran
Poreč
Treviso
Bassano d. Grappa
Vicenza
PADOVA
VENEZIA
Mestre
Lido di Venezia
Chioggia
Lido di Jesolo
VERONA
FRIULI
VENEZIA
GOLFO DI VENEZIA
Dubrovnik
Kerkira (Corfou)

MILANO
Como
Varese
Lecco
Bergamo
Brescia
Verona
Vicenza
Novara
Vigevano
Pavia
Lodi
Cremona
Mantova
Piacenza
Alessandria
Tortona
Voghera
Salsomaggiore
Fidenza
PARMA
Reggio nell' Emilia
MODENA
Carpi
Sassuolo
GENOVA
Savona
Rapallo
S. Margherita Ligure
Portofino
Chiavari
Sestri Levante
La Spezia
Portovenere
Lerici
Sarzana
Carrara
Massa
Pietrasanta
Viareggio
Lucca
Pisa
LIVORNO
Pistoia
Prato
Montecatini-Terme
Empoli
S. Gimignano
Volterra
Cecina
Rosignano Marittimo
Poggibonsi
Pontremoli
Aulla
Abetone
GOLFO DI GENOVA
MARE LIGURE
I. di Gorgona
L O M B A R D I A
E M I L I A
R O M A G N A
L I G U R I A
T O S C A N A
58
62
31

59
70
63
GOLFO DI VENEZIA
Treviso
Mestre
VENEZIA
Lido di Venezia
PADOVA
Chioggia
Rovigo
FERRARA
Comacchio
BOLOGNA
RAVENNA
Imola
Faenza
Forlì
Cesena
Cervia
Cesenatico
Rimini
Riccione
Cattolica
S. Marino
Pesaro
Fano
Senigallia
Ancona
Urbino
Jesi
Osimo
Macerata
Civitanova Marche
Porto S. Giorgio
Fermo
Ascoli
FIRENZE
Arezzo
Sansepolcro
Città di Castello
Gubbio
Fabriano
Perugia
Assisi
Lago Trasimeno
Koper
Piran
Umag
Poreč
Rovinj
Pula
Opatija
RIJEKA
CRES
Dubrovnik
Kerkira (Corfu)
Zadar
Split
Igoumenitsa
Pátra (Patrasso)

A L I G U R E
I. di Gorgona
CORSE
Cap Corse
Rogliano
Pino
Luri
Nonza
Erbalunga
Bastia
St Florent
Oletta
Calvi
l'Ile-Rousse
Belgodère
Murato
Calenzana
Muro
Ponte-Leccia
Vescovato
Morosaglia
Piedicroce
Cervione
HAUTE-CORSE
Mte Cinto
Calacuccia
Scala di Sta Regina
Corte
Col de Vergio
Golfe de Porto
Porto
les Calanche
Evisa
Piana
Venaco
Mte Rotondo
Soccia
Vizzavona
Vezzani
Col de Vizzavona
Aléria
Vico
Cargèse
CORSE-DU-SUD
Sari-d'Orcino
Bocognano
Ghisoni
Ghisonaccia
Col de Verde
Bastelica
Ajaccio
Iles Sanguinaires
Zicavo
Mte Incudine
Sta Maria-Siché
Solenzara
Petreto-Bicchisano
Col de Bavella
Aullène
Zonza
Levie
Olmeto
Propriano
Ste Lucie-de-Tallano
Sartène
Porto-Vecchio
Bonifacio
Bocche di Bonifacio
Arcipelago della Maddalena
I. Maddalena
Sta Teresa Gallura
La Maddalena
I. Caprera
Palau
Baja Sardinia
Porto Cervo
Costa Smeralda
Arzachena
Porto Rotondo
Golfo Aranci
Luogosanto
Trinità d'Agultu e V.
S. Antonio
Olbia
I. Tavolara
Aggius
Calangianus
Tempio Pausania
M. Limbara
Telti
Loiri
Monti
Padru
M. Nieddu
Isola Asinara
Golfo dell' Asinara
Falcone
Stintino
Castelsardo
Sedini
Porto Torres
Platamona Lido
Sorso
Martis
Toulon
Nice
Savona
Marseille
Porto-Torres
Livorno
Genova
Civitavecchia
Arbatax
Porto-Santo-Stefano
Pozzuoli
La Spezia
Piombino
I. di Capraia
Arcipelago Toscano
Portoferraio
Marciana Marina
Marina di Campo
Isola d'Elba
Cavo
Rio Marina
Porto Azzurro
I. Pianosa
I. d. Giglio
Giglio P.
Porto S.
I. di Montecristo
Riparbella
Solvay
Cecina
Pomarance
Larderello
Radicon
Marina di Castagneto-Donoratico
Canneto
Sassetta
Monterotondo Maritt.
Suvereto
S. Vincenzo
Massa Maritt.
Campiglia Maritt.
Venturina
Montioni
Ribolla
Piombino
Follonica
Punta Ala
Castiglione della Pescaia
Grosseto
Marina di Grosseto
Colline Metallifere
VIA AURELIA
Roma
LA GIUSTINIANA
TOMBA
NERON
OTTAVIA
TORREVECCHIA
MONTE MA
CASALOTTI
Via di Boccea
Grande Raccordo Anulare
Via della Pineta Sacchetti
Via Trionfale
Aurelia
CORVIALE
MICHELIN
Via Portuense
Via della Magliana
Autostrada Roma-Aeroporto di Fiumicino
TEVERE
Via del Mare
OSTIA ANTICA LIDO DI ROMA
CIVITAVECCHIA
A 12-CIVITAVECCHIA
FIUMICINO
V. del Casaletto
V. Trullo
Via Leone
Grego
V.LA DORIA PAMPHILI

Perugia
Assisi
Foligno
Spoleto
Terni
Rieti
L'Aquila
Ascoli Piceno
Teramo
Orvieto
Viterbo
Todi
Narni
Chianciano Terme
Montepulciano
Chiusi
Lago Trasimeno
L. di Bolsena
L. di Bracciano
Tarquinia
Civitavecchia
Ladispoli
Fregene
Fiumicino
Lido di Ostia
ROMA
Tivoli
Frascati
Marino
Albano Laziale
Castel Gandolfo
Velletri
Pomezia
Aprilia
Latina
Anzio
Nettuno
Sabaudia
S. Felice Circeo
Terracina
Sperlonga
Gaeta
Formia
Frosinone
Alatri
Fiuggi
Sora
Avezzano
Tagliacozzo
Subiaco
Sulmona
Celano
Gran Sasso d'Italia
Campo Imperatore
M. Vettore
Norcia
Cascia
Visso
Amatrice
L. di Campotosto
U M B R I A
L A Z I O
A B R U Z Z O
TEVERE
I. di Giannutri
I. Ponziane
I. Zannone
I. di Ponza
I. Ventotene
Golfo
Palestrina
Colleferro
Anagni
Ceccano
Cori
Cisterna di L.
Sezze
Priverno
Fondi
Fossanova
Civita Castellana
Monterotondo
Mentana
Guidonia
Palombara S.
Poggio Mirteto
Bracciano
Cerveteri
S. Severa
S. Marinella
Montalto di Castro
Capalbio
Orbetello
Tuscania
Montefiascone
Bolsena
Acquapendente
Pitigliano
Sorano
Manciano
Montalcino
S. Quirico d'Orcia
M. Amiata
Sinalunga
Cortona
Gubbio
Nocera Umbra
Gualdo Tadino
Bevagna
Montefalco
Trevi
Deruta
Marsciano
Città d. Pieve
Amelia
Orte
Soriano nel Cimino
Ronciglione
Sutri
Campagnano
Rignano Fl.
Fiano R.
Setteba gni
MONTE SACRO
SETTECAMINI
TOR SAPIENZA
CENTOCELLE
MICHELIN
COLOSSEO
CATACOMBE
TORRENOVA
TORRE MAURA
MORENA
CECCHIGNOLA
PRIMA PORTA
S. PAOLO FUORI LE MURA
VILLA ADA
CIAMPINO
CASTELLI ROMANI
NAPOLI
L'AQUILA AVEZZANO
PALESTRINA
Via Appia Nuova
Via Tuscolana
Via Casilina
Via Prenestina
Via Tiburtina
Via Nomentana
Via Salaria
Via Flaminia
Via Cassia
Via Aurelia
Via Laurentina
Via Ardeatina
Anulare
Raccordo
E
F
D
61
64
1
2
3
4

A
B
C
Pedaso
Ripatransone
Grottammare
S. Benedetto d. Tronto
Alba Adriatica
Giulianova
Roseto d. Abruzzi
Pineto
Silvi Marina
Montesilvano Marina
Split
Pescara
Francavilla al Mare
Ortona
Chieti
Teramo
Campli
Atri
Penne
Città S. Angelo
Loreto Aprutino
Pianella
Isola d. Gr. Sasso d'It.
Campo Imperatore
Farindola
Cepagatti
Catignano
Castel d. Monte
Barisciano
Torre de Passeri
Capestrano
Navelli
Popoli
Bucchianico
Manoppello
Lanciano
Orsogna
Guardiagrele
S. Vito Chietino
Fossacesia
Casalbordino
Punta di Penna
Vasto
Cupello
Gissi
Atessa
Termoli
Campomarino
Rocca di Mezzo
Ovindoli
Celano
Castelvecchio Subequo
Sulmona
Pratola Peligna
Forca Caruso
Pescina
Trasacco
Scanno
Maiella
Lama d. Peligni
Campo di Giove
Palena
Cansano
Valico d. Forchetta
Pescocostanzo
Rivisondoli
Roccaraso
Castel di Sangro
Capracotta
Agnone
Villetta Barrea
Barrea
Pescasseroli
Parco Nazionale d'Abruzzo
Balsorano
Sora
Forca d'Acero
Alfedena
Isernia
Forlì d. Sannio
Pescolanciano
Frosolone
Carpinone
Trivento
Lucito
Castelmauro
Larino
Ururi
Montenero di Bisaccia
Guglionesi
Palata
Montefalcone nel Sannio
Castiglione Messer Marino
Casacalenda
S. Croce di Magliano
Bonefro
Torremaggiore
Serracapriola
Lesina
Poggio Imperiale
Apricena
S. Severo
Sannicandro Garganico
Promontorio del Gargano
S. Giovanni Rotondo
Monte S. Angelo
Manfredonia
Golfo di Manfredonia
Mattinata
Vico d. Gargano
Peschici
Manacore
Rodi Garganico
Torre Mileto
L. di Lesina
L. di Varano
Cagnano Varano
S. Marco in Lamis
I. Tremiti
I. Pianosa
Palagruž
Foggia
Lucera
Castelnuovo d. Daunia
Volturara Appula
Zapponeta
Trinitapoli
S. Ferdinando di Puglia
Cerignola
Orta Nova
Troia
Ascoli Satriano
Deliceto
Candela
Rocchetta S. Antonio
Lavello
Melfi
Rapolla
Venosa
Palazzo S. Gervasio
Atella
Rionero in Vulture
Forenza
Oppido Luc.
Avigliano
Potenza
Picerno
Tito
Brienza
Marsico Nuovo
Sala Consilina
Teggiano
Montesano s. Marcellana
Campobasso
Bagnoli d. Trigno
S. Elia a Pianisi
Riccia
Jelsi
Vinchiaturo
Boiano
Campitello M.
Sepino
Colle Sannita
Montefalcone di Val Fortore
S. Marco d. Cavoti
S. Bartolomeo in Galdo
Castelfranco in Miscano
Faeto
Savignano Irpino
S. Agata di Puglia
Anzano di Puglia
Ariano Irpino
Grottaminarda
Castello d. Lago
Buonalbergo
Pontelandolfo
Morcone
Cusano Mutri
Piedimonte d'A.
Cerreto Sannita
Guardia Sanframondi
Alife
Telese
Dragoni
Caiazzo
S. Agata de' Goti
Benevento
Montesarchio
Caserta
Maddaloni
Capua
Cervinara
S. Giorgio d. Sannio
Paternopoli
Gesualdo
Frigento
Vallata
Bisaccia
Lacedonia
Andretta
S. Angelo de Lombardi
Calitri
Pescopagano
Muro Lucano
Montella
M. Cervialto
Avellino
Solofra
Baiano
Nola
Sarno
Mercato S. Severino
Nocera
Cava de' Tirreni
Salerno
Battipaglia
Pontecagnano
Montecorvino Rovella
Acerno
Campagna
Eboli
Contursi
Sicignano d. Alburni
M. Alburno
Petina
Grotte di Pertosa
Auletta
Vietri di P.
S. Rufo
Rocca d'Aspide
Capaccio
Castel S. Lorenzo
Paestum
Agropoli
Ogliastro Cilento
M. Cervati
Buonabitacolo
Sanza
Castellabate
Vallo d. Lucania
Caselle in Pittari
Golfo di Salerno
Amalfi
Positano
Maiori
Ravello
Sorrento
Vico Equense
Castellammare di Stabia
Torre Annunziata
Torre d. Greco
Ercolano
Portici
Vesuvio
Pompei
Scafati
Angri
Gragnano
Ottaviano
NAPOLI
Pozzuoli
Bacoli
Porto Vecchio
Procida
Ischia
Casamicciola Terme
Forio
I. d'Ischia
I. Ventotene
Golfo di Napoli
I. di Capri
Capri
Aversa
Giugliano in C.
Casoria
Acerra
Marano di N.
Marcianise
S. Maria Capua Vetere
Castel Volturno
Villa Literno
Mondragone
Grazzanise
Carinola
Sessa Aurunca
Teano
Roccamonfina
Caianello
Venafro
Cassino
Abbazia di Montecassino
Capriati a V.
Letino
Pratella
M. Miletto
Monti del Matese
S. Vittore d. Lazio
Pontecorvo
Pico
Ausonia
Fondi
Itri
Formia
Gaeta
Sperlonga
Golfo di Gaeta
M. Petrella
Atina
Arce
Ceprano
Isola del Liri
Abbazia di Casamari
Frosinone
Campania
Molise
Abruzzo
Catania Siracusa
Palermo
Cagliari
63
66

Napoli
0
2 km
ROMA 239 km
ROMA 236 km
CASERTA 28 km
ROMA 219 km
CASERTA 33 km
ARZANO
AFRAGOLA
CASALNUOVO DI NAPOLI
MUGNANO DI NAPOLI
CALVIZZANO
MARANO DI NAPOLI
CASORIA
AUTOSTRADA A 16
AVELLINO 56 km
BARI 261 km
Data di apertura da stabiliasi
Via Roma
SECONDIGLIANO
CHIAIANO
PISCINOLA
Via Emilio Scaglione
NAPOLI NORD
NAPOLI CAPODICHINO
CAPODICHINO
PARCO DI CAPODIMONTE
AEROSTAZIONE
TANGENZIALE
NAPOLI SUD-EST
S. CROCE
Vle dei Colli Aminei
CAPODIMONTE
ARENELLA
VOLLA
POGGIOREALE
V. Stradera
V. Nuova Poggioreale
PIANURA
CAMALDOLI
MUSEO ARCHEOLOGICO NAZIONALE
Via Argine
SOCCAVO
VOMERO
CERTOSA DI S. MARTINO
Volpicella
S. SEBASTIANO AL VESUVIO
CASTEL NUOVO
BARRA
AGNANO
FUORIGROTTA
TANGENZIALE
LA LOGGETTA
STAZIONE MERGELLINA
S. GIORGIO A CREMANO
S. GIOVANNI A TEDUCCIO
TERME DI AGNANO
MOSTRA D'OLTREMARE
SAN PAOLO
STAZIONE
CASTEL DELL'OVO
PORTO DI SANTA LUCIA
PORTO SANNAZZARO
MERGELLINA
AUTOSTRADA A 3
PORTICI
PORTICI BELLAVISTA
VESUVIO
ERCOLANO
CAMPI FLEGREI
POZZUOLI
POSILLIPO
G O L F O D I N A P O L I
STAZIONE
1
2

Barletta
Trani
Bisceglie
Molfetta
Giovinazzo
BARI
Split
Dubrovnik
Mola di Bari
Andria
Corato
Terlizzi
Bitonto
Ruvo di P.
Modugno
Capurso
Polignano a Mare
Monopoli
Rutigliano
Conversano
Castel d. Monte
Minervino Murge
Bitetto
Sannicandro di Bari
Adelfia
Casamassima
Turi
Castellana Grotte
Torre Canne
Acquaviva d. Fonti
Sammichele
Putignano
Fasano
P U G L I A
Cassano d. Murge
Alberobello
Ostuni
Carovigno
Kérkira (Corfu)
Igoumenitsa
Pátra (Patrasso)
Brindisi
Altamura
Santeramo in Colle
Noci
Locorotondo
Martina Franca
Cisternino
S. Vito d. Normanni
Gravina in Puglia
Gioia d. Colle
Ceglie Messapico
Tuturano
Mesagne
Torchiarolo
Irsina
Matera
Castellaneta
Mottola
Massafra
Grottaglie
Francavilla Fontana
Latiano
S. Pietro Vernotico
Squinzano
Surbo
S. Cataldo
Tolve
Laterza
Palagiano
Oria
S. Donaci
Trepuzzi
Tricarico
Grassano
Miglionico
Ginosa
Montescaglioso
TARANTO
S. Giorgio Ionico
Sava
Manduria
S. Pancrazio Salentino
Campi Salentina
Lecce
Accettura
S. Mauro Forte
Ferrandina
Bernalda
Avetrana
Leverano
Monteroni di Lecce
Melendugno
Lido Silvana
Copertino
Martano
Laurenzana
Stigliano
Pisticci
Lido di Metaponto
Porto Cesareo
Nardò
Galatina
Otranto
Corleto Perticara
Craco
Galatone
Maglie
Sta Cesarea Terme
Scanzano
67
Gallipoli
Parabita
Tursi
Policoro
G O L F O
Casarano
Tricase
Colobraro
Nova Siri
Rotondella
Ugento
Senise
D I T A R A N T O
Galiano d. Capo
Leuca
Capo S. Maria di Leuca
Oriolo
Latronico
D
E
F
3
4

SARDEGNA
Bonifacio
Bocche di Bonifacio
Arcipelago della Maddalena
I. Maddalena
La Maddalena
I. Caprera
Sta Teresa Gallura
Palau
Baja Sardinia
Porto Cervo
Costa Smeralda
Arzachena
Porto Rotondo
Golfo Aranci
Civitavecchia
Genova
Livorno
Arbatax
I. Tavolara
Olbia
S. Antonio
Luogosanto
Trinità d'Agultu e V.
Aggius
Calangianus
Tempio Pausania
M. Limbara
Telti
Loiri
Monti
Padru
M. Nieddu
1992
Posada
la Caletta
Isola Asinara
Golfo dell' Asinara
Toulon
Ajaccio
C. del Falcone
Stintino
Castelsardo
Porto Torres
Platamona Lido
Sedini
Sorso
Sennori
Martis
Nulvi
Osilo
Lago del Coghinas
Oschiri
Sassari
Ploaghe
Palmadula
Olmedo
Uri
Ittiri
Tramariglio
Fertilia
Alghero
Grotta di Nettuno
Villanova Monteleone
Mores
Ozieri
Pattada
Alà d. Sardi
Buddusò
Lodè
Siniscola
M. Albo
Thiesi
Romana
Bultei
Bitti
Foresta di Burgos
Bono
Orune
Pozzomaggiore
Bonorva
Cedrino
Orosei
Montresta
Nuoro
Bolotana
Oliena
Dorgali
Cala Gonone
Golfo di Orosei
Bosa
Suni
Macomer
Orani
Sarule
Ottana
Orgosolo
Cuglieri
Sedilo
Gavoi
Fonni
Genna Cruxi
M. Ferru
Abbasanta
Santu Lussurgiu
Ghilarza
Lago Omodeo
Pso di Caravai
Sta Caterina Pittinuri
Milis
Narbolia
Sorgono
Monti del Gennargentu
Desulo
P. La Marmora
Tonara
Aritzo
Tramatza
Riola Sardo
Fordongianus
Samugheo
Arbatax
Tortolì
Cabras
Tirso
Torre Grande
Simaxis
Oristano
Lanusei
S. Giovanni di Sinis
Sta Giusta
Laconi
Seulo
Seui
Jerzu
Golfo di Oristano
Nurallao
Arborea
Ales
Isili
Barumini
Terralba
Uras
Mandas
Sardara
L. Mulargia
Furtei
Ballao
Flumendosa
Guspini
S. Gavino Monreale
Sanluri
Senorbì
S. Nicolò Gerrei
Arbus
S. Andrea Frius
Villasalto
S. Vito
Muravera
Gonnosfanadiga
Serramanna
Dolianova
Fluminimaggiore
M. Linas
Villacidro
Villasor
Monastir
P. Serpeddì
S. Sperate
Mannu
Sestu
Domusnovas
Iglesias
Siliqua
Assemini
Selargius
Castiadas
Gonnesa
Villamassargia
Elmas
Quartu S. Elena
CAGLIARI
Portoscuso
Carbonia
Narcao
Villasimius
I. di S. Pietro
Carloforte
M. is Caravius
Golfo di Cagliari
Capo Carbonara
S. Giovanni Suergiu
Calasetta
S. Antioco
Giba
Sarroch
I. di S. Antioco
Pula
Napoli
Trapani-Palermo
Tunis
Teulada
Sta Margherita
Porto Pino
Capo Spartivento

TARANTO
Potenza
BASILICATA
CALABRIA
Cosenza
Catanzaro
Crotone
MESSINA
Reggio di Calabria
Golfo di Taranto
Golfo di Policastro
Golfo di S. Eufemia
Golfo di Squillace
Isole Eolie o Lipari
I. Stromboli
I. Panarea
I. Salina
I. Lipari
I. Filicudi
I. Vulcano
Sila
M. Pollino
M. Botte Donato
M. Cervati
M. Sirino
M. Alburno
Aspromonte
Paestum
Agropoli
Sapri
Maratea
Praia a Mare
Scalea
Diamante
Paola
Amantea
Pizzo
Tropea
Vibo Valentia
Gioia Tauro
Palmi
Scilla
Villa S. Giovanni
Sibari
Castrovillari
Rossano
Cariati
Cirò Marina
S. Giovanni in Fiore
Isola di Capo Rizzuto
Soverato
Stilo
Locri
Siderno
Bova Marina
Capo Spartivento
Lamezia
Nicastro
Milazzo
Capo d'Orlando
Pisticci
Metaponto
Policoro
Lagonegro
Tindari
Barcellona Pozzo di Gotto
64
65
69

A
B
C
1
2
3
4
SICILIA
MARE TIRRENO
MARE
I. di Ustica
Isole
I. Filicudi
I. Alicudi
PALERMO
Mondello
M. Pellegrino
Capo Gallo
Sferracavallo
Punta Raisi
Capaci
Carini
Cinisi
Monreale
Bagheria
Solunto
Casteldaccia
Altavilla
Trabia
Termini Imerese
Misilmeri
Piana d. Albanesi
Marineo
Villafrati
Partinico
Alcamo
Castellammare d. Golfo
Golfo di Castellammare
S. Vito lo Capo
Torre d. Impiso
Trapani
Erice
Paceco
Fulgatore
Segesta
Calatafimi
Salemi
Marsala
Birgi
Isole Egadi
I. di Levanzo
I. Favignana
I-Marèttimo
Mazara d. Vallo
Castelvetrano
Campobello di Mazara
Selinunte
Marinella
Menfi
Partanna
S. Ninfa
Sta Margherita di Belice
Sambuca di Sicilia
Chiusa Sclafani
Corleone
Prizzi
Rca Busambra
Roccapalumba
Lercara Friddi
Alia
Caltavuturo
Montemaggiore Belsito
Caccamo
Buonfornello
Cefalù
Collesano
Castelbuono
Pzo Carbonara
Petralia
Gangi
Mistretta
S. Stefano di Camastra
C. del Contrasto
Nicosia
Leonforte
Enna
Valguarnera Caropepe
Aidone
Piazza Armerina
Pietraperzia
Barrafranca
Mazzarino
Riesi
Ravanusa
Butera
Gela
Licata
Palma di Montechiaro
Campobello di Licata
Naro
Favara
Canicattì
Delia
Sommatino
Caltanissetta
S. Cataldo
Serradifalco
Montedoro
Mussomeli
Sta Caterina Villarmosa
Resuttano
Agrigento
Porto Empedocle
Aragona
Raffadali
S. Biagio Platani
Casteltermini
S. Stefano Quisquina
Alessandria d. Rocca
Caltabellotta
Ribera
Sciacca
Cagliari
Genova
Livorno
Napoli
Ustica
Tunis
Pantelleria
Trapani
Pantelleria
Tracino
I. di Pantelleria
I. di Linosa
Isole Pelagie
I. di Lampedusa
Lampedusa
Porto Empedocle
Gozo
Nadur
Victoria
Mgarr
Comino
Mellieħa
Mosta
Sliema
Valletta
MALTA
Rabat
Vittoriosa
Dingli
Zejtun
Żurrieq
Birżebbuġa
Filfola
Siracusa
A 29
A 19
A 20
S 113
S 115
S 121
S 189
S 188

Catanzaro
Golfo di Squillace
Golfo di S. Eufemia
Vibo Valentia
Reggio di Calabria
MESSINA
Taormina
M. ETNA
CATANIA
Golfo di Catania
Siracusa
Ragusa
I. Stromboli
I. Lipari
I. Vulcano
I. Salina
Palermo

Klagenfurt
Villach
Velden
Maribor
Celje
Kranj
Jesenice
Bled
LJUBLJANA
ZAGREB
Varaždin
Ptuj
Karlovac
Novo mesto
Postojna
Kočevje
TRIESTE
Koper
Gorizia
Nova Gorica
Monfalcone
Udine
Piran
Izola
Umag
Poreč
Rovinj
Pula
Opatija
RIJEKA
Crikvenica
Senj
KRK
CRES
Lošinj
Mali Lošinj
Rab
PAG
Gospić
Otočac
Plitvice
Bihać
Slunj
Ogulin
Delnice
Tolmin
Kobarid
Idrija
Vipava
Sežana
Divača
Škocjanske jame
Labin
Pazin
Motovun
Buje
Krapina
Samobor
Metlika
Rogaška Slatina
Velenje
Trbovlje
Kamnik
Škofja Loka
Vrhnika
Cerknica
Ilirska Bistrica
Karlobag
Starigrad
57
59
74
A
B
C
1
2
3
4

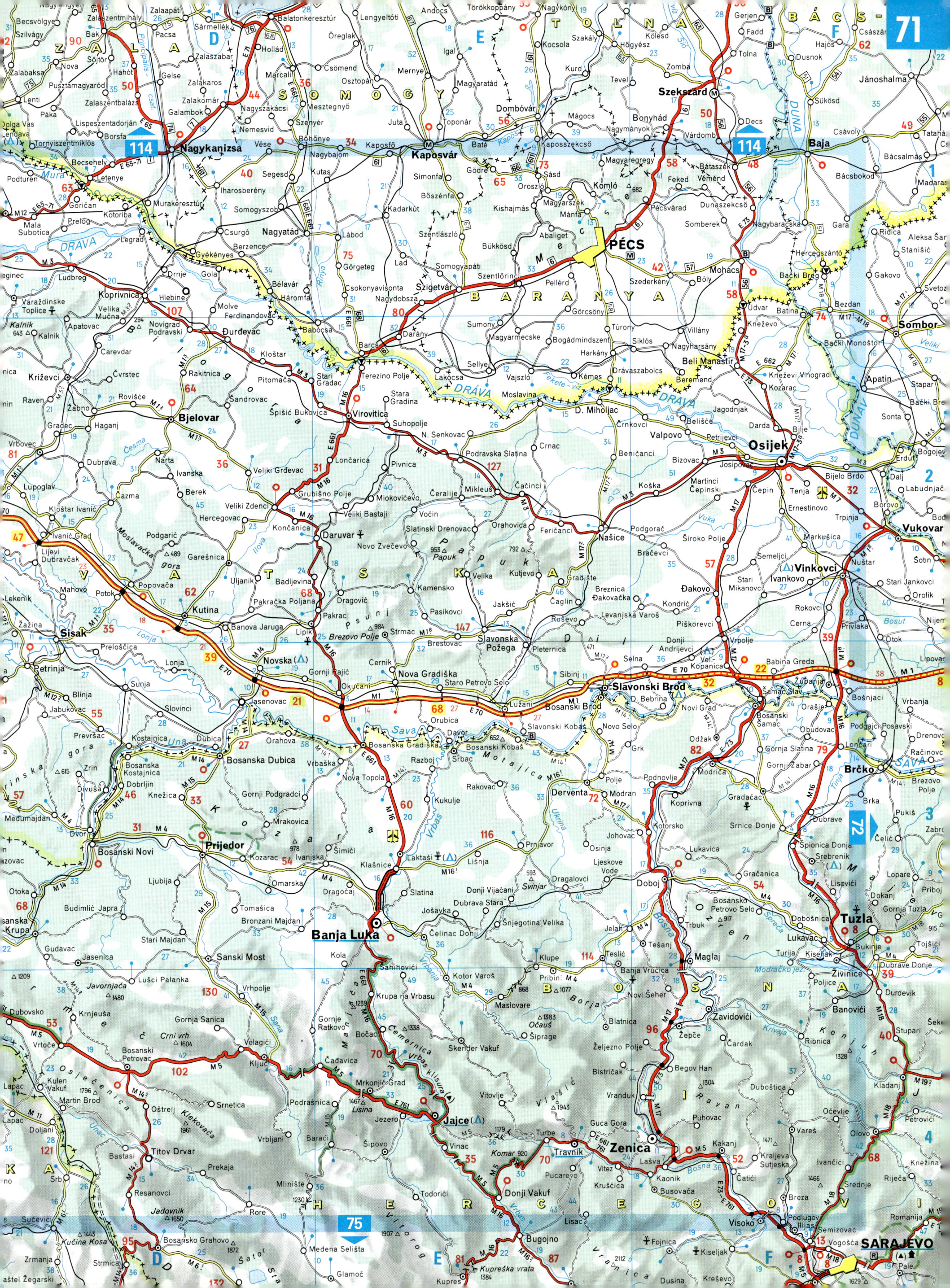

Z A L A
S O M O G Y
T O L N A
B Á C S -
B A R A N Y A
Nagykanizsa
Kaposvár
Szekszárd
Baja
PÉCS
Mohács
Sombor
Osijek
Vukovar
Vinkovci
Koprivnica
Bjelovar
Virovitica
Daruvar
Sisak
Kutina
Novska
Nova Gradiška
Slavonski Brod
Bosanski Brod
Slavonska Požega
Đakovo
Našice
Brčko
Tuzla
Doboj
Derventa
Prijedor
Bosanski Novi
Banja Luka
Jajce
Travnik
Zenica
Bugojno
Donji Vakuf
Titov Drvar
Sanski Most
Bosanski Petrovac
Ključ
Maglaj
Zavidovići
Visoko
Kakanj
SARAJEVO
DRAVA
DUNAV
DUNA
Sava
Bosna
Vrbas
Una
P a p u k
M o t a j i c a
K o z a r a
114
75
72

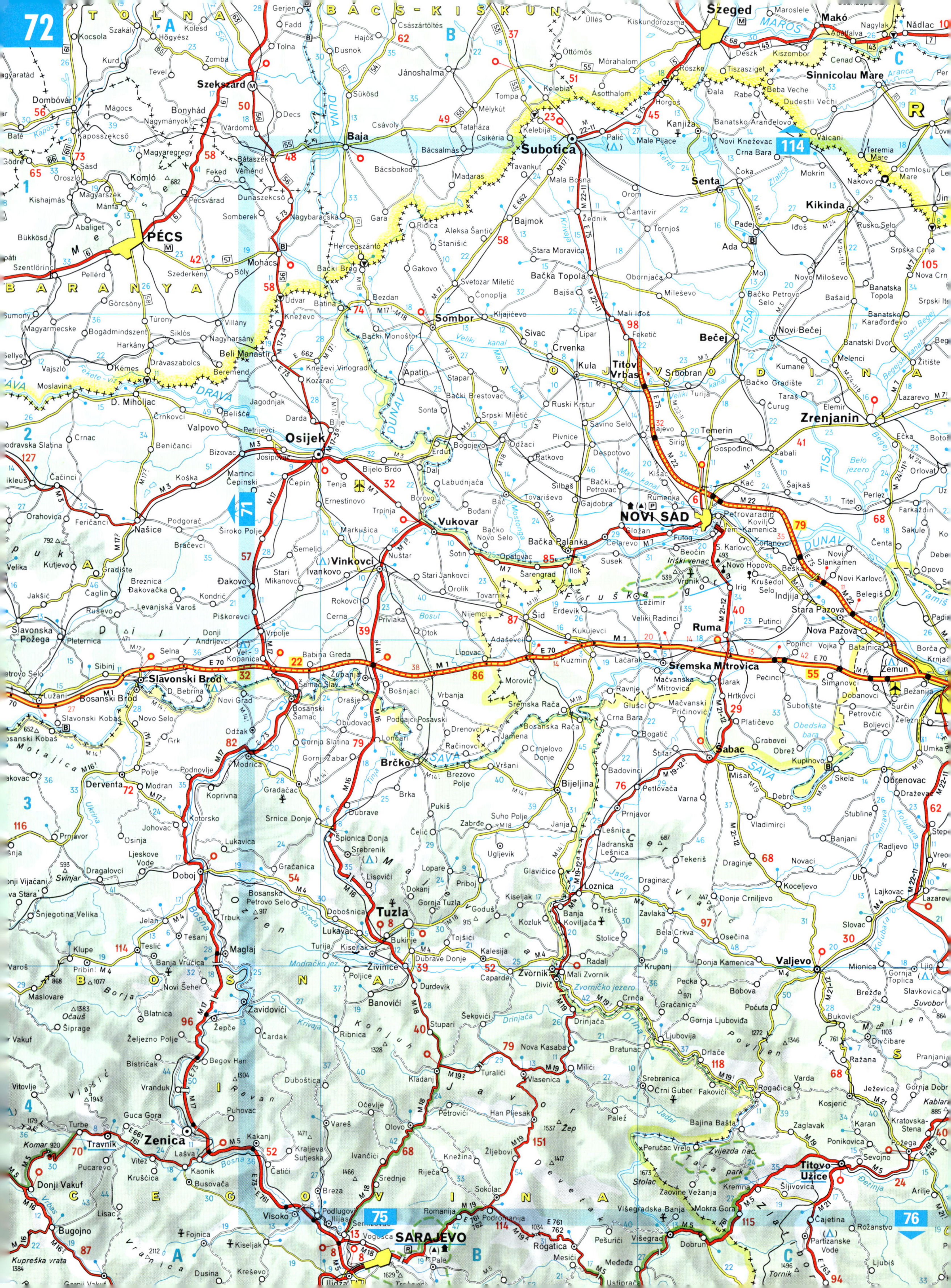
TOLNA
BÁCS-KISKUN
BARANYA
Szeged
Makó
Szekszárd
Baja
Subotica
Pécs
Mohács
Senta
Kikinda
Sombor
Bečej
Osijek
Zrenjanin
Vukovar
Vinkovci
NOVI SAD
Slavonski Brod
Sremska Mitrovica
Ruma
Zemun
Šabac
Brčko
Bijeljina
Tuzla
Zvornik
Loznica
Valjevo
Doboj
Zenica
Travnik
SARAJEVO
Titovo Užice
DUNAV
DRAVA
SAVA
TISA
DUNA
114
71
75
76

ARAD
TIMIŞOARA
MÂNIA
TIMIŞ
HUNEDOARA
Hunedoara
Deva
Simeria
ALBA
Lugoj
Petroşani
Vulcan
Lupeni
Caransebeş
Reşiţa
CARAŞ-SEVERIN
Oraviţa
Tirgu Jiu
GORJ
CARPAŢI
Parcul National Retezat
Băile Herculane
Orşova
Turnu Severin
MEHEDINŢI
Strehaia
Motru
Kladovo
Negotin
Vidin
Calafat
Pančevo
BEOGRAD
Smederevo
Požarevac
Vršac
Bela Crkva
Majdanpek
Bor
Zaječar
Kragujevac
Svetozarevo
Ćuprija
Paraćin
Kraljevo
Čačak
Kruševac
Aleksinac
Niš
Pirot
Knjaževac
Soko Banja
DUNAV
DUNĂREA
Homoljske planine
Beljanica
Kučaj
Rtanj
Ozren
Devica
Gledićske pl.
Stara Planina
BĂLGA
114
115
76
77

A
B
70
1
2
3
4
61
63
64
Zadar
Nin
Benkovac
Biograd
Dugi Otok
Kornati
Pesaro
Fano
Senigallia
Ancona
Zadar
Split
Dubrovnik
Kérkira (Corfou)
Igoumenitsa
Pátra (Patras)
Jesi
Osimo
Macerata
Civitanova Marche
Porto S. Giorgio
Fermo
S. Benedetto d. Tronto
Ascoli Piceno
Giulianova
Teramo
Pescara
Chieti
Ortona
Vasto
Termoli
Foligno
Spoleto
Terni
Rieti
L'Aquila
Avezzano
Sulmona
Tivoli
ROMA
Gran Sasso d'Italia
J A D R A N S K O M O R E
M A R C H E
A B R U Z Z O
M O L I S E
I T A L I A

SARAJEVO
Mostar
SPLIT
DUBROVNIK
Šibenik
Trogir
Omiš
Makarska
Metković
Ploče
Konjic
Jablanica
Livno
Sinj
Imotski
Knin
Drniš
Bugojno
Kupres
Prozor
Posušje
Široki Brijeg
Čitluk
Čapljina
Medjugorje
Neum
Ston
Cavtat
Trebinje
Ilidža
Hvar
Jelsa
Stari Grad
Vis
Komiža
Korčula
Vela Luka
Blato
Lastovo
Mljet
Šolta
BRAČ
HVAR
KORČULA
PELJEŠAC
Supetar
Bol
Orebić
Lopud
Koločep
Lokrum
Šipan
Palagruža
Sušac
Biševo
Svetac
I. Pianosa
I. Tremiti
Vieste
Peschici
Manfredonia
Golfo di Manfredonia
Monte S. Angelo
S. Giovanni Rotondo
S. Severo
Gargano
Promontorio del Gargano
L. di Lesina
L. di Varano
Rodi Garganico
D I N A R A
Ancona
Pescara
Bari
Venezia
Kérkira (Corfou)
Pátra
Pireás
N S K O M O R E
R I A T I Q U E)
Hvarski kanal
Viški kanal
Korčulanski kanal
Neretvanski kanal
Lastovski kanal
Mljetski kanal
D
E
F
3
4
71
76
64

SARAJEVO
Ilidža
Pale
Rogatica
Goražde
Foča
Čajniče
Pljevlja
Prijepolje
Priboj
Nova Varoš
Sjenica
Ivanjica
Novi Pazar
Tutin
Rožaje
Peć
Đakovica
Bijelo Polje
Mojkovac
Ivangrad
Andrijevica
Kolašin
Žabljak
Plužine
Nikšić
Gacko
Nevesinje
Bileća
Trebinje
Ljubinje
Stolac
DUBROVNIK
Cavtat
Hercegnovi
Kotor
Tivat
Budva
Cetinje
Titograd
Petrovac
Bar
Ulcinj
Shkodër
Lezhë
Puka
Durrës
TIRANË
Elbasan
Kavajë
SHQIPËR
CRNA GORA
Skadarsko jezero
Sinjajevina
Durmitor
Prokletije
Bari
Kérkira (Corfou)
Igoumenitsa
72
75
78
A
B
C
1
2
3
4

SOFIA
Pernik
Niš
Pirot
Dimitrovgrad
Prokuplje
Leskovac
Vranje
Priština
Titova Mitrovica
Podujevo
Gnjilane
Kumanovo
SKOPJE
Tetovo
Prizren
Kjustendil
Blagoevgrad
Kriva Palanka
Štip
Titov Veles
Kočani
Strumica
Gostivar
Kičevo
Prilep
Bitola
Ohrid
Struga
Debar
Gevgelija
Édessa
Flórina
Alexándria
Kuršumlija
Surdulica
Bujanovac
Delčevo
Berovo
Radoviš
Kavadarci
Negotino
Resen
Pogradec
Sandanski 65
Samokov
Plovdiv 156
Burgas 382
Varna 468
Vraca 116
Petrič 55
Thessaloníki 20
Thessaloníki 32
M A K E D O N I J A
H E L L Á S
Šar Planina
Ohridsko ezero
Prespansko ezero
Dojransko ezero
Osogovske planine
Babuna
Vardar
Kozuf
73
78
79
115

1
2
3
4

76

TIRANË - DURRËS
ELBASAN - BERAT
SHQIPËRIA
KORÇË
VLORË
VÓRIA PÍNDOS
TIRANË
Durrës
Elbasan
Ohrid
Korçë
Vlorë
Berat
Fier
Lushnjë
Kavajë
Shijak
Sukth
Vorë
Ndroq
Ishëm
Krujë
Laç
Burrel
Klos
Lis
Selishtë
Fushë Muhur
Peshkopi
Maqellarë
Debar
Debarska Banja Banjišta
Dolno Kosovrasti
Lazaropole
Kičevo
Izvor
Čelopec
Zajas
Mavrovi Anovi
Mavrovo
Nac. park Mavrovo
Galičnik
Jance
Pesočani
Botun
Belčište
Lešani
Mešeišta
Struga
Kosel
Bukovo
Resen
Carev Dvor
Peštani
Oteševo
Carina
Ljubaništa
Bezmisth
Goriça
Lin
Prenjas
Ćafasan
Veleshta
Lukovo
Steblevë
Shupenzë
Zerqan
Librazhd
Labinot Fushë
Bradashesh
Cërrik
Peqin
Rrogozhinë
Belsh
Divjakë
Libofshë
Roskovec
Poshnjë
Qytet Stalin
Gramsh
Kodovjat
Moglicë
Pogradec
Leshnicë
Liqenas
Maliq
Progër
Bilisht
Patos
Ballsh
Cakran
Novoselë
Selenice
Mavrove
Vajze
Gjorm
Orikum
Dukati i Ri
Dhermi
Q. e Llogarasë
Qesarat
Memaliaj
Tepelenë
Këlcyrë
Përmet
Çorovodë
Çepan
Ersekë
Leskovik
Gjirokastër
Borsh
Lukove
Delvinë
Muzine
Sarandë
Livadhe
Ktismata
Parakálamos
Kónitsa
Kalpáki
Monodéndri
Vitsa
Kípi
Flamboúrari
Grevenítio
Frangádes
Vovoússa
Skamnéli
Pápingo
Aristi
Vissani
Doliana
Delvináki
Pogoniani
Kefalóvrisso
Mázi
Melissópetra
Exohí
Amárandos
Pirsógiani
Gorgopótamos
Likórahi
Eptahóri
Drossopigí
Ag. Paraskeví
Zoúzouli
Samarína
Eléfthero
Kastaniá
Pefkos
Nestório
Komninádes
Ag. Kiriakí
Ieropigí
Mikrolímni
Vronderó
Psarádes
Píli
Sidári
Avliótes
Róda
Kassiópi
N. Othoní
N. Erikoússa
N. Mathráki
Akr. Ag. Ekaterini
Kepi i Treporteve
Laguna e Nartës
Laguna e Karavastasë
Gjiri i Rodonit
Gjiri i Lalzit
Gjiri i Durrësit
Gjiri i Karavastasë
Gjiri i Vlorës
Karaburun
Rreza e Kanalit
M. Lungarë
M. e Çikës
M. e Bratajt
Mali Gribë
Kurvelesh
Mallakastër
Myzeqe
M. Shpirag
Mali Tomorr
Çuka Partizane
M. Ostrovice
M. Valamarë
M. Rungaje
M. Lofke
M. e Qelqës
M. e Papingut
M. Bureto
M. Luce
M. Trebeshine
Zagori
Dropull
Vurg
Mali Shpat
M. Polis
Guri i Zi
Verce
Çermenikë
Mali Me Gropa
Mal i Dajt
Mal i Lopes
M. Allaman
Mal i Shebenik
Mali i Thatë
Qaf' e Shtamës
K. e Thanes
Skenderbeut
Stogovo
Jablanica
Galičica
Ohridsko ezero
Liqeni i Ohrit
Prespansko ezero
Óros Grámos
Ór. Smólikas
Ór. Tímfi
Farángi Vikou
Shkumbin
Seman
Devoll
Vjosë
Osum
Drino
Bistrice
Erzen
Ishëm
Mat
Drini i Zi
Crni Drim
Radika
Aliákmonas
Aóos
Voidomátis
Dubrovnik - Bar
Otranto - Venezia
Ancona
Brindisi
Vório Stenó Kérkiras
Passage exceptionnel
E 853
E 852
E 65
E 90
M 26

82

MAKEDONIJA
JUGOSLAVIJA
77
Bitola
Prilep
Strumica
Gevgelija
Kumanovo
Gradsko
Negotino
Kavadarci
Demir Kapija
Valandovo
Dojran
VARDAR
Ezero Tikveš
Kruševo
Makovo
Staravina
Novaci
Kremenica
Florina
Φλώρινα
FLÓRINA
Kastoriá
Αμύνταιο
Amíndeo
Édessa
Έδεσσα
Aridéa
Αριδαία
Skídra
Náoussa
Νάουσα
Véria
Βέροια
IMATHÍA
PÉLA
MAKEDONÍA
KILKÍS
Kilkís
Κιλκίς
Polikastro
Axioúpoli
Gianitsá
Γιαννιτσά
Thessaloníki
ΘΕΣΣΑΛΟΝΙΚΗ
Kólpos Thessaloníkis
Κόλπος Θεσσαλονίκης
Ptolemaída
Πτολεμαΐδα
KOZÁNI
Kozáni
Κοζάνη
Siátista
Σιάτιστα
Grevená
Γρεβενά
GREVENÁ
Neápoli
Νεάπολη
Sérvia
Σέρβια
PIERIÁ
Kateríni
Κατερίνη
Litóhoro
Λιτόχωρο
ÓROS ÓLIMBOS
ΟΡΟΣ ΟΛΥΜΠΟΣ
Mítikas
2917
Elassóna
Ελασσόνα
Deskáti
Δεσκάτη
Thermaïkós Kólpos
Θερμαϊκός Κόλπος
Aliákmonas
Alexándria
Αλεξάνδρεια
Epanomí
Néa Mihanióna
Sindos
Lagína
83
80
D
E
F

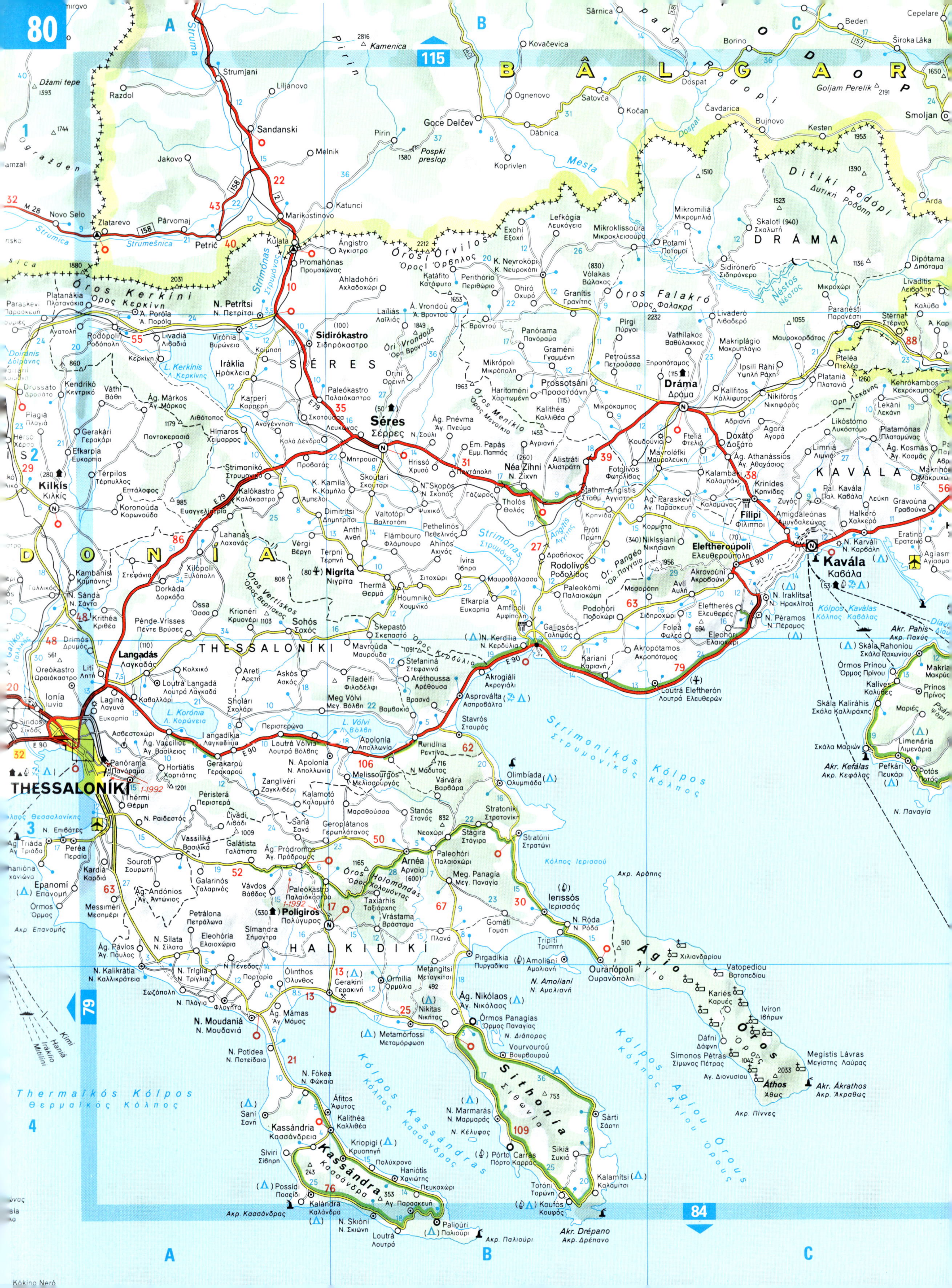
115
84
79
A
B
C
1
2
3
4
B Â L G A R I J A
Rodopi
Ditiki Rodópi
Δυτική Ροδόπη
Pirin
Struma
Mesta
Strumica
Strumešnica
Strimónas
Στρυμόνας
Nestos
Νέστος
Dospat
Óros Kerkíni
Όρος Κερκίνη
Órosi Órvilos
Όροςι Όρβηλος
Óros Falakró
Όρος Φαλακρό
Óros Meníkio
Όρος Μενοίκιο
Óros Vertískos
Όρος Βερτίσκος
Óros Kerdílio
Όρος Κερδύλιο
Óros Holomóndas
Όρος Χολομώντας
Ór. Pangéo
Όρ. Παγγαίο
L. Kerkíni
Λ. Κερκίνη
L. Korónia
Λ. Κορώνεια
L. Vólvi
Λ. Βόλβη
SÉRES
DRÁMA
KAVÁLA
THESSALONÍKI
HALKIDIKÍ
D O N I A
Sandanski
Strumjani
Petrič
Kulata
Melnik
Goce Delčev
Dospat
Smoljan
Novo Selo
Séres
Σέρρες
Dráma
Δράμα
Kavála
Καβάλα
Kilkís
Κιλκίς
Sidirókastro
Σιδηρόκαστρο
Nigríta
Νιγρίτα
Néa Zíhni
Ν. Ζίχνη
Filipi
Φίλιπποι
Eleftheroúpoli
Ελευθερούπολη
Langadás
Λαγκαδάς
THESSALONÍKI
Polígiros
Πολύγυρος
Arnéa
Αρναία
Ierissós
Ιερισσός
Ouranópoli
Ουρανόπολη
N. Moudaniá
Ν. Μουδανιά
Kassándria
Κασσάνδρεια
Kassándra
Κασσάνδρα
Sithonía
Σιθωνία
Áthos
Άθως
Ágion Óros
Καρυές
Karyés
Thermaïkós Kólpos
Θερμαϊκός Κόλπος
Strimonikós Kólpos
Στρυμονικός Κόλπος
Kólpos Kassándras
Κόλπος Κασσάνδρας
Kólpos Agíou Órous
Κόλπος Αγίου Όρους
Kólpos Kaválas
Κόλπος Καβάλας
Akr. Drépano
Ακρ. Δρέπανο
Akr. Kassándras
Ακρ. Κασσάνδρας
Akr. Akrathos
Ακρ. Άκραθος
E 79
E 90
1-1992

Kârdžali
Jaz. Kârdžali
Jaz. Studen Kladenec
Krumovgrad
Rodopi
Iztočni Rodopi
Xánthi
Komotiní
Κομοτηνή
Alexandroúpoli
Αλεξανδρούπολη
Didimótiho
Διδυμότειχο
Orestiáda
Ορεστιάδα
Souflí
Σουφλί
Féres
Φέρες
Kastaniés
Καστανιές
THRÁKI
RODÓPI
ÉVROS
XANTHI
Anatolikí Rodópi
Sápes
Σάπες
Marónia
Μαρώνεια
Ipsala
Enez
Keşan
Çanakkale
Eceabat
Kilitbahir
Gelibolu Yarımadası
Saros Körfezi
Çanakkale Boğazı
GÖKÇE ADASI
Kaleköy
Kuzu Limanı
Çınarlı
Kefaloz
Dereköy
Ayagalip
Kefalo Br.
N. SAMOTHRÁKI
Ν. ΣΑΜΟΘΡΑΚΗ
Kamariótissa
Samothráki
Thérma
Paleópoli
Lákoma
Akr. Kípos
Akr. Makrívrahos
N. THÁSSOS
Ν. ΘΑΣΟΣ
Akr. Stavrós
THRAKIKÓ PÉLAGOS
ΘΡΑΚΙΚΟ ΠΕΛΑΓΟΣ
N. LÍMNOS
Ν. ΛΗΜΝΟΣ
Mírina
Μύρινα
Moúdros
Akr. Mourdzeflos
Akr. Pláka
Kólpos Pournías
Akr. Maronías
Makri
Mésti
Lágos
L. Vistonída
Porto Lágos
Fanári
Ímeros
Nímfea
Sóstis
Iasmos
Ehínos
Kiméria
Gala G.
Pamuklu G.
Tuzla G.
Evros
Meriç N.
Ergene N.
Arda
Némos
Kápi
Kemalyeri
Kokacımen T.
Bü. Kemikli Br.
Kumkale
Truva
Intepe
Ilyas Br.
Tavşan Adaları
115
85
D
E
F
1
2
3
4

N. KÉRKIRA
N. ΚΕΡΚΥΡΑ
KÉRKIRA
ΚΕΡΚΥΡΑ
Sidári
Paleokastrítsa
Kassiópi
Gouviá
Benítses
Messongí
Lefkími
Akr. Asprókavos
N. Paxí
N. Παξοί
Gáios
Láka
Longós
N. Andípaxi
N. Αντίπαξοι
Sarandë
Buthrotum
Vurg
Konispol
Igoumenítsa
Ηγουμενίτσα
Filiátes
Parapótamos
Paramithiá
THESPROTÍA
Sívota
Pérdika
Párga
Πάργα
Kanaláki
Préveza
Πρέβεζα
PRÉVEZA
Kassópi
Nikópoli
Lefkáda
Λευκάδα
N. LEFKÁDA
N. ΛΕΥΚΑΔΑ
Nidrí
Vassilikí
Akr. Doukáto
N. Kálamos
N. Kastós
Ioánina
Ιωάννινα
IOÁNINA
Dodóni
Métsovo
Μέτσοβο
Pérama
Zagória
Monodéndri
Kónitsa
Kónitsa
Delvináki
ÍPIROS
Árta
Άρτα
ÁRTA
Filipiáda
Vónitsa
Amvrakikós Kólpos
Αμβρακικός Κόλπος
Amfilohía
Αμφιλοχία
Astakós
ETOLÍA AKARNANÍA
Agrínio
Αγρίνιο
Messolóngi
Μεσολόγγι
Etolikó
N. Itháki
Itháki
Fiskárdo
Ássos
Sámi
Argostóli
Αργοστόλι
Lixoúri
Póros
N. KEFALONIÁ
N. ΚΕΦΑΛΛΩΝΙΑ
IÓNIA
IÓNIO
78
86
Passage exceptionnel

THESSALÍA
STERÉA ELLÁDA
LÁRISSA
MAGNISSÍA
FTHIÓTIDA
FOKÍDA
VIOTÍA
KARDÍTSA
LÁRISSA ΛΑΡΙΣΑ
VÓLOS ΒΟΛΟΣ
Lamía Λαμία
Tríkala Τρίκαλα
Kardítsa Καρδίτσα
Kalambáka Καλαμπάκα
Elassóna Ελασσόνα
Tírnavos Τύρναβος
Fársala Φάρσαλα
Almirós Αλμυρός
Karpenissi Καρπενήσι
Amfissa Αμφισσα
Delfi
Itéa Ιτέα
Livadiá Λειβαδειά
Thíva Θήβα
Náfpaktos Ναύπακτος
PÁTRA ΠΑΤΡΑ
Egio Αίγιο
Kaména Voúrla Καμένα Βούρλα
Loutrá Edipsoú Λουτρά Αιδηψού
Atalándi Αταλάντη
Orhomenós Ορχομενός
Pagassitikós Kólpos Παγασητικός Κόλπος
Maliakós Kólpos Μαλιακός Κόλπος
Kólpos Itéas Κόλπος Ιτέας
Korinthiakós Kólpos Κορινθιακός Κόλπος
Óros Óssa Όρος Όσσα
Óros Pílio
Óros Óthris Όρος Όθρυς
Óros Parnassós
Óros Gióna
79
84
87

E G É O P É L A G O S
VÓRIES SPORÁDES
ΒΟΡΕΙΕΣ ΣΠΟΡΑΔΕΣ
N. Skíathos
N. Σκίαθος
N. Alónissos
N. Αλόννησος
N. Skópelos
N. Σκόπελος
N. ÉVIA
N. ΕΥΒΟΙΑ
N. SKÍROS
N. ΣΚΥΡΟΣ
N. Kirá Panagiá
N. Κυρά Παναγιά
N. Gioúra
N. Γιούρα
N. Pipéri
N. Πιπέρι
N. Peristéra
N. Περιστέρα
N. Skandzoúra
N. Σκαντζούρα
N. Ψαθούρα
N. Πράσσο
N. Αδελφοί
N. Τσουγκριά
Diavlos Pelagonissou
Diavlos Skiáthou
Diavlos Skopélou
Diavlos Alonissou
Diavlos Trikeriou
Vórios Evoikós Kólpos
Vόρειος Ευβοϊκός Κόλπος
Nótios Evoikós Kólpos
Νότιος Ευβοϊκός Κόλπος
Thessaloníki
Vólos
Kassándra
Κασσάνδρα
Possidi
Ποσείδι
Kalándra
Καλάνδρα
Akr. Kassándras
Ακρ. Κασσάνδρας
N. Skióni
N. Σκιώνη
Loutrá
Λουτρά
Haniótis
Χανιώτης
Polýhrono
Πολύχρονο
Pefkohóri
Πευκοχώρι
Ag. Paraskeví
Αγ. Παρασκευή
Palioúri
Παλιούρι
Akr. Palioúri
Ακρ. Παλιούρι
Pórto Carras
Πόρτο Καρράς
Toróni
Τορώνη
Koufós
Κουφός
Kalamítsi
Καλαμίτσι
Akr. Drépano
Ακρ. Δρέπανο
Zagorá
Ζαγορά
Horeftó
Χορευτό
Ag. Ioánis
Αγ. Ιωάννης
Tsangaráda
Τσαγκαράδα
Hánia
Χάνια
Portariá
Πορταριά
Vizítsa
Βυζίτσα
Miliés
Μηλιές
Kalamáki
Καλαμάκι
Neohóri
Νεοχώρι
K. Gadzéa
Κ. Γατζέα
Kalá Nerá
Καλά Νερά
Siki
Συκή
Áfissos
Άφυσσος
Argalasti
Αργαλαστή
Metóhi
Μετόχι
Promíri
Προμύρι
Milína
Μηλίνα
Láfkos
Λαύκος
Platania
Πλατανιά
Trikeri
Τρικέρι
Ag. Kiriakí
Skíathos
Σκίαθος
Kástro
Κάστρο
Koukounariés
Κουκουναριές
Glóssa
Γλώσσα
Loutráki
Λουτράκι
Skópelos
Σκόπελος
Agnóndas
Αγνώντας
Alónissos
Αλόννησος
Patitiri
Πατητήρι
Akr. Gérakas
Ακρ. Γέρακας
Akr. Kártsino
Ακρ. Κάρτσινο
Skíros
Σκύρος
Linariá
Λιναριά
Akr. Lithári
Ακρ. Λιθάρι
N. Σκυροπούλα
N. Βαλάξα
N. Σαρακηνό
Agriovótano
Αγριοβότανο
Akr. Artemísio
Ακρ. Αρτεμίσιο
Pefki
Πευκί
Artemísio
Αρτεμίσιο
Kanatádika
Κανατάδικα
Oreí
Ωρεοί
Istiéa
Ιστιαία
Vassiliká
Βασιλικά
Papádes
Παπάδες
Paralia Kotsikiás
Παραλία Κοτσικιάς
Agiókambos
Αγιόκαμπος
Voutás
Βουτάς
Kerassiá
Κερασιά
Edipsós
Αιδηψός
Kastaniótissa
Καστανιώτισσα
Xiró
Ξηρό
Ag. Ána
Αγ. Άννα
Angáli
Αγκάλη
Ília
Ηλία
Loutrá Edipsoú
Λουτρά Αιδηψού
Rovies
Ροβιές
Kria Vrissi
Κρύα Βρύση
Kimássi
Κυμάσι
Strofiliá
Στροφυλιά
Mandoúdi
Μαντούδι
Límni
Λίμνη
Prokópi
Προκόπι
Galatáki
Γαλατάκι
Kandíli
Κανδήλι
Sarakíniko
Σαρακήνικο
Pílio
Πήλιο
Pagóndas
Παγώντας
Ag. Sofía
Αγ. Σοφία
Óros Dírfis
Glifáda
Γλυφάδα
Kími
Κύμη
Akr. Kímis
Ακρ. Κύμης
Paralía Kímis
Παραλ. Κύμης
Órmos Kímis
Vitala
Βιτάλα
Metóhi
Μετόχι
Stavrós
Σταυρός
Átali
Άτταλη
Psahná
Ψαχνά
Politiká
Πολιτικά
Nerotriviá
Νεροτριβιά
Ágios
Άγιος
Kastélla
Καστέλλα
N. Artáki
N. Αρτάκη
Steni
Στενή
Kathení
Καθενοί
Pissónas
Πισσώνας
Mistrós
Μίστρος
Séta
Σέτα
Konistres
Κονίστρες
Oxilithos
Οξύλιθος
Ohthonía
Οχθωνιά
Akr. Ohthoniá
Monódrio
Μονόδριο
Trahíli
Τραχήλι
Halkída
Χαλκίδα
Afráti
Αφράτι
Óros Ólimbos
Vassilikó
Βασιλικό
Erétria
Ερέτρια
Gimnó
Γυμνό
Ág. Loukás
Άγ. Λουκάς
Alivéri
Αλιβέρι
Neohóri
Νεοχώρι
Ahladerí
Αχλαδερή
Lépoura
Λέπουρα
Krieza
Κριεζά
Akr. Poúnda
Ακρ. Πούντα
Ag. Apóstoli
Αγ. Απόστολοι
Vélos
Βέλος
Dístos
Δύστος
Kóskina
Κόσκινα
Amárinthos
Αμάρυνθος
Lefkandí
Λευκαντί
Akr. Kérata
Ακρ. Κέρατα
Theológos
Θεολόγος
Malessina
Μαλεσίνα
Lárimna
Λάρυμνα
Proskinás
Προσκυνάς
Martino
Μαρτίνο
Pávlos
Παύλος
Akr. Gátza
Ακρ. Γάτζα
Akr. Gáidaros
Ακρ. Γάιδαρος
Kástro
Κάστρο
Loukíssia
Λουκίσια
Drossiá
Δροσιά
Ritsóna
Ριτσώνα
Paralímni
Παραλίμνη
Iliki
Υλίκη
Mouriki
Μουρίκι
Akréfnio
Ακραίφνιο
Kopaïda
Κωπαΐδα
Aliartos
Αλίαρτος
Thíva
Θήβα
Vágia
Βάγια
Thespiés
Θεσπιές
Neohoráki
Νεοχωράκι
Tanágra
Τανάγρα
Vathí
Βαθύ
Dilessi
Δήλεσι
Inói
Οινόη
Assopía
Ασωπία
Skála Oropoú
Σκάλα Ωρωπού
Markópoulo
Μαρκόπουλο
Ag. Apóstoli
Αγ. Απόστολοι
Amfiaraío
Αμφιαράειο
Ag. Thomás
Αγ. Θωμάς
Avlóna
Αυλώνα
Melissohóri
Μελισσοχώρι
Léftkra
Λεύκτρα
Elopía
Ελλοπία
Kaparéli
Καπαρέλλι
Erithrés
Ερυθρές
Platées
Πλαταιές
Eleftherés
Ελευθερές
Skoúrta
Σκούρτα
Pili
Πύλη
Stefáni
Στεφάνη
Óros Párnitha
Πάρνηθα
Ag. Triáda
Αγ. Τριάδα
Málakasa
Μαλακάσα
Polidéndri
Πολυδένδρι
Kapandríti
Καπανδρίτι
Ramnoús
Ραμνούς
Grammatikó
Γραμματικό
Marathónas
Μαραθώνας
Ag. Marína
Αγ. Μαρίνα
N. Stira
N. Στύρα
Argiró
Αργυρό
Zárakes
Ζάρακες
Almiropótamos
Αλμυροπόταμος
Polipótamos
Πολυπόταμος
Vareléi
Βαρελαίοι
Kalérgo
Akr. Kafiréas
Ακρ. Καφηρέας
N. Kavaliani
Porto Germenó
Vília
Ag. Vassílios
Αγ. Βασίλειος
Ioánis
Livanátes
Λιβανάτες
Skála
Σκάλα
Arkítsa
Αρκίτσα
80
83
87
88
A
B
C
1
2
3
4

N. LÍMNOS
Ν. ΛΗΜΝΟΣ
Mírina
Μύρινα
Moúdros
Μούδρος
Kondopoúli
Κοντοπούλι
Bozcaada
Ezine
Ayvacık
Küçükkuyu
Bayramiç
N. Ág. Efstrátios
Ν. Άγ. Ευστράτιος
Thessaloniki
Míthimna
Μήθυμνα
N. LÉSVOS
Ν. ΛΕΣΒΟΣ
Mitilíni
Μυτιλήνη
Kalloní
Καλλονή
Sígri
Σίγρι
Eressós
Ερεσός
Plomári
Πλωμάρι
Agiássos
Αγιάσος
Polihnítos
Πολιχνίτος
N. Psará
Ν. Ψαρά
N. HÍOS
Ν. ΧΙΟΣ
Híos
Χίος
Vrondádos
Βροντάδος
Mestá
Μεστά
Pirgí
Πυργί
Çeşme
Karaburun
Alaçatı
Uzunkuyu
81
89
115
Α Ι Γ Α Ι Ο Π Ε Λ Α Γ Ο Σ

82
83

N. ZÁKINTHOS
Ν. ΖΑΚΥΝΘΟΣ
Zákinthos
Ζάκυνθος
Kólpos Laganá
Κόλπος Λαγανά
Akr. Marathiá
Ακρ. Μαραθιά
Akr. Skinári
Ακρ. Σκινάρι
Diavlos Zakinthou
Kiparissiakós Kólpos
Κυπαρισσιακός Κόλπος
Messiniakós Kólpos
Μεσσηνιακός Κόλπος
N. Strofádes
Ν. Στροφάδες
N. Sapiéndza
Ν. Σαπιέντζα
N. Shiza
Ν. Σχίζα
N. Proti
Ν. Πρώτη
N. Sfaktiria
Ν. Σφακτηρία
Akr. Akritas
Ακρ. Ακρίτας
Akr. Katákolo
Ακρ. Κατάκολο
Hlemoútsi
Χλεμούτσι
Kilíni
Κυλλήνη
Gastoúni
Γαστούνη
Amaliáda
Αμαλιάδα
Pírgos
Πύργος
Olimbía
Ολυμπία
Arhéa Olympia
Αρχ. Ολυμπία
Katákolo
Κατάκολο
K. Ahaia
Κ. Αχαΐα
Kalávrita
Καλάβρυτα
AHAÍA
ΑΧΑΪΑ
ILÍA
PELOPÓ
ARKAD
Megalópoli
Μεγαλόπολη
Andrítsena
Ανδρίτσαινα
Vassés
Βάσσες
Kiparissía
Κυπαρισσία
Filiatrá
Φιλιατρά
Gargaliáni
Γαργαλιάνοι
MESSINÍA
Messíni
Μεσσήνη
Kalamáta
Καλαμάτα
Pílos
Πύλος
Methóni
Μεθώνη
Koróni
Κορώνη
Ithómi
Ιθώμη
Athína
0
2 km
A. LIÓSSIA
AHARNES
KIFISSIÁ
IRÁKLIO
MAROÚSSI
OLIMBIAKÓ STÁDIO
PETROÚPOLI
N. LIÓSSIA
N. IONÍA
HALÁNDRI
FILOTHÉI
PERISTÉRI
PATÍSSIA
PSIHIKÓ
N. PSIHIKÓ
HOLARGÓS
DAFNÍ
HAIDÁRI
EGÁLEO
AG. VARVÁRA
NÍKEA
AKRÓPOLI
KESSARIANÍ
KALITHÉA
MOSHÁTO
PIREÁS
N. SMÍRNI
ILIOÚPOLI
AMFITHÉA
P. FÁLIRO
ARGIROÚPOLI
KALAMÁKI
ÁLIMOS
ELINIKÓ
Olympic Airways
International
FILÍ
AG-TRIADA
THESSALONÍKI
LAMÍA
PENDÉLI
RAFÍNA, VRAVRÓNA, MARATHÓNAS
ÓROS IMITÓS
GLIFÁDA, SOÚNIO, VOULIAGMÉNI
VOULIAGMÉNI, SOÚNIO
PÉRAMA, KÓRINTHOS
SKARAMANGÁS, ELEFSÍNA, KÓRINTHOS, PÁTRA

83
88
90
ATHÍNA
ΑΘΗΝΑ
PIREÁS
ΠΕΙΡΑΙΑΣ
ATIKÍ-PIREÁS
KORINTHÍA
ARGOLÍDA
LAKONÍA
Kórinthos
Κόρινθος
Loutráki
Λουτράκι
Xilókastro
Ξυλόκαστρο
Kiáto
Κιάτο
Mégara
Μέγαρα
Elefsína
Ελευσίνα
Salamína
Σαλαμίνα
Glifáda
Γλυφάδα
Vouliagméni
Βουλιαγμένη
Kifissiá
Κηφισιά
Dafní
Δαφνί
Aharnés
Αχαρνές
Asprópirgos
Ασπρόπυργος
Mikínes
Μυκήνες
Árgos
Άργος
Náfplio
Ναύπλιο
Tirintha
Τίρυνθα
Arh. Epídavros
Αρχ. Επίδαυρος
Tripoli
Τρίπολη
Nemea
Νεμέα
Méthana
Μέθανα
Póros
Πόρος
Égina
Αίγινα
Ídra
Ύδρα
Ermióni
Ερμιόνη
Kranídi
Κρανίδι
Portohéli
Πορτοχέλι
Spétses
Σπέτσες
Ástros
Άστρος
Leonídio
Λεωνίδιο
Spárti
Σπάρτη
Mistrás
Μυστράς
Géraki
Γεράκι
Monemvassía
Μονεμβασία
Neápoli
Νεάπολη
Gíthio
Γύθειο
Areópoli
Αρεόπολη
Máni
Μάνη
Moláí
Μολάοι
N. Salamína
N. Égina
N. Póros
N. Ídra
N. Spétses
N. Velopoúla
N. Falkonéra
N. Makrónisos
Hers. Methánon
Saronikós Kólpos
Argolikós Kólpos
Lakonikós Kólpos
Korinthiakós Kólpos
MIRTÓO PÉLAGOS
ΜΥΡΤΩΟ ΠΕΛΑΓΟΣ
Óros Párnonas
Óros Taígetos
Óros Párnitha
Diórigа Korínthou
Akr. Soúnio
Akr. Maléas
Akr. Ténaro
Akr. Iréo

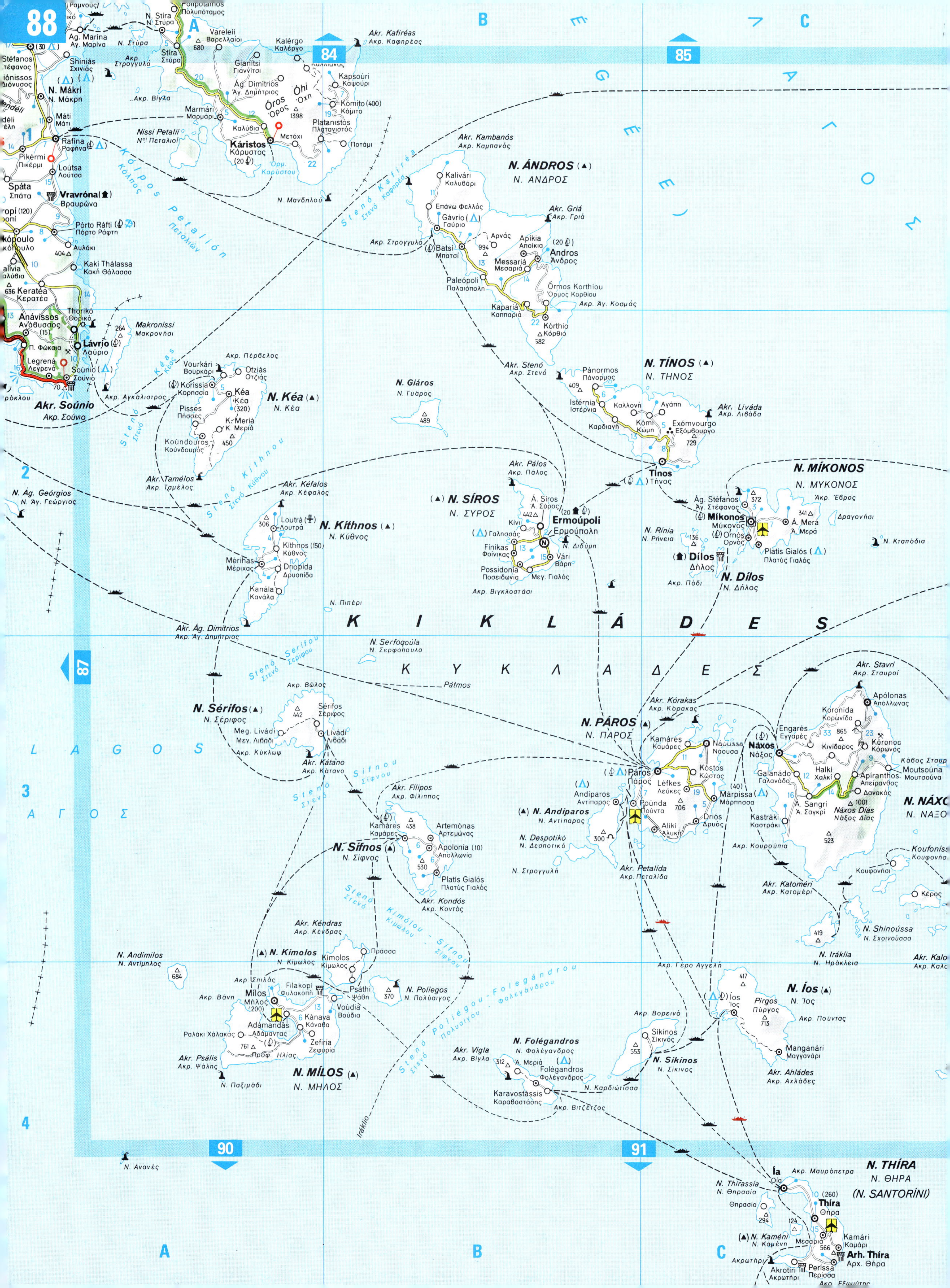

84
85
87
90
91
A
B
C
1
2
3
4
N. ÁNDROS
N. ΑΝΔΡΟΣ
N. TÍNOS
N. ΤΗΝΟΣ
N. MÍKONOS
N. ΜΥΚΟΝΟΣ
N. Kéa
N. Κέα
N. Kíthnos
N. Κύθνος
N. SÍROS
N. ΣΥΡΟΣ
N. Sérifos
N. Σέριφος
N. Sífnos
N. Σίφνος
N. MÍLOS
N. ΜΗΛΟΣ
N. Kímolos
N. Κίμωλος
N. PÁROS
N. ΠΑΡΟΣ
N. Andíparos
N. Αντίπαρος
N. NÁXOS
N. ΝΑΞΟΣ
N. Íos
N. Ίος
N. Síkinos
N. Σίκινος
N. Folégandros
N. Φολέγανδρος
N. THÍRA
N. ΘΗΡΑ
(N. SANTORÍNI)
N. Dílos
N. Δήλος
N. Giáros
N. Γυάρος
Makronissi
Μακρονήσι
K I K L Á D E S
Κ Υ Κ Λ Α Δ Ε Σ
L A G O S
Α Γ Ο Σ
Ε Γ Ε Ο
Α Ι Γ Α Ι Ο
Kólpos Petalión
Κόλπος Πεταλιών
Stenó Kafiréa
Stenó Kéas
Stenó Kíthnou
Stenó Sérifou
Stenó Sífnou
Stenó Kimólou - Sífnou
Stenó Poliégou - Folegándrou
Akr. Soúnio
Ακρ. Σούνιο
Akr. Kafiréas
Ακρ. Καφηρέας
Akr. Kambanós
Ακρ. Καμπανός
Akr. Griá
Ακρ. Γριά
Akr. Stenó
Ακρ. Στενό
Akr. Livádа
Ακρ. Λιβάδα
Akr. Tamélos
Ακρ. Ταμέλος
Akr. Kéfalos
Ακρ. Κέφαλος
Akr. Pálos
Ακρ. Πάλος
Akr. Ág. Dimítrios
Ακρ. Άγ. Δημήτριος
Akr. Kátano
Ακρ. Κάτανο
Akr. Kórakas
Ακρ. Κόρακας
Akr. Stavrí
Ακρ. Σταυρί
Akr. Petalída
Ακρ. Πεταλίδα
Akr. Katoméri
Ακρ. Κατομέρι
Akr. Kéndras
Ακρ. Κένδρας
Akr. Kondós
Ακρ. Κοντός
Akr. Filipos
Ακρ. Φίλιππος
Akr. Psális
Ακρ. Ψάλις
Akr. Vígla
Ακρ. Βίγλα
Akr. Ahládes
Ακρ. Αχλάδες
Kárístos
Κάρυστος
Rafína
Ραφήνα
Pikérmi
Πικέρμι
Loútsa
Λούτσα
Spáta
Σπάτα
Vravróna
Βραυρώνα
Pórto Ráfti
Πόρτο Ράφτη
Kaki Thálassa
Κακή Θάλασσα
Keratéa
Κερατέα
Anávissos
Ανάβυσσος
Thorikó
Θορικό
Lávrio
Λαύριο
Legrená
Λεγρενά
Soúnio
Σούνιο
Marmári
Μαρμάρι
Stíra
Στύρα
Andros
Άνδρος
Batsí
Μπατσί
Gávrio
Γαύριο
Kórthio
Κόρθιο
Tínos
Τήνος
Pánormos
Πάνορμος
Mikonos
Μύκονος
Áno Merá
Ermoúpoli
Ερμούπολη
Kéa
Κέα
Korissía
Κορησσία
Vourkári
Βουρκάρι
Pisses
Πίσσες
Koúndouros
Κούνδουρος
Loutrá
Λουτρά
Kíthnos
Κύθνος
Mérihas
Μέριχας
Dríopida
Δρυοπίδα
Kanála
Κανάλα
Sérifos
Σέριφος
Livádi
Λιβάδι
Kamáres
Καμάρες
Apolonía
Απολλωνία
Artemónas
Αρτεμώνας
Platís Gialós
Πλατύς Γιαλός
Mílos
Μήλος
Adamandás
Αδάμαντας
Filakopí
Φυλακωπή
Kímolos
Κίμωλος
Páros
Πάρος
Náoussa
Νάουσα
Léfkes
Λεύκες
Mărpissa
Μάρπισσα
Aliki
Αλυκή
Andíparos
Αντίπαρος
Náxos
Νάξος
Apóllonas
Απόλλωνας
Filóti
Apíranthos
Απείρανθος
Íos
Ίος
Folégandros
Φολέγανδρος
Karavostássis
Καραβοστάσης
Ía
Οία
Thíra
Θήρα
Kamári
Καμάρι
Perissa
Περίσσα
Akrotíri
Ακρωτήρι
Arh. Thíra
Αρχ. Θήρα
N. Thirassía
N. Θηρασία
N. Kaméni
N. Καμένη
N. Shinoússa
N. Σχοινούσα
N. Iráklia
N. Ηράκλεια
Koufoníssi
Κουφονήσι
Kéros
Κέρος
N. Políegos
N. Πολύαιγος
N. Andímilos
N. Αντίμηλος
N. Serfoqoúla
N. Σερφοπούλα
N. Despotikó
N. Δεσποτικό
N. Ananés
N. Ανανές
Pátmos
Iráklio

N. SÁMOS
Ν. ΣΑΜΟΣ
Karlovássi
Καρλοβάσι
Sámos
Σάμος
Vathí
Pithagório
Πυθαγόρειο
Paleókastro
Kokári
Vourliótes
Marathókambos
Mitilinii
Pírgos
Hóra
Spatharei
Pagóndas
Iréo
Kouméika
Ag. Kiriaki
Or. Kerketéas
Karvoúni
Léka
N. Samiopoúla
N. IKARÍA
Ν. ΙΚΑΡΙΑ
Akr. Fanári
Armenistis
Évdilos
Karavóstamo
Thérma
Ag. Kirikos
Athéras
Hristós
Hrisóstomos
Thérma Lefkádas
Amálo
Amoúdia
Karkinágri
Akr. Pápas
Thímena
Foúrni
N. Thímena
N. Foúrni
N. Ag. Minás
Agathoníssi
Meg. Horió
Arkí
N. Arkí
N. Lipsí
Lipsí
Skála
Kámpos
N. Pátmos
Pátmos
Pireás
Farmakoníssi
N. Arhángelos
Parthéni
Ag. Marina
N. Léros
Lakí
Xirókambos
Emboriós
Argiónda
Vathís
N. Télendos
Mirtiés
N. Kálimnos
Kálimnos
N. Psérimos
N. Kalólimnos
N. KOS
Kos
Tingáki
Mastihári
Andimáhia
Asfendioú
Asklipiío
Ag. Fokás
Pilio
Kardámena
Kéfalos
Ág. Ioánis
Akr. Krikelos
N. Giali
Mandráki
Páli
Nikiá
N. Nissiros
N. Pergoússa
N. Pahiá
N. Tílos
Meg. Horió
Livádia
Akr. Tráhilos
Akr. Orfós
N. Kandelioússa
N. Astipálea
Astipálea
Análipsi
Vathí
Akr. Floúda
Akr. Poúlari
Akr. Hiloús
N. Ofidoússa
N. AMORGÓS
Ν. ΑΜΟΡΓΟΣ
Katápola
Egiáli
Hozoviótissa
Amorgós
Akr. Xódoto
N. Nikouría
Arkessini
N. Donoússa
N. Levítha
N. Kínaros
N. Anáfi
Drépano
Kalamiótissa
Katelimátsa
N. Sírna
ΔΩΔΕΚΑΝΗΣΑ
DODEKÁNISS
Kuşadası Körfezi
Kusadasi
Selçuk
Efes
Pamucak
Çamlık
Ortaklar
Söke
Davutlar
Samsun Dağı
Karine
Atburgazı
Balat
Akköy
Bafa Gölü
Didim
Altınkum plajı
Tekağaç Br.
Mersinet
Mandalya Körfezi
Salih Ad.
Yalıkavak
Pazar Dağı
Ortakent
Gümüşlük
Turgutreis
Bodrum
Koca Br.
Akr. Skandári
Kara Ad.
Knidas
Claros
Değirmendere
Gümüldür
Doğanbey
Sığacık
Kiran Da.
Çılga Br.
Teke Br.
Emboriós
Kómi
Akr. Mástiho
Durmus Dağ
85
115
92
93
D
E
F

87
88
N. KÍTHIRA
Kíthira
Κύθηρα
Kapsáli
Καψάλι
Akr. Kapélo
Ακρ. Καπέλλο
Livádi
Λιβάδι
Milopótamos
Μυλοπόταμος
Aroniádika
Αρωνιάδικα
Potamós
Ποταμός
Ag. Pelagia
Αγ. Πελαγία
Karavás
Καραβάς
Frilingiánika
Φριλιγκιάνικα
Diakófti
Διακόφτι
Avlémonas
Αβλέμονας
Akr. Spathí
Ακρ. Σπαθί
Porthmós Elafonissou
Πορθμός Ελαφονήσου
Elafonissi
Ελαφονήσι
Neápoli
Νεάπολη
Velanídia
Βελανίδια
Akr. Maléas
Ακρ. Μαλέας
Ág. Andréas
Άγ. Ανδρέας
Pandánassa
Παντάνασσα
Nómia
Νόμια
Tálanda
Τάλαντα
Óros Krithína
Kólpos Epidávrou Limirás
Akr. Psális
Ακρ. Ψάλις
N. MÍLOS
Ν. ΜΗΛΟΣ
N. Ananés
Ν. Ανανές
Irakilo
KRITIKÓ PÉLAG
(MER
N. Andikíthira
Ν. Αντικύθηρα
Potamós
Ποταμός
Galanianá
Γαλανιανά
Akr. Kefáli
Ακρ. Κεφάλι
Akr. Apolitáres
Ακρ. Απολυτάρες
Kastéli
Akr. Spánda
Ακρ. Σπάντα
Diktinéon
Δικτυναίον
Akr. Voúxa
Ακρ. Βούξα
Kólpos Kissámou
Κόλπος Κισσάμου
Kólpos Hanion
Κόλπος Χανίων
Rodopós
Ροδωπός
Goniá
Γωνιά
Kolimvári
Κολυμβάρι
Kastéli
Καστέλλι
Falássarna
Φαλάσαρνα
Plátanos
Πλάτανος
Polirinia
Πολυρρηνία
Topólia
Τοπόλια
Kámbos
Κάμπος
Hrissoskalitissa
Χρυσοσκαλίτισσα
Élos
Έλος
Strovlés
Στροβλές
Kándanos
Κάντανος
Sklavopoúla
Σκλαβοπούλα
Akr. Kriós
Ακρ. Κριός
Paleohóra
Παλαιοχώρα
Rodováni
Ροδοβάνι
Soúgia
Σούγια
Máleme
Μάλεμε
Ag. Marina
Αγ. Μαρίνα
Voukoliés
Βουκολιές
Alikianós
Αλικιανός
Fournés
Φουρνές
Láki
Λάκκοι
Omalós
Ομαλός
Xilóskalo
Ξυλόσκαλο
Lefka Óri
Farángi Samariás
Ag. Rouméli
Αγ. Ρουμέλη
Haniá
Χανιά
HANIÁ
Hers. Akrotíri
Χερσ. Ακρωτήρι
Stavrós
Σταυρός
Soúda
Σούδα
Stérnes
Στέρνες
Akr. Drápano
Ακρ. Δράπανο
Mourniés
Μουρνιές
Áptera
Άπτερα
Kalíves
Καλύβες
Vrisses
Βρύσες
Askífou
Ασκύφου
Anópoli
Ανώπολη
Sfakiá
Σφακιά
Frangokástelo
Φραγκοκάστελο
Georgioúpoli
Γεωργιούπολη
Órmos Almiróu
Όρμος Αλμυρού
Réthimno
Ρέθυμνο
RÉTHIMNO
Episkopí
Επισκοπή
Argiroúpoli
Αργυρούπολη
Armeni
Αρμένοι
Sellia
Σελλιά
Plakiás
Πλακιάς
Préveli
Πρέβελη
Spíli
Σπήλι
Kissoú Kámbos
Κισσού Κάμπος
N. Paximádia
N. Gavdopoúla
Ν. Γαυδοπούλα
N. Gávdos
Ν. Γαύδος
Pireás
Thessaloníki
A
B
C
1
2
3
4

N. Astipálea
N. Αστυπάλαια
N. Síkinos
N. Σίκινος
Folégandros
Φολέγανδρος
Karavostássis
Καραβοστάσης
Akr. Vígla
Akr. Ahládes
Akr. Αχλάδες
N. Ánidros
N. Άνυδρος
88
N. THÍRA
N. ΘΗΡΑ
(N. SANTORÍNI)
Ía
N. Thirassía
N. Θηρασία
Thíra
Θήρα
Kamári
Καμάρι
Arh. Thíra
Αρχ. Θήρα
Akrotíri
Ακρωτήρι
Períssa
Περίσσα
Akr. Exomítis
Akr. Εξωμύτης
N. Kaméni
Akr. Drépano
Akr. Δρέπανο
N. Anáfi
N. Ανάφη
Kalamiótissa
Anáfi
Ανάφη
Katelimátsa
N. Makrá
N. Μακρά
N. Paheiá
N. Παχειά
N. Hristianí
N. Χριστιανή
N. Askanía
N. Ασκανία
N. Ofidoússa
N. Οφιδούσσα
Astipálea
Akr. Hilí
Iráklio
Sitía
92
N. Zafóra
N. Ζαφόρα
ΚΡΗΤΙΚΟ ΠΕΛΑΓΟΣ
(MER DE CRÈTE)
N. Hamilí
N. Χαμηλή
N. KRÍTI
N. ΚΡΗΤΗ
Avgó
Thessaloníki
Pireás
Thíra
Sífnos
N. Día
N. Δία
Kárpathos
Ródos
Lemessós (Kipros)
Haifa
Akr. Stavrós
Akr. Σταυρός
Ag. Pelagía
Αγ. Πελαγία
Balí
Μπαλί
IRÁKLIO
ΗΡΑΚΛΕΙΟ
N. Alikarnassós
N. Αλικαρνασσός
Goúrnes
Γούρνες
Limáni Hersonissou
Λιμάνι Χερσονήσου
Stalída
Σταλίδα
Mália
Μάλια
Mílatos
Μίλατος
Neápoli
Νεάπολη
Vrouhás
Βρουχάς
Akr. Ág. Ioánis
Akr. Άγ. Ιωάννης
Spinalónga
Σπιναλόγκα
Hers. Spinalónga
Eloúnda
Ελούντα
Kólpos Mirambélou
Κόλπος Μιραμπέλου
N. Pahimáda
N. Παχιμάδα
N. Dragonáda
N. Δραγονάδα
N. Gianisáda
N. Γιανυσάδα
Itanós
Ιτανός
Váï
Sitía
Σητεία
Toploú
Μονή Τοπλού
Palékastro
Παλαίκαστρο
Skopí
Σκοπή
Móhlos
Μόχλος
Ag. Nikólaos
Άγ. Νικόλαος
Kritsá
Κριτσά
Lató
Kavoússi
Καβούσι
Sfáka
Σφάκα
LASSÍTHI
Zákros
Ζάκρος
K. Zákros
Κ. Ζάκρος
Hamézi
Piskokéfalo
Πισκοκέφαλο
Handrás
Χανδράς
Zíros
Ζίρος
Kaló Horió
Καλό Χωριό
Lithínes
Λιθίνες
Makrigialós
Μακρυγιαλός
Koutsourás
Κουτσουράς
Ag. Fotiá
Αγ. Φωτιά
Goúdouras
Γούδουρας
Koufoníssi
Κουφονήσι
Ierápetra
Ιεράπετρα
N. Hrissí
N. Χρυσή
Pahiá Ámos
Παχειά Άμμος
Gourniá
Γουρνιά
Kaló Horió
Istro
Anatolí
Ανατολή
Mírtos
Μύρτος
Amoudára
Αμμουδάρα
Árvi
Άρβη
Keratókambos
Κερατόκαμπος
Á. Viánnos
Α. Βιάννος
Óros Díkti
Δίκτη
Diktéo Ándro
Δικταίο Άντρο
Psihró
Ψυχρό
Lassíthi
Ag. Geórgios
Αγ. Γεώργιος
Kastéli
Καστέλι
Potamiés
Ποταμιές
Gouves
Γούβες
Karterós
Καρτερός
Episkopí
Επισκοπή
Knossós
Κνωσός
Arhánes
Αρχάνες
Ag. Paraskiés
Αγ. Παρασκιές
Arkalohóri
Αρκαλοχώρι
IRÁKLIO
Tílissos
Τύλισος
Goúves
Vathípetro
Βαθύπετρο
Ag. Thomás
Αγ. Θωμάς
Ag. Varvára
Αγ. Βαρβάρα
Ag. Mironas
Αγ. Μύρωνας
Gioúhtas
Γιούχτας
Tefeli
Τεφέλι
Garipa
Γαρίπα
Pírgos
Πύργος
Skiniás
Σκινιάς
Ahendriás
Αχεντριάς
Óros Ídi
Όρος Ίδη
Idéo Ándro
Ιδαίο Άντρο
Anógia
Ανώγεια
Axós
Αξός
Goniés
Γωνιές
Kroussónas
Κρουσώνας
Fódele
Φόδελε
Rodiá
Ροδιά
Amoudára
Αμμουδάρα
Pérama
Πέραμα
Melidóni
Μελιδόνι
Margarítes
Μαργαρίτες
Arkádi
Αρκάδι
Zoniana
Ζωνιανά
Fourfourás
Φουρφουράς
Kamáres
Καμάρες
Vrondissi
Βροντήσι
Zarós
Ζαρός
Válsamonero
Βαλσαμόνερο
Timbáki
Τυμπάκι
Ag. Galíni
Αγ. Γαλήνη
Vóri
Βόροι
Míres
Μοίρες
Górtis
Γόρτυς
Ag. Déka
Αγ. Δέκα
Gangáles
Γκαγκάλες
Ag. Triáda
Αγ. Τριάδα
Kamiláři
Καμηλάρι
Festós
Φαιστός
Pómbia
Πόμπια
Mátala
Μάταλα
Messarás
Vagioniá
Βαγιονιά
Hárakas
Χάρακας
Asterousia
Αστερούσια
Paranímfi
Παράνυμφοι
Kapetaniana
Καπετανιανά
Lendas
Λέντας
Kalí Liménes
Καλοί Λιμένες
Antiskári
Αντισκάρι
Akr. Líthino
Akr. Λίθινο
Sitía
D
E
F
1
2
3
4

N. Síkinos
Ν. Σίκινος
Manganári
Μαγγανάρι
Akr. Ahládes
Ακρ. Αχλάδες
N. Άνυδρος
N. Astipálea
Ν. Αστυπάλαια
Akr. Floúda
Ακρ. Φλούδα
Vathí
Βαθύ
Akr. Poúlari
Ακρ. Πούλαρι
Análipsi
Ανάληψη
Astipálea
Αστυπάλαια
Λιβάδιο
Akr. Hiloús
Ακρ. Χειλούς
89
N. Οφιδούσσα
N. THÍRA
Ν. ΘΗΡΑ
(N. SANTORÍNI)
Ía
Οία
Ακρ. Μαυρόπετρα
N. Thirassía
Ν. Θηρασία
Θηρασία
Thíra
Θήρα
Kamári
Καμάρι
N. Kaméni
Ν. Καμένη
Μεσαριά
Arh. Thíra
Αρχ. Θήρα
Ακρωτήρι
Akrotíri
Ακρωτήρι
Perissa
Περίσσα
Ακρ. Εξωμύτης
Akr. Drépano
Ακρ. Δρέπανο
N. Anáfi
Ν. Ανάφη
Kalamiótissa
Καλαμιώτισσα
Anáfi
Ανάφη
Katelimátsa
Κατελιμάτσα
N. Μακρά
N. Παχειά
N. Sírna
Ν. Σύρνα
Σύρνα
N. Hristianí
Ν. Χριστιανή
N. Ασκανία
Iráklio
Sitía
N. Zafóra
Ν. Ζαφόρα
Karavónissia
Καραβόνησια
Κ Ρ Η Τ Ι Κ Ο   Π Ε Λ Α Γ Ο Σ
N. Hamilí
Ν. Χαμηλή
N. Divoúnia
Ν. Διβούνια
91
N. KRÍTI
N. ΚΡΗΤΗ
Αυγό
Thessaloníki
Pireás
Thíra
Síros
N. Día
Ν. Δία
Kárpathos
Ródos
Lemessós (Kípros)
Haifa
Ag. Pelagía
Αγ. Πελαγία
IRÁKLIO
ΗΡΑΚΛΕΙΟ
N. Alikarnassós
Ν. Αλικαρνασσός
Goúrnes
Γούρνες
Limáni Hersonissou
Λιμάνι Χερσονήσου
Knossós
Κνωσός
Karterós
Καρτερός
Goúves
Γούβες
Stalída
Σταλίδα
Mália
Μάλια
Mílatos
Μίλατος
Vrouhás
Βρουχάς
Akr. Ág. Ioánis
Ακρ. Άγ. Ιωάννης
Spinalónga
Σπιναλόγκα
Hers. Spinalónga
Χερσ. Σπιναλόγκα
Fourní
Φουρνή
Eloúnda
Ελούντα
Kólpos Mirambélou
Κόλπος Μιραμπέλλου
N. Παξιμάδα
N. Δραγονάδα
N. Γιανυσάδα
Akr. Síderos
Ακρ. Σίδερος
N. Ελάσα
Itanós
Ιτανός
Vái
Βάι
Epískopí
Επισκοπή
Arhánes
Αρχάνες
Potamiés
Ποταμιές
Neápoli
Νεάπολη
Ag. Nikólaos
Άγ. Νικόλαος
Sitía
Σητεία
Toplóu
Τοπλού
Palékastro
Παλαίκαστρο
Kastéli
Καστέλλι
Ag. Paraskiés
Αγ. Παρασκιές
Dzermiádo
Τζερμιάδο
Ag. Geórgios
Αγ. Γεώργιος
Latô
Λατώ
Kritsá
Κριτσά
Móhlos
Μόχλος
Skopí
Σκοπή
Sfáka
Σφάκα
LASSÍTHI
Kavoúsi
Καβούσι
IRÁKLIO
Arkalohóri
Αρκαλοχώρι
Díktéo Ándro
Δικταίο Άντρο
Óros Díkti
Όρος Δίκτη
Vathípetro
Βαθύπετρο
Ag. Thomás
Αγ. Θωμάς
Ag. Varvára
Αγ. Βαρβάρα
Téféli
Τεφέλι
Garipa
Γαρίπα
Gangáles
Γκαγκάλες
Pírgos
Πύργος
Skiniás
Σκινιάς
Á. Viános
Α. Βιάννος
Gourniá
Γουρνιά
Pahiá Ámos
Παχειά Άμμος
Kaló Horió
Καλό Χωριό
Stavrohóri
Σταυροχώρι
Handrás
Χανδράς
Zíros
Ζίρος
Zákros
Ζάκρος
K. Zákros
Κ. Ζάκρος
Lithines
Λιθίνες
Makrigialós
Μακρυγιαλός
Ag. Fotiá
Αγ. Φωτιά
Anatolí
Ανατολή
Ierápetra
Ιεράπετρα
Mírtos
Μύρτος
Amoudára
Αμμουδάρα
Árvi
Άρβη
Ahendriás
Αχεντριάς
Koufonissi
Κουφονήσι
N. Hrissí
Ν. Χρυσή

D
E
F
89
1
2
3
4
Akr. Krikelos
Ακρ. Κρίκελος
N. Giali
Ν. Γυαλί
Mandráki
Μανδράκι
Páli
Πάλοι
698
Nikiá
Νικιά
N. Περγούσα
N. Παχειά
N. Níssiros
Ν. Νίσυρος
N. Κανδελιούσα
Akr. Orfós
Ακρ. Ορφός
Meg. Horió
Μεγ. Χωριό
651
Μικρό Χωριό
Livádia
Λιβάδια
N. Tílos
Ν. Τήλος
N. Αντίτηλος
Akr. Tráhilos
Ακρ. Τράχηλος
N I S S
Σ A
S A
Emboriós
Εμπορειός
Nímos
Pédi
Πέδι
Sími
Σύμη
616
N. Sími
N. Σύμη
Panormitis
Πανορμίτης
Σεσκλίο
N. Sesklío
N. Σεσκλίο
RÓDOS (25)
ΡΟΔΟΣ
Akr. Zonári
Ακρ. Ζωνάρι
Iráklio
Kárpathos
Megísti
Lemessós (Kípros)
Haifa
Kremasti
Κρεμαστή
Ixiá
Ιξιά
Paradeisi
Παραδείσι
267
Triánda
Τριάντα
Filérimos
Φιλέρημος
Kalithéa
Καλλιθέα
Soroní
Σορωνή
Petaloúdes
Πεταλούδες
Kalithiés
Καλυθιές
Faliráki
Φαληράκι
Kámiros
Κάμειρος
Kalavárda
Καλαβάρδα
Psínthos
Ψίνθος
Afándou
Αφάντου
70
Prof. Ilías
Προφ. Ηλίας
798
Mandrikó
Μανδρικό
N. Alimiá
N. Αλιμιά
Αλιμιά
Απόλλωνα
Eleoússa
Ελεούσα
Tsambika
Τσαμπίκα
Kritinía
Κρητηνία
Émbonas
Έμπωνας
45
Arhángelos (160)
Αρχάγγελος
N. Hálki
N. Χάλκη
Hálki
Χάλκη
Χωριό
Akr. Mírtos
Ακρ. Μύρτος
Atáviros
Αττάβυρος
1215
Malónas
Μαλώνας
Feraklós
Φεράκλος
Σιάνα
Ág. Issídoros
Άγ. Ισίδωρος
Láerma
Λάερμα
Κάλαθος
Monólithos (290)
Μονόλιθος
Ístrios
Ίστριος
Lárdos
Λάρδος
Líndos
Λίνδος
Asklipiío
Ασκληπιείο
Apolakiá
Απολακκιά
Βάτι
Πεύκοι
Akr. Lárdos
Ακρ. Λάρδος
Messanagrós
Μεσαναγρός
Genádio
Γεννάδιο
Λαχανιά
64
Katavía
Κατταβία
Hóhlakas
Χόχλακας
N. RÓDOS
N. ΡΟΔΟΣ
Πρασονήσι
Akr. Paraspóri
Ακρ. Παρασπόρι
N. Sariá
N. Σαριά
Σαριά
630
Astakída
Αστακίδα
Hálki
TÜRKIYE
1800
Kas
Ródos
N. Ρω
Megísti
Μεγίστη
N. Megísti (Kastelórizo)
N. Μεγίστη (Καστελλόριζο)
N. Στρογγυλή
Diafáni
Διαφάνι
Ólimbos
Όλυμπος
Ródos
Messohóri
Μεσοχώρι
N. KÁRPATHOS
N. ΚΑΡΠΑΘΟΣ
Kalí Límni
Καλή Λίμνη
1215
Apéri
Απέρι
Piles
Πυλές
Kárpathos (25)
Κάρπαθος
Arkássa
Αρκάσα
Menetés
Μενετές
N. Αρμάθια
Frí
Φρυ
601
Αρβανιτοχώρι
Akr. Kastélou
Ακρ. Καστέλλου
Akr. Hélatros
Ακρ. Χέλατρος

A
B
C
1
2
3
4
Sørvær
Hasvik
Loppa
Øksfjord
Langfjordjøkelen
Nordkvaløy
Vanna
Vannavålen
Årviksand
Slettfjellet
Arnøy
Lauksundskaret
Skjervøy
Kvænangen
Rebbenesøy
Mikkelvik
Vannsundet
Skåningsbukt
Fugløysundet
Karlsøy
Hurtigrute
Kågen
Hansnes
Ringvassøy
Reinøy
Nord-Lenangen
Reisafjorden
Sørkjosen
Storslett (Nordreisa)
292
Grøtsundet
Ullsfjorden
Olderdalen
Lyngen
Djupvik
TROMSØ
Breivikeidet
Svensby
Olderdalen
Sommarøy
Eidkjosen
Tromsdalen
Hillesøy
Kvaløy
Larseng
Fagernes
Lyngseidet
Bilto
Bæccegæ
Mefjordvær
Mefjordbotn
Vikran
Jiekkevarre
Istfjellet
Skaland (Berg)
Straumsnes
Malangen
Furuflaten
Skibotn
Raisduoddarhal'di
Gryllefjord (Torsken)
Gibostad
Målsnes
Tennes
Halti-Haldi
Andenes
Senja
(Lenvik)
Finnsnes
Storsteinnes
Oteren
Nordkjosbotn
Bleik
Ånderdalen
Vangsvik
Moen (Målselv)
Heia
Mallax
Kilpisjärvi
Raittijärvi
Andøya
Andfjorden
Tranøy
Sørreisa
Solbergfjorden
Bardufoss
TROMS
Tierbmesvarri
Stonglandet
Dverberg
Skrolsvik
Brøstadbotn
Andselv
Øverbygd
Dyrøya
Målselva
Åse
Risøyhamn
Bjarkøy
Grytøya
Vågsfjorden
Myre (Øksnes)
Istindan
Kummavuopio
VESTERÅLEN
Sjøvegan (Salangen)
Setermoen (Bardu)
Saarikoski
Harstad
Andørja
Langøya
Borkenes (Kvæfjord)
Ibestad
Rolla
Myrlandshaugen
Frihetsli
Kirkestinden
Rostujaure
Straumsjøen
Sørrollnes
Lavangen
Njunis
Sortland
Flesnes
Refsnes
Kilbotn
Astafjorden
Fossbakken
Øvre Dividalen
Ishavsleden
Eidsfjorden
Sigerfjord
Grovfjord
Innset
Bø
Hinnøya
Gullesfjorden
Evenskjær (Skånland)
Gratangen
Stokmarknes
Kaljord
Melbu
Ramsund
Bogen
Bjerkvik
Vadvetjåkka
Tjeldøya
Hadselfjorden
Kongselva
Evenes
Liland
Narvik
Riksgränsen
Björkliden
Abisko
Torneträsk
Vuoskojaure
Fiskebøl
Austvågøy
Lødingen
Ofotfjorden
Eggum
Ballangen
Beisfjord
Laimoluokta
Kuortovare
Vestvågøy
Svolvær
Digermulen
Leiknes
Skarberget
Stamsund
Gravdal
Ballstad
Hurtigrute
Bognes
Kjøpsvik
Rensjön
Kungsleden
Skutvik
Hamarøy
Tysfjorden
Vistasvaggi
Engeløya
Steigen
Drag
Bjørntoppen
Sliddasjärvi
Rautas
Kebnekaise
Sagfjorden
Innhavet
Bogøy
Nikkaluokta
Kiruna
Sautusjärvi
Jukkasjärvi
Vittangiälven
Paittasjärvi
VESTFJORDEN
Nordfold
Torneälven
98
Folda
Vaisaluokta
Kallaktjåkkå
Kårsatjåkka
Stora
Svappavaara
Bonnåsjøen
Akkajaure
Kjerringøy
Sørfolda
Nieras
Kaitumälven
Sjöfallet
Fjällåsen
Festvåg
Røsvik
Rago
Vastenjaure
Vietas
Kalixälven
Padjelanta
Virihaure
Arasluokta
Stora Sjöfallet
Skaulo
BODØ
Løding
Saltoluokta
NORRBOTTENS
97

NORDKAPP
Knivskjellodden
Honningsvåg
Magerøya
Hammerfest
Kvaløya
Seiland
Alta
Porsangerhalvøya
Porsangen
Lakselv
Karasjok
FINNMARK
Finnmarksvidda
Kautokeino
Jordbruksveien
Stabbursdalen
Børselvfjellet
Nordkinnhalvøya
Mehamn
Gamvik
Berlevåg
Båtsfjord
Vardø
Varangerhalvøya
Vadsø
Varangerfjorden
Kirkenes
Tana
Nesseby
Utsjoki
Kevo
Paistunturit
Muotkatunturit
Karigasniemi
Inari
INARIJÄRVI
Ivalo
Saariselkä
Kekkosen kansallispuisto
Lemmenjoki
Øvre Anarjokka
Øvre Pasvik
Raja-Jooseppi
Nellim
Enontekiö
Pallas-Ounastunturi
Karesuando
Muonio
Kittilä
Levi
Sodankylä
Kolari
Pomokaira
Vintilankaira
LAPIN
Hurtigrute
98
99

A
B
C
1
2
3
4
66°33
Cercle polaire arctique
Norðurheimskautsbaugur
Grímsey
Hornbjarg
Ísafjarðardjúp
Bolungarvík
Ísafjörður
Drangajökull
925
Norðurfjörður
Þingeyri
Gláma
Hólmavík
Húnaflói
Patreksfjörður
Brjánslækur
Flatey
Breiðafjörður
Laugar
Búðardalur
Stykkishólmur
Grundarfjörður
Ólafsvík
Snæfellsnes
1446
Siglufjörður
Ólafsfjörður
Dalvík
Hrísey
Árskógssandur
Eyjafjörður
Skagafjörður
Sauðárkrókur
Blönduós
Varmahlíð
Akureyri
Goðafoss
Mývatn
Húsavík
Skjálfandi
Dettifoss
Jökulsá á Fjöllum
Kópasker
Raufarhöfn
Þórshöfn
Þistilfjörður
Bakkaflói
Vopnafjörður
Egilsstaðir
Seyðisfjörður
Neskaupstaður
Eskifjörður
Lagarfljót
Reyðarfjörður
Tórshavn
Askja
Dreki
Laugafell
ÍSLAND
Hofsjökull
1765
Hveravellir
Nýidalur
Langjökull
Reykholt
Húsafell
Borgarnes
Faxaflói
Akranes
Hvalfjörður
Þingvellir
914
Geysir
Gullfoss
Hvítá
Þingvallavatn
Laugarvatn
REYKJAVÍK
Garður
Sandgerði
Keflavík
Grindavík
Hveragerði
Selfoss
Þorlákshöfn
Þjórsá
Hella
Hekla
1491
Landmannalaugar
Hvolsvöllur
Mýrdalsjökull
Þórsmörk
Skógafoss
Vík
Vestmannaeyjar
Kaldakvísl
Skjálfandafljót
VATNAJÖKULL
Skaftafell
2119
Skaftá
Skeiðarársandur
Höfn
ATLANTSHAF
1 / 2 400 000
0
50 km
FØROYAR
FÆRØERNE
(DK)
Seyðisfjørður
NORÐOYAR
Viðareiði
Gjógv
Eiði
882
Kunoy
Viðoy
Oyndarfjørður
Tjørnuvík
Svínoy
Borðoy
790
Streymoy
Eysturoy
Klaksvík
Hvalvík
Leirvík
Vestmanna
Mykines
722
Vágar
Sørvágur
Toftir
Tórshavn
Kirkjubøur
Hestfjørður
Skopun
Sandoy
479
Sandur
Skálavík
Lerwick - Bergen
Hanstholm - Esbjerg
Suðuroyarfjørður
Hvalba
610
Tvøroyri
Fámjin
Suðuroy
Vágur
Sumba
0
30 km
NORSKEHAVET
Hurtigrute
Sør-Flatanger
Osen
Roan
Harsvik
100

D
E
F
Ramberg
Gravdal
Stamsund
Hurtigrute
Ballstad
Moskenesøya
Reine
Sørvågen
Moskenstraumen
Vestfjorden
Sørværøy
Røstlandet
Bognes
Kjøpsvik
Skutvik
Hamarøy
Drag
Tysfjorden
Bjørntoppen
Sliddasjávri
Innhavet
Engeløya
Steigen
Sagfjorden
Bogøy
Nordfold
Folda
Vaisaluokta
Kallaktjåkkå
Akkajaure
Sjöfallet
Bonnåsjøen
Kjerringøy
Festvåg
Røsvik
Rago
Vastenjaure
Padjelanta
Virihaure
Arasluokta
Sarek
BODØ
Løding
Vågan
Fauske
Straumen
Saltfjorden
Skjerstadfjorden
Skjerstad
Blåmannsisen
Sulitjelma
Sørarnøy
Rognan
Storfjellet
Inndyr
Beiarn
Tarrekaise
Pieskehaure
Kvikkjokk
Røkland
NORDLAND
Ørnes
Meløy
Meløyfjorden
Glomfjord
Forøy
Ågskaret
Vågaholmen
Tjong
Storglomvatnet
Snøtinden
Lønsdal
Silvervägen
Svartisen
Saltfjellet
POLARSIRKELEN
Trænfjorden
Kilboghamn
Lurøy
Lovund
MO I RANA
Dunderlandsdalen
Storforshei
Stenudden
Jäkkvik
Norra Bergnäs
Pieljekaise
Hornavan
Tomma
Sjona
Nordrana
Blå vägen
Junkeren
Dønnes
Nesna
Hemnesberget
Finneidfjord
Adolfström
Dønna
Rana
Lavong
Leland
Umbukta
Laisvall
Seløy
Silvalen
Sandnessjøen
Korgen
Ammarfjället
Overuman
Tärnasjön
Vindelfjällens N.-R.
Ammarnäs
Arjeplog
Uddjaure
Alstahaug
Mosjøen
Okstindan
Artfjället
Tjøtta
Vega
Klippen
Norra Storfjället
Hemavan
Oversjuktan
Forvik
Røssvatnet
Saga vägen
Tärnaby
Gladstad
Rørøy
Vegafjorden
Anndalsvågen
Horn
Brønnøysund
Trofors
Hattfjelldal
Vefsna
Storvindeln
Ajaureforsen
Gardiken
Gardjonas
Sorsele
Hommelstø
Berg
Sømna
Vik
Børgefjellet
Storjuktan
Vennesund
Holm
Tosenfjorden
Saga vägen
Umeälven
Blattniksele
Hortafjorden
Børgefjell
Dikanäs
Storuman
Leka
Sørgutvik
Terråk
Lyngsnes
Foldereid
Fatmomakke
Marsfjällen
Storuman
Klimpfjäll
Kultsjön
Rørvik
Kolvereid
Namsskogan
Borga-fjällen
Saxnäs
Vojmsjön
Gunnarn
Nærøy
Hofles
Salsbruket
Røyrvik
Blå vägen
Geisnes
Foldfjorden
Lund
Brekkvasselv
Namsen
Limingen
Stora Blåsjön
Jengejetneme
Abelvær
Borgafjäll
Malgomaj
VÄSTERB
Seierstad
Jormlien
Uredakke
Høylandet
Tunnsjøen
Limingen
Risback
Ølhammeren
Otterøy
Skorovatn
Bastunasfjället
Vägen sju älvar
Latikberg
Overhalla
Skage
Havdalsfjellet
Sjoutnäset
Vilhelmina
Namsos
Grong
Storsjouten
Bangsund
Sanddøla
Nordli
Gäddede
Saga vägen
Namdalseid
NORD TRØNDELAG
Norråker
Ormsjö
Ormsjön
Strömsvattudal
Hartkjølen
Munsfjället
Hotagen
Angermanälven
Gressåmoen
Snåsa
Snåsavatnet
Velde
Dorotea
Bøla
Blåfjellhatten
Fjällen
Gärdnäs
Tåsjö
Vägen sju älvar
Lillo
94
86
101

Kiruna
Kebnekaise
Nikkaluokta
Rensjön
Rautas
Jukkasjärvi
Övre Soppero
Vittangi
Svappavaara
Fjällåsen
Skaulo
Malmberget
Gällivare
Porjus
Muddus
Harsprånget
Nattavaara
Hakkas
Nilivaara
Stora Lulevatten
Sjöfallet
Stora Sjöfallet
Akkajaure
Vietas
Saltoluokta
Ruokto
Sarek
Tarrekaise
Kvikkjokk
Kungsleden
Vaisaluokta
Arasluokta
NORRBOTTENS
LÄN
Jokkmokk
POLCIRKELN
Karats
Stenudden
Jäkkvik
Hornavan
Norra Bergnäs
Gittun
Laisvall
Arjeplog
Uddjaure
Silvervägen
Vuollerim
Murjek
Pålkem
Kåbdalis
Harads
Gunnarsbyn
Moskosel
Vidsel
Storforsen
Boden
Råneå
Niemisel
Morjärv
Töre
Kalix
Överkalix
Jockfall
Korpilombolo
Tärendö
Pajala
Junosuando
Ishavsleden
Muonio
Muodoslompolo
Yli-muonio
Katkasuvanto
Kangosjärvi
Parkalompolo
Äkäslompolo
Kihlanki
Äkäsjokisuu
Kolari
Lappea
Sieppijärvi
Naamijoki
Orajärvi
Pello
Turtola
Svanstein
Juoksenki
Aavasaksa
Övertorneå
Ylitornio
Hedenäset
Karungi
Lappträsk
Vojakkala
Haparanda
Sangis
Höytiä
LULEÅ
Gammelstaden
Bergnäset
Antnäs
Klöverträsk
Älvsbyn
Vistheden
Arvidsjaur
Avaviken
Slagnäs
Sorsele
Abborrträsk
Långträsk
Öjebyn
Piteå
Bergsviken
Rosvik
Jävre
Glommersträsk
Blattnikselе
Gargnäs
Adak
Malå
Storuman
Gunnarn
Björksele
Kristineberg
Norrby
Jörn
Fallfors
Tåme
Byske
Norsjö
Boliden
Kåge
Skellefteå
Skelleftehamn
Bastuträsk
Ruskele
Kalvträsk
Bureå
Lycksele
Latikberg
Kroksjö
Amsele
Burträsk
Lövånger
Bygdsiljum
Lillögda
Hällnäs
Botsmark
Ånäset
Granön
Vindeln
Robertsfors
BOTTENVIKEN
PERÄMERI
Kalajoki
Hiekkasärkät
Himanka
Maakalla
Halju
Sautusjärvi
Torneälven
Kalixälven
Luleälven
Piteälven
Skellefteälven
Umeälven
Silver vägen
Blå vägen
Saga vägen
Harafjärden
Gunnarsfjärden
94
95
97
102

LAPIN LÄÄNI
SUOMI FINLAND
OULUN LÄÄNI
ARCTIC CIRCLE
NAPAPIIRI
ROVANIEMI
Sodankylä
Kemijärvi
Kuusamo
Taivalkoski
Pudasjärvi
Ranua
Posio
Salla
Suomussalmi
Kuhmo
Kajaani
OULU (ULEÅBORG)
Raahe
Muhos
Utajärvi
Vaala
Paltamo
Puolanka
Hyrynsalmi
Sotkamo
Vuokatti
Oulainen
Ylivieska
Haapavesi
Pyhäntä
Piippola
Pulkkila
Kestilä
Vuolijoki
Oulujärvi
Kempele
Liminka
Haukipudas
Kiiminki
Ii
Simo
Kuivaniemi
Tervola
Keminmaa
Kemijoki
Kandalakša
Kovdor
Alakurtti
Kestenga
Kalevala
Kostamukša
Pyhätunturi
Suomutunturi
Rukatunturi
Oulanka
Kitka
Pelkosenniemi
Savukoski
Luosto
Kemijärvi
Kiiminkijoki
Iijoki
Oulujoki
Hailuoto
Siikajoki
Oulunsalo
Tyrnävä
Kärsämäki
95
103

A
B
C
96
104
1
2
3
4
NORGE
Frohavet
Hustadvika
Frøya
Hitra
Smøla
Kristiansund
Molde
Ålesund
Åndalsnes
Sunndalsøra
Orkanger
TRONDHEIM
Melhus
Støren
Oppdal
Trollheimen
MØRE OG ROMSDAL
SØR TRØN
Trollstigveien
Dovrefjell
Snøhetta
Geiranger
Stryn
Loen
Olden
Nordfjordeid
Volda
Ørsta
Måløy
Florø
Førde
Sandane
Jostedalsbreen
Sognefjell
Jotunheimen
Galdhøpiggen
Glittertind
Lom
Vågåmo
Otta
Rondane
SOGN OG FJORDANE
Sognefjorden
Høyanger
Sogndal
Hermansverk
Lærdalsøyri
Valdres
Fagernes
OPPLAND
Gudbrandsdalen
Lillehammer
Gjøvik
Hamar
Mjøsa
Voss
HORDALAND
Hardangerjøkulen
Geilo
Gol
Hallingdal
BUSKERUD
Tynset
Dombås
Lesja
Romsdalen
Sunndalen

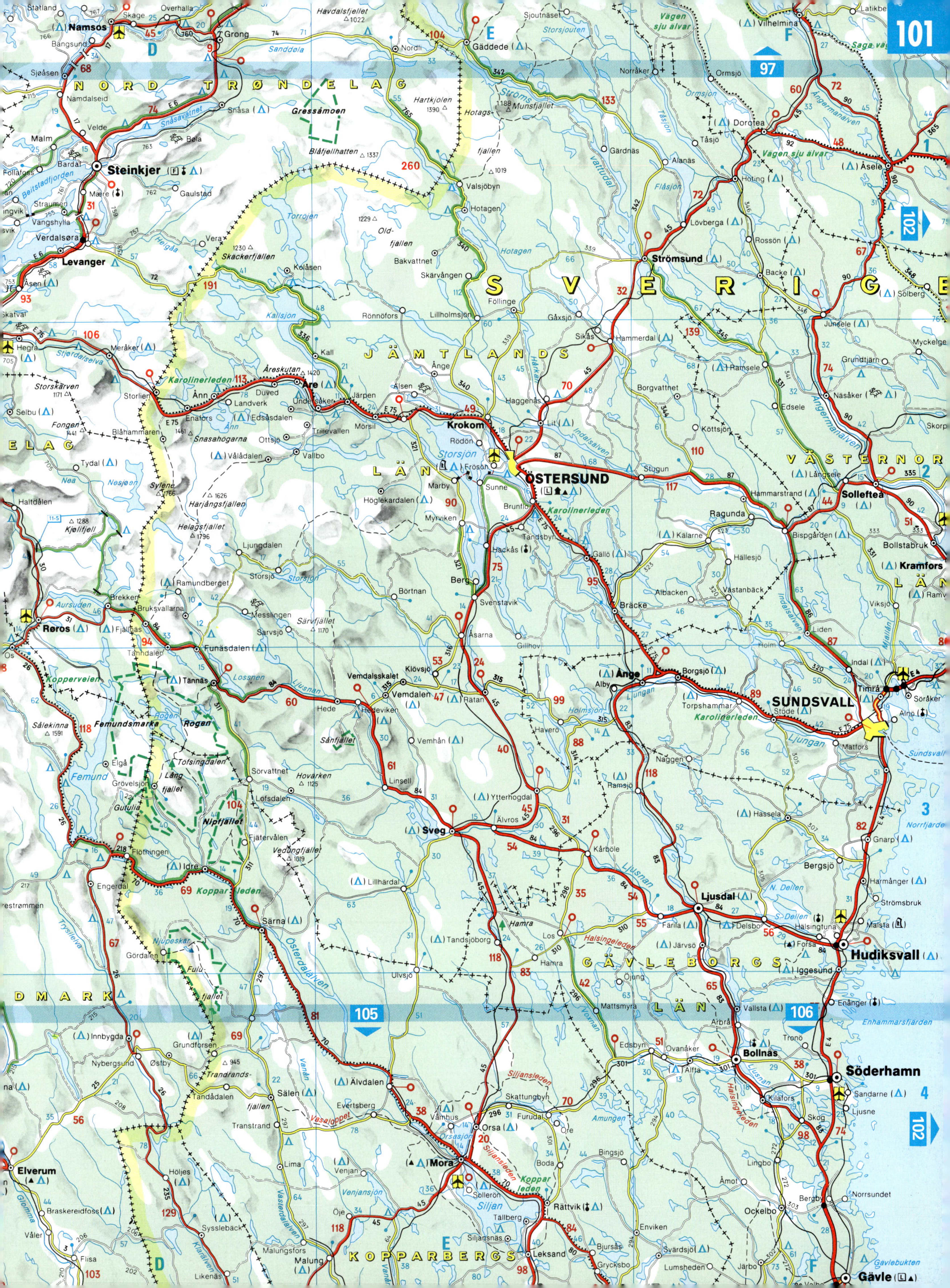
Namsos
Grong
Steinkjer
Levanger
Verdalsøra
Gressåmoen
Skackerfjällen
Kallsjön
Åreskutan
Åre
Storlien
Krokom
Östersund
Storsjön
Frösön
Hammerdal
Strömsund
Hotagen
Föllinge
Valsjöbyn
Gäddede
Dorotea
Åsele
Vilhelmina
Sollefteå
Kramfors
Bispgården
Ragunda
Hammarstrand
Stugun
Bräcke
Gällö
Ånge
Sundsvall
Timrå
Alnö
Matfors
Ljungan
Hudiksvall
Iggesund
Ljusdal
Delsbo
Järvsö
Bollnäs
Söderhamn
Gävle
Edsbyn
Ovanåker
Sveg
Ytterhogdal
Hede
Vemdalen
Funäsdalen
Tännäs
Røros
Femundsmarka
Rogen
Idre
Särna
Sälen
Älvdalen
Mora
Orsa
Siljan
Rättvik
Leksand
Malung
Elverum
Karolinerleden
Kopparleden
Siljansleden
Hälsingleden
Vasaloppet
Österdalälven
Ljusnan
Indalsälven
Ångermanälven
NORD TRØNDELAG
SVERIGE
JÄMTLANDS LÄN
VÄSTERNORRLANDS LÄN
GÄVLEBORGS LÄN
KOPPARBERGS LÄN
HEDMARK
97
102
105
106

98
101
106
Lycksele
Umeå
Vindeln
Vännäs
Bjurholm
Robertsfors
Bygdeå
Holmsund
Nordmaling
Örnsköldsvik
Härnösand
Bureå
Kokkola
Karleby
Jakobstad
Pietarsaari
Nykarleby
Uusikaarlepyy
Vaasa
Vasa
Korsholm
Mustasaari
Seinäjoki
Lapua
Kurikka
Alavus
Kauhava
Kalajoki
Ylivieska
Oulainen
Kristinestad
Kristiinankaupunki
Kaskinen
Kaskö
Närpes
Närpiö
Virrat
Parkano
Kankaanpää
Pori
(Björneborg)
Tampere
Rauma
Uusikaupunki
Huittinen
Loimaa
Forssa
Valkeakoski
Hämeenlinna
Laitila
Mynämäki
Norra Kvarken
Merenkurkku
Bottenhavet
Bottniska viken
Pohjanlahti
(Golfe de Botnie)
Selkämeri
Vaasan lääni
Turun ja Porin lääni
Häme

99
107
Kajaani
OULUJÄRVI
Kuhmo
Sotkamo
Vuokatti
Paltaniemi
Otanmäki
Hiidenportti
Nurmes
Valtimo
Lieksa
PIELINEN
Koli
Pankakoski
Patvinsuo
Iisalmi
Sonkajärvi
Vieremä
Kiuruvesi
Pyhäsalmi
Pihtipudas
Viitasaari
Keitele
Kuopio
KUOPION LÄÄNI
Siilinjärvi
Maaninka
Juankoski
Nilsiä
Outokumpu
Joensuu
POHJOIS-KARJALAN LÄÄNI
Ilomantsi
Liperi
Polvijärvi
Kontiolahti
Tuusniemi
Suonenjoki
Rautalampi
Konnevesi
Äänekoski
Suolahti
KESKI-SUOMEN LÄÄNI
Jyväskylä
Jämsä
Varkaus
Leppävirta
Heinävesi
Valamo
Pieksämäki
Joroinen
Rantasalmi
Savonlinna
Punkaharju
Kerimäki
Kitee
Tohmajärvi
Värtsilä
Sortavala
Parikkala
MIKKELIN LÄÄNI
Mikkeli
Kangasniemi
Juva
Sulkava
Puumala
Ristiina
Mäntyharju
Heinola
Sysmä
PÄIJÄNNE
Lahti
Hollola
Orimattila
Kouvola
Kuusankoski
Anjalankoski
KYMEN LÄÄNI
Kotka
Hamina
Vaalimaa
Lappeenranta
Imatra
Joutseno
Taipalsaari
Saimaa
Vyborg
Priozërsk
Sosnovo
Kamenka
Primorsk
Zelenogorsk
Pervomajskoe
Ladožskoe
R S F S R
Hyvinkää
Riihimäki
Järvenpää
Mäntsälä
Loviisa
Pernå
Mänttä

SOGN OG FJORDANE
HORDALAND
ROGALAND
AUST-AGDER
VEST-AGDER
TELEMARK
BUSKERUD
VESTFOLD
OPPLAND
BERGEN
STAVANGER
SKIEN
Flora
Førde
Sandane
Haugesund
Sandnes
Egersund
Flekkefjord
Mandal
Kristiansand
Arendal
Grimstad
Lillesand
Porsgrunn
Larvik
Sandefjord
Drammen
Kongsberg
Notodden
Horten
Kragerø
Risør
Voss
Odda
Sauda
Granvin
Eidfjord
Geilo
Gol
Rjukan
Sogndal
Lom
Vågåmo
Otta
Fagernes
Jostedalsbreen
Jotunheimen
Hardangervidda
Hardangerfjorden
Sognefjorden
Valdres
Hallingdal
Numedal
Setesdal
Jæren
Newcastle
Hanstholm
Hirtshals
Frederikshavn
Kiel-København
Amsterdam
Lerwick
100
108

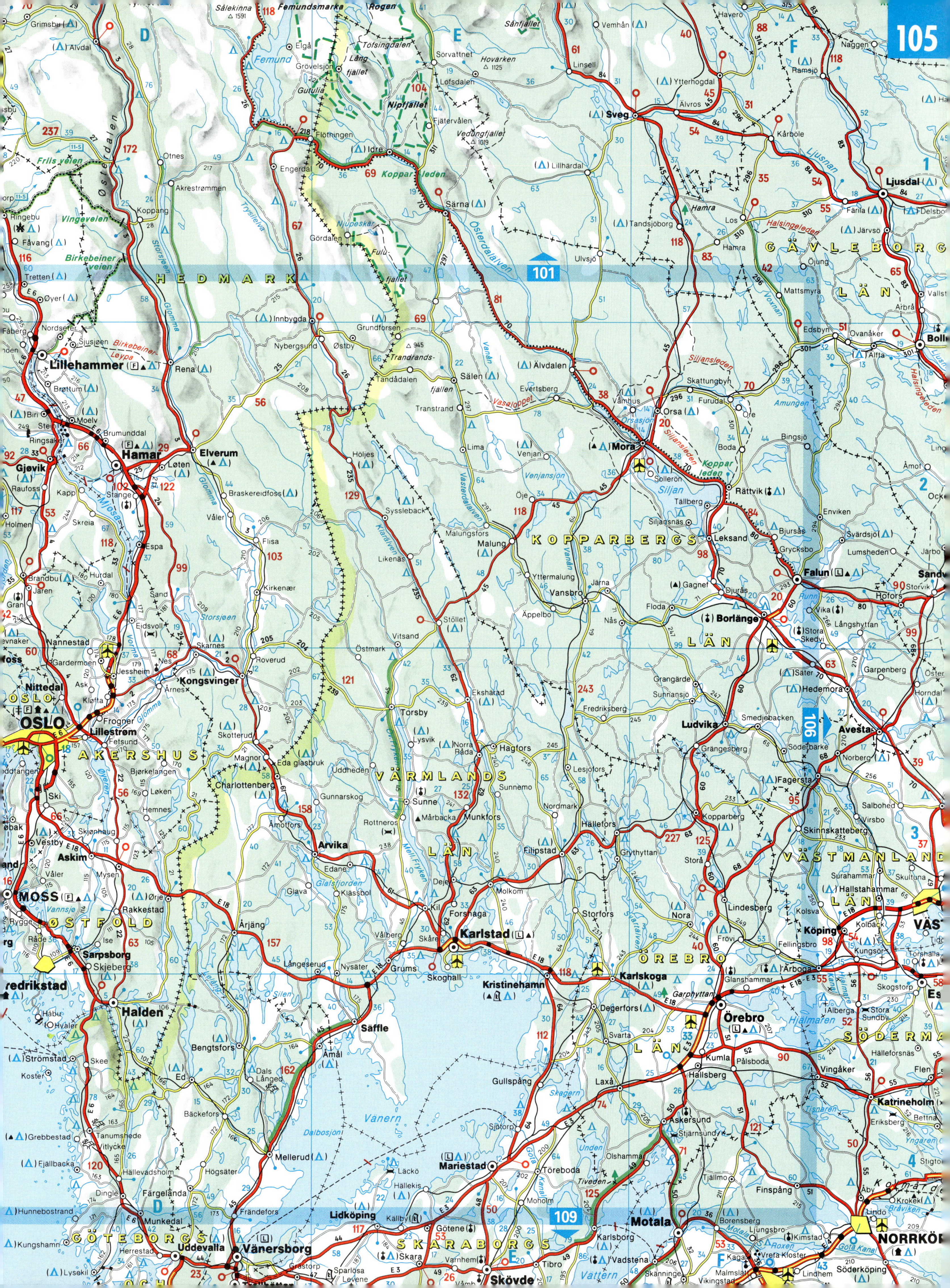
HEDMARK
GÄVLEBORG
LÄN
KOPPARBERGS
LÄN
VÄRMLANDS
LÄN
ÖREBRO
LÄN
VÄSTMANLAND
LÄN
SÖDERMANLAND
AKERSHUS
ØSTFOLD
GÖTEBORGS
SKARABORGS
Sveg
Ljusdal
Hamar
Lillehammer
Gjøvik
Elverum
Oslo
Lillestrøm
Kongsvinger
Moss
Sarpsborg
Fredrikstad
Halden
Mora
Orsa
Rättvik
Leksand
Falun
Borlänge
Ludvika
Hedemora
Avesta
Fagersta
Köping
Arboga
Örebro
Karlskoga
Kristinehamn
Karlstad
Arvika
Säffle
Åmål
Mariestad
Lidköping
Skövde
Motala
Vänersborg
Uddevalla
Norrköping
Katrineholm
Vänern
Siljan
101
106
109

SUNDSVALL
Sundsvallsbukten
Ljungan
Mattfors
Naggen
Ramsjö
Ytterhogdal
Älvros
Kårbole
Ljusnan
Hassela
Norrfjärden
Gnarp
Bergsjö
Harmånger
Strömsbruk
Ljusdal
N. Dellen
S. Dellen
Färila
Järvsö
Delsbo
Hälsingtuna
Malsta
Forsa
Hudiksvall
Iggesund
Hamra
Los
Hälsingeleden
GÄVLEBORGS
LÄN
Öjung
Mattsmyra
Voxnan
Vallsta
Arbrå
Enånger
Enhammarsfjärden
Edsbyn
Ovanåker
Alfta
Bollnäs
Trönö
Söderhamn
Sandarne
Ljusne
Kilafors
Skog
Siljansleden
Skattungbyn
Furudal
Orsa
Amungen
Ore
Boda
Bingsjö
Lingbo
Åmot
Bergby
Norrsundet
Ockelbo
Kopparleden
Siljan
Rättvik
Tällberg
Leksand
Enviken
Bjursås
Gryckbo
Svärdsjö
Lumsheden
Jädraås
Falun
Sandviken
Valbo
Gävle
Gävlebukten
Storvik
Hofors
Runn
Gagnef
Djurås
Borlänge
Vika
Stora Skedvi
Långshyttan
Lövstabukten
Skutskär
Älvkarleby
Skarplinge
Öregrundsgrepen
Arsunda
Mehedeby
Lövstabruk
Söderfors
Tierp
Öregrund
Garpenberg
Österfärnebo
Säter
Hedemora
Horndal
Gysinge
UPPSALA
LÄN
Östhammar
Gimo
Österbybruk
Månkarbo
Ludvika
Smedjebacken
Avesta
Dalälven
Östervåla
Vendel
Viksta
Grisslehamn
Grängesberg
Söderbärke
Norberg
Fagersta
Björklinge
Salsta
Vattholma
Rasbo
Hallstavik
Väddö
Sala
Heby
Gävsta
Edsbro
Kopparberg
Salbohed
Virsbo
UPPSALA
Skinnskatteberg
Fjärdhundra
Sävja
Norrtälje
Kapellskär
Storå
VÄSTMANLANDS
LÄN
Surahammar
Hallstahammar
Skultuna
Tillberga
Örsundsbro
Skokloster
Knivsta
Rimbo
Märsta
Arlanda
Lindesberg
Kolsva
Västerås
Enköping
Sigtuna
Upplands-Väsby
Vallentuna
Åkersberga
STOCKHOLMS
LÄN
Nora
Frövi
Fellingsbro
Köping
Kolbäck
Kungsör
Torshälla
Tidö
Jäder
Bålsta
Bro
Sollentuna
Täby
Lidingö
Arboga
Glanshammar
Skogstorp
Eskilstuna
Strängnäs
Drottningholm
Stora Sundby
Mariefred
Gripsholm
Sturehov
Turinge
Boo
Tyresö
STOCKHOLM
Garphyttan
Örebro
Hjälmaren
Alberga
Åkers styckebruk
Tumba
Södertälje
Namdö
SÖDERMANLANDS
LÄN
Kumla
Pålsboda
Hällefors
Malmköping
Nykvarn
Järna
Jordbro
Västerhaninge
Hallsberg
Vingåker
Flen
Stjärnhov
Gnesta
Sorunda
Ösmo
Mysingen
Askersund
Tisnaren
Katrineholm
Bettna
Vagnhärad
Tullgarn
Nynäshamn
Stjärnsund
Eriksberg
Yngaren
Runtuna
Trosa
Stigtomta
Tjällmo
Finspång
Åby
Kolmården
Jönåker
Nyköping
Krokek
Oxelösund
Lindö
Bråviken
Nävekvarn
Borensberg
Ljungsbro
Motala
Kimstad
Roxen
Vreta Kloster
Norrköping
Göta Kanal
Kaga
Malmslätt
Lindhem
Söderköping
Vikingstad
BOTTENHAVET
BOTTNISKA VIKEN
POH
(GOLFE DE BOTNIE
SELKÄMERI
LANDSKAPET
ÅLAND
Åland
Ahvenanmaa
Geta
Saltvik
Finström
Sund
Kumlinge
Hammarland
Godby
Kastelholms
Vårdö
Delet Teili
Storby
Eckerö
Jomala
Lumparland
Sottunga
Lumparn
Mariehamn
Maarianhamina
Lemland
Föglö
Kokarsfjärden
Kristiinan
Tallinn
Helsinki
Leningrad
(MERI)
ÄMER
BALT
Gotska Sandön
101
102
105
109

PORI
BJÖRNEBORG
Rauma
TAMPERE
Hämeenlinna
LAHTI
Heinola
Kouvola
Kotka
Mikkeli
Forssa
Loimaa
Salo
TURKU
ÅBO
Naantali
Pargas
Lohja
Espoo
Vantaa
HELSINKI
HELSINGFORS
Porvoo
Borgå
Hanko
Hangö
Ekenäs
Tammisaari
Hyvinkää
Riihimäki
Järvenpää
Kerava
Valkeakoski
Toijala
Huittinen
Kankaanpää
Parkano
Virrat
Mänttä
Jämsä
Orivesi
Nokia
Urjala
Somero
Mynämäki
Laitila
Uusikaupunki
Anjalankoski
Loviisa
Mäntyharju
Sysmä
Padasjoki
HÄMEEN LÄÄNI
TURUN JA PORIN LÄÄNI
UUDENMAAN LÄÄNI
MIKKELIN LÄÄNI
KYMEN LÄÄNI
Päijänne
Skärgårdshavet
Saaristomeri
Stockholm
Travemünde
Gdansk
Lübeck
Nynäshamn
Naissaar
TALLINN
Paldiski
Rakvere
Loksa
Tapa
EESTI
Hiumaa
Saaremaa
Itäinen Suomenlahti
Sipoonselkä
Suomenlinna
Kauniainen
Grankulla
Espoo
Esbo
Vantaa
Vanda
Tikkurila
Malmi
Kehä Ring III
Kehä Ring I
Otaniemi
Lauttasaari
Munkkiniemi
Herttoniemi
Vuosaari
Östersundom
Santahamina
HELSINKI
HELSINGFORS
Kouvola, Kotka
0
5 km

Kristiansand
104
SKAGERRAK
Hirtshals
Hjørring
Skagen
Frederikshavn
Læsø
Brønderslev
Hanstholm
Thisted
ÅLBORG
Ålborg Bugt
Himmerland
Limfjorden
Mors
Nykøbing M
Skive
Viborg
Randers
Grenå
Djursland
Holstebro
Struer
Ringkøbing
Herning
Silkeborg
J Y L L A N D
D A N M A R K
ÅRHUS
Ebeltoft
Horsens
Vejle
Esbjerg
Ribe
Kolding
Fredericia
Haderslev
Åbenrå
Tønder
Sønderborg
Flensburg
Schleswig
Kiel
Kieler Bucht
ODENSE
Nyborg
Svendborg
Langeland
Ærøskøbing
Kalundborg
Holbæk
Slagelse
Sorø
Roskilde
KØBENHAVN
Køge
Ringsted
Næstved
Vordingborg
Nykøbing F
Maribo
Lolland
Falster
Hillerød
Helsingør
Helsingborg
MALMÖ
Landskrona
Trelleborg
KATTEGAT
Anholt
Halmstad
Falkenberg
Varberg
GÖTEBORG
Kungälv
Borås
Uddevalla
Vänersborg
Trollhättan
Kungsbacka
Sylt
Fanø
Rømø

SKARABORGS
Skara
Skövde
Tibro
Hjo
Vättern
Vadstena
Falköping
Tidaholm
JÖNKÖPING
Huskvarna
Gränna
Mullsjö
Habo
Bankeryd
Taberg
Nässjö
Tranås
Eksjö
Aneby
Forserum
Ödeshög
Mjölby
ÖSTERGÖTLANDS LÄN
Linköping
LINKÖPING
Söderköping
Norrköping
Vreta Kloster
Boxholm
Kisa
Åtvidaberg
Björsäter
Valdemarsvik
Överum
Gamleby
Västervik
Österbymo
Norra Kvill
Vimmerby
Mariannelund
Ankarsrum
Storebro
Hultsfred
Vetlanda
JÖNKÖPINGS LÄN
Vaggeryd
Skillingaryd
Gnosjö
Gislaved
Anderstorp
Värnamo
Reftele
Smålands-stenar
Sävsjö
Korsberga
Virserum
Kristdala
Oskarshamn
Fårbo
Åseda
Fågelfors
Högsby
Blå Jungfrun
Byxelkrok
Böda
Löttorp
KALMAR LÄN
Lenhovda
Rottne
Grönskåra
Mönsterås
Lammhult
Växjö
Alvesta
Lagan
Ljungby
KRONOBERGS LÄN
Bolmen
Hovmantorp
Lessebo
Eriksmåla
Orrefors
Bäckebo
Nybro
Lindsdal
Kalmar
Smedby
Borgholm
Köpingsvik
Gärdslösa
Öland
Färjestaden
Gårdby
Resmo
Karlevi
Mörbylånga
Stora Alvaret
Emmaboda
Tingsryd
Urshult
Ryd
Almhult
Strömsnäsbruk
Markaryd
Lönsboda
Osby
Vittsjö
Broby
Sibbhult
Olofström
Mörrum
BLEKINGE LÄN
Bräkne-Hoby
Kallinge
Ronneby
Karlshamn
Karlskrona
Rödeby
Söderåkra
Torsås
Grönhögen
Nättraby
Jämjö
Björketorp
Sölvesborg
Bromölla
Bäckaskog
Hässleholm
Perstorp
Finja
Kristianstad
Tollarp
Rinkaby
Åhus
Hanöbukten
Höör
Bosjökloster
Everöd
Hörby
Kristinehov
Brösarp
Vitaby
Ovedskloster
Sjöbo
Tryde
St Olof
Sövdeborg
Simrishamn
Tomelilla
Valleberga
Ystad
Świnoujście
København
Hammershus
Allinge-Sandvig
Christiansø
BORNHOLM (DK)
Gudhjem
Hasle
Svaneke
Åkirkeby
Rønne
Nexø
Pedersker
Travemünde
Arkona
Saßnitz
Kappelshamnsviken
Lärbro
Othem
Slite
Visby
Bro
Dalhem
Gothem
GOTLANDS LÄN
Väte
Hejde
Klintehamn
Garde
Etelhem
Ljugarn
Lojsta
Lye
Grötlingbo
Burgsviken
Burgsvik
Vamlingbo
Fårö
Fårösund
Gotland

Bottenhavet
Åland (SF)
SF
Turku
Naantali
Uusikaupunki
Loimaa
Salo
Pargas
Lohja
Karkkila
Hyvinkää
Järvenpää
Kerava
Porvoo
Loviisa
Kotka
Espoo
HELSINKI
Ekenäs
Hanko
Mariehamn
Eckerö
Kappelskär Stockholm
Stockholm Travemünde
Gävle
Ockelbo
Sandviken
Gräsö
Vendel
Östhammar
Björkö
Avesta
Fagersta
Sala
Uppsala
Skokloster
Norrtälje
Kappelskär
Turku
Enköping
Västerås
Mälaren
STOCKHOLM
Helsinki Leningrad
Drottningholm
Eskilstuna
Strängnäs
Gripsholm
Södertälje
Flen
Nynäshamn
Katrineholm
Nyköping
Oxelösund
Kolmården
Norrköping
Linköping
Valdemarsvik
Västervik
Vimmerby
Gotska Sandön (S)
Fårö
Fårösund
Slite
Visby
Klintehamn
Ljugarn
Gotland
Burgsvik
Byxelkrok
Oskarshamn
Högsby
Borgholm
Nybro
Kalmar
Öland
Grönhögen
Karlskrona
Bornholm (DK)
BALTIC SEA
MER BALTIQUE
Finskij Zaliv
TALLINN
Paldiski
Kohtla-Järve
Rakvere
Tapa
Mustvee
Paide
Jõgeva
Türi
Põltsamaa
Vormsi
Hiiumaa
Kärdla
Haapsalu
ESTONIJA
Muhu
Virtsu
Pärnu
Viljandi
Tartu
Saaremaa
Orissaare
Kuressaare
Kilingi-Nõmme
Võrtsjärv
Võru
Rūjiena
Valga
Rižskij Zaliv
Salacgrīva
Valmiera
Smiltene
Kolkasrags
Kolka
Irbes Šaurums
Cēsis
Gauja
Sigulda
Ventspils
Talsi
RĪGA
Jūrmala
Tukums
Ogre
Madona
LATVIJA
Kuldīga
Jelgava
Stučka
Jēkabpils
Saldus
Dobele
Bauska
Daugava
Liepāja
Venta
Mažeikiai
Joniškis
Biržai
Rokiškis
Skuodas
Kuršėnai
Šiauliai
Telšiai
Panevėžys
Palanga
Plungė
Radviliškis
Utena
LITVA
Klaipėda
Raseiniai
Ukmergė
Kėdainiai
Šilutė
Tauragė
Neris
Nemunas
Jurbarkas
Vilnius
Kuršskij Zaliv
Sovetsk
Neman
Kaunas
Trakai
Svetlogorsk
Polessk
Kaliningrad
Čern'achovsk
Gusev
Vilkaviškis
Prienai
Kapsukas
Alytus
Eišiškės
Baltijsk
Gvardejsk
Pravdinsk
Bagrationovsk
Mamonovo
Braniewo
Zatoka Gdańska
Zalew Wiślany
Władysławowo
Łeba
Wejherowo
Gdynia
Sopot
GDAŃSK
Lębork
Ustka
Słupsk
Kartuzy
Darłowo
Sławno
Koszalin
Kołobrzeg
Bytów
Kościerzyna
Tczew
Elbląg
Malbork
Miastko
Białogard
Czersk
Starogard Gdański
Kwidzyn
Połczyn-Zdrój
Szczecinek
Chojnice
Człuchów
Świecie
Grudziądz
Drawsko Pomorskie
Jastrowie
Chełmno
Brodnica
Iława
Ostróda
Olsztyn
Lidzbark Warmiński
Kętrzyn
Węgorzewo
Jezioro Mamry
Giżycko
Mrągowo
Mazury
Jezioro Śniardwy
Ełk
Szczytno
Suwałki
Augustów
Grajewo
Druskininkai
Grodno
Lida
Ščučin
Mosty
Volkovysk
Łomża
Ostrołęka
Białystok
Narew
Mława
Przasnysz
Bielsk Podlaski
Puszcza
106
109
49
112
165
308
476
523
352
485
185

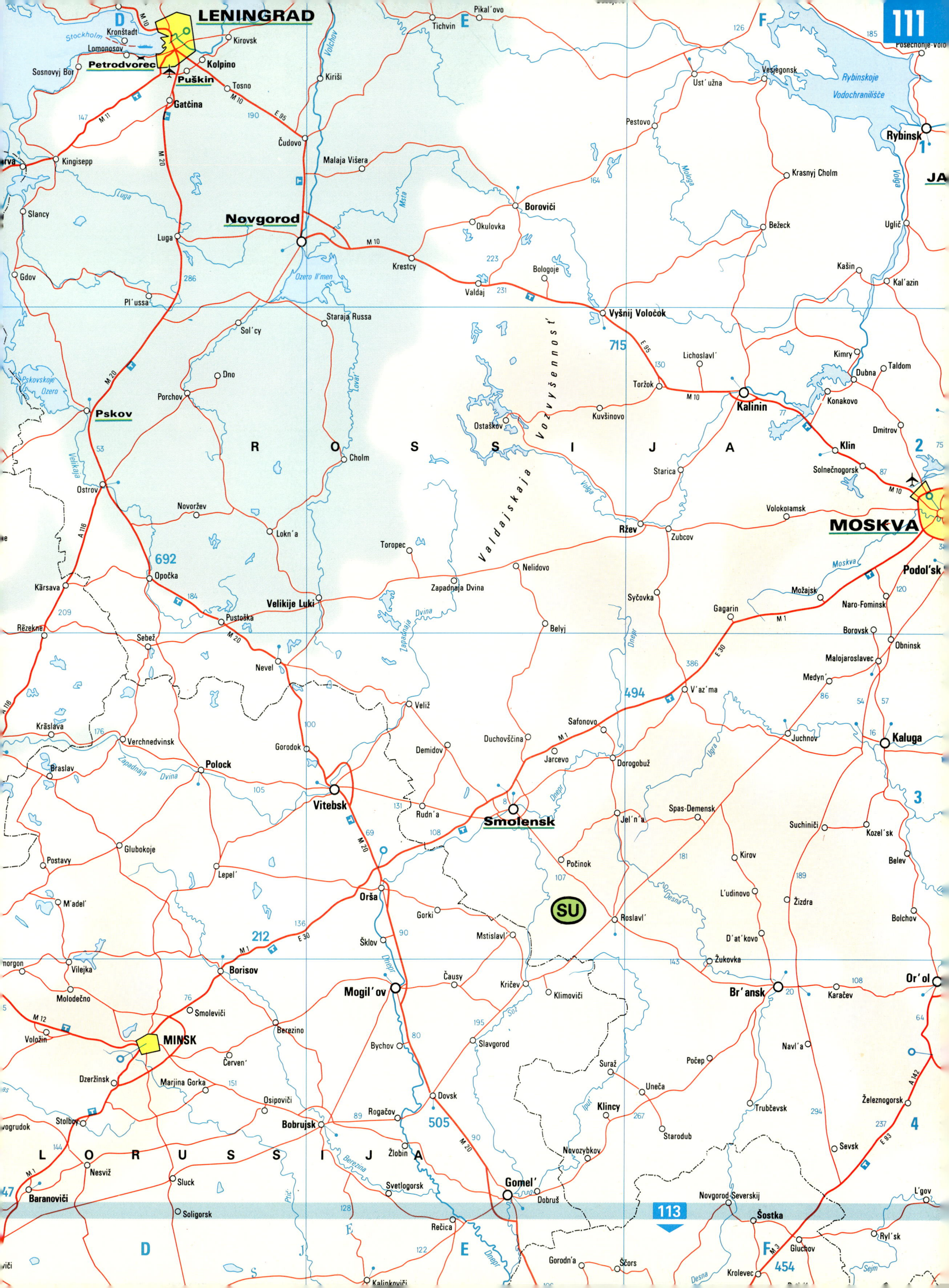
LENINGRAD
Kronštadt
Lomonosov
Petrodvorec
Puškin
Kolpino
Kirovsk
Tosno
Gatčina
Sosnovyj Bor
Kingisepp
Slancy
Gdov
Luga
Pl'ussa
Novgorod
Čudovo
Kiriši
Tichvin
Pikal'ovo
Malaja Višera
Krestcy
Valdaj
Okulovka
Boroviči
Bologoje
Vyšnij Voloček
Pestovo
Ust'užna
Vesjegonsk
Rybinskoje Vodochranilišče
Rybinsk
Krasnyj Cholm
Bežeck
Uglič
Kašin
Kal'azin
Kimry
Dubna
Taldom
Lichoslavl'
Toržok
Kalinin
Konakovo
Dmitrov
Klin
Solnečnogorsk
MOSKVA
Volokolamsk
Podol'sk
Naro-Fominsk
Možajsk
Gagarin
Borovsk
Obninsk
Malojaroslavec
Medyn'
Juchnov
Kaluga
Suchiniči
Kozel'sk
Belev
Bolchov
Žizdra
Or'ol
Karačev
Br'ansk
Kirov
L'udinovo
D'at'kovo
Žukovka
Navl'a
Počep
Trubčevsk
Železnogorsk
Sevsk
L'gov
Ryl'sk
Gluchov
Šostka
Krolevec
Novgorod-Severskij
Starica
Ržev
Zubcov
Syčovka
Kuvšinovo
Ostaškov
Valdajskaja Vozvyšennost'
Staraja Russa
Sol'cy
Dno
Porchov
Pskov
Pskovskoje Ozero
Ozero Il'men
Ostrov
Novoržev
Cholm
Lokn'a
Toropec
Nelidovo
Zapadnaja Dvina
Belyj
Opočka
Kārsava
Rēzekne
Pustoška
Velikije Luki
Sebež
Nevel
Veliž
Krāslava
Verchnedvinsk
Braslav
Polock
Gorodok
Vitebsk
Demidov
Duchovščina
Safonovo
Jarcevo
Dorogobuž
V'az'ma
Smolensk
Rudn'a
Jel'n'a
Spas-Demensk
Počinok
Roslavl'
Orša
Gorki
Šklov
Mstislavl'
Kričev
Klimoviči
Čausy
Mogil'ov
Bychov
Slavgorod
Dovsk
Rogačov
Žlobin
Svetlogorsk
Rečica
Gomel'
Dobruš
Surаž
Uneča
Klincy
Starodub
Novozybkov
Gorodn'a
Ščors
Kalinkoviči
Glubokoje
Postavy
Lepel'
M'adel'
Vilejka
Molodečno
Borisov
Smoleviči
MINSK
Voložin
Červen'
Berezino
Dzeržinsk
Marjina Gorka
Osipoviči
Bobrujsk
Stolbcy
Nesviž
Sluck
Soligorsk
Baranoviči
R O S S I J A
B E L O R U S S I J A
SU
Volga
Dnepr
Desna
Zapadnaja Dvina
Berezina
Velikaja
Lovat'
Msta
Mologa
Moskva
Ugra
M 10
M 20
M 1
E 95
E 30
113

110
49
53
57
114
PL
H
WARSZAWA
POZNAŃ
WROCŁAW
ŁÓDŹ
KRAKÓW
Gdańsk
Toruń
Bydgoszcz
Białystok
Lublin
Radom
Częstochowa
Katowice
Opole
Kielce
Rzeszów
Przemyśl
Brest
L'VOV
Hradec Králové
Brno
Olomouc
Ostrava
Kroměříž
Macocha
Wieliczka
Dobšiná
Baradla
Košice
Prešov
Užgorod
WIEN
Bratislava
Győr
Esztergom
Eger
Miskolc
Debrecen
BUDAPEST
Szolnok
Székesfehérvár
Veszprém
Balaton
Kecskemét
Szeged
Pécs
Sopron
Szombathely
Graz
Maribor
Oradea
Cluj-Napoca
Arad
Subotica
Krkonoše
Tatry
Malbork
Olsztyn
Grodno
Lwów
K A R P A T Y
Puszcza Białowieska
Roztocze
Góry Świętokrzyskie
Nízke Beskydy
Slovenské Rudohorie
Mátra
Bakony
Donautal
M a r a m u r
Mazury
Vistula
Warta
Odra
Bug
Wisła
Duna
Tisza
Drava
Mureș

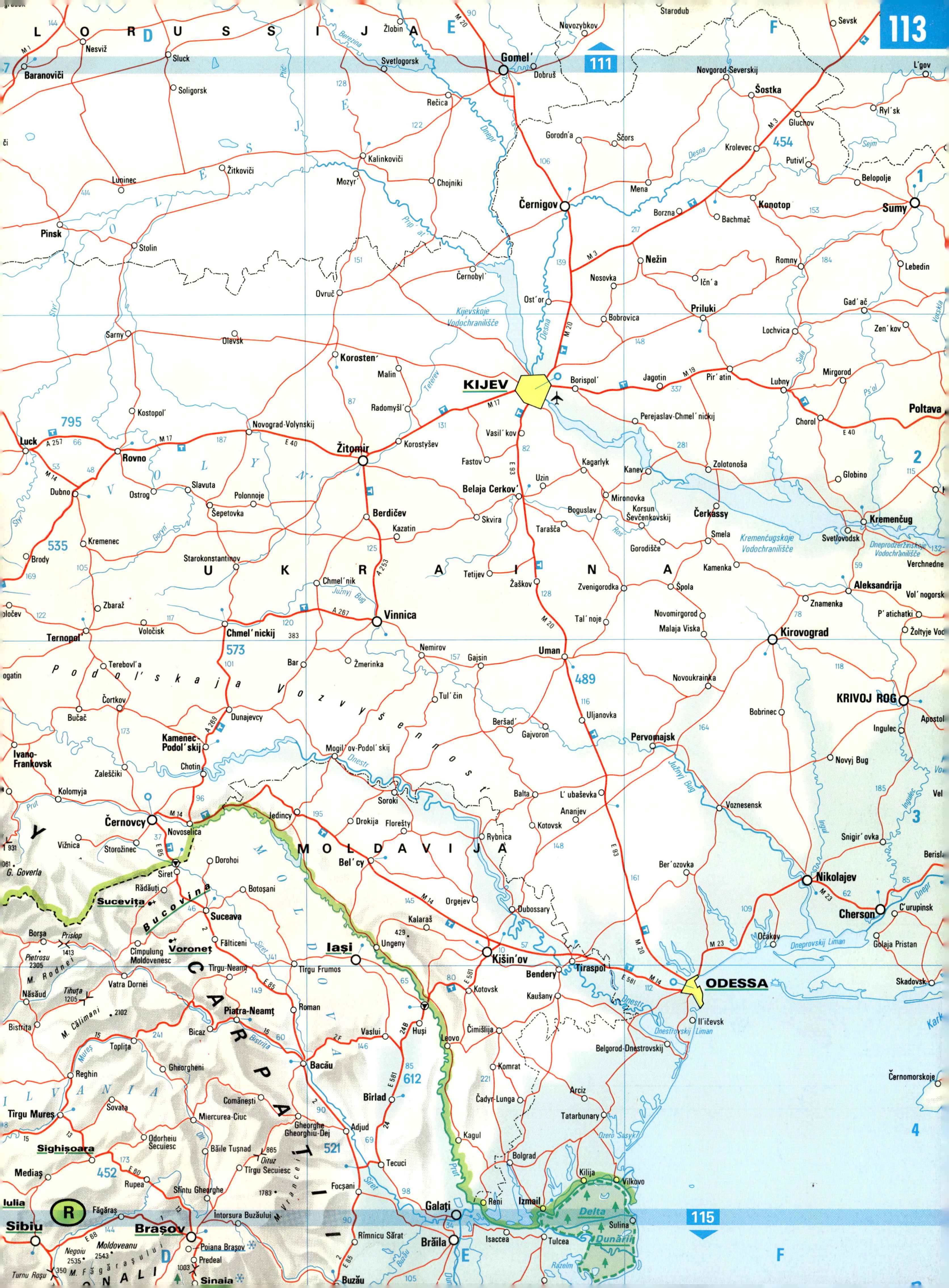

111
115
Gomel'
Baranoviči
Nesviž
Sluck
Soligorsk
Svetlogorsk
Žlobin
Novozybkov
Starodub
Sevsk
Dobruš
Novgorod-Severskij
Šostka
L'gov
Ryl'sk
Gluchov
Rečica
Kalinkoviči
Mozyr'
Chojniki
Žitkoviči
Luninec
Pinsk
Stolin
Gorodn'a
Ščors
Krolevec
Putivl'
Belopolje
Sumy
Černigov
Mena
Borzna
Konotop
Bachmač
Nežin
Nosovka
Romny
Lebedin
Černobyl'
Ovruč
Ost'or
Ičn'a
Priluki
Gad'ač
Bobrovica
Lochvica
Zen'kov
Kijevskoje Vodochranilišče
Sarny
Olevsk
Korosten'
Malin
Radomyšl'
KIJEV
Borispol'
Jagotin
Pir'atin
Lubny
Mirgorod
Poltava
Kostopol'
Novograd-Volynskij
Žitomir
Korostyšev
Vasil'kov
Perejaslav-Chmel'nickij
Chorol
Luck
Rovno
Dubno
Ostrog
Slavuta
Polonnoje
Šepetovka
Fastov
Kagarlyk
Kanev
Zolotonoša
Globino
Uzin
Belaja Cerkov'
Mironovka
Korsun Ševčenkovskij
Boguslav
Čerkassy
Kremenčug
Berdičev
Kazatin
Skvira
Tarašča
Smela
Kremenčugskoje Vodochranilišče
Svetlovodsk
Dneprodzeržinskoje Vodochranilišče
Kremenec
Brody
Starokonstantinov
Gorodišče
Kamenka
Verchnedneprovsk
U K R A I N A
Chmel'nik
Tetijev
Žaškov
Zvenigorodka
Špola
Aleksandrija
Zbaraž
Vinnica
Tal'noje
Novomirgorod
Znamenka
Vol'nogorsk
P'atichatki
Ternopol'
Voločisk
Chmel'nickij
Malaja Viska
Kirovograd
Žoltyje Vody
Terebovl'a
Bar
Žmerinka
Nemirov
Gajsin
Uman
Podol'skaja Vozvyšennost'
Čortkov
Bučač
Tul'čin
Uljanovka
Novoukrainka
Krivoj Rog
Bobrinec
Apostolovo
Dunajevcy
Kamenec-Podol'skij
Beršad'
Gajvoron
Pervomajsk
Ingulec
Ivano-Frankovsk
Mogil'ov-Podol'skij
Novyj Bug
Zaleščiki
Chotin
Kolomyja
Soroki
Balta
L'ubaševka
Ananjev
Voznesensk
Černovcy
Novoselica
Jedincy
Drokija
Floreštу
Rybnica
Kotovsk
Snigir'ovka
Vižnica
Storožinec
MOLDAVIJA
Dorohoi
Bel'cy
Ber'ozovka
Nikolajev
Siret
Rădăuţi
G. Goverla
Botoşani
Suceviţa
Bucovina
Suceava
Orgejev
Dubossary
Cherson
C'urupinsk
Borşa
Prislop
Voroneţ
Fălticeni
Kalaraš
Ungeny
Iaşi
Kišin'ov
Očakov
Golaja Pristan
Cîmpulung Moldovenesc
Pietrosu 2305
M. Rodnei
Tîrgu-Neamţ
Tîrgu Frumos
Bendery
Tiraspol
ODESSA
Năsăud
Tihuţa 1205
Vatra Dornei
CARPAŢII
Kotovsk
Kaušany
Skadovsk
Piatra-Neamţ
Roman
Bistriţa
M. Călimani 2102
Bicaz
Toplita
Vaslui
Huşi
Leovo
Čimišlija
Il'ičevsk
Dnestrovskij Liman
Belgorod-Dnestrovskij
Bacău
Reghin
Gheorgheni
Komrat
Bîrlad
Čadyr-Lunga
Arciz
Černomorskoje
Sovata
Comăneşti
Tîrgu Mureş
Miercurea-Ciuc
Gheorghe Gheorghiu-Dej
Adjud
Kagul
Tatarbunary
Odorheiu Secuiesc
Băile Tuşnad
Oituz
Tîrgu Secuiesc
Sighişoara
Tecuci
Bolgrad
Mediaş
Rupea
Sfîntu Gheorghe
Focşani
Kilija
Vilkovo
Făgăraş
Întorsura Buzăului
Galaţi
Reni
Izmail
Delta Dunării
Sulina
Sibiu
Braşov
Poiana Braşov
Predeal
Rîmnicu Sărat
Brăila
Isaccea
Tulcea
Negoiu 2535
Moldoveanu 2543
Turnu Roşu
Sinaia
Buzău
Dnepr
Desna
Pripjat
Dnestr
Prut
Siret
Južnyj Bug
Ingulec

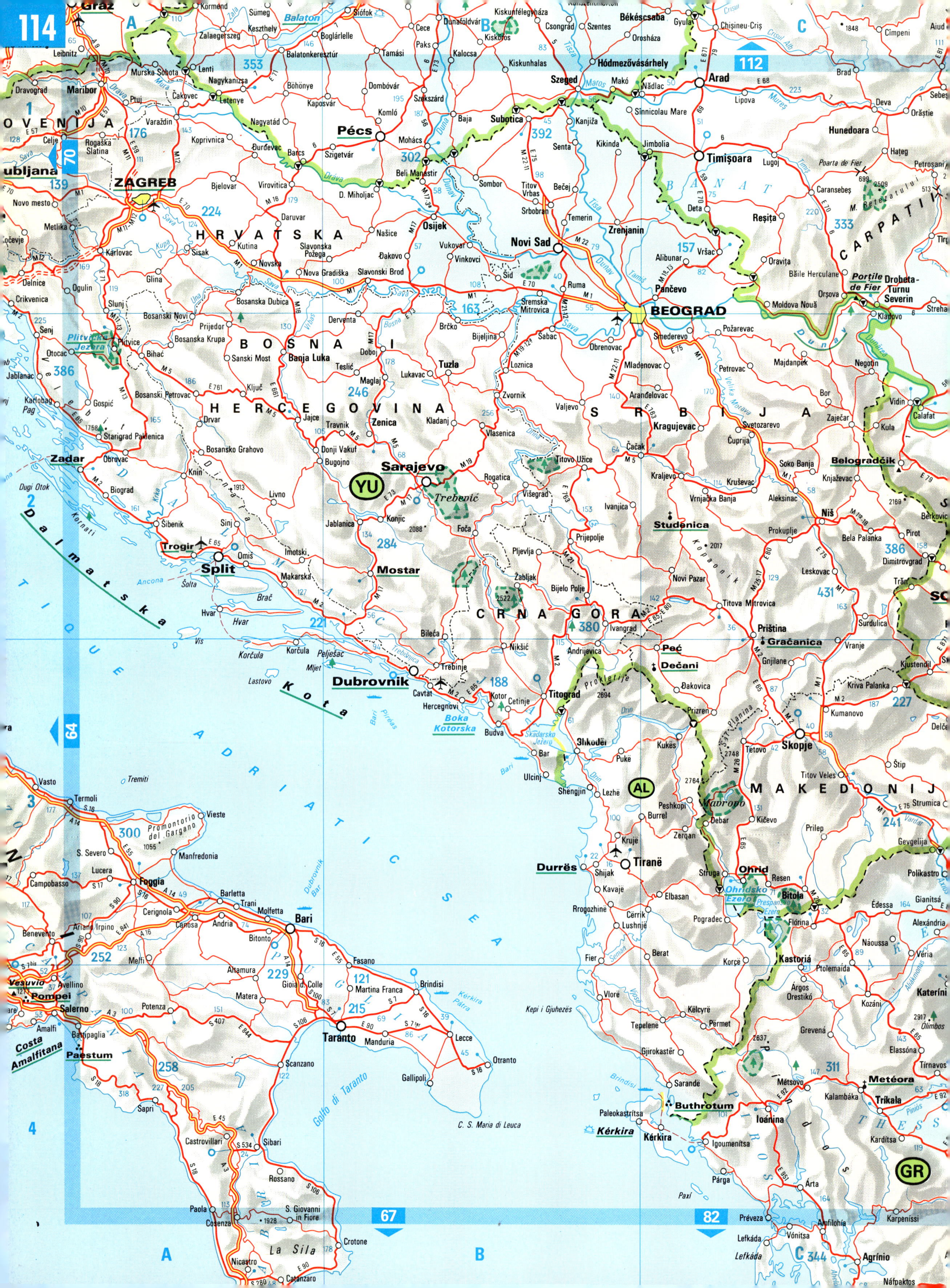
112
70
64
67
82
SLOVENIJA
Ljubljana
ZAGREB
HRVATSKA
BOSNA I HERCEGOVINA
Sarajevo
YU
SRBIJA
BEOGRAD
Novi Sad
CRNA GORA
Titograd
MAKEDONIJA
Skopje
AL
Tiranë
Durrës
GR
CARPATI
Graz
Maribor
Pécs
Szeged
Arad
Timişoara
Balaton
Osijek
Banja Luka
Tuzla
Zenica
Mostar
Split
Trogir
Zadar
Dubrovnik
Kotorska
Boka
Plitvička Jezera
Dalmatska
Kota
ADRIATIC SEA
Studenica
Gračanica
Dečani
Peć
Priština
Niš
Kragujevac
Ohrid
Ohridsko Ezero
Bitola
Kastoriá
Ioánina
Metéora
Trikala
Kérkira
Buthrotum
Foggia
Bari
Brindisi
Taranto
Lecce
Otranto
Salerno
Pompei
Vesuvio
Paestum
Costa Amalfitana
Golfo di Taranto
Promontorio del Gargano
La Sila
C. S. Maria di Leuca
Portile de Fier
Drobeta-Turnu Severin
Belogradčik
Trebević
Skadarsko Jezero
Shkodër

MER NOIRE
BLACK SEA
Marmara Denizi
AEGEAN SEA
Thrakikó Pélagos
Vóries Sporádes
BUCUREȘTI
İSTANBUL
Sighișoara
Mediaș
Sibiu
Brașov
Făgăraș
Sinaia
Ploiești
Pitești
Rîmnicu Vîlcea
Buzău
Focșani
Galați
Brăila
Izmail
Tulcea
Kilija
Vilkovo
Sulina
Delta Dunării
Histria
Constanța
Mamaia
Eforie
Mangalia
Cernavodă
Slobozia
Urziceni
Călărași
Oltenița
Giurgiu
Alexandria
Roșiori de Vede
Turnu Măgurele
Craiova
Caracal
Slatina
Drăgășani
Ruse
Silistra
Dulovo
Razgrad
Tutrakan
Tolbuhin
Albena
Balčik
Zlatni Pjasăci
Varna
Devnja
Madara
Šumen
Tărgovište
Preslav
Popovo
Bjala
Svištov
Nikopol
Zimnicea
Pleven
Loveč
Lukovit
Veliko Tărnovo
Gorna Orjahovica
Sevlievo
Gabrovo
Trojan
Kotel
Elena
Sliven
Jambol
Karnobat
Ajtos
Burgas
Nesebăr
Slănčev Brjag
Obzor
Pomorie
Sozopol
Mičurin
Ahtopol
Malko Tărnovo
Kazanlăk
Šipka
Stara Zagora
Nova Zagora
Karlovo
Sopot
Hisarja
Rosovo dolina
Sredna Gora
Stara Planina
Plovdiv
Pazardžik
Asenovgrad
Haskovo
Dimitrovgrad
Harmanli
Bačkovo
Kărdžali
Smoljan
Pamporovo
Rila
Samokov
Botevgrad
Vraca
Mezdra
Ihtiman
Kostenec
Velingrad
Batak
Blagoevgrad
Razlog
Goce Delčev
Sandanski
Petrič
Ruse
Elhovo
Edirne
Svilengrad
Kırklareli
Yıldız Dağları
Derekoy
Lüleburgaz
Saray
Çorlu
Silivri
Tekirdağ
Uzunköprü
Keşan
İpsala
Alexandroúpoli
Komotiní
Xánthi
Dráma
Kavála
Sérres
Sidirókastro
Thássos
Samothráki
Kilkís
Nigríta
THESSALONÍKI
Políghiros
Halkidikí
Ágio Óros
Thermaïkós Kólpos
Límnos
Mírina
Gökçe
Lésvos
Mithimna
Mitilíni
Plomári
Gelibolu
Eceabat
Çanakkale
Biga
Karabiga
Erdek
Bandırma
Gönen
Susurluk
Balıkesir
Ezine
Ayvacık
Edremit
Burhaniye
Ayvalık
Bergama
Soma
Kırkağaç
Akhisar
Manisa
Turgutlu
Salihli
Alaşehir
Foça
Karaburun
Çeşme
Urla
İzmir
Bayındır
Ödemiş
Tire
Selçuk
Efes
Kuşadası
Söke
Aydın
Nazilli
Sultanhisar
Denizli
Pamukkale
Sarayköy
Aphrodisias
Çardak
Yeşilova
Acıpayam
Bozdoğan
Buldan
Çal
Çivril
Dinar
Kula
Uşak
Sivaslı
Demirci
Gediz
Simav
Sındırgı
Emet
Çavdarhisar
Kütahya
Tavşanlı
Bursa
Uludağ
Mudanya
Gemlik
İznik
Yalova
Bilecik
Bozüyük
Eskişehir
Gebze
Kartal
Üsküdar
Kilyos
Şile
Kandıra
İzmit
Adapazarı
Sapanca
Geyve
Göynük
Karasu
Akçakoca
Vólos
Almirós
Skiathos
Skópelos
Skiros
Halkída
Kími
Évia
Kaména Voúrla
Loutrá Edipsoú
Delfí
Livadiá
Thíva
Itéa
Hios
BG
TR
R

Index Register Índice Indice

F Lorsqu'un nom figure plusieurs fois dans l'index, une précision est ajoutée entre parenthèses pour permettre de l'identifier plus facilement: pays, région ou ville la plus proche, élément géographique d'après les abréviations ci-dessous.

NL Bij namen die meermalen in het register voorkomen, staat tussen haakjes een aanduiding ter verklaring: het land, de streek, de dichtstbijgelegen stad of een geografisch gegeven (zie de afkortingen hieronder).

GB Where there are two or more identical place names, the name of the distinguishing country or region or nearest large town is given in brackets; geographical features are indicated by the abbreviations below.

E Para poder localizar más fácilmente un nombre que figura varias veces en el índice, se añade entre paréntesis el país, la región o ciudad más cercana, o un elemento geográfico, con las abreviaturas siguientes.

D Tritt ein Name mehrfach im Register auf, wird er durch eine in Klammern gesetzte nähere Bestimmung genauer definiert. Sie finden folgende Zusätze: Land, Region oder nächstgelegene Stadt, geographische Gegebenheiten, ggf. abgekürzt

I Quando un nome figura più volte nell'indice, una precisazione viene aggiunta tra parentesi per permettere d'identificarlo più facilmente: nazione, regione o città la più vicina, elemento geografico come da abbreviazioni qui di seguito.

Abbr.	
Ákr	Ákra, Akrotírion
B	Bay, Baie, Bucht, Bahía, Baía, Bukt(en), Bugt, Bukhta
Bgem	Barragem
C	Cape, Cap, Cabo, Capo
Co	County
Ch	Chaîne
Chan	Channel
Dépt	Département
Emb	Embalse
Ez	Ezero
G	Gulf, Golfe, Golfo
Gges	Gorges
I(s), *I(s)*	Isle(s), Island(s), Ile(s), Ilha(s), Isla(s), Isola(e)
Jez	Jezero, Jezioro
K	Kanal, Kanaal
L, *L*	Lake, Loch, Lough, Llyn, Lac, Laguna, Lago, Límni

Abbr.	
Liq	Liquen
Meg	Méga, Megál, -a, -i, -o
Mikr.	Mikr-í, -ón
Mgne(s)	Montagne(s)
M, Mte(s)	Maj, Maj'e, Monte(s)
Mt(s), *Mt(s)*	Mount(s), Mountain(s), Mont(s)
Mti	Monti, Muntii
Nac	Nacional(e)
Nat	National
Naz	Nazionale
N	Nissí, Nissos
Ni	Nissiá, Nissi
Os	Ostrov(a)
Ot	Otok(i), Otoci
Oz	Ozero(a)
P	Pass
Pal	Paleós, á, ó
Pen	Peninsula, Penisola

Abbr.	
Pk	Park
Pl	Planina
Pque	Parque
Prov	Province
Pso	Passo
Pt(e)	Point(e)
Rib	Ribeirão
R, *R*	River, Rivière, Rio, Ria, Rijeka
Reg	Region, Région
Res	Reservoir, Reservoire
Sa	Sierra, Serra
Sd	Sound, Sund
St	Saint, Sankt, Sint
Ste(s)	Sainte(s)
Teh L	Tehnití Límni
V	Valley, Vale, Vallée, Val, Valle, Vall

A

Aachen **51** D3
Aalen **55** E2
Aalsmeer **16** C2
Aalst **50** B3
Aalten **17** D3
Aalter **50** B3
Äänekoski **103** D2
Aapajärvi **95** F4
Aarau **27** F2
Aarberg **27** E2
Aarburg **27** F2
Aare **58** A3
Aargau **27** F2
Aarlen **21** D2
Aarschot **50** C3
Aavasaksa **98** C2
Abades **40** A1
Abadiño **36** B1
A Baiuca **34** A1
Abanilla **45** D2
Abano Terme **61** D1
Abbadia San Salvatore **63** D1
Abbasanta **66** B3
Abbazia di Casamari **63** F3
Abbazia di Fossanova **63** F3
Abbazia di Montecassino **64** A3
Abbazia San Clemente a Casauria **64** A2
Abbeville **19** E2
Abbeyfeale **14** B3
Abbeyleix **12** C4
Abbey Town **5** D4
Abbiategrasso **60** A1
Abborrträsk **98** B3
Abbots Bromley **6** C3
Abbotsbury **9** D3
Abcoude **16** C2
Abejar **36** B3
Abejuela **41** E3
Abela **42** A1
Abelvær **97** D4
Abenberg **55** E2
Abenójar **39** F4
Åbenrå **108** A4
Abensberg **55** F2
Aberaeron **8** C1
Aberdar **8** C2
Aberdare **8** C2
Aberdaron **6** A3
Aberdaugleddau **8** B2
Aberdeen **3** E4
Aberdovey **6** A3
Aberfeldy **4** C1
Aberfoyle **4** C2
Abergavenny **9** D2
Abergele **6** B2
Abergwaun **8** B1
Aberhonddu **8** C1
Aberlady **5** D2
Aberpennar **8** C2
Aberporth **8** B1
Abersoch **6** A3
Abertawe **8** C2
Aberteifi **8** B1
Abertillery **9** D2
Aber-Wrac'h, l' **22** A2
Aberystwyth **8** C1
Abetone **60** C3
Abiego **37** E3
Abingdon **9** E2
Abington **5** D3
Abisko **94** B3
Abisko (Nat park) **94** B4
Abla **44** B3
Ablis **19** E4
Åbo **107** D2
Abondance **27** E3
Abony **112** B4
Aboyne **3** E4
Abrantes **38** B3
Abreschviller **21** E4
Abrets, les **30** C1
Abriès **31** E2
Abruzzo **63** F2
Abruzzo, Parco Nazionale d' **64** A2
Abstadt-Tailfingen **55** D3
Abtenau **59** E1
Åby **105** F4
Åbybro **108** B2
A Caniza **34** A3
Acceglio **31** E2
Accettura **65** D4
Acciaroli **67** D1
Accous **37** D1
Accrington **6** C2
Acebo **39** D2
Acedo **36** B2
Acehuche **39** D3
Acerno **64** B4
Acerra **64** B4
Aceuchal **39** D4
Ache **59** E1
Achenkirch **59** D1
Achenpaß **56** A4
Achensee **59** D1
Achern **54** C3
Acheux **19** F2
Achill I **12** A2
Achim **17** F1
Achnacroish **4** B1
Achnasheen **2** C3
A'Chràlaig **2** C4
Aci Castello **69** D3
Acıpayam **115** F4
Acireale **69** D3
Aci Trezza **69** D3
Acle **7** F3
A Coruña **34** B1
Acqualagna **61** E4
Acquapendente **63** D1
Acquasanta Terme **63** F1
Acquasparta **63** E1
Acquaviva delle Fonti **65** D3
Acqui-Terme **60** A2
Acri **67** E2
Ada **72** C1
Adaja, R **39** F2
Adak **98** A3
Ådalsel **104** C2
Adamandás **88** A4
Adamclisi **115** E1
Adamello **58** C3
Adamello Brenta, Parco Naturale **58** C3
Adamello, Mont' **58** C3
Adamuz **43** F2
Adanero **39** F1
Adapazarı **115** F3
Adare **14** B3
Adaševci **72** B3
Adda **60** B2
Adelboden **27** E3
Adelfia **65** D3
Adelsheim **55** D1
Ademuz **41** D3
Adenau **51** E4
Ádendro **79** F3
Adéres, Óros **87** E2
Adiça, Sa da **42** C1
Adige **61** D1
Adjud **113** E4
Admont **57** D3
Adolfström **97** F3
Adorf **53** D3
Adour **28** B4
Adra **44** B4
Adradas **36** B4
Adrall **32** A3
Adrano **69** D3
Adria **61** D2
Adriatic Sea **114** A3
Adzaneta **41** E3
Aegean Sea **115** E4
Aenona **74** C1
Aerinó **83** F2
Ærø **108** B4
Ærøskøbing **108** B4
A Estrada **34** A2
Aetópetra **82** B1
Aetós (Kefaloniá) **82** B4
Aetós (Makedonía) **79** D3
Aetós (Stereá Eláda) **82** C3
Äetsä **107** D2
Afándou **93** F1
Åfarnes **100** B2
Aféa **87** F2
Affi **60** C1
Afiónas **82** A1
Áfissos **83** F2
Áfitos **80** B4
Afjord **100** C1
Åfjorden **104** A1
Aflenzer Seeberg **57** E3
Aflenz Kurort **57** E3
Afráti **84** B4
Afsluitdijk **16** C1
A Garda **34** A3
Agathoníssi **89** E2
Agay **31** E4
Agazzano **60** B2
Agde **30** A4
Agdenes **100** C1
Agen **28** C3
Àger **37** F3
Ager **56** C3
Ageranós **87** D4
Agerbæk **108** A3
Agger **17** E4
Aggius **66** B1
Aggsbach-Dorf **57** E2
Aggsbach-Markt **57** E2
Agiá **83** F1
Agiá, Akr **83** F4
Agía Ána (Évia) **84** A3
Agía Ána (Viotía) **83** F4
Agía Efimía **82** B4
Agía Efthimía **83** E4
Agía Ekateríni, Akr **82** A1
Agía Fotiá **91** F4
Agía Galíni **91** D4
Agía Kiriakí (Makedonía) **78** C3
Agía Kiriakí (Pelopónissos) **86** B3
Agía Kiriakí (Sámos) **89** E2
Agía Lávra **86** C1
Agía Marína (Égina) **87** F2
Agía Marína (Kríti) **90** B3
Agía Marína (Léros) **89** E3
Agía Marína (Stereá Eláda) **83** E3
Agía Marína (Stereá Eláda) **88** A1
Agía Paraskeví (Lésvos) **85** F2
Agía Paraskeví (Makedonía) **80** C2
Agía Paraskiés **91** E4
Agía Pelagía (Kíthira) **90** A1
Agía Pelagía (Kríti) **91** D3
Agía Rouméli **90** B4
Agíasma **80** C2
Agiásmata **85** E4
Agía Sofía (Évia) **84** B3
Agía Sofía (Pelopónissos) **87** D2
Agía Sotíra **87** E1
Agiássos **85** F2
Agía Triáda (Kríti) **91** D4
Agía Triáda (Makedonía) **79** F3
Agía Triáda (Pelopónissos) **86** C1
Agía Triáda (Stereá Eláda) **87** F1
Agía Varvára **91** D4
Agiófilo **83** D1
Agiókambos (Évia) **83** F3
Agiókambos (Thessalía) **83** F1
Agionóri **87** E2
Ágio Óros **80** C4
Agiopigí **83** D2
Ágios **84** A3
Ágios Anárgiri (Pelopónissos) **87** D3
Ágios Anárgiri (Thessalía) **83** E2
Ágios Andónios **80** A3
Ágios Andréas (Arkadía) **87** D2
Ágios Andréas (Lakonía) **87** E4
Ágios Apóstoli (Évia) **84** B4
Ágios Apóstoli (Pelopónissos) **87** E4

Ágios Apóstoli (Stereá Eláda) 84 B4
Ágios Athanássios (Dráma) 80 C2
Ágios Athanássios (Péla) 79 D2
Ágios Avgoustínos 86 C3
Ágios Déka 91 D4
Ágios Dimítrios, Akr 88 A3
Ágios Dimítrios (Évia) 88 A1
Ágios Dimítrios (Lakonía) 87 D3
Ágios Dimítrios (Makedonía) 79 E4
Ágios Dimítrios (Messinía) 87 D4
Ágios Dimítrios (Stereá Eláda) 83 D3
Ágios Dionissios 79 E4
Ágios Efstrátios, N 85 D2
Ágios Fokás 89 F3
Ágios Fokás, Akr 85 F3
Ágios Geórgios (Évia) 83 F3
Ágios Geórgios, N 87 F2
Ágios Geórgios (Lassíthi) 91 E4
Ágios Geórgios (Stereá Eláda) 83 D3
Ágios Geórgios (Zákinthos) 86 A1
Ágios Geórgiou, Órmos 87 E3
Ágios Germanós 79 D2
Ágios Górdis 82 A1
Ágios Harálambos 81 E2
Ágios Ioánis, Akr 91 F3
Ágios Ioánis (Dodekánissa) 89 F4
Ágios Ioánis (Pelopónissos) 87 E2
Ágios Ioánis (Stereá Eláda) 83 F4
Ágios Ioánis (Thessalía) 83 F3
Ágios Ioánis (Thessalía) 83 F2
Ágios Irínis, Akr 85 D1
Ágios Issídoros 93 E2
Ágios Kírikos 89 D2
Ágios Konstandínos (Stereá Eláda) 83 F3
Ágios Konstandínos (Thessalía) 83 E2
Ágios Kosmás (Grevená) 79 D4
Ágios Kosmás (Kavála) 80 C2
Ágios Léon 86 A1
Ágios Loukás 84 B4
Ágios Mámas 80 A4
Ágios Márkos 80 A2
Ágios Mathéos 82 A2
Ágios Míronas 91 D4
Ágios Nikítas 82 B3
Ágios Nikólaos (Etolía-Akarnanía) 82 B3
Ágios Nikólaos (Fokída) 83 E4
Ágios Nikólaos (Fthiótida) 83 F3
Ágios Nikólaos (Hers.Methánon) 87 E2
Ágios Nikólaos (Ípiros) 82 B1
Ágios Nikólaos (Kríti) 91 E4
Ágios Nikólaos (Lakonía) 87 D3
Ágios Nikólaos (Makedonía) 80 B4
Ágios Nikólaos (Messinía) 86 C3
Ágios Pandeleímonos 79 D3
Ágios Pángalos, Akr 83 E4
Ágios Paraskeví (Ípiros) 78 C4
Ágios Paraskeví (Makedonía) 79 F2
Ágios Pávlos 80 A3
Ágios Pétros 87 D2
Ágios Pnévma 80 B2
Ágios Pródromos 80 A3
Ágios Sóstis 83 E3
Ágios Stéfanos (Kiklådes) 88 C2
Ágios Stéfanos (Stereá Eláda) 87 F1
Ágios Theódori (Makedonía) 79 D4
Ágios Theódori (Pelopónissos) 87 E1
Ágios Theódori (Thessalía) 83 F3
Ágios Thomás (Kríti) 91 D4
Ágios Thomás (Stereá Eláda) 84 B4
Ágios Vassílios (Makedonía) 80 A3
Ágios Vassílios (Stereá Eláda) 84 A4
Ágios Vissários 83 E2
Agíou Órous, Kólpos 80 C4
Agira 68 C3
Agly 32 B2
Ágnanda 82 C2
Agnanderó 83 D2
Ágnandi 83 F3
Agnóndas 84 B3
Agnone 64 B2
Agnoúnda 87 E2
Agon-Coutainville 18 B3
Agorá 80 C2
Agordo 59 D3
Agost 45 E1
Agout 29 D4
Agrafiótis 83 D2
Agramunt 37 F3
Agrate Br. 60 A1
Agreda 36 C3
Agreliá 83 D1
Agri 65 D4
Agriá 83 F2
Agrigento 68 B4
Agriliá 82 C4
Agriliá, Akr 85 F3
Agrilos 86 B3
Agrínio 82 C3
Agriovótano 83 F3
Agropoli 64 B4
Agskaret 97 E2
Aguadulce (Almeria) 44 B4
Aguadulce (Sevilla) 43 E3
Aguas Vivas, R 37 D4
Aguaviva 41 E2
A Gudiña 34 C3
Agudo 39 F4
Agueda 38 B1
Agueda, R 39 D2
Aguiar 42 B1
Aguiar da Beira 38 C1
Aguilafuente 40 A1
Aguilar 43 F2
Aguilar de Campóo 35 F2
Aguilar del Alfambra 41 E2
Aguilar, Emb de 35 F2
Águilas 44 C3
Ahaia 86 C1
Aharnés 87 F1
Ahaus 17 E3
Åheim 100 A3
Ahelóos 82 C4
Ahendriás 91 E4
Ahérondas 82 B2
Ahigal 39 D2
Ahilio (Kérkira) 82 A1
Ahilio (Thessalía) 83 E2
Ahinós 80 B2
Ahjärvi 103 F3
Ahladerí 84 B4
Ahládes, Akr 88 C4
Ahladohóri 80 B1
Ahlainen 102 B3
Ahlbeck 49 E2
Ahlen 17 E3
Ahlhorn 17 F1
Ahrensbök 48 B2
Ahrensburg 48 B2
Ahrweiler 51 E4
Ähtäri 102 C2
Ähtärinjärvi 102 C2
Ähtävänjoki 102 C2
Ahtopol 115 E2
Ahun 25 E4
Åhus 109 D3
Ahvenanmaa 106 C3
Ahvenselkä 99 E1
Aichach 55 F3
Aidenbach 56 B2
Aidone 68 C3
Aigen 56 C2
Aigle 27 E3
Aigle, Bge de l' 29 E1
Aigle, l' 19 D4
Aignan 28 C4
Aignay-le-Duc 26 C2
Aigoual, Mt 29 F3
Aigre 24 C4
Aigrefeuille-d'Aunis 24 B4
Aigrefeuille-sur-Maine 24 B3
Aiguablava 32 C3
Aiguebelette 30 C1
Aiguebelle 31 D1
Aigueperse 26 A4
Aigues 30 C3
Aigues-Mortes 30 B4
Aigües Tortes, Parque Nac de 37 F2
Aiguilles 31 E2
Aiguillon 28 C3
Aiguillon, l' 24 B4
Aigurande 25 E4
Ailefroide 31 D2
Aillant 26 A1
Ailly-le-Haut-locher 19 E2
Ailly-sur-Noye 19 F2
Ailsa Craig 4 B3
Aimargues 30 B4
Aime 31 D1
Ain 27 D3
Ain (Dépt) 26 C4
Ainhoa 28 A4
Ainsa 37 E2
Ainsdale 6 B2
Ainzón 36 C3
Airaines 19 E2
Airasca 31 E2
Airdrie 4 C2
Aire *R* 7 D2
Aire 19 F1
Aire, I del 45 F2
Aire, Sa de 38 B3
Aire-sur-l'Adour 28 B4
Airisto 107 D3
Airolo 58 A3
Airvault 24 C3
Aisne 20 A3
Aisne (Dépt) 20 A2
Aitana 45 E1
Aiterhofen 56 B2
Aitrach 55 E3
Aitzgorri 36 B1
Aiud 112 C4
Aix-d'Angillon, les 26 A2
Aixe 29 D1
Aix-en-Othe 26 B1
Aix-en-Provence 30 C4
Aix, I d' 24 B4
Aix-les-Bains 27 D4
Aizenay 24 B3
Ajaccio 33 E4
Ajaureforsen 97 F3
Ajdanovac 77 D1
Ajdovščina 70 A2
Ajka 112 A4
Ajo 35 F1
Ajo, C de 36 A1
Ajos 99 D3
Ajtos 115 E2
Akarnaniká, Óri 82 C3
Äkäsjokisuu 95 D4
Äkäskero 95 D4
Äkäslompolo 95 D4
Akçakoca 115 F3
Aken 53 D1
Åkersberga 106 B3
Akershus 105 D3
Åkers styckebruk 106 B4
Akhisar 115 F4
Åkirkeby 109 D4
Akkajaure 94 B4
Akkerhaugen 104 C3
Akku 95 E3
Akranes 96 A2
Akráta 87 D1
Ákrathos, Akr 80 C4
Akréfnio 83 F4
Åkrehamn 104 A3
Akrestrømmen 100 C3
Akritas 79 D2
Akritas, Akr 86 C4
Akrogiáli 80 B3
Akropótamos 80 B3
Akrotíri 91 E1
Akrovoúni 80 C2
Aktí Apólona 87 F2
Akujärvi 95 F3
Akureyri 96 B1
Ål 104 C2
Ala 60 C1
Ala di Stura 31 E1
Alà dei Sardi 66 B2
Alaejos 35 E4
Alagí 86 C3
Alagna Valsesia 27 F4
Alagnon 29 F2
Alagón 37 D3
Alagón, R 39 D2
Alagonía 86 C3
Alahärmä 102 C2
Ala-Honkajoki 102 B3
Alaior 45 F2
Alajärvi 102 C2
Alakylä 99 D1
Alalkomenés 83 F4
Alameda 43 F3
Alamillo 43 F1
Alanäs 101 F1
Aland 48 C3
Åland 106 C3
Alandroal 38 C4
Alange 39 D4
Alange, Emb de 39 D4
Alanis 43 E2
Alapitkä 103 E2
Alaraz 39 E1
Alarcón 40 C3
Alarcón, Emb de 40 C3
Alar del Rey 35 F3
Alaşehir 115 F4
Alassio 31 F3
Alastaro 107 D2
Alatoz 41 D4
Alatri 63 F3
Alavieska 102 C1
Ala-Vuokki 99 F4
Alavus 102 C2
Alba 31 F2
Alba Adriatica 64 A1
Albacete 40 C4
Albacken 101 F2
Alba de Tormes 39 E1
Albæk 108 B1
Albaida 45 E1
Albaida, Pto de 45 E1
Alba Iulia 114 C1
Albaladejo 44 B1
Albalate de Cinca 37 E3
Albalate del Arzobispo 37 D4
Albalate de las Nogueras 40 C2
Alban 29 E3
Albánchez 44 C3
Albano di Lucania 65 D4
Albano Laziale 63 E3
Albarca 37 F4
Albarella, I 61 D1
Albares 35 D2
Albarracín 41 D2
Albarracín, Sa de 41 D2
Albatana 45 D1
Albatera 45 D2
Albena 115 E2
Albenga 31 F3
Albens 27 D4
Alberche, R 39 F2
Alberga 105 F4
Albergaria-a-Velha 38 B1
Alberique 41 E4
Albernoa 42 B1
Alberobello 65 E3
Albersdorf 48 A2
Albert 19 F2
Albert Kanaal 50 C3
Albertville 27 D4
Albestroff 21 E3
Albi 29 E3
Albiano 31 F1
Albinia 63 D2
Albino 58 B4
Albisola Marina 60 A3
Albocácer 41 F2
Albolodúy 44 B3
Albolote 44 A3
Albo, M 66 C2
Alborea 41 D4
Ålborg 108 B2
Ålborg Bugt 108 B2
Albox 44 C3
Albstadt-Ebingen 55 D3
Albufeira 42 A3
Albujón 45 D2
Albulapass 58 B3
Albuñol 44 A4
Alburno, Mte 64 C4
Alburquerque 38 C3
Alby (F) 27 D4
Alby (S) 101 E3
Alcácer do Sál 42 A1
Alcáçovas 42 B1
Alcadozo 44 C1
Alcafozes 38 C2
Alcains 38 C2
Alcalá de Chivert 41 F2
Alcalá de Guadaira 43 D3
Alcalá de Henares 40 B2
Alcalá de la Selva 41 E2
Alcalá del Júcar 41 D4
Alcalá de los Gazules 43 D4
Alcalá del Río 43 D2
Alcalá la Real 44 A3
Álcamo 68 B3
Alcampel 37 E3
Alcanadre, R 37 E3
Alcanar 41 F2
Alcanede 38 A3
Alcanena 38 B3
Alcanhões 38 B3
Alcañices 34 C4
Alcañiz 37 E4
Alcántara 39 D3
Alcántara, Emb de 39 D3
Alcantarilha 42 A2
Alcantarilla 45 D2
Alcaracejos 43 E1
Alcaraz 44 B1
Alcaraz, Sa de 44 C1
Alcaria do Cume 42 B2
Alcaria Ruiva 42 B2
Alcarrache, R 42 C1
Alcarràs 37 E4
Alcaudete 43 F3
Alcaudete de la Jara 39 F3
Alcázar de San Juan 40 B4
Alceda 35 F2
Alcester 9 E1
Alcoba 39 F4
Alcobaça 38 A3
Alcoba de los Montes 39 F4
Alcobendas 40 B2
Alcoceber 41 F3
Alcochete 38 A4
Alcolea 43 F2
Alcolea de Cinca 37 E3
Alcolea del Pinar 36 B4
Alcolea del Río 43 E2
Alconchel 42 C1
Alcora 41 E3
Alcorisa 41 E2
Alcorlo, Emb de 40 B1
Alcoutim 42 B2
Alcover 37 F4
Alcoy 45 E1
Alcubierre 37 D3
Alcubierre, Sa de 37 D3
Alcubilla de Avellaneda 36 A3
Alcublas 41 E3
Alcudia 45 F2
Alcudia de Crespins 41 E4
Alcudia de Guadix 44 B3
Alcuéscar 39 D4
Aldeacentenera 39 E3
Aldeadávila, Emb de 34 C4
Aldea del Cano 39 D3
Aldea del Fresno 40 A2
Aldea del Rey 44 A1
Aldeanueva de Ebro 36 C3
Aldeanueva de la Vera 39 E2
Aldeanueva del Camino 39 E2
Aldeburgh 11 E1
Aldeia da Ponte 39 D2
Aldeia Nova de São Bento 42 C1
Alderney 18 A2
Aldershot 9 F3
Aldinci 77 E3
Aldocer 40 C2
Aledo 44 C2
Aleksandrija 113 F2
Aleksandrovac (Srbija) 73 D3
Aleksandrovac (Srbija) 77 D1
Aleksa Šantić 72 B1
Aleksinac 73 E4
Alençon 23 F3
Alenquer 38 A3
Alentejo 42 B1
Alepohóri (Pelopónissos) 87 D2
Alepohóri (Stereá Eláda) 87 E1
Aléria 33 F3
Alès 30 B3
Ales 66 B3
Aleşd 112 C4
Alessandria 60 A2
Alessandria d. Rocca 68 B3
Ålestrup 108 A2
Ålesund 100 A2
Aletschhorn 27 F3
Alexandria (GB) 4 C2
Alexándria (GR) 79 F3
Alexandria (RO) 115 D2
Alexandroúpoli 81 E2
Alf 51 E4
Alfajarín 37 D3
Alfambra (E) 41 D2
Alfambra (P) 42 A2
Alfambra, R 41 E2
Alfândega da Fé 34 C4
Alfaro 36 C3
Alfarrás 37 E3
Alfaz del Pi 45 E1
Alfedena 64 A2
Alfeizerão 38 A3
Alfeld (Bayern) 55 F1
Alfeld (Niedersachsen) 52 B1
Alfiós 86 B2
Alfonsine 61 D2
Alfonso XIII, Emb de 44 C2
Alford (Grampian) 3 E4
Alford (Lincs) 7 E3
Alfreton 7 D3
Alfta 101 F4
Algaida 45 F3
Algar 43 D4
Ålgård 104 A4
Algar de Palancia 41 E3
Algarinejo 43 F3
Algarrobo 43 F4
Algarve 42 B2
Algatocín 43 E4
Algeciras 43 D4
Algemesí 41 E4
Alghero 66 A2
Alginet 41 E4
Algodonales 43 E3
Algodor, R 40 A3
Algora 40 C1
Algorta 36 B1
Algoz 42 A2
Alhama de Almería 44 B3
Alhama de Aragón 36 C4
Alhama de Granada 43 F3
Alhama de Murcia 45 D2
Alhambra 40 B4
Alhamilla, Sa 44 B3
Alhaurín el Grande 43 E4
Alhóndiga 40 B2
Alia (E) 39 E3
Alia (I) 68 C3
Aliaga 41 E2
Aliaguilla 41 D3
Aliákmona, L 79 E4
Aliákmonas 79 D4
Alíartos 83 F4
Alibunar 73 D2
Alicante 45 E2
Alicudi, I 68 C2
Alicún de Ortega 44 B2
Alife 64 B3
Alijó 34 B4
Alikés 86 A1
Alikianós 90 B3
Alikí (Kiklådes) 88 C3
Alikí (Thássos) 81 D3
Alimiá, N 93 E1
Alingsås 108 C1
Alinyà 32 A3
Aliseda 39 D3
Alise-Ste-Reine 26 B2
Aliste, R 35 D4
Alistráti 80 B2
Ali Terme 69 D2
Alivéri 84 B4
Aljezur 42 A2
Aljibe 43 D4
Aljucén 39 D4
Aljustrel 42 B1
Alkionídon, Kólpos 87 E1
Alkmaar 16 C2
Allaire 22 C4
Allaman, M 76 C4
Allanche 29 E2
Alland 57 E3
Allariz 34 B3
Alleen 104 B4
Alleghe 59 D3
Allègre 29 F2
Allen, L 12 C2
Allensbach 55 D4
Allentsteig 57 E2
Allepuz 41 E2
Aller 48 A4
Allersberg 55 F1
Allershausen 55 F3
Alleuze 29 F2
Allevard 31 D1
Allier (Dépt) 26 A3
Allier *R* 26 A3
Allinge-Sandvig 109 D4
Allo 36 C2
Alloa 5 D2
Allonnes 23 F4
Allos 31 D3
Allos, Col d' 31 D3
Alloza 41 E1
Allstedt 52 C2
Almacelles 37 E3
Almáchar 43 F3
Almada 38 A4
Almadén 39 F4
Almadén de la Plata 43 D2
Almadenejos 43 F1
Almagro 40 A4
Almajano 36 B3
Almansa 45 D1
Almansil 42 B3
Almanza 35 E2
Almanzora, R 44 B3
Almanzor, Pico 39 E3
Almaraz 39 E3
Almargen 43 E3
Almarza 36 B3
Almazán 36 B4
Almazora 41 E3
Almedinilla 43 F3
Almeida (E) 35 D4
Almeida (P) 39 D1
Almeirim 38 B3
Almelo 17 D2
Almenar 37 E3
Almenara 41 E3
Almenaras 44 B1
Almenara, Sa de la 44 C3
Almenar de Soria 36 B3
Almendra, Emb de 35 D4
Almendral 38 C4

Alkmaar
Purmerend
Harlingen
Volendam
Zaandijk
Zaanse Schans
Assendelft
Polder Oostzaan
Het Kalf
De Haal
Ilpendam
Monnickendam
Westzaan
Polder
Koog- a/d Zaan
Zaanstad
De Heul
Het Twiske
Den Ilp
Ilperveld
Overleek
Westzaan
Zaandam
Oostzaan
Landsmeer
Waterland
Watergang
Broek in Waterland
Zuiderwoude
Nauerna
Westzaner-Overtoom
Broekervaart
N 247
A 10
Noordzeekanaal
Amerikahaven
Westhaven
Hemhaven
Coentunnel
Coenhaven
Molenwijk
Kadoelen
Tuindorp Oostzaan
W A T E R L A N D
Holysloot
Zunderdorp
Ruigoord
Bijksloot
Nieuwendam
Ransdorp
Spaarnwoude
N 202
Basisweg
Sloterdijk
Het IJ
W. H. Vliegenbos
Schellingwoude
Durgerdam
IJdoorn
N 5
Haarlemmerweg
Halfweg
Centraal Station
IJ. tunnel
Oranjesluizen
Schellingwouderbrug
Slotermeer
Burgemeester Röell straat
Geuzenveld
Dam
Buiten IJ
AMSTERDAM
Zwanenburg
Artis
Zeeburgerdijk
Rembrandt park
Overtoomseveld
Oosterpark
Flevopark
IJmeer
Osdorp
Slotervaart
Vondelpark
Rijksmuseum
Watergraafsmeer
Lijnden
Plesman laan
Sloten
Beatrixpark
Amstel station
Diemen
P.E.N. Over-Diemen
Badhoevedorp
Over-Amstel
Duivendrecht
E 231
Buitenveldert
Nieuwe Meer
Amsterdam Zuidoost
Amsterdamse bos
Bijlmermeer
Gaasperpark
Driemond
SCHIPHOL
Amstelveen
Gaasperdam
Aviodome
Bulle Wijk
Ouderkerk a/d Amstel
Bovenkerk
Oosteinderpoel
Polder de Rondehoep
Rozenburg
Oosteinde
Oude Meer
Noorder Legmeer polder
Waardhuizen
Voetangel
Abcoude
Nigtevecht
Rijnkanaal
1/100 000
Aalsmeer
Uithoorn
Hilversum Utrecht
Den Haag
Rotterdam
Haarlem
IJmuiden
Zandvoort
Amersfoort Apeldoorn
Bussum

Almendralejo 39 D4
Almere-Stad 16 C2
Almeria 44 B4
Almeria, G de 44 B4
Almerimar 44 B4
Almese 31 E1
Almhult 109 D2
Almijara, Sa de 44 A3
Almiri 87 E1
Almiró 86 C3
Almiropótamos 84 B4
Almirós 83 F2
Almiróu, Órmos 90 C3
Almodôvar 42 B2
Almodóvar del Campo 43 F1
Almodóvar del Pinar 40 C3
Almodóvar del Rio 43 E2
Almogia 43 F3
Almoguera 40 B2
Almoharin 39 D4
Almonacid de la Sierra 36 C4
Almonacid de Toledo 40 A3
Almonacid de Zorita 40 B2
Almonaster la Real 42 C2
Almonte 42 C3
Almoradi 45 D2
Almorox 40 A2
Almourol 38 B3
Almsee 56 C3
Almudébar 37 D3
Almuñecar 44 A4
Almuradiel 44 A1
Alness 2 C3
Alnö 101 F3
Alnwick 5 E3
Alónia 79 F3
Alónissos 84 B2
Alónissos, N 84 B2
Alora 43 E3
Alorines, Pto de 45 D1
Alosno 42 C2
Alost 50 B3
Alozaina 43 E4
Alp 32 A3
Alpalhão 38 C3
Alpbach 59 D1
Alpe-d'Huez, l' 31 D1
Alpedrinha 38 C2
Alpera 41 D4
Alpes-de-Haute-Provence 31 D3
Alpes-Maritimes 31 E3
Alpe Veglia 58 A3
Alphen aan den Rijn 16 C3
Alpi Apuane 60 B3

Alpiarça 38 B3
Alpignano 31 E1
Alpi Orobie 58 B3
Alpirsbach 54 C3
Alpua 99 D4
Alqueva 42 B1
Alqueva, Bgem de 42 B1
Alquézar 37 E3
Als 108 B2
Als (Reg) 108 B4
Alsasua 36 B2
Alsdorf 17 D4
Alsen 101 E2
Alsfeld 52 A3
Alstahaug 97 D3
Alston 5 E4
Alta 95 D2
Altaelva 95 D2
Altafjorden 95 D2
Altamura 65 D3
Alta, Sa 41 D2
Altastenberg 17 F4
Altaussee 56 C3
Altavilla 68 B3
Altdöbern 53 E1
Altdorf (CH) 58 A2
Altdorf (D) 55 F1
Altea 45 E1
Altedo 61 D2
Altena 17 E4
Altenahr 51 E4
Altenau 52 B2
Altenberg 53 E3
Altenberge 17 E3
Altenburg 53 D3
Altenholz 48 A1
Altenhundem 17 F4
Altenkirchen (Mecklenburg-Vorpommern) 49 D1
Altenkirchen (Rheinland-Pfalz) 51 E3
Altenmarkt (D) 56 B3
Altenmarkt (Salzburg) 59 F1
Altenmarkt (Steiermark) 57 D3
Altenstadt 55 E3
Altensteig 54 C3
Altentreptow 49 D2
Altenwalde 47 F2
Alte Oder 49 E3
Alter do Chão 38 C3
Altglashütten 54 C4
Altheim 56 C3
Althofen 70 B1
Altkirch 27 E1
Altlandsberg 49 E4
Altlengbach 57 E2
Altmühl 55 F2
Altmühlsee 55 E2
Altmünster 56 C3
Altnaharra 2 C2
Alto Campó 35 F2
Alto Cruz 36 C4
Alto de Allariz 34 B3
Alto de Barazar 36 B1
Alto de Covelo 34 C3
Alto de Estividas 34 B3
Alto de Fumaces 34 B3
Alto del Couso 34 B3
Alto del Portalé 37 E4
Alto del Rodicio 34 B3
Alto de Santo Domingo 34 B2
Alto do Cañizo 34 C3
Alto Laza 37 D2
Altomira 40 B2
Alton 9 F3
Altopascio 60 C3
Alto Rabagão, Bgem do 34 B3
Altorricon 37 E3
Altotero 36 A2
Altötting 56 B3
Altrincham 6 C2
Alt Ruppin 49 D3
Altshausen 55 D4
Altstätten 58 B2
Altura 41 E3
Altweilnau 51 F4
Alustante 41 D2
Alva 4 C2
Alvaiázere 38 B2
Alvalade 42 A1
Alvão, Sa de 34 B4
Alva, R 38 B2
Alvdal 100 C3
Älvdalen 101 E4
Alvelos, Sa de 38 B2
Alverca do Ribatejo 38 A4
Alvesta 109 D2
Alvignac 29 D2
Ålvik 104 B2
Alvito 42 B1
Alvito, Bgem do 42 B1
Älvkarleby 106 B2
Alvor 42 A2
Älvros 101 E3
Älvsborgs Län 108 C1
Älvsbyn 98 B3
Alyth 5 D1
Alytus 110 C4
Alz 56 B3
Alzenau 52 A4
Alzey 54 C1
Alzira 41 E4
Alzola 36 B1
Alzon 29 F3
Alzonne 32 B1
Amadora 38 A4
Åmål 105 E4
Amalfi 64 B4
Amaliáda 86 B1
Amaliápoli 83 F2
Amálo 89 D2
Amance 27 D1
Amancey 27 D2
Amandola 61 F4
Amantea 67 E3
Amárandos (Ípiros) 78 C4
Amárandos (Thessalía) 83 D2
Amarante 34 B4
Amareleja 42 C1
Amares 34 A4
Amárinthos 84 B4
Amatrice 63 F1
Amay 50 C4
Amaya 35 F3
Ambarès-et-Lagrave 28 B2
Ambasaguas 35 E2
Ambazac 25 E4
Ambelákia (Thessalía) 83 E1
Ambelákia (Thráki) 81 F1
Ambelia 83 E2
Ambelikó 85 F3
Ambelióna 86 C2
Ambelónas 83 E1
Amberg 55 F1
Ambérieu-en-Bugey 26 C4
Ambert 29 F1
Ambès 28 B2
Ambierle 26 B4
Amble 5 E3
Ambleside 5 D4
Amblève 51 D4
Amboise 25 D2
Ambra 61 D4
Ambrières-les-Vallées 18 C4
Ameixial 42 B2
Ameland 16 C1
Amelia 63 E2
Amélie-les-Bains-Palalda 32 B3
Amelinghausen 48 B3
Amer 32 B3
A Merca 34 B3
Amerongen 16 C3
Amersfoort 16 C3
Amersham 9 F2
Amesbury 9 E3
A Mezquita 34 C3
Amfiaraio 84 B4
Amfiklia 83 E3
Amfilohia 82 C3
Amfipoli 80 B2
Ámfissa 83 E4
Amiata, Mont' 63 D1
Amiens 19 F2
Amigdaleónas 80 C2
Amigdaliá 83 E4
Amindeo 79 D3
Åmli 104 B4
Amlwch 6 A2
Ammanford 8 C2
Ämmänsaari 99 E3
Ammarfjället 97 F3
Ammarnäs 97 F3
Ammel 56 A4
Ammersattel 55 F4
Ammersee 56 A3
Amohóri 79 D3
Amoliani 80 B4
Amorbach 55 D1
Amorebieta 36 B1
Amorgós 89 D3
Amorgós, N 89 D3
Amório 81 F1
Åmot (Buskerud) 104 C3
Åmot (S) 105 F2
Åmot (Telemark) 104 B3
Åmotfors 105 D3
Amótopos 82 C2
Amou 28 B4
Amoudára 91 D3
Amoudára 91 E4
Amoúdia 89 D2
Ampezzo 59 E3
Ampfing 56 B3
Amphion 27 D3
Amplepuis 26 B4
Amposta 41 F2
Ampthill 9 F2
Ampudia 35 E4
Ampuero 36 A1
Amriswil 58 B1
Amrum 47 F1
Amsele 98 B4
Amstelveen 16 C2
Amsterdam 16 C2
Amstetten 57 D3
Amungen 101 E4
Amurrio 36 B1
Amusco 35 F3
Amvrakia, L 82 C3
Amvrakikós Kólpos 82 C3
Anadia 38 B1
Anáfi 91 E1
Anafi, N 91 F1
Anafonítria 86 A1
Anagni 63 F3
Anáktora Néstoros 86 B3
Análipsi 83 F4
Análipsi 92 C1
Análipsis 86 C3
Ananjev 113 E3
Anaráhi 79 D3
Anárgiri 79 D3
Änarjohka 95 E2
Anascaul 14 A3
Ånaset 102 B1
Åna Sira 104 A4
Anatolí (Ípiros) 82 C1
Anatolí (Kríti) 91 E4
Anatolí (Thessalía) 83 F1
Anatolikí Rodópi 81 D2
Anatolikó 79 D3
Änättijärvi 99 F4
Anávatos 85 E4
Anávissos 87 F2
Anávra (Kardítsa) 83 E2
Anávra (Magníssia) 83 E3
An Cabhán 13 D3
Ancares, Sa de 34 C2
Ancenis 23 D4
Ancerville 20 C4
Anchuras 39 F3
An Clochán 12 A3
An Cóbh 14 C4
Ancona 61 F3
Ancy-le-Franc 26 B1
Anda 100 A3
Andalo 58 C3
Åndalsnes 100 B2
Andalucía 43 E2
Andarax, R 44 B3
Andartikó 79 D2
Andebu 104 C3
Andelot 26 C1
Andelys, les 19 E3
Andenes 94 A3
Andenne 50 C4
Anderlues 50 B4
Andermatt 58 A3
Andernach 51 E4
Andernos 28 A2
Anderstorp 109 D2
Andfjorden 94 B3
Andigonos 79 D3
Andikíra 83 E4
Andikíras, Kólpos 83 E4
Andikíthira, N 90 A2
Andimáhia 89 F3
Andímilos, N 88 A4
Andinítsa 83 E3
Andíparos 88 B3
Andíparos, N 88 B3
Andípaxi, N 82 B2
Andípsara, N 85 E4
Andírio 83 D4
Ándissa 85 E2
Andoain 36 C1
Andorno Micca 31 F1
Andorra 41 E1
Andorra la Vella 32 A2
Andosilla 36 C2
Andover 9 E3
Andøya 94 A3
Andratx 45 E3
Andravída 86 B1
Andretta 64 C3
Andrézieux-Bouthéon 30 B1
Andria 65 D3
Andrijevica 76 C2
Andrítsena 86 C2
Andros 88 B1
Ándros, N 88 B1
Androússa 86 C3
Andselv 94 B3
Andújar 43 F2
Anduze 30 B3
Aneby 109 D1
Ånes 100 B2
Anet 19 E4
Aneto, Pico de 37 E2
Angáli 84 A3
Ånge (Jämtlands Län) 101 E2
Ånge (Västernorrlands Län) 101 E3
Angeja 38 B1
Ängelholm 108 C3
Angeli 95 E3
Angelohóri 79 E3
Angelókastro (Pelopónissos) 87 E2
Angelókastro (Stereá Eláda) 82 C4
Anger 57 E4
Angera 58 A4
Ångermanälven 101 F2
Angermünde 49 E3
Angern 57 F2
Angers 23 E4
Angerville 25 E1
Ängesån 98 C2
Anghiari 61 D4
Angistis, Stathmós 80 B2
Angístri 87 E2
Angístri, N 87 E2
Ángistro 80 B1
Angitis 80 B2
Angles 25 D3
Anglès (E) 32 B3
Anglès (F) 32 B1
Anglesey, I of 6 A2
Anglesola 37 F3
Anglet 28 A4
Anglure 20 B4
Angoulême 28 C1
Angri 64 B4
Ängsö 106 C3
Angüés 37 E3
Anguiano 36 B2
Anguillara Veneta 61 D1
Angvik 100 B2
Anholt 108 C2
Aniane 30 A4
Aniche 20 A1
Aniene 63 F2
Ánixi 79 D4
Anizy-le-Château 20 A3
Anjalankoski 107 F2
Anjum 47 D3
Ankaran 70 A3
Ankarsrum 109 E1
Anklam 49 E2
Ankogel 59 E2
An Longfort 12 C3
An Muileann gCearr 13 D3
Ånn 101 D2
Ånn L 101 D2
Annaberg 57 E3
Annaberg-Buchholz 53 E3
Annaburg 53 E1
Annan 5 D3
Annan R 5 D3
Anndalsvågen 97 D3
Annecy 27 D4
Annemasse 27 D4
Annevoie-Rouillon 50 C4
Annonay 30 B1
Annone Veneto 59 E4
Annot 31 D3
Annweiler 54 C2
Áno Drossiní 81 E2
Anógia 87 D3
Anógia 91 D3
Áno Hóra 83 D4
Anoia, R 32 A4
Áno Kalendíni 82 C2
Áno Kalíniki 79 D2
Áno Kómi 79 E4
Áno Lefkími 82 A2
Áno Melás 79 D3
Áno Merá 88 C2
Anópoli 90 C4
Áno Polidéndri 83 F1
Áno Poróia 80 A2
Áno Rodákino 90 C4
Áno Sangrí 88 C3
Áno Síros 88 B2
Añover de Tajo 40 A3
Áno Viános 91 E4
Áno Vrondoú 80 B2
Áno Zervohóri 79 E3
Ansbach 55 E1
Anse 26 C4
Ansedonia 63 D2
Ansião 38 B2
Ansnes 100 C1
Ansó 37 D2
Anstruther 5 D2
An tAonach 12 C4
Antas 44 C3
Antegnate 60 B1
Antemil 34 A1
Antequera 43 F3
Anterselva 59 D2
Ánthia 81 E2
Anthíli 83 E3
Anthis 80 B2
Antholz 59 D2
Anthótopos 83 E2
Antibes 31 E4
Antifer, Cap d' 19 D3
An tInbhear Mór 15 E3
Antnäs 98 C3
Antraigues 30 B2
Antrain 18 B4
Antrim 13 E2
Antrim (Co) 13 E2
Antrim Coast 13 E1
Antrim Mts 13 E1
Antrodoco 63 F2
Anttola 103 E3
Antwerpen 50 B3
Antwerpen (Prov) 50 C3
An Uaimh 13 D3
Anvers 50 B3
Anzano di Puglia 64 C3
Anzio 63 E3
Anzola d'Ossola 58 A4
Anzy-le-Duc 26 B4
Aoiz 36 C2
Aóos 78 C4
Aosta 27 E4
Aoste 27 E4
Apatin 72 B2
Apatovac 71 D2
Apecchio 61 E4
Apeldoorn 17 D2
Apen 47 E3
Apéri 93 D3
Aphrodisias 115 F4
Apidiá 87 D3
Apikia 88 B1
Apíranthos 88 C3
Apolakiá 93 E2
Apolda 52 C3
Apolitáres, Akr 90 A2
Apólonas 88 C3
Apolonía (Kikládes) 88 B3
Apolonía (Makedonía) 80 B3
A Pontenova Villaodriz 34 C1
Apóstoli 90 C4
Äppelbo 105 E2
Appenweier 54 C3
Appenzell 58 B2
Appiano 59 D3
Appingedam 47 D3
Appleby 5 D4
Aprica 58 C3
Apricena 64 C2
Aprilia 63 E3
Ápsalos 79 E2
Apt 30 C3
Áptera 90 C3
Aquileia 59 F3
Aquitaine, L' 25 E2
Arabba 59 D3
Aracena 42 C2
Aracena, Emb de 43 D2
Aracena, Sa de 42 C2
Aračinovo 77 E3
Arad 112 C4
Åradalsfjorden 104 B1
Arada, Sa de 38 B1
Aragón 37 D3
Aragona 68 B4
Aragón, R 36 C2
Arahnéo, Óros 87 E2
Aráhova (Etolía-Akarnanía) 83 D3
Aráhova (Viotía) 83 E4
Arákinthos, Óros 83 D4
A Ramallosa 34 A3
Aramits 37 D1
Aranda de Duero 36 A3
Aranđelovac 73 D3
Aran I 12 C1
Aran Is 12 A4
Aranjuez 40 B3
Arantzazu 36 B1
Aran, Vall d' 37 F2
Araquil, R 36 C2
Ara, R 37 E2
Aras de Alpuente 41 D3
Arasluokta 97 F1
Árahthos 82 C2
Áratos 81 E2
Aravaca 40 A2
Aravis, Col des 27 D4
Aravissós 79 E2
Áraxos 86 B1
Áraxos, Akr 86 B1
Arazede 38 B2
Arba, R 36 C3
Arbatax 66 C3
Arbeca 37 F4
Arbesbach 57 D2
Arboga 105 F3
Arbois 27 D3
Arbon 58 B1
Arbón, Emb de 34 C1
Arborea 66 B3
Arborio 31 F1
Arbrå 101 F4
Arbroath 5 E1
Arbresle, l' 26 B4
Arbúcies 32 B4
Arbus 66 B3
Arc 31 D1
Arcachon 28 A2
Arce 64 A3
Arcen 17 D3
Arc-en-Barrois 26 C1
Arceniega 36 A1
Arcevia 61 E4
Archena 45 D2
Arches 27 D1
Archiac 28 B1
Archidona 43 F3
Arcidosso 63 D1
Arcipelago Toscano 62 B1
Arcis 20 B4
Arciz 113 E4
Arco 58 C4
Arco de Baúlhe 34 B4
Arcos 35 F3
Arcos de Jalón 36 B4
Arcos de la Frontera 43 D3
Arcos de Valdevez 34 A3
Arcouest, Pte de l' 22 C2
Arcs, les (Savoie) 31 D1
Arcs, les (Var) 31 D4
Arcusa 37 E2
Arda 115 E3
Ardales 43 E3
Årdalstangen 104 B1
Ardánio 81 F2
Ardara 12 C1
Árdas 81 F1
Ardbeg 4 B2
Ardèche (Dépt) 30 B2
Ardèche R 30 B2
Ardèche, Gges de l' 30 B3
Ardee 13 D3
Ardennes (Dépt) 20 B3
Ardennes, Canal des 20 C3
Ardentes 25 E3
Ardentinny 4 C2
Ardes 29 F1
Ardez 58 B2
Ardglass 13 E2
Ardila, R 42 C1
Ardila, Rib de 42 C1
Ardisa 37 D3
Ardlussa 4 B2
Ardmore 14 C4
Ardrahan 12 B4
Ardres 19 E1
Ardrishaig 4 B2
Ardrossan 4 C2
Ards Pen 13 E2
Arduaine 4 B1
Ardvasar 2 B4
Åre 101 D2
Arenas de Cabrales 35 E2
Arenas de Iguña 35 F2
Arenas de San Juan 40 B4
Arenas de San Pedro 39 F2
Arendal 104 C4
Arendonk 50 C3
Arendsee 48 C3
Arenos, Emb de 41 E3
Arenys de Mar 32 B4
Arenzano 60 A3
Areópoli 87 D4
Arès 28 A2
Ares (Galicia) 34 B1
Ares (Valencia) 41 E2
Ares, Col des 37 F2
Ares, Pto de 32 B3
Åreskutan 101 D2
Aréthoussa 80 B3
Aretí 80 A3
Arévalo 39 F1
Arez 38 C3
Arezzo 61 D4
Arfará 86 C3
Argalastí 83 F2
Argamasilla de Alba 40 B4
Argamasilla de Calatrava 44 A1
Arganda 40 B2
Arganil 38 B2
Arga, R 36 C2
Argássi 86 A2
Argelès 32 B2
Argelès-Gazost 37 E1
Argens 31 D4
Argent 25 F2
Argenta 61 D2
Argentan 19 D4
Argentario, Mte 63 D2
Argentat 29 D2
Argente 41 D2
Argentera 31 E3
Argentière 27 E4
Argentière-la-Bessée, l' 31 D2
Argentona 32 B4
Argenton-Château 24 C3
Argenton-sur-Creuse 25 E3

Bergen op Zoom
4°20
Roosendaal
Breda
51°20
Brecht
Schilde
Turnhout
Turnhout Hasselt
Ranst Nijlen
Lier
Mechelen
Bruxelles-Brussel
Brussel
Boom
Temse
Gent
Gent St.-Niklaas
Hulst St.-Niklaas
Kieldrecht
ANTWERPEN
(ANVERS)
De Kalmthoutse Heide
Kalmthout
Heide
Heikant
Putte
Rijmakersbos
Kijkuit
Platluis
Noordhoek
Stadshoek
Steenovens
Zandvliet
B.A.S.F.
AIR LIQUIDE
Kanaaldok B 3
Zandvlietsluis
Berendrechtsluis
Berendrecht
Driehoek
Ertbrand
Kapellenbos
Withof
Maria ter Heide
Stabroek
Heuvels
Mastenhof
Starrenhof
BELGIAN REFINING CORPORATION
SOLVAY
NAFTA
Kanaaldok B 2
Delwaidedok
KERNCENTRALE DOEL
Doel
SCHELDE
MONSANTO
GAMATEX
DEGUSSA
Molen
Frans Tijsmanstunnel
Lillo-Fort
Lillobrug
BAYER
Pekgat
Krekelberg
Hoevenen
Kapellen
St.-Jozefkapel
Hoogboom
Mishaegen
Bethanie
Hoge Kaart
Drijhoek
Luizenfort
Lage Kaart
Het Zand
Brasschaat
Leugenberg
St.-Mariaburg
Vormingsstation Antwerpen-Noord
GENERAL MOTORS
CARGILL
Kanaaldok B 1
AQUALON BELGIUM
Liefkenshoek
Geslecht
HALTERMANN
Industriegebied : werk in uitvoering
Zone industrielle : en cours de réalisation
BAYER
RHONE-POULENC
Churchilldok
De Grote Put
Ekeren
Hof de Bist
Donk
Vriesdonck
Peerdsbos
Elshout
Zeurt
Koningshof
Boudewijnsluis
Van Cauwelaertsluis
Zesde Havendok
Hansadok
FORD
Gas Terminal
FINA
Petroleumbrug
FINANESTE
ESSO
MERCANTILE-BELIARD
Wilmarsdonkbrug
Leopolddok
Oosterweelbrug
Albertdok
Vierde Havendok
NYNAS-P
UNIVERSAL-REFFINING
Vijfde Havendok
GENERAL MOTORS
Luchtbal
Oude Barreel
Donk
Schotenhof
Schoten
De Villers
EBES
Fort Ste Marie
Steenland
Kallo
PETROCHIM
TEXACO
Dijk gracht
BP
EXXON
POLYSAR
Noordkasteel
Boerinnesluis
Royerssluis
Kattendijksluis
Kattendijkdok
Merksem
IJzerbrug
Deurnebrug
Merksembrug
Wetschof
Hoogmolenbrug
Broekstraat
Albert Kanaal
Put van Fien
UNION CARBIDE
Melseledijk
Briel
Kalishoek
Neerstraathoek
Smoutpot
Zwijndrecht
Antwerpen Linkeroever
Gaverland
Krabbenhoek
Melsele
Bosuil
Bisschoppenhof
Lakbors
Krabbershoek
Wijnegem
Waasland tunnel
Steen
Grote Markt
Kathedraal
Museum Plantin-Moretus
Centraal
Deurne
Erbrugge
Witte Brug
Beemdkant
Rivierenhof
Sterckshof
Schijn
Groot Schijn
Borgerhout
Cortewalle
Beveren
Vendoorn
Zwijndrecht-Fort
Ponjaart
Schaarbeek
Galgenweel
Burchtse Weel
Kennedy tunnel
Museum voor Schone Kunsten
Bolivar-Plaats
Oost
Immerseel
Kallement
Kandonklaar
Wommelgem
Doornboom
De Puithoek
Molen
Burcht
Oeverkant
A.B.P.
Vormingsstation Antwerpen-Kiel
Zuid
Boelaer park
Boekenberg park
Hulgenrode
Borsbeek
Kast Hof ter Saksen
Puiput
Kiel
Berchem
ANTWERPEN DEURNE
Nachtegalen park
Middelheim park
Es
Wilde Haan
Sterhoek
Zwaantjes
Toefelhoek
Vremde
Haasdonk
De Vitshaag
Schiphoek
Hoboken
Luithagen
Cantecroy
Spokenhof
Mosselbank
Doorn
COCKERILL YARDS
Koornbloem
Bist
Wilrijk
Oude God
Mortsel
Kruibeke
Molenberg
Schoonselhof
Edegem
Schaliehoeve
Eggerseel
Barbier
Hove
Boechout
Beestenhoek
Kemphoek
Klaverblad
Neerland
Boechout
1/100 000
A12: 12-1992
A1-E19
A 13-E 34
A 14-E 17
E19
N 49
N 49A
N 70

Argentré-du-Plessis 23 E3
Arginónda 89 F3
Argirádes 82 A2
Argiró 84 B4
Argiropoúlio 83 E1
Argiroúpoli 90 C3
Argithéa 83 D2
Argolída 87 E2
Argolikós Kólpos 87 E2
Árgos 87 D2
Árgos Orestikó 79 D3
Argos, R 44 C2
Argostóli 82 B4
Arguedas 36 C3
Argueil 19 E3
Arguellite 44 B1
Arguis 37 D2
Argyll 4 B1
Argyll Forest Park 4 C2
Arhánes 91 D4
Arhángelos (Makedonía) 79 E2
Arhángelos (Ródos) 93 F1
Arhéa Epidavros 87 E2
Arhéa Kleonés 87 D1
Arhéa Kórinthos 87 E1
Arhéa Neméa 87 D1
Arhéa Olympía 86 C2
Arhéa Thíra 91 E1
Århus 108 B3
Arianá 81 E2
Ariano Irpino 64 B3
Ariano nel Polesine 61 D2
Aridéa 79 E2
Ariège (Dépt) 32 A2
Ariège *R* 32 A2
Arija 35 F2
Arild 108 C3
Arilje 72 C4
Arinagour 2 B4
Aríni 86 C2
Ariño 37 D4
Arinthod 27 D3
Arisaig 2 B4
Arisaig, Sd of 2 B4
Arísti 78 C4
Aristoménis 86 C3
Arísvi 81 E2
Aritzo 66 B3
Arive 36 C2
Ariza 36 B4
Årjäng 105 D3
Arjeplog 98 A3
Arjona 44 A2
Arkádi 91 D3
Arkadía 86 C2
Arkaig, L 2 C4
Arkalohóri 91 E4
Arkássa 93 D3
Arkessíni 89 D3
Arkí, N 89 E2
Arkítsa 83 F3
Arklow 15 E3
Arkona, Kap 49 D1
Arkoúdi, N 82 B4
Arlaban, Pto de 36 B1
Arlanc 29 F1
Arlanda 106 B3
Arlanza, R 36 A3
Arlanzón 36 A2
Arlanzón, R 35 F3
Arlbergpaß 58 B2
Arlberg-Straßentunnel 58 B2
Arlempdes 30 A2
Arles (Bouches-du-Rhône) 30 B4
Arles (Pyrénées-Orientales) 32 B3
Arlesheim 27 E2
Arlon 21 D2
Arlsleben 52 C2
Armação de Pêra 42 A3
Armadale 5 D2
Arma di Taggia 31 F3
Armagh 13 D2
Armagh (Co) 13 D2
Armamar 34 B4
Arméni 90 C3
Armenií 86 C3
Armenistís 89 D2
Armentières 19 F1
Armilla 44 A3
Armólia 85 E4
Armunia 35 D3
Árna 87 D3
Arnac-Pompadour 29 D1
Arnay-le-Duc 26 B2
Arnéa 80 B3
Arneburg 48 C4
Arnedillo 36 B3
Arnedo 36 C3
Arnes 41 F2
Årnes 105 D3
Arnhem 17 D3
Arni 60 B3
Árnissa 79 E2
Arno 60 C4
Arnoldstein 59 F2
Arnon 25 F3
Arnøy 94 C2
Arnsberg 17 F3
Arnstadt 52 C3
Arnstein 52 B4
Aroanía, Óri 86 C1
Aroche 42 C2
Aroche *Mt* 42 C1
Arogí 81 D2
Arolsen 52 A2
Arona 58 A4
Aroniádika 90 A1
Aronkylä 102 B3
Åros 104 C3
Arosa 58 B2
Arouca 38 B1
Arousa, I de 34 A2
Årøysund 104 C3
Arpajon 19 F4
Arpela 99 D3
Arquata del Tronto 63 F1
Arques (Pas-de-Calais) 19 F1
Arques (Seine-Maritime) 19 E2
Arquillos 44 A2
Arrabal 34 A3
Arrábida, Sa da 38 A4
Arracourt 21 D4
Arraiolos 38 B4
Arran 4 B2
Arras 19 F2
Arrasate-Mondragon 36 B1
Arreau 37 E2
Arrecife 42 C4
Arredondo 36 A1
Arrée, Mts d' 22 B2
Arrens 37 E2
Arrifana 38 C1
Arrigorriaga 36 B1
Arriondas 35 E1
Arrochar 4 C2
Arromanches 18 C3
Arronches 38 C4
Arroux 26 B3
Arrow, L 12 C2
Arroyo de la Luz 39 D3
Arroyo del Ojanco 44 B1
Arroyo de San Serván 39 D4
Arroyomolinos de León 43 D1
Arroyomolinos de Montánchez 39 D4
Arruda dos Vinhos 38 A3
Års 108 A2
Ars (Charente-Maritime) 24 B4
Ars (Moselle) 21 D3
Arsié 59 D3
Arsiero 59 D4
Árs Kógssanður 96 B1
Arsunda 106 B2
Arsy 19 F3
Artà 45 F2
Árta 82 C2
Artajona 36 C2
Árta (Nomos) 82 C2
Arta Terme 59 E3
Arteaga, G de 36 B1
Artemissía 86 C3
Artemissío (Évia) 83 F3
Artemissío (Pelopónissos) 87 D2
Artemónas 88 B3
Artena 63 F3
Artenay 25 E1
Artern 52 C2
Artesa de Segre 37 F3
Artessianó 83 D2
Artfjället 97 E3
Arth (CH) 58 A2
Arth (D) 56 B2
Arthurstown 15 D4
Arties 37 F2
Artjärvi 107 F2
Artotína 83 D3
Artruix, C de 45 F2
A Rúa 34 C3
Arucas 42 B4
Arudy 37 D1
Arundel 9 F3
Arve 27 E4
Árvi 91 E4
Arvidsjaur 98 A3
Årvik 100 A2
Arvika 105 E3
Årviksand 94 C2
Arzachena 66 B1
Arzacq-Arraziguet 28 B4
Arzano 22 B3
Aržano 75 E1
Arzberg 53 D4
Arzignano 60 C1
Árzos 81 F1
Arzúa 34 B2
As 50 C3
Aš 53 D4
Åsa 108 C2
Asamati 77 D4
Åsarna 101 E2
Åsarp 109 D1
Ascain 28 A4
Ascha 56 B2
Aschach 56 C2
Aschaffenburg 52 A4
Aschau 56 B3
Aschbach Markt 57 D3
Ascheberg (Nordrhein-Westfalen) 17 E3
Ascheberg (Schleswig-Holstein) 48 B2
Aschendorf 17 E1
Aschersleben 52 C2
Asciano 61 D4
Ascione, Colle d' 67 F3
Asco 33 F3
Ascó 37 E4
Ascoli Piceno 63 F1
Ascoli Satriano 64 C3
Ascona 58 A3
Åse 94 A3
Åseda 109 E2
Åsele 101 F1
Åsen 101 D1
Asenovgrad 115 D3
Åseral 104 B4
Asfáka 82 B1
Asfeld 20 B3
Åsgårdstrand 104 C3
Ashbourne (GB) 6 C3
Ashbourne (IRL) 13 D3
Ashburton 8 C4
Ashby de la Zouch 6 C3
Ashford 11 D3
Ashington 5 E3
Ashton-under-Lyne 6 C2
Asiago 59 D4
Asikkala 107 F2
Asin 37 D3
Asinara, G dell' 66 B1
Asinara, I 66 A1
Ask 105 D3
Askainen 107 D2
Askeaton 14 B3
Askersund 105 F4
Askífou 90 C3
Askim 105 D3
Áskio, Óros 79 D3
Askja 96 C2
Asklipiío (Dodekánissa) 89 F3
Asklipiío (Ródos) 93 E2
Askola 107 F2
Askós 80 A3
Askøy 104 A2
Askvoll 104 A1
Asmunti 99 D3
Asnæs 108 B3
Asnen 109 D2
As Neves 34 A3
Asola 60 B1
Asolo 59 D4
Aspang 57 F3
Aspatria 5 D4
Aspe 45 D2
Aspe, Gave d' 37 D1
Asperg 55 D2
Aspet 37 F2
Aspin, Col d' 37 E2
As Ponte de Garcia Rodriguez 34 B1
Áspra Spítia 83 E4
Aspres 30 C2
Áspro 79 E3
Aspróhoma 86 C3
Asprókavos, Akr 82 A2
Aspromonte 67 E4
Asprópirgos 87 F1
Asprovalta 80 B3
Asse 50 B3
Assemini 66 B4
Assen 17 D1
Assens 108 B3
Assergi 63 F2
Assini 87 E2
Assisi 63 E1
Aßmannshausen 51 F4
Assomáton 91 D3
Assopía 84 A4
Assopós (Korinthía) 87 D1
Assopós (Lakonía) 87 E4
Assopós *R* 87 E1
Ássos (Ípiros) 82 B2
Ássos (Kefaloniá) 82 B4
Astaffort 28 C3
Astafjorden 94 B3
Astakída, N 93 D2
Astakós 82 C4
Asten 57 D3
Asti 31 F2
Astipálea 92 C1
Astipálea, N 92 C1
Astorga 35 D3
Åstorp 108 C3
Ástros 87 D2
Astudillo 35 F3
Asturias 34 C2
Asvestádes 81 F1
Asvestohóri 82 B1
Asvestópetra 79 D3
Atalaia 38 A3
Atalándi 83 F3
Atalaya de la Calzada 44 A1
Atalayassa 45 D4
Átali 84 B3
Ataquines 39 F1
Atarfe 44 A3
Atáviros 93 E2
Ateca 36 C4
Atella 64 C3
Atessa 64 B2
Ath 50 B4
Athamánon, Óri 82 C2
Athánio 82 B3
Athboy 13 D3
Athenry 12 B3
Athéras 89 D2
Athéras, Akr 82 B4
Atherstone 9 E1
Athína 87 F1
Áthira 79 F2
Athlone 12 C3
Áthos 80 C4
Athy 13 D4
Atienza 36 B4
Atikí-Piréas 87 F1
Atina 64 A3
Átokos, N 82 C4
Atouguia da Baleia 38 A3
Ätran 108 C2
Ätran *R* 108 C2
Atri 64 A1
Atsikí 85 D1
Attendorn 17 F4
Attersee 56 C3
Attersee *L* 56 C3
Attigliano 63 E2
Attigny 20 B3
Attleborough 11 D1
Attnang 56 C3
Åtvidaberg 109 E1
Au 55 F2
Aub 55 E1
Aubagne 30 C4
Aubange 21 D2
Aube 20 B4
Aube (Dépt) 20 B4
Aubenas 30 B2
Aubenton 20 B2
Auberive 26 C1
Aubeterre 28 C1
Aubigny (Cher) 25 F2
Aubigny (Pas-de-Calais) 19 F2
Aubin 29 E3
Aubisque, Col d' 37 E1
Aubonne 27 D3
Aubrac 29 F2
Aubrac, Mts d' 29 F2
Aubusson 25 F4
Auch 28 C4
Auchencairn 4 C3
Auchterarder 5 D1
Auchtermuchty 5 D1
Aude (Dépt) 32 B2
Aude *R* 32 B1
Audenge 28 A2
Audeux 27 D2
Audierne 22 A3
Audincourt 27 E2
Audlem 6 C3
Audruicq 19 F1
Audun-le-Roman 21 D3
Audun-le-Tiche 21 D3
Aue *R* 48 A4
Aue 53 D3
Auer 59 D3
Auerbach (Bayern) 55 F1
Auerbach (Sachsen) 55 D3
Auffach 59 D1
Aughnacloy 13 D2
Aughrim 13 D4
Augsburg 55 F3
Augusta 69 D4
Augustenborg 108 B4
Augustów 110 C4
Augustusburg 53 E3
Aukan 100 B2
Aukra 100 B2
Aulanko 107 E2
Auletta 64 C4
Aulla 60 B3
Aullène 33 F4
Aulnay 24 C4
Aulne 22 B3
Aulnoye-Aymeries 20 B2
Ault 19 E2
Aulus-les-Bains 37 F2
Auma 53 D3
Aumale 19 E2
Aumetz 21 D3
Aumont-Aubrac 29 F2
Aunay-sur-Odon 18 C3
Auneau 19 E4
Auneuil 19 E3
Auning 108 B2
Aups 31 D4
Aura 107 D2
Aurajoki 107 D2
Auray 22 C4
Aurdal 104 C2
Aure 100 B2
Aurich 47 E3
Aurignac 37 F1
Aurillac 29 E2
Aurland 104 B2
Auron 31 E3
Auron *R* 25 F3
Auronzo di Cadore 59 E2
Auros 28 B3
Aursjøen 100 B3
Aursuden 101 D2
Ausonia 64 A3
Außernbrünst 56 C2
Ausso Corno 59 F3
Aust-Agder 104 B4
Austbygd 104 C3
Austvågøy 94 A3
Auterive 37 F1
Authie 19 F2
Autol 36 C3
Autrans 30 C1
Autrey 26 C2
Auttoinen 107 E1
Autun 26 B3
Auvézère 28 C2
Auvillar 28 C3
Auxerre 26 A1
Auxi-le-Château 19 E2
Auxonne 26 C2
Auzances 25 F4
Auzon 29 F1
Availles-Limouzine 25 D4
Avala 73 D3
Avaldsnes 104 A3
Avallon 26 B2
Avaloirs, Mt des 23 E3
Ávas 81 E2
Avaviken 98 A3
Ávdira 81 D2
Avebury 9 E2
A Veiga 34 C3
Aveiras de Cima 38 A3
Aveiro 38 B1
Aveiro, R de 38 B1
Avellino 64 B4
Aven Armand 29 F3
Aven d'Orgnac 30 B3
Averøya 100 B2
Aversa 64 B4
Avesnes 20 B2
Avesnes-le-Comte 19 F2
Avesta 105 F3
Avetrana 65 E4
Aveyron 29 D3
Aveyron (Dépt) 29 E3
Avezzano 63 F2
Avgerinós 79 D4
Avgó 82 C2
Avía 86 C3
Aviano 59 E3
Aviémonas 90 A2
Aviemore 3 D4
Aviés 79 E4
Avigliana 31 E1
Avigliano 64 C4
Avignon 30 B3
Ávila 39 F2
Ávila, Sa de 39 F2
Avilés 35 D1
Aviño 34 B1
Avintes 34 A4
Avión 34 B2
Avioth 20 C3
Avis 38 B4
Avisio 59 D3
Avize 20 B3
Avlákia 89 E1
Avlí 80 C2
Avliótes 82 A1
Avlóna 84 B4
Avlum 108 A2
Avola 69 D4
Avon (Co) 9 D2
Avon *R* (Hants) 9 E1
Avon *R* (Warw) 9 E3
Avonmouth 9 D2
Avord 25 F3
Avoriaz 27 E4
Avranches 18 B4
Avre 19 D4
Avtovac 76 A2
Awe, L 4 B1
Axams 59 D2
Axat 32 B2
Axiohóri 79 F2
Axiós 79 F3
Axioúpoli 79 F2
Ax-les-Thermes 32 A2
Axminster 9 D3
Axós 91 D3
Ay 20 B3
Ayamonte 42 B2
Aydin 115 F4
Ayedo 36 B3
Ayerbe 37 D3
Aylesbury 9 F2
Ayllón 36 A4
Ayllón, Sa de 36 A4
Aylsham 7 F3
Ayna 44 C1
Ayora 41 D4
Ayr 4 C3
Ayre, Pt of 6 A1
Ayvacık 115 E4
Ayvalık 115 E4
Aywaille 51 D4
Azáceta, Pto de 36 B2
Azaila 37 D4
Azambuja 38 A3
Azanja 73 D3
Azaruja 38 B4
Azay-le-Ferron 25 E3
Azay-le-Rideau 25 D2
Azinheira dos Barros 42 A1
Azkoitia 36 B1
Aznalcázar 43 D3
Aznalcóllar 43 D2
Azpeitia 36 B1
Azuaga 43 E1
Azuara 37 D4
Azuer, R 40 A4
Azuqueca de Henares 40 B2
Azután, Emb de 39 F3
Azzano Decimo 59 E3

B

Baad 58 B2
Baal 17 D4
Baamonde 34 B1
Baarle-Nassau 16 C4
Baarn 16 C2
Baba 77 E4
Babadag 113 E4
Babajevo 111 E1
Babelsberg 49 D4
Babenhausen (Bayern) 55 E3
Babenhausen (Hessen) 52 A4
Babina Greda 71 F3
Babin Kal 73 F4
Babin Most 77 D2
Babino Polje 75 F2
Babin Potok 70 C4
Babljak 76 B2
Babuna 77 E3
Babušnica 77 E1
Bač 72 B2
Bački Breg 72 B1
Bacau 113 D4
Baccarat 21 E4
Bæccegæhal'di 94 C2
Baceno 58 A3
Bacharach 51 E4
Bächistock 58 A2
Bachmač 113 F1
Bačina 73 E4
Bačka Palanka 72 B2
Bäckaskog 109 D3
Bačka Topola 72 B1
Backe 101 F1
Bäckebo 109 E2
Bäckefors 105 D4
Bački Breg 71 F1
Bački Brestovac 72 B2
Bački Monoštor 72 B2
Bački Petrovac 72 B2
Backnang 55 D2
Bačko Gradište 72 C2
Bačko Novo Selo 72 B2
Bačko Petrovo Selo 72 C1
Bačkovo 115 D3
Bacoli 64 A4
Bacqueville 19 D2
Baczyna 49 F3
Bad Aibling 56 B3
Badajoz 38 C4
Badalona 32 B4
Bad Aussee 56 C3
Bad Bentheim 17 E2
Bad Bergzabern 54 C2
Bad Berka 52 C3
Bad Berleburg 17 F4
Bad Berneck 53 D4
Bad Bertrich 51 E4
Bad Bevensen 48 B3
Bad Bibra 52 C2
Bad Blankenburg 52 C3
Bad Brambach 53 D4
Bad Bramstedt 48 A2
Bad Brückenau 52 B4
Bad Buchau 55 D3
Bad Camberg 51 F4
Bad Deutsch Altenburg 57 F2
Bad Doberan 48 C2
Bad Driburg 52 A2
Bad Düben 53 D2
Bad Dürkheim 54 C1
Bad Dürrenberg 53 D2
Bad Durrheim 54 C3
Bad Elster 53 D4
Bad Ems 51 E4
Baden (A) 57 F3
Baden (CH) 27 F2
Baden-Baden 54 C2
Bad Endorf 56 B3
Badenweiler 54 C4
Baden-Württemberg 55 D3
Baderna 70 A3
Bad Essen 17 F2
Bad Frankenhausen 52 C2
Bad Freienwalde 49 E3
Bad Friedrichshall 55 D2
Bad Gandersheim 52 B1
Badgastein 59 E2
Bad Gleichenberg 57 F4
Bad Godesberg 51 E3
Bad Goisern 56 C3
Bad Gottleuba 53 E3
Bad Griesbach 56 C2
Bad Grund 52 B2
Bad Hall 57 D3
Bad Harzburg 52 B1
Bad Herrenalb 54 C2
Bad Hersfeld 52 B3
Bad Hofgastein 56 C4
Bad Homburg 51 F4
Bad Honnef 51 E3
Bad Honnigen 51 E4
Badia Polesine 61 D2
Badia Tedalda 61 D3
Bad Iburg 17 F2
Badija 75 E2
Bad Ischl 56 C3
Bad Karlshafen 52 A2
Bad Kissingen 52 B4
Bad Kleinen 48 C2
Bad Kleinkirchheim 59 F2
Bad König 55 D1
Bad Königshofen 52 B4
Bad Kösen 52 C2
Bad Kreuznach 54 B1
Bad Krozingen 54 C4
Bad Laasphe 17 F4
Bad Langensalza 52 B3
Bad Lauchstädt 53 D2
Bad Lausick 53 D2
Bad Lauterberg 52 B2
Bad Leonfelden 57 D2
Bad Liebenstein 52 B3
Bad Liebenwerda 53 E2
Bad Liebenzell 54 C2
Bad Lippspringe 17 F3
Badljevina 71 D2
Bad Meinberg 52 A2
Bad Mergentheim 55 D1
Bad Mitterndorf 56 C4
Bad Münder 52 A1
Bad Münster am Stein-Ebernburg 54 B1
Bad Münstereifel 51 E4
Bad Muskau 53 F1
Bad Nauheim 52 A4
Bad Nenndorf 52 A1
Bad Neuenahr-Ahrweiler 51 E4
Bad Neustadt 52 B4
Bad Oeynhausen 17 F2
Badolato 67 F3
Badolatosa 43 F3
Bad Oldesloe 48 B2
Badonviller 21 E4
Bad Orb 52 A4
Badovinci 72 B3
Bad Peterstal-Griesbach 54 C3
Bad Pyrmont 52 A1
Bad Radkersburg 70 C1
Bad Ragaz 58 B2
Bad Rappenau 55 D2
Bad Reichenhall 56 B3
Bad Rippoldsau-Schapbach 54 C3
Bad Rothenfelde 17 F2
Bad Saarow-Pieskow 49 E4
Bad Sachsa 52 B2
Bad Säckingen 54 C4
Bad St Leonhard 57 E4
Bad Salzdetfurth 52 B1
Bad Salzschlirf 52 B3
Bad Salzuflen 17 F2
Bad Salzungen 52 B3
Bad Schallerbach 56 C3
Bad Schandau 53 F2
Bad Schmiedeberg 53 D1
Bad Schönborn 54 C2
Bad Schussenried 55 D3
Bad Schwalbach 51 F4
Bad Schwartau 48 B2
Bad Segeberg 48 B2
Bad Soden 51 F4
Bad Soden-Salmünster 52 A4
Bad Sooden-Allendorf 52 B2
Bad Sulza 52 C2
Bad Sülze 49 D2
Bad Tatzmannsdorf 57 F4
Bad Tennstedt 52 C2
Bad Tölz 56 A4
Badules 36 C4
Bad Urach 55 D3
Bad Vibel 52 A4
Bad Vöslau 57 F3
Bad Waldsee 55 D4
Bad Wiessee 56 A4
Bad Wildungen 52 A3
Bad Wilsnack 48 C3
Bad Wimpfen 55 D2
Bad Windsheim 55 E1
Bad Wörishofen 55 E3
Bad Wurzach 55 E4
Bad Zwischenahn 47 E3
Bae Colwyn 6 B2
Baena 43 F2
Baeza 44 A2
Bagà 32 A3
Bâgé-le-Châtel 26 C4
Bagenalstown 15 D3
Bagenkop 108 B4
Bagheria 68 B3
Bagnacavallo 61 D2
Bagnara Calabra 67 E4
Bagnères-de-Bigorre 37 E1
Bagnères-de-Luchon 37 E2
Bagni del Masino 58 B3
Bagni di Lucca 60 C3
Bagno a Ripoli 61 D3
Bagno di Romagna 61 D3
Bagnoles-de-l'Orne 18 C4
Bagnoli del Trigno 64 B2
Bagnolo Mella 60 B1
Bagnols-les-Bains 29 F3
Bagnols-sur-Cèze 30 B3
Bagnoregio 63 E1
Bagolino 58 C4
Bagrationovsk 110 B4
Bagrdan 73 E4
Baia Mare 112 C3
Baiano 64 B4
Baião 34 B4
Baiersbronn 54 C3
Baignes-Ste-Radegonde 28 B1
Baigneux-les-Juifs 26 C2
Baile Átha Cliath 13 E4
Baile Átha Luain 12 C3
Băile Herculane 114 C1
Bailén 44 A2
Băile Tuşnad 113 D4
Bailieborough 13 D3
Bailleul 19 F1
Bain-de-Bretagne 23 D3
Bains-les-Bains 27 D1
Baio 34 A1

Barcelona
0
2 km
LA JONQUERA 149 km
GIRONA/GERONA 96 km
PUIGCERDÀ 169 km
VIC 66 km
TERRASSA/TARRASSA 27 km
MATARÓ 28 km
TERRASSA/TARRASA 28 km
S. CUGAT DEL VALLÈS 19 km
STA COLOMA DE GRAMENET
BADALONA
S. ANDREU
S. ADRIÀ DE BESÒS
VALL D'HEBRON
TIBIDABO
(532)
VALLVIDRERA
Parque Güell
Pl. de Lesseps
SAGRADA FAMILIA
Pl. de les Glòries Catalanes
PLAZA DE TOROS MONUMENTAL
DIAGONAL
Pl. Francesc. Macià
Monasterio de Pedralbes
ESPLUGUES DE LLOBREGAT
S. JUST DESVERN
Ciudad Universitaria
DIAGONAL
Estación Barcelona Sants
Pl. d'Espanya
PL. DE TOROS LAS ARENAS
PARQUE DE LA CIUDADELA
Pl. de Catalunya
CATEDRAL
BARRIO GÒTICO
Estación Barcelona Término
PARC DE MAR
MAR
MEDITERRÁNEO
ESTACIÓN MARÍTIMA
PUERTO
PLAYA
MONTJUÏC
Parque de Atracciones
CASTILLO DE MONTJUÏC
FERIA
L'HOSPITALET DE LLOBREGAT
CORNELLÀ DE LLOBREGAT
CASTELLDEFELS C 245
108 km TARRAGONA
169 km LLEIDA/LÉRIDA
AEROPUERTO, CASTELLDEFELS 23 km
SITGES 42 km
MICHELIN
BALEARES
GENOVA
Pl. Cerdà
Via Favència
Meridiana
Av. del Paral. lel
Gran Via
Carret. Reial
Collblanc
Sants
Sta Eulàlia

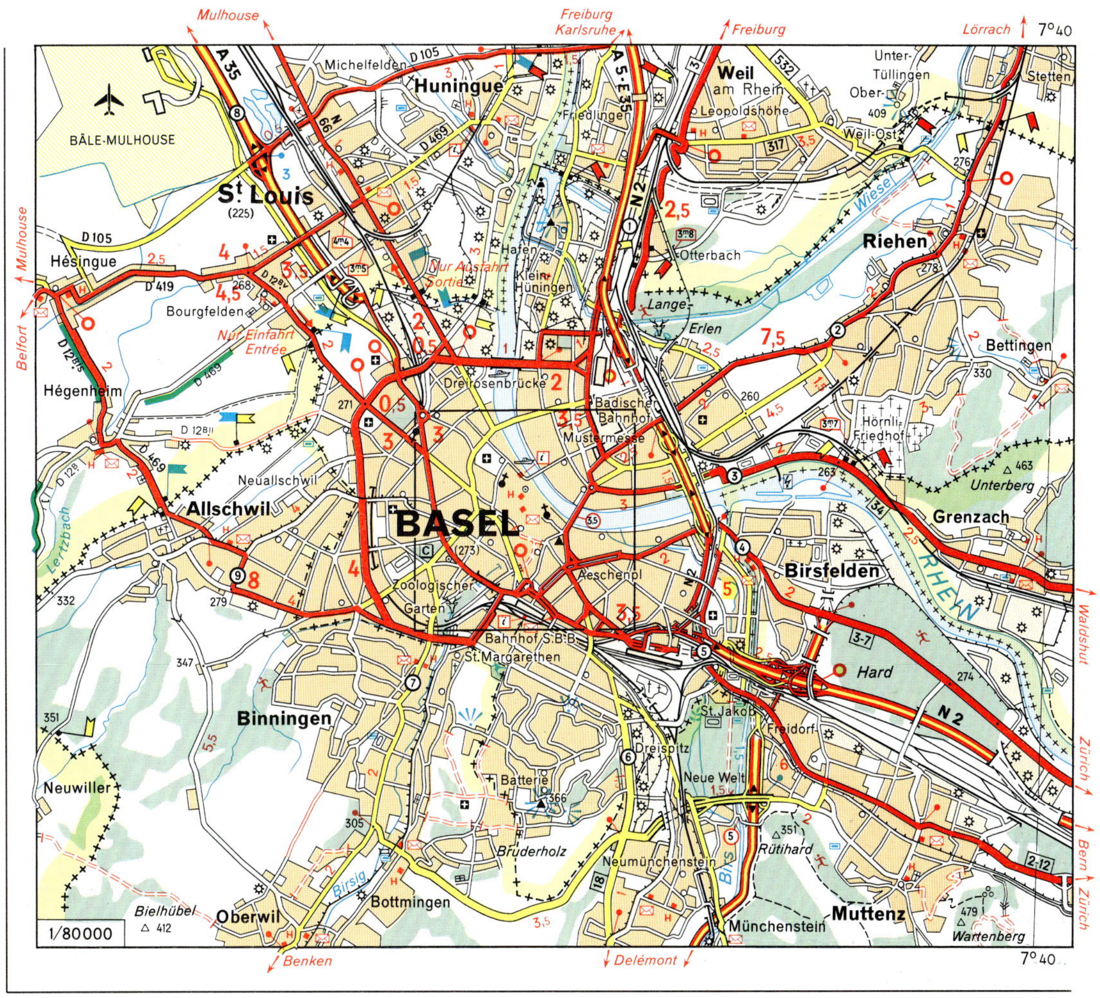
Mulhouse
Freiburg
Karlsruhe
Freiburg
Lörrach
7°40
BÂLE-MULHOUSE
Huningue
Weil am Rhein
Leopoldshöhe
Unter-Tüllingen
Ober-
Weil-Ost
Stetten
St Louis
Hésingue
Riehen
Otterbach
Bourgfelden
Lange
Erlen
Bettingen
Hégenheim
Dreirosenbrücke
Badischer Bahnhof
Mustermesse
Hörnli Friedhof
Neuallschwil
Allschwil
BASEL
Unterberg
Grenzach
Birsfelden
RHEIN
Zoologischer Garten
Aeschenpl
Bahnhof S.B.B.
St.Margarethen
Hard
Binningen
St. Jakob
Freidorf
Dreispitz
Neuwiller
Neue Welt
Batterie
Rütihard
Bruderholz
Neumünchenstein
Birsig
Birs
Bottmingen
Oberwil
Bielhübel
Münchenstein
Muttenz
Wartenberg
1/80000
Benken
Delémont
Waldshut
Zürich
Bern
Zürich
Belfort
Mulhouse
N 2
A 35

Baiono 34 A3
Bais 23 E3
Baïse 28 C3
Baïse-Darré 37 E1
Baja 114 B1
Baja Sardinia 66 B1
Bajgora 77 D1
Bajina Bašta 72 C4
Bajmok 72 B1
Bajram Curri 76 C2
Bajša 72 B1
Bajzë 76 B3
Bakar 70 B3
Bakarac 70 B3
Bakewell 6 C3
Bakio 36 B1
Bakkaflói 96 C1
Bakony 112 A4
Bakvattnet 101 E1
Bala 6 B3
Balaguer 37 F3
Balanegra 44 B4
Balaruc 30 A4
Balassagyarmat 112 B3
Balaton 112 A4
Balatonfüred 112 B4
Balatonkeresztúr 112 A4
Balazote 40 C4
Balbigny 26 B4
Balbriggan 13 E3
Balčik 115 E2
Balderschwang 55 E4
Baldock 9 F2
Baldo, Mte 58 C4
Bale 70 A4
Baleal 38 A3
Baleizão 42 B1
Balerma 44 B4
Balestrand 100 A3
Balí 91 D3
Balikesir 115 E4
Bälinge 106 B3
Balingen 55 D3
Balivanich 2 A3
Ballachulish 2 C4
Ballaghaderreen 12 C3
Ballangen 94 B3
Ballantrae 4 B3
Ballao 66 B3
Ballater 3 D4
Ballaugh 6 A1
Ballenstedt 52 C2
Balleroy 18 C3
Ballerup 108 C3
Ballina 12 B2
Ballinamore 12 C3
Ballinasloe 12 C3
Ballingarry 14 C3
Ballinrobe 12 B3
Ballintober 12 B3
Ballobar 37 E4
Ballon 23 F3
Ballon d'Alsace 27 E1
Ballstad 97 E1
Ballybay 13 D2
Ballybofey 12 C1
Ballybunnion 12 A4
Ballycastle (IRL) 12 B2
Ballycastle (N Ire) 13 E1
Ballyclare 13 E2
Ballyconnell 12 C2
Ballycotton 14 C4
Ballycroy 12 B2
Ballyduff 14 B3
Ballyforan 12 C3
Ballygawley 13 D2
Ballyhaunis 12 B3
Ballyheige 14 A3
Ballyjamesduff 13 D3
Ballymahon 12 C3
Ballymena 13 E2
Ballymoe 12 C3
Ballymoney 13 E1
Ballymore 12 C3
Ballymote 12 C2
Ballynahinch 13 E2
Ballysadare 12 C2
Ballyshannon 12 C2
Ballyvaughan 12 B4
Balmaseda 36 A1
Balme 31 E1
Balmoral Castle 3 D4
Balneario de Panticosa 37 E2
Balsareny 32 A3
Balsfjorden 94 B2
Balsicas 45 D2
Balsorano 63 F2
Bålsta 106 B3
Balsthal 27 E2
Balta 113 E3
Baltanás 35 F4
Baltar 34 B3
Baltic Sea 110 B2
Baltijsk 110 B4
Baltinglass 13 D4
Baltrum 47 E3
Bambalió 82 C3
Bamberg 52 C4
Bambíni 82 C3
Bamburgh 5 E3
Bampton 8 C3
Banagher 12 C4
Banat 114 C1
Banatska Palanka 73 D2
Banatska Topola 72 C1
Banatski Brestovac 73 D3
Banatski Dvor 72 C2
Banatski Karlovac 73 D2
Banatsko Aranđđelovo 72 C1
Banatsko Karađorđevo 72 C2
Banatsko Novo Selo 73 D2
Banbridge 13 E2
Banbury 9 E1
Banchory 3 E4
Bande 34 B3
Bandak 104 B2
Bandırma 115 E3
Bandol 30 C4
Bandon 14 B4
Bandon R 14 B4
Bañeres 45 E1
Banff 3 E3
Bangor (IRL) 12 B2
Bangor (N Ire) 13 E2
Bangor (Wales) 6 A2
Bangsund 97 D4
Banie 49 E3
Banja (Srbija) 73 D3
Banja (Srbija) 76 B1
Banja Koviljača 72 B3
Banja Luka 71 E3
Banjani 72 C3
Banja Vrućica 71 F3
Banjska 76 C1
Bankeryd 109 D1
Bann (N Ire) 13 D1
Bann (Wexford) 15 D3
Bannalec 22 B3
Banon 30 C3
Bañón 41 D2
Baños de Cerrato 35 F4
Baños de la Encina 44 A2
Baños de la Fuensanta 44 C2
Baños de Molgas 34 B3
Baños de Montemayor 39 E2
Baños de Fuensanta 35 E1
Banova Jaruga 71 D2
Banovići 71 F4
Banque de Fraiture 51 D4
Banque Michel 51 D4
Bansin 49 E2
Banská-Bystrica 112 B3
Banská-Štiavnica 112 B3
Bansko 77 F3
Bantry 14 B4
Bantry B 14 A4
Bañuela 43 F1
Banyalbufar 45 E2
Banyoles 32 B3
Banyuls 32 C3
Bao, Emb de 34 C3
Bapaume 19 F2
Bar (SU) 113 D3
Bar (YU) 76 B3
Baracaldo 36 B1
Barać i 71 E4
Baradla 112 B3
Barahona 36 B4
Barajas 40 B2
Barajas de Melo 40 B3
Barajevo 73 D3
Baralla 34 C2
Barane 76 C2
Baranoviči 111 D4
Baraqueville 29 E3
Barasona, Emb de 37 E3
Barbadillo del Mercado 36 A3
Barban 70 A3
Barbarano Vicentino 61 D1
Barbarušince 77 E2
Barbastro 37 E3
Barbat 70 B4
Barbate de Franco 43 D4
Barbate, Emb de 43 D4
Barbazan 37 F2
Barberino di Mugello 60 C3
Barbezieux 28 B1
Barbizon 19 F4
Barbotan 28 B3
Barby 52 C1
Barca de Alva 39 D1
Barca, Emb de la 35 D1
Barcarrota 42 C1
Barcellona Pozzo di Gotto 69 D2
Barcelona 32 B4
Barcelonnette 31 D2
Barcelos 34 A4
Barcena, Emb de 34 C2
Barchfeld 52 B3
Barcis 59 E3
Barcones 36 B4
Barcs 114 A1
Bardal 101 D1
Bardejov 112 B3
Bardi 60 B2
Bardineto 31 F3
Bardolino 60 C1
Bardonecchia 31 D1
Bardu 94 B3
Bardufoss 94 B3
Bare 76 B1
Barèges 37 E2
Barentin 19 D3
Barenton 18 C4
Bares, Estaca de 34 B1
Barfleur 18 B2
Barfleur, Pte de 18 B2
Bargas 40 A3
Bargoed 9 D2
Bargteheide 48 B2
Bari 65 D3
Barić Draga 70 C4
Barisciano 63 F2
Barjac 30 B3
Barjols 31 D4
Barlby 7 D2
Bar, le 31 E3
Bar-le-Duc 20 C4
Barletta 65 D3
Barlinek 49 F3
Barlovento 42 A4
Barmouth 6 A3
Barmstedt 48 A2
Barna 12 B3
Barnard Castle 5 E4
Bärnau 53 D4
Barneveld 16 C3
Barneville 18 B3
Barnsley 7 D2
Barnstaple 8 C3
Barnstorf 17 F1
Barntrup 52 A1
Barovo 77 E3
Barqueiro 38 B2
Barr 21 E4
Barra 2 A4
Barracas 41 E3
Barrachina 41 D2
Barraco 39 F2
Barrafranca 68 C4
Barra Head 2 A4
Barrancos 42 C1
Barranco Velho 42 B2
Barranda 44 C2
Barra, Sd of 2 A4
Barrax 40 C4
Barrea 64 A2
Barre-des-Cévennes 29 F3
Barreiro 38 A4
Barrême 31 D3
Barrhead 4 C2
Barrhill 4 C3
Barri 9 D2
Barrow 13 D4
Barrow-in-Furness 6 B1
Barrow, R 15 D3
Barruecopardo 39 D1
Barruelo de Santullán 35 F2
Barry 9 D2
Barsinghausen 52 A1
Bar-sur-Aube 26 B1
Bar-sur-Seine 26 B1
Barth 49 D1
Barthe-de-Neste, la 37 E1
Barton-upon-Humber 7 D2
Barumini 66 B3
Baruth 53 E1
Barvas 2 B2
Barycz 112 A2
Barzio 58 B4
Bašaid 72 C1
Bàscara 32 B3
Baschi 63 E1
Basconcillos del Tozo 35 F2
Basel 27 E2
Baselga di Pinè 59 D3
Bas-en-Basset 30 B1
Basento 65 D4
Basildon 11 D2
Basilicata 65 D4
Basingstoke 9 E3
Baška 70 B3
Bæskades 95 D2
Baška Voda 75 E2
Baške Oštarije 70 C4
Baslow 6 C3
Basovizza 59 F4
Bas-Rhin 21 E4
Bassano del Grappa 59 D4
Bassée, la 19 F1
Bassella 37 F3
Bassens 28 B2
Bassum 17 F1
Båstad 108 C3
Bastasi 71 D4
Bastelica 33 F3
Bas'tevarri 95 D3
Bastia 33 F2
Bastide-de-Sérou, la 37 F2
Bastogne 20 C2
Bastunäsfjället 97 E4
Bastuträsk 98 B4
Bataille, Col de la 30 C2
Batajnica 72 C3
Batak 115 D3
Batalha 38 B3
Batea 41 F1
Bath 9 D2
Bathgate 5 D2
Bâtie-Neuve, la 31 D2
Batina 72 B1
Batlava 77 D1
Batočina 73 D3
Båtsfjord 95 F1
Batsí 88 B1
Battaglia Terme 61 D1
Battenberg 17 F4
Battice 51 D3
Battipaglia 64 B4
Battle 11 D3
Batz (Finistère) 22 B2
Batz (Loire-Atlantique) 24 A2
Baud 22 C3
Baugé 23 E4
Baugy 26 A2
Baule, la 24 A2
Baume, Cirque de 27 D3
Baume-les-Dames 27 D2
Baumholder 54 B1
Bauska 110 C3
Bautzen 53 F2
Baux, les 30 B3
Bavanište 73 D2
Bavay 20 B1
Bavella, Col de 33 F4
Båven 106 B4
Baveno 58 A4
Bawtry 7 D2
Bayard, Col 31 D2
Bayerisch Eisenstein 56 C1
Bayerischer Wald 56 B2
Bayern 55 F2
Bayeux 18 C3
Bayhirivagh 2 A4
Bayındır 115 F4
Bayon 21 D4
Bayonne 28 A4
Bayreuth 52 C4
Bayrischzell 56 B4
Baza 44 B3
Bazas 28 B3
Baza, Sa de 44 B3
Bazoches-sur-Hoëne 19 D4
Bazzano 60 C2
Beachy Head 10 C3
Beaconsfield 9 F2
Béal an Átha 12 B2
Béal Átha na Sluaighe 12 C3
Beaminster 9 D3
Beanntrai 14 B4
Beara 14 A4
Beariz 34 B2
Beas 42 C2
Beasain 36 C1
Beas de Segura 44 B2
Beattock 5 D3
Beaucaire 30 B3
Beaufort (Jura) 26 C3
Beaufort (Savoie) 27 E4
Beaufort-en-Vallée 23 E4
Beaugency 25 E2
Beaujeu 26 C4
Beaulieu (Alpes-Maritime) 31 E3
Beaulieu (Corrèze) 29 D2
Beaulieu (GB) 9 E3
Beaumaris 6 A2
Beaumesnil 19 D3

Londonderry
Larne
Carrickfergus
Millbank
Mossley
Monkstown
Greenisland
Ballymartin Water
Mallusk
Carnmoney
Jordanstown
Whiteabbey
Hyde Park
NEWTOWNABBEY
Glengormley
Rathcoole
BELFAST LOUGH
Liverpool
Douglas (Isle of Man)
Ulster Way
Craigavad
Transport Museum
The Ulster Folk Museum
Bangor
Boghil
Bellevue Zoological Gardens
Whitehouse
Greencastle
Holywood
Belfast Airport
Flush
Cave Hill
Squires Hill
Back Burn
Belfast Castle
BELFAST
Fortwilliam
Ballysillan
Skegoney
Legoniel
Clady Water
Forth
Oldpark
Ardoyne
Cliftonville
BELFAST HARBOUR AIRPORT
Redburn
Crons Hill
Craigantlet
Knocknagoney
Ballygomartin
Divis
Blackmountain
Woodvale
Shankill
Victoria Park
Sydenham
Parliament House
Stormont
Dundonald
Newtownards
Whiterock
Falls
City Hall
Ballymacarrett
Belmont
Ballyhackmore
Church House
Bloomfield
Tullycarnet
Hannahstown
Black Hill
Queen's University
Ormeau
Orangefield
Shandon
Gilnahirk
Milltown
Ulster Museum
Botanic Gardens
Willowfield
Castlereagh
Enler
Andersontown
Suffolk
Windsor
Cregagh
Braniel
Colin
Ballynafeigh
Rosetta
Ladybrook
Malone
Stranmillis
Comber
Poleglass
Balmoral
Finaghy
Taughmonagh
Crossnacreevy
Belvoir Park Forest
Newtownbreda
Gransha
Ballystockart
Twinbrook
Lisleen
Dunmurry
Belvoir
Lagan
Derryaghy
Upper Malone
Giants Ring
Purdysburn
Moneyreagh
Lagan Valley Regional Park
Dallylesson
Lambeg
Drumbeg
1/120 000
2 km
1 mile
Lisburn Craigavon
Enniskillen Dublin
Downpatrick Newcastle

Beaumetz-lès-Loges 19 F2
Beaumont (B) 50 B4
Beaumont (Dordogne) 28 C2
Beaumont (Manche) 18 B2
Beaumont (Val d'Oise) 19 F3
Beaumont-de-Lomagne 28 C3
Beaumont-le-Roger 19 D3
Beaumont-sur-Sarthe 23 F3
Beaune 26 C2
Beaune-la-Rolande 25 F1
Beaupréau 24 C2
Beauraing 50 C4
Beaurepaire 30 C1
Beaurepaire-en-Bresse 26 C3
Beausset, le 31 D4
Beauvais 19 E3
Beauvoir (Deux-Sèvres) 24 C4
Beauvoir (Vendée) 24 A3
Bebington 6 B2
Bebra 52 B3
Beccles 11 E1
Becedas 39 E2
Beceite 41 F2
Bečej 72 C2
Becerreá 34 C2
Bec-Hellouin, le 19 D3
Bécherel 23 D3
Bechet 115 D2
Bechhofen 55 E2
Bečići 76 B3
Becilla de Valderaduey 35 E3
Beckenried 58 A2
Beckington 9 D3
Beckum 17 F3
Bečov 53 E4
Bedale 6 C1
Bédarieux 30 A4
Beddgelert 6 A3
Bederkesa 47 F3
Bedford 9 F1
Bedfordshire 9 F1
Bedlington 5 E3
Bedmar 44 A2
Bednja 70 C1
Bedonia 60 B3
Bedum 47 D3
Bedwas 9 D2
Bedworth 9 E1
Beeford 7 E2
Beelitz 49 D4
Beerfelden 55 D1
Beeskow 49 E4
Beetzendorf 48 B4
Bégard 22 C2
Begejci 72 C2
Begejski kanal 72 C2
Beg-Meil 22 B3
Begna 104 C2
Begov Han 71 F4
Bégude-de-Mazenc, la 30 C2
Begues 32 A4
Begur 32 C3
Behalúa de Guadix 44 B3
Behobia 28 A4
Behringersmühle 52 C4
Beiarn 97 E2
Beilen 17 D1
Beilingries 55 F2
Beinn a'Ghlò 3 D4
Beinn an Oir 4 B2
Beinn Bheigeir 4 B2
Beinn Dearg 2 C3
Beira Alta 38 B1
Beira Baixa 38 C2
Beira Litoral 38 B1
Beisfjord 94 B3
Beith 4 C2
Beitostølen 104 C1
Beitstadfjorden 101 D1
Beiuș 112 C4
Beja 42 B1
Béjar 39 E2
Béjar, Pto de 39 E2
Békés 112 C4
Békéscsaba 112 C4
Bel 41 F2
Bělá 56 B1
Bélâbre 25 E3
Bela Crkva (Srbija) 72 C3
Bela Crkva (Vojvodina) 73 D2
Belaja Cerkov' 113 E2
Belalcázar 43 E1
Belanovce 77 E2
Belanovica 73 D3
Bela Palanka 77 E1
Belasica 77 F3
Belcaire 32 A2
Belchen 54 C4
Belchite 37 D4
Belčište 77 D4
Belcoo 12 C2
Bel'cy 113 E3
Belec 70 C2
Belecke 17 F3
Belegiš 72 C2
Belej 70 B4
Beleña, Emb de 40 B1
Belesar, Emb de 34 B2
Belev 111 F3
Bele Vode 76 C1
Belfast 13 E2
Belfast L 13 E2
Belford 5 E3
Belfort 27 E2
Belforte all'Isauro 61 E3
Belgern 53 E2
Belgie 16 B3
Belgique 50 B3
Belgodère 33 F3
Belgorod-Dnestrovskij 113 F4
Belianes 37 F4
Belice 68 B3
Beli Drim 76 C2
Beli Manastir 71 F2
Belin-Béliet 28 B3
Beli Potok 73 F4
Belišće 71 F2
Beli Timok 73 F4
Beljakovce 77 E2
Beljanica 73 E3
Beljina 73 D3
Bellac 25 D4
Bellagio 58 B4
Bellano 58 B4
Bellaria 61 E3
Bellcaire d'Urgell 37 F3
Belledonne, Chaîne de 31 D1
Belleek 12 C2
Bellegarde (Ain) 27 D4
Bellegarde (Gard) 30 B3
Bellegarde (Loiret) 25 F1
Bellegarde-en-Marche 25 F4
Belle-Ile 22 B4
Belle-Isle-en-Terre 22 B2
Bellême 23 F3
Bellencombre 19 E2
Bellerive 26 A4
Belleville 26 C4
Belley 27 D4
Bellinzona 58 A3
Bell-lloc d'Urgell 37 F3
Bello 41 D1
Bellpuig 37 F4
Belluno 59 E3
Bellver 45 E3
Bellver de Cerdanya 32 A3
Bélmez 43 E1
Belmont (F) 26 B4
Belmont (GB) 3 F1
Belmonte (Asturias) 35 D1
Belmonte (Castilla-la-Mancha) 40 C3
Belmonte (P) 38 C2
Belmont-sur-Rance 32 B1
Belmullet 12 A2
Belo Brdo 76 C1
Belogradčik 114 C2
Belo jez 72 C2
Beloljin 77 D1
Belœil 50 B4
Belo Polje 76 C2
Belopolje 113 F1
Belorado 36 A2
Belorussija 111 D4
Belpech 32 A2
Belper 6 C3
Belsay 5 E3
Belsh 76 C4
Beltinci 70 C1
Belturbet 13 D2
Belušić 73 E4
Belvedere Marittimo 67 E2
Belver 37 E3
Belvès 28 C2
Belvis de la Jara 39 F3
Belyj 111 E2
Belz 22 C4
Belzig 53 D1
Bembézar, Emb
Bembézar, Emb de 43 E2
Bembibre 35 D2
Bemposta 38 B3
Bemposta, Bgem da 34 C4
Benabarre 37 E3
Benaguacil 41 E3
Benahadux 44 B3
Ben Alder 2 C4
Benalmádena 43 F4
Benalúa de las Villas 44 A3
Benamargosa 43 F3
Benamaurel 44 B2
Benamejí 43 F3
Benamocarra 43 F4
Benaoján 43 E4
Ben Armine 3 D2
Benasal 41 E2
Benasque 37 E2
Benavente (E) 35 D3
Benavente (P) 38 A4
Benavides 35 D3
Benbecula 2 A3
Ben Chonzie 4 C1
Ben Cruachan 4 B1
Bendery 113 E4
Bendorf 51 E4
Benediktbeuern 56 A4
Benešov (Severočeský) 53 F3
Benešov (Středočeský) 53 F4
Bénévent-l'Abbaye 25 E4
Benevento 64 B3
Benfeld 21 E4
Benfleet 11 D2
Bengtsfors 105 D4
Ben Hope 2 C2
Beničanci 71 E2
Benicarló 41 F2
Benicasim 41 F3
Benidorm 45 E1
Benifaió 41 E4
Beninar, Emb de 44 B3
Benissa 45 E1
Benitses 82 A1
Ben Klibreck 2 C2
Benkovac 74 C1
Ben Lawers 4 C1
Ben Lomond 4 C1
Ben Macdui 3 D4
Ben More (Grampian) 4 C1
Ben More (Mull) 4 B1
Ben More Assynt 2 C2
Benneckenstein 52 B2
Ben Nevis 2 C4
Bénodet 22 B3
Benquerencia de la Serena 43 E1
Bensberg 17 E4
Bensersiel 47 E3
Bensheim 54 C1
Bentley 7 D2
Ben Vorlich 4 C1
Ben Wyvis 2 C3
Bény-Bocage, le 18 C3
Beočin 72 C2
Beograd 73 D3
Bérarde, la 31 D2
Berat 114 C3
Berbegal 37 E3
Berberana 36 B1
Berberia, C de 45 D4
Berceto 60 B3
Berching 55 F2
Berchtesgaden 56 C4
Berck-Plage 19 E1
Berdičev 113 E2
Beregovo 112 C3
Bereguardo 60 A2
Bere I 14 A4
Berek 71 D2
Bere Regis 9 D3
Beret 37 F2
Berettyóújfalu 112 C4
Berezina 111 E4
Berezino 111 D4
Berg (A) 57 F2
Berg (Nordland) 97 D3
Berg (S) 101 E2
Berg (Troms) 94 B2
Berga (D) 52 C2
Berga (E) 32 A3
Bergama 115 E4
Bergamo 60 B1
Bergara 36 B1
Bergby 106 B2
Bergedorf 48 B3
Bergen (B) 50 B4
Bergen (D) 49 D1
Bergen (N) 104 A2
Bergen (Niedersachsen) 48 A4
Bergen (Niedersachsen) 48 B3
Bergen (NL) 16 C2
Bergen aan Zee 16 C2
Bergen op Zoom 16 B4
Bergerac 28 C2
Berggießhübel 53 F2
Berghamn fjärden 107 D3
Bergheim 17 D4
Bergisch Gladbach 17 E4
Bergnäset 98 C3
Bergneustadt 17 E4
Bergö 102 B2
Berg-Rudolphstein 53 D3
Bergsjö 101 F3
Bergsviken 98 B3
Bergues 19 F1
Bergum 47 D3
Bergün 58 B3
Beringel 42 B1
Beringen 50 C3
Berja 44 B4
Berka 52 B3
Berkåk 100 C2
Berkel 17 D2
Berkhamsted 9 F2
Berkheim 55 E3
Berkhof 48 A4
Berkovica 114 C2
Berkovići 75 F2
Berkshire 9 E2
Berlaimont 20 A2
Berlanga 43 D1
Berlanga de Duero 36 B4
Berlebeck 17 F3
Berlenga, I 38 A3
Berlevåg 95 F1

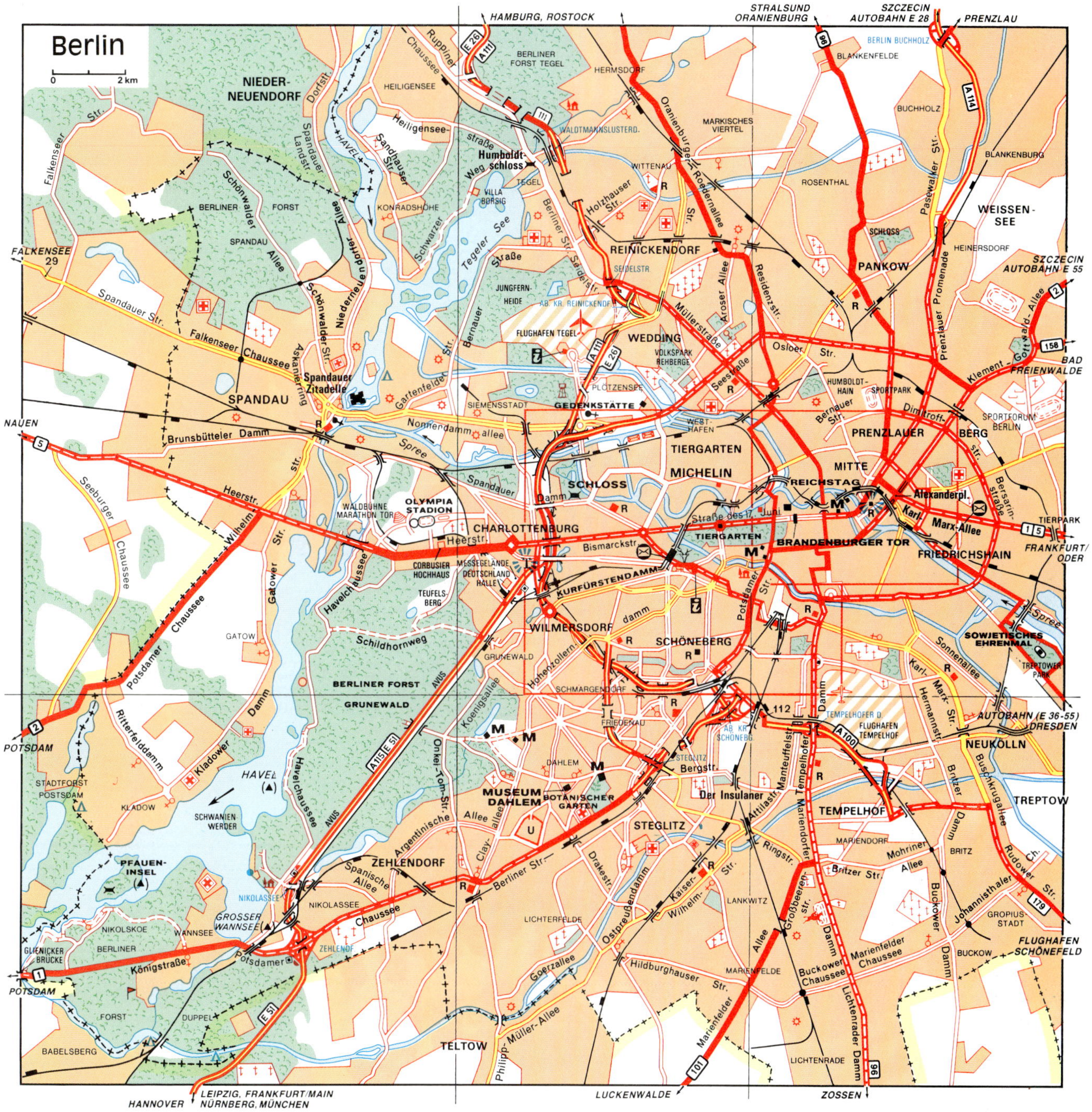
Berlin
0
2 km
HAMBURG, ROSTOCK
STRALSUND ORANIENBURG
SZCZECIN AUTOBAHN E 28
PRENZLAU
NIEDER-NEUENDORF
HEILIGENSEE
BERLINER FORST TEGEL
HERMSDORF
BLANKENFELDE
BUCHHOLZ
BLANKENBURG
WEISSEN-SEE
HEINERSDORF
SZCZECIN AUTOBAHN E 55
ROSENTHAL
MÄRKISCHES VIERTEL
WITTENAU
TEGEL
Humboldt-schloss
KONRADSHÖHE
FALKENSEE
SPANDAU
Spandauer Zitadelle
FLUGHAFEN TEGEL
JUNGFERN-HEIDE
REINICKENDORF
WEDDING
PANKOW
PRENZLAUER BERG
BAD FREIENWALDE
NAUEN
SIEMENSSTADT
GEDENKSTÄTTE
TIERGARTEN
MICHELIN
MITTE
SCHLOSS
REICHSTAG
Alexanderpl.
Marx-Allee
FRIEDRICHSHAIN
TIERPARK
FRANKFURT/ODER
OLYMPIA STADION
CHARLOTTENBURG
BRANDENBURGER TOR
KURFÜRSTENDAMM
WILMERSDORF
SCHÖNEBERG
GATOW
BERLINER FORST
GRUNEWALD
HAVEL
POTSDAM
SOWJETISCHES EHRENMAL
TREPTOWER PARK
AUTOBAHN (E 36-55) DRESDEN
NEUKÖLLN
TREPTOW
TEMPELHOF
FLUGHAFEN TEMPELHOF
MUSEUM DAHLEM
BOTANISCHER GARTEN
STEGLITZ
ZEHLENDORF
PFAUEN-INSEL
NIKOLASSEE
WANNSEE
LICHTERFELDE
LANKWITZ
MARIENDORF
BRITZ
GROPIUS STADT
FLUGHAFEN SCHÖNEFELD
BUCKOW
MARIENFELDE
LICHTENRADE
TELTOW
BABELSBERG
HANNOVER
LEIPZIG, FRANKFURT/MAIN NÜRNBERG, MÜNCHEN
LUCKENWALDE
ZOSSEN

Berlin (Ost) 49 E4
Berlin (West) 49 D4
Bermejales, Emb 43 F3
Bermeja, Sa 43 E4
Bermeo 36 B1
Bermillo 35 D4
Bern 27 E2
Bernalda 65 D4
Bernardsthal 57 F1
Bernartice 57 D1
Bernau (Baden-Württemberg) 54 C4
Bernau (Bayern) 56 B3
Bernau (Brandenburg) 49 E4
Bernaville 19 F2
Bernay 19 D3
Bernburg 52 C1
Berndorf 57 E3
Berne 47 F3
Bernesga, R 35 D2
Bernina, Piz 58 B3
Bernina, Pso del 58 B3
Bernkastel-Kues 54 B1
Bernsdorf 53 F2
Bernstein 57 F3
Beroun 53 F4
Berounka 53 F4
Berovo 77 F3
Ber'oza 112 C1
Ber'ozovka 113 F3
Berra 61 D2
Berre 30 C4
Berre, Etang de 30 C4
Beršad' 113 E3
Bersenbrück 17 E2
Bertamirans 34 A2
Bertinoro 61 D3
Bertrix 20 C2
Berwang 58 C1
Berwick-upon-Tweed 5 E2
Berwyn 6 B3
Berzocana 39 E3
Berzosa 39 D1
Besalú 32 B3
Besançon 27 D2
Besande 35 E2
Besaya, R 35 F2
Besbre 26 B3
Besigheim 55 D2
Beška 72 C2
Besna Kobila 77 E2
Besse 29 E1
Bességes 30 B3
Besse-sur-Issole 31 D4
Bessines 25 E4
Betancuria 42 C4
Betanzos 34 B1
Betelu 36 C1
Bétera 41 E3
Beteta 40 C2
Bétharram, Grottes de 37 E1
Bethesda 6 A2
Béthune 19 F1
Béthune R 19 E2
Bettna 106 A4
Bettola 60 B2
Bettolle 61 D4
Bettyhill 3 D2
Betws-y-Coed 6 A3
Betz 19 F3
Betzdorf 51 F3
Beuil 31 E3
Beura 58 A4
Beuron 55 D3
Beuvray, Mont 26 B3
Beuvron 25 E2
Beuzeville 19 D3
Bevagna 63 E1
Beveren-Waas 50 B3
Beverley 7 D2
Beverstedt 47 F3
Beverungen 52 A2
Beverwijk 16 C2
Bewdley 9 D1
Bex 27 E3
Bexhill 11 D3
Beynac 29 D2
Beynat 29 D2
Bežanija 72 C3
Bézards, les 26 A1
Bezas 41 D2
Bezdan 72 B1
Bezdrep 57 D1
Bežeck 111 F1
Béziers 30 A4
Bezmisht 77 D4
Béznar 44 A3
Biała Podlaska 112 C1
Białowieska 112 C1
Białystok 112 C1
Biancavilla 69 D3
Bianco 67 E4
Bianco, M 27 E4
Biandrate 31 F1
Biar 45 D1
Biarritz 28 A4
Biasca 58 A3
Bibbiena 61 D4
Biberach 54 C3
Biberach an der Riß 55 E3
Bibinje 74 C1
Bibione 59 F4
Bibury 9 E2
Bicaj 76 C3
Bicaz 113 D4
Bicester 9 E2
Bichl 56 A4
Bidache 28 A4
Bidart 28 A4
Bidasoa, R 36 C1
Biddendon 11 D3
Bidean nam Bian 4 C1
Bideford 8 C3
Biebelried 55 E1
Biedenkopf 17 F4
Biel 27 E2
Bielefeld 17 F2
Bielerhöhe 58 B2
Biella 31 F1
Bielsa 37 E2
Bielsa, Tunnel de 37 E2
Bielsko-Biała 112 B3
Bielsk Podlaski 112 C1
Bienne R 27 D3
Bienne 27 E2
Bientina 60 C4
Bienvenida 43 D1
Bierné 23 E4
Bierre 26 B2
Biesbosch 16 C3
Biescas 37 D2
Biese 48 C4
Biesenthal 49 E3
Bietigheim-Bissingen 55 D2
Biferno 64 B2
Biga 115 E3
Biggar 5 D2
Biggleswade 9 F1
Bignasco 58 A3
Bihać 70 C3
Bihorului, M 112 C4
Bijele Poljane 76 B2
Bijeljani 75 F2
Bijeljina 72 B3
Bijelo Brdo 71 F2
Bijelolasica 70 B3
Bijelo Polje 76 B2
Bilbao 36 B1
Bileća 76 A2
Bilecik 115 F3
Bilećko jez 76 A2
Biłgoraj 112 C2
Bilina 53 E3
Biljača 77 E2
Biljanovac 76 C1
Bilje 71 F2
Billerbeck 17 E3
Billericay 11 D2
Billingham 5 E4
Billingshurst 10 C3
Billom 29 F1
Billund 108 A3
Bilo 77 E1
Bilogora 71 D2
Bilto 94 C2
Bilzen 50 C3
Binaced 37 E3
Binačka Morava 77 D2
Binasco 60 A1
Binche 50 B4
Binéfar 37 E3
Bingen 51 F4
Bingham 7 D3
Bingley 6 C2
Bingsjö 101 E4
Binic 22 C2
Binz 49 D1
Bioča 76 C2
Bioče 76 B2
Biograd 74 C1
Biogradsko, nac park 76 B2
Biokovo 75 E2
Bionaz 27 E4
Biot, le 27 E3
Birchington 11 D2
Birgi 68 A3
Biri 105 D2
Birkebeiner veien 104 C1
Birkeland 104 B4
Birkenfeld 54 B1
Birkenhead 6 B2
Birkenwerden 49 D4
Birkerød 108 C3
Birkfeld 57 E4
Bîrlad 113 E4
Birmingham 9 E1
Birnau 55 D4
Birr 12 C4
Biržai 110 C3
Birzebugga 68 B4
Bisaccia 64 C3
Biscarrosse 28 A3
Biscarrosse-Plage 28 A3
Bisceglie 65 D3
Bischofsgrün 53 D4
Bischofsheim 52 B4
Bischofshofen 59 E1
Bischofswerde 53 F2
Bischofswiesen 56 C4
Bischofszell 58 A1
Bischwiller 21 F4
Bisenti 63 F1
Biševo 75 D2
Bishop Auckland 5 E4
Bishop's Castle 9 D1
Bishop's Stortford 10 C2
Bisignano 67 E2
Bisko 75 D1
Bismark 48 C4
Bismo 100 B3
Bispgården 101 F2
Bispingen 48 A3
Bistar 77 E2
Bistra pl 77 D3
Bistrica (Crna Gora) 76 B2
Bistrica (Srbija) 76 B1
Bistrica ob S. 70 C2
Bistričak 71 E4
Bistrița 113 D4
Bistrița R 113 D4
Bitburg 54 A1
Bitche 21 E3
Bitetto 65 D3
Bitola 77 E4
Bitonto 65 D3
Bitovnja 75 F1
Bitterfeld 53 D2
Bitti 66 B2
Bizákos 82 C3
Bizau 58 B2
Bizovac 71 F2
Bjala 115 D2
Bjarkøy 94 B3
Bjästa 102 A2
Bjelašnica 75 F1
Bjelašnica 76 A2
Bjelovar 71 D2
Bjerkreim 104 A4
Bjerkvik 94 B3
Bjerringbro 108 B2
Bjørkelangen 105 D3
Björketorp 109 E3
Bjorkfjället 97 F3
Björkliden 94 B3
Björklinge 106 B3
Björköby 102 B2
Björksele 98 A4
Bjorli 100 B3
Björna 102 A2

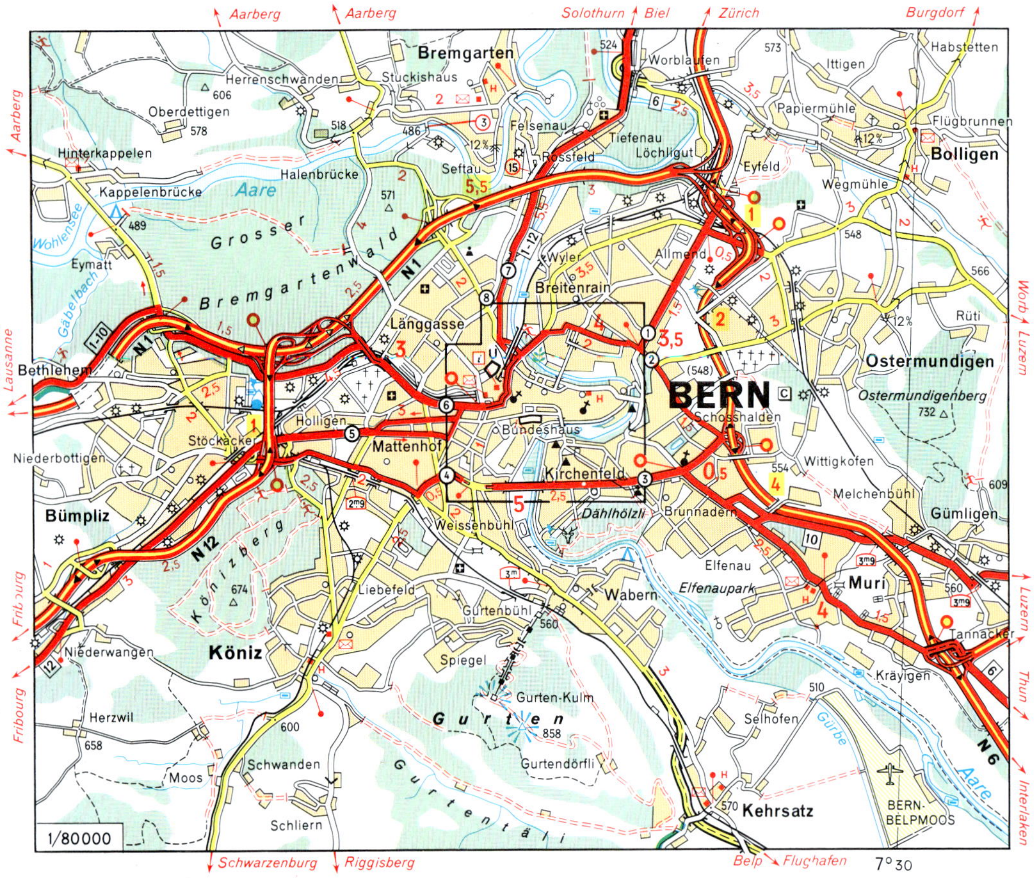
Aarberg
Aarberg
Solothurn
Biel
Zürich
Burgdorf
Bremgarten
Herrenschwanden
Stuckishaus
Oberdettigen
Hinterkappelen
Kappelenbrücke
Halenbrücke
Aare
Wohlensee
Eymatt
Grosser Bremgartenwald
Gäbelbach
Bethlehem
Bümpliz
Niederbottigen
Stöckacker
Holligen
Mattenhof
Länggasse
Breitenrain
Wyler
Felsenau
Seftau
Tiefenau
Löchligut
Worblaufen
Ittigen
Papiermühle
Habstetten
Flugbrunnen
Bolligen
Eyfeld
Wegmühle
Allmend
BERN
Schosshalden
Ostermundigen
Ostermundigenberg
Rüti
Wittigkofen
Melchenbühl
Gümligen
Bundeshaus
Kirchenfeld
Dählhölzli
Brunnadern
Elfenau
Elfenaupark
Muri
Tannacker
Kräyigen
Weissenbühl
Wabern
Liebefeld
Gurtenbühl
Könizberg
Köniz
Niederwangen
Herzwil
Spiegel
Gurten-Kulm
Gurten
Gurtendörfli
Selhofen
Kehrsatz
BERN-BELPMOOS
Schwanden
Moos
Schlieren
Gurtentäli
1/80000
Worb
Luzern
Thun
Interlaken
Belp
Flughafen
Schwarzenburg
Riggisberg
Fribourg
Neuchâtel
Lausanne
7°30

Bjørnafjorden 104 A2
Björneborg 107 D1
Bjørnevatn 95 F2
Bjørntoppen 97 F2
Björsäter 109 E1
Bjurholm 102 A1
Bjursås 101 E4
Bjuv 108 C3
Blace 77 D1
Blackburn 6 C2
Black Head 12 B4
Black Isle 2 C3
Black Mt 8 C2
Black Mts 9 D2
Blackpool 6 B2
Black Sea 115 F2
Blacksod B 12 A2
Blackstairs Mts 15 D3
Blackwater 15 D3
Blackwaterfoot 4 B2
Blackwater, R 14 C4
Blackwater Res 2 C4
Blaenau Ffestiniog 6 A3
Blaenavon 9 D2
Blåfjellhatten 101 E1
Blagaj 75 F2
Blagnac 29 D4
Blagoevgrad 115 D3
Blåhammaren 101 D2
Blåhø 100 C2
Blain 23 D4
Blainville 21 D4
Blair Atholl 3 D4
Blairgowrie 5 D1
Blå Jungfrun 109 E2
Blakeney 7 F3
Blakstad 104 B4
Blåmannsisen 97 F2
Blâmont 21 E4
Blanca 45 D2
Blanc, C 45 E3
Blanc, le 25 D3
Blanc, Mont 27 E4
Blanco, R 43 E3
Blandford Forum 9 D3
Blanes 32 B4
Blangy 19 E2
Blangy-le-Château 19 D3
Blankenberge 50 A3
Blankenburg 52 C2
Blankenheim 51 D4
Blankernhain 52 C3
Blanquefort 28 B2
Blanquilla 44 B2
Blansko 57 F1
Blanzac 28 C1
Blanzy 26 B3
Blåøret 100 C2
Blarney 14 B4
Blatná 56 C1
Blatnica 71 E4
Blato 75 E1
Blattniksele 98 A3
Blaubeuren 55 D3
Blauen 54 C4
Blaufelden 55 E2
Blaustein 55 E3
Blavet 22 C3
Blaye 28 B2
Blaževo 77 D1
Bleckede 48 B3
Bled 70 A2
Blefjell 104 C3
Bleiburg 70 B1
Bleicherode 52 B2
Bleik 94 A3
Bleiloch-Talsperre 53 D3
Blekinge Län 109 D3
Blendija 73 E4
Bléneau 26 A2
Blenheim Palace 9 E2
Blénod 21 D3
Bléone 31 D3
Blérancourt 19 F3
Bléré 25 D2
Blesle 29 F1
Bletchley 9 F2
Bletterans 26 C3
Blexen 47 F3
Bleymard, le 29 F3
Blidinje jez 75 E1
Blieskastel 54 B2
Bligny 26 C2
Blinisht 76 C3
Blinja 71 D3
Bloemendaal 16 B2
Blois 25 E2
Blokhus 108 B2
Blomberg 52 A1
Blönduós 96 B1
Blonville 19 D3
Bloody Foreland Head 12 C1
Blosenberg 53 D3
Bloška Polica 70 B2
Blovice 56 C1
Bludenz 58 B2
Blue Stack Mts 12 C2
Blumberg (Baden-Württemberg) 54 C4
Blumberg (Brandenburg) 49 E4
Blyth 5 E3
Bø (Telemark) 104 C3
Bø (Vesterålen) 94 A3
Boadella, Emb de 32 B3
Boal 34 C1
Boan 76 B2

Bologna

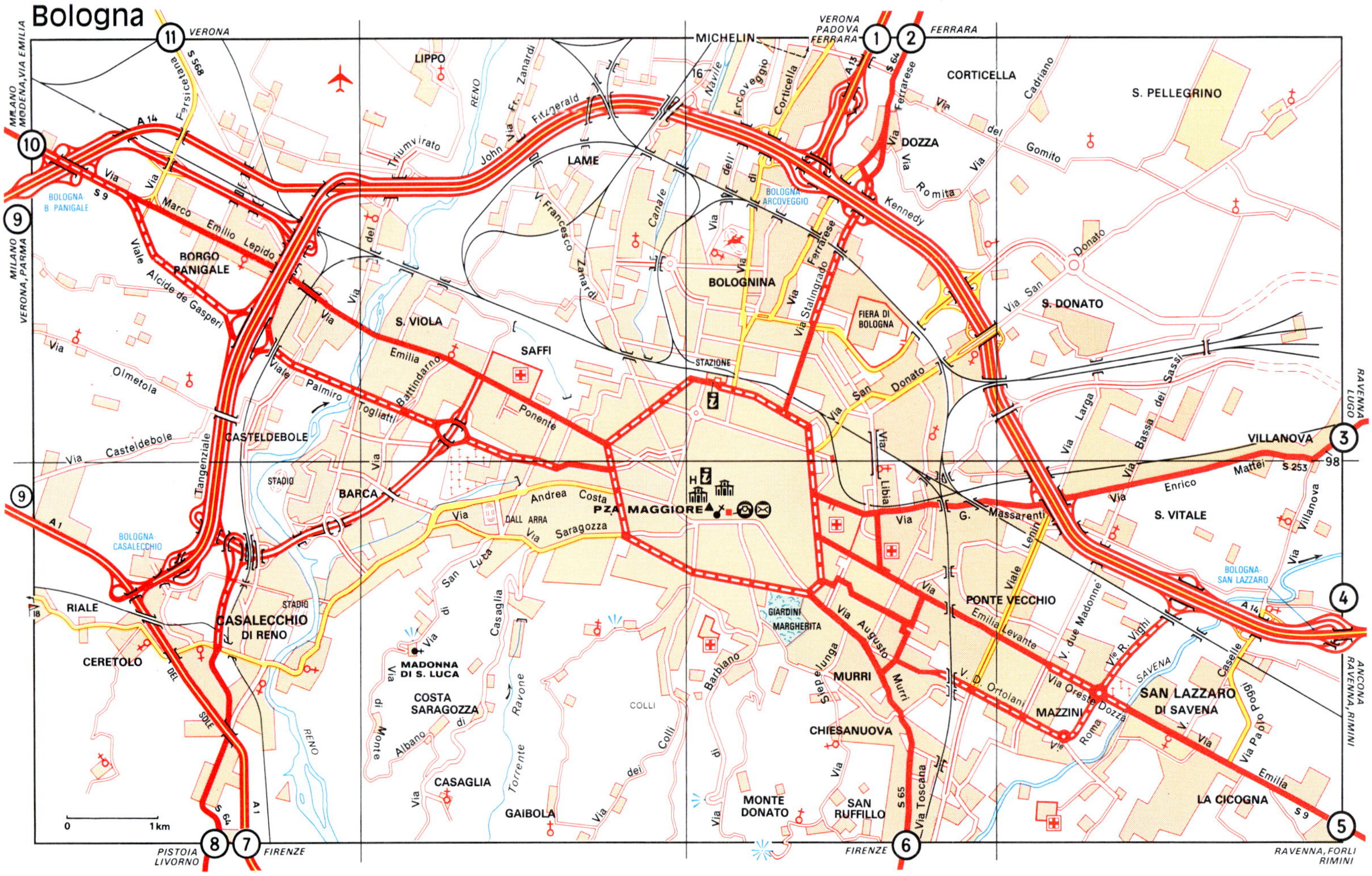
VERONA
MICHELIN
VERONA PADOVA FERRARA
FERRARA
MILANO MODENA, VIA EMILIA
MILANO VERONA, PARMA
CORTICELLA
S. PELLEGRINO
LIPPO
DOZZA
LAME
BOLOGNA B. PANIGALE
BOLOGNA ARCOVEGGIO
BORGO PANIGALE
BOLOGNINA
S. VIOLA
SAFFI
S. DONATO
FIERA DI BOLOGNA
STAZIONE
CASTELDEBOLE
STADIO
BARCA
PZA MAGGIORE
VILLANOVA
S. VITALE
BOLOGNA CASALECCHIO
BOLOGNA SAN LAZZARO
PONTE VECCHIO
RIALE
CASALECCHIO DI RENO
CERETOLO
MADONNA DI S. LUCA
COSTA SARAGOZZA
CASAGLIA
GAIBOLA
COLLI
GIARDINI MARGHERITA
MURRI
MAZZINI
SAN LAZZARO DI SAVENA
CHIESANUOVA
MONTE DONATO
SAN RUFFILLO
LA CICOGNA
RAVENNA LUGO
ANCONA RAVENNA, RIMINI
RAVENNA, FORLI RIMINI
PISTOIA LIVORNO
FIRENZE
FIRENZE
0 1 km

Stafford
Manchester
Stafford
2°
Stafford, Stoke-on-Trent
Ashbourne
Derby
1° 40
52° 40
52° 20
Cannock
Lichfield
Tamworth
Brownhills
Aldridge
WOLVERHAMPTON
WALSALL
Sutton Coldfield
West Bromwich
DUDLEY
SANDWELL
BIRMINGHAM
Stourbridge
Halesowen
Solihull
Kidderminster
Stourport-on-Severn
Bromsgrove
1/200000
3 km
2 miles
Worcester
Bristol
Worcester
Redditch
Redditch
Evesham, Stratford-upon-Avon
Warwick
Telford, Shrewsbury
Whitchurch
Bridgnorth
Bridgnorth
Telford, Shrewsbury
Leominster
Northampton
Nottingham
London
Coventry
Warwick
BIRMINGHAM AIRPORT
N.E.C.
BRITISH LEYLAND
BRITISH STEEL
AUSTIN MORRIS GROUP

Boara Pisani	61	D1
Bobbio	60	A2
Bobigny	19	F4
Bobingen	55	F3
Böblingen	55	D2
Boblitz	53	E1
Boborás	34	B2
Bobova	72	C4
Bóbr	53	F1
Bobrinec	113	F3
Bobrovica	113	E2
Bobrujsk	111	E4
Bočac	71	E4
Bocairent	45	E1
Bocca Trabaria	61	E4
Bocche di Bonifacio	33	F4
Bocco, Pso del	60	B3
Boceguillas	36	A4
Bocholt	17	D3
Bochov	53	E4
Bochum	17	E3
Bockel	48	A3
Bockenem	52	B1
Böckstein	59	E2
Bockum-Hövel	17	E3
Bocognano	33	F3
Boda	101	E4
Böda	109	F2
Bodafors	109	D2
Bodđani	72	B2
Bode	52	C1
Bodegraven	16	C3
Boden	98	B3
Bodenmais	56	B1
Bodensee	58	B1
Bodenteich	48	B4
Bodenwerder	52	A1
Bodenwöhr	56	B1
Bodman-Radolfzell	55	D4
Bodmin	8	B4
Bodø	97	E1
Boecillo	35	E4
Boëge	27	D4
Boën	26	B4
Boeza	35	D2
Boffalora	60	A1
Bogarra	44	C1
Bogatić	72	C3
Bogdanci	77	F3
Bogdaniec	49	F3
Bogë	76	C2
Bogen (D)	56	B2
Bogen (N)	94	B3
Bogense	108	B3
Bogetići	76	B2
Boglárlelle	112	B4
Bognanco	27	F4
Bognes	94	A4
Bognor Regis	9	F3
Bogodol	75	F1
Bogojevo	72	B2
Bogomila	77	E3
Bogomolje	75	E2
Bogorodika	77	F4
Bogovina	73	E4
Bogøy	97	E1
Boguslav	113	E2
Bogutovac	73	D4
Bohain-en-Verman-dois	20	A2
Boherboy	14	B3
Bohinjska Bistrica	70	A2
Bohinjsko jez	70	A2
Böhlen	53	D2
Böhme	48	A4
Böhmenkirch	55	E2
Böhmer Wald	56	B1
Bohmte	17	F2
Böhönye	114	A1
Boiano	64	B3
Boiro	34	A2
Bois-d'Amont	27	D3

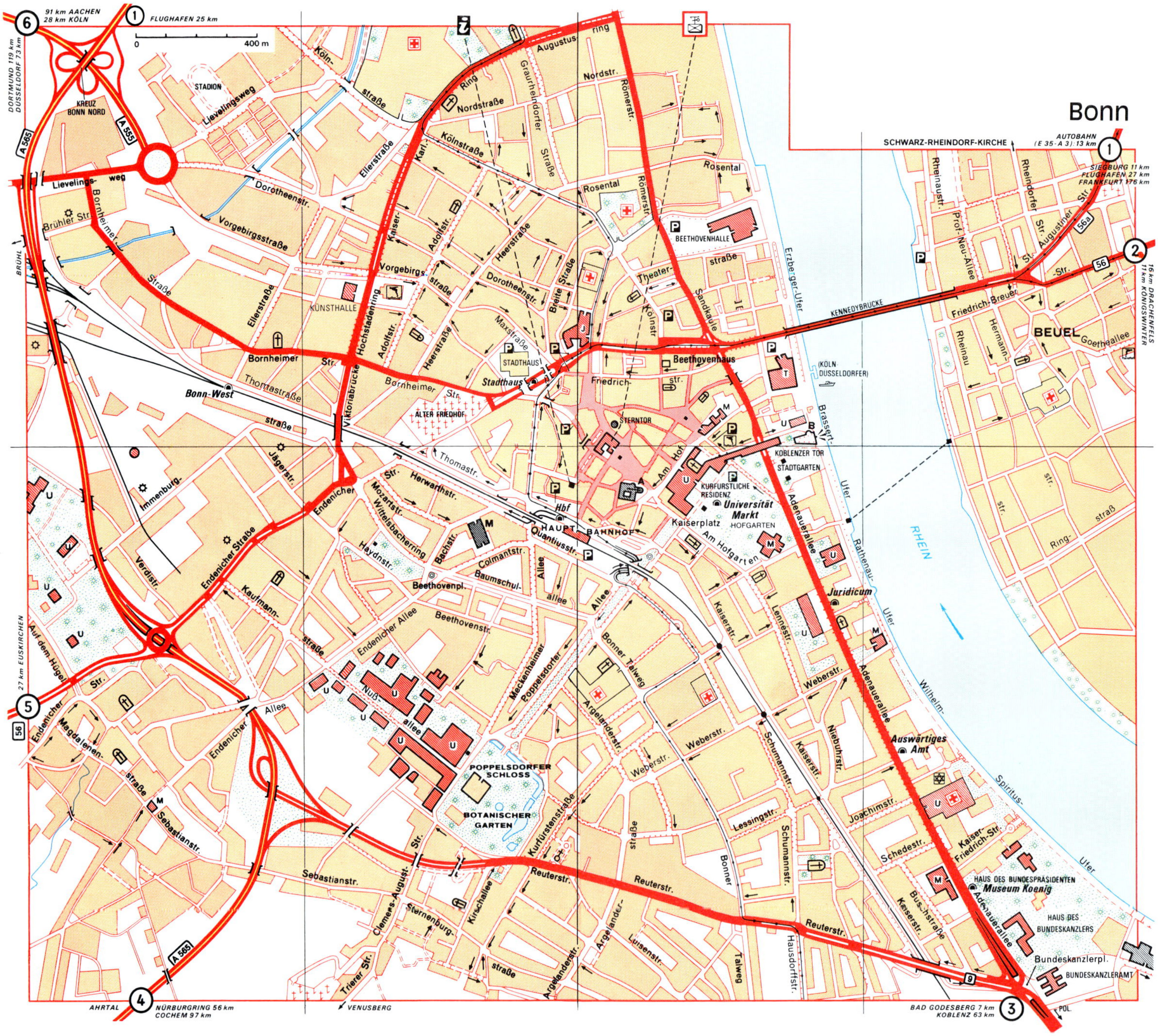
Bonn
91 km AACHEN
28 km KÖLN
FLUGHAFEN 25 km
DORTMUND 119 km
DÜSSELDORF 73 km
KREUZ BONN NORD
STADION
Lievelingsweg
Dorotheenstr.
Vorgebirgsstraße
Brühler Str.
Bornheimer Str.
Ellerstraße
KUNSTHALLE
Hochstadenring
Viktoriabrücke
Kaiser-Karl-Ring
Kölnstraße
Nordstraße
Augustusring
Römerstr.
Rosental
BEETHOVENHALLE
Theaterstr.
Sandkaule
Beethovenhaus
Friedrichstr.
STADTHAUS
Stadthaus
ALTER FRIEDHOF
Bonn-West
Thomastraße
Immenburgstr.
Endenicher Straße
Herwarthstr.
Quantiusstr.
HAUPTBAHNHOF
Hbf
STERNTOR
KOBLENZER TOR
STADTGARTEN
KURFÜRSTLICHE RESIDENZ
Universität
Markt
HOFGARTEN
Kaiserplatz
Am Hofgarten
Adenauerallee
Juridicum
Beethovenpl.
Poppelsdorfer Allee
Meckenheimer Allee
Nußallee
POPPELSDORFER SCHLOSS
BOTANISCHER GARTEN
Auswärtiges Amt
HAUS DES BUNDESPRÄSIDENTEN
Museum Koenig
HAUS DES BUNDESKANZLERS
Bundeskanzlerpl.
BUNDESKANZLERAMT
Reuterstr.
Sebastianstr.
Kaufmannstraße
Verdistr.
RHEIN
Erzberger-Ufer
Brassert-Ufer
KENNEDYBRÜCKE
SCHWARZ-RHEINDORF-KIRCHE
AUTOBAHN (E 35 - A 3) 13 km
SIEGBURG 11 km
FLUGHAFEN 27 km
FRANKFURT 176 km
BEUEL
Friedrich-Breuer-Str.
Goetheallee
16 km DRACHENFELS
11 km KÖNIGSWINTER
27 km EUSKIRCHEN
AHRTAL
NÜRBURGRING 56 km
COCHEM 97 km
VENUSBERG
BAD GODESBERG 7 km
KOBLENZ 63 km
POL

Boitzenburg	49	E3
Bóixols	37	F3
Boizenburg	48	B3
Bojana	76	B3
Bøjden	108	B4
Bojnik	77	D1
Boka Kotorska	76	A3
Bøkfjorden	95	F2
Bokn	104	A3
Boknafjorden	104	A3
Bol	75	E2
Bøla	101	D1
Bolbec	19	D3
Bolchov	111	F3
Bolera, Emb de la	44	B2
Bolesławiec	112	A2
Boleszkowice	49	E3
Bolgrad	113	E4
Boliden	98	B4
Boliqueime	42	B2
Boljanići	76	B1
Boljevac	73	E4
Boljevci	72	C3
Boljkovci	73	D4
Boljuni	75	F2
Bolkesjø	104	C3
Bollebygd	108	C1
Bollène	30	B3
Bollnäs	101	F4
Bollstabruk	101	F2
Bollullos de la Mitación	43	D2
Bollullos par del Condado	42	C2
Bolmen	109	D2
Bolnâos de Calatrava	40	A4
Bologna	60	C2
Bologne	26	C1
Bologoje	111	E1
Bolos	40	B4
Bolotana	66	B2
Bolsena	63	D1
Bolsena, L di	63	D2
Bolsward	16	C1
Boltaña	37	E2
Boltenhagen	48	B2
Bolton	6	C2
Bolungarvik	96	A1
Bolus Head	14	A4
Bolzano	59	D3
Bombarral	38	A3
Bomenzien	48	C3
Bom Jesus	34	A4
Bømlo	104	A3
Bonaigua, Pto de la	37	F2
Boñar	35	E2
Bonar Bridge	2	C3
Bonares	42	C2
Bonassola	60	B3
Bondeno	60	C2
Bondone, Mte	58	C3
Bonefro	64	B2
Bo'-Ness	5	D2
Bonete	45	D1
Bonette, Col de la	31	D3
Bonhomme, Col du	27	E1
Bonifacio	33	F4
Bonn	51	E3
Bonnåsjøen	97	F1
Bonnat	25	E4
Bonndorf	54	C4
Bonnétable	23	F3
Bonneuil-Matours	25	D3
Bonneval (Eure-et-Loir)	25	E1
Bonneval (Savoie)	31	E1
Bonneville	27	D4
Bonneville, la	19	E4
Bonnières	19	E3
Bonnieux	30	C3
Bono	66	B2
Bonorva	66	B2
Bønsnes	104	C3
Boo	106	B4
Boom	50	B3
Boos	19	E3
Bootle	6	B2
Bopfingen	55	E2
Boppard	51	E4
Bor (CS)	53	E4
Bor (YU)	73	E3
Boračko jez	75	F1
Borås	108	C1
Borba	38	C4
Borbollón, Emb de	39	D2
Borbona	63	F1
Borča	72	C3
Borci	75	F1
Bordeaux	28	B2
Bordeira	42	A2
Bordères-Louron	37	E2
Border Forest Park, The	5	D3
Borders Region	5	D3
Bordesholm	48	A2
Bordighera	31	E3
Borðoy	96	A3
Bore	60	B2
Borello	61	D3
Borensberg	105	F4
Boréon, le	31	E3
Borga	107	F2
Borgafjäll	97	E4
Borga-fjällen	97	E4
Borgarnes	96	A2
Børgefjell	97	E3
Børgefjellet	97	E3
Borger	17	D1
Börger	17	E1
Borghetto	63	E2
Borghetto S.S.	31	F3
Borgholm	109	E2
Borgholzhausen	17	F2
Borghorst	17	E2
Borgia	67	F3
Borgomanero	58	A4
Borgone	31	E1
Borgonovo Val Tidone	60	B2
Borgorose	63	F2
Borgo San Dalmazzo	31	E2
Borgo San Lorenzo	61	D3
Borgosesia	58	A4
Borgo Tufico	61	E4
Borgo Val di Taro	60	B3
Borgo Valsugana	59	D3
Borgsjö	101	F3
Borgund	104	B1
Borgvattnet	101	F2
Boričje	76	B2
Borisov	111	D4
Borispol'	113	E2
Borja (E)	36	C3
Borja (YU)	71	E4
Borken	17	E3
Borkenes	94	A3
Børkop	108	B3
Borkum	47	D3
Borlänge	105	F2
Bormes-les-Mimosas	31	D4
Bormida	60	A2
Bormio	58	C3
Born	48	C1
Borna	53	D2
Bornes	34	C4
Bornes, Sa de	34	C4
Bornholm	109	D4
Bornhöved	48	B2
Börnicke	49	D4
Bornos	43	D3
Bornos, Emb de	43	D3
Boroughbridge	7	D1
Borovec	115	D3
Boroviči	111	E1
Borovnica	70	B2
Borovo	72	B2
Borovsk	111	F2
Borre	104	C3
Borriol	41	E3
Borris	15	D3
Borrisokane	12	C4
Borşa	113	D3
Børselv	95	E1
Børselva	95	E2
Børselvfjellet	95	E2
Bórsio	86	B1
Bort-les-Orgues	29	E1
Börtnan	101	E2
Borzna	113	F1
Borzonasca	60	A3
Bosa	66	A2
Bosanci	70	C3
Bosanska Dubica	71	D3
Bosanska Gradiška	71	E3
Bosanska Kostajnica	71	D3
Bosanska Krupa	71	D3
Bosanska Rača	72	B3
Bosanski Brod	71	E3

Bosanski Kobaš 71 E3
Bosanski Novi 71 D3
Bosanski Petrovac 71 D4
Bosanski Šamac 71 F3
Bosansko Grahovo 71 D4
Bosansko Petrovo Selo 71 F3
Bosco 61 E4
Bosco Chiesanuova 59 D4
Bosilegrad 77 E2
Bosiljevo 70 C3
Bosjökloster 109 D3
Boskoop 16 C3
Bosna 71 F4
Bosna i Hercegovina 71 E4
Bošnjace 77 E1
Bošnjaci 72 B3
Bossòst 37 F2
Bostan 75 E2
Boštanj 70 B2
Boston 7 E3
Bosut 72 B2
Botev 115 D2
Botevgrad 115 D2
Bothel 5 D4
Boticas 34 B4
Botley 9 E3
Botngård 100 C
Botnie, G de 102 A3
Botoš 72 C2
Botoşani 113 D3
Botrange 51 D4
Botsmark 102 A1
Botte Donato, Mte 67 F2
Bottenhavet 102 A3
Bottniska Viken Pohjanlahti 102 A3
Bottrop 17 E3
Botun 77 D4
Bouaye 24 B2
Boucau 28 A4
Bouchain 20 A2
Bouches-du-Rhône 30 B4
Boudry 27 E2
Bouillon 20 C2
Bouilly 26 B1
Boúka 86 C3
Boulay-Moselle 21 D3
Boulogne (Haute-Garonne) 37 F1
Boulogne (Pas-de-Calais) 19 E1
Boulogne R 24 B3
Bouloire 23 F3
Boulou, le 32 B2
Boumort 37 F3
Bourbon-Lancy 26 B3
Bourbon-l'Archambault 26 A3
Bourbonne-les-Bains 27 D1
Bourboule, la 29 E1
Bourbourg 19 F1
Bourbriac 22 C2
Bourdeaux 30 C2
Bourdeilles 28 C1
Bourg 28 B2
Bourg-Achard 19 D3
Bourganeuf 25 E4
Bourg-Argental 30 B1
Bourg-de-Péage 30 C2
Bourg-de-Visa 28 C3
Bourg-d'Oisans, le 31 D2
Bourg-en-Bresse 26 C4
Bourges 25 F3
Bourget, le 30 C1
Bourg-Lastic 29 E1
Bourg-Madame 32 A3
Bourgneuf-en-Retz 24 B3
Bourgogne 26 C2
Bourgoin-Jallieu 30 C1
Bourg-St-Andéol 30 B3
Bourg-St-Maurice 31 D1
Bourgtheroulde 19 D3
Bourgueil 25 D2
Bourmont 26 C1
Bourne 7 D3
Bourne, Gges de la 30 C2
Bournemouth 9 E3
Bourniá, Akr 87 E3
Bousquet-d'Orb, le 30 A4
Boussac 25 F4
Boussens 37 F1
Boutonne 24 C4
Bouxwiller 21 E3
Bouzonville 21 D3
Bovalino Marina 67 F4
Bova Marina 67 E4
Bovan 73 E4
Bovec 70 A2
Bóveda 34 B2
Bøverdal 100 B3
Boves 19 F2
Boves 31 E3
Bovey Tracy 8 C3
Bovolone 60 C1
Bowes 5 E4
Bowness 6 B1
Bowness-on-Solway 5 D3
Boxholm 109 E1
Boxmeer 17 D3
Boxtel 16 C3
Boyle 12 C2
Boyne 13 D3
Božaj 76 B3
Božava 74 C1
Bozdoğan 115 F4
Bozel 31 D1
Bozen 59 D3
Božica 77 E2
Boži Dar 53 E3
Bozouls 29 E3
Bozüyük 115 F3
Bozzolo 60 C2
Bra 31 F2
Brabant 50 B3
Brač 75 E2
Bracadale 2 B3
Bracadale, L 2 B3
Bracciano 63 E2
Bracciano, L di 63 E2
Bracco, Pso del 60 B3
Bračevci 71 F2
Bracieux 25 E2
Bräcke 101 E2
Brackenheim 55 D2
Brackley 9 E2
Bracknell 9 F2
Brackwede 17 F3
Brad 112 C4
Bradano 65 D4
Bradashesh 76 C4
Bradford 6 C2
Bradford-on-Avon 9 D2
Bradina 75 F1
Brading 9 E3
Bradwell-on-Sea 11 D2
Braemar 3 D4
Braga 34 A4
Bragança 34 C3
Braguia, Pto de 35 F2
Braies, L di 59 D2
Brăila 113 E4
Braine 20 A3
Braine-le-Comte 50 B4
Braintree 11 D2
Brake 47 F3
Brakel 52 A2
Bräkne-Hoby 109 D3
Brallo di Pregola 60 A2
Brálos 83 E3
Bramming 108 A3
Brampton 5 D3
Bramsche 17 E2
Brancaleone 67 E4
Brancion 26 C3
Brand 58 B2
Brandbu 105 D2
Brande 108 A3
Brandenburg 49 D4
Brandenburg (Land) 49 D3
Brand-Erbisdorf 53 E3
Brander, Pass of 4 B1
Brandis 53 D2
Brändö 107 D2
Brandon 11 D1
Brandon Head 14 A3
Brandon Mt 14 A3
Brandýs Stará Boleslav 53 F3
Braničevo 73 E3

Bordeaux

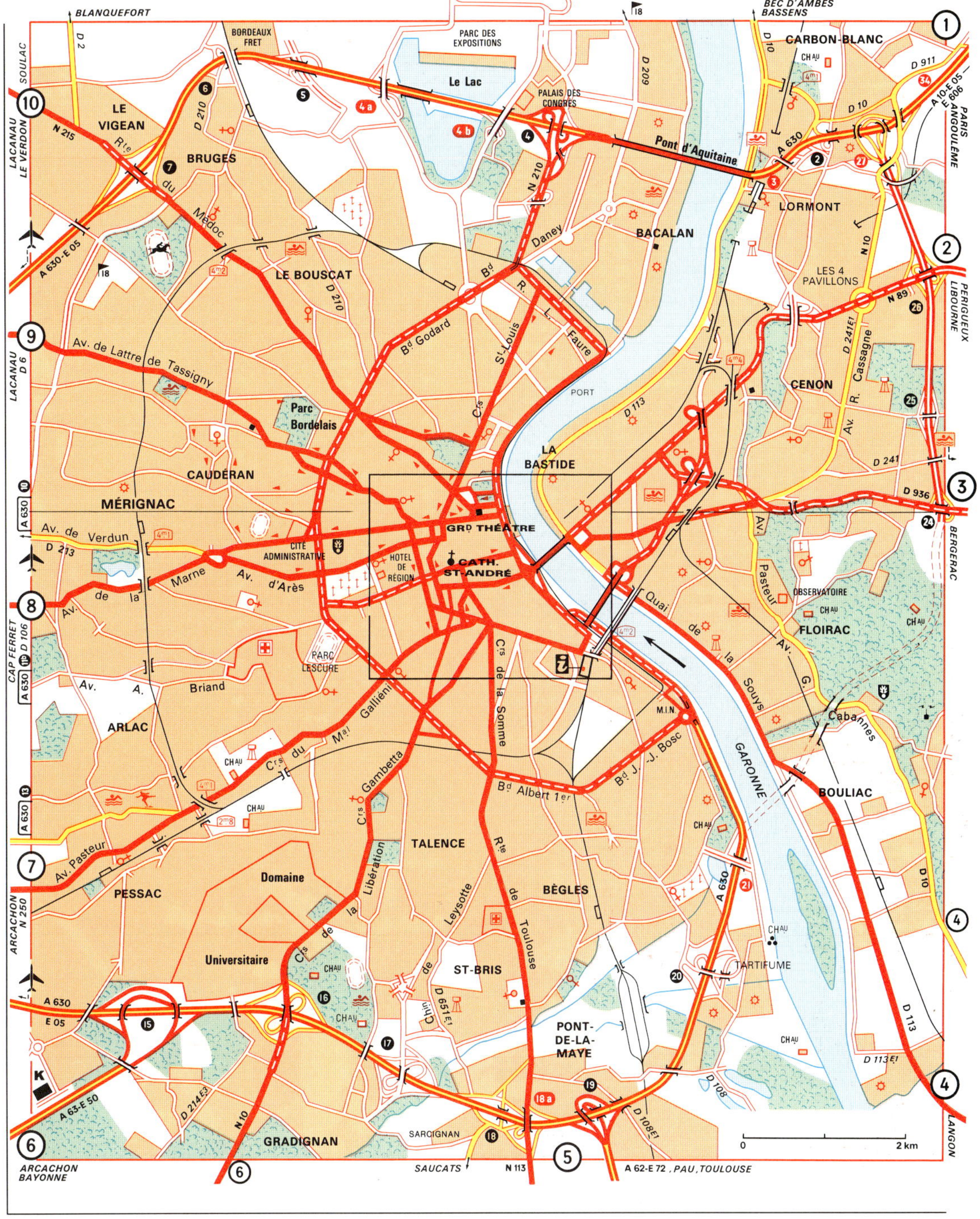
BLANQUEFORT
BEC D'AMBES BASSENS
CARBON-BLANC
LE VIGEAN
BRUGES
Le Lac
PALAIS DES CONGRES
PARC DES EXPOSITIONS
BORDEAUX FRET
Pont d'Aquitaine
LORMONT
BACALAN
LE BOUSCAT
LES 4 PAVILLONS
CENON
Parc Bordelais
CAUDÉRAN
LA BASTIDE
MÉRIGNAC
GRD THÉÂTRE
CATH. ST ANDRÉ
CITE ADMINISTRATIVE
HOTEL DE REGION
PARC LESCURE
FLOIRAC
ARLAC
GARONNE
BOULIAC
TALENCE
PESSAC
Domaine Universitaire
BÈGLES
ST-BRIS
PONT-DE-LA-MAYE
GRADIGNAN
SARCIGNAN
TARTIFUME
ARCACHON BAYONNE
SAUCATS
A 62-E 72, PAU, TOULOUSE
LANGON
BERGERAC
PERIGUEUX LIBOURNE
PARIS ANGOULEME
LACANAU LE VERDON
SOULAC
CAP FERRET
0 2 km

Braniewo 110 B4
Branne 28 B2
Braño Caballo 35 D2
Brañosera 35 F2
Br'ansk 111 E4
Brantôme 28 C1
Braskereidfoss 105 D2
Braslav 111 D3
Brasov 113 D4
Brassac-les-Mines 29 F1
Brasschaat 50 B3
Bratislava 112 A3
Brattvåg 100 A2
Bratunac 72 B4
Braubach 51 E4
Braunau 56 C3
Braunfels 51 F4
Braunlage 52 B2
Braunsbedra 53 D2
Braunschweig 52 B1
Braunton 8 C3
Braus, Col de 31 E3
Bravães 34 A3
Bravuogn 58 B3
Bray (IRL) 13 E4
Bray (Seine-et-Marne) 20 A4
Bray (Somme) 19 F2
Bray-Dunes 19 F1
Brazatortas 43 F1
Brbinj 74 C1
Brčko 72 B3
Brda 110 A4
Brđani 73 D4
Brea 36 C4
Brécey 18 B4
Brechin 3 E4
Brecht 50 C3
Břeclav 57 F1
Brecon 8 C1
Brecon Beacons Nat Pk 8 C2
Breda (E) 32 B4
Breda (NL) 16 C3
Bredbyn 102 A2
Bredelar 17 F3
Bredstedt 47 F1
Bree 50 C3
Bregalnica 77 F3
Breganze 59 D4
Bregenz 58 B1
Bréhal 18 B4
Bréhat, I de 22 C2
Breiðafjörður 96 A2
Breil-sur-Roya 31 E3
Breisach 54 B4
Breitengüßbach 52 C4
Breitungen 52 B3
Breivikbotn 95 D1
Breivikeidet 94 C2
Brekke 104 A1
Brekken 101 D2
Brekkvasselv 97 D4
Brekstad 100 C1
Bremanger Landet 100 A3
Bremen 47 F3
Bremerhaven 47 F3
Bremervörde 47 F3
Bremsnes 100 B2
Breña, Emb de la 43 E2
Brenes 43 D2
Brenna 53 D2
Brenner 59 D2
Brennilis 22 B3
Breno 58 C4
Brénod 26 C4
Brentwood 10 C2
Brescia 60 B1
Breskens 16 B4
Bresle 19 E2
Bresles 19 F3
Bressanone 59 D2
Bressay 3 F2
Bresse, la 27 E1
Bressuire 24 C3
Brest (F) 22 A2
Brest (SU) 112 C1
Brest R 23 D4
Brestanica 70 C2
Brestova 70 B3
Brestovac (Hrvatska) 71 E2
Brestovac (Srbija) 73 E3
Brestovac (Srbija) 77 D1
Brestovac (Srbija) 77 E1
Brestovačka Banja 73 E3
Bretenoux 29 D2
Breteuil (Eure) 19 D4
Breteuil (Oise) 19 F3
Bretten 54 C2
Breuil-Cervinia 27 F4
Brevik 104 C4
Breza 71 F4
Brežđe 72 C4
Brežice 70 C2
Breznica 70 C2
Breznica Đakovačka 71 F2
Březnice 56 C1
Brezno 112 B3
Brezolles 19 E4
Brezovica 77 D2
Brezovo Polje (Bosna i Hercegovina) 72 B3
Brezovo Polje (Hrvatska) 71 E2
Briançon 31 D2
Briare 26 A2
Bribirske Mostine 75 D1
Bricquebec 18 B3
Brides 31 D1
Bridgend (Scotland) 4 A2
Bridgend (Wales) 8 C2
Bridge of Allan 4 C2
Bridgnorth 9 D1
Bridgwater 9 D3
Bridlington 7 E1
Bridport 9 D3
Briec 22 B3
Brie-Comte-Robert 19 F4
Brielle 16 B3
Brienne-le-Château 20 B4
Brienon 26 A1
Brienz 27 F3
Brienza 64 C4
Briey 21 D3

Brig 27 F3
Brigg 7 D2
Brighouse 6 C2
Brightlingsea 11 D2
Brighton 10 C3
Brignogan 22 A2
Brignoles 31 D4
Brihuega 40 B2
Briksdal 100 A3
Brilon 17 F3
Brimnes 104 B2
Brinches 42 B1
Brindisi 65 F3
Brinon 26 A2
Brioni 70 A4
Brionne 19 D3
Brioude 29 F1
Brioux 24 C4
Briouze 18 C4
Brisighella 61 D3
Brissac-Quincé 24 C2
Brissago 58 A3
Bristol 9 D2
Bristol Chan 8 C2
Brive-la-Gaillarde 29 D2
Briviesca 36 A2
Brixen 59 D2
Brixham 8 C4
Brixlegg 59 D1
Brjánslækur 96 A1
Brka 72 B3
Brna 75 E2
Brnaze 75 D1
Brno 57 F1
Bro (Gotlands Län) 109 F4
Bro (Stockholms Län) 106 B3
Broad B 2 B2
Broadford (GB) 2 B3
Broadford (IRL) 12 B4
Broad Haven 12 B2
Broad Law 5 D3
Broadstairs 11 D3
Broadway 9 E1
Broager 108 A4
Broby 109 D3
Brocken 52 B2
Brod (Bosna i Hercegovina) 76 A1
Brod (Makedonija) 77 D3
Brodarevo 76 B1
Brodica 73 E3
Brodick 4 B2
Brod na Kupi 70 B3
Brodnica 112 B1
Brody (PL) 53 F1
Brody (SU) 113 D2
Broglie 19 D3
Brohl-Lützing 51 E4
Brolo 69 D2
Bromarv 107 D3
Brombachsee 55 E2
Brome 48 B4
Bromölla 109 D3
Bromsgrove 9 E1
Bromyard 9 D1
Bronchales 41 D2
Brønderslev 108 B2
Broni 60 A2
Brønnøysund 97 D3
Brøns 108 A3
Bronte 69 D3
Bronzani Majdan 71 D3
Broom, L 2 C2
Broons 22 C3
Brora 3 D3
Brösarp 109 D3
Brossac 28 B1
Brøstadbotn 94 B3
Brotas 38 B4
Broto 37 E2
Brotton 5 F4
Brøttum 105 D2
Brou (Ain) 26 C4
Brou (Eure-et-Loir) 25 E1
Brouage 24 B4
Brough 5 E4
Brough Head 3 D1
Broughshane 13 E1
Broughton-in-Furness 6 B1
Brouis, Col de 31 E3
Brovst 108 B2
Brownhills 9 E1
Brozas 39 D3
Bruay-en-Artois 19 F1
Bruay-sur-l'Escaut 20 A1
Bruchsal 54 C2
Brück 53 D1
Bruck (D) 56 B1
Bruck (Niederösterreich) 57 F2
Bruck (Salzburg) 59 E1
Bruck an der Mur 57 E4
Brückl 70 B1
Bruckmühl 56 B3
Brüel 48 C2
Bruès 34 B2
Bruges 50 A3
Brugg 27 F2
Brügge 17 E4
Brugge 50 A3
Brühl 17 E4
Brújula, Pto de la 36 A2
Bruksvallarna 101 D2
Brûlon 23 E3
Brumath 21 E4
Brummen 17 D3
Brumunddal 105 D2
Bruneck 59 D2
Brunete 40 A2
Brunflo 101 E2
Brunico 59 D2
Brünigpass 27 F3
Bruniquel 29 D3
Brunkeberg 104 B3
Brunnen 58 A2
Brunsbüttel 47 F2
Brunssum 17 D4
Bruntál 112 A3
Bruravik 104 B2
Brus 77 D1
Brusand 104 A4
Brušane 70 C4
Brusasco 31 F1
Brusnik 73 F3
Brussel 50 B3
Brusson 27 F4
Brüssow 49 E2
Bruton 9 D3
Bruvno 70 C4
Bruxelles 50 B3
Bruyères 27 D1
Brvenik 76 C1
Bryne 104 A4
Brynmawr 9 D2
Brzan 73 D3
Brza Palanka 73 F3
Brzeće 77 D1
Brzeg 112 A2
Buarcos 38 B2
Buavåg 104 A3
Bubry 22 C3
Bučač 113 D3
Buçaco 38 B2
Buccheri 69 D4
Bucchianico 64 A2
Bucelas 38 A4
Buchan Ness 3 E3
Büchen 48 B3
Buchen 55 D1
Buchenwald 52 C3
Buchholz 48 A3
Buchloe 55 E3
Buchs 58 B2
Buchy 19 E3
Bucine 61 D4
Bučje 73 F4
Bückeburg 52 A1
Buckfastleigh 8 C4
Buckhaven 5 D2
Buckie 3 D3
Buckingham 9 F2
Buckinghamshire 9 F2
Buckovička Banja 73 D3
Buckow 49 E4
Bückwitz 49 D3
Bučovice 57 F1
Bucovina 113 D3
Bucureşti 115 D1
Bud 100 B2
Budapest 112 B4
Búðardalur 96 A2
Buddon Ness 5 D1
Buddusò 66 B2
Bude 8 B3
Büdelsdorf 48 A2
Budimlić Japra 71 D3
Büdingen 52 A4
Budinšćina 70 C2
Budleigh Salterton 8 C3
Budrio 61 D2
Budva 76 B3
Budyně nad Ohře 53 F3
Buenache de Alarcón 40 C3
Buen Amor 39 E1
Buenavista de Valdavia 35 E3
Buendia 40 C2
Buendia, Emb de 40 C2
Buet, Mt 27 E4
Bueu 34 A2
Bug 112 C1
Bugeat 29 D1
Bugojno 71 E4
Bugøynes 95 F2
Bugue, le 28 C2
Bühl 54 C3
Builth Wells 9 D1
Buin, Piz 58 B2
Buis-les-Baronnies 30 C3

Brugge

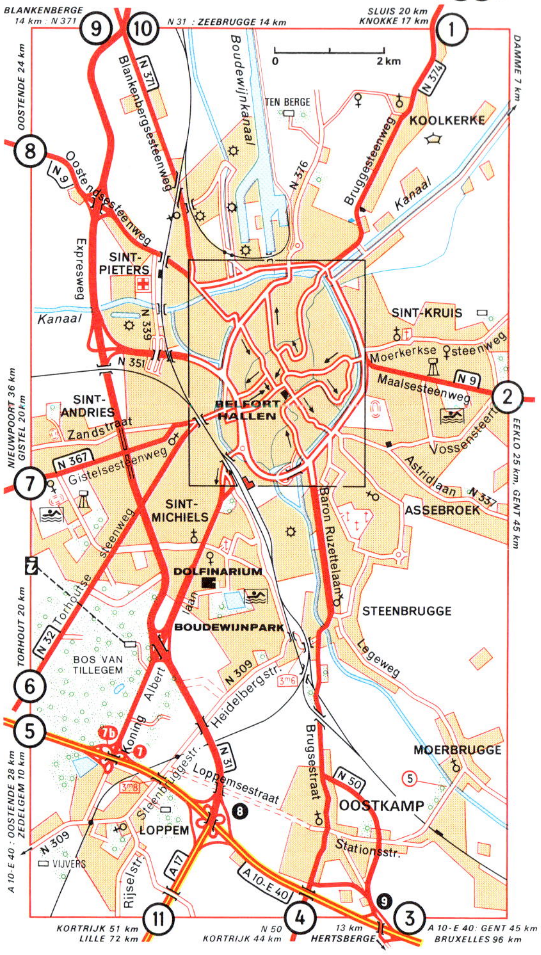
BLANKENBERGE 14 km : N 371
N 31 : ZEEBRUGGE 14 km
SLUIS 20 km
KNOKKE 17 km
DAMME 7 km
OOSTENDE 24 km
0
2 km
TEN BERGE
KOOLKERKE
Kanaal
Boudewijnkanaal
Blankenbergsesteenweg
Oostendsesteenweg
Brugsesteenweg
Expresweg
SINT-PIETERS
SINT-KRUIS
Moerkerkse steenweg
Maalsesteenweg
BELFORT HALLEN
NIEUWPOORT 36 km
GISTEL 20 km
SINT-ANDRIES
Zandstraat
Gistelsesteenweg
Vossensteert
Astridlaan
ASSEBROEK
EEKLO 25 km, GENT 45 km
SINT-MICHIELS
Torhoutse steenweg
Baron Ruzettelaan
DOLFINARIUM
BOUDEWIJNPARK
STEENBRUGGE
TORHOUT 20 km
BOS VAN TILLEGEM
Legeweg
Heidelbergstr.
Koning Albert
MOERBRUGGE
A 10 - E 40 : OOSTENDE 28 km
ZEDELGEM 10 km
Loppemsestraat
Brugsestraat
OOSTKAMP
LOPPEM
Stationsstr.
VIJVERS
Rijselstr.
KORTRIJK 51 km
LILLE 72 km
N 50
KORTRIJK 44 km
13 km
HERTSBERGE
A 10 - E 40 : GENT 45 km
BRUXELLES 96 km

Esztergom
Vác
Košice, Miskolc
Hatvan, Košice
M 3
Békásmegyer
Káposztásmegyer
DUNA
MOGYORÓD
PILISVÖRÖSVÁR
ÚJPEST
ÜRÖM
Rákospalota
CSÖMÖR
KEREPESTARCSA
SOLYMÁR
Arany-hegyi-p.
RÓMAIFÜRDŐ
Dorog, Komárom
Harmashatár-hegy
495
Óbudai-sz
Nagytarcsa
Pesthidegkút
ÓBUDA
ANGYALFÖLD
ÚJPALOTA
Rákosszentmihály
Cinkota
Margit-sz
Sashalom
Mátyasföld
ZUGLÓ
RÁKOSLIGET
PÉCEL
BUDAKESZI
Városliget
Népstadion
Rákos Patak
János-hegy
527
PARLAMENT
Hungexpo
Rákoscsaba
BUDAPEST
Rákoskeresztúr
Jászberény
MÚZEUM
KŐBÁNYA
Rákoskert
Budai-Hegység
KONGRESS PALAST
ZITADELLE
Nepliget
Rákoshegy
Ecser
Ferencváros
SASAD
FERIHEGY 1
FERIHEGY 2
KIPEST
PESTLŐRINC
BUDAÖRS
KELENFÖLD
Ráckevei (Soroksári) Duna
Győr, Wien
M 1
VECSÉS
PEST-ERZSÉBET
TÖRÖKBÁLINT
Anna-hegy
267
Tétényi-Fennsík
Budafok
PESTIMRE
CSEPEL
GYÁL
Székesfehérvár
M 7
SOROKSÁR
Budatétény
M 0
M 5
Debrecen, Szolnok
Millenniumtelep
1/200 000
NAGYTÉTÉNY
Pécs, Barcs
Kecskemét
Baja, Kalocsa
Érd
Szeged, Beograd

1/100 000
BRUSSEL
BRUXELLES
Schaerbeek
Schaarbeek
Anderlecht
St.-Agatha-Berchem
Berchem-Ste Agathe
Koekelberg
St.-Jans-Molenbeek
Molenbeek-St Jean
St. Josse-Ten-Noode
St.-Joost-Ten-Node
St. Lambrechts-Woluwe
Woluwe-St Lambert
Woluwe-St Pierre
St.-Pieters-Woluwe
Etterbeek
Ixelles
Elsene
St. Gilles
St.-Gillis
Forest
Vorst
Uccle
Ukkel
Watermael-Boitsfort
Watermaal-Bosvoorde
Auderghem
Oudergem
Evere
Jette
Ganshoren
Dilbeek
Zellik
Wemmel
Strombeek-Bever
Grimbergen
Vilvoorde
(Vilvorde)
Machelen
Diegem
Zaventem
Kortenberg
Steenokkerzeel
Melsbroek
BRUSSEL NATIONAAL
BRUXELLES NATIONAL
Kraainem
Wezembeek-Oppem
Sterrebeek
Tervuren
Overijse
Hoeilaart
Linkebeek
Drogenbos
Beersel
Ruisbroek
St.-Pieters-Leeuw
Lot
Alsemberg
Wolvertem
Meise
Beigem
Sterrebeek
FORÊT DE SOIGNES
ZONIËNWOUD
Merchtem
Londerzeel
St.-Niklaas
Nieuwenrode
Eppegem
Antwerpen
Mechelen
Halle
Mons
Charleroi
Dworp
Braine l'Alleud
St.-Genesius-Rode
Waterloo
Genval
Namur
E 42
4°20
50°50

Buitrago del Lozoya 40 B1
Bujalance 43 F2
Bujanovac 77 E2
Bujaraloz 37 E4
Buje 70 A3
Bujeo, Pto del 43 D4
Bukinje 71 F3
Bukova Gora 75 E1
Bukovi 72 C4
Bukovo 77 D4
Bülach 58 A1
Buldan 115 F4
Bulgnéville 27 D1
Bullas 44 C2
Bulle 27 E3
Büllingen 51 D4
Bully 19 F1
Bultei 66 B2
Buna 75 F2
Bunclody 15 D3
Buncrana 13 D1
Bünde 17 F2
Bunde 47 E3
Bun Dobhráin 12 C2
Bundoran 12 C2
Bunë 76 B3
Bunessan 4 B1
Bungay 11 D1
Bunić 70 C4
Bunmahon 14 C4
Buñol 41 E4
Bunratty Castle 12 B4
Buntingford 9 F2
Buñuel 36 C3
Buonabitacolo 67 D1
Buonalbergo 64 B3
Buonconvento 61 D4
Buonfornello 68 C3
Burbach 51 F3
Burbáguena 41 D1
Burdalo, R 39 E4
Bure 7 F3
Bureå 98 B4
Burela 34 C1
Büren 17 F3
Buren 47 D3
Burfjord 95 D2
Burford 9 E2
Burg (Sachsen-Anhalt) 48 C4
Burg (Schleswig-Holstein) 48 B1
Burgas 115 E2
Burgau 55 E3
Burgbernheim 55 E1

Burgdorf (CH) 27 E2
Burgdorf (D) 48 B4
Bürgel 52 C3
Burgenland 57 F4
Burgess Hill 10 C3
Burggrub 52 C4
Burghasungen 52 A2
Burghausen 56 B3
Burgjoß 52 B4
Burgkunstadt 52 C4
Burglengenfeld 55 F1
Burgohondo 39 F2
Burgos 35 F3
Burgsinn 52 B4
Burgstädt 53 E3
Burg Stargard 49 D2
Burgsvik 109 F4
Burgsviken 109 F4
Burguete 36 C1
Burgui 37 D2
Burguillo, Emb de 39 F2
Burguillos del Cerro 43 D1
Burhaniye 115 E4
Burhave 47 F3
Burie 28 B1
Burjassot 41 E4
Burk 53 F2
Burkau 53 F2
Burnham 9 D3
Burnham-on-Crouch 11 D2
Burnley 6 C2
Burntisland 5 D2
Buronzo 31 F1
Burrel 76 C3
Burriana 41 E3
Burrow Head 4 C4
Burry Port 8 C2
Bursa 115 F3
Burscheid 17 E4
Bürstadt 54 C1
Burton-upon-Trent 6 C3
Burträsk 98 B4
Burwick 3 E1
Bury 6 C2
Buryn' 113 F1
Bury St Edmunds 11 D1
Busalla 60 A3
Busambra, Rca 68 B3
Busca 31 E2
Buševa pl 77 D3
Buševec 70 C2
Bushat 76 C3
Bushmills 13 E1
Buskerud 104 C2
Buško Blato 75 E1
Busko-Zdrój 112 B2
Busovača 71 F4
Bussang 27 E1
Busseto 60 B2
Bussière-Badil 28 C1
Bussolengo 60 C1
Bussum 16 C2
Busto Arsizio 60 A1
Busto de Bureba 36 A2
Büsum 47 F2
Bute 4 B2
Butera 68 C4
Buthrotum 114 C4
Buttermere 5 D4
Buttevant 14 B3
Butt of Lewis 2 B2
Buttstädt 52 C2
Butzbach 51 F4
Bützow 48 C2
Buxtehude 48 A3
Buxton 6 C3
Buxy 26 C3
Buzançais 25 E3
Buzancy 20 C3
Buzău 113 E4
Buzău *R* 113 E4
Buzet 70 A3
Bužim 70 C3
Bychov 111 E4
Bydgoszcz 112 A1
Bygdeå 102 B1
Bygdin 100 B3
Bygdin *L* 100 B3
Bygdsiljum 102 B1
Bygland 104 B4
Byglandsfjord 104 B4
Byglandsfjord *L* 104 B4
Bykle 104 B3
Bykleheiene 104 B3
Bylderup-Bov 108 A4
Byrkjelo 100 A3
Byske 98 B4
Byskeälven 98 B3
Bytom 112 B2
Bytów 110 A4
Byxelkrok 109 E2

C

Cabañaquinta 35 D2
Cabañas 44 B2
Cabanes 41 F3
Cabannes, les 32 A2
Čabar 70 B3
Cabeceiras 34 B4
Cabeço de Vide 38 C3
Cabella Ligure 60 A2
Cabeza del Buey 39 E4
Cabezas Rubias 42 C2
Cabezo Gordo 42 C2
Cabezón 35 E4
Cabezón de la Sal 35 F2
Cabezuela del Valle 39 E2
Cabo de Gata 44 C4
Cabourg 18 C3
Cabra 43 F2
Cabra del Santo Cristo 44 A2
Cabras 66 A3
Cabre, Col de 30 C2
Cabreira, Sa da 34 B4
Cabreiros 34 B1
Cabrejas, Pto de 40 C3
Cabrejas, Sa de 36 A3
Cabréra 36 C4
Cabrera, I de 45 F3
Cabrera, Sa de la 34 C3
Cabrerets 29 D3
Cabriel, R 41 D3
Cabril, Bgem do 38 B2
Cabrillas 39 E1
Cabrito, Pto del 43 D4
Cabuérniga 35 F2
Čabulja 75 E1
Cacabelos 34 C2
Čačak 73 D4
Caccamo 68 B3
Cacela 42 B3
Cáceres 39 D3
Cachafeiro 34 A2
Cachopo 42 B2
Čačinci 71 E2
Cadabo 34 C2
Cadalso de los Vidrios 40 A2
Cadaqués 32 C3
Cadarache 30 C3
Cadaval 38 A3
Čađavica 71 E4
Čadca 112 B3
Cadelbosco di Sopra 60 C2
Cadenabbia 58 B4
Cadena, Pto de la 45 D2
Cadenberge 47 F2
Cadenet 30 C3
Cader Idris 6 A3
Cádiar 44 A3
Cadillac 28 B2
Cadipietra 59 D2
Cadi, Serra del 32 A3
Cádiz 43 D4
Cádiz, B de 43 D4
Cádiz, G de 42 C3
Cadouin 28 C2
Čadyr-Lunga 113 E4
Caen 18 C3
Caerdydd 9 D2
Caerfyrddin 8 C2
Caergybi 6 A2
Caernarfon 6 A3
Caernarfon B 6 A3
Caerphilly 9 D2
Caersws 9 D1
Cafasan 77 D4
Cagli 61 E4
Cagliari 66 B4
Cagliari, G di 66 B4
Čaglin 71 E2
Cagnano Varano 64 C2
Cagnes 31 E3
Caha Mts 14 A4
Caher 14 C3
Cahersiveen 14 A4
Cahore Pt 15 E3
Cahors 29 D3
Caia, Bgem do 38 C4
Caianello 64 A3
Caión 34 A1
Cairn Gorm 3 D4
Cairngorm Mts 3 D4
Cairnryan 4 B3
Cairo Montenotte 31 F2
Caiseal 14 C3
Caisleán an Bharraigh 12 B3
Caistor 7 D2
Caivano 64 B4
Cajarc 29 D3
Čajetina 72 C4
Čajniče 76 B1
Čakor 76 C2
Čakovec 70 C1
Čakovice 53 F3
Çal 115 F4
Calabor 34 C3
Calabria 67 E2
Calaceite 41 F1
Calacuccia 33 F3
Cala d'Or 45 F3
Cala, Emb de la 43 D2
Calaf 37 F3
Calafat 114 C2
Calafell 37 F4
Calafort Ros Láir 15 D4
Cala Gonone 66 C2
Calahonda 44 A4
Calahorra 36 C2
Calais 19 E1
Calamocha 41 D1
Calañas 42 C2
Calanche, les 33 E3
Calanda 41 E1
Calanda, Emb de 41 E2
Calangianus 66 B1
Cala'n Porter 45 F2
Calar Alto 44 B3
Călărași 115 E1
Cala Ratjada 45 F2
Calasetta 66 A4
Calasparra 44 C2
Calatafimi 68 B3
Calatañazor 36 B3
Calatayud 36 C4
Calatorao 36 C4
Calau 53 E1
Calazzo 64 B3
Calbe 52 C1
Calcena 36 C3
Caldaro 59 D3
Caldarola 61 F4
Caldas da Rainha 38 A3
Caldas das Taipas 34 A4
Caldas de Reis 34 A2
Caldas de Vizela 34 A4
Caldeirão, Sa do 42 B2
Caldelas 34 A3
Caldera de Taburiente, Pque Nac de la 42 A4
Calderina 40 A4
Caldes de Boí 37 F2
Caldes de Malavella 32 B3
Caldes de Montbui 32 A4
Caldirola 60 A2
Caledonian Canal 2 C4
Calella (Palamós) 32 C3
Calella (Pinedo de Mar) 32 B4
Calenzana 33 F3
Calera de León 43 D1
Calera y Chozas 39 F3
Caleruega 36 A3
Caletta, la 66 C2
Cálig 41 F2
Călimănești 115 D1
Călimani, M 113 D4
Calitri 64 C3
Calizzano 31 F3
Callac 22 B3
Callan 15 D3
Callander 4 C1
Calla, Pso della 61 D3
Callington 8 C4
Callosa de Ensarría 45 E1
Callosa de Segura 45 D2
Calmazzo 61 E3
Calmbach 54 C2
Calne 9 E2
Calolziocorte 58 B4
Calonge 32 B3
Calpe 45 E1
Caltabellotta 68 B3
Caltagirone 69 D4
Caltanissetta 68 C3
Caltavuturo 68 C3
Caluso 31 E1
Calvados 18 C3
Calvi 33 E3
Calvitero 39 E2
Calvörde 48 C4
Calw 54 C2
Calzada de Calatrava 44 A1
Calzada de Valdunciel 39 E1
Cam 9 F1
Camacho, Pto 44 A3
Camaiore 60 C3
Camaldoli 61 D3
Camaleño 35 E2
Camarasa 37 F3
Camarasa, Emb de 37 F3
Camarat, Cap 31 D4
Camarena 40 A2
Camarès 32 B1
Camaret 22 A3
Camarillas 41 E2
Camarillas, Emb de 44 C1
Camariñas 34 A1
Camarzana 35 D3
Camas 43 D2
Cambados 34 A2
Cambas 38 C2
Camberley 9 F2
Cambil 44 A2
Cambo-les-Bains 28 A4
Camborne 8 B4
Cambrai 20 A2
Cambre 34 B1
Cambremer 19 D3
Cambrian Mts 8 C1
Cambridge 10 C1
Cambridgeshire 10 C1
Cambrils de Mar 37 F4
Camburg 52 C3
Camelford 8 B3
Camerino 61 E4
Camigliatello Silano 67 E2
Caminha 34 A3
Caminomorisco 39 D2
Caminreal 41 D2
Camogli 60 A3
Campagna 64 C4
Campagne-lès-Hesdin 19 E2
Campan 37 E1
Campana 67 F2
Campanario 39 E4
Campania 64 B4
Campaspero 35 F4
Campbeltown 4 B3
Campello 45 E1
Campi Bisenzio 60 C3
Campiglia Marittima 62 C1
Campilhas, Bgem de 42 A1
Campillo de Altobuey 41 D3
Campillo de Aragón 36 C4
Campillo de Arenas 44 A2
Campillo de Llerena 43 D1
Campillos 43 E3
Campione 58 A4
Campi Salentina 65 F4
Campitello M 64 B3
Campli 63 F1
Campo 37 E2
Campobasso 64 B3
Campobello di Licata 68 C4
Campobello di Mazara 68 A3
Campo Carlo Magno 58 C3
Campo de Beisteros 38 B1
Campo de Caso 35 E2
Campo de Criptana 40 B4
Campo di Fiori 58 A4
Campo di Giove 64 A2
Campodonico 61 E4
Campoformido 59 F3
Campogalliano 60 C2
Campo Imperatore 63 F1
Campo Ligure 60 A3
Campo Maior 38 C4
Campomanes 35 D2
Campomarino 64 B2
Campora San Giovanni 67 E3
Camporredondo, Emb de 35 E2
Camporrobles 41 D3
Campos 45 F3
Camposampiero 59 D4
Campos, Canal de 35 E4
Campotosto, L di 63 F1
Campo Tures 59 D2
Camprodon 32 B3
Camucia 61 D4
Camuñas 40 B3
Cañada de Benatanduz 41 E2
Cañadas, Pto 43 D1
Çanakkale 115 E3
Çanakkale Boğazı 115 E3
Canal du Nord 19 F2
Canal du Rhône au Rhin 27 E2
Canales de la Sierra 36 A3
Canals 41 E4
Canal San Bovo 59 D3
Cañamero 39 E3
Canarias, Is 42 B4
Canas de Senhorim 38 C1
Cañaveral 39 D3
Cañaveral de León 43 D2
Cañaveras 40 C2
Canazei 59 D3
Cancale 18 B4
Cancárix 45 D1
Canche 19 E1
Cancon 28 C2
Candanchu 37 D2
Candas 35 D1
Candasnos 37 E4
Candé 23 E4
Candeeiros, Sa dos 38 A3
Candela 64 C3
Candelaria, Sa 39 E2
Candelario 39 E2
Candelaro 64 C2
Candeleda 39 F2
Candes 25 D2
Canelles, Emb de 37 F3
Canelli 31 F2
Canero 35 D1
Canet de Mar 32 B4
Cañete 41 D3
Cañete de las Torres 43 F2
Cañete la Real 43 E3
Canet-Plage 32 B2
Canfranc-Estación 37 D2
Cangas 34 A3
Cangas de Narcea 34 C2
Cangas de Onís 35 E1
Canha 38 B4
Canicattì 68 C4
Canicattini Bagni 69 D4
Canigou, Pic du 32 B2
Cañigral 41 D3
Caniles 44 B3
Canin, M 59 F3
Canino 63 D2
Canis 18 B3
Cañizal 39 E1
Canjáyar 44 B3
Canna 2 B4
Cannero Riviera 58 A4
Cannes 31 E4
Canneto 60 C4
Cannich 2 C3
Cannobio 58 A4
Cannock 9 E1
Canonbie 5 D3
Canosa di Puglia 64 C3
Canourgue, la 29 F3
Cansano 64 A2
Cansiglio 59 E3
Cantabria 35 F2
Cantal (Dépt) 29 E2
Cantal, Mts du 29 E2
Cantalapiedra 39 F1
Cantalejo 40 A1
Cantalpino 39 E1
Cantanhede 38 B2
Cantavieja 41 E2
Čantavir 72 B1
Canterbury 11 D3
Cantillana 43 D2
Cantoira 31 E1
Cantoral 35 E2
Cantoria 44 C3
Cantù 60 A1
Canvey I 11 D2
Cany-Barville 19 D2
Caorle 59 E4
Caorso 60 B2
Capaccio 64 C4
Capaci 68 B3
Capalbio 63 D2
Capannelle, Pso delle 63 F1
Caparde 72 B4
Caparroso 36 C2
Capbreton 28 A4
Cap Corse 33 F2
Cap-d'Agde, le 30 A4
Cap d'Antibes 31 E4
Capdenac-Gare 29 E2
Capel Curig 6 A3
Capelle, la 20 B2
Capendu 32 B2
Capestang 30 A4
Capestrano 64 A2
Capileira 44 A3
Capistrello 63 F2
Čapljina 75 F2
Capmany 32 B3
Cappelle sul Tavo 64 A1
Cappoquin 14 C4
Capracotta 64 A2
Capraia, I di 62 B1
Caprera, I 66 B1
Capri 64 B4
Capriati a Volturno 64 A3
Capri, I di 64 B4
Captieux 28 B3
Capua 64 B3
Capurso 65 D3
Capvern 37 E1
Caracal 115 D2
Caracuel 40 A4
Caragh, L 14 A4
Caraman 29 D4
Caramanico Terme 64 A2
Caramulo 38 B1
Caramulo, Sa do 38 B1
Caransebeș 114 C1
Carantec 22 B2
Caravaca de la Cruz 44 C2
Caravai, Pso di 66 B3
Caravius, M. is 66 B4
Carbajales de Alba 35 D4
Carballiño 34 B2
Carballo 34 A1
Carbayo 35 D2
Carbonara, C 66 C4
Carbonara, Pzo 68 C3
Carbon-Blanc 28 B2
Carboneras 44 C3
Carboneras de Guadazaón 41 D3
Carbonero el Mayor 40 A1
Carbonia 66 B4
Carbonin 59 E2
Carbonne 37 F1
Carcaboso 39 D2
Carcabuey 43 F3
Carcaixent 41 E4
Carcans 28 A2
Carcans-Plage 28 A2
Carcare 31 F2
Carcassonne 32 B1
Carcastillo 36 C2
Carcès 31 D4
Carche 45 D1
Čardak 71 F4
Çardak 115 F4
Cardedeu 32 B4
Cardeña 43 F1
Cardener, R 32 A4
Cardenete 41 D3
Cardiff 9 D2
Cardigan 8 B1
Cardigan B 8 B1
Cardona 32 A3
Carei 112 C3
Carentan 18 B3
Cares, R 35 E2
Carevdar 71 D2
Carev Dvor 77 D4
Cargèse 33 E3
Carhaix-Plouguer 22 B3
Caria 38 C2
Cariati 67 F2
Caričin Grad 77 D1
Carignan 20 C2
Carignano 31 E2
Carina 77 D4
Cariñena 36 C4

Carini 68 B3
Cariño 34 B1
Carinola 64 A3
Carisio 31 F1
Carlet 41 E4
Carling 21 D3
Carlingford 13 E3
Carlingford L 13 E3
Carlisle 5 D3
Carlit, Pic 32 A2
Carloforte 66 A4
Carlow 13 D4
Carlow (Co) 13 D4
Carloway 2 B2
Carluke 4 C2
Carmagnola 31 E2
Carmarthen 8 C2
Carmarthen B 8 B2
Carmaux 29 E3
Carmona 43 E2
Carna 12 A3
Carnac 22 C4
Carnaio, Pso del 61 D3
Carn Ban 2 C4
Carndonagh 13 D1
Carnedd Llewelyn 6 A3
Carn Eige 2 C3
Carneros, Pto de los 39 F4
Carnew 15 D3
Carnforth 6 B1
Carnia 59 F3
Carnia (Reg) 59 E3
Carnlough 13 E1
Carnon 30 B4
Carnota 34 A2
Carnoustie 5 D1
Carnsore Pt 15 D4
Carnwath 5 D2
Caroch 41 D4
Carolles 18 B4
Carovigno 65 E3
Carpaneto Piacentino 60 B2
Carpaţii Meridionali 114 C1
Carpenedolo 60 B1
Carpentras 30 C3
Carpi 60 C2
Carpignano Sesia 58 A4
Carpineti 60 C3
Carpineto Romano 63 F3
Carpinone 64 A3
Carquefou 24 B2
Carqueiranne 31 D4
Carracedelo 34 C2
Carradale 4 B2
Carraig na Siúire 14 C3
Carral 34 B1
Carrantuohill 14 A4
Carranza 36 A1
Carrara 60 B3
Carrascal 41 E2
Carrascosa del Campo 40 C3
Carrascoy 45 D2
Carrasqueta, Pto de la 45 E1
Carrazeda de Ansiães 34 B4
Carrazedo de Montenegro 34 B4
Carrbridge 3 D4
Carregado 38 A3
Carregal do Sal 38 B2
Carreña de Cabrales 35 E1
Carrickfergus 13 E2
Carrickmacross 13 D3
Carrick-on-Shannon 12 C3
Carrick-on-Suir 14 C3
Carrigart 12 C1
Carrio 34 B1
Carrión de Calatrava 40 A4
Carrión de los Condes 35 E3
Carrión, R 35 E3
Carrizo de la Ribera 35 D2
Carro 30 C4
Carrouges 18 C4
Carrù 31 F2
Carry-le-Rouet 30 C4
Carsoli 63 F2
Cartagena 45 D3
Cártama 43 F4
Cartaxo 38 A3
Cartaya 42 C2
Carter Bar 5 D3
Carteret 18 B3
Carvajal 43 F4
Carviçais 39 D1
Carvin 19 F1
Carvoeira 42 A3
Carvoeiro, C 38 A3
Casabermeja 43 F3
Casa Branca (Alentejo) 42 A1
Casa Branca (Ribatejo) 38 B4
Casacalenda 64 B2
Casalarreina 36 B2
Casalbordino 64 B2
Casalbuttano 60 B1
Casal di Principe 64 A4
Casalecchio di Reno 60 C2
Casale Monferrato 31 F1
Casale sul Sile 59 E4
Casalmaggiore 60 B2
Casalpusterlengo 60 B2
Casamassima 65 D3
Casamicciola Terme 64 A4
Casa Nuevas 44 C2
Casarabonela 43 E3
Casarano 65 F4
Casar de Cáceres 39 D3
Casares 43 E4
Casares de las Hurdes 39 D2
Casariche 43 E3
Casarsa 59 E3
Casas de Don Pedro 39 E4
Casas de Fernando Alonso 40 C4
Casas de Juan Núñez 41 D4
Casas del Puerto 45 D1
Casas de Luján 40 B3
Casas de Miravete 39 E3
Casas Ibáñez 41 D4
Casasimarro 40 C4
Casatejada 39 E3
Casavieja 39 F2
Cascais 38 A4
Cascante 36 C3
Cascia 63 E1
Casciana Terme 60 C4
Cascina 60 C4
Casei Gerola 60 A2
Caselle in Pittari 67 D1
Caselle Torinese 31 E1
Caserio del Puente 35 D3
Caserta 64 B3
Casetas 37 D3
Cas-gwent 9 D2
Cashel 14 C3
Casicas del Rio Segura 44 B2
Casillas 39 D2
Casina 60 C2
Casinos 41 E3
Casnewydd 9 D2
Casoio 34 C3
Casola in Lunigiana 60 B3
Casoli 64 A2
Casoria 64 B4
Caspe 37 E4
Cassà de la Selva 32 B3
Cassagnes-Begonhès 29 E3
Cassano allo Ionio 67 E2
Cassano delle Murge 65 D3
Cassel 19 F1
Cassino 64 A3
Cassis 30 C4
Castalla 45 D1
Castanet-Tolosan 29 D4
Castanheira de Pêra 38 B2
Castaños, Pto de los 39 D3
Castasegna 58 B3
Casteggio 60 A2
Castejón 36 C3
Castejón de Monegros 37 E4
Castejón de Sos 37 E2
Castejón de Valdejasa 37 D3
Castelbuono 68 C3
Casteldaccia 68 B3
Casteldelfino 31 E2
Castel del Monte (Abruzzo) 63 F2
Castel del Monte (Puglia) 65 D3
Castel del Rio 61 D3
Castel di Sangro 64 A2
Castelfidardo 61 F4
Castelfiorentino 60 C4
Castelfranco Emilia 60 C2
Castelfranco in Miscano 64 B3
Castelfranco Veneto 59 D4
Castel Gandolfo 63 E3
Casteljaloux 28 B3
Castellabate 67 D1
Castellamare di Stabbia 64 B4
Castellammare d. Golfo 48 B3
Castellammare, G di 68 B3
Castellamonte 31 E1
Castellana Grotte 65 E3
Castellane 31 D3
Castellaneta 65 E4
Castellar de la Muela 41 D2
Castellar del Vallès 32 A4
Castellar de Santiago 44 B1
Castellar de Santisteban 44 B2
Castell' Arquato 60 B2
Castelldans 37 F4
Castelldefels 32 A4
Castell de Ferro 44 A4
Castelleone 60 B1
Castellfollit de la Roca 32 B3
Castellina in Chianti 61 D4
Castell-nedd 8 C2
Castelló de la Plana 41 F3
Castello del Lago 64 B3
Castelló d'Empúries 32 B3
Castelloli 32 A4
Castellón de la Plana 41 F3
Castellón de Rugat 45 E1
Castellote 41 E2
Castello Tesino 59 D3
Castellterçol 32 A4
Castelluccio 63 F1
Castel Madama 63 F2
Castelmassa 60 C2
Castelmauro 64 B2
Castelmoron 28 C3
Castelnaudary 32 A1
Castelnau-de-Médoc 28 B2
Castelnau-de-Montmiral 29 D3
Castelnau-Magnoac 37 E1
Castelnau-Montratier 29 D3
Castelnau-Rivière-Basse 28 B4
Castelnovo ne' Monti 60 B3
Castelnuovo Berardenga 61 D4
Castelnuovo Bocca d'Adda 60 B2
Castelnuovo della Daunia 64 B3
Castelnuovo di Garfagnana 60 C3
Castelnuovo di Porto 63 E2
Castelnuovo Scrivia 60 A2
Castelo Branco 38 C2
Castelo de Bode, Bgem do 38 B3
Castelo de Paiva 34 A4
Castelo de Vide 38 C3
Castelraimondo 61 E4
Castelrotto 59 D3
Castel San Giovanni 60 A2
Castel San Lorenzo 64 C4
Castel San Pietro Terme 61 D3
Castelsardo 66 B1
Castelsarrasin 29 D3
Castelserás 41 E1
Casteltermini 68 B3
Castelvecchio Subequo 63 F2
Castelvetrano 68 A3
Castel Volturno 64 A4
Castets 28 A3
Castiadas 66 C4
Castiglioncello 60 C4
Castiglione d'Adda 60 B2
Castiglione dei Pepoli 60 C3
Castiglione del Lago 61 D4
Castiglione della Pescaia 62 C1
Castiglione delle Stiviere 60 C1
Castiglione in Teverina 63 E1
Castiglione Messer Marino 64 B2
Castiglione Olona 60 A1
Castiglion Fiorentino 61 D4
Castilblanco 39 F4
Castilblanco de los Arroyos 43 D2
Castilla, Canal de 35 E4
Castilla-La Mancha 40 A4
Castilla-León 35 F4
Castilla, Mar de 40 C2
Castilleja del Campo 43 D2
Castilléjar 44 B2
Castillejo 39 E1
Castillejo de Martin Viejo 39 D1
Castillo de Loarre 37 D2
Castillo de Locubin 43 F2
Castillon, Bge de 31 D3
Castillon-en-Couserans 37 F2
Castillon-la-Bataille 28 B2
Castillonnès 28 C2
Castillo, Pto del 44 A3
Castillo y Elejabeitia 36 B1
Castilruiz 36 C3
Castions di Strada 59 F3
Castlebar 12 B3
Castlebay 2 A4
Castlebellingham 13 D3
Castleblayney 13 D3
Castlecomer 13 D4
Castledawson 13 D2
Castlederg 13 D2
Castledermot 13 D4
Castle Douglas 4 C3
Castleford 7 D2
Castleisland 14 B3
Castlemaine 14 A3
Castlepollard 13 D3
Castlerea 12 C3
Castlerock 13 D1
Castleton 6 C2
Castletownbere 14 A4
Castletown (I of Man) 6 A1
Castletown (Scotland) 3 D2
Castlewellan 13 E2
Castocalbón 35 D3
Castrejón 39 F1
Castrejón, Emb de 40 A3
Castres 32 B1
Castries 30 B4
Castril 44 B2
Castrillo de la Reina 36 A3
Castrillo de Villavega 35 F3
Castro 34 B2
Castro Caldelas 34 B3
Castrocaro Terme 61 D3
Castrocontrigo 35 D3
Castro Daire 38 C1
Castro del Río 43 F2
Castrogeriz 35 F3
Castro Laboreiro 34 B3
Castro Marim 42 B2
Castromonte 35 E4
Castronuevo 35 D4
Castronuño 35 E4
Castropol 34 C1
Castrop-Rauxel 17 E3
Castroreale 69 D2
Castroreale Terme 69 D2
Castrotierra 35 E3
Castro Urdiales 36 A1
Castroverde 34 C2
Castro Verde 42 B2
Castroverde de Campos 35 E3
Castrovillari 67 E2
Castuera 39 E4
Cataluña 32 A3
Catalunya 37 F3
Catania 69 D3
Catania, G di 69 D3
Catanzaro 67 F3
Catanzaro Lido 67 F3
Catarroja 41 E4
Cateau, le 20 A2
Catelet, le 20 A2
Catenanuova 69 D3
Catež 70 C2
Cathair na Mart 12 B3
Čatići 71 F4
Catignano 64 A2
Catoira 34 A2
Catoute 35 D2
Catral 45 D2
Catria, Mte 61 E4
Cattenom 21 D3
Cattolica 61 E3
Catus 29 D2
Caudebec 19 D3
Caudete 45 D1
Caudiel 41 E3
Caudry 20 A2
Caulnes 23 D3
Caulonia 67 F4
Caumont-l'Eventé 18 C3
Caunes 32 B1
Caussade 29 D3
Čausy 111 E4
Cauterets 37 E2
Cava de' Tirreni 64 B4
Cávado, R 34 A4
Cavaglià 31 F1
Cavaillon 30 C3
Cavalaire 31 D4
Cavalerie, la 29 F3
Cavalese 59 D3
Cavalière 31 D4
Cavan 13 D3
Cavan (Co) 13 D3
Cavarzere 61 D1
Cavazzo 59 E3
Çavdarhisar 115 F4
Cavero, Pto de 36 C4
Cavezzo 60 C2
Cavo 62 C1
Cavo, Mte 63 E3
Cavour 31 E2
Cavtat 76 A3
Caya 38 C4
Cayeux 19 E2
Caylar, le 29 F3
Caylus 29 D3
Cayolle, Col de la 31 E3
Cayres 29 F2
Cazalla de la Sierra 43 D2
Cazals 29 D2
Cazaubon 28 B3
Cazaux 28 A2
Cazères 37 F1
Cazin 70 C3
Čazma 71 D2
Cazorla 44 B2
Cazorla, Sa de 44 B2
Cea 34 B2
Ceanannus Mor 13 D3
Cea, R 35 E3
Ceatharlach 13 D4
Cebolla 39 F3
Cebollera 36 B3
Cebreros 40 A2
Ceccano 63 F3
Cece 112 B4
Cechy 53 F4
Cecina 60 C4
Cecina R 60 C4
Cecita, L di 67 F2
Ceclavín 39 D3
Cedeira 34 B1
Cedillo, Bgem de 38 C3
Cedrillas 41 E2
Cedrino 66 C2
Cedynia 49 E3
Cefalù 68 C3
Cega, R 40 A1
Cegléd 112 B4
Ceglie Messapico 65 E3
Čegrane 77 D3
Cehegín 44 C2
Čehotina 76 A1
Ceira, R 38 C2
Čejč 57 F1
Celákovice 53 F3
Celano 63 F2
Celanova 34 B3
Celavevo 72 B2
Čelebić 75 D1
Čelebići 76 B1
Celemín, Emb de 43 D4
Čelić 72 B3
Čelinac Donji 71 E3
Celje 70 B2
Cella 41 D2
Celle 48 B4
Celle Ligure 60 A3
Celles 24 C4
Čelopeci 77 D3
Celorico 34 B4
Celorico da Beira 38 C1
Čemerna pl 73 D4
Čemernica 71 E4
Čemerno 76 A2
Cenajo, Emb del 44 C1
Cencenighe 59 D3
Cenicero 36 B2
Čenta 72 C2
Centelles 32 B4
Cento 60 C2
Cento Croci, Pso 60 B3
Central Region 4 C1
Centre, Canal du 26 B3
Centuripe 69 D3
Cepagatti 64 A2
Čepin 71 F2
Ceppo 63 F1
Ceprano 63 F3
Cer 72 C3
Čeralije 71 E2
Cerbère 32 C3
Cercal (Alentejo) 42 A1
Cercal (Estremadura) 38 A3
Cercedilla 40 A2
Cerchiara di Calabria 67 E2
Cerchov 56 B1
Cerdedo 34 A2
Cerdeira 39 D2
Cère 29 E2
Cerea 60 C1
Cereda, Pso di 59 D3
Čerepovec 111 F1
Ceres 31 E1
Ceresole Reale 31 E1
Céret 32 B3
Cerezo de Abajo 36 A4
Cerezo de Riotirón 36 A2
Cerignola 64 C3
Cérilly 26 A3
Cerisiers 26 A1
Cerisy-la-Salle 18 B3
Cerizay 24 C3
Čerkassy 113 F2
Cerknica 70 B2
Cerkniško jez 70 B2
Cerkno 70 A2
Cerler 37 E2
Černá 56 C2
Cerna 71 F2
Cernache de Bonjardim 38 B2
Čern'achovsk 110 B4
Cernadilla, Emb de 34 C3
Cernavodă 115 E1
Cernay 27 E1
Černigov 113 E1
Černik 71 E3
Cernobbio 58 B4
Černobyl' 113 E1
Černomorskoje 113 F4
Černovcy 113 D3
Cerreto, Pso del 60 B3
Cerreto Sannita 64 B3
Cerrigydrudion 6 B3
Čerrik 76 C4
Certaldo 60 C4
Certosa di Pavia 60 A2
Cervales 39 E3
Cervaro 64 C3
Cervati, Mte 67 D1
Cervatos 35 F2
Cervatos de la Cueza 35 E3
Červen' 111 D4
Cervera 37 F3
Cervera de la Cañada 36 C4
Cervera del Río Alhama 36 C3
Cervera de Pisuerga 35 F2
Cerveteri 63 E2
Cervia 61 E3
Cervialto, Mte 64 C4
Cervignano del Friuli 59 F3
Cervinara 64 B3
Cervino 27 E4
Cervione 33 F3
Cervo 34 C1
Červonograd 112 C2
Cesana Torinese 31 D2
Cesarica 70 C4
Cesarò 69 D3
Cesena 61 D3
Cesenatico 61 E3
Cēsis 110 C2
Česka Kamenice 53 F2
Česká Lípa 53 F3
České Budějovice 57 D1
České Velenice 57 D2
Český Krumlov 57 D2
Česma 71 D2
Çeşme 115 E4
Cespedosa 39 E2
Cessalto 59 E4
Cetina (E) 36 C4
Cetina R (YU) 75 D1
Cetinje 76 B3
Cetraro 67 E2
Ceuti 45 D2
Ceva 31 F2
Cevedale, Mte 58 C3
Cévennes, Parc Nat des 29 F3
Cevico de la Torre 35 F4
Čevo 76 B2
Ceyrat 29 F1
Ceyzériat 26 C4
Cèze 30 B3
Chabanais 25 D4
Chablis 26 B1
Chabreuil 30 C2
Chabris 25 E2
Chagny 26 C3
Chailland 23 E3
Chaillé 24 B3
Chaise-Dieu, la 29 F1
Chalabre 32 A2
Chalais 28 C1
Chalamont 26 C4
Chalampé 27 E1
Chalindrey 26 C1
Challans 24 B3
Challes 31 D1
Chalonnes 24 C2
Châlons-sur-Marne 20 B3
Chalon-sur-Saône 26 C3

Châlus 28 C1
Cham 56 B1
Chambéry 31 D1
Chambley 21 D3
Chambly 19 F3
Chambon, Bge du 31 D2
Chambon-Feugerol-les, le 30 B1
Chambon-sur-Lac 29 E1
Chambon-sur-Lignon, le 30 B2
Chambon-sur-Voueize 25 F4
Chambord 25 E2
Chambre, la 31 D1
Chamonix 27 E4
Champagnac-de-Belair 28 C1
Champagne-Mouton 25 D4
Champagnole 27 D3
Champdeniers 24 C3
Champeaux 23 D3
Champéry 27 E4
Champex 27 E4
Champlitte 26 C2
Champlon, Bre.de 50 C4
Champoluc 27 F4
Champorcher 31 E1
Champs-sur-Tarentaine 29 E1
Champtoceaux 24 B2
Chamrousse 31 D1
Chamusca 38 B3
Chanac 29 F3
Chanas 30 B1
Chança, R 42 C2
Chantada 34 B2
Chantelle 26 A4
Chantemerle 31 D2
Chantilly 19 F3
Chantonnay 24 B3
Chanza, Emb del 42 B2
Chaource 26 B1
Chapel-en-le-Frith 6 C2
Chapelle-d'Angillon, la 25 F2
Chapelle-de-Guinchay, la 26 C4
Chapelle-en-Valgaudemar, la 31 D2
Chapelle-en-Vercors, la 30 C2
Chapinería 40 A2
Charbonnières 26 C4
Charco Redondo, Emb de 43 D4
Chard 9 D3
Charente 28 B1
Charente (Dépt) 28 C1
Charente-Maritime 24 B4
Charenton-du-Cher 25 F3
Charité, la 26 A2
Charleroi 50 B4
Charlestown 12 B3
Charleville 14 B3
Charleville-Mézières 20 C2
Charlieu 26 B4
Charlottenberg 105 D3
Charly 20 A3
Charmes 21 D4
Charny (Meuse) 20 C3
Charny (Yonne) 26 A1
Charolles 26 B3
Chârost 25 E3
Charquemont 27 E2
Charroux 25 D4
Chartre, la 23 F4
Chartres 19 E4
Châs 38 B1
Chasseneuil 28 C1
Chasseral la Neuveville 27 E2
Chasseron, le 27 D3
Châtaigneraie, la 24 C3
Château-Arnoux 31 D3
Châteaubourg 23 D3
Châteaubriant 23 D4
Château-Chinon 26 B2
Château-de-Bonaguil 29 D2
Château de Ventadour 29 E1
Château d'Oex 27 E3
Château-du-Loir 23 F4
Châteaudun 25 E1
Châteaugiron 23 D3
Château-Gontier 23 E4
Château-Landon 25 F1
Château-la-Vallière 25 D2
Château, le 24 B4
Châteaulin 22 B3
Châteaumeillant 25 F3
Châteauneuf (Charente) 28 B1
Châteauneuf (Ille-et-Vilaine) 18 B4
Châteauneuf de Randon 29 F2
Châteauneuf-du-Faou 22 B3
Châteauneuf-du-Pape 30 B3
Châteauneuf-en-Thymerais 19 E4
Châteauneuf-la-Forêt 29 D1
Châteauneuf-les-Bains 26 A4
Châteauneuf-sur-Cher 25 F3
Châteauneuf-sur-Loire 25 F1
Châteauneuf-sur-Sarthe 23 E4
Châteauponsac 25 E4
Château-Porcien 20 B3
Château-Queyras 31 D2
Château-Regnault 20 C2
Châteaurenard (Loiret) 25 F1
Châteaurenard (Vaucluse) 30 B3
Château-Renault 25 D2
Châteauroux 25 E3
Château-Salins 21 D4
Château-Thierry 20 A3
Châteauvillain 26 C1
Châtel 27 E3
Châtelaillon-Plage 24 B4
Châtelard, le 27 D4
Châtelaudren 22 C2
Châteldon 26 A4
Châtelet 50 C4
Châtelet, le (Cher) 25 F3
Châtelet, le (Seine-et-Marne) 19 F4
Châtelguyon 26 A4
Châtellerault 25 D3
Châtel-Montagne 26 B4
Châtel-St-Denis 27 E3
Châtel-sur-Moselle 21 D4
Châtelus-Malvaleix 25 E4
Châtenois 27 D1
Chatham 11 D2
Châtillon 27 F4
Châtillon-Coligny 26 A1
Châtillon-en-Bazois 26 B2
Châtillon-en-Diois 30 C2
Châtillon-sur-Chalaronne 26 C4
Châtillon-sur-Indre 25 E3
Châtillon-sur-Loire 26 A2
Châtillon-sur-Marne 20 B3
Châtillon-sur-Seine 26 B1
Châtre, la 25 E3
Chatsworth House 6 C3
Chatteris 9 F1
Chaudes-Aigues 29 F2
Chauffailles 26 B4
Chaufour 19 E4
Chaulnes 19 F2
Chaumergy 26 C3
Chaumont-en-Vexin 19 E3
Chaumont (Haute-Marne) 26 C1
Chaumont (Loir-et-Cher) 25 E2
Chauny 20 A2
Chausey, I 18 B4
Chaussin 26 C3
Chauvigny 25 D3
Chaux-de Fonds, la 27 E2
Chaves 34 B3
Chazelles 30 B1
Cheb 53 D4
Cheddar Gorge 9 D3
Chef-Boutonne 24 C4
Cheles 42 C1
Chełm 112 C2
Chełmno 112 A1
Chelmsford 11 D2
Cheltenham 9 E2
Chelva 41 D3
Chemillé 24 C2
Chemin 26 C3
Chemnitz 53 E3
Chénérailles 25 F4
Chenonceaux 25 E2
Chepstow 9 D2
Cher 25 F3
Cher (Dépt) 25 F2
Chera 41 D3
Cherbourg 18 B2
Chéroy 26 A1
Cherson 113 F3
Chert 41 F2
Cheshire 6 C2
Cheshunt 9 F2
Chesne, le 20 C3
Cheste 41 E4
Chester 6 B3
Chesterfield 7 D3
Chester-le-Street 5 E4
Chevagnes 26 A3
Chevillon 20 C4
Cheviot Hills, The 5 E3
Cheviot, The 5 E3
Chèvre, Cap de la 22 A3
Chevreuse 19 E4
Cheylard, le 30 B2
Chèze, la 22 C3
Chiampo 59 D4
Chianciano Terme 63 D1
Chianti 61 D4
Chiaramonte Gulfi 69 D4
Chiaravalle 61 F3
Chiaravalle Centrale 67 F3
Chiari 60 B1
Chiasso 58 A4
Chiavari 60 A3
Chiavenna 58 B3
Chichester 9 F3
Chiclana de la Frontera 43 D4
Chieming 56 B3
Chiemsee 56 B3
Chieri 31 E1
Chiers 20 C3
Chiesa in Valmalenco 58 B3
Chiesina Uzz. 60 C3
Chieti 64 A2
Chiltern Hills 9 F2
Chimay 50 B4
Chimorra 43 E1
Chinchilla de Monte Aragón 41 D4
Chinchón 40 B2
Chinon 25 D2
Chioggia 61 D1
Chioula, Col de 32 A2
Chipiona 42 C3
Chippenham 9 E2
Chipping Campden 9 E1
Chipping Norton 9 E2
Chipping Sodbury 9 D2
Chirivel 44 C2
Chişineu-Criş 112 C4
Chisone 31 E2
Chiusa 59 D2
Chiusa di Pesio 31 E2
Chiusa Sclafani 68 B3
Chiusatorte 59 F3
Chiusi 63 D1
Chiva 41 E4
Chivasso 31 F1
Chlum u Třeboně 57 D1
Chmel'nickij 113 D2
Chmel'nik 113 E2
Chociwel 49 F2
Chodov 53 E4
Chojna 49 E3
Chojnice 110 A4
Chojniki 113 E1
Cholet 24 C3
Chollerford 5 E3
Cholm 111 E2
Chomutov 53 E3
Chorges 31 D2
Chorley 6 C2
Chorol 113 F2
Choszczno 49 F3
Chotin 113 D3
Chouto 38 B3
Chrastava 53 F2
Christchurch 9 E3
Christiansfeld 100 A3
Christiansø 109 D4
Chur 58 B2
Church Stretton 9 D1
Chust 112 C3
Ciamarella 31 E1
Cians, Gorges du 31 E3
Ćićarija 70 A3
Čičavica 77 D2
Cicciano 64 B4
Ćićevac 73 E4
Čičevo 76 A2
Cidacos, R 36 B3
Cidade Nova de Santo André 42 A1
Cidones 36 B3
Ciechanów 112 B1
Ciechocinek 112 B1
Ciempozuelos 40 B2
Cíes, Is 34 A3
Cieszyn 112 B3
Cieza 45 D2
Cifuentes 40 C2
Cigliano 31 F1
Cigüela R 40 B3
Cíjara, Emb de 39 F4
Cijevna 76 B3
Cilavegna 60 A1
Čilipi 76 A3
Cill Airne 14 B4
Cillas 36 C4
Cill Chainnigh 15 D3
Cilleros 39 D2
Cilleruelo de Bezana 35 F2
Cill Mhantáin 13 E4
Cima Brenta 58 C3
Cima d'Asta 59 D3
Cimadolmo 59 E4
Cima Presanella 58 C3
Cimišlija 113 E4
Cimone, Mte 60 C3
Cîmpeni 112 C4
Cîmpina 115 D1
Cîmpulung 115 D1
Cîmpulung Moldovenesc 113 D3
Cinca, R 37 E3
Cincar 75 E1
Cinctorres 41 E2
Ciney 50 C4
Cinfães 34 A4
Cingoli 61 F4
Cinigiano 63 D1
Cinisi 68 B3
Cinovec 53 E3
Cinque Terre 60 B3
Cintegabelle 32 A1
Cinto, M 33 F3
Cintruénigo 36 C3
Ciórraga 36 B1
Ciotat, la 30 C4
Čiovo 75 D2
Cirencester 9 E2
Cirey 21 E4
Ciria 36 C3
Ciriè 31 E1
Cirò 67 F2
Cirò Marina 67 F2
Čirpan 115 D2
Cisa, Pso della 60 B3
Cisneros 35 E3
Čista 74 C1
Cista Provo 75 E1
Cisterna di Latina 63 F3
Cisternino 65 E3
Cistierna 35 E2
Čitluk (Mostar) 75 F2
Čitluk (Posušje) 75 E1
Cittadella 59 D4
Città del Pieve 63 D1
Città di Castello 61 E4
Cittaducale 63 F2
Cittanova 67 E4
Cittareale 63 F1
Città Sant' Angelo 64 A1
Ciudad Encantada 40 C3
Ciudad Real 40 A4
Ciudad Rodrigo 39 D1
Ciutadella de Menorca 45 F1
Cividale del Friuli 59 F3
Civita Castellana 63 E2
Civitanova Marche 61 F4
Civitavecchia 63 D2
Civitella del Tronto 63 F1
Civitella Roveto 63 F2
Civray 25 D4
Çivril 115 F4
Clacton-on-Sea 11 D2
Clain 25 D4
Clairvaux-les-Lacs 27 D3
Clamecy 26 A2
Claonaig 4 B2
Clapham 6 C1
Clara 12 C4
Clare 11 D1
Clare 12 B3
Clare (Co) 12 B4
Clare I 12 A3
Claremorris 12 B3
Claudy 13 D1
Clausthal-Zellerfeld 52 B2
Claut 59 E3
Claviere 31 D2
Clavin, Pto de 39 D3
Clay Cross 6 C3
Claye-Souilly 19 F4
Clayette, la 26 B4
Clear I 14 A4
Clécy 18 C4
Clefmont 26 C1
Cléguérec 22 C3
Clelles 30 C2
Clères 19 E3
Clermont 19 F3
Clermont-en-Argonne 20 C3
Clermont-Ferrand 29 F1
Clermont-l'Hérault 30 A4
Clervaux 21 D2
Cléry 25 E2
Cles 58 C3
Clevedon 9 D2
Cleveland Hills 7 D1
Cleveleys 6 B2
Clew B 12 B3
Clifden 12 A3
Clisham 2 B2
Clisson 24 B2
Clitheroe 6 C2
Cloghan 12 C4
Clogheen 14 C3
Clogherhead 13 E3
Clogher Head 14 A3
Clogh Mills 13 E1
Clonakilty 14 B4
Clonbur 12 B3
Clondalkin 13 D4
Clones 13 D2
Clonfert 12 C4
Clonmacnoise 12 C4
Clonmel 14 C3
Cloppenburg 17 E1
Clovelly 8 B3
Cloyes 25 E1
Cluain Meala 14 C3
Cluj-Napoca 112 C4
Clun 9 D1
Cluny 26 C3
Clusaz, la 27 D4
Cluse de Pontarlier 27 D3
Cluses 27 E4
Clusone 58 B4
Clwyd 6 B3
Clyde 4 C2
Clydebank 4 C2
Clyde, Firth of 4 B2
Coachford 14 B4
Coalisland 13 D2
Coalville 9 E1
Coaña 34 C1
Côa, R 39 D2
Coatbridge 4 C2
Cobeña 40 B2
Cobh 14 C4
Coburg 52 C4
Coca 40 A1
Coca, Pso di 58 B3
Cocentaina 45 E1
Cochem 51 E4
Cockburnspath 5 E2
Cockermouth 5 D4
Codevigo 61 D1
Codigoro 61 D2
Codogno 60 B2
Codos 36 C4
Codroipo 59 E3
Coesfeld 17 E3
Coevorden 17 D2
Cofrentes 41 D4
Coghinas, L del 66 B2
Cognac 28 B1
Cogne 31 E1
Cogolin 31 D4
Cogolludo 40 B1
Coigach 2 C2
Coimbra 38 B2
Coin 43 E4
Coina 38 A4
Čoka 72 C1
Col 70 A2
Colares 38 A4
Colbe 17 F4
Colchester 11 D2
Coldbackie 2 C2
Colditz 53 D2
Coldstream 5 E2
Coleford 9 D2
Coleraine 13 D1
Colfiorito 63 E1
Colico 58 B3
Coligny 26 C3
Colindres 36 A1
Colintraive 4 B2
Coll 2 A4
Collado Bajo 41 D2
Coll de Nargó 37 F3
Collecchio 60 B2
Colle di Val d'Elsa 60 C4
Colleferro 63 F3
Colle Isarco 59 D2
Colle Salvetti 60 C4
Colle Sannita 64 B3
Collesano 68 C3
Colli a Volturno 64 A3
Collina, Pso della 60 C3
Collinée 22 C3
Colline Metallifere 60 C4
Collio 58 C4
Collioure 32 B2
Collobrières 31 D4
Collodi 60 C3
Collonges 27 D4
Collonges-la-Rouge 29 D2
Colmar 27 E1
Colmars 31 D3
Colmenar 43 F3
Colmenar de Oreja 40 B3
Colmenar Viejo 40 A2
Colnabaichin 3 D4
Colne 6 C2
Colobraro 65 D4
Cologna Veneta 60 C1
Cologne 28 C4
Colombey-les-Belles 21 D4
Colombey-les-Deux-Eglises 26 C1
Colombière, Col de la 27 D4
Colombres 35 F1
Colomera 44 A3
Colonsay 4 A2
Colorno 60 B2
Colosimi 67 F3
Columbretes, I 41 F3
Colunga 35 E1
Colwyn Bay 6 B2
Comacchio 61 D2
Comănesti 113 D4
Coma-ruga 37 F4
Combarro 34 A2
Combeaufontaine 27 D1
Combe Laval 30 C2
Combe Martin 8 C3
Comber 13 E2
Combloux 27 E4
Combourg 18 B4
Combronde 26 A4
Comeglians 59 E2
Comeragh Mts 14 C3
Comillas 35 F1
Comines 19 F1
Comino 68 B4
Comiso 69 D4
Commentry 26 A4
Commercy 20 C4
Como 58 B4
Como, L di 58 B3
Cómpeta 43 F3
Compiègne 19 F3
Comporta 38 A4
Comps-sur-Artuby 31 D3
Comunanza 63 F1
Concarneau 22 B3
Conches 19 D4
Concordia sulla Secchia 60 C2
Condat 29 E1
Condé 20 A1
Conde, Emb del 43 E3
Condé-en-Brie 20 A3
Condeixa-a-Nova 38 B2
Condé-sur-Noireau 18 C4
Condom 28 C3
Condrieu 30 B1
Conegliano 59 E3
Conejeros, Pto de los 38 C4
Conflans 21 D3
Confolens 25 D4
Cong 12 B3
Congleton 6 C3
Congost de Tresponts 32 A3
Congosto de Valdavia 35 E2
Congresbury 9 D2
Conil de la Frontera 43 D4
Conisbrough 7 D2
Coniston 5 D4
Conlie 23 F3
Conliège 26 C3
Connaught 12 B3
Connel 4 B1
Connemara 12 A3
Connerré 23 F3
Conn, L 12 B2
Čonoplja 72 B1
Conques 29 E2
Conquet, le 22 A2
Conquista 43 F1
Conselice 61 D2
Conselve 61 D1
Consett 5 E4
Constância 38 B3
Constanta 115 E1
Constantina 43 E2
Consuegra 40 A3
Consuma 61 D3
Contamines, les 27 E4
Contarina 61 D2
Conthey 27 E3
Contigliano 63 E2
Contin 2 C3
Contrasto, C del 68 C3
Contraviesa, Sa de la 44 B4
Contreras, Emb de 41 D3
Contres 25 E2
Contrexéville 27 D1
Contursi 64 C4
Conty 19 F2
Convento de Calatrava 44 A1
Conversano 65 E3
Conwy 6 A2
Cookstown 13 D2
Cootehill 13 D3
Čop 112 C3
Cope 45 D3

Cope, C 45 D3
Copertino 65 F4
Copparo 61 D2
Corabia 115 D2
Cora Droma Rúisc 12 C3
Corato 65 D3
Coray 22 B3
Corbeil-Essonnes 19 F4
Corbie 19 F2
Corbigny 26 B2
Corbola 61 D2
Corbones, R 43 E2
Corbridge 5 E3
Corby 9 F1
Corcaigh 14 B4
Corcieux 27 E1
Córcoles, R 40 C4
Corconte 35 F2
Corcubión 34 A1
Cordes 29 D3
Córdoba 43 F2
Cordobilla de Lácara 39 D4
Cordobilla, Emb de 43 F3
Corduente 40 C2
Corella 36 C3
Coreses 35 D4
Corfe Castle 9 E3
Corgo 34 B2
Cori 63 F3
Coria 39 D2
Coria del Río 43 D3
Corias 34 C2
Corigliano Calabro 67 F2
Corinaldo 61 E3
Coripe 43 E3
Cork 14 B4
Cork (Co) 14 B4
Corlay 22 C3
Corleone 68 B3
Corleto Perticara 65 D4
Çorlu 115 E3
Cormatin 26 C3
Cormeilles 19 D3
Cormery 25 D2
Cormons 59 F3
Cornago 36 C3
Cornellana 35 D1
Corniche des Cévennes 29 F3
Corniglio 60 B3
Cornimont 27 E1
Cornuda 59 D4
Cornus 29 F3
Cornwall 8 B4
Corps 31 D2
Corraes 34 C3
Corral de Almaguer 40 B3
Corral de Cantos 39 F3
Corralejo 42 C4
Corrales 35 D4
Corran 2 C4
Corraun 12 B2
Corredoiras 34 B2
Correggio 60 C2
Corrèze 29 D1
Corrèze (Dépt) 29 D1
Corrèze *R* 29 D2
Corrib, L 12 B3
Corridonia 61 F4
Corrofin 12 B4
Corse 33 E2
Corse-du-Sud 33 F3
Corsham 9 D2
Čortanovci 72 C2
Corte 33 F3
Corte de Peleas 39 D4
Cortegada 34 B3
Cortegana 42 C2
Cortemaggiore 60 B2
Cortemilia 31 F2
Corteolona 60 A2
Cortes de Aragón 41 E1
Cortes de Baza 44 B2
Cortes de la Frontera 43 E4
Cortijos Nuevos 44 B2
Cortina d'Ampezzo 59 E3
Čortkov 113 D3
Cortona 61 D4
Coruche 38 B4
Corvara in Badia 59 D3
Corvera 45 D2
Corvera Toranzo 35 F2
Corwen 6 B3
Cosenza 67 E2
Cosham 9 E3
Cosne 26 A2
Cosne-d'Allier 26 A3
Cossato 31 F1
Cossé-le-Vivien 23 E3
Cosson 25 E2
Cossonay 27 D3
Costa Blanca 45 E2
Costa Brava 32 C3
Costa da Caparica 38 A4
Costa del Sol 44 A4
Costa de Santo André 42 A1
Costalunga, Pso di 59 D3
Costa Smeralda 66 B1
Costa Vasca 36 B1
Costa Verde 35 D1
Costigliole d'Asti 31 F2
Coswig (Sachsen) 53 E2
Coswig (Sachsen-Anhalt) 53 D1
Côte-d'Or (Dépt) 26 C2
Côtes-d'Armor 22 C3
Côte-St-André, la 30 C1
Cotignac 31 D4
Cottbus 53 F1
Coubet, Collado de 32 B3
Coubre, Pointe de la 28 A1
Couches 26 B3
Couço 38 B4
Coucy-le-Château-Auffrique 20 A3
Couesnon 23 D3
Couhé 25 D4
Couilly 19 F4
Couiza 32 B2
Coulanges 26 A2
Coulanges-la-Vineuse 26 A2
Coulommiers 19 F4
Coulon 24 C4
Coulonges 24 C3
Coupar Angus 5 D1
Couptrain 18 C4
Courchevel 31 D1
Cour-Cheverny 25 E2
Courçon 24 C4
Courmayeur 27 E4
Couronne, la 28 C1
Courpière 29 F1
Cours 26 B4
Coursan 32 B1
Coursegoules 31 E3
Courseulles 18 C3
Courson-les-Carrières 26 A2
Courtenay 26 A1
Courthézon 30 C3
Courtine, la 29 E1
Courtomer 19 D4
Courtown 15 E3
Courtrai 50 A3
Courville 19 E4
Cousin 26 B2
Coussey 20 C4
Coutances 18 B3
Coutras 28 B2
Couvertoirade, la 29 F3
Couvin 50 C4
Couze 25 E4
Cova da Iria 38 B3
Covadonga 35 E1
Covadonga, Pque Nac de la Sa de 35 E2
Covarrubias 36 A3
Coventry 9 E1
Covilhã 38 C2
Cowbridge 8 C2
Cowdenbeath 5 D2
Cowes 9 E3
Cowfold 10 C3
Cozes 28 B1
Craco 65 D4
Craigavon 13 E2
Craigellachie 3 D3
Craighouse 4 B2
Craigievar Castle 3 E4
Craignure 4 B1
Crail 5 D2
Crailsheim 55 E2
Craiova 115 D2
Cranborne 9 E3
Crans 27 E3
Craon 23 E3
Craonne 20 B3
Craponne 29 F1
Crathes Castle 3 E4
Crati 67 E2
Crato 38 C3
Craughwell 12 B4
Crau, la 31 D4
Craven Arms 9 D1
Crawinkel 52 C3
Crawley 10 C3
Creag Meagaidh 2 C4
Creagorry 2 A3
Crécy 20 A2
Crécy-en-Ponthieu 19 E2
Crécy-la-Chapelle 19 F4
Crediton 8 C3
Creegh 12 B4
Creeslough 12 C1
Creglingen 55 E1
Creil 19 F3
Crema 60 B1
Crémieu 26 C4
Cremona 60 B2
Créon 28 B2
Crepaja 73 D2
Crépy-en-Valois 19 F3
Cres 70 B4
Cres *I* 70 B4
Crescentino 31 F1
Crespino 61 D2
Crest 30 C2
Cresta 58 B3
Cresta del Gallo 45 D2
Créteil 19 F4
Crêtes, Route des 27 E1
Creully 18 C3
Creuse 25 E4
Creuse (Dépt) 25 E4
Creusot, le 26 B3
Creußen 53 D4
Creutzwald 21 D3
Creuzburg 52 B3
Crevacuore 58 A4
Crevalcore 60 C2
Crèvecœur-le-Grand 19 E3
Crevillente 45 D2
Crewe 6 C3
Crewkerne 9 D3
Crianlarich 4 C1
Criccieth 6 A3
Crickhowell 9 D2
Cricklade 9 E2
Crieff 4 C1
Criel 19 E2
Crikvenica 70 B3
Crimmitschau 53 D3
Crinan 4 B2
Criquetot-l'Esneval 19 D3
Crissolo 31 E2
Crişu Alb 112 C4
Crişu Negru 112 C4
Crişu Repede 112 C4
Crivitz 48 C2
Crkvice 76 A2
Crmljan 76 C2
Črmošnjice 70 B2
Črna 70 B1
Crna Bara (Srbija) 72 B3
Crna Bara (Vojvodina) 72 C1
Crnac (Hrvatska) 71 E2
Crnac (Srbija) 76 C1
Crna Gora 76 B2
Crna gora 77 E2
Crna reka 77 E4
Crna Trava 77 E1
Crnča 72 B4
Crni Drim 77 D4
Crni Guber 72 C4
Crni Lug (Bosna i Hercegovina) 75 D1
Crni Lug (Hrvatska) 70 B3
Crni Timok 73 E4
Crni vrh *Mt* (Bosna i Hercegovina) 71 D4
Črni vrh *Mt* (Slovenija) 70 B1
Crni vrh *Mt* (Srbija) 76 B1
Črni vrh (Slovenija) 70 A2
Crnivec 70 B2
Crnjelovo Donje 72 B3
Črnkovci 71 F2
Crno jez 76 B2
Črnomelj 70 B3
Croagh Patrick 12 B3
Croce dello Scrivano, Pso 64 C4
Croce Domini, Pso di 58 C4
Crocello, Pso di 64 C4
Crocq 25 F4
Croisic, le 24 A2
Croisière, la 25 E4
Croix de Fer, Col de la 31 D1
Croix Haute, Col de la 30 C2
Croix-Valmer, la 31 D4
Crolly 12 C1
Cromarty 3 D3
Cromer 7 F3
Crook 5 E4
Croom 14 B3
Cross Fell 5 D4
Cross Hands 8 C2
Crosshaven 14 C4
Crossmaglen 13 D3
Crossmolina 12 B2
Crotone 67 F3
Crotoy, le 19 E2
Crowborough 10 C3
Crowland 9 F1
Crowle 7 D2
Croyde 8 C3
Croydon 9 F2
Crozant 25 E4
Crozon 22 A3
Cruden Bay 3 E3
Crudgington 6 C3
Crumlin 13 E2
Cruseilles 27 D4
Crussol 30 B2
Cruz 40 B3
Cruzamento de Pegões 38 A4
Cruz da Légua 38 A3
Cruz de Tejeda 42 B4
Crven Grm 75 E2
Crvenka 72 B2
Crymmych 8 B1
Csongrád 112 B4
Csorna 112 A4
Cuacos 39 E2
Cualedro 34 B3
Cuba 42 B1
Cubel 36 C4
Cucalón, Sa de 41 D1
Cuckfield 10 C3
Cudillero 35 D1
Čudovo 111 D1
Čudskoje Ozero 110 C1
Cuéllar 35 F4
Cuenca 40 C3
Cuenca, Serr de 40 C3
Cuerda 41 D3
Cuerda del Pozo, Emb de la 36 B3
Cuers 31 D4
Cuerva 40 A3
Cueva de la Pileta 43 E4
Cueva de la Vieja 41 D4
Cueva de Nerja 44 A4
Cueva Foradada, Emb de 41 E1
Cueva, Sa do 35 E1
Cuevas de Altamira 35 F1
Cuevas de Artà 45 F3
Cuevas de Canalobre 45 E1
Cuevas del Aguila 39 F2
Cuevas del Amanzora 44 C3
Cuevas del Becerro 43 E3
Cuevas del Campo 44 B2
Cuevas del Drac 45 F3
Cuevas del Valle 39 F2
Cuevas de San Clemente 35 F3
Cuevas de San Marcos 43 F3
Cuevas de Valporquero 35 D2
Cuevas de Vinromá 41 F2
Cuglieri 66 A3
Cuijk 17 D3
Cuillin Sd 2 B4
Cuillins, The 2 B3
Cuiseaux 26 C3
Cuisery 26 C3
Culan 25 F3
Culdaff 13 D1
Culebra, Sa de la 34 C3
Culemborg 16 C3
Cúllar Baza 44 B2
Cullen 3 E3
Cullera 41 E4
Cullompton 8 C3
Culoz 27 D4
Culross 5 D2
Cumbernauld 4 C2
Cumbre Alta 39 F3
Cumbres Mayores 42 C1
Cumbria 5 D4
Cumbrian Mts 5 D4
Cumiana 31 E2
Čumić 73 D3
Cumnock 4 C3
Cunault 24 C2
Cuneo 31 E2
Cunlhat 29 F1
Čunski 70 B4
Cuorgnè 31 E1
Cupar 5 D1
Cupello 64 B2
Cupramontana 61 E4
Cuprija 73 E4
Cure 26 B2
Cure, la 27 D3
Curia 38 B1
Currane, L 14 A4
Curtea de Argeş 115 D1
Curtis 34 B1
Čurug 72 C2
C'urupinsk 113 F3
Cusano Mutri 64 B3
Cushendall 13 E1
Cushendun 13 E1
Cusna, Mte 60 C3
Cusset 26 A4
Cutro 67 F3
Cuxhaven 47 F2
Cvikov 53 F3
Čvrsnica 75 E1
Čvrstec 71 D2
Cwmbrân 9 D2
Cybinka 49 F4
Cysoing 20 A1
Czarnków 112 A1
Czersk 110 A4
Częstochowa 112 B2
Człuchów 112 A1

D

Dabar 70 C3
Dąbie 49 E2
Dabie, Jez 49 E2
Dabilje 77 F3
Dabo 21 E4
Dachau 55 F3
Dachsteingruppe 59 F1
Dačice 57 E1
Dadiá 81 F2
Dáfnes 86 C1
Dáfni (Límnos) 85 D1
Dáfni (Makedonía) 80 C4
Dáfni (Pelopónissos) 86 C1
Dáfni (Stereá Eláda) 83 D4
Dafní (Stereá Eláda) 87 F1
Dáfnio 87 D3
Dafnónas (Stereá Eláda) 83 D3
Dafnónas (Thráki) 80 C2
Dafnotí 82 C2
Dafnoúdi, Akr 82 B4
Dagali 104 C2
Dagebüll 47 F1
Dagenham 10 C2
Dahlen 53 E2
Dahlenburg 48 B3
Dahme (D) 48 B2
Dahme (DDR) 53 E1
Dahme *R* 53 E1
Dahn 54 B2
Daimiel 40 A4
Daimuz 41 E4
Dajt, Mal i 76 C4
Đakovica 76 C2
Đakovo 71 F2
Đala 72 C1
Dalälven 106 A3
Dalane 104 A4
Dalbeattie 4 C3
Dalbosjön 105 E4
Dalby 109 D3
Dale (Hordaland) 104 A2
Dale (Sogn og Fjordane) 104 A1
Dalen 104 B3
Dalhem 109 F4
Dalías 44 B4
Daliburgh 2 A3
Dalj 72 B2
Dalkeith 5 D2
Dalkey 13 E4
Dalmally 4 C1
Dalmellington 4 C3
Dalmine 60 B1
Dalry 4 C2
Dalsbruk 107 D3
Dalsfjorden 104 A1
Dalsjöfors 109 D1
Dals Långed 105 D4
Dalton 6 B1
Daluis, Gorges de 31 E3
Dalvik 96 B1
Dalwhinnie 2 C4
Damaskiniá 79 D3
Damássi 83 E1
Damazan 28 C3
Damelevières 21 D4
Damgan 22 C4
Damianó 79 F2
Dammartin-en-Goële 19 F3
Damme 17 F2
Damnjane 76 C2
Dampierre 27 D2
Dampierre-sur-Salon 27 D2
Damville 19 E4
Damvillers 20 C3
Dangé 25 D3
Danilovgrad 76 B2
Dannemarie 27 E2
Dannenberg 48 B3
Dão, R 38 C1
Daoulas 22 B3
Darda 71 F2
Dardesheim 52 C1
Darfo Boario Terme 58 C4
Dargilan, Grotte de 29 F3
Dargun 49 D2
Darlington 5 E4
Darłowo 110 A4
Darmstadt 54 C1
Darney 27 D1
Daroca 36 C4
Darque 34 A3
Darß 48 C1
Dartford 10 C2
Dartmoor Nat Pk 8 C3
Dartmouth 8 C4
Daruvar 71 E2
Darwen 6 C2
Dasburg 51 D4
Dasing 55 F3
Dassel 52 B2
Dassohóri 81 D2
Dassow 48 B2
D'at'kovo 111 F3
Datteln 17 E3
Daugava 110 C3
Daugavpils 110 C3
Daun 51 E4
Dava 3 D3
Davat 77 D4
Daventry 9 E1
Davia 87 D2
Davidovac 73 F2
Dávlia 83 F4
Davor 71 E3
Davos 58 B2
Dawlish 8 C3
Dax 28 A4
Deádnu 95 E2
Deal 11 D3
Deauville 19 D3
Deba 36 B1
Debar 77 D3
Debarska Banja Banjišta 77 D3
Debeli Lug 73 E3
Debeli vrh 70 B2
Debeljača 72 C2
Dębica 112 B2
De Bilt 16 C3
Dęblin 112 C2
Dębno 49 F3
Debrc 72 C3
Debrecen 112 C4
Dečani 76 C2
Decazeville 29 E2
Děčín 53 F3
Decize 26 A3
Dedemsvaart 17 D2
Dee (Scotland) 3 D4
Dee (Wales/Eng) 6 B3
Degaña 34 C2
Degebe, R 38 B4

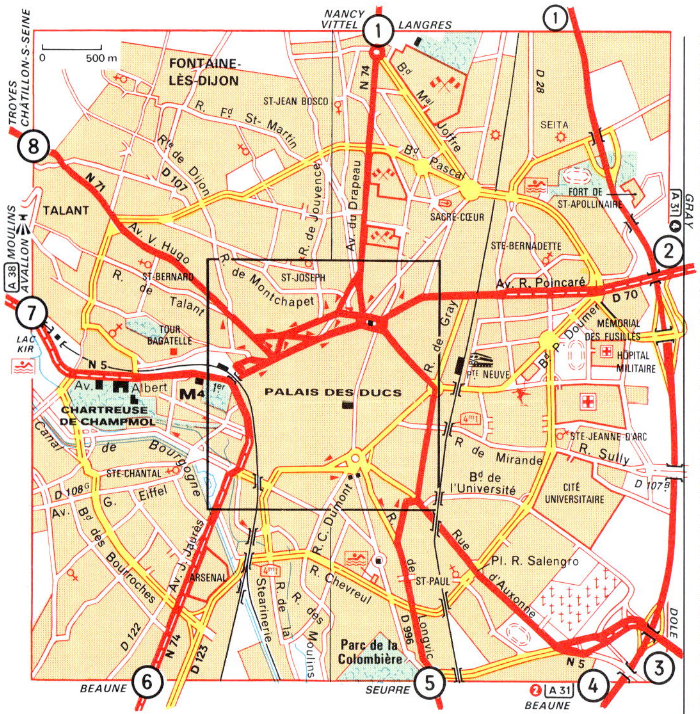
NANCY
VITTEL
LANGRES
TROYES
CHÂTILLON-S-SEINE
FONTAINE-LÈS-DIJON
TALANT
PALAIS DES DUCS
CHARTREUSE DE CHAMPMOL
ST-JOSEPH
SACRÉ-CŒUR
STE-BERNADETTE
ST-BERNARD
TOUR BAGATELLE
STE-CHANTAL
ARSENAL
ST-PAUL
STE-JEANNE-D'ARC
CITÉ UNIVERSITAIRE
MÉMORIAL DES FUSILLÉS
HÔPITAL MILITAIRE
FORT DE ST-APOLLINAIRE
SEITA
Parc de la Colombière
Pl. R. Salengro
GRAY
DOLE
BEAUNE
SEURRE
MOULINS
AVALLON
0 500 m

Dijon

Degerfjärden 102 A2
Degerfors 105 E4
Degerndorf 56 B4
Deggendorf 56 B2
Dego 31 F2
Degracias 38 B2
De Haan 50 A3
Dehesa de Montejo 35 F2
Deià 45 E2
Deidesheim 54 C1
Deinze 50 B3
Deiva Marina 60 B3
Dej 112 C4
Deje 105 E3
Dejë, Mal 76 C3
De Koog 16 C1
Delčevo 77 F2
Delden 17 D2
Deleitosa 39 E3
Delémont 27 E2
Deléria 83 E1
Delet Teili 106 C3
Delfi 83 E4
Delft 16 B3
Delfzijl 47 D3
Delia 68 C4
Delianuova 67 E4
Deliblato 73 D2
Deliblatska Peščara 73 D2
Deliceto 64 C3
Delimeđe 76 C1
Delitzsch 53 D2
Delle 27 E2
Dellen, N 101 F3
Dellen, S 101 F3
Delme 21 D3
Delmenhorst 47 F3
Delnice 70 B3
Delsbo 101 F3
Delta Dunării 113 E4
Delvin 13 D3
Delvináki 82 B1
Demanda, Sa de la 36 B2
Demer 50 C3
Demidov 111 E3
Demirci 115 F4
Demir Kapija 77 F3
Demmin 49 D2
Demoiselles, Grotte des 29 F3
Demonia 87 E4
Denain 20 A1
Denbigh 6 B3
Den Burg 16 C1
Dendermonde 50 B3
Dendre 50 B4
Dendrohóri 79 D3
Denekamp 17 E2
Den Haag 16 B3
Den Helder 16 C1
Denia 45 E1
Denizli 115 F4
Denkendorf 55 F2
Dennington 11 D1
Denny 4 C2
Den Oever 16 C1
Dent de Vaulion 27 D3
De Panne 50 A3
Đeravica 76 C2
Derby 6 C3
Derbyshire 6 C3
Der Chantecoq, L du 20 C4
Đerdap, H.E. 73 F2
Đerdap, Klisura 73 E3
Derekoy 115 E2
Derenburg 52 C1
Derg, L (Clare) 12 C4
Derg, L (Donegal) 12 C2
Der Grabow 49 D1
Dermatás, Akr 83 F1
Dermbach 52 B3
Derneburg 52 B1
Derravaragh, L 13 D3
Derrynasaggart Mts 14 B4
Derryveagh Mts 12 C1
Deruta 63 E1
Dervaig 4 B1
Derval 23 D4
Dervéni 87 D1
Derventa 71 E3
Derviziana 82 B2
Derwent (Derbys) 6 C3
Derwent (Durham) 5 E4
Derwent (Yorks) 7 D1
Derwent Water 5 D4
Desborough 9 F1
Descartes 25 D3
Desenzano 60 B1
Desertas 42 A3
Desfiladero de Despeñaperros 44 A1
Desfiladero de la Hermida 35 F2
Desfiladero de los Beyos 35 E2
Desfiladero del Teverga 35 D2
Desfina 83 E4
Desimirovac 73 D4
Desio 60 A1
Deskáti 83 D1
Desna 111 F3
Despotikó, N 88 B3
Despotovac 73 E3
Despotovo 72 B2
Dessau 53 D1
Destriana 35 D3
Desulo 66 B3
Desvres 19 E1
Deta 114 C1
Đetinja 72 C4
Detmold 52 A1
Dettelbach 55 E1
Dettifoss 96 C1
Deurne 17 D3
Deutsche Alpenstraße 55 E4
Deutsche Bucht 47 E2
Deutschkreutz 57 F3
Deutschlandsberg 70 B1
Deutsch-Wagram 57 F2
Deux-Alpes, les 31 D2
Deux-Sèvres 24 C3
Deva 114 C1
Deve Bair 77 E2
Deventer 17 D2
Deveron 3 E3
Devetak 72 B4
Devil's Bridge 8 C1
Devil's Elbow 3 D4
Devizes 9 E2
Devnja 115 E2
Dewsbury 6 C2
Deza 36 C4
Diablerets, les 27 E3
Diablerets, les *Mt* 27 E3
Diafáni 93 D2
Diakófti 90 A1
Diakoftó 86 C1
Diamante 67 E2
Dia, N 91 E3
Diano Marina 31 F3
Diápora Nissiá 87 E1
Diavlos Alonissou 84 B2
Diavlos Oreón 83 F3
Diavlos Pelagonissou 84 B2
Diavlos Skiáthou 84 A2
Diavlos Skopélou 84 A2
Diavlos Trikeriou 83 F3
Diavlos Zákinthou 86 A1
Diavolitsi 86 C3
Diavolo, Pso del 64 A2
Diavolórema 81 E2
Dibbersen 48 A3
Dicmo 75 D1
Dicomano 61 D3
Dídima 87 E2
Dídimo, Óros 87 E2
Didimótiho 81 F1
Die 30 C2
Dieburg 52 A4
Diedorf 52 B2
Diego Alvaro 39 E2
Diekirch 21 D2
Diemel 52 A2
Diemelstadt 52 A2
Diepholz 17 F2
Dieppe 19 E2
Dierdorf 51 E4
Dieren 17 D3
Diesdorf 48 B4
Dießen 56 A3
Diest 50 C3
Dietenheim 55 E3
Dietfurt 55 F2
Dietikon 27 F2
Dietmannsried 55 E4
Dieulefit 30 C2
Dieulouard 21 D4
Dieuze 21 D4
Diez 51 F4
Diezma 44 A3
Differdange 21 D3
Digerkampen 100 B3
Digermulen 94 A4
Dignano 59 E3
Digne-les-Bains 31 D3
Digoin 26 B3
Dijle 50 C3
Dijon 26 C2
Dikanäs 97 F3
Dikea 81 F1
Díkela 81 E2
Diksmuide 50 A3
Diktéo Ándro 91 E4
Diktinéon 90 B3
Díkti, Óros 91 E4
Dilessi 84 B4
Dilináta 82 B4
Dilj 71 E2
Dillenburg 51 F3
Dillingen (Bayern) 55 E2
Dillingen (Saarland) 54 A2
Dilofos 81 F1
Dílos 88 C2
Dílos, N 88 C2
Dimena 87 E2
Dímitra 83 E1
Dimitritsi 80 B2
Dimitrovgrad (BG) 115 D3
Dimitrovgrad (YU) 77 F1
Dimitsána 86 C2
Dinami 67 E4
Dinan 18 B4
Dinant 50 C4
Dinar 115 F4
Dinara *Mt* 75 D1
Dinara (Reg) 75 D1
Dinard 18 B4
Dinbych 6 B3
Dinbych-y-pysgod 8 B2
Dingelstädt 52 B2
Dingle 14 A3
Dingle 105 D4
Dingle (Reg) 14 A3
Dingle B 14 A3
Dingli 68 B4
Dinglingen 54 C3
Dingolfing 56 B2
Dingwall 2 C3
Dinjiška 70 C4
Dinkelsbühl 55 E2
Dinklage 17 F2
Dinslaken 17 D3
Dío 79 F4
Diónissos 87 F1
Dióriga Korinthou 87 E1
Dipótama 80 C1
Dippoldiswalde 53 E2
Dirráhio 86 C3
Dírfis, Óros 84 B3
Disentis 58 A3
Disgrazia, Mte 58 B3
Dispílio 79 D3
Diss 11 D1
Dissen 17 F2
Distomo 83 E4
Distos 84 B4
Ditiki Rodópi 80 C1
Dittaino 69 D3
Ditzingen 55 D2
Divača 70 A3
Divaráta 82 B4
Divčibare 72 C4
Dives 18 C3
Dives *R* 18 C3
Divič 72 B4
Divjakë 76 C4
Divljana 77 E1
Divonne 27 D3
Divor, Bgem do 38 B4
Divor, Rib de 38 B4
Divoúnia, Ni 92 C2
Dívri 83 E3
Divuša 71 D3
Djupini 96 A3
Djupvik 94 C2
Djurås 105 F2
Djursland 108 B2
Dmitrov 111 F2
Dnepr 111 E3
Dneprodzeržinsk-oje Vodochranilišče 113 F2
Dneprovskij Liman 113 F3
Dnestr 112 C3
Dnestrovskij Liman 113 F4
Dno 111 D2
Dobanovci 72 C3
Dobbiaco 59 E2
Dobel 54 C2
Dobele 110 C3
Döbeln 53 E2
Doberlug-Kirchhain 53 E1
Döbern 53 F1
Dobersberg 57 E1
Dobieszczyn 49 E2
Doboj 71 F3
Dobošnica 71 F3
Dobra (PL) 49 F2
Dobra (YU) 73 E3
Dobra *R* 70 C3
Dobra Voda 73 D4
Dobra Voda *Mt* 77 D3
Dobrašinci 77 F3
Dobratsch 59 F2
Dobrčane 77 D2
Döbriach 59 F2
Dobrica 73 D2
Dobričevo 73 D2
Dobri Do 77 D1
Dobrinj 70 B3
Dobříš 53 F4
Dobrljin 71 D3
Dobrna 70 B1
Dobromani 75 F2
Dobro Polje 76 A1
Dobrovnik 70 C1
Dobrun 72 C4
Dobruš 111 E4
Dobruševo 77 E4
Dobrzany 49 F2
Dobšiná 112 B3
Docksta 102 A2
Doc Penfro 8 B2
Dodekánissa 89 E3
Dodóni 82 B1
Doesburg 17 D3
Doetinchem 17 D3
Doganović 77 D2
Dogliani 31 F2
Doiráni 79 F2
Doiránis, L 79 F2
Doiras, Emb de 34 C1
Dojransko Ez 77 F3
Dokanj 72 B3
Dokka 104 C2
Dokkum 47 D3
Dokós, N 87 E3
Doksy 53 F3
Dolac 76 C2
Dol-de-Bretagne 18 B4
Dole 26 C2
Dôle, la 27 D3
Dølemo 104 B4
Dolenci 77 D4
Dolenja Vas 70 B2
Dolenjske Toplice 70 B2
Dolga Vas 71 D1
Dolgellau 6 A3
Doliana 78 C4
Dolianova 66 B4
Dolihi 79 E4
Dolina 112 C3
Doljani 71 D4
Doljevac 77 D1
Dolla 12 C4
Döllach 59 E2
Dollar 5 D2
Dolle 48 C4
Dolní Dvořiště 57 D2
Dolno Kosovrasti 77 D3
Dolo 61 D1
Dolomiti 59 D3
Dolomiti Bellunesi, Parco Naz dello 59 D3
Dolores 45 D2
Dolovo 73 D2
Dol Poustevna 53 F2
Domaševo 75 F2
Domažlice 56 B1
Dombås 100 B3
Dombasle 21 D4
Dombóvár 114 B1
Domburg 16 B3
Domène 30 C1
Doméniko 83 E1
Domèvre-en-Haye 21 D4
Domfront 18 C4
Dömitz 48 C3
Domme 29 D2
Dommitzsch 53 D2
Domnista 83 D3
Domodossola 58 A4
Domokós 83 E2
Dompaire 27 D1
Dompierre 26 B3
Domrémy 20 C4
Domusnovas 66 B4
Domžale 70 B2
Don (England) 7 D2
Don (Scotland) 3 E4
Donaghadee 13 E2
Doña María Ocaña 44 B3
Doña Mencía 43 F2
Doñana, Parque Nac de 43 D3
Donau 56 C2
Donaueschingen 54 C4
Donauwörth 55 E2
Donawitz 57 E4
Don Benito 39 E4
Doncaster 7 D2
Donegal 12 C2
Donegal B 12 C2
Donegal (Co) 12 C1
Dongen 16 C3
Donges 23 D4
Donington 7 E3
Donja Bebrina 71 F3
Donja Brela 75 E2
Donja Brezna 76 B2
Donja Bukovica 76 B2
Donja Kamenica 72 C3
Donja Šatornja 73 D3
Donje Crnljevo 72 C3
Donje Dragovlje 77 E1
Donje Ljupče 77 D2
Donji Andrijevci 71 F3
Donji Barbeš 77 E1
Donji Kanzanci 75 D1
Donji Lapac 71 D4
Donji Malovan 75 E1
Donji Miholjac 71 E2
Donji Milanovac 73 E3
Donji Ruzani 75 D1
Donji Seget 75 D2
Donji Vakuf 71 E4
Donji Vijačani 71 E3
Donji Zemunik 74 C1
Donjon, le 26 B3
Dønna 97 D3
Donnemarie-Dontilly 20 A4
Donnersbachwald 57 D4
Dønnes 97 D2
Donon 21 E4
Donon, Col du 21 E4
Donostia-San Sebastián 36 C1
Donoússa, N 89 D3
Donzenac 29 D2
Donzère 30 B2
Donzy 26 A2
Doorn 16 C3
Doornik 50 A4
Dora Baltéa 27 E4
Dora Riparia 31 E1
Dorat, le 25 D4
Đorče Petrov 77 D3
Dorchester 9 D3
Dordives 25 F1
Dordogne 29 E1
Dordogne (Dépt) 28 C2
Dordogne *R* 28 B2
Dordrecht 16 C3
Dore 29 F1
Dorfen 56 B3
Dorfmark 48 A4
Dorgali 66 C2
Dório 86 C3
Dorkáda 80 A2
Dorking 10 C3
Dormagen 17 E4
Dormans 20 A3
Dornbirn 58 B2
Dornburg 52 C3
Dorndorf 52 B3
Dornes 26 A3
Dornie 2 B3
Dornoch 3 D3
Dornoch Firth 3 D3
Dornstetten 54 C3
Dornum 47 E3
Dorog 112 B4
Dorogobuž 111 E3
Dorohoi 113 D3
Dorotea 101 F1
Dörpstedt 48 A1
Dorset 9 D3
Dorsten 17 E3
Dortan 27 D3
Dortmund 17 E3
Dortmund-Ems-Kanal 17 E2
Dorum 47 F3
Dörzbach 55 D1
Dosbarrios 40 B3
Dos Hermanas 43 D3
Dosse 49 D3
Douai 19 F2
Douarnenez 22 A3
Doubs 26 C3
Doubs (Dépt) 27 D2
Doucier 27 D3
Doudeville 19 D2
Doué 24 C2
Douglas (I of Man) 6 A1
Douglas (Scotland) 4 C2
Doukáto, Akr 82 B3
Doulaincourt 20 C4
Doulevant-le-Château 20 C4
Doullens 19 F2
Doulus Head 14 A4
Doune 4 C2
Doupov 53 E3
Dourdan 19 E4
Dourgne 32 A1
Douro 34 A4
Douro, R 34 A4
Douvaine 27 D3
Douve 18 B3
Douvres 18 C3
Dover 11 D3
Dover, Str of 11 D3
Dovre 100 C3
Dovrefjell 100 C3
Dovsk 111 E4
Down 13 E2
Downham Market 10 C1
Downpatrick 13 E2
Dowra 12 C2
Doxarás 83 E2
Doxáto 80 C2
Dozulé 19 D3
Drac 30 C2
Dračevo 77 E3
Drachten 17 D1
Drag 94 A4
Dragalovci 71 E3
Dragaš 77 D3
Drăgăşani 115 D1
Dragaši 76 B1
Draginac 72 C3
Draginje 72 C3
Dragočaj 71 E3
Dragocvet 73 D4
Dragoevo 77 E3

DUBLIN / BAILE ÁTHA CLIATH
DUBLIN BAY
Dún Laoghaire
Howth / Binn Éadair
North Bull Island
Phœnix Park
Finglas / Fionnghlas
Blanchardstown / Baile Bhalainséir
Clondalkin / Cluain Dolcáin
Tallaght / Tamhlacht
Dundrum / Dún Droma
Blackrock / An Charraig Dhubh
Dalkey / Deilginis
Killiney / Cill Iníon Léinín
Killiney Bay
Shankill / Seanchill
Stillorgan / Stigh Lorgan
Three Rock Mountain
Kilmashogue Mountain
Tribadden Mountain
Cruagh Mountain
Two Rock Mountain
Ireland's Eye
Dalkey Island
Sorrento Point
James Joyce Tower
Baily Lighthouse
Drumleck Point
Holyhead
Liverpool
Douglas (I. of Man)
Monaghan
Drogheda
Malahide
Navan
Lucan
Naas
Baltinglass
Enniskerry
Wicklow
Bray
6°20
53°20
1/120 000
2 km
1mile

Düsseldorf
2 km
NEUSS
HOFGARTEN
KÖNIGSALLEE
HAFEN
RHEIN
OBERKASSEL
NIEDERKASSEL
GOLZHEIM
DERENDORF
MÖRSENBROICH
GRAFENBERG
GERRESHEIM
FLINGERN
OBERBILK
FRIEDRICH-STADT
HAMM
UNTERRATH
RATH
D. RATH
AAPERWALD
WILDPARK
LIERENFELD
STOFFELN
WERSTEN
HOLTHAUSEN
ELLER
UNTERBACH
VOLMERSWERTH
FLEHE
MEERBUSCH
LÖRICK
HEERDT
RHEINSTADION
MESSE GELÄNDE
NORDPARK
Südring
Brüsseler Str.
Bergische Landstr.
Erkrather Str.
Kölner Str.
Hellweg
Theodorstr.
Bonner Str.
WESEL DUISBURG
AUTOBAHN (E 35-A 3) (AB-Kreuz Breitscheid)
ESSEN MÜLHEIM
AUTOBAHN (E-35-A 3)
WUPPERTAL AUTOBAHN (E 35-A 3) (Düsseldorf-Mettmann)
NIJMEGEN KREFELD
MÖNCHEN GLADBACH
AACHEN MÖNCHENGLADBACH
KÖLN KOBLENZ
NEUSS KÖLN
AUTOBAHN (A 59) KÖLN
SCHLOSS BENRATH (PARK)

Name	Page	Grid
Dragoman	114	C2
Dragonera, I	45	E3
Dragoni	64	B3
Dragør	108	C3
Dragoš	77	E4
Dragotiná	82	A2
Dragović	71	E2
Dragovića Polje	76	B2
Dragozetići	70	B3
Dragsfjärd	107	D3
Dragsvik	100	A3
Draguignan	31	D4
Dráma	80	C2
Dráma (Nomos)	80	C1
Drammen	104	C3
Drammen selva	104	C3
Drangajökull	96	A1
Drangedal	104	C3
Dranske	49	D1
Drápano, Akr	90	C3
Drasenhofen	57	F1
Drau	59	F2
Dráva	71	E2
Dravograd	70	B1
Drawno	49	F2
Drawsko Pomorskie	112	A1
Draženov	56	B1
Draževac	72	C3
Drebkau	53	F1
Dreki	96	C2
Drenewydd	9	D1
Drenovac	77	E2
Drenovci	72	B3
Drenovo	77	E3
Drenthe	17	D1
Drépano (Makedonía)	79	E3
Drépano (Pelopónissos)	87	E2
Drépano, Akr (Anáfi)	91	E1
Drépano, Akr (Makedonía)	80	B4
Dresden	53	E2
Dreux	19	E4
Drežnik-Grad	70	C3
Driebergen	16	C3
Driebes	40	B2
Driméa	83	E3
Drimós	79	F3
Drin	76	C3
Drina	76	A1
Drini i Zi	77	D3
Drinit, Gjiri i	76	B3
Drinjača	72	B4
Drinjača *R*	72	B4
Drinovci	75	E2
Driopída	88	A2
Driós	88	C3
Drisht	76	C3
Driva	100	B2
Drlače	72	C4
Drnholec	57	F1
Drniš	75	D1
Drnje	71	D1
Drnovo	70	C2
Drøbak	105	D3
Drobeta-Turnu Severin	114	C1
Drochtersen	48	A2
Drogheda	13	D3
Drogobyč	112	C3
Droichead Átha	13	D3
Droichead Nua	13	D4
Droitwich	9	E1
Drokija	113	E3
Dromcolliher	14	B3
Drôme (Dépt)	30	C2
Drôme *R*	30	C2
Dromore (Down)	13	E2
Dromore (Tyrone)	13	D2
Dronero	31	E2
Dronfield	7	D2
Drongaráti	82	B4
Dronne	28	C1
Dronninglund	108	B2
Dronten	16	C2
Drosendorf Stadt	57	E1
Drossáto	79	F2
Drosseró	79	E2
Drossiá	84	A4
Drossohóri	83	E4
Drossopigí (Árta)	82	C2
Drossopigí (Ioánina)	78	C4
Drossopigí (Makedonía)	79	D3
Drottningholm	106	B4

Droué 25 E1
Drulingen 21 E3
Drumkeeran 12 C2
Drummore 4 B4
Drumnadrochit 2 C3
Drumochter, Pass of 2 C4
Drumshanbo 12 C2
Drusenheim 21 F4
Druskininkai 110 C4
Druten 16 C3
Drvenik (Hrvatska) 75 D2
Drvenik (Hrvatska) 75 E2
Dryburgh 5 D3
Drymen 4 C2
Duben 53 E1
Dubi 53 E3
Dubica 71 D3
Dublin 13 E4
Dublin (Co) 13 D4
Dubna 111 F2
Dubňany 57 F1
Dubno 113 D2
Dubona 73 D3
Dubossary 113 E3
Duboštica 71 F4
Dubovac 73 D2
Dubovsko 71 D4
Dubrava (Hrvatska) 71 D2
Dubrava (Pelješac) 75 F2
Dubrava Stara 71 E3
Dubrave 71 F3
Dubrave Donje 72 B3
Dubravica 73 D3
Dubrovnik 76 A2
Ducey 18 B4
Ducherow 49 E2
Duchkov 53 E3
Duchovščina 111 E3
Duclair 19 D3
Dudelange 21 D3
Duderstadt 52 B2
Dudley 9 E1
Dudweiler 54 B2
Dueñas 35 E4
Duero, R 35 D4
Duesund 104 A1
Dufftown 3 D3
Duga Poljana 76 C1
Duga Resa 70 C3
Dugi Otok 74 C1
Dugi Rat 75 D2
Dugo Selo 70 C2
Duingt 27 D4
Duino 59 F3
Duisburg 17 D3
Dukagjin 76 C2
Dukat 77 E2
Duleek 13 D3
Dulje 77 D2
Dülken 17 D4
Dülmen 17 E3
Dulnain Bridge 3 D4
Dulovo 115 E2
Dumbarton 4 C2
Dumbria 34 A1
Dumfries 4 C3
Dumfries and Galloway 4 C3
Dun 20 C3
Dunaföldvár 112 B4
Dunajevcy 113 D3
Dunărea 113 E4
Dunaújváros 112 B4
Dunav 72 B2
Dunav 114 D2
Dunbar 5 E2
Dunblane 4 C2
Duncansby Head 3 E2
Dundalk 13 D3
Dundalk B 13 E3
Dun Dealgan 13 D3
Dundee 5 D1
Dundonnell 2 C3
Dundrum B 13 E2
Dunfanaghy 12 C1
Dunfermline 5 D2
Dungannon 13 D2
Dún Garbhán 14 C4
Dungarvan 14 C4
Dungarvan Harbour 14 C4
Dungeness 11 D3
Dungiven 13 D1
Dunglow 12 C1
Dunje 77 E4
Dunkeld 5 D1
Dunkerque 19 F1
Dún Laoghaire 13 E4
Dun-le-Palestel 25 E4
Dunmanus B 14 A4
Dunmanway 14 B4
Dunmore 12 B3
Dunmore East 15 D4
Dunnamanagh 13 D1
Dún na nGall 12 C2
Dunnet 3 D2
Dunnet Head 3 D2
Dunoon 4 C2
Duns 5 E2
Dunshaughlin 13 D3
Dunstable 9 F2
Dunster 8 C3
Dun-sur-Auron 25 F3
Dunvegan 2 B3
Dunvegan Head 2 B3
Duolbbadasgai'sa 95 E1
Đurakovac 76 C2
Durance 30 C3
Durango 36 B1
Duran, Pso 59 D3
Duras 28 C2
Duratón, R 40 A1
Durban-Corbières 32 B2
Durbuy 50 C4
Dúrcal 44 A3
Đurđđevac 71 D2
Đurđđevića Tara 76 B1
Durdevik 72 B4
Düren 51 D3
Durham 5 E4
Durham (Co) 5 E4
Durlach 54 C2
Durlas 14 C3
Durmanec 70 C2
Durmitor 76 B2
Durness 2 C2
Dürnkrut 57 F2
Dürnstein 57 E2
Durrës 76 C4
Durrësit, Gjiri i 76 C4
Durrow 12 C4
Dursey I 14 A4
Dursley 9 D2
Durtal 23 E4
Duruelo de la Sierra 36 B3
Dusina 75 F1
Düsseldorf 17 E4
Duved 101 D2
Duvno 75 E1
Duži (Bosna i Hercegovina) 75 F2
Duži (Bosna i Hercegovina) 76 A2
Dverberg 94 A3
Dvor 71 D3
Dyfed 8 C1
Dyje 57 E1
Dyrnes 100 B1
Dyrøya 94 B3
Džami tepe 77 F3
Džanići 75 F1
Džep 77 E1
Dzermiádo 91 E4
Dzeržinsk 111 D4
Dzierżoniów 112 A2
Dziwńw 49 E1
Džumajlija 77 E3
Dźwirzyno 49 F1

E

Eaglescliffe 5 E4
Eaní 79 D4
Earith 10 C1
Earlston 5 D2
Earn 5 D1
Easingwold 7 D1
Easky 12 B2
Eastbourne 10 C3
East Dereham 7 F3
Easter Ross 2 C3
East Grinstead 10 C3
East Kilbride 4 C2
Eastleigh 9 E3
East Linton 5 D2
East Retford 7 D2
East Sussex 10 C3
Eaux-Bonnes 37 D2
Eauze 28 B3
Ebbw Vale 9 D2
Ebeleben 52 C2
Ebeltoft 108 B3
Eben 59 F1
Ebenfurth 57 F3
Ebensee 56 C3
Eberbach 55 D1
Ebermannstadt 52 C4
Ebern 52 C4
Eberndorf 70 B1
Ebersbach 53 F2
Ebersberg 56 B3
Eberstein 70 B1
Eberswalde 49 E3
Ebmath 53 D3
Eboli 64 C4
Ebrach 52 C4
Ebreichsdorf 57 F3
Ebreuil 26 A4
Ebro, Emb del 35 F2
Ebro, R 37 D4
Ebstorf 48 B3
Eccleshall 6 C3
Eceabat 115 E3
Echallens 27 D3
Echarmeaux, les 26 B4
Echarri-Aranaz 36 C2
Echegárate, Pto de 36 B1
Echelles, les 30 C1
Echt 17 D4
Echte 52 B2
Echternach 21 D2
Écija 43 E2
Ečka 72 C2
Eckartsberga 52 C2
Eckernförde 48 A1
Eckerö 106 C3
Ecommoy 23 F4
Ecos 19 E3
Ecouché 18 C4
Ecrins, les 31 D2
Ecrins, Massif des 31 D2
Ecrins, Parc Nat des 31 D2
Ecueillé 25 E3
Ed 105 D4
Eda glasbruk 105 D3
Edam 16 C2
Edane 105 E3
Eday 3 E1
Eddrachillis B 2 C2
Ede 16 C3
Edelény 112 B3
Edelweißspitze 59 E2
Eden 5 D4
Edenderry 13 D4
Edenkoben 54 C2
Eder 52 A3
Eder-Stausee 52 A3
Édessa 79 E3
Edewecht 47 E3
Edgeworthstown 12 C3
Edinburgh 5 D2
Edipsós 83 F3
Edirne 115 E3
Edland 104 B3
Edolo 58 C3
Edremit 115 E4
Edsåsdalen 101 D2
Edsbro 106 B3
Edsbyn 101 E4
Edsele 101 F2
Eeklo 50 B3
Eelde 47 D3
Eemshaven 47 D3
Eferding 56 C2
Efes 115 E4
Efira 86 B1
Efkarpía (Makedonía) 79 F2
Efkarpía (Makedonía) 80 B2
Eforie 115 E1
Efxinoúpoli 83 F2
Egadi, Is 68 A3
Ega, R 36 C2
Egeln 52 C1
Egéo Pélagos 84 A1
Eger 112 B3
Egersund 104 A4
Egeskov 108 B4
Egestorf 48 A3
Egg 58 B1
Eggenburg 57 E2
Eggenfelden 56 B2
Eggesin 49 E2
Eggum 94 A3
Eghezée 50 C4
Egiáli 89 D3
Egie 87 D4
Egilsstaðir 96 C2
Égina 87 F2
Égina, N 87 F2
Eginio 79 F3
Égio 83 E4
Égira 87 D1
Egletons 29 D1
Eglinton 13 D1
Egloffstein 55 F1
Egmond aan Zee 16 C2
Egósthena 87 E1
Egremont 5 D4
Egtved 108 A3
Egués 36 C2
Eguzon 25 E3
Ehinádes Nissiá 82 C4
Ehingen 55 D3
Ehinos 81 D2
Ehra-Lessien 48 B4
Ehrang-Pfalzel 54 A1
Ehrenberg 52 B3
Ehrenhausen 70 C1
Ehrwald 58 C1
Eibar 36 B1
Eibenstock 53 D3
Eibiswald 70 B1
Eichstätt 55 F2
Eide 100 B2
Eider 48 A2
Eidfjord 104 B2
Eidfjorden 104 B2
Eiði 96 A3
Eidkjosen 94 B2
Eidsborg 104 B3
Eidsbugarden 100 B3
Eidsdal 100 B2
Eidsfjorden 94 A3
Eidsfoss 104 C3
Eidsvåg 100 B2
Eidsvoll 105 D2
Eigg 2 B4
Eikelandsosen 104 A2
Eiken 104 B4
Eikeren 104 C3
Eikesdal 100 B2
Eilean Donan Castle 2 B3
Eilenburg 53 D2
Eilsleben 52 C1
Einbeck 52 B2
Eindhoven 16 C4
Einsiedeln 58 A2
Eisenach 52 B3
Eisenberg 53 D3
Eisenerz 57 D3
Eisenerzer Alpen 57 D4
Eisenhüttenstadt 49 F4
Eisenkappel 70 A1
Eisenstadt 57 F3
Eisfeld 52 C3
Eišiškės 110 C4
Eisleben 52 C2
Eislingen 55 D2
Eisriesenwelt-Höhle 59 E1
Eitorf 51 E3
Eivissa 45 D4
Ejea de los Caballeros 37 D3
Ejulve 41 E2
Ekára 83 E2
Ekenäs 107 E3
Ekshärad 105 E3
Eksjö 109 D1
Elafohóri 81 F1
Elafonissi 87 E4
Élafos 82 B2
El Algar 45 D2
El Almendro 42 C2
El Aquián 44 B4
El Arahal 43 E3
El Arenal 45 E3
Elassóna 83 E1
El Atazar, Emb de 40 B1
Eláti (Makedonía) 79 E4
Eláti (Thessalía) 83 D2
Eláti *Mt* 82 B3
Elátia 83 F3
Elatohóri 79 E3
Elatoú 83 D4
Elatóvrissi 83 D3
Elba, Isola d' 62 C2
El Barco de Ávila 39 E2
Elbasan 76 C4
Elbe 48 B3
Elbe-Lübeck-Kanal 48 B2
El Berrón 35 D1
Elbe-Seitenkanal 48 B4
Elbeuf 19 D3
Elbigenalp 58 C2
Elbingerode 52 C2
Elbląg 110 B4
El Bodón 39 D2
El Bonillo 40 C4
El Bosque 43 E3
Elburg 17 D2
El Burgo 43 E3
El Burgo de Osma 36 A3
El Burgo Ranero 35 E3
El Cabaco 39 E2
El Caló 45 D4
El Campo de Peñaranda 39 F1
El Carpio 43 F2
El Carpio de Tajo 39 F3
El Casar de Talamanca 40 B2
El Castillo de las Guardas 43 D2

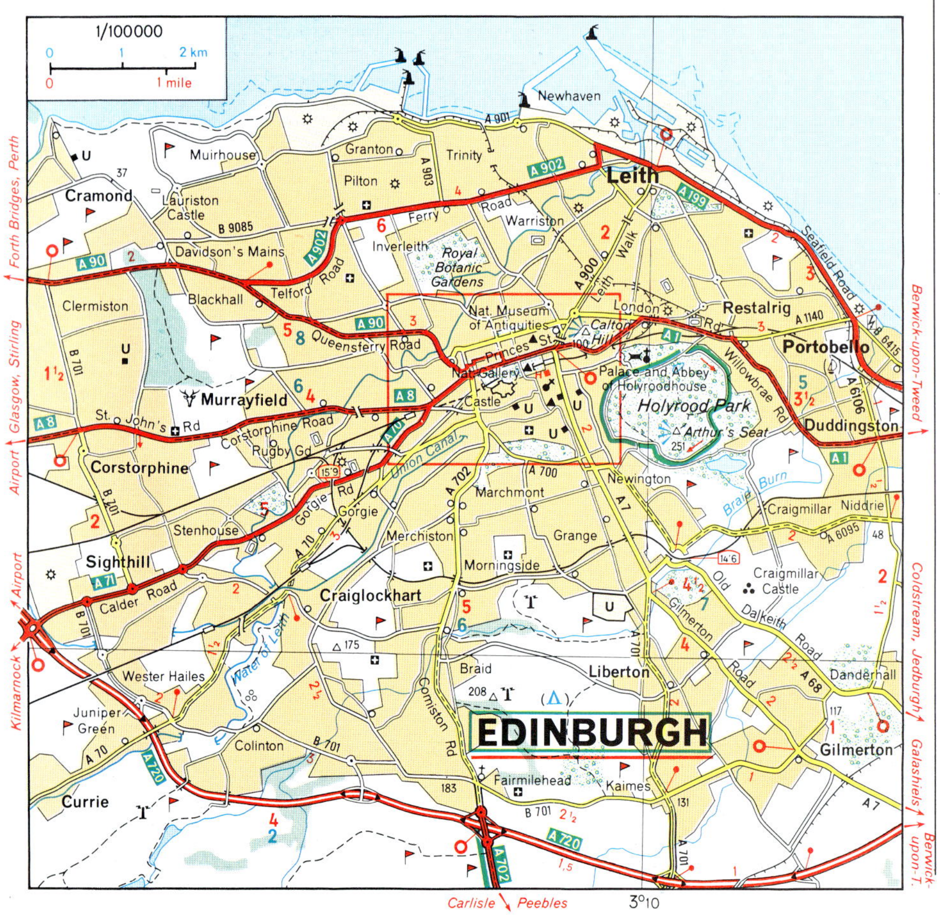

1/100000
0 1 2 km
0 1 mile
EDINBURGH
Newhaven
Leith
Granton
Trinity
Pilton
Muirhouse
Cramond
Lauriston Castle
Davidson's Mains
Inverleith
Royal Botanic Gardens
Warriston
Restalrig
Portobello
Blackhall
Clermiston
Nat. Museum of Antiquities
Calton Hill
Princes St
Nat. Gallery
Castle
Palace and Abbey of Holyroodhouse
Holyrood Park
Arthur's Seat
Duddingston
Murrayfield
Corstorphine
Stenhouse
Gorgie
Sighthill
Merchiston
Marchmont
Newington
Grange
Morningside
Craigmillar
Craigmillar Castle
Niddrie
Craiglockhart
Liberton
Braid
Wester Hailes
Juniper Green
Colinton
Currie
Fairmilehead
Kaimes
Gilmerton
Danderhall
Seafield Road
Queensferry Road
Ferry Road
Telford Road
St. John's Rd
Corstorphine Road
Union Canal
Calder Road
Water of Leith
Comiston Rd
Gilmerton Road
Dalkeith Road
Willowbrae Rd
Leith Walk
Braid Burn
Forth Bridges, Perth
Glasgow, Stirling
Airport
Kilmarnock
Berwick-upon-Tweed
Coldstream, Jedburgh
Galashiels
Carlisle
Peebles
A 90
A 902
A 901
A 199
A 1
A 8
A 71
A 70
A 702
A 720
A 7
A 68
A 6095
B 9085
3°10

El Centenillo 44 A1
El Cerro de Andévalo 42 C2
Elche 45 D2
Elche de la Sierra 44 C1
El Coronil 43 D3
El Cubillo 41 D3
El Cubo de Don Sancho 39 D1
El Cubo de Tierra del Vino 39 E1
El Cuervo 43 D3
Elda 45 D1
Elde 48 C3
Eldena 48 C3
Elefsína 87 F1
Eleftherés (Makedonía) 80 C2
Eleftherés (Stereá Eláda) 87 E1
Eleftherés (Thessalía) 83 E1
Eléfthero 78 C4
Eleftherohóri 79 D4
Eleftheroúpoli 80 C2
El Ejido 44 B4
Elemir 72 C2
Elena 115 D2
Eleófito 82 C3
Eleohóri 80 C3
Eleohória 80 A3
Eleónas 83 E4
Eleoússa 93 F1
El Escorial 40 A2
El Espinar 40 A2
El Figueró 32 B4
El Formigal 37 D2
Elgå 100 D3
Elgin 3 D3
Elgóibar 36 B1
Elgol 2 B4
El Grado 37 E3
El Grado, Emb de 37 E3
El Grao 41 E4
El Grau 41 F3
Elhovo 115 E2
El Hoyo de Pinares 40 A2
Eliá 87 D4
Elie 5 D2
Elikónas, Óros 83 F4
Elimäki 107 F2
Elinikó 86 C2
Elinohóri 81 F1
Elizondo 36 C1
Ełk 110 C4
Ellesmere 6 B3
Ellesmere Port 6 B2
Ellingen 55 E2
Ellon 3 E4
Ellös 108 C1
Ellrich 52 B2
Ellwangen 55 E2
El Madroño 42 C2
El Maestrazgo 41 E2
Elmas 66 B4
El Masnou 32 B4
El Molar 40 B2
El Molinillo 40 A3
El Moral 44 C2
Elmshorn 48 A2
Elne 32 B2
Elnesvågen 100 B2
Elóna 87 D3
Elopía 83 F4
Elorn 22 B2
Élos (Kríti) 90 B3
Élos (Pelopónissos) 87 D4
Eloúnda 91 E3
Eloyes 27 D1
El Pardo 40 A2
El Paular 40 A1
El Pedernoso 40 B3
El Pedroso 43 D2
El Perelló (Catalunya) 41 F2
El Perelló (Valencia) 41 E4
Elphin 12 C3
El Picazo 40 C4
El Pinell de Brai 41 F1
El Pobo de Dueñas 41 D2
El Pont d'Armentera 37 F4
El Portal 43 D4
El Port de la Selva 32 C3
El Port de Llança 32 B3
El Prat de Llobregat 32 A4
El Puente 36 A1
El Puente del Arzobispo 39 F3
El Puerto de Sagunto 41 E3
El Puerto de Santa María 43 D4
El Real de la Jara 43 D2
El Real de San Vicente 39 F2
El Remolcador, Pto 41 E3
El Robledo 39 F4
El Rocío 42 C3
El Romeral 40 B3
El Rompido 42 C3
El Ronquillo 43 D2
El Royo 36 B3
El Rubio 43 E3
Elsa 60 C4
El Saler 41 E4
El Salobral 40 C4
El Saucejo 43 E3
Elsdorf 17 D4
Elserdorf 55 F2
El Serrat 32 A2
Elsfleth 47 F3
Elsterberg 53 D3
Elsterwerda 53 E2
El Tiemblo 40 A2
Eltisley 9 F1
Eltmann 52 C4
El Toboso 40 B3
El Torcal 43 F3
Eltz 51 E4
El Vado, Emb de 40 B1
Elvanfoot 4 C3
Elvas 38 C4
Elvekrok 100 B3
El Vellón, Emb de 40 A2
Elven 22 C4
El Vendrell 37 F4
Elverum 105 D2
El Vicario, Emb de 40 A4
El Villar de Arnedo 36 C2
El Viso 43 E1
El Viso del Alcor 43 D2
Elx 45 D2
Ely 10 C1
Elygsfors 109 E2
Elzach 54 C3
Elze 52 B1
Emån 109 E2
Embessós 82 C3
Embid 41 D1
Embid de Ariza 36 C4
Émbonas 93 E1
Emboriós (Híos) 89 D1
Emboriós (Sími) 93 E1
Embrun 31 D2
Emden 47 E3
Emet 115 F4
Emilia-Romagna 60 C3
Emlichheim 17 E2
Emmaboda 109 E2
Emmeloord 16 C2
Emmen 17 E1
Emmendingen 54 C3
Emmerich 17 D3
Emocriós 89 F3
Em. Papás 80 B2
Empoli 60 C4
Empúries 32 C3
Ems 17 E1
Emsdetten 17 E2
Ems-Jade-Kanal 47 E3
Emskirchen 55 E1
Enafors 101 D2
Enajärvi 103 E4
Enånger 101 F4
Encamp 32 A2
Encausse 37 E1
Encinas de Abajo 39 E1
Encinasola 42 C1
Encinedo 34 C3
Endelave 108 B3
Endrinal 39 E2
Enego 59 D3
Enfesta 34 A2
Eng 59 D1
Engadin 58 B3
Engarés 88 C3
Engelberg 27 F3
Engelhartszell 56 C2
Engeløya 97 E1
Engelsdorf 53 D2
Engelskirchen 17 E4
Engen 58 A1
Enger 17 F2
Engerdal 101 D3
Enghien 50 B3
England 9 F1
English Channel 10 A4
Engstingen 55 D3
Enguera 41 E4
Enguídanos 41 D3
Enhammarsfjärden 101 F4
Enipéas 83 E2
Enkhuizen 16 C2
Enköping 106 B3
Enna 68 C3
Enneberg 59 D2
Ennell, L 12 C3
Ennepetal 17 E4
Ennezat 26 A4
Ennis 12 B4
Enniscorthy 15 D3
Enniskerry 13 D4
Enniskillen 13 D2
Ennistimon 12 B4
Enns 57 D3
Enns R 57 D3
Eno 103 F2
Enol, L 35 E2
Enonkoski 103 F3
Enontekiö 95 D3
Énos, Óros 86 A1
Enschede 17 E2
Ensisheim 27 E1
Entlebuch 27 F2
Entraygues-sur-Truyère 29 E2
Entredichos 40 C3
Entre-os-Rios 34 A4
Entrepeñas, Emb de 40 C2
Entrevaux 31 E3
Entrèves 27 E4
Entroncamento 38 B3
Envalira, Pto de 32 A2
Envermeu 19 E2
Enviken 101 E4
Enz 54 C2
Enza 60 B2
Enzklösterle 54 C2
Eochaill 14 C4
Eolie o Lipari, Is 69 D2
Eo, R 34 C1
Epanomí 79 F3
Epe 17 D2
Epernay 20 B3
Epernon 19 E4
Epidávrou, Kólpos 87 E2
Epidávrou Limirás, Kólpos 87 E4
Épila 36 C3
Epinac 26 B3
Epinal 27 D1
Epine, l' 20 B3
Episkopí (Kríti) 90 C3
Episkopí (Kríti) 91 E3
Episkopí (Makedonía) 79 E3
Episkopí (Pelopónissos) 87 E3
Epitálio 86 B2
Eppan 59 D3
Epping 10 C2
Eppingen 55 D2
Epsom 10 C3
Eptahóri 78 C4
Eptálofos 83 E3
Epte 19 E3
Epworth 7 D2
Eraclea 59 E4
Eraclea-Mare 59 E4
Eräjärvi 103 D3
Erásmio, N. 81 D2
Eratiní 83 E4
Eratinó 80 C2
Erátira 79 D3
Erba 58 B4

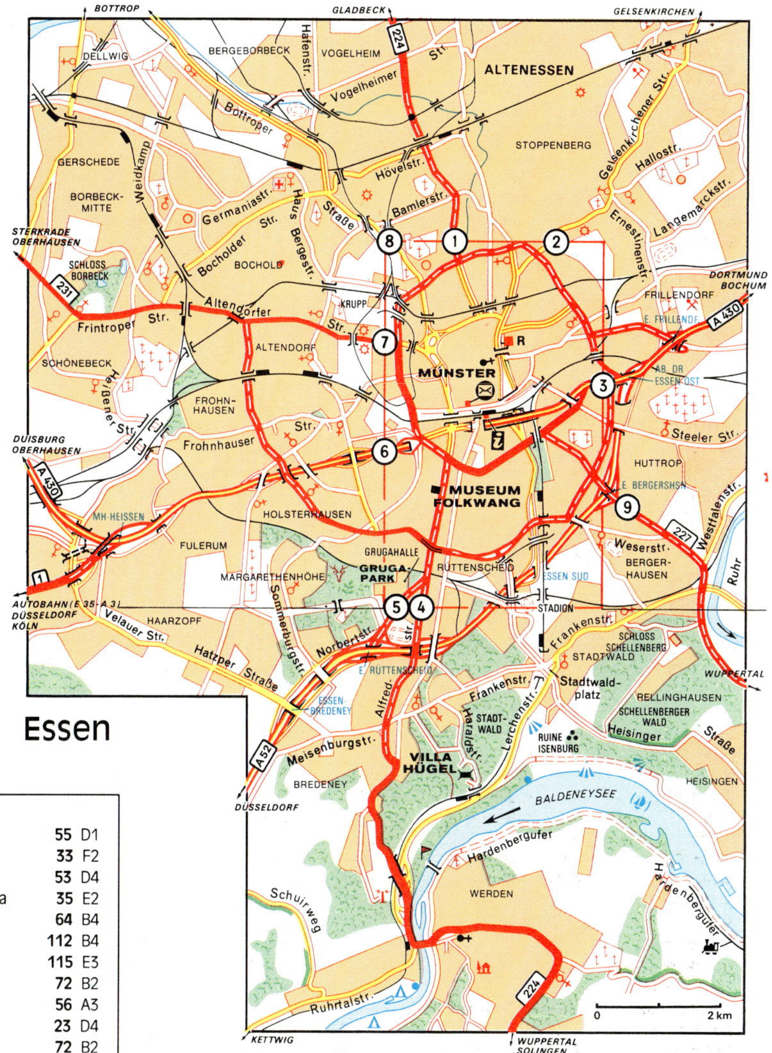
BOTTROP
GLADBECK
GELSENKIRCHEN
DELLWIG
BERGEBORBECK
VOGELHEIM
ALTENESSEN
GERSCHEDE
STOPPENBERG
BORBECK-MITTE
STERKRADE OBERHAUSEN
SCHLOSS BORBECK
BOCHOLD
DORTMUND BOCHUM
FRILLENDORF
KRUPP
ALTENDORF
SCHÖNEBECK
MÜNSTER
FROHNHAUSEN
DUISBURG OBERHAUSEN
HUTTROP
MUSEUM FOLKWANG
HOLSTERHAUSEN
FULERUM
GRUGAHALLE
GRUGA-PARK
RÜTTENSCHEID
MARGARETHENHÖHE
BERGERHAUSEN
AUTOBAHN (E 35-A 3) DÜSSELDORF KÖLN
HAARZOPF
STADION
SCHLOSS SCHELLENBERG
STADTWALD
WUPPERTAL
RELLINGHAUSEN
SCHELLENBERGER WALD
RUINE ISENBURG
VILLA HÜGEL
BREDENEY
HEISINGEN
DÜSSELDORF
BALDENEYSEE
WERDEN
KETTWIG
WUPPERTAL SOLINGEN
2 km

Essen

Erbach 55 D1
Erbalunga 33 F2
Erbendorf 53 D4
Ercina, L de la 35 E2
Ercolano 64 B4
Érd 112 B4
Erdek 115 E3
Erdevik 72 B2
Erding 56 A3
Erdre 23 D4
Erdut 72 B2
Eresma, R 40 A1
Eressós 85 E2
Erétria 84 B4
Erezée 50 C4
Erfde 48 A2
Erft 17 D4
Erftstadt 51 E3
Erfurt 52 C3
Erges, R 39 D2
Ergoldsbach 56 B2
Eriboll, L 2 C2
Erice 68 A3
Ericeira 38 A3
Ericht, L 2 C4
Erikoússa, N 78 A4
Eriksberg 106 A4
Eriksmåle 109 E2
Erillas 43 E1
Erímanthos 86 C2
Erímanthos, Óros 86 C1
Eripol, Pto del 37 E3
Erithrés 87 E1
Erkelenz 17 D4
Erkner 49 E4
Erla 37 D3
Erlangen 55 F1
Erlsbach 59 E2
Ermenonville 19 F3
Ermidas-Aldeia 42 A1
Ermióni 87 E2
Ermoúpoli 88 B2
Ermsleben 52 C2
Erndtebrück 17 F4
Erne 13 D3
Ernée 23 E3
Erne, R 12 C2
Ernestinovo 71 F2
Ernstbrunn 57 F2
Erquy 22 C2
Errazu 36 C1
Errigal Mt 12 C1
Erris Head 12 A2
Erskine Bridge 4 C2
Erstein 21 E4
Ervenik 75 D1
Ervidel 42 B1
Ervy 26 B1
Erwitte 17 F3
Erzberg 57 D3
Erzen 76 C4
Erzgebirge 53 E3
Esbjerg 108 A3
Esblada 37 F4
Esbo 107 E3
Escabas, R 40 C2
Escairón 34 B2
Escalada 35 F2
Escalante 36 A1
Escaldes, les 32 A2
Escalona 40 A2
Escalonilla 40 A3
Escalos de Cima 38 C2
Escandón, Pto de 41 D2
Esca, R 37 D2
Escarène, l' 31 E3
Escároz 37 D2
Escatrón 37 D4
Escaut (B) 50 B3
Escaut (F) 20 A2
Esch (D) 51 F4
Esch (L) 21 D2
Eschede 48 B4
Eschenbach 53 D4
Eschershausen 52 B1
Eschwege 52 B2
Eschweiler 51 D3
Escombreras 45 D3
Escorihuela 41 E2
Escudo, Pto del 35 F2
Escúllar 44 B3
Escurial 39 E4
Esens 47 E3
Esera, R 37 E2
Esgueva 35 F4
Esguevillas de Esgueva 35 F4
Esher 9 F2
Esino 61 E4
Esk 5 D3
Eskifjörður 96 C2
Eskilstuna 106 A4
Eskisehir 115 F3
Eskoriatza 36 B1
Esla, R 35 D4
Eslarn 56 B1
Eslohe 17 F4
Eslöv 109 D3
Espa 105 D2
Espadañedo 34 C3
Espadán, Sa de 41 E3
Espalion 29 E3
Esparreguera 32 A4
Espedal 100 C3
Espejo 43 F2
Espelette 28 A4
Espelkamp 17 F2
Espenschied 51 F4
Espera 43 D3
Esperó, Pta 45 F2
Espichel, C 38 A4
Espiel 43 E1
Espigüete 35 E2
Espinama 35 E2
Espinho 34 A4
Espinilla 35 F2
Espinosa de Cerrato 35 F4
Espinosa de los Monteros 36 A1
Espoo 107 E3
Esporles 45 E3
Esposende 34 A4
Espot 37 F2
Espuña, Sa de 44 C2
Esquedas 37 D3
Esquivias 40 A2
Essarts, les 24 B3
Esse 102 C1
Essen (Niedersachsen) 17 E2
Essen (Nordrhein-Westfalen) 17 E3
Essenbach 56 B2
Essex 11 D2
Essími 81 E2
Esslingen 55 D2
Essonne 25 F1
Essoyes 26 B1
Est, Canal de l' 27 D1
Estaca, Pto de la 42 A4
Estacas de Trueba, Pto de las 35 F2
Estadilla 37 E3
Estagel 32 B2
Estaires 19 F1
Estarreja 38 B1
Estats, Pic d' 37 F2
Estavayer 27 E3
Este 61 D1
Estella 36 C2
Estepa 43 E3
Estepona 43 E4
Esteras de Medina 36 B4
Esterel 31 E4
Esternay 20 A4
Esterri d'Àneu 37 F2
Estissac 26 B1
Estói 42 B3
Estonija 110 C2
Estoril 38 A4
Estrela, Sa da 38 C2
Estrella 44 A1
Estremadura 38 A3
Estremoz 38 C4
Estret de Collegats 37 F3
Estrées-St-Denis 19 F3
Esztergom 112 B4
Etables 22 C2

Etain 20 C3
Etampes 19 F4
Etaples 19 E1
Etel 22 B4
Etelhem 109 F4
Etive, L 4 B1
Etna, M 69 D3
Etne 104 A3
Etolia-Akarnania 82 C3
Etolikó 82 C4
Etrépagny 19 E3
Etretat 19 D2
Ettelbruck 21 D2
Etten 16 C3
Ettenheim 54 C3
Ettington 9 E1
Ettlingen 54 C2
Eugénie-les-Bains 28 B4
Eume, Emb del 34 B1
Eume, R 34 B1
Eupen 51 D4
Eura 107 D2
Eurajoki 107 D2
Euratsfeld 57 D3
Eure 19 E4
Eure (Dépt) 19 E3
Eure-et-Loir 25 E1
Europabrücke 59 D2
Europoort 16 B3
Euskadi 36 B2
Euskirchen 51 E3
Eußenhausen 52 B3
Eutin 48 B2
Evangelismós 83 E1
Evangelístria 83 F4
Evaux-les-Bains 25 F4
Évdilos 89 D2
Evendorf 48 B3
Evenes 94 B3
Evenskjær 94 B3
Evergem 50 B3
Everöd 109 D3
Evertsberg 101 E4
Evesham 9 E1
Evian 27 D3
Évia, N 84 B3
Evijärvi 102 C2
Evinohóri 83 D4
Évinos 83 D3
Evisa 33 F3
Evje 104 B4
Évlalo 81 D2
Evolène 27 E4
Évora 38 B4
Évoramonte 38 B4
Evran 18 B4
Evrecy 18 C3
Evreux 19 E3
Evritania 83 D2
Evron 23 E3
Evropós 79 F2
Évros 81 F2
Évros R 81 F2
Evrostína 87 D1
Evrótas 87 D3
Evry 19 F4
Évzoni 79 F2
Exaplátanos 79 E2
Éxarhos 83 F4
Excideuil 29 D1
Exe 8 C3
Exeter 8 C3
Exmes 19 D4
Exmoor Nat Pk 8 C3
Exmouth 8 C3
Exohí (Ípiros) 78 C4
Exohí (Makedonía) 79 E3
Exohí (Makedonía) 80 B1
Exómvourgo 88 C2
Exter 17 F2
Extremadura 39 E4
Eydehavn 104 C4
Eye 9 F1
Eyemouth 5 E2
Eye Pen 2 B2
Eygues 30 C2
Eyguières 30 C4
Eygurande 29 E1
Eyjafjörður 96 B1
Eymet 28 C2
Eymoutiers 29 D1
Eyre 28 B3
Eyrieux 30 B2
Eysturoy 96 A3
Eyzies, les 29 D2
Ezcaray 36 B2
Eze 31 E3
Ezine 115 E4

F

Faak 59 F2
Fabara 37 E4
Fåberg 105 D2
Fabero 34 C2
Fåborg 108 B4
Fabriano 61 E4
Fábricas de Riópar 44 C1
Fabro 63 D1
Facinas 43 D4
Facture 28 A2
Faenza 61 D3
Færøerne 96 A3
Faeto 64 B3
Fafe 34 A4
Făgăras 113 D4
Făgărașului, M 113 D4
Fågelfors 109 E2
Fagernes (Oppland) 104 C2
Fagernes (Troms) 94 C2
Fagersta 105 F3
Fairford 9 E2
Fair Head 13 E1
Fair I 3 F3
Fakenham 7 E3
Fakovići 72 C4
Fakse 108 C4
Fakse Ladeplads 108 C4
Falaise 18 C4
Falakró, Óros 80 C1
Falássarna 90 B3
Falcade 59 D3
Falces 36 C2
Falconara Marittima 61 F3
Falcone 69 D2
Falcone, C del 66 A1
Falerna 67 E3
Faliráki 93 F1
Falkefjellet 95 F1
Falkenberg (D) 53 E2
Falkenberg (S) 108 C2
Falkensee 49 D4
Falkenstein 53 D3
Falkirk 4 C2
Falkland 5 D2
Falkonéra, N 87 F3
Falköping 109 D1
Fallersleben 48 B4
Fällfors 98 B4
Fallingbostel 48 A4
Falmouth 8 B4
Falset 37 F4
Falster 108 C4
Falterona Mte 61 D3
Fălticeni 113 D3
Falun 105 F2
Falzarego, Pso 59 D3
Fámjin 96 A4
Fanad Head 13 D1
Fanári (Pelopónissos) 87 E2
Fanári (Pelopónissos) 86 C2
Fanári (Thessalía) 83 D2
Fanári (Thráki) 81 D2
Fanári, Akr 89 D2
Fanefjord 108 C4
Fani i Madh 76 C3
Fani i Vogël 76 C3
Fanjeaux 32 A1
Fannich, L 2 C3
Fano 61 E3
Fanø 108 A3
Fanø Bugt 108 A3
Fanós 79 F2
Faouët, le 22 B3
Faou, le 22 B3
Farángi Samariás 90 B4
Farángi Víkou 78 C4
Fara Novarese 58 A4
Fårbo 109 E2
Fardes, R 44 A3
Fareham 9 E3
Fårevejle 108 B3
Färgelanda 105 D4
Färila 101 F3
Farindola 63 F1
Faringdon 9 E2
Farini d'Olmo 60 B2
Färjestaden 109 E2
Farkadóna 83 E1
Farkaždin 72 C2
Farlete 37 D3
Farmakonissi 89 F2
Farnborough 9 F3
Farnese 63 D2
Farnham 9 F3
Faro 42 B3
Fårö 109 F3
Fårösund 109 F3
Farra d'Alpago 59 E3
Fársala 83 E2
Farsø 108 A2
Farsund 104 A4
Farum 108 C3
Fasano 65 E3
Fašku Vaskojoki 95 E3
Fastov 113 E2
Fátima 38 B3
Fatmomakke 97 E4
Faucille, Col de la 27 D3
Faucogney 27 D1
Faulquemont 21 D3
Fauquembergues 19 E1
Fauske 97 F2
Fauville 19 D3
Fåvang 100 C3
Favara 68 C4
Favareta 41 E4
Faverges 27 D4
Faverney 27 D1
Faversham 11 D3
Favignana, I 68 A3
Fawley 9 E3
Faxaflói 96 A2
Fayence 31 D4
Fayl-Billot 26 C1
Fayón 37 E4
Fay-sur-Lignon 30 B2
Fažana 70 A4
Feale 14 B3
Fécamp 19 D2
Féclaz, la 31 D1
Feda 104 B4
Feggesund 108 A2
Fehmarn 48 B1
Fehmarnbelt 48 B1
Fehmarnsund 48 B1
Fehrbellin 49 D3
Fehring 57 F4
Fejø 108 B4
Feketić 72 B2
Felanitx 45 F3
Felbertauern-tunnel 59 E2
Feld 59 F2
Feldafing 56 A3
Feldbach 57 F4
Feldberg (Baden-Württemberg) 54 C4
Feldberg (Mecklenburg-Vorpommern) 49 D3
Feldkirch 58 B2
Feldkirchen 59 F2
Felgueiras 34 A4
Felixstowe 11 D2
Fellbach 55 D2
Felletin 25 F4
Fellingsbro 105 F3
Felton 5 E3
Feltre 59 D3
Femer Bælt 108 B4
Femundsmarka 101 D3
Fene 34 B1
Fener 59 D3
Fenestrelle 31 E1
Fénétrange 21 E3
Feolin Ferry 4 B2
Fer à Cheval, Cirque du 27 E4
Feraklós 93 F2
Ferbane 12 C4
Ferdinandovac 71 D1
Ferdinandshof 49 E2
Fère-Champenoise 20 B4
Fère-en-Tardenois 20 A3
Fère, la 20 A2
Ferentino 63 F3
Féres 81 F2
Feria 43 D1
Feričanci 71 E2
Ferlach 70 A1
Fermanagh 12 C2
Fermo 61 F4
Fermoselle 34 C4
Fermoy 14 C4
Fernancaballero 40 A4
Fernán Núñez 43 F2
Ferney-Voltaire 27 D4
Fernpaß 58 C1
Ferrandina 65 D4
Ferrara 61 D2
Ferreira 34 C1
Ferreira do Alentejo 42 B1
Ferreira do Zêzere 38 B3
Ferreiras 42 A3
Ferreras de Abajo 35 D3
Ferreries 45 F2
Ferreruela de Huerva 41 D1
Ferret, Cap 28 A2
Ferrette 27 E2
Ferriere 60 B2
Ferrières 25 F1
Ferrol 34 B1
Ferru, M 66 B3
Ferté-Alais, la 19 f4
Ferté-Bernard, la 23 F3
Ferté-Frênel, la 19 D4
Ferté-Gaucher, la 20 A4
Ferté-Macé, la 18 C4
Ferté-Milon, la 20 A3
Ferté-St-Aubin, la 25 E2
Ferté-sous-Jouarre, la 20 A3
Ferté-Vidame, la 19 D4
Fertilia 66 A2
Fervenza, Emb de 34 A1
Festós 91 D4
Festre, Col du 30 C2
Festvåg 97 E1
Fethard 14 C3
Fetlar 3 F1
Fetsund 105 D3
Feucht 55 F1
Feuchtwangen 55 E2
Feunte Dé 35 E2
Feurs 26 B4
Feyzin 30 B1
Ffestiniog 6 A3
Fflint 6 B2
Fiano R. 63 E2
Fiastra 61 F4
Ficarolo 60 C2
Fichtel-gebirge 53 D4
Fidenza 60 B2
Fieberbrunn 59 E1
Fier 114 B3
Fiera di Primiero 59 D3
Fierzës, Liq i 76 C3
Fiesole 61 D3
Fife 5 D2
Fife Ness 5 D1
Figália 86 C2
Figeac 29 E2
Figline Valdarno 61 D4
Figueira da Foz 38 B2
Figueira de Castelo Rodrigo 39 D1
Figueiró dos Vinhos 38 B2
Figueras 32 B3
Figueres 32 B3
Figueruela de Arriba 34 C3
Fihtio 87 D2
Filabres, Sa de los 44 B3
Filadélfi 80 B3
Filadelfia 67 F3
Filáki 83 E2
Filákio 81 F1
Filakopí 88 A4
Filérimos 93 F1
Filey 7 E1
Filfola 68 B4
Filí 87 F1
Filía (Lésvos) 85 F2
Filía (Pelopónissos) 86 C1
Filiátes 82 B1
Filiatrá 86 B3
Filicudi, I 68 C2
Filiouri 81 E2
Filipi 80 C2
Filipiáda 82 C2
Filipjakov 74 C1
Filipos, Akr 88 B3
Filipstad 105 E3
Filira 81 E2
Fillan 100 C1
Fille-fjell 104 B1
Filo 83 E2
Filótas 79 D3
Filottrano 61 F4
Finale Emilia 60 C2
Finale Ligure 31 F3
Fiñana 44 B3
Finca de la Concepción 43 F3

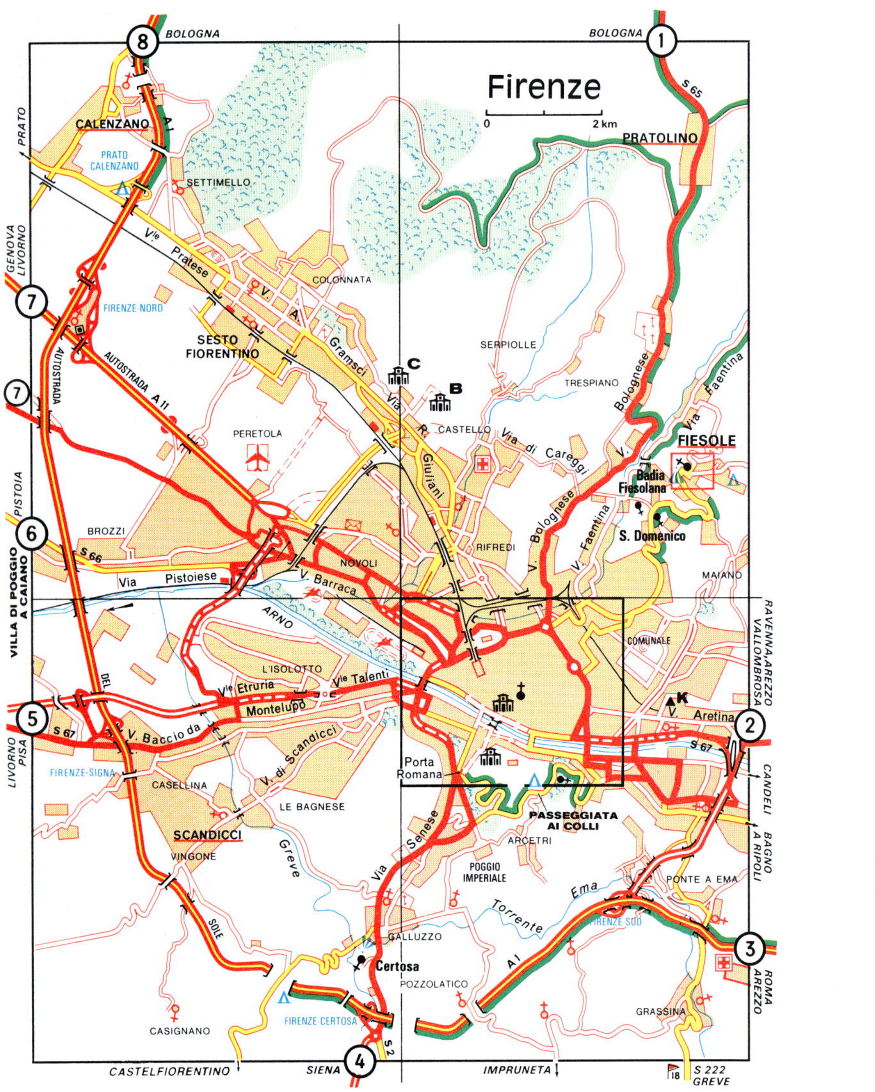

Firenze
0
2 km
BOLOGNA
BOLOGNA
CALENZANO
PRATO
SETTIMELLO
PRATOLINO
GENOVA LIVORNO
SESTO FIORENTINO
FIRENZE-NORD
COLONNATA
PERETOLA
SERPIOLLE
TRESPIANO
CASTELLO
FIESOLE
Badia Fiesolana
S. Domenico
BROZZI
NOVOLI
RIFREDI
MAIANO
PISTOIA
VILLA DI POGGIO A CAIANO
Via Pistoiese
ARNO
L'ISOLOTTO
Monteluppo
COMUNALE
Aretina
RAVENNA, AREZZO VALLOMBROSA
LIVORNO PISA
FIRENZE-SIGNA
CASELLINA
LE BAGNESE
Porta Romana
PASSEGGIATA AI COLLI
SCANDICCI
VINGONE
ARCETRI
POGGIO IMPERIALE
PONTE A EMA
CANDELI
BAGNO A RIPOLI
GALLUZZO
Certosa
POZZOLATICO
FIRENZE-CERTOSA
GRASSINA
ROMA AREZZO
CASIGNANO
CASTELFIORENTINO
SIENA
IMPRUNETA
S 222 GREVE

Finchingfield 11 D2
Findhorn 3 D3
Finikas 88 B2
Finikoúndas 86 C4
Finistère 22 B3
Finisterre, Emb de 40 A3
Finja 109 D3
Finn 13 D1
Finneidfjord 97 E3
Finnentrop 17 F4
Finnmark 95 D2
Finnmarksvidda 95 D3
Finnøy 104 A3
Finnsnes 94 B3
Finow 49 E3
Finowfurt 49 E3
Finskij Zaliv 110 C1
Finspång 105 F4
Finsteraarhorn 27 F3
Finsterau 56 C2
Finsterwalde 53 E1
Finström 106 C3
Fintona 13 D2
Fintown 12 C1
Fionnphort 4 A1
Fiorenzuola d'Arda 60 B2
Firenze 60 C3
Firenzuola 61 D3
Firminy 30 B1
Firmo 67 E2
Fischamend Markt 57 F2
Fischbach 55 F1
Fischbeck 48 C4
Fischen 55 E4
Fishbourne 9 E3
Fishguard 8 B1
Fiskárdo 82 B4
Fiskari 107 E3
Fiskebøl 94 A3
Fismes 20 A3
Fissini 85 D1
Fisterra 34 A2
Fitero 36 C3
Fities 82 C3
Fitjar 104 A2
Fiuggi 63 F3
Fiumicino 63 E3
Fivemiletown 13 D2
Fivizzano 60 B3
Fjällåsen 94 C4
Fjällbacka 105 D4
Fjällnäs 101 D2
Fjärdhundra 106 B3
Fjærland 100 A3
Fjätervålen 101 D3
Fjelie 108 C3
Fjellerup 108 B2
Fjerritslev 108 A2
Fjerze 76 C3
Flå 104 C2
Fladså 108 A3
Fladungen 52 B3
Flaine 27 E4
Flakk 100 C2
Flåm 104 B2
Flamborough Head 7 E1
Flambourári 82 C1
Flámbouro (Makedonía) 79 D3
Flámbouro (Makedonía) 80 B2
Flamignano 63 F2
Flamouriá 79 E3
Flannan I 2 A2
Flåsjön 101 F1
Flåten 94 C2
Flatey 96 A1
Flatråker 104 A2
Flattnitz 59 F2
Flatval 100 C1
Flèche, la 23 E4
Fleetwood 6 B1
Flekkefjord 104 A4
Flen 106 A4
Flensborg Fjord 108 A4
Flensburg 48 A1
Flers 18 C4
Flesberg 104 C3
Flesnes 94 A3
Fleurance 28 C4
Fleurier 27 D3
Fleurus 50 C4
Fleury 19 F4
Fleury-sur-Andelle 19 E3
Flèves, N 87 F2
Flevoland 16 C2
Flexenpaß 58 B2
Flims Waldhaus 58 B2
Flint 6 B2
Flisa 105 D2
Flix 37 E4
Flixecourt 19 F2
Flize 20 C2
Floda 105 F2
Flogny 26 B1
Flöha 53 E3
Flomohóri 87 D4
Flora 77 F3
Florac 29 F3
Flor da Rosa 38 C3
Florennes 50 C4
Florensac 30 A4
Florenville 20 C2
Floreşty 113 E3
Floriáda 82 C2
Floridia 69 D4
Flórina 79 D2
Flórina (Nomos) 79 D3
Florø 104 A1
Flörsheim-Dalsheim 54 C1
Flötningen 101 D3
Floúda, Akr 92 C1
Floúnda 91 E3
Flüelapass 58 B2
Flüelen 58 A2
Flühli 27 F3
Flumendosa 66 C3
Flumen, R 37 D3
Flumet 27 D4
Fluminimaggiore 66 A4
Flums 58 B2
Fluvià, R 32 B3
Foča 76 A1
Foça 115 E4
Foce Verde 63 F3
Fochabers 3 D3
Fockbek 48 A2
Focşani 113 E4
Fódele 91 D3
Foggia 64 C3
Föglö 106 C3
Fohnsdorf 57 D4
Föhr 47 F1
Foiano della Chiana 61 D4
Foinaven 2 C2
Foix 32 A2
Fojnica (Bosna i Hercegovina) 75 F1
Fojnica (Bosna i Hercegovina) 75 F2
Fokí 83 E4
Fokstuhø 100 C3
Folda 97 E1
Foldereid 97 D4
Foldfjorden 97 D4
Foleá 80 C2
Folégandros 91 D1
Folégandros, N 91 D1
Følen 104 A3
Folgaria 59 D4
Folgefonna 104 B2
Folgoët, le 22 A2
Folgoso de la Ribera 35 D2
Foligno 63 E1
Folkestad 100 A3
Folkestone 11 D3
Follafoss 101 D1
Folldal 100 C3
Follebu 104 C1
Follina 59 E3
Föllinge 101 E1
Follonica 62 C1
Folmava 56 B1
Folói 86 C2
Fombellida 35 F4
Fond-de-France, le 31 D1
Fondevila 34 B3
Fondi 63 F3
Fondo 59 D3
Fonfría (Aragón) 37 D4

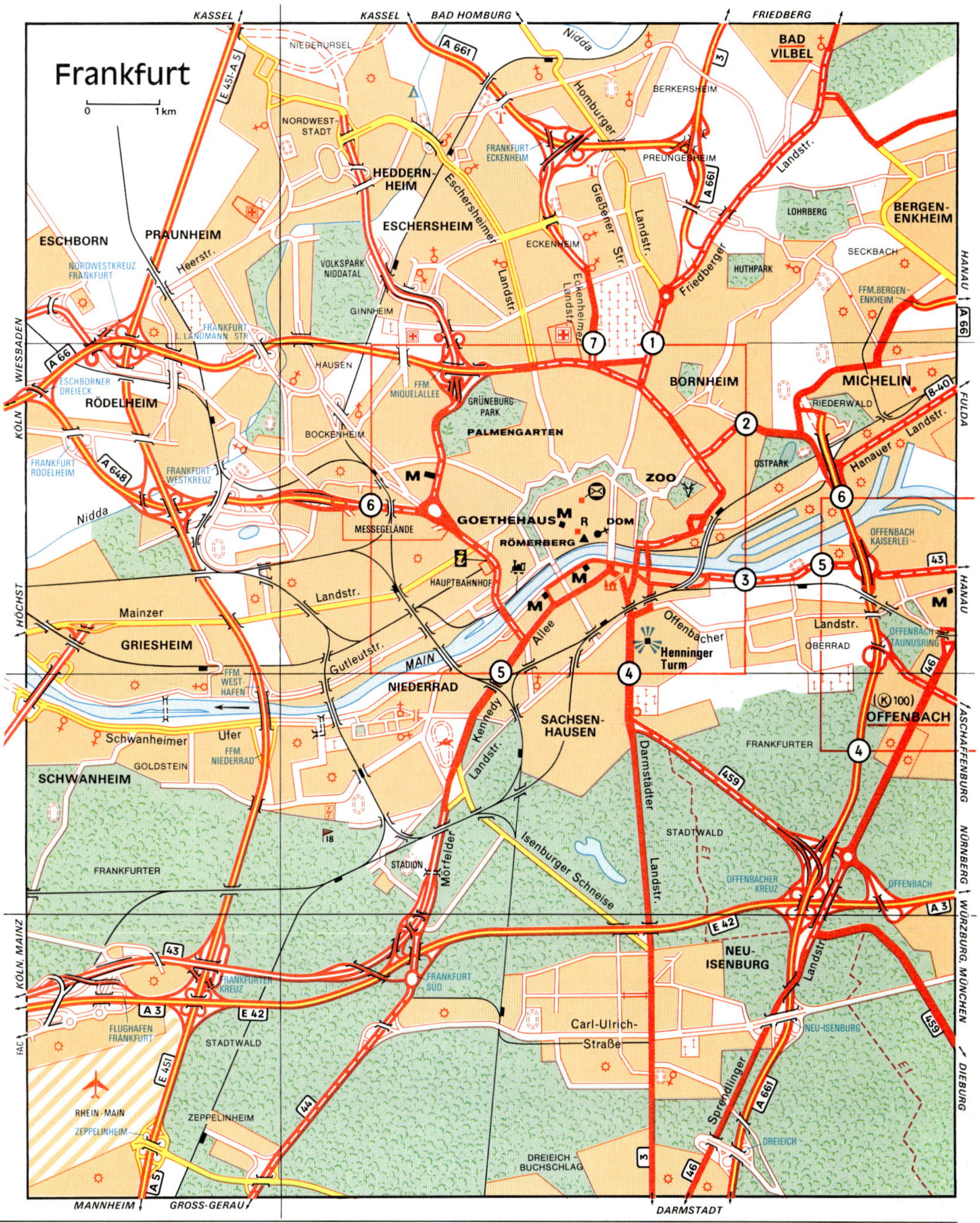

Frankfurt
0 1 km
KASSEL
BAD HOMBURG
FRIEDBERG
BAD VILBEL
HANAU
FULDA
ASCHAFFENBURG
NÜRNBERG
WÜRZBURG, MÜNCHEN
DIEBURG
DARMSTADT
MANNHEIM
GROSS-GERAU
KÖLN, MAINZ
HÖCHST
KÖLN
WIESBADEN
ESCHBORN
PRAUNHEIM
HEDDERN-HEIM
ESCHERSHEIM
NORDWEST-STADT
BERKERSHEIM
PREUNGESHEIM
BERGEN-ENKHEIM
SECKBACH
BORNHEIM
RÖDELHEIM
BOCKENHEIM
PALMENGARTEN
MESSEGELÄNDE
GOETHEHAUS
RÖMERBERG
DOM
ZOO
OSTPARK
MICHELIN
HAUPTBAHNHOF
MAIN
Mainzer Landstr.
GRIESHEIM
NIEDERRAD
SACHSEN-HAUSEN
Henninger Turm
OBERRAD
OFFENBACH
SCHWANHEIM
STADTWALD
STADION
Isenburger Schneise
NEU-ISENBURG
Carl-Ulrich-Straße
ZEPPELINHEIM
RHEIN-MAIN
FLUGHAFEN FRANKFURT
DREIEICH BUCHSCHLAG
Darmstädter Landstr.
Mörfelder Landstr.
Kennedy Allee
Gutleutstr.
Eschersheimer Landstr.
Homburger Landstr.
Friedberger Landstr.
Hanauer Landstr.
Offenbacher Landstr.
Sprendlinger Landstr.
A 661
A 66
A 648
A 5
A 3
E 42
E 451

Fonfría (Castilla-León) 35 D4
Fongen 101 D2
Fonn 100 A3
Fonni 66 B3
Fonollosa 32 A4
Fonsagrada 34 C2
Fontaine 27 E1
Fontainebleau 19 F4
Fontaine-de-Vaucluse 30 C3
Fontaine-Française 26 C2
Fontaine-Henry 18 C3
Fontaine-le-Dun 19 D2
Fontanigorda 60 A3
Fonte Longa 34 B4
Fontenay 26 B2
Fontenay-le-Comte 24 C3
Fontenay-Trésigny 19 F4
Fontevraud-l'Abbaye 25 D2
Fontfroide, Abbaye de 32 B2
Fontgombault 25 D3
Fontibre 35 F2
Fontiveros 39 F1
Fontoy 21 D3
Font-Romeu 32 A2
Fontvieille 30 B4
Fonz 37 E3
Fonzaso 59 D3
Foppolo 58 B3
Forata, Emb de 41 E4
Forbach 21 E3
Forca Canapine 63 F1
Forca Caruso 64 A2
Forca d'Acero 64 A2
Forcall 41 E2
Forcalquier 30 C3
Forcarei 34 A2
Forchheim 55 F1
Forclaz, Col de la 27 E4
Forcola di Mte Rest 59 E3
Førde 100 A3
Førdefjorden 104 A1
Förderstedt 52 C1
Fordingbridge 9 E3
Fordongianus 66 B3
Foreland 9 F3
Forenza 64 C3
Foresta di Burgos 66 B2
Føresvik 104 A3
Forêt d'Orient, Lac de la 26 B1
Forez, Monts du 29 F1
Forfar 5 D1
Forges-les-Eaux 19 E3
Forggensee 55 F4
Forio 64 A4
Forlì 61 D3
Forlì del Sannio 64 A2
Forlimpopoli 61 D3
Formazza 58 A3
Formby 6 B2
Formentera 45 D4
Formentor, C 45 F2
Formerie 19 E3
Formia 64 A3
Formigine 60 C2
Fornaci di Barga 60 C3
Fornells 45 F1
Forni Avoltri 59 E2
Forni di Sopra 59 E3
Forno di Zoldo 59 E3
Fornos de Algodres 38 C1
Fornovo di Taro 60 B2
Forøy 97 E2
Forøyar 96 A3
Forres 3 D3
Forsa 101 F3
Forserum 109 D1
Forshaga 105 E3
Forsnes 100 B1
Forssa 107 E2
Forst 53 F1
Fort Augustus 2 C4
Forte dei Marmi 60 B3
Forth 55 F1
Forth R 4 C2
Forth Bridges 5 D2
Forth, Firth of 5 D2
Fort-Mahon 19 E2
Fortore 64 B2
Fortrose 3 D3
Fortuna 45 D2
Fortuneswell 9 D4
Fort William 2 C4
Forvik 97 D3
Fos (Ariège) 37 F2
Fos (Bouches-du-Rhône) 30 C4
Foscagno, Pso di 58 C3
Fosnavåg 100 A2
Fossacesia 64 B2
Fossano 31 E2
Fossat, le 37 F1
Fossbakken 94 B3
Fosses 50 C4
Fossli 104 B2
Fossombrone 61 E3
Fotiná 79 E4
Fotolívos 80 B2
Fouesnant 22 B3
Foug 21 D4
Fougères 23 D3
Fougerolles 27 D1
Foula 3 E2
Foulness Pt 11 D2
Fountains Abbey 6 C1
Fouras 24 B4
Fourchambault 26 A2
Fourfourás 91 D4
Foúrka 83 E3
Fourmies 20 B2
Fourná 83 D3
Fournels 29 F2
Fournés 90 B3
Foúrni (Dodekánissa) 89 E2
Fourní (Kríti) 91 E3
Foúrni (Pelopónissos) 87 E2
Fourniá, Akr 85 E2
Foúrni, N 89 E2
Fours 26 B3
Fousseret, le 37 F1
Foústani 79 E2
Fowey 8 B4
Foxford 12 B2
Foyers 2 C4
Foyle, L 13 D1
Foyle, R 13 D1
Foz 34 C1
Foz do Arelho 38 A3
Foz do Douro 34 A4
Foz Giraldo 38 C2
Frabosa Soprana 31 F3
Fraddon 8 B4
Fraga 37 E4
Frailes 44 A3

Fraize 27 E1
Fram 70 C1
Frammersbach 52 B4
Fræna 100 B2
Francavilla al Mare 64 A1
Francavilla di Sicilia 69 D3
Francavilla Fontana 65 E4
Francavilla in Sinni 65 D4
Francker 16 C1
Francofonte 69 D4
Francoli, R 37 F4
Francorchamps 51 D4
Frändefors 105 D4
Frangádes 82 C1
Frangísta 83 D3
Frangokástelo 90 C4
Frangy 27 D4
Frankenberg (Hessen) 52 A3
Frankenberg (Sachsen) 53 E3
Frankenburg 56 C3
Frankenmarkt 56 C3
Frankenstein 54 C1
Frankenthal 54 C1
Frankfurt am Main 52 A4
Frankfurt an der Oder 49 F4
Fránk Rezat 55 E2
Fránk Saale 52 B4
Františkovy Lázně 53 D4
Franzburg 49 D1
Franz-Josephs-Höhe 59 E2
Frascati 63 E3
Frascineto 67 E2
Frasdorf 56 B3
Fraserburgh 3 E3
Frasno, Pto del 36 C4
Fratel 38 C3
Fratta Polesine 61 D2
Frauenfeld 58 A1
Frauenkirchen 57 F3
Frauenstein 53 E3
Frechen 17 E4
Frechilla 35 E3
Freckenhorst 17 F3
Fredensborg 108 C3
Fredericia 108 B3
Frederikshavn 108 B1
Frederikssund 108 C3
Frederiksværk 108 C3
Fredrika 102 A1
Fredriksberg 105 E3
Fredrikstad 105 D3
Fregenal de la Sierra 42 C1
Fregene 63 E3
Fréhel, Cap 22 C2
Frei 100 B2
Freiberg 53 E3
Freiberger Mulde 53 D2
Freiburg (Baden-Württemberg) 54 C4
Freiburg (Niedersachsen) 48 A2
Freienhufen 53 E1
Freilassing 56 C3
Freilingen 51 F4
Freising 55 F3
Freistadt 57 D2
Freital 53 E2
Freiwalde 53 E1
Freixedas 38 C1
Freixido 34 C3
Freixo de Espada à Cinta 39 D1
Fréjus 31 D4
Fréjus, Tunnel du 31 D1
Frenchpark 12 C3
Frêne, Col du 31 D1
Freren 17 E2
Freshford 12 C4
Freshwater 9 E3
Fresnay-sur-Sarthe 23 F3
Fresne-St-Mamès 27 D2
Fresnes-en-Woëvre 20 C3
Fresno Alhándiga 39 E1
Fresvikbreen 104 B1
Freudenberg (Baden-Württemberg) 55 D1
Freudenberg (Nordrhein-Westfalen) 17 F4
Freudenstadt 54 C3
Frévent 19 F2
Freyburg 52 C2
Freyenstein 48 C3
Freyung 56 C2
Frí 93 D3
Frías 36 A2
Frías de Albarracín 41 D2
Fribourg 27 E3
Fridingen 55 D3
Friedberg (A) 57 F3
Friedberg (Bayern) 55 F3
Friedberg (Hessen) 52 A4
Friedeberg 47 E3
Friedersdorf 49 E4
Friedland (Niedersachsen) 52 B2
Friedland (Mecklenburg-Vorpommern) 49 D2
Friedrichroda 52 B3
Friedrichshafen 55 D4
Friedrichskoog 47 F2
Friedrichsort 48 A1
Friedrichstadt 47 F1
Friedrichsthal 54 B2
Friesach 57 D4
Friesack 49 D4
Friesland 16 C1
Friesoythe 17 E1
Frigiliana 44 A4
Frihetsli 94 c3
Friis veien 100 C3
Frikes 82 B4
Frilingiánika 90 A1
Frinton-on-Sea 11 D2
Friol 34 B2
Fristad 109 D1
Fritsla 108 C1
Fritzlar 52 A3
Friuli-Venezia Giulia 59 E3
Frizington 5 D4
Frodsham 6 B2
Frogner 105 D3
Frohavet 100 C1
Frohburg 53 D2
Frohnleiten 57 E4
Froissy 19 F3
Froitzheim 51 D3
Frome 9 D3
Fromentine 24 A3
Frómista 35 F3
Fronteira 38 C4
Frontenay-Rohan-Rohan 24 C4
Frontenhausen 56 B2
Frontera 42 A4
Frontignan 30 A4
Fronton 29 D3
Frosinone 63 F3
Frosolone 64 B3
Fröson 101 E2
Frosta 100 C1
Frostavallen 109 D3
Frøstrup 108 A2
Frouard 21 D4
Froússa 82 C2
Frövi 105 F3
Frøya 100 B1
Frøyfjorden 100 B1
Frøysjøen 100 A3
Fruges 19 F1
Fruška 72 b2
Frutigen 27 E3
Frýdek-Místek 112 B3
Fteliá 80 C2
Ftéri (Makedonía) 79 E4
Ftéri (Pelopónissos) 86 C1
Fthiótida 83 E3
Fucecchio 60 C4
Fuencaliente (Castilla-la-Mancha) 43 F1
Fuencaliente (Is Canarias) 42 A4
Fuendejalón 36 C3
Fuendetodos 37 D4
Fuengirola 43 F4
Fuenlabrada 40 A2
Fuenlabrada de los Montes 39 F4
Fuenmayor 36 B2
Fuensalida 40 A3
Fuensanta de Martos 43 F2
Fuensanta, Emb de la 44 C1
Fuente-Alamo 45 D1
Fuente Alamo 45 D2
Fuentecén 35 F4
Fuente de Cantos 43 D1
Fuente del Maestre 43 D1
Fuente de Pedro Naharro 40 B3
Fuente de Piedra 43 E3
Fuente el Fresno 40 A4
Fuenteguinaldo 39 D2
Fuente la Higuera 45 D1
Fuentelapeña 39 E1
Fuente Obejuna 43 E1
Fuente Palmera 43 E2
Fuentepinilla 36 B3
Fuentesauco 39 E1
Fuentes de Andalucía 43 E2
Fuentes de Ayódar 41 E3
Fuentes de Ebro 37 D4
Fuentes de León 43 D1
Fuentes de Nava 35 E3
Fuentes de Oñoro 39 D1
Fuentes de Ropel 35 D3
Fuentes de Valdepero 35 F3
Fuentidueña 35 F4
Fuentidueña de Tajo 40 B3
Fuerte del Rey 44 A2
Fuerteventura 42 C4
Fügen 59 D1
Fuglebjerg 108 B4
Fugløysundet 94 C2
Fulda 52 B3
Fulda *R* 52 B3
Fulgatore 68 A3
Fulpmes 59 D2
Fulufjället 101 D4
Fumay 20 B2
Fumel 28 C3
Funäsdalen 101 D2
Funchal 42 A3
Fundão 38 C2
Funes 59 D2
Fuorn, Pso dal 58 C3
Furadouro 38 B1
Furci 64 B2
Furkapass 58 A3
Furnace 4 B2
Furnás 45 D3
Fürstenau 17 E2
Fürstenberg 49 D3
Fürstenfeld 57 F4
Fürstenfeldbruck 55 F3
Fürstenlager 54 C1
Fürstenwalde 49 E4
Fürstenwerder 49 E3
Fürstenzell 56 C2
Furtei 66 B3
Fürth 55 E1
Furth 56 B1
Furtwangen 54 C3
Furudal 101 E4
Furuflaten 94 C2
Fuscaldo 67 E2
Fusch 59 E1
Fuschl 56 C3
Fuseta 42 B3
Fushë Arrez 76 C3
Fushë Muhur 76 C3
Fusignano 61 D2
Füssen 55 E4
Fustiñana 36 C3
Futa, Pso della 60 C3
Futog 72 C2
Futrikelv 94 B2
Fuzine 70 B3
Fyn 108 B4
Fyne, L 4 B2
Fynshav 108 B4
Fyresdal 104 B3
Fyresvatn 104 B3
Fyrkat 108 B2

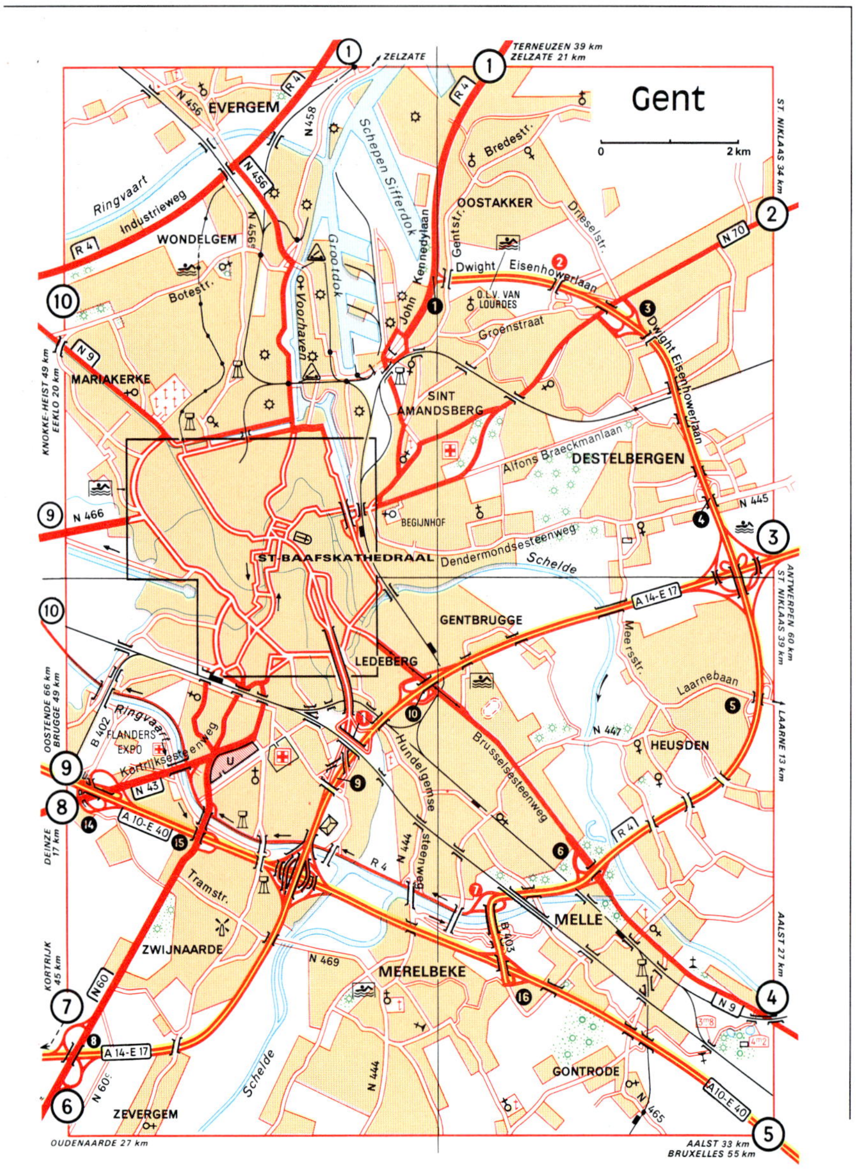

Gent
0
2 km
ZELZATE
TERNEUZEN 39 km
ZELZATE 21 km
EVERGEM
WONDELGEM
OOSTAKKER
MARIAKERKE
SINT AMANDSBERG
DESTELBERGEN
ST-BAAFSKATHEDRAAL
GENTBRUGGE
LEDEBERG
HEUSDEN
MELLE
MERELBEKE
ZWIJNAARDE
GONTRODE
ZEVERGEM
FLANDERS EXPO
OUDENAARDE 27 km
AALST 33 km
BRUXELLES 55 km

G

Gaaldorf 57 D4
Gabarret 28 B3
Gabela 75 F2
Gaberl-Sattel 57 E4
Gabia la Grande 44 A3
Gabicce Mare 61 E3
Gabriel y Galán, Emb de 39 E2
Gabrovka 70 B2
Gabrovo 115 D2
Gacé 19 D4
Gacilly, la 23 D4
Gacko 76 A2
Gad'ač 113 F1
Gäddede 97 E4
Gadebusch 48 B2
Gádor 44 B3
Gádor, Sa de 44 B3
Gadžin Han 77 E1
Găeşti 115 D1
Gaeta 64 A3
Gaeta, Golfo di 64 A3
Gagarin 111 F2
Gaggenau 54 C2
Gagnef 105 F2
Gail 59 E2
Gailbergsattel 59 E2
Gaildorf 55 D2
Gailey 9 E1
Gaillac 29 D3
Gaillimh 12 B3
Gaillon 19 E3
Gainsborough 7 D2
Gairloch 2 B3
Gaj 73 D2
Gajdobra 72 B2
Gajsin 113 E3
Gajvoron 113 E3
Gakovo 72 B1
Galan 37 E1
Galanádo 88 C3
Galanianá 90 A2
Galanta 112 A3
Galapagar 40 A2
Galarinós 80 A3
Galaroza 42 C2
Galashiels 5 D2
Galatádes 79 E3
Galatáki 84 A3
Galatás (Argolída) 87 E2
Galatás (Korinthía) 87 D1
Galaţi 113 E4
Galatina 65 F4
Galatiní 79 D3
Galátista 80 A3
Galatone 65 F4
Galaxídi 83 E4
Galdakao 36 B1
Galdhøpiggen 100 B3
Galeata 61 D3
Galegos 38 C3
Galende 34 C3
Galera 44 B2
Galiano del Capo 65 F4
Galibier, Col du 31 D1
Galicia 34 B2
Galičica 77 D4
Galičnik 77 D3
Galikós 79 F3
Galipsós 80 B2
Galisteo 39 D2
Galiz, Pto de 43 D4
Gallarate 60 A1
Gallardon 19 E4
Gallargues 30 B3
Gállego, R 37 D3
Galley Head 14 B4
Galliate 60 A1
Gallipoli 65 F4
Gällivare 98 B2
Gallneukirchen 57 D2
Gällö 101 E2
Gallo, C 68 B2
Gallocanta, L de 41 D1
Gallo, R 41 D2
Galloway Forest Park 4 C3
Gallspach 56 C3
Gallur 36 C3
Gälöfjärden 106 B4
Galston 4 C2
Galten 108 B3
Galtür 58 C2
Galty Mts 14 C3
Galveias 38 B3
Gálvez 40 A3
Galway 12 B3
Galway (Co) 12 B3
Galway B 12 B4
Gamaches 19 E2
Gambarie d'Aspromonte 67 E4
Gaming 57 D3
Gamleby 109 E1
Gammelstaden 98 C3
Gammertingen 55 D3
Gampenjoch 58 C3
Gams 58 B2
Gamvik 95 E1
Gamzigrad 73 E4
Ganacker 56 B2
Gand 50 B3
Gándara 34 B1
Ganderkesee 17 F1
Gandesa 41 F1
Gandia 41 E4
Gandino 58 B4
Gandria 58 A4
Gangáles 91 D4
Ganges 29 F3
Gangi 68 C3
Gangkofen 56 B2
Gannat 26 A4
Gänserndorf 57 F2
Gañuelas 45 D2
Gap 31 D2
Garabit, Viaduc de 29 F2
Garajonay 42 A4
Garajonay (Parque Nac) 42 A4
Gara, L 12 C3
Garching 56 B3
Garcia 37 E4

Garcia de Sola, Emb de 39 F4
Garciaz 39 E3
Gard (Dépt) 30 B3
Gard *R* 30 B3
Garda 60 C1
Garda, L di 58 C4
Gardanne 30 C4
Gårdby 109 E2
Garde 109 F4
Garde-Freinet, la 31 D4
Gardelegen 48 C4
Gardermoen 105 D3
Gardiken 97 F3
Gardiki 83 D3
Garding 47 F2
Gardjönäs 97 F3
Gärdnäs 101 E1
Gardone Riviera 60 C1
Gardone Val Trompia 60 B1
Gärdslösa 109 E2
Gardunha, Sa da 38 C2
Garður 96 A2
Garešnica 71 D2
Garessio 31 F3
Garforth 7 D2
Gargaliáni 86 B3
Gargano, Promontorio del 64 C2
Garganta 44 B2
Garganta del Chorro 43 E3
Garganta del Escalar 37 E2
Garganta la Olla 39 E2
Gargantas 40 C2
Gargantas del Sil 34 B2
Gargellen 58 B2
Gargilesse 25 E3
Gargnano 58 C4
Gargnäs 98 A3
Garigliano 64 A3
Gariglione, Mte 67 F3
Garípa 91 E4
Garlasco 60 A2
Garlin 28 B4
Garlstorf 48 B3
Garmisch-Partenkirchen 55 F4
Garona, R 37 F2
Garonne 28 B2
Garpenberg 105 F3
Garphyttan 105 F4
Garraf 32 A4
Garrafe de Torio 35 D2
Garray 36 B3
Garrel 17 E1
Garrovillas 39 D3
Garrucha 44 C3
Gars 57 E2
Gartempe 25 E4
Gartow 48 C3
Gartz 49 E3
Garvagh 13 D1
Garvão 42 A2
Garve 2 C3
Garynahine 2 B2
Garz 49 D1
Gaschurn 58 B2
Gassino Torinese 31 E1
Gastoúni 86 B1
Gata (Extremadura) 39 D2
Gata (Valencia) 45 E1
Gata, C de 44 C4
Gata, Sa de 39 D2
Gatčina 111 D1
Gatehouse of Fleet 4 C3
Gateshead 5 E3
Gattinara 31 F1
Gattorna 60 A3
Gatwick Airport 10 C3
Gaucín 43 E4
Gauja 110 C2
Gaula 100 C2
Gauldalen 100 C2
Gaulstad 101 D1
Gausta 104 C3
Gauting 56 A3
Gavà 32 A4
Gavardo 60 B1
Gavarnie 37 E2
Gavarnie, Cirque de 37 E2
Gavdopoúla, N 90 B4
Gávdos, N 90 C4
Gave d'Oloron 28 A4
Gavi 60 A2
Gavião 38 B3
Gavia, Pso di 58 C3
Gavirate 58 A4
Gävle 106 B2

1/80000
GENÈVE
LAC LÉMAN
Ferney-Voltaire
Meyrin
Vernier
Lancy
Carouge
Onex
Chêne-Bougeries
Chêne-Bourg
Thônex
Cologny
Vandœuvres
Veyrier
Palais des Nations
Palais des Expositions
GENÈVE-COINTRIN
Plan-les-Ouates
Confignon
Bernex
Perly-Certoux
Troinex
Gaillard
Monnetier
Collonge-Bellerive
Pregny-Chambésy
RHÔNE
Arve
A 40-E 25

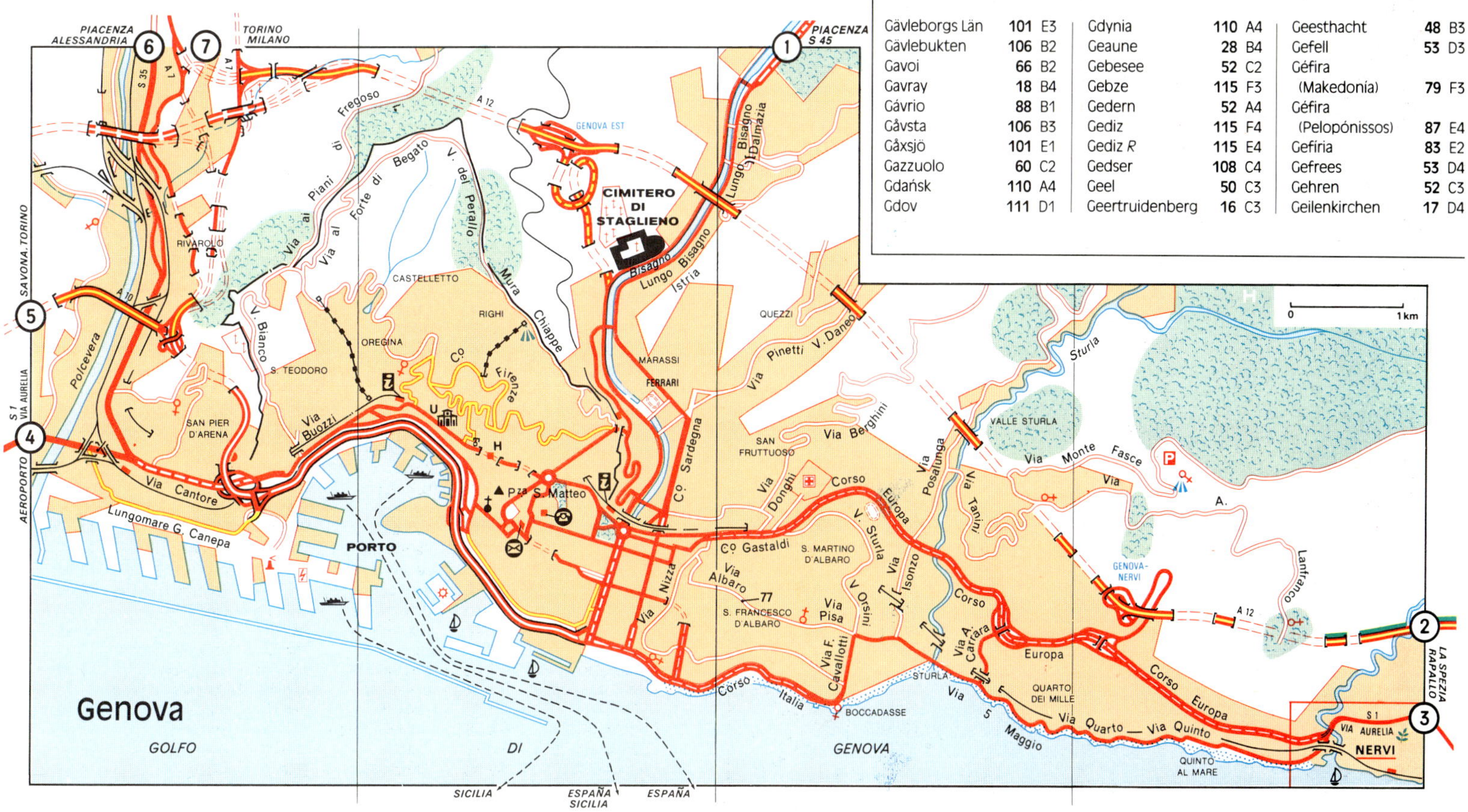

Genova
GOLFO DI GENOVA
PORTO
CIMITERO DI STAGLIENO
NERVI
PIACENZA ALESSANDRIA
TORINO MILANO
PIACENZA S 45
SAVONA, TORINO
AEROPORTO
LA SPEZIA RAPALLO
GENOVA EST
GENOVA-NERVI

Gävleborgs Län 101 E3
Gävlebukten 106 B2
Gavoi 66 B2
Gavray 18 B4
Gávrio 88 B1
Gåvsta 106 B3
Gåxsjö 101 E1
Gazzuolo 60 C2
Gdańsk 110 A4
Gdov 111 D1
Gdynia 110 A4
Geaune 28 B4
Gebesee 52 C2
Gebze 115 F3
Gedern 52 A4
Gediz 115 F4
Gediz *R* 115 E4
Gedser 108 C4
Geel 50 C3
Geertruidenberg 16 C3
Geesthacht 48 B3
Gefell 53 D3
Géfira (Makedonía) 79 F3
Géfira (Pelopónissos) 87 E4
Gefíria 83 E2
Gefrees 53 D4
Gehren 52 C3
Geilenkirchen 17 D4

4°20
4°
Stirling
Kincardine
Kilpatrick Hills
Cochno Loch
Loch Humphrey
Jaw Resr.
Mugdock
Mugdock Resr.
Craigmaddie Resr.
Blairskaith
Milton of Campsie
Birdston
Kelvin
Dullatur
Croy
Eastfield
Cumbernauld
Palacerigg
Fannyside Lochs
Luggiebank
Twechar
Kirkintilloch
Waterside
Condorrat
Torrance
Balmore
Milngavie
Bowling
Old Kilpatrick
Duntocher
Faifley
Erskine Bridge
Hardgate
Bearsden
Bardowie
Antonine Wall
Cadder
Lenzie
Moodiesburn
Mollinsburn
Annathill
Greengairs
Wattston
Longriggend
Bishopton
Erskine
Drumchapel
Bishopbriggs
Auchinloch
Muirhead
Riggend
Stand
Clydebank
Temple
Lumloch
Stepps
Garnkirk
Gartcosh
Marnock
Glenboig
Glenmavis
Caldercruix
Inchinnan
Georgetown
Glasgow Airport
Yoker
Springburn
Plains
Renfrew
Clyde Tunnel
Partick
Govan
Linwood
GLASGOW
Coatbridge
Airdrie
Coatdyke
Craigneuk
Roughrigg Resr.
Elderslie
Johnstone
PAISLEY
Pollokshields
Shettleston
Baillieston
Old Monkland
Calderbank
Chapelhall
Salsburgh
Newhouse
Burrell Collection
Rutherglen
Birkenshaw
North Calder
Caterpillar
Viewpark
Mossend
Glenburn
Pollokshaws
Carmyle
Newton
Holytown
Newarthill
Gleniffer Braes
Nitshill
Thornliebank
Cambuslang
Uddingston
Castle
Bothwell
Bellshill
New Stevenston
Cleland
Barrhead
Giffnock
Flemington
Strathclyde
Nether Kirkton
Carmunnock
Stonefield
Motherwell
Ravenscraig
Newmains
Neilston
Balgray Resr.
Clarkston
Busby
Rogerton
Nerston
High Blantyre
Craigneuk
Uplawmoor
Netherplace
Newton Mearns
Waterfoot
Neilston Pad
Harelaw Dam
Thorntonhall
Hamilton
Wishaw
Waterloo
Bogside
East Kilbride
Meikle Earnock
Low Waters
Overtown
Jackton
Calder Glen
Cadzow Resr.
Long Loch
Eaglesham
Law
Lochcraig Resr.
Quarter
Millheugh
Larkhall
Ballageich Hill
Auldhouse
Limekilnburn
Ashgill
Dalserf
1/200000
3 km
2 miles
Crianlarich
Greenock
Largs
Irvine
Kilmarnock
Strathaven
Dumfries, Carlisle
M 74, Kilmarnock
Edinburgh
Peebles
55°50

Geilo 104 C2
Geiranger 100 B3
Geirangerfjorden 100 B3
Geisa 52 B3
Geiselhöring 56 B2
Geisenfeld 55 F2
Geisenhausen 56 B2
Geising 53 E3
Geisingen 54 C4
Geislingen 55 E2
Geismar 52 B2
Geisnes 97 D4
Geithain 53 D2
Gela 68 C4
Gelderland 17 D2
Geldern 17 D3
Geldrop 16 C4
Geleen 17 D4
Gelibolu 115 E3
Gelnhausen 52 A4
Gelsa 37 D4
Gelsdorf 51 E4
Gelsenkirchen 17 E3
Gelting 48 A1
Gembloux 50 C4
Gemeaux 26 C2
Gémenos 30 C4
Gemert 17 D3
Gemlik 115 F3
Gemona del Friuli 59 F3
Gémozac 28 B1
Gemünd 51 D4
Gemünden (Bayern) 52 B4
Gemünden (Hessen) 52 A3
Gemünden (Rheinland-Pfalz) 54 B1
Genádio 93 E2
Gençay 25 D4
Generalísimo, Emb del 41 D3
Generalski Stol 70 C3
General-Toševo 115 E2
Generoso, Mte 58 A4
Genève 27 D4
Genil, R 43 E2
Genisséa 81 D2
Génissiat, Barrage de 27 D4
Genk 50 C3
Genlis 26 C2
Genna Cruxi 66 C3
Gennargentu, Mti del 66 B3
Gennep 17 D3
Gennes 24 C2
Génolhac 29 F3
Genova 60 A3
Genova, Golfo di 60 A4
Genova, Val di 58 C3
Gent 50 B3
Genthin 49 D4
Gentioux 29 D1
Genzano di Lucania 64 C3
Genzano di Roma 63 E3
Georgianí 79 E3
Georgioúpoli 90 C3
Georgitsi 87 D3
Gera 53 D3
Geraardsbergen 50 B3
Gerabronn 55 E2
Gerace 67 F4
Gerakári (Kriti) 90 C4
Gerakári (Makedonía) 79 F2
Gerakaroú 80 A3
Gerakás 87 E4
Gérakas, Akr 84 B2
Geráki 87 D3
Gerakiní 80 B4
Gerakovoúni 83 F3
Gerania 87 E1
Gérardmer 27 E1
Geras 57 E2
Gerbéviller 21 D4
Gerbier de Jonc 30 B2
Gerbini 69 D3
Gerbstedt 52 C2
Gerena 43 D2
Gerês 34 B3
Gerês, Sa do 34 B3
Geretsried 56 A3
Gérgal 44 B3
Geringswalde 53 E2
Gerlitzen 59 F2
Gerlos 59 D2
Gerlospaß 59 D1
Gérmas 79 D3
Germering 55 F3
Germersheim 54 C2
Gernika-Lumo 36 B1
Gernrode 52 C2
Gernsbach 54 C2
Gernsheim 54 C1
Gerola Alta 58 B3
Geroliménas 87 D4
Gerolstein 51 D4
Gerolzhofen 52 B4
Gerona 32 B3
Geroplátanos 80 B3
Gerovo 70 B3
Gerri de la Sal 37 F3
Gers 28 C3
Gers (Dépt) 28 C4
Gersau 58 A2
Gersfeld 52 B4
Gerstetten 55 E2
Gersthofen 55 E3
Gerswalde 49 E3
Gesäuse 57 D3
Gescher 17 E3
Geseke 17 F3
Gesualdo 64 B3
Geta 106 C2
Getafe 40 A2
Gets, les 27 E4
Gettorf 48 A1
Gevelsberg 17 E4
Gevgelija 77 F4
Gévora, R 38 C4
Gevrey-Chambertin 26 C2
Gex 27 D3
Geysir 96 B2
Geyve 115 F3
Gföhl 57 E2
Ghedi 60 B1
Gheorghe Gheorghiu-Dej 113 D4
Gheorgheni 113 D4
Ghilarza 66 B3
Ghisonaccia 33 F3
Ghisoni 33 F3
Giali, N 89 F4
Giáltra 83 F3
Gianitsá 79 E3
Gianitsi 84 C4
Giannádes 82 A1
Giannutri, I di 63 D2
Gianoúli 81 F2
Giant's Causeway 13 E1
Giardini 69 D3
Giáros, N 88 B2
Giarratana 69 D4
Giarre 69 D3
Giat 29 E1
Giaveno 31 E1
Giba 66 B4
Gibostad 94 B2
Gibraleón 42 C2
Gibraltar 43 E4
Gideå 102 A2
Gideälven 102 A2
Gieboldehausen 52 B2
Gien 26 A2
Giengen 55 E2
Giens 31 D4
Gießen 51 F3
Giethoorn 17 D2
Gifhorn 48 B4
Gigha I 4 B2
Giglio, I del 62 C2
Giglio Porto 62 C2
Gignac 30 A4
Gijón 35 D1
Gilching 56 A3
Gilford 13 E2
Giljevo 76 C1
Gilleleje 108 C3
Gillhov 101 E2
Gillingham (Dorset) 9 D3
Gillingham (Kent) 11 D2
Gill, L 12 C2
Gilze 16 C3
Gimenells 37 E3
Gimnó 84 B4
Gimo 106 B3
Gimont 28 C4
Gingst 49 D1
Ginosa 65 D4
Ginzling 59 D2
Giogo di Scarperia 61 D3
Gioia del Colle 65 E3
Gioia Tauro 67 E4
Gióna, Óros 83 E3
Gioúhtas 91 D4
Gioúra, N 84 B2
Giovinazzo 65 D3
Giovi, Pso dei 60 A3
Girifalco 67 F3
Giromagny 27 E1
Girona 32 B3
Gironde 28 B1
Gironde (Dépt) 28 B2
Gironella 32 A3
Girvan 4 C3
Gisburn 6 C2
Gislaved 109 D2
Gisors 19 E3
Gissi 64 B2
Gistel 50 A3
Githio 87 D4
Gittun 98 A2
Giugliano in Campo 64 B4
Giulianova 64 A1
Giurgiu 115 D2
Give 108 A3
Givors 30 B1
Givry 26 C3
Givry-en-Argonne 20 C3
Gizéla 81 D2
Giżycko 110 B4
Gjalicë, M 77 D3
Gjendesheim 100 B3
Gjermundshavn 104 A2
Gjesvær 95 D1
Gjirokastër 114 C4
Gjøra 100 C2
Gjöv 96 A3
Gjøvik 105 D2
Gjuhezës, Kepi i 114 B4
Gla 83 F4
Gladbeck 17 E3
Gladenbach 17 F4
Gladstad 97 D3
Glafsfjorden 105 E3
Gláma 96 A1
Glamis 5 D1
Glamis Castle 5 D1
Glamoč 71 E4
Glamorgan 8 C2
Glamsbjerg 108 B3
Glan 54 B1
Glandon, Col du 31 D1
Glandorf 17 F2
Glan-Münchweiler 54 B1
Glanshammar 105 F4
Glarus 58 A2
Glasgow 4 C2
Glas Maol 3 D4
Glastonbury 9 D3
Glauchau 53 D3
Glava 105 D3
Glavatičevo 75 F1
Glavičice 72 B3
Glavnik 77 D1
Gledić 73 D4
Gledićske pl 73 D4
Gleinalmtunnel 57 E4
Gleisdorf 57 E4
Glen Albyn 2 C4
Glenamoy 12 B2
Glénan, I de 22 B4
Glenariff 13 E1
Glenarm 13 E1
Glenbeigh 14 A4
Glen Carron 2 C3
Glen Coe 4 C1
Glencolumbkille 12 C1
Glendalough 13 D4
Glenelg 2 B4
Glenfinnan 2 B4
Glengarriff 14 A4
Glenluce 4 C3
Glen More 2 C4

Glen More Forest Park 3 D4
Glennamaddy 12 C3
Glenrothes 5 D2
Glenties 12 C1
Glifa 83 F3
Glifáda (Atikí-Piréas) 87 F1
Glifáda (Fokída) 83 D4
Glikí 82 B2
Glikóvrissi 87 D4
Glina 70 C3
Glittertind 100 B3
Gliwice 112 B2
Globino 113 F2
Globočica 77 D2
Gloggnitz 57 E3
Głogów 112 A2
Glomfjord 97 E2
Glomma 105 D3
Glommersträsk 98 B3
Gloppet 102 B2
Glossop 6 C2
Gloucester 9 D2
Gloucestershire 9 D2
Gložan 72 B2
Głubczyce 112 A2
Glubokoje 111 D3
Głuchołazy 112 A2
Gluchov 113 F1
Glücksburg 48 A1
Glückstadt 48 A2
Glumsø 108 C4
Glušci 72 C3
Glyn Ebwy 9 D2
Gmund (D) 56 A4
Gmünd (Kärnten) 59 F2
Gmünd (Nieder-österreich) 57 D2
Gmunden 56 C3
Gnarp 101 F3
Gnesta 106 B4
Gniezno 112 A1
Gnjilane 77 D2
Gnoien 49 D2
Gnosjö 109 D3
Goat Fell 4 B2
Goce Delčev 115 D3
Goch 17 D3
Goðafoss 96 B1
Godalming 9 F3
Godby 106 C3
Godelheim 52 A2
Goderville 19 D3
Godmanchester 9 F1
Gödöllő 112 B4
Godović 70 A2
Goduš 72 B3
Goeree 16 B3
Goes 16 B3
Göggingen 55 F3
Göhren 49 D1
Goirle 16 C3
Góis 38 B2
Goito 60 C1
Gokčanica 73 D4
Gokçe 115 E3
Gol 104 C2
Gola 71 D1
Golada 34 B2
Golaja Pristan' 113 F3
Golczewo 49 F2
Goldbach 52 A4
Goldberg 48 C2
Goldenstedt 17 F1
Golegã 38 B3
Golema reka 77 D3
Golemo Selo 77 E2
Goleniów 49 F2
Goleš 77 E2
Golfe-Juan 31 E4
Golfo Aranci 66 C1
Goli 70 B4
Golija (Crna Gora) 76 A2
Golija (Srbija) 76 C1
Goljak 77 D2
Goljaki, M. 70 A2
Goljam Perelik 115 D3
Göllersdorf 57 E2
Golling 59 E1
Golo 33 F3
Golpejas 39 E1
Golspie 3 D3
Golßen 53 E1
Golubac 73 E3
Golubovci 76 B3
Golubovec 70 C2
Golzow 49 D4
Gómara 36 B3
Gomáti 80 B3
Gombrèn 32 A3
Gomecello 39 E1
Gomel' 111 E4
Gomera 42 A4
Gómfi 83 D2
Gommern 52 C1
Goncelin 31 D1
Gondomar (P) 34 A4
Gondomar (E) 34 A3
Gondrecourt 20 C4
Gönen 115 E3
Góni 83 E1
Goniá 90 B3
Goniés 91 D3
Gonnesa 66 B4
Gonnosfanadiga 66 B4
Goole 7 D2
Goor 17 D2
Goppenstein 27 F3
Göppingen 55 D2
Gora 70 C3
Goražde 76 A1
Gördalen 101 D3
Gordes 30 C3
Gorenja Vas 70 A2
Gorey (GB) 18 B3
Gorey (IRL) 15 D3
Gorgona, I di 60 B4
Gorgonzola 60 A1
Gorgopótamos 78 C4
Gorica (Bosna i Hercegovina) 75 E2
Gorica (Makedonija) 77 D4
Goričan 71 D1
Gorice 70 B3
Gorinchem 16 C3
Goritsá 87 D3
Gorizia 59 F3
Gorjanci 70 C2
Gorki 111 E3
Gorleston-on-Sea 7 F4
Gorlice 112 B3
Görlitz 53 F2
Gorna Orjahovica 115 D2
Gornja Dobrinja 72 C4
Gornja Grabovica 75 F1
Gornja Kamenica 73 F4
Gornja Klina 77 D2
Gornja Ljubovidđa 72 C4
Gornja Ljuta 75 F1
Gornja Ploča 70 C4
Gornja Radgona 70 C1
Gornja Sabanta 73 D4
Gornja Sanica 71 D4
Gornja Slatina 71 F3
Gornja Toplica 72 C4
Gornja Toponica 73 E4
Gornja Tuzla 72 B3
Gornje Dubočke 76 A2
Gornje Ratkovo 71 E4
Gornje Selo 75 D2
Gornji Grad 70 B2
Gornji Kokoti 76 B3
Gornji Kosinj 70 C4
Gornji Lapac 71 D4
Gornji Lukavac 76 A2
Gornji Milanovac 73 D4
Gornji Petrovci 70 C1
Gornji Podgradci 71 D3
Gornji Rajić 71 E3
Gornji Stepoš 73 E4
Gornji Vakuf 75 E1
Gornji Zabar 71 F3
Gorno Orizari 77 E3
Goro 61 D2
Gorodišče 113 F2
Gorodn'a 111 E4
Gorodok (Belorussija) 111 D3
Gorodok (Ukraina) 112 C2
Gorredijk 17 D1
Gorron 23 E3
Gort 12 B4
Gorteen 12 C3
Gortin 13 D2
Górtis 91 D4
Gortmore 12 B3
Gorumna I 12 B3
Goryn' 113 D2
Góry Świętokrzyskie 112 B2
Görzke 53 D1
Gorzów Wielkopolski 49 F3
Gosaldo 59 D3
Gosau 59 F1
Gosausee 59 F1
Göschenen 58 A3
Gościno 49 F1
Gosforth 5 D4
Goslar 52 B1
Gospić 70 C4
Gospođinci 72 C2
Gosport 9 E3
Gößl 56 C3
Gossau 58 B2
Gosselies 50 B4
Gossensass 59 D2
Gößnitz 53 D3
Gössweinstein 52 C4
Gostivar 77 D3
Göstling 57 D3
Gostyń 112 A2
Götaälv 108 C1
Göta Kanal 105 E4
Göteborg 108 C1
Göteborgs och Bohus Län 108 C1
Götene 105 E4
Gotha 52 C3
Gothem 109 F4
Gotland 109 F4
Gotlands Län 109 F4
Gotska Sandön 106 C4
Göttingen 52 B2
Gottwaldov 112 A3
Götzis 58 B2
Gouarec 22 C3
Gouda 16 C3
Gouménissa 79 F2
Goumois 27 E2
Goúra 87 D1
Gourdon 29 D2
Gourin 22 B3
Gournay-en-Bray 19 E3
Goúrnes 91 E3
Gourniá 91 E4
Gourock 4 C2
Gouveja 38 C2
Goúves 91 E3
Gouviá 82 A1
Gouzon 25 F4
Goveđari 75 E2
Goverla 113 D3
Gowienica 49 F2
Göynük 115 F3
Gozd 70 A1
Gozo 68 B4
Gozzano 58 A4
Graal-Müritz 48 C1
Graben-Neudorf 54 C2
Grabenstätt 56 B3
Grabovac 75 E2
Grabovci 72 C3
Grabow 48 C3
Gračac 70 C4
Gračanica (Bosna i Hercegovina) 71 F3
Gračanica (Crna Gora) 76 B2
Gračanica (Kosovo) 77 D2
Gračanica (Srbija) 72 C4
Graçay 25 E2
Grächen 27 F4
Gradac (Crna Gora) 76 B1
Gradac (Hrvatska) 75 E2
Gradac (Srbija) 76 C1
Gradačac 71 F3
Gradara 61 E3
Gradče, Ez 77 F2
Gradec 71 D2
Gradefes 35 E2
Gradeška pl 77 F3
Gradina 77 F1
Gradisca d'Isonzo 59 F3
Gradište (Hrvatska) 71 E2
Gradište (Makedonija) 77 E2
Grado (E) 35 D1
Grado (I) 59 F4
Gradsko 77 E3

Uddevalla, Oslo
Trollhättan
GÖTEBORG
Hisingen
Torslanda
Björlanda
Harestad
Säve
Surte
Lövgärdet
Gårdsten
Bergum
Gråbo
Olstorp
Stannum
Floda
Olofstorp
Angered
Bergsjön
Kortedala
Kåhög
Jonsered
Lerum
Aspen
Öxeryd
Partille
Sävedalen
Härlanda
Örgryte
Öjersjö
Landvetter
Härryda
Delsjöarna
Nordre älv
Nordre älvs fjord
Björkö
Tolered
Lundby
Backa
Tuve
Biskopsgården
Newcastle
Sandvik
Amsterdam
Harwich
Fredrikshavn
Kiel
Dana fjord
Älvsborg
Annedal
Mölndal
Råda
Mölnlycke
LANDVETTER
Asperö
Frölunda
Brännö
Askim
Styrsö
Donsö
Benareby
Kållered
Askims fjord
Vrångö
Billdal
Hällesaker
Inserös
Jäxviken
Lindome
Alvsåker
St Härsjön
Rådasjön
0
5 km
E 6
Helsingborg, Malmö
Örebro, Stockholm
Borås, Jönköping

Gradskovo 73 F3
Grafelfing 56 A3
Grafenau 56 C2
Gräfenberg 55 F1
Gräfenhainichen 53 D1
Grafenwöhr 55 F1
Grafing 56 B3
Gragnano 64 B4
Grahovo (Bosna i Hercegovina) 76 A2
Grahovo (Slovenija) 70 A2
Graiguenamanagh 15 D3
Grain 11 D2
Grainau 55 F4
Grajewo 110 C4
Gram 108 A3
Gramat 29 D2
Gramatikó 83 E2
Gramatikoú 83 D4
Graméni 80 B2
Graméno 82 B1
Grametten 57 D1
Grammichele 69 D4
Grámos, Óros 78 C3
Grampian 3 E4
Grampian Mts 4 C1
Gramsh 77 D4
Gramzow 49 E3
Gran 105 D2
Granada 44 A3
Granadella 37 E4
Granadilla de Abona 42 B4
Granard 12 C3
Gran Canaria 42 B4
Grancey-le-Château 26 C2
Grandas 34 C1
Grand Ballon 27 E1
Grand Bois, Col du 30 B1
Grand-Bornand, le 27 D4
Grand-Bourg 25 E4
Grandcamp-Maisy 18 C3
Grand Canal d'Alsace 27 E1
Grand Canyon du Verdon 31 D3
Grand-Champ 22 C4
Grand-Colombier 27 D4
Grand-Combe, la 30 B3
Grand Combin 27 E4
Grand-Couronne 19 D3
Grand-Croix 30 B1
Grande Casse 31 D1
Grande de Europa, Punta 43 E4
Grande Dixence, Bge de la 27 E4
Grande-Motte, la 30 B4
Grande Sassière 31 E1
Grandes Rousses 31 D1
Grand-Fougeray 23 D4
Grand-Lemps, le 30 C1
Grand Lieu, L de 24 B3
Grand-Lucé, le 23 F4
Grand Morin 20 A4
Grândola 42 A1
Grandpré 20 C3
Grand-Pressigny, le 25 D3
Grand Rhône 30 B4
Grandrieu 29 F2
Grand-Serre, le 30 C1
Grands Goulets 30 C2
Grandval, Bge de 29 F2
Grandvilliers 19 E3
Grañén 37 D3
Grangärde 105 F3
Grangemouth 5 D2
Grange-Over-Sands 6 B1
Grängesberg 105 F3
Granges-sur-Vologne 27 E1
Granier, Col du 30 C1
Granitis 80 B1
Granitsa 83 D2
Granja (Alentejo) 42 C1
Granja (Douro) 34 A4
Granja de Torrehermosa 43 E1
Granja, Pto de la 43 D1
Gränna 109 D1
Granollers 32 A4
Granön 102 A1
Gran Paradiso 31 E1
Gran San Bernardo, Colle del 27 E4
Gran San Bernardo, Traforo del 27 E4
Gran Sasso d'Italia 63 F1
Gransee 49 D3
Gran Tarajal 42 C4
Grantham 7 D3
Grantown-on-Spey 3 D3
Granville 18 B4
Granvin 104 B2
Grappa, Mte 59 D3
Grasleben 52 C1
Grasmere 5 D4
Grassano 65 D4
Grasse 31 E3
Gråstenn 108 A4
Grästorp 108 C1
Gratangen 94 B3
Gratini 81 E2
Gratkorn 57 E4
Graubünden 58 B2
Grau-du-Roi, le 30 B4
Graulhet 29 D4
Graus 37 E3
Gravalos 36 C3
Gravdal 97 E1
Grave 17 D3
Gravedona 58 B3
Grave, la 31 D1
Gravelines 19 F1
Gravellona-Toce 58 A4
Grave, Pointe de 28 A1
Gravesend 11 D2
Graviá 83 E3
Gravina in Puglia 65 D3
Gravona 33 F3
Gravoúna 80 C2
Gray 26 C2
Grays Thurrock 10 C2
Graz 57 E4
Grazalema 43 E3
Grazzanise 64 A3
Grdelica 77 E1
Great Blasket I. 14 A3
Great Driffield 7 D1
Great Dunmow 11 D2
Great Grimsby 7 E2
Great Malvern 9 D1
Great Ormes Head 6 A2
Great Ouse 7 E3
Great Torrington 8 C3
Great Yarmouth 7 F4
Grebbestad 105 D4
Greccio 63 E2
Greding 55 F2
Gredos 39 F2
Gredos, Sa de 39 F2
Greenhead 5 D3
Greenlaw 5 E2
Greenock 4 C2
Greenodd 6 B1
Greggio 31 F1
Gregolimano 83 F3
Greifenburg 59 E2
Greiffenberg 49 E3
Greifswald 49 D1
Greifswalder Bodden 49 D1
Grein 57 D2
Greiz 53 D3
Grenå 108 B2
Grenade (Haute-Garonne) 29 D4
Grenade (Landes) 28 B4
Grenchen 27 E2
Grenoble 30 C1
Grense Jakobselv 95 F2
Gréoux-les-Bains 31 D3
Gressåmoen 101 E1
Gresse 30 C2
Gressoney-la-Trinite 27 F4
Gressoney-St-Jean 27 F4
Gresten 57 D3
Grésy 31 D1
Greußen 52 C2
Greve 61 D4
Greven 17 E2
Grevená 79 D4
Grevená (Nomos) 79 D4
Grevenbroich 17 D4
Grevenbrück 17 F4
Grevenítio 82 C1
Grevesmühlen 48 B2
Greve Strand 108 C3
Greyabbey 13 E2
Greystones 13 E4
Grez-en-Bouère 23 E3
Grezzana 60 C1
Grgur 70 B4
Griá, Akr 88 B1
Grianan of Aileach 13 D1
Griebenow 49 D2
Gries 59 D2
Gries im Sellrain 58 C2
Grieskirchen 56 C3
Griffen 70 B1
Grignan 30 B2
Grigno 59 D3
Grignols 28 B3
Grimaldi 67 E3
Grimaud 31 D4
Grimma 53 D2
Grimmen 49 D2
Grimone, Col de 30 C2
Grimsbu 100 C3
Grimselpass 27 F3
Grimsey 96 B1
Grimstad 104 B4
Grindaheim 104 C2
Grindavik 96 A2
Grindelwald 27 F3
Grindsted 108 A3
Griñón 40 A2
Grintavec 70 B2
Gripsholm 106 B4
Grisignano 61 D1
Gris Nez, Cap 19 E1

Grisolles 29 D4
Grisslehamn 106 B3
Gríva 79 E2
Grizáno 83 D1
Grk 71 F3
Grljan 73 F3
Grmec 71 D4
Grøa 100 B2
Gröbming 59 F1
Grocka 73 D3
Gröditz 53 E2
Grodno 110 C4
Groenlo 17 D3
Gröer Arber 56 B1
Groitzsch 53 D2
Groix 22 B4
Groix, I de 22 B4
Grömitz 48 B2
Gronau 17 E2
Grönenbach 55 E4
Grong 97 D4
Grönhögen 109 E3
Groningen 47 D3
Groningen (Prov) 47 D3
Gröningen 52 C1
Grönskåra 109 E2
Grønsund 108 C4
Gropello Cairoli 60 A2
Groscavallo 31 E1
Grosio 58 C3
Grosne 26 C3
Gross Beerberg 52 C3
Gross Bösenstein 57 D4
Großbreitenbach 52 C3
Großburgwedel 48 A4
Großenbrode 48 B1
Großenhain 53 E2
Großenzersdorf 57 F2
Grosse Pierre 27 E1
Grosse Röder 53 E2
Grosser Plöner See 48 B2
Grosseto 62 C1
Gross Feldberg 51 F4
Gross-Gerau 54 C1
Groß Gerungs 57 D2
Großglockner Hochalpenstraße 59 E2
Großglockner 59 E2
Großhabersdorf 55 E1
Groß Ötscher 57 E3
Großpetersdorf 57 F4
Gross Priel 57 D3
Gross Rachel 56 C2
Großraming 57 D3
Großraschen 53 E1
Groß Reken 17 E3
Großröhrsdorf 53 F2
Groß Rosennock 59 F2
Grossschönau 53 F2
Groß-Schönebeck 49 E3
Groß Siegharts 57 E2
Gross-Umstadt 55 D1
Großvenediger 59 E2
Großweil 56 A4
Grostenquin 21 D3
Grosuplje 70 B2
Grötlingbo 109 F4
Grøtsundet 94 C2
Grotta di Nettuno 66 A2
Grottaglie 65 E4
Grottaminarda 64 B3
Grottammare 61 F4
Grotte di Pertosa 64 C4
Grotteria 67 F4
Grouin, Pte du 18 B4
Grove 34 A2
Grövelsjön 101 D3
Grovfjord 94 B3
Grubišno Polje 71 D2
Gruda 76 A3
Grude 75 E2
Grudziądz 112 B1
Gruinard B 2 C3
Gruissan 32 B2
Grums 105 E3
Grünau 56 C3
Grünberg 52 A3
Grünburg 57 D3
Grundarfjörður 96 A2
Grundforsen 101 D4
Grundlsee 56 C3
Grundlsee *L* 56 C3
Grundsund 108 C1
Grundtjärn 101 F2
Grünstadt 54 C1
Grünwald 56 A3
Grupčin 77 D3
Gruyères 27 E3
Gruža 73 D4
Gruža *R* 73 D4
Grycksbo 105 F2
Gryfice 49 F2
Gryfino 49 E3
Gryllefjord 94 B2
Grythyttan 105 E3
Grytøya 94 B3
Grza 73 E4
Gschütt, Paß 59 F1
Gstaad 27 E3
Gstadt 56 B3
Guadahortuna 44 A2
Guadaira, R 43 E3
Guadajira, R 39 D4
Guadajoz, R 43 F2
Guadalajara 40 B2
Guadalaviar 41 D2
Guadalaviar, R 41 D2
Guadalcacín, Emb de 43 D3
Guadalcanal 43 D1
Guadalén, Emb de 44 A1
Guadalén, R 44 B1
Guadalest 45 E1
Guadalete, R 43 D4
Guadalfeo, R 44 A4
Guadalhorce, R 43 E4
Guadalimar, R (Andalucía) 43 D3
Guadalimar, R (Andalucía) 44 B2
Guadalmellato, Emb de 43 F2
Guadalmena, Emb de 44 B1
Guadalmena, R 44 B1
Guadalmez, R 43 F1
Guadalope, R 41 E2
Guadalquivir, R 43 D3
Guadal, R 44 B2
Guadalteba-Guadalhorce, Emb del 43 E3
Guadalupe 39 E3
Guadalupe, Sa de 39 E3
Guadarrama 40 A2
Guadarrama, Pto de 40 A2
Guadarrama, R 40 A2
Guadarrama, Sa de 40 A1
Guadarranque, Emb del 43 E4
Guadasuar 41 E4
Guadazaón, R 40 C3
Guadiamar, R 43 D3
Guadiana Menor, R 44 B2
Guadiana, R 39 F4
Guadiaro 43 E4
Guadiaro, R 43 E4
Guadiato, R 43 E2
Guadiela, R 40 C2
Guadix 44 B3
Guajaraz, Emb de 40 A3
Gualdo Tadino 61 E4
Guara, Sa de 37 E3
Guarda 38 C1
Guardamar del Segura 45 D2
Guardiagrele 64 A2
Guardia Sanframondi 64 B3
Guardias Viejas 44 B4
Guardo 35 E2
Guareña 39 D4
Guarrizas, R 44 A1
Guarromán 44 A2
Guastalla 60 C2
Gubbio 61 E4
Guben 53 F1
Guberevac 73 D4
Gubin 53 F1
Guča 73 D4
Guca Gora 71 E4
Gúdar, Sa de 41 E2
Gudavac 71 D3
Gudbrandsdalen 100 C3
Guderup 108 A4
Gudhjem 109 D4
Gudingen 109 E1
Gudow 48 B3
Gudvangen 104 B2
Guebwiller 27 E1
Guémené 22 B3
Guémené-Penfao 23 D4
Güeñes 36 B1
Guer 23 D3
Guérande 22 C4
Guerche-de-Bretagne, la 23 D3
Guerche, la 26 A3
Guéret 25 E4
Guérigny 26 A2
Guerlédan, L de 22 C3
Guernsey 18 A3
Guéthary 28 A4
Gueugnon 26 B3
Güglingen 55 D2
Guglionesi 64 B2
Guía 42 B4
Guía de Isora 42 A4
Guichen 23 D3
Guidonia 63 E2
Guignes 19 F4
Guijo de Granadilla 39 D2
Guijuelo 39 E2
Guildford 9 F3
Guillaumes 31 E3
Guillena 43 D2
Guillestre 31 D2
Guillon 26 B2
Guilvinec 22 A3
Güimar 42 B4
Guimarães 34 A4
Guimiliau 22 B2
Guînes 19 E1
Guingamp 22 C2
Guipavas 22 A2
Guisborough 5 F4
Guiscard 19 F3
Guise 20 A2
Guissona 37 F3
Guist 7 F3
Guitiriz 34 B1
Guitres 28 B2
Gujan-Mestras 28 A2
Gulbene 110 C2
Guldborg Sund 108 C4
Gullesfjorden 94 A3
Gullfoss 96 B2
Gullkrona fjärd 107 D3
Gullspång 105 E4
Gumiel de Hizán 36 A3
Gummersbach 17 E4
Gundelfingen 55 E3
Gundelsheim 55 D2
Gunnarn 97 F4
Gunnarsbyn 98 B3
Gunnärsfjärden 98 C3
Gunnarskog 105 E3
Gunten 27 F3
Günterode 52 B2
Guntín de Pallares 34 B2
Günzburg 55 E3
Gunzenhausen 55 E2
Gurk 70 A1
Gurk *R* 59 F2
Gurrea de Gállego 37 D3
Gusev 110 B4
Gusinje 76 C2
Guspini 66 B3
Güssing 57 F4
Güsten 52 C1
Güstrow 48 C2
Gutcher 3 F1
Gutenstein 57 E3
Gütersloh 17 F3
Gutulia 100 D3
Gützkow 49 D2
Guyhirn 10 C1
Gvardejsk 110 B4
Gvarv 104 C3
Gvozd 76 B2
Gweebarra B 12 C1
Gwent 9 D2
Gwynedd 6 A3
Gy 27 D2
Gyöngyös 112 B4
Győr 112 A4
Gysinge 106 A3
Gyula 112 C4

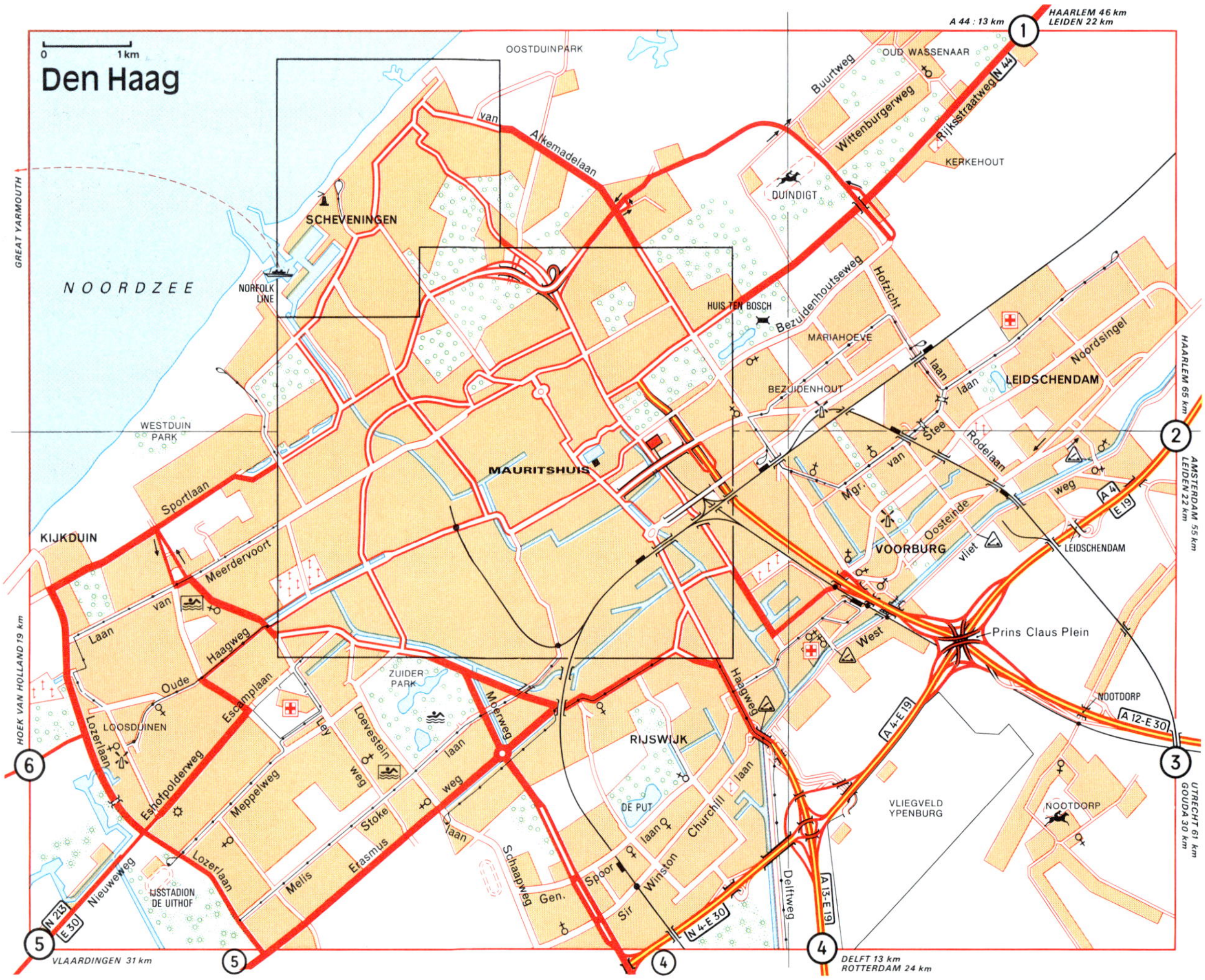
Den Haag
0
1 km
NOORDZEE
SCHEVENINGEN
NORFOLK LINE
OOSTDUINPARK
Alkemadelaan
OUD WASSENAAR
Wittenburgerweg
Rijksstraatweg
KERKEHOUT
DUINDIGT
HUIS TEN BOSCH
Bezuidenhoutseweg
Hofzicht
MARIAHOEVE
BEZUIDENHOUT
LEIDSCHENDAM
Noordsingel
MAURITSHUIS
WESTDUIN PARK
KIJKDUIN
Sportlaan
Meerdervoort
Haagweg
Oude
Escamplaan
LOOSDUINEN
Lozerlaan
Erasmus
Melis
Stoke
Moerweg
RIJSWIJK
Churchill
Winston
Sir
DE PUT
Schaapweg
VOORBURG
Oosteinde
Vliet
West
Prins Claus Plein
NOOTDORP
VLIEGVELD YPENBURG
Delftweg
ZUIDER PARK
IJSSTADION DE UITHOF
Nieuweweg
A 44 : 13 km
HAARLEM 46 km
LEIDEN 22 km
HAARLEM 65 km
AMSTERDAM 55 km
LEIDEN 22 km
UTRECHT 61 km
GOUDA 30 km
DELFT 13 km
ROTTERDAM 24 km
VLAARDINGEN 31 km
HOEK VAN HOLLAND 19 km
GREAT YARMOUTH
A 4-E 19
A 12-E 30
A 13-E 19
N 4-E 30
N 44

H

Haag (A) 57 D3
Haag (D) 56 B3
Haag am Hausruck 56 C3
Haaksbergen 17 D2
Haamstede 16 B3
Haapajärvi 103 D1
Haapajärvi *L* 103 D1
Haapakoski 103 E2
Haapamäki (Keski-Suomen Lääni) 102 C3
Haapamäki (Oulun Lääni) 103 D1
Haapavesi 103 D1
Haapsalu 110 B2
Haar 56 A3
Haaren 17 F3
Haarlem 16 B2
Habay 20 C2
Habo 109 D1
Habsheim 27 E1
Hachenburg 51 F3
Hachmühlen 52 A1
Hackås 101 E2
Hadamar 51 F4
Haddington 5 D2
Hadersdorf 57 E2
Haderslev 108 A4
Hadleigh 11 D2
Hadmersleben 52 C1
Hadrian's Wall 5 E3
Hadselfjorden 94 A3
Hadsten 108 B2
Hadsund 108 B2
Hadžići 75 F1
Haganj 71 D2
Hægebostad 104 B4
Hagen (Niedersachsen) 47 F3
Hagen (Nordrhein-Westfalen) 17 E4
Hagenow 48 B3
Hagetmau 28 B4
Hagfors 105 E3
Häggdånger 101 F3
Haggenås 101 E2
Hagondange 21 D3

Hague, Cap de la 18 B2
Haguenau 21 E3
Hahn 47 F3
Hahnbach 55 F1
Haigerloch 55 D3
Hailsham 10 C3
Hailuoto 99 D4
Hainaut 50 B4
Hainburg 57 F2
Hainfeld 57 E3
Hainichen 53 E2
Hajdúböszörmény 112 C4
Hajdučica 73 D2
Hajdúszoboszló 112 C4
Hajla 76 C2
Hajnówka 112 C1
Hakarp 109 D1
Hakkas 98 B2
Häkkilä 103 D2
Halámky 57 D2
Halandritsa 86 C1
Halbe 53 E1
Halberstadt 52 C1
Halden 105 D4
Haldensleben 48 C4
Halesowen 9 E1
Halesworth 11 E1
Halhjem 104 A2
Halifax 6 C2
Halikko 107 E2
Halju 95 D4
Halkeró 80 C2
Hálki (Dodekánissa) 93 E1
Halkí (Kikládes) 88 C3
Hálki (Thessalía) 83 E1
Halkiádes 83 E2
Halkída 84 B4
Halkidikí 80 B3
Hálki, N 93 E1
Halkidóna 79 F3
Halkió 85 F4
Halkío 87 D1
Halkodóni, Óros 83 E2
Hallands Län 108 C2
Halle (B) 50 B3
Halle (Nordrhein-Westfalen) 17 F2
Halle (Sachsen-Anhalt) 53 D2
Hällefors 105 E3
Hälleforsnäs 105 F4
Hallein 56 C3
Hällekis 105 E4
Hallenberg 17 F4
Hallencourt 19 E2
Halle-Neustadt 53 D2
Hällesjö 101 F2
Hällevadsholm 105 D4
Halligen 47 F1
Hallingdal 104 C2
Hallingskarvet 104 B2
Hall in Tirol 59 D1
Hällnäs 102 A1
Hallsberg 105 F4
Hallstadt 52 C4
Hallstahammar 105 F3
Hallstatt 59 F1
Hallstavik 106 B3
Halluin 19 F1
Halmstad 108 C2
Hals 108 B2
Halsa 100 B2
Halsafjorden 100 B2
Hälsingtuna 101 F3
Halsskov 108 B3
Halstead 11 D2
Halsteren 16 B3
Halsua 102 C2
Haltdålen 101 D2
Haltern 17 E3
Halti-Haldi 94 C3
Halver 17 E4
Ham 19 F2
Hamar 105 D2
Hamarøy 94 A4
Hamburg 48 A3
Hambye 18 B4
Hamdorf 48 A2
Hämeenkyrö 102 C3
Hämeen Lääni 102 C3
Hämeenlinna 107 E2
Hämelerwald 52 B1
Hameln 52 A1
Hamersleben 52 C1
Hamilí, N 92 C2
Hamilton 4 C2
Hamina 103 F4
Hamm 17 E3
Hammarland 106 C3
Hammarstrand 101 F2
Hammaslahti 103 F2
Hammel 108 B3
Hammelburg 52 B4
Hammerdal 101 E2
Hammerfest 95 D1
Hammershus 109 D4
Hamneidet 94 C2
Hamningberg 95 F1
Hamoir 50 C4
Hampshire 9 E3
Hamra 101 E3
Hamra (Reg) 101 E3
Hamre 104 B4
Hamzali 77 F3
Hamzići 75 F2
Hanákia 86 B2
Hanau 52 A4
Handrás 91 F4
Hanerau-Hademarschen 48 A2
Hangö 107 E3
Hangon läntinenselkä 107 D3
Hangö västra fjärd 107 D3
Haniá (Haniá) 90 B3
Hánia (Lakonía) 87 D3
Haniá (Nomos) 90 B3
Hánia (Thessalía) 83 F2
Hani i Hotit 76 B3
Hanion, Kólpos 90 B3
Haniótis 80 B4
Hankamäki 103 E1
Hankasalmen as 103 D3
Hankasalmi 103 D3
Hankensbüttel 48 B4
Hanko 107 E3
Hannover 48 A4
Hannut 50 C4
Hanöbukten 109 D3
Han Pijesak 72 B4
Hansnes 94 C2
Han-sur-Lesse 50 C4
Hanstedt 48 A3
Hanstholm 108 A2
Haparanda 98 C3
Harads 98 B3
Harafjärden 98 C3
Haraldshaugen 104 A3
Haranes 97 D4
Haravgí 79 E3
Harburg (Bayern) 55 E2
Harburg (Hamburg) 48 A3
Hårby 108 B4
Hardangerfjorden 104 A2
Hardangerjøkulen 104 B2
Hardangervidda 104 B2
Hardbakke 104 A1
Hardegg 57 E1
Hardegsen 52 B2
Hardelot 19 E1
Hardenberg 17 D2
Harderwijk 16 C2
Hardheim 55 D1
Hardwick Hall 7 D3
Hareid 100 A2
Harelbeke 50 A3
Haren (D) 17 E1
Haren (NL) 47 D3
Harewood 6 C2
Haria 42 C3
Haringvlietdam 16 B3
Haritoméni 80 B2
Härjångsfjällen 101 D2
Harjavalta 107 D2
Harjunpää 107 D1
Hårkan 101 E2
Härkmeri 102 B3
Harlech 6 A3
Harlesiel 47 E3
Harleston 11 D1
Harlingen 16 C1
Harlow 10 C2
Harmånger 101 F3
Harmanli 115 E3
Härnösand 101 F3
Haro 36 B2
Harokopió 86 C4
Haroldswick 3 F1
Haroué 21 D4
Harøyfjorden 100 A2
Harpenden 9 F2
Harplinge 108 C2
Harpstedt 17 F1
Harris 2 A2
Harrislee 47 F1
Harris, Sd of 2 A3
Harrogate 6 C1
Härryda 108 C1
Harsefeld 48 A3
Harsprånget 98 B2
Harstad 94 B3
Harsvik 96 C4
Hartberg 57 F4
Hårteigen 104 B2
Hartha 53 E2
Hartkjölen 101 E1
Hartland Pt 8 B3
Hartlepool 5 F4
Hartmannsdorf 53 E3
Hartola 103 D3
Harwich 11 D2
Harz 52 B2
Harzgerode 52 C2
Hase 17 E2
Haselünne 17 E2
Haskovo 115 D3
Haslach (A) 56 C2
Haslach (D) 54 C3
Hasle 109 D4
Haslemere 9 F3
Haslev 108 C4
Hasparren 28 A4
Hassela 101 F3
Hasselfelde 52 C2
Hasselt 50 C3
Haßfurt 52 C4
Hássia, Óri 83 D1
Hässleholm 109 D3
Hastière 50 C4
Hastings 11 D3
Hasvik 95 D1
Hatě 57 E1
Haţeg 114 C1
Hatfield 9 F2
Hatherleigh 8 C3
Hattem 17 D2
Hattfjelldal 97 E3
Hattingen 17 E3
Hattula 107 E2
Hattuvaara (Lieksa) 103 F1
Hattuvaara (Ilomantsi) 103 F2
Hatvan 112 B4
Hatvik 104 A2
Hatzí 82 C2
Haubourdin 19 F1
Hauge 104 A4
Haugesund 104 A3
Hauho 107 E2
Haukelifjell 104 B2
Haukeligrend 104 B3
Haukipudas 99 D3
Haukivesi 103 E3
Haukivuori 103 E3
Haunstetten 55 F3
Haus 59 F1
Hausach 54 C3
Hausham 56 A4
Hausjärvi 107 E2
Hautajärvi 99 E2
Hautecombe 27 D4
Haute-Corse 33 F3
Hautefort 29 D1
Haute-Garonne 29 D4
Haute-Loire 29 F2
Haute-Marne 26 C1
Hautes-Alpes 31 D2
Haute-Saône 27 D1
Haute-Savoie 27 D4
Haute-Vienne (Dépt) 29 D1
Hauteville-Lompnes 27 D4
Hautmont 20 B2
Haut-Rhin (Dept) 27 E1
Havant 9 F3
Havári 86 B1
Havdalsfjellet 97 E4
Havdáta 82 B4
Havel 49 D4
Havelange 50 C4
Havelberg 48 C3
Haverfordwest 8 B2
Haverhill 11 D1
Haverö 101 E3
Havneby 108 A4
Havøysund 95 D1
Havraň 53 E3
Havre, Le 19 D3
Hawes 6 C1
Hawick 5 D3
Hawkhurst 11 D3
Hayange 21 D3
Haye-du-Puits, la 18 B3
Haye-Pesnel, la 18 B4
Hayle 8 A4
Hay-on-Wye 9 D1
Haywards Heath 10 C3
Hazebrouck 19 F1
Headford 12 B3
Heanor 7 D3
Héas 37 E2
Heathfield 10 C3
Heathrow Airport 9 F2
Hebrides, Outer 2 A2
Hebrides, Sea of the 2 A3
Heby 106 B3
Hechingen 55 D3
Hecho 37 D2
Hechtel 50 C3
Hecklingen 52 C1
Hedal 104 C2
Heddal 104 C3
Hédé 23 D3
Hede 101 E3
Hedemora 105 F3
Hedenäset 98 C2
Hedensted 108 B3
Hedesundafjärdarna 106 B3
Hedeviken 101 E3
Hedmark 104 C1
Hedon 7 E2
Heemstede 16 C2
Heerde 17 D2
Heerenveen 17 D1
Heerlen 51 D3
Heeze 16 C4
Hegge 104 C1
Hegra 101 D2
Heia 94 C3
Heide 47 F2
Heidelberg 54 C1
Heidenau 53 E2
Heidenheim 55 E2
Heidenreichstein 57 D1
Heikendorf 48 A1
Heikkila 99 F2
Heilbronn 55 D2
Heiligenberg 55 D4
Heiligenblut 59 E2
Heiligenhafen 48 B1
Heiligenkirchen 17 F3
Heiligenkreuz 57 F4
Heiligenstadt 52 B2
Heilsbronn 55 E1
Heimari 103 E3
Heimdal 100 C2
Heimertingen 55 E3
Heinävaara 103 F2
Heinävesi 103 E2
Heinola 107 F1
Heinolan mlk 107 F1
Heinsberg 17 D4
Heist 50 A3
Heist-op-den-Berg 50 C3
Hejde 109 F4
Hekla 96 B2
Hekuravë, Maj'e 76 C2
Helagsfjället 101 D2
Hélatros, Akr 93 D3
Heldeburg 52 C4
Heldrungen 52 C2
Helechal 43 E1
Helensburgh 4 C2
Helgåa (N) 101 D1
Helgaå (S) 109 D3
Helgasjön 109 D2
Helgoland 47 E2
Hella *Is* 96 B2
Hella *N* 104 B1
Hellemofjorden 97 F1
Hellendoorn 17 D2
Hellesylt 100 A3
Hellevoetsluis 16 B3
Hellin 44 C1
Hellvik 104 A4
Helmbrechts 53 D4
Helme 52 C2
Helmond 17 D3
Helmsdale 3 D2
Helmsley 7 D1
Helmstadt 55 D1
Helmstedt 52 C1
Helpter Berge 49 E2
Helsa 52 B2
Helsingborg 108 C3
Helsinge 108 C3
Helsingfors 107 F3
Helsingør 108 C3
Helsinki 107 F3
Helston 8 B4
Helvetinjärvi 102 C3
Helvick Head 14 C4
Hemau 55 F2
Hemavan 97 E3
Hemel Hempstead 9 F2
Hemer 17 E3
Hemme 100 C2
Hemmoor 48 A2
Hemnefjorden 100 C1
Hemnes 105 D3
Hemnesberget 97 E2
Hemsedal 104 C2
Hemsedal *V* 104 C2
Henares, R 40 B2
Hendaye 28 A4
Hengelo 17 D2
Hengersberg 56 B2
Hengstpaß 57 D3
Hénin-Beaumont 19 F1
Henley 9 E1
Henley-on-Thames 9 F2

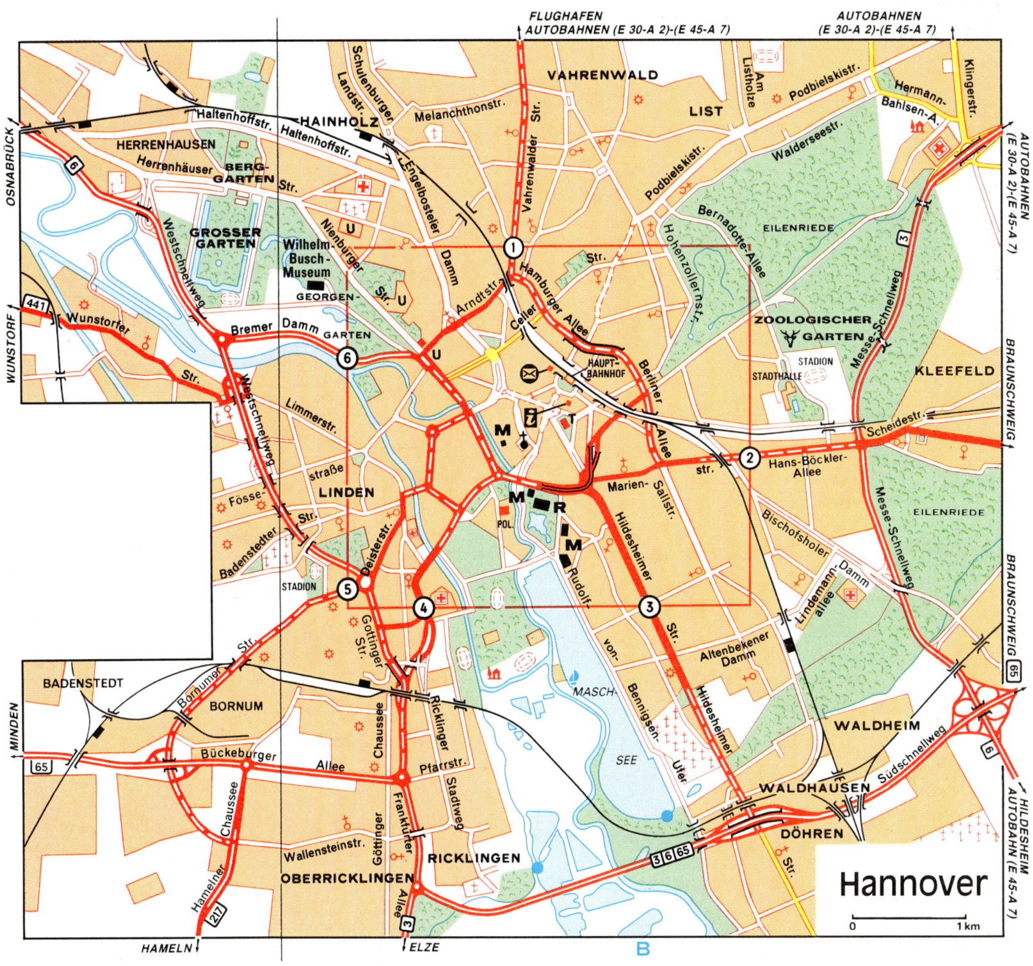
FLUGHAFEN
AUTOBAHNEN (E 30-A 2)-(E 45-A 7)
AUTOBAHNEN (E 30-A 2)-(E 45-A 7)
VAHRENWALD
LIST
HAINHOLZ
HERRENHAUSEN
BERG-GARTEN
GROSSER GARTEN
Wilhelm-Busch-Museum
GEORGEN-GARTEN
EILENRIEDE
ZOOLOGISCHER GARTEN
STADION
KLEEFELD
LINDEN
BADENSTEDT
BORNUM
MASCH-SEE
RICKLINGEN
OBERRICKLINGEN
WALDHEIM
WALDHAUSEN
DÖHREN
OSNABRÜCK
WUNSTORF
MINDEN
BRAUNSCHWEIG
HILDESHEIM AUTOBAHN (E 45-A 7)
HAMELN
ELZE
Hannover
0 1 km

Henneberg 52 B3
Hennebont 22 B3
Hennef 51 E3
Hennigsdorf 49 D4
Henrichemont 25 F2
Henstedt-Ulzburg 48 A2
Henstridge 9 D3
Hepoköngäs 99 E4
Heppenheim 54 C1
Heraclea 77 E4
Hérault 29 F4
Hérault (Dépt) 30 A4
Herbault 25 E2
Herbertingen 55 D3
Herbiers, les 24 B3
Herbignac 22 C4
Herbolzheim 54 C3
Herborn 51 F3
Herbrechtingen 55 E2
Herbstein 52 A3
Herceg Novi 76 A3
Hercegovac 71 D2
Hercegov Goleša 76 B1
Hereford 9 D1
Hereford and Worcester 9 D1
Herencia 40 B4
Herentals 50 C3
Herford 17 F2
Héricourt 27 E2
Heringsdorf 49 E2
Herisau 58 B2
Hérisson 26 A3
Hérisson, Cascades du 27 D3
Herk 50 C3
Herleshausen 52 B3
Hermagor 59 F2
Herma Ness 3 F1
Hermannsburg 48 B4
Hermansverk 104 B1
Hermenault, l' 24 C3
Herment 29 E1
Hermeskeil 54 B1
Hermigua 42 A4
Hermsdorf 53 D3
Hernani 36 C1
Hernansancho 39 F1
Herne 17 E3
Herne Bay 11 D3
Herning 108 A3
Heroldsberg 55 F1
Herónia 83 F4
Herøy 100 A2
Herrala 107 F2
Herre 104 C3
Herrenberg 55 D3
Herrenchiemsee 56 B3
Herrera (Andalucía) 43 E3
Herrera (Aragón) 37 D4
Herrera *Mt* 37 D4
Herrera de Alcántara 38 C3
Herrera del Duque 39 F4
Herrera de Pisuerga 35 F3
Herrera, Pto de 36 B2
Herreruela 39 D3
Herrestad 108 C1
Herrieden 55 E2
Herrljunga 109 D1
Herrnburg 48 B2
Herrnhut 53 F2
Herrsching 56 A3
Herrskog 102 A2
Hersbruck 55 F1
Herselt 50 C3
Hérso 79 F2
Hersónissos Akrotíri 90 C3
Hersónissos Methánon 87 E2
Hersónissos Spinalónga 91 E3
Herstal 51 D3
Herten 17 E3
Hertford 9 F2
Hertfordshire 9 F2
Hervás 39 E2
Herzberg (Brandenburg) 53 E1
Herzberg (Niedersachsen) 52 B2
Herzogenaurach 55 E1
Herzogenburg 57 E2
Herzsprung 49 D3
Hesdin 19 E2
Hesel 47 E3
Hessen 52 A3
Hesseng 95 F2
Hessisch-Lichtenau 52 B2
Hessisch Oldendorf 52 A1
Hestfjørður 96 A4
Hetekylä 99 E3
Hetin 72 C1
Hettange 21 D3
Hettstedt 52 C2
Heubach 55 E2
Heuchin 19 F1
Heukuppe 57 E3
Hevlín 57 F1
Hexham 5 E3
Heyrieux 30 C1
Heysham 6 B1
Hiddensee 49 D1
Hieflau 57 D3
Hiekkasarkät 102 C1
Hierbas 41 E3
Hierro 42 A4
Hiersac 28 C1
Hietaniemi 95 F4
Higham Ferrers 9 F1
Highland 2 C3
High Peak 6 C2
High Willhays 8 C3
High Wycombe 9 F2
Higuera de Arjona 44 A2
Higuera de la Serena 43 E1
Higuera de la Sierra 43 D2
Higuera de Vargas 42 C1
Higuera la Real 42 C1
Higueruela 41 D4
Hiidenportti 103 E1
Hiiumaa 110 B1
Híjar 37 D4
Hilchenbach 17 F4
Hildburghausen 52 C3
Hilden 17 E4
Hilders 52 B3
Hildesheim 52 B1
Hiliomódi 87 E1
Hillegom 16 B2
Hillerød 108 C3
Hillesøy 94 B2
Hillswick 3 F1
Hiloús, Akr 92 C1
Hilpoltstein 55 F2
Hiltula 103 E3
Hilvarenbeek 16 C4
Hilversum 16 C2
Himanka 102 C1
Himaros 80 A2
Himmerland 108 B2
Hinckley 9 E1
Hindelang 55 E4
Hindhead 9 F3
Hindsholm 108 B3
Hinnøya 94 A3
Hinodejo 36 B3
Hinojares 44 B2
Hinojosa de Duero 39 D1
Hinojosa del Duque 43 E1
Hinterrhein 58 B3
Hintersee (Bayern) 56 B4
Hintersee (Meckenburg-Vorpommern) 49 E2
Hinterstoder 57 D3
Hintertux 59 D2
Hinterweidenthal 54 B2
Hios 85 F4
Hios, N 85 E4
Hirschau 55 F1
Hirschberg 53 D3
Hirschegg 58 B2
Hirsingue 27 E2
Hirson 20 B2
Hirşova 115 E1
Hirtshals 108 B1
Hirvasvaara 99 E2
Hirvensalmi 103 E3
Hirvilahti 103 E2
Hirwaun 8 C2
Hisarja 115 D2
Histria 115 E1
Hitchin 9 F2
Hitra 100 C1
Hitzacker 48 B3
Hjälmaren 105 F4
Hjartdal 104 C3
Hjellestad 104 A2
Hjelmeland 104 A3
Hjelmsøya 95 D1
Hjo 109 D1
Hjørring 108 B1
Hjørundfjorden 100 A2
Hlebine 71 D1
Hlemoútsi 86 B1
Hlomó, Óros 83 F3
Hluboká 57 D1
Hobro 108 B2
Höchberg 55 D1
Hochdorf 27 F2
Hochfeiler 59 D2
Hochfelden 21 E4
Hochgolling 59 F1
Hochgrabe 59 E2
Hochosterwitz 70 B1
Hochreichart 57 D4
Hochschober 59 E2
Hochschwab 57 D3
Hochspeyer 54 C1
Höchst 55 D1
Höchstadt 55 E1
Höchstädt 55 E2
Hochtannbergpaß 58 B2
Hochtor (Osttirol) 59 E2
Hochtor (Steiermark) 57 D3
Hockenheim 54 C2
Hoddesdon 9 F2
Hodenhagen 48 A4
Hœdic 22 C4
Hódmezővásárhely 114 B1
Hodnet 6 B3
Hodonín 57 F1
Hodoš 70 C1
Hodovo 75 F2
Hoedekenskerke 16 B4
Hoek van Holland 16 B3
Hoemsbu 100 B2
Hof 53 D4
Hofgeismar 52 A2
Hofheim 52 B4
Hofles 97 D4
Höfn 96 C2
Hofolding 56 A3
Hofors 105 F2
Hofsjökull 96 B2
Höganäs 108 C3
Høgebru 100 A3
Höglekardalen 101 E2
Högsäter 105 D4
Högsby 109 E2
Høgset 100 B2
Hohe Acht 51 E4
Hohenau 57 F2
Hohenberg 57 E3
Hohenems 58 B2
Hohengandern 52 B2
Hohenlimburg 17 E4
Hohenlinden 56 B3
Hohenlockstedt 48 A2
Hohenmölsen 53 D2
Hohenpeißenberg 56 A4
Hohenseeden 48 C4
Hohenstein 53 D3
Hohentauern 57 D4
Hohenwestedt 48 A2
Hohenzollern 55 D3
Hoher Zinken 56 C3
Hohe Tauern 59 E2
Hohe Tauern, Nat Pk 59 E2
Hóhlakas 93 E2
Hohneck 27 E1
Hohwachter Bucht 48 B1
Hohwald, le 21 E4
Højer 108 A4
Hokksund 104 C3
Hol 104 C2
Holbæk 108 C3
Holbeach 7 E3
Holdorf 17 F2
Holíč 57 F1
Höljäkkä 103 E1
Höljes 101 D4
Hollabrunn 57 E2
Høllen 104 B4
Hollenstedt 48 A3
Höllental 57 E3
Holles 97 D4
Hollfeld 52 C4
Hollingsholm 100 B2
Hollola 107 F2
Hollum 16 C1
Hollywood 13 D4
Holm (N) 97 D3
Holm (S) 101 F2
Hólmavík 96 A1
Holmec 70 B1
Holmen 105 D2
Holmestrand 104 C3
Holmfirth 6 C2
Holmön 102 B1
Holmsjön 101 E3
Holmslands Klit 108 A3
Holmsund 102 B1
Holomóndas, Óros 80 B3
Holstebro 108 A2
Holsted 108 A3
Holsworthy 8 C3
Holt 7 F3
Holwerd 47 D3
Holycross Abbey 14 C3
Holyhead 6 A2
Holy I (Anglesey) 6 A2
Holy I (Northumberland) 5 E2
Holywell 6 B2
Holywood 13 E2
Holzappel 51 F4
Holzgau 58 C2
Holzkirchen 56 A3
Holzleitner Sattel 58 C2
Holzminden 52 A2
Homberg (Hessen) 52 A3
Homberg (Nordrhein-Westfalen) 17 D3
Homburg 54 B2
Hommelstø 97 D3
Hommelvik 100 C2
Hommersåk 104 A3
Homoljske planine 73 E3
Hondarribia Fuenterrabia 36 C1
Hondón de las Nieves 45 D2
Hönebach 52 B3
Hønefoss 104 C3
Honfleur 19 D3
Høng 108 B3
Hónikas 87 D2
Honiton 9 D3
Honkajoki 102 B3
Honningsvåg 95 E1
Honrubia 40 C3
Honrubia de la Cuesta 36 A3
Hontalbilla 40 A1
Hontoria del Pinar 36 A3
Hooge 47 F1
Hoogeveen 17 D2
Hoogezand 47 D3
Hoogstraten 50 C2
Hook Head 15 D4
Höör 109 D3
Hoorn 16 C2
Hopetoun House 5 D2
Hopfgarten 59 D1
Hopperstad 104 B1
Hóra (Dodekánissa) 89 E2
Hóra (Pelopónissos) 86 C3
Hora Svatého Šebestiána 53 E3
Horažd'ovice 56 C1
Horb 54 C3
Hörby 109 D3
Horcajo de los Montes 39 F4
Horcajo de Santiago 40 B3
Horcajo de Trevélez 44 A3
Horcajo-Medianero 39 E2
Horche 40 B2
Hordaland 104 B2
Horden 5 E4
Horeftó 83 F2
Horezu 115 D1
Horgen 58 A2
Horgoš 72 C1
Horley 10 C3
Horn (A) 57 E2
Horn (Baden-Württemberg) 55 D4
Horn (N) 97 D3
Horn (Nordrhein-Westfalen) 52 A2
Hornachos 43 D1
Hornachuelos 43 E2
Hornavan 98 A2
Hornberg 54 C3
Hornbjarg 96 A1
Hornburg 52 B1
Horncastle 7 E3
Horndal 106 A3
Horneburg 48 A3
Hörnefors 102 A2
Hörnerkirchen 48 A2
Hornet 100 C2
Hornindal 100 A3
Hornindalsvatn 100 A3
Hørning 108 B3
Horni Počernice 53 F3
Hornisgrinde 54 C3
Horni Slavkov 53 E4
Hornos 44 B2
Hornoy 19 E2
Hornsea 7 E2
Hörnum 47 F1
Hořovice 53 F4
Horsens 108 B3
Horsham 10 C3
Hørsholm 108 C3
Horšovký Týn 56 B1
Horst 48 B3
Horstmar 17 E2
Hortafjorden 97 D3
Horten 104 C3
Hortezuela 36 B4
Hortiátis 80 A3
Hospental 58 A3
Hospital 14 C3
Hospital de Orbigo 35 D3
Hossa 99 F3
Hossegor 28 A4
Hostalric 32 B4
Hotagen 101 E1
Hotagen *L* 101 E1
Hotagsfjällen 101 E1
Hoting 101 F1
Hotton 50 C4
Houat 22 C4
Houches, les 27 E4
Houdain 19 F1
Houdan 19 E4
Houeillès 28 B3
Houffalize 51 D4
Houghton-le-Spring 5 E4
Houlgate 18 C3
Houmnikó 80 B2
Hoúni 83 D3
Hourtin 28 A2
Houtskär 107 D3
Hov 108 B3
Hovärken 101 D3
Hovden 104 B3
Hove 10 C3
Hovet 104 B2
Hovmantorp 109 E2
Høvringen 100 C3
Howden 7 D2
Howth 13 E4
Höxter 52 A2
Hoy 3 D1
Hoya 17 F1
Høyanger 100 A3
Hoyerswerda 53 F2
Hoylake 6 B2
Høylandet 97 D4
Hoym 52 C1
Hoyos 39 D2
Höytiäinen 103 F2
Hoz de Beteta 40 C2
Hozoviótissa 89 D3
Hracholuská přehr nádrž 53 E4
Hradec-Králove 112 A2
Hrádek 57 E1
Hrádek nad Nisou 53 F2
Hranice (Severomoravský) 112 A3
Hranice (Západočeský) 53 D4
Hrasnica 75 F1
Hrastnik 70 B2
Hrastovlje 70 A3
Hřensko 53 F2
Hrísey 96 B1
Hrissafa 87 D3
Hrissí, N 91 E4
Hrissó 80 B2
Hrissoskalítissa 90 B3
Hrissoúpoli 80 C2
Hrissovítsi 86 C2
Hristiani, N 91 D1
Hristianó 86 C3
Hristós 89 D2
Hrómio 79 D4
Hrtkovci 72 C3
Hrušovany 57 F1
Hrvace 75 D1
Hrvatska 70 C2
Hückeswagen 17 E4
Hucknall 7 D3
Hucqueliers 19 E1
Huddersfield 6 C2
Hude 47 F3
Hudiksvall 101 F3
Huebra, R 39 E1
Huedin 112 C4
Huélago 44 A3
Huélamo 40 C2
Huelgoat 22 B3
Huelma 44 A2
Huelva 42 C2
Huelva, Riv. de 43 D2
Huércal-Overa 44 C3
Huérguina 41 D3
Huerta del Rey 36 A3
Huerta de Valdecarábanos 40 A3
Huertahernando 40 C2
Huerto 37 E3
Huerva, R 37 D4
Huesa 44 B2
Huesca 37 D3
Huéscar 44 B2
Huesna, Emb de 43 D2
Huete 40 B3
Huétor-Santillán 44 A3
Huétor-Tájar 43 F3
Hüfingen 54 C4
Huftarøy 104 A2
Huisne 23 F3
Huittinen 107 D2
Huizen 16 C2
Hulst 16 B4
Hultsfred 109 E2
Humada 35 F3
Humanes 40 B1
Humber Bridge 7 D2
Humber, R 7 E2
Humberside 7 D2
Humberside (Airport) 7 D2
Humenné 112 C3
Humppila 107 E2
Hundested 108 C3
Hundorp 100 C3
Hunedoara 114 C1
Hünfeld 52 B3
Hungerford 9 E2
Hunnebostrand 105 D4
Húnsflói 96 A1
Hunspach 21 F3
Hunsrück 54 B1
Hunstanton 7 E3
Hunte 17 F1
Huntingdon 9 F1
Huntly 3 E3
Hurdal 105 D2
Huriel 25 F4
Hurones, Emb de los 43 D3
Hurskaala 103 E3
Hürth 17 E4
Hurum 104 C1
Hurup 108 A2
Husafell 96 B2
Húsavík *Is* 96 B1
Husavik (N) 104 A2
Husbands Bosworth 9 F1
Hushinish 2 A2
Huşi 113 E4
Huskvarna 109 D1
Husnes 104 A2
Hustadvika 100 B2
Hustopeče 57 F1
Husum (D) 47 F1
Husum (S) 102 A2
Hutovo 75 F2
Hutovo Blato 75 F2
Hüttenberg 57 D4
Hüttschlag 59 E1
Huttula 103 D3
Huttwil 27 F2
Huy 50 C4
Hvalba 96 A4
Hvalfjörður 96 A2
Hvalpsund 108 A2
Hvalvík 96 A3
Hvar 75 D2
Hvar *I* 75 E2
Hvarski kan 75 D2
Hveragerði 96 A2
Hveravellir 96 B2
Hvidbjerg 108 A2
Hvide Sande 108 A3
Hvítá 96 B2
Hvittingfoss 104 C3
Hvitträsk 107 E3
Hvolsvöllur 96 B3
Hwlffordd 8 B2
Hyde 6 C2
Hyen 100 A3
Hyères 31 D4
Hyères, Iles d' 31 D4
Hylsfjorden 104 A3
Hyltebruk 108 C2
Hyrynsalmi 99 E4
Hythe 11 D3
Hyvinkää 107 E2
Hyypiö 99 D2

I

Ía 91 E1
Ialomiţa 115 E1
Iaşi 113 E3
Íasmos 81 D2
Ibañeta, Pto 36 C1
Ibar 73 D4
Ibbenbüren 17 E2
Ibestad 94 B3
Ibi 45 E1
Ibias, R 34 C2
Ibiza 45 D4
Ibiza *I* 45 D3
Iblei, Mti 69 D4
Ičn'a 113 F1
Icod de los Vinos 42 A4
Idanha a Nova 38 C2
Idar-Oberstein 54 B1
Idéo Ándro 91 D4
Ídi, Óros 91 D4
Idoméni 79 F2
Iđđoš 72 C1
Ídra 87 F2
Ídra, N 87 F3
Ídras, Kólpos 87 E2
Idre 101 D3
Idrigill Pt 2 B3
Idrija 70 A2
Idrijca 70 A2
Idro 58 C4
Idstein 51 F4
Ielsi 64 B3
Ieper 50 A3
Ierápetra 91 E4
Ierissós 80 B3
Ieropigí 78 C3
If, Château d' 30 C4
Ifestía 85 D1
Ifjord 95 E1
Ifjordfjellet 95 E1
Igalo 76 A3
Iga Vas 70 B2
Iggesund 101 F3
Iglesias 66 B4
Igls 59 D2
Igoumenítsa 82 B2
Igrane 75 E2
Igualada 37 F4
Ihtiman 115 D2
Ii 99 D3
Iijarvi 95 E2
Iijoki 99 D3
Iisalmi 103 E1
Iisvesi 103 E2
IJmuiden 16 B2
IJssel 17 D3
IJsselmeer 16 C2
IJsselmuiden 17 D2
IJzendijke 16 B4
Ijzer 50 A3
Ikaalinen 102 C3
Ikaría, N 89 D2
Ikast 108 A3
Ilandža 73 D2
Ilanz 58 B3
Ilche 37 E3
Ilchester 9 D3
Ile-Bouchard, l' 25 D3
Ile-Rousse, l' 33 F2
Ilfracombe 8 C3
Ílhavo 38 B1
Ília 83 F3
Ilía 86 B1
Il'ičevsk 113 F4
Ílida 86 B1
Ilidža 75 F1
Ilijas 71 F4
Ilíki 84 A4
Ilíki, L 84 A4
Iliókastro 87 E2
Ilirska Bistrica 70 B3
Ilkeston 7 D3
Ilkley 6 C2
Illana 40 B2
Illano 34 C1
Illar 44 B3
Ille 23 D3
Ille et Rance, Canal d' 23 D3
Ille-et-Vilaine 23 D3
Iller 55 E4
Illertissen 55 E3
Illescas 40 A2
Ille-sur-Têt 32 B2
Illhæusern 27 E1
Illiers 25 E1
Illingen 55 D2
Illmitz 57 F3
Illora 44 A3
Illueca 36 C4
Ilm 52 C3
Ilmajoki 102 C2
Ilmenau *R* 48 B3
Ilmenau 52 C3
Il'men, Ozero 111 D1
Ilminster 9 D3
Ilok 72 B2
Ilomantsi 103 F2
Ilova 71 D2
Ilovik 70 B4
Ilsenburg 52 B1
Ilsfeld 55 D2
Imathía 79 E3
Imatra 103 F4
Ímeros 81 E2
Imitós 87 F1
Immenstaad 55 D4
Immenstadt 55 E4
Immingham 7 E2
Immingham Dock 7 E2
Imola 61 D3
Imotski 75 E1
Imperia 31 F3
Imphy 26 A3
Impruneta 61 D4
Imst 58 C2
Ina 49 F3
Inari 95 E3
Inarijärvi 95 E3
Inarijoki 95 E3
Inca 45 F2
Inchnadamph 2 C2
Inchtree 2 C4
Incisa in Val d'Arno 61 D4
Incudine, M 33 F4
Indal 101 F3
Indalsälven 101 E2
Indija 72 C2
Indre 25 D2
Indre (Dépt) 25 E3
Indre-et-Loire 25 D2
Infiesto 35 E1
Ingå 107 E3
Ingelmunster 50 A3
Ingleton 6 C1
Ingolstadt 55 F2
Ingrandes 23 E4
Ingul 113 F3
Ingulec 113 F3
Ingulec *R* 113 F3
Ingwiller 21 E3
Iniesta 41 D4
Iniö 107 D2
Iniön aukko 107 D2
Inis 12 B4
Inis Córthaidh 15 D3
Inishbofin 12 A3
Inishcrone 12 B2
Inisheer 12 B4
Inishkea 12 A2
Inishmaan 12 B4
Inishmore 12 B4
Inishmurray 12 C2
Inishowen 13 D1
Inishowen Head 13 D1
Inishshark 12 A3
Inishtrahull 13 D1
Inishturk 12 A3
Inkee 99 E3
Inkoo 107 E3
Inn (CH) 58 B3
Inn (D) 56 B3
Innbygda 104 C1
Inndyr 97 E2
Innellan 4 B2
Innerleithen 5 D2
Inner Sd 2 B3
Innfield 13 D3
Innhavet 97 F1
Innichen 59 E2
Inning 56 A3
Innsbruck 59 D2
Innset 94 B3
Innvik 100 A3
Inói (Pelopónissos) 86 B1
Inói (Stereá Eláda) 84 A4
Inoússes 85 F4
Inoússes, N 85 F4
Inowrocław 112 A1
Ins 27 E2
Ińsko 49 F2
Interlaken 27 F3
Întorsura Buzăului 113 D4
Inveraray 4 B1
Inverbervie 3 E4
Invergarry 2 C4
Invergordon 3 D3
Inverkeithing 5 D2
Invermoriston 2 C4
Inverness 2 C3
Inverurie 3 E4
Inzell 56 B3
Ioánina 82 C1
Ioánina (Nomos) 82 B1
Ioanínon, L 82 C1
Iona 4 A1
Ionia 79 F3
Iónia Nissiá 82 A2
Íos 88 C4
Íos, N 88 C4
Ipáti 83 E3
Ipéria 83 E2
Iphofen 55 E1
Ípiros 82 B2
Ipsilí Ráhi 80 C2
Ípsos 82 A1
Ipsoúnda 86 C2
Ipswich 11 D2
Iput' 111 E4
Iráklia (Makedonía) 80 A2
Iráklia (Stereá Eláda) 83 E3
Iráklia, N 88 C3
Iráklio 91 D3
Iráklio (Nomos) 91 D4
Irati, R 36 C2
Irbes Šaurums 110 B2
Irdning 57 D4
Iregua, R 36 B2
Iréo (Argolída) 87 D2
Iréo (Dodekánissa) 89 E2
Iréo (Korinthía) 87 E1
Iréo, Akr 87 E1
Iría 87 E2
Irig 72 C2
Irish Sea 13 F3
Iriški venac 72 C2
Irixoa 34 B1
Irnijärvi 99 E3
Iron-Bridge 9 D1
Irschenberg 56 B3
Irsina 65 D4
Irún 36 C1
Irurzun 36 C2
Irvine 4 C2
Irvinestown 12 C2
Irxleben 52 C1
Isaba 37 D2
Isaccea 113 E4
Ísafjarðardjúp 96 A1
Ísafjörður 96 A1
Isala 115 E3
Isane 100 A3

Kilyos
Sariyer
Beykoz
E 80
Kavakcik
Kanlica
Bebek
Alibeyköy
Kâğithane
Anadolu Hisari
E 80
Edirne
Keşan
Saray
Arnavutköy
Kandilli
Siâhdarağa
Ortaköy
Vaniköy
20
MECIDIYEKÖY
Boğaziçi
BESIKTAS
Çengelköy
Halicioğlu
EYÜP
Hasköy
Taksim
BEYOĞLU
Dolmabahçe
BEYLERBEYI
Atikali
Haliç
Galata Kulesi
KUZGUNCUK
Süleymaniye Camii
SALACAK
20
FATIH
ÜMRANIYE
Topkapi Sarayi
ÜSKÜDAR
Şile
Kapali Çarşi
Sehrenini
Ayasofya
Validebagi
Sultan Ahmet Camii
Harem
HAYDARPASA
ISTANBUL
Fikirtepe
E 80
KADIKÖY
Kiziltoprak
Izmit
FENERBAHÇE
Göztepe
ERENKÖY
MARMARA
DENIZI
1/150000
Izmit

Isar 56 B2
Isarco 59 D2
Isbister 3 F1
Iscar 35 E4
Ischgl 58 C2
Ischia 64 A4
Ischia, I d' 64 A4
Ise 105 D3
Isefjord 108 C3
Iselle 58 A3
Iselsberg 59 E2
Iseo 60 B1
Iseo, L d' 58 B4
Iseran, Col de l' 31 E1
Isère (Dépt) 30 C1
Isère (R) 30 C1
Iserlohn 17 E3
Isernia 64 A3
Isfjellet 94 C2
Isfjorden 100 B2
Ishavsleden 94 C3
Ishëm 76 C4
Ishëm *R* 76 C4
Isigny 18 C3
Isili 66 B3
Iskăr 115 D2
Is'kuras 95 E2
Isla 3 D4
Isla 36 A1
Isla Cristina 42 C3
Isla Mayor 43 D3
Island Magee 13 E2
Islay 4 A2
Isle 28 C2
Isle-Adam, l' 19 F3
Isle-de-Noé, l' 28 C4
Isle-en-Dodon, l' 37 F1
Isle-Jourdain, l' (Gers) 28 C4
Isle-Jourdain, l' (Vienne) 25 D4
Isle of Man 6 A1
Isle of Portland 9 D4
Isle of Whithorn 4 C4
Isle of Wight 9 E4
Isleornsay 2 B4
Isles of Scilly 8 A4
Isle-sur-la-Sorgue, l' 30 C3
Isle-sur-le-Doubs, l' 27 D2
Isle-sur-Serein, l' 26 B2
Ismaning 55 F3
Isnäs 107 F2
Isny 55 E4
Iso-Evo 107 E2
Isojärvi 103 D3
Isojoki 102 B3
Isokylä 99 E2
Isokyrö 102 B2
Isola 31 E3
Isola del Gran Sasso d'Italia 63 F1
Isola della Scala 60 C1
Isola del Liri 64 A3
Isola di Capo Rizzuto 67 F3
Isona 37 F3
Isonzo 59 F3
Isorella 60 B1
Iso-Syöte 99 E3
Ispica 69 D4
Issambres, les 31 D4
Issel 17 D3
Issigeac 28 C2
Issoire 29 F1
Issóva, M. 86 C2
Íssoma 86 C1
Issoudun 25 E3
Is-sur-Tille 26 C2
Issy-l'Evêque 26 B3
Ist 74 B1
Istán 43 E4
İstanbul 115 F3
Istarske Toplice 70 A3
Istérnia 88 B2
Istha 52 A2
Isthmía 87 E1
Istibanja 77 F2
Istiéa 83 F3
Istindan 94 B3
Istok 76 C2
Istres 30 C4
Ístrios 93 E2
Isturits et d'Oxocelhaya, Grottes d' 28 A4
Itä-Aure 102 C3
Itäinen Suomenlahti 107 F2
Itanós 91 F3
Itéa (Flórina) 79 D2
Itéa (Grevená) 79 D4
Itéa (Stereá Eláda) 83 E4
Itéa (Thessalía) 83 E2
Itéas, Kólpos 83 E4
Itháki 82 B4
Itháki, N 82 B4
Ithómi 86 C3
Iti 83 E3
Ítilo 87 D4
Íti, Óros 83 E3
Iton 19 E3
Itri 64 A3
Itta 52 B3
Ittiri 66 A2
Itz 52 C4
Itzehoe 48 A2
Ivacevići 112 C1
Ivajlovgrad 115 E3
Ivalo 95 E3
Ivalojoki Avvil 95 E3
Ivančice 57 F1
Ivančići 71 F4
Ivančna Gorica 70 B2
Ivanec 70 C1
Ivangrad 76 C2
Ivanić Grad 71 D2
Ivanjica 73 D4
Ivanjska 71 E3
Ivankovo 71 F2
Ivano-Frankovsk 113 D3
Ivanščica 70 C2
Ivan Sedlo 75 F1
Ivanska 71 D2
Iveland 104 B4
Iveragh 14 A4
Ívira 80 B2
Iviron 80 C4
Ivrea 31 F1
Ivry-la-Bataille 19 E4
Ixiá 93 F1
Ixworth 11 D1
Iž 74 C1
Izeda 34 C4
Izegem 50 A3
Izernore 26 C4
Izlake 70 B2
Izmail 113 E4
İzmir 115 E4
İzmit 115 F3
Iznájar 43 F3
Iznájar, Emb de 43 F3
Iznallos 44 A3
İznik 115 F3
İznik Gölü 115 F3
Izoard, Col d' 31 D2
Izola 70 A3
Iz Veli 74 C1
Izvor (Makedonija) 77 D4
Izvor (Makedonija) 77 F3
Izvor (Srbija) 73 E4

J

Jaala 107 F2
Jääsjärvi 103 D3
Jabalón, R 44 A1
Jabbeke 50 A3
Jablanac 70 B4
Jablan Do 76 A2
Jablanica 75 F1
Jablanica (Reg) 77 D4
Jablanica *R* 77 D1
Jablaničko jez 75 F1
Jablonec nad Nisou 112 A2
Jablonné v Podještědí 53 F3
Jabugo 42 C2
Jabuka (Bosna i Hercegovina) 76 A1
Jabuka (Srbija) 76 B1
Jabuka (Vojvodina) 73 D2
Jabuka, I 74 C2
Jabukovac (Hrvatska) 71 D3
Jabukovac (Srbija) 73 F3
Jabukovik 77 E1
Jaca 37 D2
Jáchymov 53 E3
Jadar (Bosna i Hercegovina) 72 C4
Jadar (Srbija) 72 B3
Jäder 106 A3
Jaderberg 47 F3
Jadovik 76 B1
Jadovnik 71 D4
Jadranska Lešnica 72 B3
Jadransko More 74 B2
Jadraque 40 B1
Jaén 44 A2
Jagodnjac 71 F2
Jagotin 113 F2
Jagst 55 E2
Jagsthausen 55 D2
Jahorina 76 A1
Jahorina (Reg) 76 A1
Jajce 71 E4
Jäkkvik 97 F2
Jakobselv 95 F2
Jakobstad 102 C1
Jakšić 71 E2
Jakupica 77 E3
Jalasjärvi 102 C3
Jaligny 26 A3
Jalón, R 36 C3
Jalovik Izvor 73 F4
Jambol 115 E2
Jamena 72 B3
Jämijärvi 102 C3
Jäminkipohja 102 C3
Jämjö 109 E3
Jammerbugten 108 A2
Jamnička Kiselica 70 C2
Jämsä 103 D3
Jämsänkoski 103 D3
Jämtlands Län 101 E2
Janakkala 107 E2
Janče 77 D3
Jandía, Pta de 42 C4
Jándula, Emb del 44 A1
Jandula, R 44 A1
Jänisselkä 103 F2
Janja 72 B3
Janjevo 77 D2
Janjina 75 E2
Jankov kamen 76 C1
Jañona 39 D2
Jantra 115 D2
Janville 25 E1
Janzé 23 D3
Japetić 70 C2
Jäppilä 103 E2
Jaraba 36 C4
Jarafuel 41 D4
Jaraicejo 39 E3
Jaráiz 39 E2
Jarak 72 C3
Jarama, R 40 B2
Jarandilla de la Vera 39 E2
Järbo 106 A2
Jarcevo 111 E3
Jard 24 B3
Jæren 104 A4
Jaren 105 D2
Jargeau 25 E1
Jarkovac 73 D2
Jarmen 49 D2
Jarmenovci 73 D3
Jarnac 28 B1
Jarnages 25 E4
Järna (Kopparbergs Län) 105 E2
Järna (Stockholms Län) 106 B4
Jarny 21 D3
Jarocin 112 A2
Jaroměřice 57 E1
Jarosław 112 C2
Järpen 101 E2
Jarrow 5 E3
Järvelä 107 F2
Järvenpää 107 E2
Järvsö 101 F3
Jaša Tomić 73 D2
Jasenak 70 B3
Jasenica (Bosna i Hercegovina) 71 D3
Jasenica (Srbija) 73 D3
Jasenovac 71 D3
Jasenovo (Crna Gora) 76 B2
Jasenovo (Srbija) 76 B1
Jasenovo (Vojvodina) 73 D2
Jasień 53 F1
Jasika 73 E4
Jasikovo 73 E3
Jasło 112 C3
Jasmund 49 D1
Jastrebarsko 70 C2
Jastrowie 112 A1
Jászberény 112 B4
Jau, Col de 32 B2
Jaufenpass 59 D2
Jaunay-Clan 25 D3
Jaunpass 27 E3
Jausiers 31 D2
Javalambre 41 D3
Javalambre, Sa de 41 E3
Javalón 41 D2
Javea 45 E1
Jävenitz 48 C4
Javie, la 31 D3
Javor 76 C1
Javořice 57 D1
Javornjača 71 D4
Javorov 112 C2
Jävre 98 B4
Javron 23 E3
Jedburgh 5 D3
Jedincy 113 D3
Jędrzejów 112 B2
Jeesiö 95 E4
Jeetze 48 B3
Jegun 28 C4
Jegunovce 77 D3
Jēkabpils 110 C3
Jektevik 104 A2
Jelah 71 E3
Jelašca 76 A1
Jelenia Góra 112 A2
Jelenje 70 B3
Jelgava 110 C3
Jelling 108 A3
Jel'n'a 111 E3
Jelsa (N) 104 A3
Jelsa (YU) 75 E2
Jemnice 57 E1
Jena 52 C3
Jenbach 59 D1
Jengejetneme 97 E4
Jennersdorf 57 F4
Jeppo 102 C2
Jerez de la Frontera 43 D3
Jerez de los Caballeros 42 C1
Jérica 41 E3
Jerichow 49 D4
Jerisjärvi 95 D4
Jerpoint Abbey 15 D3
Jersey 18 A3
Jerte 39 E2
Jerte, R 39 E2
Jerxheim 52 B1
Jerzu 66 C3
Jesenice (CS) 53 E4
Jesenice (YU) 70 A1
Jesenik 112 A2
Jesi 61 F4
Jesolo 59 E4
Jessen 53 D1
Jessheim 105 D3
Jeßnitz 53 D2
Jetzelsdorf 57 E2
Jeumont 20 B1
Jevenstedt 48 A2
Jever 47 E3
Jevišovice 57 E1
Jevnaker 105 D2
Jezerane 70 C3
Jezerce 77 D2
Jezercë, M 76 C2
Jezero 71 E4
Jezero Šćit 75 E1
Jezersko 70 B1
Ježevica 72 C4
Jičín 112 A2
Jiekkevarre 94 C2
Jihlava 57 E1
Jihlava *R* 57 E1
Jijona 45 E1
Jiloca, R 41 D2
Jílové u Prahy 53 F4
Jimbolia 114 C1
Jimena 44 A2
Jimena de la Frontera 43 E4
Jindřichovice 53 D3
Jindřichuv Hradec 57 D1
Jirkov 53 E3
Jiu 115 D2
Jizera 53 F3
Joachimsthal 49 E3
Jockfall 98 C2
Jódar 44 A2
Jodoigne 50 C3
Joensuu 103 F2
Jogeva 110 C1
Johanngeorgenstadt 53 D3
John o'Groats 3 D2
Johnstone 4 C2
Johovac 71 F3
Joigny 26 A1
Joinville 20 C4
Jokela 107 E2
Jokijärvi 99 E3
Jokikylä 99 E4
Jokioinen 107 E2
Jokkmokk 98 B2
Jökulsá-á Fjöllum 96 C1
Joloskylä 99 D3
Jølstravatnet 100 A3
Jomala 106 C3
Jönåker 106 A4
Jondal 104 B2
Jongunjärvi 99 E3
Joniškis 110 C3
Jönköping 109 D1
Jönköpings Län 109 D2
Jonzac 28 B1
Jordbro 106 B4
Jordbruksveien 95 D2
Jormlien 97 E4
Jörn 98 B4
Joroinen 103 E3
Jørpeland 104 A3
Jørstadmoen 105 D2
Jošanica 73 E4
Jošanička Banja 76 C1
Jošavka 71 E3
Josenfjorden 104 A3
Jose Toran, Emb de 43 E2
Josipdol 70 C3
Josipovac 71 F2
Josselin 22 C3
Jostedalsbreen 100 A3
Jotunheimen 100 B3
Jou, Coll de 32 A3
Joué 25 D2
Jougne 27 D3
Joutjärvi 107 F2
Joutsa 103 D3
Joutseno 103 E4
Joutsijärvi 99 E2
Joyeuse 30 B2
Juankoski 103 E2
Juan-les-Pins 31 E4
Júcar, R 41 E4
Jüchen 17 D4
Juchnov 111 F3
Judaberg 104 A3
Judenau 57 E2
Judenburg 57 D4
Judio 43 F1
Juelsminde 108 B3
Jugenheim 54 C1
Jugon 22 C3
Jugorje 70 B2
Juillac 29 D1
Juist 47 E3
Jukkasjärvi 94 C4
Jülich 17 D4
Julierpass 58 B3
Jullouville 18 B4
Jumaliskylä 99 F4
Jumeaux 29 F1
Jumièges 19 D3
Jumilhac-le-Grand 29 D1
Jumilla 45 D1
Jumilla, Pto de 45 D1
Juminen 103 E1
Jumisko 99 E2
Juneda 37 F4
Jungfrau 27 F3
Junik 76 C2
Juniville 20 B3
Junkeren 97 E2
Junosuando 95 D4
Junsele 101 F2
Juntusranta 99 F3
Juojärvi 103 E2
Juoksenki 98 C2
Juorkuna 99 E4
Jura 4 B2
Jura (Canton) 27 E2
Jura (Dépt) 27 D3
Jura, Sd of 4 B2
Jurbarkas 110 C3
Jurjevo 70 B4
Jurmala 110 C2
Jurmofjärden 107 D3
Jurmu 99 E3
Juromenha 38 C4
Jurva 102 B2
Jussey 27 D1
Justel 34 D3
Jüterbog 53 E1
Juuka 103 E2
Juupajoki 103 D3
Juurusvesi 103 E2
Juva (Mikkelin Lääni) 103 E3
Juva (Turun ja Porin Lääni) 107 D2
Juvigny-le-Tertre 18 C4
Juvigny-sous-Andaine 18 C4
Juvola 103 E3
Juzennecourt 26 C1
Južna Morava 73 E4
Južnyj Bug 113 E2
Jyderup 108 B3
Jylland 108 A3
Jyrkkä 103 E1
Jyväskylä 103 D3

K

Kaakamo 99 D3
Kaamanen 95 E3
Kaamaskoki 95 E2
Kaaresuvanto 95 D3
Kaarina 107 D2
Kaatsheuvel 16 C3
Kaavi 103 E2
Kaavinjärvi 103 E2
Kåbdalis 98 B3
Kablart 72 C4
Kać 72 C2
Kačanik 77 D2
Kačarevo 73 D2
Kačikol 77 D2
Kadaň 53 E3
Kadi Bogaz 73 F4
Kadrifakovo 77 E3
Kafiréas, Akr 84 C4
Kafiréa, Stenó 88 B1
Kåfjord 95 E1
Kåfjorden 94 C2
Kaga 106 A4
Kagarlyk 113 F2
Kagul 113 E4
Kahla 52 C3
Kaiáfas 86 B2
Kailbach 55 D1
Kaimaktsalán 79 E2
Kainasto 102 B3
Kaindorf 57 E4
Kaipola 103 D3
Kairala 95 F4
Kaisergebirge 59 D1
Kaiserslautern 54 B1
Kaisheim 55 E2
Kaitumälven 94 C4
Kaluđerovo 73 E2
Kajaani 99 E4
Kakan 74 C1
Kakanj 71 F4
Kaki Thálassa 88 A1
Kakí Vígla 87 F1
Kakslauttanen 95 E3
Kalajoki 102 C1
Kalajoki *R* 102 C1
Kalak 95 E1
Kalamáki (Lárissa) 83 F2
Kalamáki (Magnissía) 84 A2
Kalamáki, Akr 85 D2
Kalamáta 86 C3
Kalambáka 83 D1
Kalambáki 80 C2
Kalámi 89 E1
Kalamiótissa 91 F1
Kalamítsi (Makedonía) 80 B4
Kalamítsi (Stereá Eláda) 82 B3
Kálamos, N 82 C3
Kalamoti 85 F4
Kalamotó 80 A3
Kalándra 80 A4
Kalá Nerá 83 F2
Kalá Nissiá 87 E1
Kalanti 107 D2
Kalapódi 83 F3
Kalaraš 113 E3
Kälarne 101 F2
Kalavárda 93 E1
Kalávrita 86 C1
Kal'azin 111 F1
Kalbe 48 C4
Kalce 70 A2
Kaldakvísl 96 B2
Kaléndzi (Ípiros) 82 C2
Kaléndzi (Pelopónissos) 86 C1
Kalenić 73 D4
Kalérgo 84 C4
Kalesija 72 B3
Kali 74 C1
Kaliakoúda 83 D3
Kaliáni 87 D1
Kalídromo, Óros 83 E3
Kalifitos 80 C2
Kali Liménes 91 D4
Kalí Límni 93 D3
Kalimassiá 85 F4
Kalimenci, Ez 77 F2
Kálimnos 89 F3
Kálimnos, N 89 E3
Kalinin 111 F2
Kaliningrad 110 B4
Kalinkoviči 113 E1
Kalinovik 75 F1
Kalipéfki 79 E4
Kalirâhi 79 D4
Kalithéa (Dodekánissa) 93 F1
Kalithéa (Ilía) 86 C2
Kalithéa (Makedonía) 80 B2
Kalithéa (Messinía) 86 C3
Kalithéa (Stereá Eláda) 83 D3
Kalithéa (Thessalía) 80 B4
Kalithiés 93 F1
Kalithiro 83 D2
Kalivári 88 B1
Kalíves (Kriti) 90 C3
Kalíves (Thássos) 80 C3
Kalívia (Ahaïa) 86 C1
Kalívia (Atikí-Piréas) 87 F1
Kalívia (Etolía-Akarnanía) 82 C3
Kalívia (Korinthía) 87 D1
Kalívia Varikoú 79 F4
Kalix 98 C3
Kalixälven 98 C2
Kaljord 94 A3
Kalkar 17 D3
Kalkkinen 107 F1
Kall 101 D2
Kallaktjåkkå 94 B4
Kallavesi 103 E2
Kållby 102 C1
Källby 105 E4
Kallinge 109 E3
Kallio 102 C3
Kalliojoki 99 F4
Kallislahti 103 E3
Kallmünz 55 F2
Kallsjön 101 D1
Kalmar 109 E2
Kalmar Län 109 E2
Kalmar sund 109 E2
Kalmit 54 C2
Kalna 73 F4
Kalnik 71 D2
Kalnik *Mt* 71 D2
Kalocsa 112 B4
Kalogerikoú 87 D2
Kalogriá 86 B1
Kalohóri 83 D1
Kaló Horió 91 E4
Kalókastro 80 A2
Kaló Neró 86 C3
Kaloní (Lésvos) 85 F2
Kaloní (Pelopónissos) 87 E2
Kalonís, Kólpos 85 F2
Kaloskopí 83 E3
Kalotássi, Akr 89 D4
Kalø Vig 108 B3
Kalpáki 78 C4
Kals 59 E2
Kalsdorf 57 E4
Kaltbrunn 58 A2
Kaltenkirchen 48 A2
Kaltennordheim 52 B3
Kaltern 59 D3
Kaltezés 87 D2
Kaluga 111 F3
Kalundborg 108 B3
Kaluš 112 C3
Kalvåg 104 A1
Kalvehave 108 C4
Kälviä 102 C1
Kalvola 107 E2
Kalvträsk 98 B4
Kamáres (Kriti) 91 D4
Kamarés (Páros) 88 C3
Kamáres (Pelopónissos) 83 D4
Kamáres (Sífnos) 88 B3
Kamári 91 E1
Kamariótissa 81 E3
Kambanós, Akr 88 B1
Kambiá 85 E4
Kámbos (Kriti) 90 B3
Kámbos (Pelopónissos) 86 C3
Kámbos (Stereá Eláda) 83 D4
Kamčija 115 E2
Kamen 17 E3
Kamenari 76 A3
Kaména Voúria 83 F3
Kamenec-Podol'skij 113 D3
Kamenica 77 F2
Kamenice 57 D1
Kaméni, N 91 E1
Kamenjak, Rt 70 A4
Kamenka 113 F2
Kamensko (Hrvatska) 71 E2
Kamensko (Hrvatska) 75 E1
Kamenz 53 F2
Kamień Pomorski 49 E2
Kamieński, Zalew 49 E2
Kamilári 91 D4
Kaminia 86 B1
Kámiros 93 E1
Kamnik 70 B2
Kamp 57 E2
Kamp-Bornhofen 51 E4
Kampen (D) 47 F1
Kampen (NL) 17 D2
Kamp-Lintfort 17 D3
Kanal 70 A2
Kanála 88 A2
Kanal Dunav-Tisa-Dunav 73 D2
Kanália 55 D4
Kanatádika 83 F3
Kánava 88 A4
Kándanos 90 B3
Kandel 54 C2
Kandel *Mt* 54 C3
Kandern 54 C4
Kandersteg 27 F3
Kándia 87 E2
Kandíla (Pelopónissos) 87 D2
Kandíla (Stereá Eláda) 82 C3
Kandíli 84 A3
Kandira 115 F3
Kandrše 70 B2
Kanestraum 100 B2
Kanev 113 F2
Kanfanar 70 A3
Kangádio 86 B1
Kangasala 107 E1
Kangaslampi 103 E2
Kangasniemi 103 D3
Kangosjärvi 95 D4
Kanjiža 72 C1
Kankaanpää 102 C3
Kannonkoski 103 D2
Kannus 102 C1
Kannusjärvi 103 E4
Kanturk 14 B3
Kaona 73 D4
Kaonik (Bosna i Hercegovina) 71 F4

Kaonik (Srbija) 73 E4
Kapandriti 87 F1
Kaparéli 83 F4
Kapariá 88 B2
Kapele, Vrh 70 C3
Kapellskär 106 C3
Kapélo, Akr 90 A2
Kapfenberg 57 E3
Kaplice 57 D2
Kaposvár 114 B1
Kapp 105 D2
Kappel 51 E4
Kappeln 48 A1
Kappelshamnsviken 109 F3
Kaprije 74 C1
Kaprun 59 E1
Kapsáli 90 A2
Kápsas 87 D2
Kapsoúri 88 B1
Kapsukas 110 C4
Kapuvár 112 A4
Karabiga 115 E3
Karaburun 115 E4
Karačev 111 F4
Karadeniz Boğazi 115 F3
Karan 72 C4
Karasjåkka 95 E2
Karasjok 95 E2
Karasu 115 F3
Karats 98 A2
Karavás 90 A1
Karavómilos 83 F3
Karavónissia 92 C2
Karavostássis 91 D1
Kårböle 101 E3
Karcag 112 B4
Kardámena 89 F3
Kardámila 85 E4
Kardamili 86 C3
Kardeljevo 75 E2
Kärdla 110 B1
Kardítsa 55 D4
Kardítsa (Nomos) 55 D4
Kărdžali 115 D3
Karerpass 59 D3
Karesuando 95 D3
Karfás 85 F4
Karhukangas 99 D4
Karhula 103 F4
Karhunkierros 99 F2
Karhutunturi 95 F4
Kariá (Pelopónissos) 87 D2
Kariá (Stereá Eláda) 83 F3
Kariés (Makedonía) 80 C4
Kariés (Pelopónissos) 87 D3
Karigasniemi 95 E2
Karijoki 102 B3
Karinainen 107 D2
Kariótisa 79 E3
Karis 107 E3
Káristos 88 A1
Karítena 86 C2
Karjaa 107 E3
Karjalohja 107 E3
Karkaloú 86 C2
Karkinágri 89 D2
Karkku 107 D1
Kärkölä 107 E2
Karleby 102 C1
Karlevi 109 E3
Karlino 49 F1
Karlobag 70 C4
Karlovac 70 C3
Karlovássi 89 E1
Karlovo 115 D2
Karlovy Vary 53 E4
Karlsborg 105 E4
Karlsburg 49 D2
Karlsfeld 55 F3
Karlshamn 109 D3
Karlshuld 55 F2
Karlskoga 105 E4
Karlskrona 109 E3
Karlsøy 94 C2
Karlsruhe 54 C2
Karlstad 105 E3
Karlstadt 52 B4
Karlštejn 53 F4
Karlstift 57 D2
Karmøy 104 A3
Karnezéika 87 E2
Karnobat 115 E2
Kärnten 59 F2
Karolinerleden 101 E2
Karow 48 C2
Kärpankylä 99 F2
Kárpathos 93 D3
Kárpathos, N 93 D3
Karpenissi 83 D3
Karperí 80 A2
Karperó 79 D4
Kärsämäki 103 D1
Kårsatjåkka 94 B4
Karsava 111 D2
Karstädt 48 C3
Karstula 103 D2
Kartal 115 F3
Kartéri (Ípiros) 82 B2
Kartéri (Pelopónissos) 87 D1
Karterós 91 D3
Kártsino, Akr 84 C3
Karttula 103 E2
Kartuzy 110 A4
Karungi 98 C3
Karunki 98 C3
Karup 108 A2
Karvala 102 C2
Kärväskylä 103 D2
Karvia 102 C3
Karviná 112 B3
Karvoskylä 103 D1
Karvounári 82 B2
Karwendelgebirge 59 D1
Kašalj 76 C1
Kašin 111 F1
Kašina 70 C2
Kaskinen 102 B3
Kasko 102 B3
Káspakas 85 D1
Kašperské Hory 56 C1
Kassándra 80 B4
Kassándras, Kólpos 80 B4
Kassándria 80 A4
Kassel 52 A2
Kassiópi 82 A1
Kassópi 82 B2
Kássos, N 93 D3
Kastaniá (Makedonía) 79 E3
Kastaniá (Pelopónissos) 87 D1
Kastaniá (Thessalía) 82 C1
Kastaniá (Thessalía) 83 D2
Kastaniés 81 F1
Kastaniótissa 83 F3
Kastéla 84 B4
Kastelhoms 106 C3
Kastéli (Kríti) 90 B3
Kastéli (Kríti) 91 E4
Kastellaun 51 E4
Kastelórizo 93 F2
Kastélou, Akr 93 D3
Kastelruth 59 D3
Kaštel Stari 75 D1
Kaštel Žegarski 75 D1
Kasterlee 50 C3
Kastl 55 F1
Kastorf 48 B2
Kastóri 87 D3
Kastoriá 79 D3
Kastoriá (Nomos) 78 C3
Kastoriás, L 79 D3
Kastós, N 82 C4
Kastráki (Kikládes) 88 C3
Kastráki (Stereá Eláda) 82 C3
Kastráki (Thessalía) 83 D1
Kastrakíou, Teh L 82 C3
Kastrí (Pelopónissos) 87 D2
Kastrí (Stereá Eláda) 83 E3
Kastrí (Thessalía) 83 F1
Kástro (Pelopónissos) 86 B1
Kástro (Skiathos) 84 A2
Kástro (Stereá Eláda) 83 F4
Kastrossikiá 82 B2
Katafígio 79 E4
Katáfito 80 B1
Katáfourko 82 C3
Katahás 79 F3
Katákolo 86 B2
Katálako 85 D1
Kátano, Akr 88 A3
Katápola 89 D3
Katára 82 C1
Katastári 86 A1
Katavía 93 E2
Katelimátsa 91 F1
Kateliós 86 A1
Kateríni 79 F4
Katerloch 57 E4
Katharó 91 E4
Katheni 84 B4
Katići 76 C1
Kätkäsuvanto 95 D4
Katlanovo 77 E3
Katlanovska Banja 77 E3
Katlenburg-Duhm 52 B2
Káto Ahaïa 86 B1
Káto Alissós 86 B1
Káto Asséa 87 D2
Káto Doliana 87 D2
Káto Figália 86 C2
Káto Gadzéa 83 F2
Katohí 82 C4
Káto Kamíla 80 B2
Káto Klinés 79 D2
Káto Makrinoú 83 D4
Katoméri, Akr 88 C3
Káto Moussounitsa 83 E3
Káto Nevrokópi 80 B1
Káto Ólimbos 83 E1
Káto Tithoréa 83 E4
Katoúna (Lefkáda) 82 B3
Katoúna (Stereá Eláda) 82 C3
Káto Vassilikí 83 D4
Káto Vérga 86 C3
Káto Vérmio 79 E3
Káto Vlassía 86 C1
Katowice 112 B2
Káto Zahlorou 86 C1
Káto Zákros 91 F4
Katrineholm 106 A4
Katschberg 59 F2
Katschberg-Tunnel 59 F2
Kattegat 108 C2
Katwijk aan Zee 16 B2
Kaub 51 F4
Kaufbeuren 55 E3
Kauhajärvi 102 C2
Kauhajoki 102 B3
Kauhaneva-Pohjankangas 102 C3
Kauhava 102 C2
Kaukonen 95 E4
Kaunas 110 C3
Kaupanger 104 B1
Kaušany 113 E4
Kaustinen 102 C2
Kautokeino 95 D3
Kautokeinoelva 95 D3
Kauttua 107 D2
Kavadarci 77 E3
Kavajë 76 C4
Kavála 80 C2
Kavála (Nomos) 80 C2
Kaválas, Kólpos 80 C2
Kavarna 115 E2
Kavili 81 F1
Kavirio-Hlói 81 E4
Kävlinge 108 C3
Kávos 82 A2
Kavoússi 91 F4
Käylä 99 E2
Kaysersberg 27 E1
Kazan 73 E2
Kažani 77 E4
Kazanlăk 115 D2
Kazárma 86 C3
Kazatin 113 E2
Kazimierz Dolny 112 C2
Kazincbarcika 112 B3
Kdyně 56 B1
Kéa 88 A2
Keadew 12 C2
Keady 13 D2
Keähkkiljohka 95 D3
Keal, L na 4 B1
Kéa Meriá 88 A2
Kéa, N 88 A2
Kéas, Stenó 88 A2
Kebnekaise 94 B4
Kebnekaise *Mt* 94 B4
Kebock Head 2 B2
Kecskemét 112 B4
Kėdainiai 110 C3
Kédros 83 D2
Kędzierzyn-Koźle 112 B2
Keel 12 A2
Keerbergen 50 C3
Kefalári 87 D2
Kefálas, Akr 80 C3
Kefáli, Akr 90 A2
Kefaloniá, N 82 B4
Kéfalos 89 F4
Kéfalos, Akr 88 A2
Kefalóvrisso (Ípiros) 78 C4
Kefalóvrisso (Pelopónissos) 86 C3
Kefalóvrisso (Stereá Eláda) 82 C4
Kefalóvrisso (Thessalía) 83 D1
Keflavík 96 A2
Kehl 54 C3
Kehlstein 56 C4
Kehrókambos 80 C2
Kéhros 81 E2
Keighley 6 C2
Keimaneigh, Pass of 14 B4
Keitele 103 D2
Keitele *L* 103 D2
Keith 3 D3
Kéla 79 D2
Kelankylä 99 E3
Kelberg 51 E4
Kelbra 52 C2
Këlcyrë 114 C4
Kelebija 72 B1
Kelefá 87 D4
Kelheim 55 F2
Kellinghusen 48 A2
Kellojärvi 99 F4
Kellokoski 107 E2
Kells 13 D3
Kelso 5 E2
Kelujärvi 95 E4
Kemberg 53 D1
Kembs 27 E1
Kemi 99 D3
Kemihaara 95 F4
Kemijärvi 99 E2
Kemijärvi *L* 99 E2
Kemijoki 99 D2
Keminmaa 99 D3
Kemiö 107 D3
Kemnath 53 D4
Kempele 99 D4
Kempen 17 D4
Kempenich 51 E4
Kempten 55 E4
Kendal 6 B1
Kéndras, Akr 88 B3
Kendrikó 79 F2
Kenilworth 9 E1
Kenmare 14 A4
Kenmare River 14 A4
Kennacraig 4 B2
Kenoúrgio 83 D3
Kent 11 D3
Kentallen 4 B1
Kenzingen 54 C3
Keramía 85 F2
Keramidi 83 F2
Keramítsa 82 B1
Kéramos 85 E4
Keramotí 81 D2
Kerassiá (Évia) 84 A3
Kerassiá (Thessalía) 83 F2
Kerassiés 79 E2
Kerassohóri 83 D3
Kerassóna 82 C2
Keráta, Akr 83 F3
Keratéa 87 F2
Kerava 107 E2
Kerdília, N 80 B3
Kérés 72 C1
Keri 86 A2
Kerimäki 103 F3
Kerken 17 D3
Kerketéas, Óros 89 E1
Kerkétio, Óri 83 D2
Kerkíni, Óros 80 A1
Kerkínis, L 80 A2
Kérkira 82 A1
Kérkira, N 82 A1
Kerkonkoski 103 D2
Kerkrade 51 D3
Kernascléden 22 B3
Kéros, N 88 C3
Kerpen 17 D4
Kerrera 4 B1
Kerry 14 B3
Kerry Head 14 A3
Kerteminde 108 B3
Kértezi 86 C1
Kerzers 27 E2
Kesälahti 103 F3
Keşan 115 E3
Kesch, Piz 58 B3
Kesh 12 C2
Keski-Suomen Lääni 103 D2
Kessariani 87 F1
Kestilä 99 D4
Keswick 5 D4
Keszthely 112 A4
Kętrzyn 110 B4
Kettering 9 F1
Kettletoft 3 E1
Kettwig 17 E4
Ketzin 49 D4
Keukenhof 16 B2
Keurusselkä 103 D3
Keuruu 102 C3
Kevelaer 17 D3
Kevo 95 E2
Kevo (Nat Pk) 95 E2
Key, L 12 C3
Keynsham 9 D2
Kežmarok 112 B3
Kianí 81 F1
Kiantajärvi 99 F3
Kiáto 87 D1
Kiberg 95 F1
Kičevo 77 D3
Kidderminster 9 D1
Kidlington 9 E2
Kidsgrove 6 C3
Kidwelly 8 C2
Kiefersfelden 56 B4
Kiekinkoski 99 F4
Kiel 48 A1
Kielce 112 B2
Kielder Reservoir 5 E3
Kieler Bucht 48 A1
Kiental 27 F3
Kierinki 99 D1
Kietz 49 F4
Kifissiá 87 F1
Kifissos 83 F4
Kifjord 95 E1
Kihlanki 95 D4
Kihniö 102 C3
Kihti Skiftet 107 D3
Kiihtelysvaara 103 F2
Kiikala 107 E2
Kiikka 107 D2
Kiikoinen 107 D1
Kiimanen 99 E4
Kiiminginjoki 99 D3
Kiiminki 99 D3
Kiiskilä 102 C1
Kiistala 95 E4
Kijev 113 E2
Kijevo (Hrvatska) 75 D1
Kijevo (Kosovo) 77 D2
Kijevskoje Vodochranilišče 113 E2
Kikinda 72 C1
Kikládes 88 B2
Kil 105 E3
Kíla 79 D3
Kiláda (Makedonía) 79 E3
Kiláda (Pelopónissos) 87 E2
Kilafors 101 F4
Kilbaha 12 A4
Kilbeggan 12 C4
Kilbirnie 4 C2
Kilboghamn 97 E2
Kilbotn 94 B3
Kilbrannan Sd 4 B2
Kilchoan 2 B4
Kilcock 13 D4
Kilcormac 12 C4
Kilcreggan 4 C2
Kilcullen 13 D4
Kildare 13 D4
Kildare (Co) 13 D4
Kildorrery 14 C3
Kilfenora 12 B4
Kilgarvan 14 B4
Kilija 113 E4
Kilingi-Nõmme 110 C2
Kilíni 86 B1
Kilíni, Óros 87 D1
Kilkee 12 A4
Kilkeel 13 E3
Kilkenny 15 D3
Kilkenny (Co) 15 D3
Kilkhampton 8 B3
Kilkieran B 12 A3
Kilkís 79 F2
Kilkís (Nomos) 79 F2
Killadysert 12 B4
Killala B 12 B2
Killaloe 12 B4
Killarney 14 B4
Killary Harbour 12 A3
Killashandra 12 C3
Killenaule 14 C3
Killimer 12 B4
Killin 4 C1
Killinkoski 102 C3
Killorglin 14 A3
Killybegs 12 C2
Killyleagh 13 E2
Kilmaine 12 B3
Kilmallock 14 B3
Kilmarnock 4 C2
Kilmartin 4 B2
Kilmore Quay 15 D4
Kilmurry 12 B4
Kilninver 4 B1
Kilnsea 7 E2
Kilpisjärvi 94 C3
Kilpisjärvi *L* 94 C3
Kilrea 13 D1
Kilronan 12 B4
Kilrush 12 B4
Kilsyth 4 C2
Kiltamagh 12 B3
Kiltealy 15 D3
Kilwinning 4 C2
Kilyos 115 F3
Kimássi 84 A3
Kiméria 81 D2
Kími 84 B3
Kimina 79 F3
Kimis, Órmos 84 B4
Kimísseos Theotókou 87 D2
Kimito 107 D3
Kímolos 88 B4
Kímolos, N 88 B4
Kimólou Sífnou, Stenó 88 B3
Kimry 111 F2
Kimstad 105 F4
Kínaros, N 89 D3
Kinbrace 3 D2
Kincardine 5 D2
Kindberg 57 E3
Kindelbrück 52 C2
Kinéta 87 E1
Kingisepp 111 D1
Kingissepp 110 B2
Kingsbridge 8 C4
Kingscourt 13 D3
King's Lynn 7 E3
Kingston 9 F2
Kingston-upon-Hull 7 E2
Kingswear 8 C4
Kington 9 D1
Kingussie 3 D4
Kínira 81 D3
Kinlochbervie 2 C2
Kinlochewe 2 C3
Kinloch Rannoch 4 C1
Kinna 108 C1
Kinnairds Head 3 E3
Kinnasniemi 103 F2
Kinnegad 13 D3
Kinnitty 12 C4
Kinnula 103 D2
Kinross 5 D2
Kinsale 14 B4
Kinsarvik 104 B2
Kintaus 103 D3
Kintore 3 E4
Kintyre 4 B2
Kinvarra 12 B4
Kinzig 54 C3
Kióni 82 B4
Kiparíssi 87 E3
Kiparissía 86 C3
Kiparissiakós Kólpos 86 B2
Kiparissías, Óri 86 C3
Kipárissos 83 E2
Kípi (Ípiros) 78 C4
Kípi (Thráki) 81 F2
Kipinä 99 D3
Kípos, Akr 81 E3
Kipourío 79 D4
Kippure 13 D4
Kipséli 83 E2
Kir 76 C3
Kirá Panagiá, N 84 B2
Kirchbach 57 E4
Kirchberg (Rheinland-Pfalz) 54 B1
Kirchberg (Sachsen) 53 D3
Kirchberg (Nieder österreich) 57 E2
Kirchberg (Tirol) 59 E1
Kirchberg an der Pielach 57 E3
Kirchdorf 57 D3
Kirchenlamitz 53 D4
Kirchenthumbach 53 D4
Kirchhain 52 A3
Kirchheim (Baden-Württemberg) 55 D2
Kirchheim (Hessen) 52 B3
Kirchheimbolanden 54 C1
Kirchheim unter teck 55 D2
Kirchhundem 17 F4
Kirchlengern 17 F2
Kirchmöser 49 D4
Kirchschlag 57 F3
Kiriakí 81 F1
Kiriáki 83 F4
Kiriši 111 E1
Kırkağaç 115 E4
Kirkby Lonsdale 6 C1
Kirkby Stephen 5 E4
Kirkcaldy 5 D2
Kirkcolm 4 B3
Kirkcudbright 4 C3
Kirkenær 105 D2
Kirkenes 95 F2
Kirkeøy 105 D4
Kirkestinden 94 B3
Kirkham 6 B2
Kirki 81 E2
Kirkintilloch 4 C2
Kirkjubøur 96 A4
Kirkkonummi 107 E3
Kırklareli 115 E3
Kirkonmaanselkä 103 F4
Kirkwall 3 E1
Kirn 54 B1
Kirov 111 F3
Kirovograd 113 F2
Kirovsk 111 D1
Kirriemuir 5 D1
Kirtorf 52 A3
Kiruna 94 C4
Kisa 109 E1
Kisac 72 C2
Kiseljak (Loznica) 72 B3
Kiseljak (Sarajevo) 75 F1
Kiseljak (Tuzla) 71 F3
Kišin'ov 113 E3
Kisko 107 E3
Kiskőrös 112 B4
Kiskunfélegyháza 112 B4
Kiskunhalas 114 B1
Kissámou, Kólpos 90 B3
Kißlegg 55 E4
Kissoú Kámbos 90 C4
Kistanje 75 D1
Kisújszállás 112 B4
Kisvárda 112 C3
Kita 87 D4
Kitee 103 F3
Kíthira 90 A2
Kíthira, N 90 A2
Kíthnos 88 A2

Kithnos, N 88 A2
Kithnou, Stenó 88 A2
Kitinen 95 E4
Kitka 99 E2
Kitriés, Akr 86 C3
Kittilä 95 E4
Kittsee 57 F2
Kitzbühel 59 E1
Kitzingen 55 E1
Kiukainen 107 D2
Kiuruvesi 103 D1
Kiutaköngäs 99 E2
Kivalo 99 D3
Kivéri 87 D2
Kivi 88 B2
Kivijärvi 103 D2
Kivijärvi *L* 103 D2
Kivijärvi *L* 103 E4
Kivilahti 103 F2
Kivitaipale 99 D2
Kivotós 79 D4
Kizário 81 E2
Kjellerup 108 A2
Kjerringøy 97 E1
Kjerringvåg 100 C1
Kjerringvik 101 D1
Kjølifjell 101 D2
Kjøllefjord 95 E1

ÄNGELHOLM
Oslo, Göteborg
Jönköping, Stockholm
Ängelholm
Ystad
Kristianstad
Frederiksværk, Århus
Frederiksværk
Roskilde, Kalundborg
Rødbyhavn, Odense
STURUP
Trelleborg
Dronningmølle
Hornbæk
Ålsgårde
Hittarp
Sofiero
Helsingborg
Kronborg
Helsingør
Snekkersten
Espergærde
Humlebæk
Esbønderup
Gurre Sø
Esrum Sø
Tikøb
Nødebo
Fredensborg
Sletten
Frederiksborg
Grønholt
Hillerød
Karlebo
Niverød
Nivå Bugt
Ny Hammershholt
Kokkedal
Rungsted
Rungstedlund
Allerød
Blovstrød
Hørsholm
Lillerød
Sjælsø
Brådebæk
Vedbæk
Trørød
Birkerød
Holte
Skodsborg
Nærum
Farum
Søllerød
Furesø
Virum
Eremitagen
Tårbæk
Værløse
Frederiksdal
Lyngby-Tårbæk
Hareskovby
Ordrup
Klampenborg
Bagsværd
Charlottenlund
Gentofte
Herlev
Gladsaxe
Ballerup
Skovlunde
Bispebjerg
Islev
Brønshøj
KØBENHAVN
Herstedt
Vanløse
Rødovre
Frederiksberg
Christianshavn
Albertslund
Glostrup
Valby
Sundbyerne
Hvidovre
Avedøre
Kastrup
Tåstrup
Brøndby
Kalvebo-derne
Tårnby
KASTRUP
Ishøj
Ishøj Strand
Avedøre Holme
Amager
Hundige
Greve Strand
Køge Bugt
Dragør
Søvang
Mörarp
Bjuv
Billesholm
N. Vram
Ljungbyhed
Söderåsen
Risekatslösa
Hässlunda
Stenestad
Påarp
Bårslöv
Kågeröd
Gantofta
Fjärestad
Ekeby
Konga
Rydebäck
Vallåkra
Halmstad
Härslöv
Glumslöv
Sireköpinge
S:t Ibb
Ven
Bäckviken
Tågarp
Tirup
Svalöv
Torrlösa
Asmundtorp
Billeberga
Landskrona
Marieholm
Trollenäs
Häljarp
Teckomatorp
Annelöv
Svanabacken
Lundåkrabukten
Ålstorp
Dösjebro
St. Harrie
Hofterup
Kävlinge
Harrie
Örtofta
Barsebäck
Håstad
Barsebäckshamn
Lödde-köpinge
Furulund
Stångby
Borgeby
Fjelie
Vallkärra
Bjärred
Flädie
Lund
ÖRESUND
Saltholm
Hjärup
Lomma
Lommabukten
Åkarp
Staffanstorp
Burlöv
MALMÖ
Limhamn
S. Sallerup
Bara
Torup
Bunkeflostrand
Kristineberg
Oxie
Skabersjö
Norra Klagshamn
Kaglinge
Sjödiken
Tygelsjö
Södra Klagshamn
Svedala
Gässie villastad
V Ingelstad
Hököpinge
Vellinge
Ö Grevie
Grenå
Oslo
Rønne
0
5
10 km
13°

Kjøpsvik 94 B4
Kjustendil 114 C3
Klæbu 100 C2
Kladanj 72 B4
Kladnica 76 C1
Kladnice 75 D1
Kladno 53 F4
Kladovo 73 F2
Klagenfurt 70 A1
Klaipėda 110 B3
Klaksvik 96 A3
Klana 70 B3
Klanac 70 C4
Klanxbüll 47 F1
Klarälven 105 E2
Klašnice 71 E3
Klässbol 105 E3
Klášterec 53 E3
Klasvik 96 A3
Klatovy 56 C1
Klaukkala 107 E2
Klausen 59 D2
Klausenpass 58 A2
Klazienaveen 17 E2
Kleinhaugsdorf 57 E2
Kleinheubach 55 D1
Kleinwalsertal 55 E4
Klekovača 71 D4
Klenike 77 E2
Klenovica 70 B3
Kleppe 104 A3
Kleppestø 104 A2
Kleve 17 D3
Kličevac 73 D2
Klimoviči 111 E4
Klimpfjäll 97 E4
Klin 111 F2
Klina 76 C2
Klinča Selo 70 C2
Klincy 111 E4
Klingenbach 57 F3
Klingenthal 53 D3
Klinovec 53 E3
Klintehamn 109 F4
Klippan 108 C3
Klippen 97 E3
Klippitztörl 57 D4
Klis 75 D1
Klissoúra 79 D3
Klisura (Makedonija) 77 F3
Klisura (Srbija) 77 E1
Klitoria 86 C1
Klitten 53 F2
Klixbüll 47 F1
Kljajićevo 72 B2
Ključ 71 D4
Kłodzko 112 A2
Kløfta 105 D3
Klokkarvik 104 A2
Klokočevac 73 F3
Klos 76 C4
Kloštar 71 D2
Kloštar Ivanić 71 D2
Klösterle 58 B2
Klosterneuburg 57 F2
Klosters 58 B2
Kloten 58 A2
Klötze 48 C4
Klöverträsk 98 B3
Klövsjö 101 E3
Kluczbork 112 A2
Klupe 71 E3
Klütz 48 B2
Knapdale 4 B2
Knappogue Castle 12 B4
Knäred 109 D2
Knaresborough 6 C1
Knarvik 104 A2
Kneginec 71 D1
Kneža 115 D2
Knežak 70 B3
Kneževi Vinogradi 71 F2
Kneževo 71 F2
Knežica 71 D3
Knežina 72 B4
Knić 73 D4
Knidi 79 D4
Knighton 9 D1
Knight's Town 14 A4
Knin 75 D1
Knittelfeld 57 D4
Knivskjellodden 95 D1
Knivsta 106 B3
Knjaževac 73 F4
Knockmealdown Mts 14 C3
Knokke-Heist 50 A3
Knole House 10 C3
Knossós 91 D3
Knutsford 6 C2
Koarvikodds 95 E3
Kobarid 70 A2
Kobbfjorden 95 D1
Kobel'aki 113 F2
København 108 C3
Kobern-Gondorf 51 E4
Kobišnica 73 F3
Koblenz 51 E4
Kobrin 112 C1
Koca D 115 F3
Kočani 77 F2
Koceljevo 72 C3
Kočerin 75 E2
Kočevje 70 B2
Kočevski rog 70 B2
Kochel 56 A4
Kocher 55 E2
Kodiksami 107 D2
Kodisjoki 107 D2
Köflach 57 E4
Køge 108 C3
Køge Bugt 108 C3
Kohtla-Järve 110 C1
Koikkala 103 E3
Koirakoski 103 E1
Koitajoki 103 F2
Koitelainen 95 E4
Koitere 103 F2
Koivujärvi 103 D1
Koivusuo 103 F2
Kokála 87 D4
Kokar 106 C3
Kokári 89 E1
Kokarsfjärden 106 C3
Kokemäenjoki 107 D1
Kokemäki 107 D2
Kokin Brod 76 B1
Kókino Neró 83 F1
Kokkola 102 C1
Kokotí 83 F3
Koksijde-Bad 50 A3
Kola 71 E3
Koláka 83 F4
Kolari (SF) 98 C1
Kolari (YU) 73 D3
Kolåsen 101 D1
Kolašin 76 B2
Kolbäck 105 F3
Kołbacz 49 F2
Kołbaskowo 49 E2
Kolbermoor 56 B3
Kolby Kås 108 B3
Kolding 108 A3
Kolho 103 D3
Koli 103 F2
Kolima 103 D2
Kolimvári 90 B3
Kolín 112 A3
Kolindrós 79 F3
Kolínes 87 D3
Kolka 110 B2
Kolkanlahti 103 D2
Kolkasrags 110 B2
Kölleda 52 C2
Kolmården 106 A4
Köln 17 E4
Koło 112 B1
Kołobrzeg 49 F1
Koločep 75 F2
Kolomyja 113 D3
Koloveč 56 B1
Kolovrat 76 B1
Kolpino 111 D1
Kolsva 105 F3
Kolubara 72 C3
Kolvereid 97 D4
Komagfjord 95 D2
Kómanos 79 D3
Komar 71 E4
Kómara 81 F1
Komarnica 76 B2
Komárno 112 B4
Kombóti 82 C2
Koméno 82 C3
Kómi (Kiklådes) 88 B2
Kómi (Hios) 89 D1
Komílio 82 B3
Komin 70 C2
Kómito 88 B1
Komiža 75 D2
Komló 114 B1
Komninádes 78 C3
Komniná (Makedonía) 79 D3
Komniná (Thráki) 81 D2
Komorane 77 D2
Komotiní 81 E2
Komovi 76 B2
Komrat 113 E4
Komulanköngäs 99 E4
Konak 73 D2
Konakovo 111 F2
Končanica 71 D2
Kondiás 85 D1
Kondopoúli 85 D1
Kondós, Akr 88 B3
Kondovázena 86 C1
Kondrić 71 F2
Konečka pl 77 E3
Køng 108 C4
Köngernheim 54 C1
Konginkangas 103 D2
Kongsberg 104 C3
Kongselva 94 A3
Kongsfjord 95 F1
Kongsvinger 105 D3
Kœnigsbourg 27 E1
Königsbrück 53 E2
Königsbrunn 55 F3
Königsee 52 C3
Königsfeld 54 C3
Königslutter 52 B1
Königsschlösser 55 F4
Königssee 56 C4
Königssee *L* 56 C4
Königstein (Hessen) 51 F4
Konigstein (Sachsen) 53 F2
Königswiesen 57 D2
Königswinter 51 E3
Königs-Wusterhausen 49 E4
Konin 112 A1
Koniskós 83 D1
Konístres 84 B4
Kónitsa 78 C4
Konj 75 E1
Konjevrate 75 D1
Konjic 75 F1
Konjsko 76 A2
Konjuh 71 F4
Konkämäälven 94 C3
Könnern 52 C2
Konnevesi 103 D2
Konnevesi *L* 103 D2
Könönpelto 103 E3
Konopište 77 E3
Konotop 113 F1
Konsko 77 F4
Konsmo 104 B4
Konstantinovy Lázně 53 E4
Konstanz 55 D4
Kontich 50 B3
Kontiolahti 103 F2
Kontiomäki 99 E4
Konttajärvi 98 C2
Konz 54 A1
Kopaida 83 F4
Kopáni 82 C2
Kopanós 79 E3
Kopaonik 77 D1
Koparnes 100 A2
Kópasker 96 C1
Köpenick 49 E4
Koper 70 A3
Kopervik 104 A3
Köping 105 F3
Köpingsvik 109 E2
Koplik 76 B3
Köpmanholmen 102 A2
Koporiće 77 D1
Koppang 100 C3
Kopparberg 105 F3
Kopparbergs Län 105 E2
Kopparleden 101 E2
Kopperby 48 A1
Kopperveien 100 D3
Koprivna 71 F3
Koprivnica (Bosna i Hercegovina) 71 D1

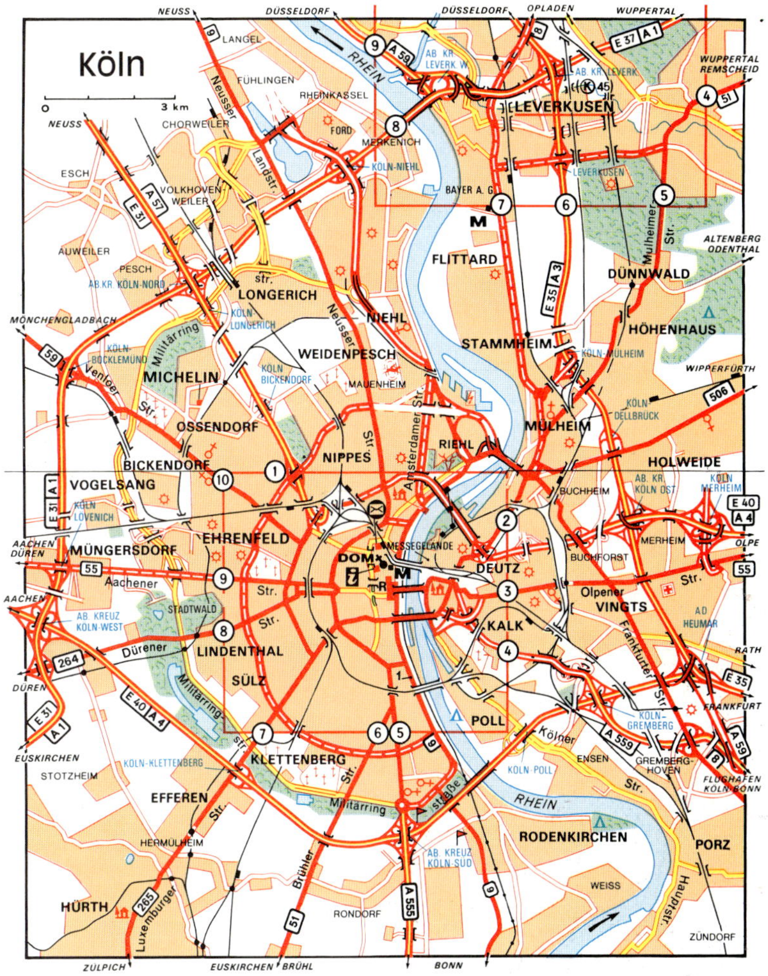

Köln
0 3 km
NEUSS
DÜSSELDORF
OPLADEN
WUPPERTAL
LEVERKUSEN
RHEIN
FLITTARD
DÜNNWALD
LONGERICH
NIEHL
STAMMHEIM
HÖHENHAUS
WEIDENPESCH
MICHELIN
OSSENDORF
NIPPES
RIEHL
MÜLHEIM
HOLWEIDE
BICKENDORF
VOGELSANG
EHRENFELD
MÜNGERSDORF
DEUTZ
KALK
VINGTS
LINDENTHAL
SÜLZ
POLL
KLETTENBERG
EFFEREN
RODENKIRCHEN
PORZ
HÜRTH
ZÜLPICH
EUSKIRCHEN
BRÜHL
BONN

Koprivnica (Srbija) 73 F3
Korab 77 D3
Kórakas, Akr 88 C3
Koralpe 70 B1
Korana 70 C3
Korbach 52 A2
Korbevac 77 E2
Korbovo 73 F2
Korçë 114 C3
Korčula 75 E2
Korčula *I* 75 E2
Korčulanski kan 75 E2
Korensko sedlo 70 A1
Kórfos 87 E2
Korgåsen 95 F2
Korgen 97 E3
Koria 107 F2
Korifássi 86 C3
Korikío Ándro 83 E4
Kórimvos 81 F1
Koríni 83 F4
Korinós 79 F4
Korinthía 87 D1
Korinthiakós Kólpos 87 D1
Kórinthos 87 E1
Korissía 88 A2
Korissós 79 D3
Korita (Bosna i Hercegovina) 76 A2
Korita (Crna Gora) 76 B2
Korita (Mljet) 75 F2
Koríthi 86 A1
Koritnik 76 C1
Koritnik, M. 77 D3
Korkeakangas 103 F3
Korkeakoski 103 D2
Körmend 112 A4
Kornat 74 C1
Kornati 74 C1
Korneuburg 57 F2
Kornofoléa 81 F2
Kornwestheim 55 D2
Koromacno 70 B4
Koróna 79 F2
Koróni 86 C4
Korónia 83 F4
Korónia, L 80 A3
Koronída 88 C3
Koronissía 82 C3
Korónos 88 C3
Koronoúda 80 A2
Koropí 87 F1
Körös 112 B4
Korosten' 113 E2
Korostyšev 113 E2
Korouoma 99 E2
Korpilahti 103 D3
Korpilombolo 98 C2
Korpo 107 D3
Korppoo 107 D3
Korsberga 109 E2
Korsfjorden 104 A2
Korsholm 102 B2
Korsnäs 102 B2
Korsør 108 B4
Korsun-Ševčenkovskij 113 F2
Korsvoll 100 B2
Kortesjärvi 102 C2
Kórthio 88 B2
Kortrijk 50 A3
Kortteenperä 99 D2
Korvala 99 D2
Korvaluoma 102 C3
Korvatunturi 95 F3
Kos 89 F3
Kosančić 77 D1
Kosanica 76 B1
Kościan 112 A2
Kościerzyna 110 A4
Kosel 77 D4
Koserow 49 E1
Košice 112 C3
Kosjerić 72 C4
Koška 71 F2
Koskenkorva 102 B2
Koskenpää 103 D3
Koski (Hameen Lääni) 107 E2
Koski (Turun ja Porin Lääni) 107 D2
Kóskina 84 B4
Koskue 102 C3
Kosmaj 73 D3
Kosmás 87 D3
Kósmio 81 E2
Kos, N 89 F3
Kosovo 77 D2
Kosovo Polje 77 D2
Kosovska Kamenica 77 D2
Kössen 59 E1
Kósta 87 E3
Kostajnica 71 D3
Kostanjevac 70 C2
Kostanjevica 70 C2
Kostenec 115 D3
Koster 105 D4
Kostolac 73 D3
Kostonjärvi 99 E3
Kostopol' 113 D2
Kóstos 88 C3
Kostrzyn 49 F4
Kosturino 77 F3
Kosula 103 E2
Koszalin 110 A4
Kőszeg 112 A4
Kotala (Keski-Suomen Lääni) 102 C3
Kotala (Lapin Lääni) 99 E1
Kótas 79 D3
Kotel 115 E2
Köthen 53 D1
Kotka 103 F4
Kotor 76 B3
Kotoriba 71 D1
Kotorsko 71 F3
Kotor Varoš 71 E4
Kotovsk (Moldavija) 113 E4
Kotovsk (Ukraina) 113 E3
Kotraža 73 D4
Kótronas 87 D4
Kotroniá 81 F2
Kötschach-Mauthen 59 E2
Köttsjön 101 F2
Kötzting 56 B1
Koufália 79 F3
Koufoníssi (Kiklådes) 88 C3
Koufoníssi (Kríti) 91 F4
Koufós 80 B4
Kouklií 82 B1
Koukounariés 84 A2
Koúla 81 D1
Kouméika 89 E2
Koúndouros 88 A2
Kounoupéli 86 B1
Koura 102 C2
Koúrenda 82 B1
Kourkoulí 84 A3
Kournás 90 C3
Kouroúta 86 B2
Koutselió 82 C1
Koutsó 81 D2
Koutsóhero 83 E1
Kouvola 107 F2
Kovačica 72 C2
Kovel' 112 C2
Kovero 103 F2
Kovin 73 D3
Köyliö 107 D2
Kozáni 79 D3
Kozáni 79 D3
Kozara 71 D3
Kozarac (Bosna i Hercegovina) 71 D3
Kozarac (Hrvatska) 71 F2
Kožel'sk 111 F3
Kozica 75 E2

Kozina 70 A3
Kozjak 77 E4
Kozluk 72 B3
Kožuf 77 F4
Kragenæs 108 B4
Kragerø 104 C4
Kragujevac 73 D4
Krajišnik 73 D2
Krajkovac 77 D1
Krajn 76 C3
Krajnik Dln 49 E3
Krakhella 104 A1
Krakow 48 C2
Kraków 112 B2
Kraljeva Sutjeska 71 F4
Kraljevica 70 B3
Kraljevo 73 D4
Kralovice 53 E4
Kralupy 53 F3
Kramfors 101 F2
Kranenburg 17 D3
Krani 77 E4
Kraniá Elassónas 79 E4
Kraniá (Makedonia) 79 D4
Kraniá (Thessalía) 82 C1
Kranichfeld 52 C3
Kranidi 87 E2
Kranj 70 A2
Kranjska Gora 70 A1
Krapina 70 C2
Krapinske Toplice 70 C2
Krašić 70 C2
Krāslava 111 D3
Kraslice 53 D3
Krasná Lipa 53 F2
Kraśnik 112 C2
Krasno Polje 70 C4
Krasnyj Cholm 111 F1
Krasnystaw 112 C2
Kráthio 87 D1
Krátigos 85 F3
Kratovo 77 E2
Kratovska-Stena 72 C4
Krauchenwies 55 D3
Krautheim 55 D1
Kravarsko 70 C2
Krefeld 17 D4
Kremasti (Pelopónissos) 87 E3
Kremasti (Ródos) 93 F1
Kremastón, Teh L 83 D3
Kremenčug 113 F2
Kremenčugskoje Vodochranilišče 113 F2
Kremenec 113 D2
Kremidi, Akr 87 E4
Kremmen 49 D3
Kremna 72 C4
Kremnica 112 B3
Krems 57 E2
Kremsmünster 57 D3
Krepoljin 73 E3
Kreševo 75 F1
Krestcy 111 E1
Kréstena 86 B2
Kreuth 56 A4
Kreuzbergpass 59 E2
Kreuzlingen 58 A1
Kreuztal 17 F4
Kria Vrissi (Évia) 84 A3
Kria Vrissi (Makedonia) 79 E3
Kričev 111 E4
Krieglach 57 E3
Kriens 27 F2
Krikelo 83 D3
Krikelos 82 C3
Krikelos, Akr 89 F4
Krimml 59 D2
Krimmler Wasserfälle 59 D2
Krimpen 16 C3
Krinides 80 C2
Krionéri (Makedonia) 80 A2
Krionéri (Pelopónissos) 86 C3
Krionéri (Pelopónissos) 87 D1
Kriopigí 80 B4
Kriós, Akr 90 B4
Kristalopigí 78 C3
Kristdala 109 E2
Kristiansand 104 B4
Kristianstad 109 D3
Kristianstads Län 109 D3
Kristiansund 100 B2
Kristiinankaupunki 102 B3
Kristineberg 98 A4
Kristinehamn 105 E4
Kristinehov 109 D3
Kristinestad 102 B3
Krithéa 79 F2
Krithina, Óros 87 E4
Kritikó Pélagos 90 B2
Kriti, N 91 E3
Kritinia 93 E1
Kritsá 91 E4
Kriva Feja 77 E2
Krivaja (Bosna i Hercegovina) 71 F4
Krivaja (Vojvodina) 72 B1
Kriva Palanka 77 E2
Kriva reka 77 E2
Krivogaštani 77 E4
Krivoj Rog 113 F3
Krivolak 77 E3
Křižanov 57 E1
Križevci 71 D2
Krk 70 B3
Krk *I* 70 B3
Krka 70 B2
Krka *R* 75 D1
Krkonoše 112 A2
Krmčine 74 C1
Krn 70 A2
Krnjača 72 C3
Krnjak 70 C3
Krnjeuša 71 D4
Krnjevo 73 D3
Krnov 112 A3
Krnovo 76 B2
Krøderen 104 C2
Krokeés 87 D3
Krokeide 104 A2
Krokek 106 A4
Krokilio 83 D4
Krokom 101 E2
Krókos 79 E4
Kroksjö 98 A4
Krolevec 113 F1
Kröller Müller 17 D3
Kroměříž 112 A3
Kronach 52 C4
Kronobergs Län 109 D2
Kronoby 102 C1
Kronshagen 48 A1
Kronštadt 111 D1
Kröpelin 48 C2
Kropp 48 A1
Kroppenstedt 52 C1
Krosno 112 C3
Krosno Odrzańskie 53 F1
Krotoszyn 112 A2
Kroussónas 91 D4
Krovili, Pal. 81 E2
Krrabe, M 76 C3
Krško 70 C2
Krstac 76 A2
Krstača 76 C2
Krstinja 70 C3
Kruë i Fushës 76 C3
Kruiningen 16 B4
Krujë 76 C4
Krumbach 55 E3
Krumpendorf 70 A1
Krün 55 F4
Krupà 53 E4
Krupac (Bosna i Hercegovina) 75 F1
Krupac (Crna Gora) 76 B2
Krupac (Srbija) 77 E1
Krupaja 73 E3
Krupa na Vrbasu 71 E4
Krupanj 72 C3
Krupište 77 E3
Krupka 53 E3
Kruså 108 A4
Krušćica 71 E4
Krušćica, Jezero 70 C4
Krušedol Selo 72 C2
Kruševac 73 E4
Kruševica 73 D3
Kruševo 77 E4
Krute 76 B3
Kruunupyy 102 C1
Krvavec 70 B2
Krynica 112 B3
Krzeszyce 49 F4
Kteniás, Óros 87 D2
Ktismata 82 B1
Kubitzer Bodden 49 D1
Küblis 58 B2
Kučaj 73 E4
Kučevište 77 D2
Kučevo 73 E3
Kuchl 59 E1
Kučina Kosa 71 D4
Kućište 75 E2
Kućište 76 C2
Kudowa-Zdrój 112 A2
Kufstein 59 D1
Kühlungsborn 48 C2
Kuhmalahti 103 D3
Kuhmo 99 F4
Kuhmoinen 103 D3
Kuivajärvi 99 F4
Kuivajoki 99 D3
Kuivalahti 107 D2
Kuivaniemi 99 D3
Kuivasjärvi 102 C3
Kuivi 95 E2
Kuk 70 C4
Kukavica 77 E1
Kukës 76 C3
Kukkia 107 E1
Kukko 102 C2
Kukujevci 72 B2
Kukulje 71 E3
Kula (BG) 114 C2
Kula (TR) 115 F4
Kula (YU) 72 B2
Kuldīga 110 B3
Kulennoinen 103 F3
Kulen Vakuf 71 D4
Kulina 73 E4
Kulju 107 E1
Kulkjica 74 C1
Kullaa 107 D1
Kulm 27 F2
Kulmbach 52 C4
Kuloharju 99 E2
Külsheim 55 D1
Kultakero 99 E1
Kultsjön 97 E4
Kum 70 B2
Kumane 72 C2
Kumanovo 77 E2
Kumla 105 F4
Kumlinge 106 C3
Kummavuopio 94 C3
Kummerower See 49 D2
Kumputunturi 95 E4
Kumrovec 70 C2
Kungälv 108 C1
Kungsbacka 108 C1
Kungshamn 105 D4
Kungsör 105 F3
Kunoy 96 A3
Kunrau 48 B4
Kunszentmárton 112 B4
Künzelsau 55 D2
Kuolimo 103 E4
Kuolio 99 E3
Kuopio 103 E2
Kuopion Lääni 103 E2
Kuorboaivi 95 E2
Kuorevesi 103 D3
Kuortane 102 C2
Kuortovare 94 C4
Kuortti 103 D3
Kupa 70 B3
Kupa 70 C3
Kupferzell 55 D2
Kupinova Glava 73 E3
Kupinovo 72 C3
Kupres 75 E1
Kupreška vrata 75 E1
Kurfar 59 D3
Kurikka 102 B2
Kuřim 57 F1
Kuršėnai 110 C3
Kuršskij Zaliv 110 B3
Kursu 99 E2
Kuršumlija 77 D1
Kuršumlijska Banja 77 D1
Kurtakko 95 D4
Kuru 102 C3
Kusadak 73 D3
Kuşadasi 115 E4
Kusel 54 B1
Küsnacht 58 A2
Küssnacht 58 A2
Kustavi 107 D2
Küstenkanal 17 E1
Kütahya 115 F3
Kutina 71 D2
Kutjevo 71 E2
Kutná-Hora 112 A3
Kutno 112 B1
Kuttanen 95 D3
Kuttura 95 E3
Kúty 57 F2
Kuumu 99 F4
Kuusamo 99 E2
Kuusamojärvi 99 F2
Kuusankoski 107 F2
Kuusjärvi 103 E2
Kuusjoki 107 E2
Kuvšinovo 111 E2
Kuzma 70 C1
Kuzmin 72 B3
Kvæfjord 94 A3
Kvaløy 94 B2
Kvaløya 95 D1
Kvalsund 95 D1
Kvalvøg 100 B2
Kvam 100 C3
Kvænangen 94 C2
Kvænangsbotn 95 D2
Kvanndal 104 B2
Kvanne 100 B2
Kværndrup 108 B4
Kvarner 70 B4
Kvarnerić 70 B4
Kvernes 100 B2
Kvevlax 102 B2
Kvikkjokk 98 A2
Kvikne 100 C2
Kvina 104 B4
Kvinesdal 104 B4
Kvinesdal *V* 104 B4
Kvisvik 100 B2
Kviteseid 104 B3
Kvitnes 100 B2
Kvitsøy 104 A3
Kwidzyn 110 B4
Kyjov 57 F1
Kyläinpää 102 B2
Kylänlahti 103 F1
Kyleakin 2 B3
Kyle of Lochalsh 2 B3
Kyle of Tongue 2 C2
Kylerhea 2 B3
Kylestrome 2 C2
Kyll 51 D4
Kyllburg 51 D4
Kylmäkoski 107 E2
Kylmälä 99 D4
Kymen Lääni 103 F4
Kynsivesi 103 D3
Kyritz 49 D3
Kyrksæterøra 100 C2
Kyrkslätt 107 E3
Kyrönjoki 102 C2
Kyröjärvi 102 C3
Kyselka 53 E3
Kyšice 53 F4
Kyyjärvi 102 C2
Kyyvesi 103 E3

L

Laa an der Thaya 57 F2
La Adrada 39 F2
Laage 48 C2
Laakajärvi 103 E1
La Alberca 39 E2
La Alberca de Záncara 40 C3
La Alberguería de Argañán 39 D2
La Albuera 38 C4
La Albufera 41 E4
La Alcarria 40 C2
La Algaba 43 D2
La Almarcha 40 C3
La Almunia de Doña Godina 36 C4
La Antillas 42 C3
La Azohia 45 D3
Labacolla 34 A2
La Baells, Emb de 32 A3
Labajos 40 A1
La Bañeza 35 D3
La Barca de la Florida 43 D3
Labasheeda 12 B4
Labastida 36 B2
Labastide-Clairence 28 A4
Labastide-Murat 29 D2
Labastide-Rouairoux 32 B1
Labe 53 F3
Labin 70 A3
Labinot Fushë 76 C4
La Bisbal de Falset 37 E4
La Bisbal d'Empordà 32 B3
Laboe 48 A1
Labouheyre 28 A3
Labouret, Col du 31 D3
La Bóveda de Toro 35 D4
La Brède 28 B2
Labrit 28 B3
Labruguière 32 B1
Labudnjača 72 B2
Laç 76 C4
La Cabrera 40 B1
Lacalahorra 44 B3
La Campana 43 E2
Lacanau 28 A2
Lacanau-Océan 28 A2
Lacapelle-Marival 29 D2
Laćarak 72 B3
La Carlota 43 E2
La Carolina 44 A1
Lacaune 32 B1
Lacaune, Mts de 32 B1
La Cava 41 F2
La Cazada de Oropesa 39 E3
Lacedonia 64 C3
Läckö 105 E4
Lac Léman 27 E3
La Codosera 38 C3
Laconi 66 B3
La Coronada 39 E4
La Coruña 34 B1
Lacq 28 B4
La Cumbre 39 E3
La Espina 35 D1
Ladbergen 17 E2
Ládi 81 F1
Ladispoli 63 E2
Ladoeiro 38 C3
Ladožskoje Ozero 111 D1
Laérma 93 E2
La Felguera 35 D1
Laferté 27 D1
Laffrey 30 C2
Láfka 87 D1
Láfkos 83 F2
Lafnitz 57 F4
La Franca, 35 E1
Lafrançaise 29 D3
La Fregeneda 39 D1
La Frontera 40 C2
La Fuente de San Esteban 39 D1
Lagan 109 D2
Lagan *R* 109 D2
Laganá, Kólpos 86 A2
Laganás 86 A2
Lagarfljót 96 C2
La Garganta 34 C1
La Garriga 32 B4
Lagartera 39 E3
Lagastrello, Pso di 60 B3
Lage 17 F3
Lagen 100 C3
Lågen (Buskerud) 104 C3
Lågen (Oppland) 100 C3
Laggan 2 C4
Laggan, L 2 C4
Laginá (Makedonia) 79 F3
Laginá (Thráki) 81 F2
La Gineta 40 C4
Lagnieu 26 C4
Lagny 19 F4
Lago 67 E3
Lagoa 42 A2
Lagoaça 34 C4
Lagonegro 65 D4
Lagonissi 87 F2
Lagos 42 A2
Lágos 81 D2
Łagów 49 F4
La Granjuela 43 E1
Lagrasse 32 B2
Laguardia 36 B2
La Guardia 40 B3
La Guardia de Jaén 44 A2
Laguarres 37 E3
Laguarta 37 E2
Laguiole 29 E2
Laguna de Duero 35 E4
Lahanás 80 A2
La Hermida 35 E2
La Herradura 44 A4
Lahinch 12 B4
Lahn 17 F4
Lahnstein 51 E4
Laholm 108 C2
Laholmsbukten 108 C2
La Horcajada 39 E2
La Horra 35 F4
Lahr 54 C3
Lahti 107 F2
Laichingen 55 D3
Laide 2 B3
La Iglesuela del Cid 41 E2
Laignes 26 B1
Laigueglia 31 F3
Laihia 102 B2
Lailiás 80 B2
Laimbach 57 D2
Laimoluokta 94 C3
Lainate 60 A1
Lainioälven 95 D4
Lairg 2 C2
Laissac 29 E3
Laísta 78 C4
Laisvall 97 F3
Laitikkala 107 E2
Laitila 107 D2
La Jana 41 F2
Lajkovac 72 C3
La Jonquera 32 B3
Laká 82 A2
Lakavica 77 E3
Lake District Nat Pk 5 D4
Lakí 89 E3
Láki 90 B3
Lákmos, Óri 82 C1
Lákoma 81 E3
Lákones 82 A1
Lakonía 87 D3
Lakonikós Kólpos 87 D4
Lakópetra 86 B1
Laksefjorden 95 E1
Lakselv 95 D2
Laktaši 71 E3
La Laguna 42 B4
La Lantejuela 43 E3
Lálas 86 C2
Lalbenque 29 D3
L'Alcudia 41 E4
L'Aldea 41 F2
Lalín 34 B2
Lalinac 73 F4
Lalinde 28 C2
La Línea de la Concepción 43 E4
Laliótis 87 D1
Lalm 100 C3
La Losa 44 B2
Lalouvesc 30 B1
Lalueza 37 E3
La Luisiana 43 E2
Lalzit, Gjiri i 76 C4
Lam 56 B1
Lama dei Peligni 64 A2
La Magdalena 35 D2
Lamalou 30 A4
La Manche 10 A4
La Manga del Mar Menor 45 D2
Lamarche 27 D1
La Marmora, P 66 B3
Lamarque 28 B2
Lamastre 30 B2
Lambach 56 C3
Lamballe 22 C3
Lambesc 30 C4
Lámbia 86 C1
Lambiri 83 D4
Lámbou Míli 85 F2
Lambrecht 54 C2
Lamego 34 B4
La Mesa Roldán 44 C3
Lamia 83 E3
Lamlash 4 B2
Lammermuir Hills 5 D2
Lammhult 109 D2
Lammi 107 E2
La Molina 32 A3
Lamotte-Beuvron 25 E2
Lampaul 22 A2
Lampedusa 68 A4
Lampedusa, I di 68 A4
Lampertheim 54 C1
Lampeter 8 C1
L'Ampolla 41 F2
Lamstedt 47 F3
La Mudarra 35 E4
La Muela 37 D4
Lamure 26 B4
Lana 58 C3
Lanaja 37 D3
Lanaken 51 D3
Lanark 4 C2
La Nava de Ricomalillo 39 F3

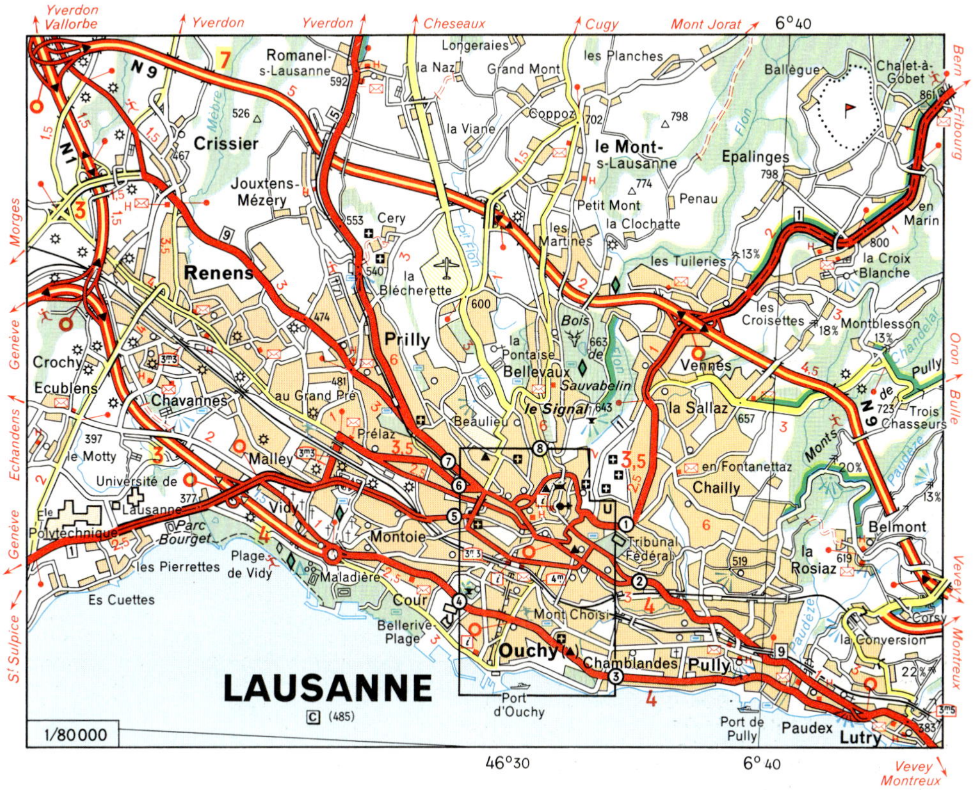
LAUSANNE
1/80 000
Yverdon Vallorbe
Yverdon
Cheseaux
Cugy
Mont Jorat
Morges
Genève
Echandens
St Sulpice
Vevey Montreux
Oron
Bulle
Bern Fribourg
Romanel-s-Lausanne
Crissier
Jouxtens-Mézery
Renens
Prilly
le Mont-s-Lausanne
Epalinges
Longeraies
Grand Mont
les Planches
Ballègue
Chalet-à-Gobet
Petit Mont
la Clochatte
Penau
Cery
la Blécherette
les Tuileries
la Croix Blanche
Montblesson
Vennes
la Sallaz
Bellevaux
Sauvabelin
le Signal
Beaulieu
Crochy
Ecublens
Chavannes
au Grand Pré
Prélaz
Malley
le Motty
Université de Lausanne
Polytechnique
Parc Bourget
les Pierrettes
Plage de Vidy
Vidy
Es Cuettes
Montoie
Maladière
Cour
Bellerive Plage
Tribunal Fédéral
Mont Choisi
Ouchy
Chamblandes
Pully
Port d'Ouchy
Port de Pully
Paudex
Lutry
Chailly
Belmont
la Rosiaz
la Conversion
Fontanettaz
Trois Chasseurs
46°30
6°40

La Nava de Santiago 39 D4
Lancashire 6 B2
Lancaster 6 B1
Lanchester 5 E4
Lanciano 64 A2
Landau (Bayern) 56 B2
Landau (Rheinland-Pfalz) 54 C2
Landeck 58 C2
Landerneau 22 B2
Landes 28 B3
Landes de Lanvaux 22 C3
Landete 41 D3
Landévennec 22 A3
Landivisiau 22 B2
Landivy 18 C4
Landmannalaugar 96 B2
Landquart 58 B2
Landrecies 20 A2
Landriano 60 A1
Landsberg 53 D2
Landsberg 56 A3
Land's End 8 A4
Landshut 56 B2
Landskapet Åland 106 C2
Landskrona 108 C3
Landstuhl 54 B2
Landverk 101 D2
Lanersbach 59 D2
Lanesborough 12 C3
Langáda (Híos) 85 F4
Langáda (Pelopónissos) 87 D4
Langadás 79 F3
Langádas 87 D3
Langa de Duero 36 A3
Langádia 86 C2
Langadíkia 80 A3
Langangen 104 C4
Langeac 29 F2
Langeais 25 D2
Langeland 108 B4
Langelandsbælt 108 B4
Langelmäki 103 D3
Langelmävesi 103 D3
Langelsheim 52 B1
Langenargen 55 D4
Langenau 55 E3
Langenberg 53 D3
Langenbruck 55 F2
Langenburg 55 D2
Langeneß 47 F1
Langenfeld 17 E4
Längenfeld 58 C2
Langenhagen 48 A4
Langenhahn 51 F3
Langen (Hessen) 52 A4
Langen (Niedersachsen) 47 F3
Langenlois 57 E2
Langenthal 27 F2
Langenwang 57 E3
Langenzenn 55 E1
Langeoog 47 E3
Långeserud 105 E3
Langeskov 108 B3
Langesund 104 C4
Langevåg 100 A2
Langevåg 104 A3
Långfjället 101 D3
Langfjord 95 D2
Langfjorden 95 E1
Langfjordjøkelen 94 C2
Langforden 100 B2
Langhirano 60 B2
Langholm 5 D3
Langjökull 96 B2
Langnau 27 F2
Langogne 29 F2
Langon 28 B2
Langøya 94 A3
Langport 9 D3
Langres 26 C1
Langrune 18 C3
Långsele 101 F2
Långshyttan 105 F2
Långträsk 98 B3
Lanjarón 44 A3
Lanke 49 E3
Länkipohja 103 D3
Lanmeur 22 B2
Lannemezan 37 E1
Lannilis 22 A2
Lannion 22 B2
Lanouaille 29 D1
Lans-en-Vercors 30 C1
Lanslebourg 31 E1
Lanta 29 D4
Lantosque 31 E3
La Nuez de Arriba 35 F3
Lanusei 66 C3
Lanvollon 22 C2
Lanzahita 39 F2
Lanzarote 42 C3
Lanzo Torinese 31 E1
Laois 12 C4
La Oliva (Is Canarias) 42 C4
La Oliva (Navarra) 36 C2
Laon 20 A3
La Orotava 42 B4
La Paca 44 C2
Lapalisse 26 B4
La Palma 42 A4
La Palma del Condado 42 C2
La Panadella 37 F4
Lápas 86 B1
Lapa, Sa da 38 C1
Laperdiguera 37 E3
La Pinilla 36 A4
Lapinjärvi 107 F2
Lapin Lääni 95 E4
Lapinlahti 103 E2
La Platja d'Aro 32 B4
La Plaza 35 D2
Lapleau 29 E1
Laplume 28 C3
La Pobla 41 E4
La Pobla de Lillet 32 A3
La Pobla de Massaluca 37 E4
La Pobla de Segur 37 F3
La Pobla de Vallbona 41 E3
Lapoutroie 27 E1
Lapovo 73 D3
Lappajärvi 102 C2
Lappajärvi *L* 102 C2
Lappalaisten-Kesätuvat 95 D3
Lappea 98 C2
Lappeenranta 103 F4
Lappfjärd 102 B3
Lappfors 102 C2
Lappi 107 D2
Lappoå 102 C2
Lappohja 107 E3
Lappträsk 98 C3
Lappträsk 107 F2
Lappvesi 106 C3
Lapua 102 C2
Lapuanjoki 102 C2
La Puebla de Almoradiel 40 B3
La Puebla de Cazalla 43 E3
La Puebla de Híjar 37 D4
La Puebla de los Infantes 43 E2
La Puebla del Río 43 D3
La Puebla de Montalbán 39 F3
La Puebla de Valverde 41 D2
La Pueblanueva 39 F3
La Puerta de Segura 44 B1
Lapväärtti 102 B3
L'Aquila 63 F2
La Rábida 42 C3
La Rábita 44 B4
Laracha 34 A1
Laragh 13 D4
Laragne-Montéglin 30 C3
La Rambla 43 F2
Lärbro 109 F3
Larche (Alpes-de-Haute-Provence) 31 E2
Larche (Corrèze) 29 D2
Larche, Col de 31 E2
Lærdalsøyri 104 B1
Lardarello 60 C4
Lárdos 93 F2
Lárdos, Akr 93 F2
Laredo 36 A1
Laren 16 C2
Largentière 30 B2
Largs 4 C2
Lárimna 84 A4
La Rinconada 43 D2
Larino 64 B2
La Rioja 36 B2
Lárissa 83 E1
Lárissa (Nomos) 83 E2
Larmor 22 B4
Larne 13 E2
La Robla 35 D2
La Roca 32 B4
La Roca de la Sierra 39 D4
Larochette 21 D2
La Roda (Andalucía) 43 E3
La Roda (Castilla-la-Mancha) 40 C4
Laroles 44 B3
Laroquebrou 29 E2
Laroque-d'Olmes 32 A2
Laroque-Timbaut 28 C3
Larouco 34 B3
Larraga 36 C2
Larrau, Pto de 37 D2
Larseng 94 B2
Larsmo 102 C1
Laruns 37 D2
Larv 109 D1
Larvik 104 C4
Lasalle 29 F3
Las Alpujarras 44 A3
Las Arenas 36 B1
Lasarte 36 C1
Las Batuecas 39 E2
Las Cabezas de San Juan 43 D3
Las Cabrillas, Pto de 41 E2
Las Caldas de Besaya 35 F2
Las Campanas 36 C2
Lascaux, Grotte de 29 D2
La Seca 35 E4
La Selva del Camp 37 F4
La Sénia 41 F2
La Seu d'Urgell 32 A3
Las Huelgas Reales 35 F3
Lasinjski Sjeničak 70 C3
Laško 70 B2
Las Mesas 40 B4
Las Mestas 39 E2
Las Minas 44 C1
Las Navas de la Concepción 43 E2
Las Navas del Marqués 40 A2
Las Negras 44 C4
Læsø 108 B2
La Solana 40 B4
Las Pajanosas 43 D2
Las Palmas de Gran Canaria 42 B4
Las Pedroñeras 40 C4
Las Pedrosas 37 D3
La Spezia 60 B3
Las Portas, Emb de 34 B3
Las Rozas 40 A2
Lassan 49 E2
Lassay 23 E3
Lassigny 19 F3
Lassíthi 91 E4
Lassíthi (Nomos) 91 F4
Lastovo 75 E3
Lastovo *I* 75 E3
Lastovski kan 75 E2
Lastra a Signa 60 C3
Lastres 35 E1
Lastrup 17 E1
Lastva 76 A2
Lašva 71 F4
Las Veguillas 39 E1
Las Ventas con Peña Aguilera 40 A3
Las Vertientes 44 B3
Las Viñas 43 F2
Lätäseno 95 D3
Laterza 65 D4
Lathen 17 E1
Latheron 3 D2
Latiano 65 E3
Latikberg 97 F4
Latina 63 F3
Latisana 59 E3
Lató 91 E4
La Torre del Valle 35 D3
Latour-de-France 32 B2
Latronico 65 D4
Latronquière 29 E2
Latvija 110 C3
Lauchhammer 53 E2
Lauder 5 D2
Lauenau 52 A1
Lauenburg 48 B3
Lauenstein 53 E3
Lauf 55 F1
Laufen (CH) 27 E2
Laufen (D) 56 B3
Laufenburg 54 C4
Lauffen 55 D2
Laugafell 96 B2
Laugar 96 A2
Laugarvatn 96 B2
Lauhanvuori 102 B3
Lauingen 55 E2
Laujar de Andarax 44 B3
Laukaa 103 D3
Lauksundskaret 94 C2
Launceston 8 B3
La Unión 45 D3
Laupheim 55 E3
Lauragh 14 A4
Laureana di Borrello 67 E4
Laurencekirk 3 E4
Laurenzana 65 D4
Lauria 67 E1
Laurière 25 E4
Lausanne 27 D3
Lauta 53 E2
Lautaret, Col du 31 D2
Lautenthal 52 B1
Lauter 54 C2
Lauterbach 52 A3
Lauterbourg 21 F3
Lauterbrunnen 27 F3
Lauterecken 54 B1
Lautrec 32 A1
Lauttakylä 107 D2
Lauvstad 100 A2
Lauvvik 104 A3
Lauzerte 29 D3
Lauzet-Ubaye, le 31 D2
Lauzun 28 C2
Lavagna 60 A3
Laval 23 E3
Lavamünd 70 B1
Lavandou, le 31 D4
Lavangen 94 B3
Lavant 70 B1
Lávara 81 F2
Lavardac 28 C3
La Vecilla 35 E2
Lavelanet 32 A2
La Vellés 39 E1
Lavello 64 C3
Lavelsloh 17 F2
Lavenham 11 D1
Laveno 58 A4
Lavéra 30 C4
La Verna 61 D3
Lavia 102 C3
Laviano 64 C4
Lavik 104 A1
La Villa de Don Fadrique 40 B3
Lavinio Lido di Enea 63 E3
La Virgen del Camino 35 D2
Lavis 59 D3
Lavit 28 C3
Låvong 97 E3
Lavour 29 D4
Lavoûte-Chilhac 29 F2
Lavre 38 B4
Lávrio 88 A2
Lavvuoai'vi 95 D3
Laxå 105 E4
Laxe 34 A1
Laxford Bridge 2 C2
Laxo 3 F1
Lay 24 B3
La Yesa 41 D3
Layos 40 A3
Laza 34 B3
Lazarevac 72 C3
Lazarev Krst 76 B2
Lazarevo 72 C2
Lazaropole 77 D3
Lazio 63 E2
Lazise 60 C1
Lázně Kynžvart 53 D4
Laznica 73 E3
Leadenham 7 D3
Leamington Spa, Royal 9 E1
Leane, L 14 B4
Łeba 110 A4
Lebach 54 B2
Lebane 77 E1
Lebedin 113 F1
Lebesby 95 E1
Lębork 110 A4
Lebrija 43 D3
Lebus 49 F4
Lecce 65 F4
Lecco 58 B4
Lécera 37 D4
Lećevica 75 D1
Lech (A) 58 B2
Lech (D) 55 E2
Léchère, la 31 D1
Lechlade 9 E2
Leciñena 37 D3
Leck 47 F1
Lecques, les 30 C4
Lectoure 28 C3
Lecumberri 36 C1
Ledaña 41 D4
Ledanca 40 B1
Ledbury 9 D1
Ledesma 39 E1
Lédignan 30 B3
Ledmore 2 C2
Lee 14 B4
Leeds 6 C2
Leek 6 C3
Leenane 12 B3
Leer 47 E3
Leerdam 16 C3
Leese 48 A4
Leeuwarden 16 C1
Lefkáda 82 B3
Lefkáda, N 82 B3
Lefkádia 79 E3
Lefkadíti 83 E3
Lefkandí 84 B4
Lefká Óri 90 B3
Léfkara 79 E4
Léfkes 88 C3
Lefkími 81 F2
Lefkími, Akr 82 A2
Lefkógia 80 B1
Lefkopigí 79 D4
Léfktra 83 F4
Legan 48 A2
Leganés 40 A2
Legé 24 B3
Legnago 60 C1
Legnano 60 A1
Legnica 112 A2
Legrad 71 D1
Legrená 87 F2
Léguevin 29 D4
Legutiano 36 B1
Le Havre 19 D3
Lehená 86 B1
Lehnin 49 D4
Lěhovo 79 D3
Lehrberg 55 E1
Lehre 52 B1
Lehrte 52 B1
Lehtimäki 102 C2
Lehtovaara (Lapin Lääni) 99 D1
Lehtovaara (Oulun Lääni) 103 E1

Tongeren
Houtain-St Siméon
Glons
Antwerpen
Maastricht
Maastricht
Othée (Elch)
Xhendremael
Villers-St Siméon
Juprelle
Hermée
Oupeye
Hermalle-s/s-Argenteau
Argenteau
Vivegnis
Wixhou
Sarolay
ESPERANCE LONGDOZ
Chertal
MEUSE
Voroux-lez-Liers
Liers
zone industrielle des Hauts-Sarts
Sabare
Aux Communes
Milmort
Pontisse
Cheratte
Lantin
Rocourt
les Monts
Housse
Hoignée
Waroux
Alleur
Parc industriel d'Alleur
Hombroux
Vottem
Herstal
la Préalle
Wandre
Fort
Loncin
Thier-à-Liège
Rabosée
Sur les Heids
Xhavée
Saive
Awans
Bierset
Ste Walburge
Ans
Ile Monsin
Souverain-Wandre
Citadelle
Parc industriel de Grâce-Hollogne
Wasseige
Glain
Bellaire
Parfondvaux
Droixhe
Liège-Bierset
Grâce-Hollogne
Montegnée
LIÈGE (Luik)
Bressoux
Jupille-s-Meuse
Queue-du-Bois
Robermont
Berleur
St Nicolas
St Gilles
la Chartreuse
Bois-de-Breux
Moulin-s/s-Fléron
Crotteux Hollogne
Lamay
Grivegnée
Beyne-Heusay
Mons-lez-Liège
Mabotte
Bruyères
Fléron
Ruy
Bois-de-Mont
Tilleur
Cointe
les Thiers
Chênée
Ste Anne
Romsée
Jemeppe
S.A. COCKERILL OUGRÉE PROVIDENCE
Sclessin
Kinkempois
Angleur
Vaux-s/s-Chèvremont
Magnée
Souxhon
Grande
Flémalle-Haute
MEUSE
Seraing
Renory
Streupas
Méhagne
Bouny
Basilique de Chèvremont
El' Heur
Lize
Ougrée
Sauheid
Au Pairay
Val St Lambert
CRISTAL DU VAL-St-LAMBERT
Bois de St Jean
Sart-Tilman
Embourg
Chaudfontaine
Casino
Fonds de Forêt
Ivoz-Ramet
Bois de l'Abbaye
les Communes
Bois de la Marchandise
Université de Liège
Ninane
la Brouck
Prayon
Boncelles
Colonster
Sainval
Vesdre
Au Thier
Sur-le-Mont
les Cours
la Lonhienne
Arboretum
le Sart-Haguet
Sur Cortil
Chau de l'Abbaye
Bois de la Neuville
Bois de la Vequée
les Fréhisses
les Gonhis
Tilff
Brialmont
Beaufays
Péry
Avister
Grotte de Tilff
Méry
Bou-Bou
Neuville-en-Condroz
la Roche aux Faucons
Fechereux
1/100 000
St Truiden
Bruxelles
Hannut
Namur
Huy
Namur
St Rémy
Verviers
Micheroux
Aachen
Verviers
Verviers
Dinant
Marche-en-Famenne
Dinant
Ouffet
Esneux
Bastogne
Spa
50° 40
5° 40

Leibnitz 70 B1
Leicester 9 F1
Leicestershire 9 E1
Leiden 16 B3
Leie 50 B4
Leighton Buzzard 9 F2
Leikanger 100 A3
Leiknes 97 F1
Leine 48 A4
Leinefelde 52 B2
Leini 31 E1
Leipheim 55 E3
Leipzig 53 D2
Leira (Møre og Romsdal) 100 B2
Leira (Oppland) 104 C2
Leirbotn 95 D2
Leiria 38 B2
Leiro 34 B2
Leirpollskogen 95 F1
Leirvåg 104 A1
Leirvik (Færøerne) 96 A3
Leirvik (Hordaland) 104 A3
Leirvik (Sogn og Fjordane) 104 A1
Leisnig 53 E2
Leiston 11 E1
Leitáriegos, Pto de 34 C2
Leith 5 D2
Leitha 57 F2
Leitir Ceanainn 12 C1
Leitrim 12 C3
Leitzkau 52 C1
Leivonmäki 103 D3
Leiza 36 C1
Lek 16 C3
Léka 89 E1
Leka 97 D3
Lekáni 80 C2
Lekeitio 36 B1
Lekenik 71 D2
Leknes (Møre og Romsdal) 100 A2
Leknes (Nordland) 97 E1
Łeknica 53 F1
Leksand 101 E4
Leksvik 100 C1
Leland 97 D3
Lelång 105 D4
Lelija 76 A1
Lelystad 16 C2
Lelystad-Haven 16 C2
Léman, Lac 27 E3
Le Mans 23 F3
Lembach 21 E3
Lembeye 28 B4
Lemförde 17 F2
Lemgo 17 F2
Lemgow 48 C3
Lemi 103 E4
Lemland 106 C3
Lemmenjoki 95 E3
Lemmenjoki (Nat Pk) 95 E3
Lemmenjoki *R* 95 E3
Lemmer 16 C1
Lemonodássos 87 F2
Lempäälä 107 E1
Lempdes 29 F1
Lemvig 108 A2
Lenart 70 C1
Lencloître 25 D3
Lend 59 E1
Léndas 91 D4
Lendava 71 D1
Lendava *R* 70 C1
Lendinara 61 D2
Lengefeld 53 E3
Lengenfeld 53 D3
Lengerich 17 E2
Lenggries 56 A4
Lenhovda 109 E2
Leningrad 111 D1
Lenk 27 E3
Lenne 17 F4
Lennestadt 17 F4
Lens 19 F2
Lensahn 48 B2
Lentföhrden 48 A2
Lenti 114 A1
Lentiira 99 F4
Lenting 55 F2
Lentini 69 D3
Lentua 99 F4
Lenvik 94 B3
Lenzburg 27 F2
Lenzen 48 C3
Lenzerheide Valbella 58 B3
Lenzkirch 54 C4
Leoben 57 E4
Leobersdorf 57 F3
Leogang 59 E1
Leominster 9 D1
Léon 28 A3
León 35 D2
León, Mtes de 35 D2
Leonberg 55 D2
Léoncel 30 C2
Leondári (Pelopónissos) 86 C2
Leondári (Thessalía) 83 E2
Leóndio 87 D2
Leonessa 63 E1
Leonforte 68 C3
Leonídio 87 E3
León, Pto del 43 F3
Leopoldsburg 50 C3
Leopoldsdorf 57 F2
Leopoldsteinersee 57 D3
Leovo 113 E4
Lepel' 111 D3
Lepenoú 80 C3
Lepenski vir 73 E3
Lepetane 76 B3
Lepoglava 70 C1
Leposavić 77 D1
Lépoura 84 B4
Leppäjärvi 95 D3
Leppävirta 103 E2
Leptokariá (Makedonía) 79 F4
Leptokariá (Thráki) 81 E2
Lercara Friddi 68 B3
Léré 26 A2
Lerici 60 B3
Lérida 37 E4
Lerin 36 C2
Lérins 31 E4
Lerma 35 F3
Lermoos 58 C1
Lérni 87 D2
Léros, N 89 E3
Lerum 108 C1
Lerwick 3 F2
Les 37 F2
Lešak 76 C1
Lešani 77 D4
Les Borges Blanques 37 F4
L'Escala 32 C3
Lescar 28 B4
Lesce 70 A2
Lešće 70 C3
Lescun 37 D2
Leshnicë 77 D4
Lesima, Mte 60 A2
Lesina 64 C2
Lesina, L di 64 C2
Lesja 100 B3
Lesjöfors 105 E3
Leskovac 77 E1
Les Llosses 32 A3
Lesneven 22 B2
Lešnica 72 B3
Lesparre-Médoc 28 A1
L'Espina 41 F2
L'Espluga de Francolí 37 F4
Les Portes de Fer 73 E3
L'Espunyola 32 A3
Lessay 18 B3
Lessebo 109 E2
Lessines 50 B3
Lessini 82 C4
L'Estartit 32 C3
Lestelle-Bétharram 37 E1
Lestijärvi 102 C2
Lestijoki 102 C1
Lestkov 53 E4
Lésvos, N 85 F2
Leszno 112 A2
Letchworth 9 F2
Letenye 114 A1
Letino 64 A3
Letmathe 17 E4
Letterfrack 12 A3
Letterkenny 12 C1
Lettermullan 12 A3
Letur 44 C1
Letuš 70 B1
Letzlingen 48 C4
Leuca 65 F4
Leuchars 5 D1
Leuk 27 F3
Leukerbad 27 E3
Leuna 53 D2
Leutenberg 52 C3
Leutershausen 55 E1
Leutkirch 55 E4
Leutschach 70 B1
Leuven 50 C3
Leuze 50 B4
Levajok 95 E2
Levanger 101 D1
Levanjska Varoš 71 F2
Levant, I du 31 D4
Levanto 60 B3
Levanzo, I di 68 A3
Levásjoki 102 B3
Levene 108 C1
Leven (England) 7 D2
Leven (Scotland) 5 D2
Levens 31 E3
Leverano 65 F4
Leverburgh 2 A3
Leverkusen 17 E4
Levet 25 F3
Levi 95 E4
Levice 112 B3
Levico Terme 59 D3
Levidi 87 D2
Levie 33 F4

Levier 27 D3
Levítha, N 89 E3
Levoča 112 B3
Levroux 25 E3
Lévy, Cap 18 B2
Lewes 10 C3
Lewis 2 B2
Leyburn 6 C1
Leyland 6 B2
Leyre 37 D2
Leysdown-on-Sea 11 D2
Leysin 27 E3
Lézardrieux 22 C2
Lézat 37 F1
Lezay 24 C4
Lezhë 76 C3
Lézignan-Corbières 32 B2
Ležimir 72 C2
Lezoux 29 F1
Lezuza 40 C4
L'gov 111 F4
L'Hospitalet de l'Infant 37 F4
Liabygda 100 B2
Liákoura 83 E4
Lianokládi 83 E3
Liathach 2 C3
Liberec 112 A2
Libochovice 53 F3
Libourne 28 B2
Librazhd 77 D4
Librilla 45 D2
Licata 68 C4
Licciana Nardi 60 B3
Lich 52 A4
Lichfield 9 E1
Lichoslavl' 111 F2
Lichtenberg 53 D3
Lichtenfels 52 C4
Lichtenstein 53 D3
Lichtenvoorde 17 D3
Lička Jesenica 70 C3
Lički Osik 70 C4
Ličko Lešće 70 C4
Lida 110 C4
Liddel Water 5 D3
Liden 101 F2
Lidhult 109 D2
Lidingö 106 B4
Lidköping 105 E4
Lido degli Estensi 61 D2
Lido delle Nazioni 61 D2
Lido di Camaiore 60 B3
Lido di Classe 61 E3
Lido di Jesolo 59 E4
Lido di Metaponto 65 E4
Lido di Ostia 63 E3
Lido di Savio 61 E3
Lido di Spina 61 D2
Lido di Venezia 61 D1
Lidoriki 83 E4
Lido Silvana 65 E4
Lidzbark Warmiński 110 B4
Liebenwalde 49 D3
Lieberose 53 F1
Liège 51 D4
Liège (Prov) 51 D4
Lieksa 103 F1
Lienz 59 E2
Liepāja 110 B3
Lier 50 C3
Liérganes 35 F2
Liernais 26 B2
Lieser 59 F2
Liesjärvi 107 E2
Liestal 27 E2
Lieto 107 D2
Liétor 44 C1
Lieurey 19 D3
Lievestuore 103 D3
Liévin 19 F1
Liezen 57 D3
Liffey 13 D4
Liffol-le-Grand 20 C4
Lifford 13 D1
Liffré 23 D3
Lifjell 104 C3
Ligiá 86 B1
Lignano Sabbiadoro 59 F4
Ligné 23 D4
Lignières 25 F3
Ligny-en-Barrois 20 C4
Ligny-le-Châtel 26 B1
Ligourió 87 E2
Ligueil 25 D3
Liguria 60 A3
Liháda 83 F3
Liikasenvaara 99 E2
Lijeva Rijeka 76 B2
Lijevi Dubravčak 71 D2
Lika 70 C4
Likenås 105 E2
Likeo, Óri 86 C2
Likódimo, Óros 86 C3
Likófos 81 F2
Likoporiá 87 D1
Likórahi 78 C4
Likóstomo 80 C2
Likouría 86 C1
Liland 94 B3
Lilea 83 E3
Lilienfeld 57 E3
Liljendal 107 F2
Lilla Edet 108 C1
Lillby 102 C2
Lille 19 F1
Lille Bælt 108 A3
Lillebonne 19 D3
Lillehammer 105 D2
Lillerød 108 C3
Lillers 19 F1
Lillesand 104 B4
Lillestrøm 105 D3
Lillhärdal 101 E3
Lillo 40 B3
Lillögda 102 A1
Lillsholmsjön 101 E1
Lim 76 B1
Lima 101 D4
Limáni Hersonissou 91 E3
Limáni Litohórou 79 F4
Lima, R 34 A3
Limavady 13 D1
Limbach 53 D3
Limbara, M 66 B2
Limburg (B) 50 C3
Limburg (D) 51 F4
Limburg (NL) 17 D4
Limenária 80 C3
Limerick 14 B3
Limerick (Co) 14 B3
Limfjorden 108 A2
Limia, R 34 B3
Limingen 97 E4
Liminka 99 D4
Liminpuro 99 E4
Limljani 76 B3
Límnes 87 E2
Límni 84 A3
Limniá 80 C2
Límnitsa 83 D4
Límnos, N 85 D1
Limoges 29 D1
Limogne 29 D3
Limone Piemonte 31 E3
Limonest 26 C4
Limours 19 E4
Limoux 32 B2
Lin 77 D4
Linares 44 A2
Linares del Arroyo, Emb de 36 A3
Linares de Mora 41 E2
Linares de Riofrio 39 E2
Linariá 84 C3
Linas, M 66 B4
Lincoln 7 D3
Lincolnshire 7 D3
Lindås 104 A2
Lindau 55 D4
Linden 52 C4
Lindenberg 55 E4
Linderhof 55 F4
Lindesberg 105 F3
Lindesnes 104 B4
Lindhem 106 A4
Lindö 106 A4
Líndos 93 F2
Lindoso 34 B3
Lindow 49 D3
Lindsdal 109 E2
Lingbo 106 A2
Linge 100 B2
Lingen 17 E2
Linguaglossa 69 D3
Linken 49 E2
Linköping 106 A4
Linlithgow 5 D2
Linnansaari 103 E3
Linnhe, L 4 B1
Linosa, I di 68 A4
Linsell 101 E3
Linslade 9 F2
Linthal 58 A2
Linyola 37 F3
Linz 51 E4
Linz 57 D2
Lion 18 C3
Lion-d'Angers, le 23 E4
Lioni 64 C4
Lióprasso 83 D1
Lioran, le 29 E2
Lipar 72 B2
Lipari 69 D2
Lipari, I 69 D2
Lipenská přehr nádrž 56 C2
Liperi 103 F2
Lipiany 49 F3
Lipica 70 A3
Lipik 71 D2
Lipkovo 77 E2
Lipljan 77 D2
Lipno 57 D2
Lipova 112 C4
Lipovac 72 B3
Lippe 17 E3
Lippstadt 17 F3
Lipsí 89 E2
Lipsí, N 89 E2
Liptovský Mikuláš 112 B3
Liqenas 77 D4
Lírkia 87 D2
Lis 76 C3
Lisac 71 E4
Lisboa 38 A4
Lisburn 13 E2
Liscia 66 B1
Lisdoonvarna 12 B4
Lisieux 19 D3
Lisina 71 E4
Liskeard 8 B4
Lisková 56 B1
Lisle 29 D3
Lismore (GB) 4 B1
Lismore (IRL) 14 C4
Lisnaskea 13 D2
Lišnja 71 E3
Lisovići 71 F3
Lisse 16 C2
List 47 F1
Listafjorden 104 A4
Lištica 75 E2
Listowel 14 B3
Lit 101 E2
Lit-et-Mixe 28 A3
Lithakiá 86 A2
Lithári, Akr 84 C3
Lithines 91 F4
Líthino, Akr 91 D4
Lithio 85 E4
Litî 79 F3
Litija 70 B2
Litóhoro 79 F4
Litoměřice 53 F3
Litomyšl 112 A3
Litschau 57 D1
Littlehampton 10 C3
Little Minch, The 2 A3
Little Moreton Hall 6 C3
Littleport 10 C1
Litva 110 C3
Litvínov 53 E3
Livaara 99 F3
Liváda, Akr 88 C2
Livade 70 A3
Livaderó (Dráma) 80 C2
Livaderó (Kozáni) 79 E4
Livádi (Kíthira) 90 A2
Livádi (Makedonía) 80 A3
Livádi (Sérifos) 88 A3
Livádi (Thessalía) 79 E4
Livadiá (Makedonía) 80 A2
Livadiá (Stereá Eláda) 83 F4
Livádia (Tílos) 89 F4
Livadítis 80 C1
Livadohóri 85 D1
Livanátes 83 F3
Livari 76 B3
Livarot 19 D4
Livenza 59 E4
Liverá 79 D3
Liverdun 21 D4

Lille

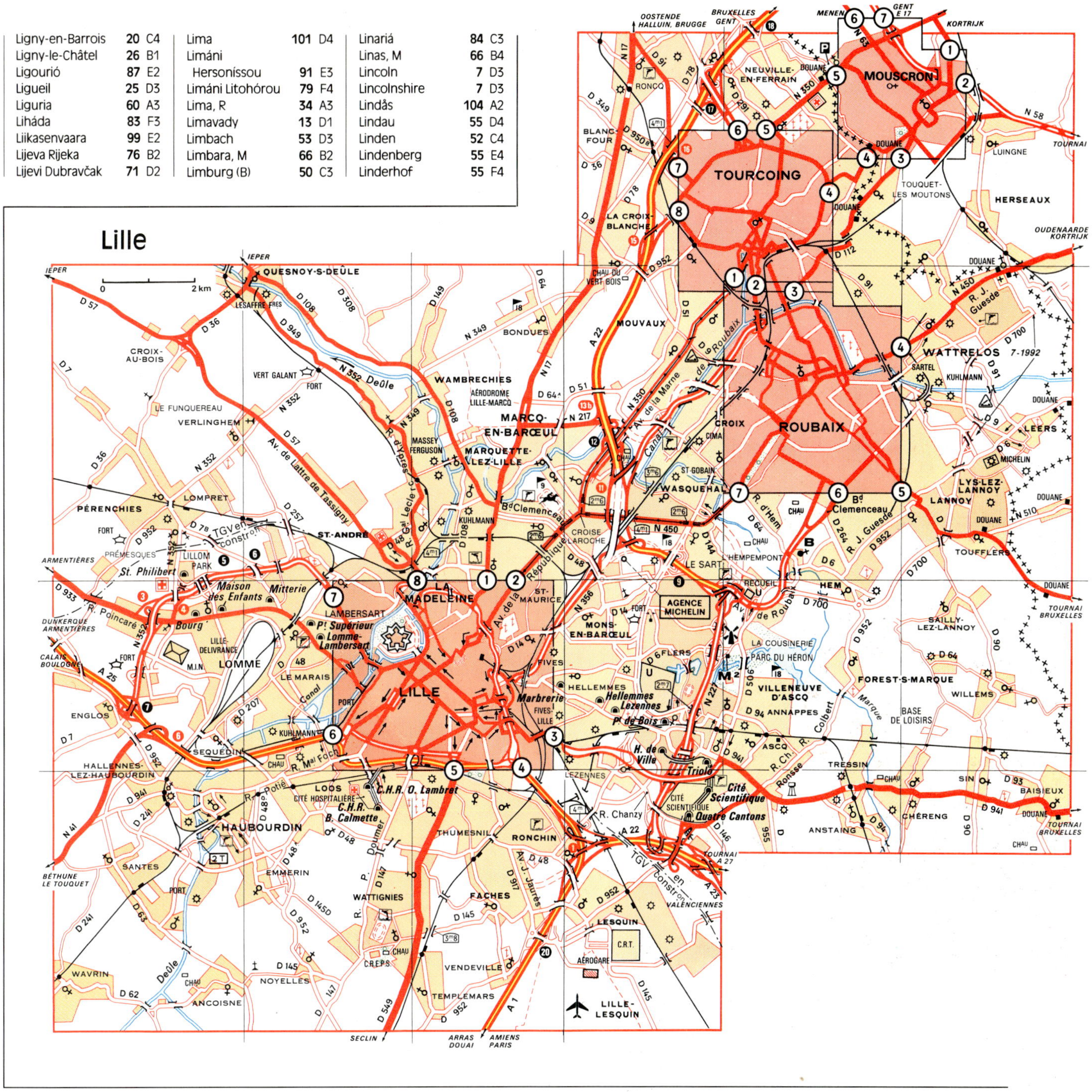
Lille
TOURCOING
MOUSCRON
ROUBAIX
WATTRELOS
LILLE
LA MADELEINE
MARCQ-EN-BARŒUL
WAMBRECHIES
LOMME
HAUBOURDIN
LOOS
RONCHIN
LESQUIN
LILLE-LESQUIN
MONS-EN-BARŒUL
VILLENEUVE D'ASCQ
CROIX
HEM
LYS-LEZ-LANNOY
LANNOY
MOUVAUX
FACHES
WATTIGNIES
SEQUEDIN
PÉRENCHIES
LOMPRET
QUESNOY-S-DEÛLE
HERSEAUX
FOREST-S-MARQUE
ANSTAING
CHÉRENG
TRESSIN
BAISIEUX
WAVRIN
NOYELLES
ANCOISNE
TEMPLEMARS
VENDEVILLE
SECLIN
ARRAS DOUAI
AMIENS PARIS
IEPER
OOSTENDE HALLUIN, BRUGGE
BRUXELLES GENT
KORTRIJK
TOURNAI BRUXELLES
AGENCE MICHELIN
0 2 km

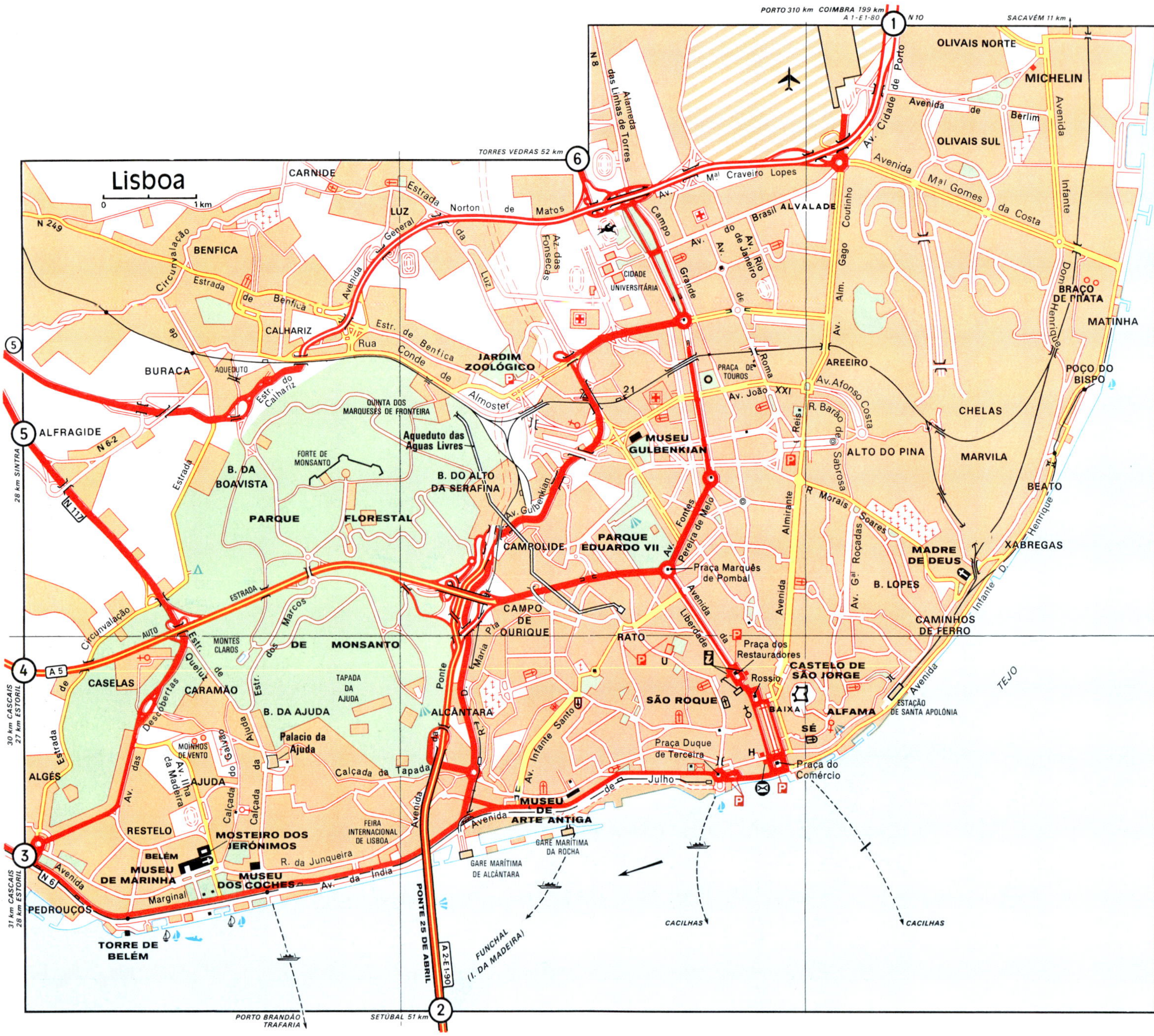
Lisboa
0 1 km
PORTO 310 km COIMBRA 199 km
A 1-E 1-80
N 10
SACAVÉM 11 km
TORRES VEDRAS 52 km
OLIVAIS NORTE
MICHELIN
OLIVAIS SUL
CARNIDE
LUZ
BENFICA
ALVALADE
CIDADE UNIVERSITÁRIA
BRAÇO DE PRATA
MATINHA
CALHARIZ
BURACA
AQUEDUTO
JARDIM ZOOLÓGICO
AREEIRO
PRAÇA DE TOUROS
POÇO DO BISPO
ALFRAGIDE
QUINTA DOS MARQUESES DE FRONTEIRA
Aqueduto das Águas Livres
MUSEU GULBENKIAN
CHELAS
ALTO DO PINA
MARVILA
FORTE DE MONSANTO
B. DA BOAVISTA
B. DO ALTO DA SERAFINA
BEATO
PARQUE FLORESTAL DE MONSANTO
PARQUE EDUARDO VII
CAMPOLIDE
MADRE DE DEUS
XABREGAS
Praça Marquês de Pombal
B. LOPES
CAMPO DE OURIQUE
CAMINHOS DE FERRO
MONTES CLAROS
RATO
Praça dos Restauradores
CASTELO DE SÃO JORGE
Rossio
CASELAS
TAPADA DA AJUDA
SÃO ROQUE
BAIXA
ALFAMA
ESTAÇÃO DE SANTA APOLÓNIA
TEJO
CARAMÃO
B. DA AJUDA
ALCÂNTARA
SÉ
Palacio da Ajuda
MOINHOS DE VENTO
Praça Duque de Terceira
Praça do Comércio
ALGÉS
AJUDA
MUSEU DE ARTE ANTIGA
RESTELO
MOSTEIRO DOS JERÓNIMOS
FEIRA INTERNACIONAL DE LISBOA
GARE MARÍTIMA DA ROCHA
GARE MARÍTIMA DE ALCÂNTARA
BELÉM
MUSEU DE MARINHA
MUSEU DOS COCHES
PEDROUÇOS
TORRE DE BELÉM
PONTE 25 DE ABRIL
A 2-E 1-90
FUNCHAL (I. DA MADEIRA)
CACILHAS
PORTO BRANDÃO TRAFARIA
SETÚBAL 51 km
28 km SINTRA
30 km CASCAIS 27 km ESTORIL
31 km CASCAIS 28 km ESTORIL

Livernon 29 D2
Liverpool 6 B2
Liverpool B 6 B2
Livigno 58 C3
Livingston 5 D2
Livno 75 E1
Livo 99 E3
Livojärvi 99 E2
Livojoki 99 E3
Livold 70 B3
Livorno 60 C4
Livorno Ferraris 31 F1
Livron 30 B2
Lixoúri 82 B4
Lizard 8 B4
Lizard Pt 8 B4
Lizy 19 F3
Lizzano in Belvedere 60 C3
Ljeskove Vode 71 E3
Ljig 72 C3
Ljubaništá 77 D4
Ljubata, D 77 E2
Ljubelj 70 A1
Ljubija 71 D3
Ljubinje 75 F2
Ljubiš 72 C4
Ljubišnja 76 B1
Ljubljana 70 B2
Ljubno 70 B1
Ljubojno 77 E4
Ljubostinja 73 D4
Ljuboten 77 D2
Ljubovija 72 C4
Ljubuša 75 E1
Ljubuški 75 E2
Ljugarn 109 F4
Ljungan 101 F3
Ljungby 109 D2
Ljungbyhed 109 D3
Ljungdalen 101 D2
Ljungsbro 105 F4
Ljungskile 108 C1
Ljusdal 101 F3
Ljusnan 101 E3
Ljusne 101 F4
Ljutići 76 B1
Ljutoglav 77 D2
Ljutomer 70 C1
Llagostera 32 B3
Llanberis 6 A3
Llanca 32 C3
Llandeilo 8 C2
Llandovery 8 C1
Llandrindod Wells 9 D1
Llandudno 6 A2
Llandysul 8 C1
Llanelli 8 C2
Llanerchymedd 6 A2
Llanes 35 E1
Llanfairfechan 6 A2
Llanfair-ym-Muallt 9 D1
Llanfyllin 6 B3
Llangadog 8 C2
Llangefni 6 A2
Llangollen 6 B3
Llangurig 8 C1
Llanidloes 8 C1
Llano, Pto 39 E3
Llanrhystud 8 C1
Llanrwst 6 A3
Llanwrtyd-Wells 8 C1
Llanymyddyfri 8 C1
Llarga 41 E4
Llavorsi 37 F2
Lleida 37 E4
Llera 43 D1
Llerena 43 D1
Lles 32 A3
Llessui 37 F2
Lleyn Pen 6 A3
Llíria 41 E3
Llívia 32 A2
Llobregat, R 32 A3
Llodio 36 B1
Lloret de Mar 32 B4
Llucmajor 45 F3
Llynclys 6 B3
Lnáre 56 C1
Loanhead 5 D2
Loano 31 F3
Löbau 53 F2
Löbejün 53 D2
Lobenstein 52 C3
Łobez 49 F2
Löbnitz 49 D1
Lobo 36 A4
Lobón 39 D4
Loburg 53 D1
Locana 31 E1
Locarno 58 A3
Lochaline 4 B1
Lochboisdale 2 A3
Lochcarron 2 B3
Lochearnhead 4 C1
Lochem 17 D2
Loches 25 D3
Loch Garman 15 D3
Lochgelly 5 D2
Lochgilphead 4 B2
Lochinver 2 C2
Lochmaben 5 D3
Lochmaddy 2 A3
Loch Ness 2 C3
Lochranza 4 B2
Lochvica 113 F2
Lochy, L 2 C4
Lockenhaus 57 F3
Lockerbie 5 D3
Löcknitz 49 E2
Locle, le 27 E2
Locmariaquer 22 C4
Locminé 22 C3
Locorotondo 65 E3
Locquirec 22 B2
Locri 67 F4
Locronan 22 B3
Loctudy 22 B3
Lodè 66 C2
Lodève 30 A4
Lodi 60 B1
Løding 97 E1
Lødingen 94 A3
Lodosa 36 C2
Łódź 112 B2
Loeches 40 B2
Loen 100 A3
Løfallstrand 104 A2
Lofário 81 E2
Lofer 59 E1
Löffingen 54 C4
Lofoten 97 E1
Lofsdalen 101 D3
Lofthus 104 B2
Loftus 5 F4
Log 70 A2
Logarska dolina 70 B1
Logatec, D. 70 A2
Logroño 36 B2
Logrosán 39 E3
Løgstør 108 A2
Løgten 108 B3
Løgumkloster 108 A4
Lohals 108 B4
Lohberg 56 B1
Lohilahti 103 E3
Lohiniva 99 D1
Lohja 107 E3
Lohjanjärvi 107 E2
Lohne 17 F2
Löhne 17 F2
Lohr 52 B4
Lohtaja 102 C1
Loiano Rioveggio 60 C3
Loibltunnel 70 A1
Loimaa 107 E2
Loimaan kunta 107 D2
Loimijoki 107 D2
Loing 26 A2
Loir 25 E1
Loire 23 E4
Loire (Dépt) 29 F1
Loire-Atlantique 23 D4
Loir-et-Cher 25 E2
Loiret 25 E1
Loiri 66 B1
Loiron 23 E3
Loitz 49 D2
Loja 43 F3
Lojsta 109 F4
Lokalahti 107 D2
Lokan Tekojärvi 95 F4
Løken 105 D3
Lokeren 50 B3
Loket 53 E4
Lokka 95 F4
Løkken (N) 100 C2
Løkken (S) 108 B1
Lokn'a 111 D2
Lokrum 76 A2
Lokve (Hrvatska) 70 B3
Lokve (Slovenija) 70 A2
Lokve (Vojvodina) 73 D2
Lolland 108 B4
L'Olleria 45 E1
Lom (BG) 115 D2

1/200 000
0 1 2 3 km
0 1 2 miles
Southport
Preston
Skelmersdale
Southport
Preston
Wigan
Belfast
Douglas (Isle of Man)
Dún Laoghaire
Crosby Channel
Maghull
Kirkby
Crosby
Bootle
Litherland
Wallasey
Hoylake
BIRKENHEAD
LIVERPOOL
ST. HELENS
Knowsley
Roby
Huyton
Prescot
Rainford
Billinge
Ashton-in-Makerfield
Golborne
Haydock
Newton-le-Willows
WARRINGTON
Widnes
Runcorn
Speke
LIVERPOOL AIRPORT
RIVER MERSEY
Bebington
Ellesmere Port
Manchester Ship Canal
Frodsham
Helsby
Neston
Heswall
West Kirby
WIRRAL
RIVER DEE/AFON DYFRDWY
Flint
Fflint
Queensferry
Chester
Chester
Whitchurch
Nantwich
Manchester
Stoke-on-Trent
Manchester
Macclesfield
Stockport
Stockport

Lom (CS) 53 E3
Lom (N) 100 B3
Loma Negra 36 C3
Lomazzo 60 A1
Lombarda, Colle della 31 E3
Lombardia 60 A1
Lombez 28 C4
Lomello 60 A2
Lomen 104 C1
Lomma 108 C3
Lommatzsch 53 E2
Lommel 50 C3
Lomond, L 4 C2
Lomonosov 111 D1
Lomont, Mts du 27 E2
Lompolo 95 E4
Łomża 112 B1
Lonato 60 B1
Lončari 71 F3
Lončarica 71 E2
Londinières 19 E2
London 9 F2
Londonderry 13 D1
Londonderry (Co) 13 D1
Longá 86 C3
Longádes 82 C1
Longaníkos 87 D3
Longares 36 C4
Longarone 59 E3
Long Eaton 7 D3
Longeau 26 C1
Longford 12 C3
Longford (Co) 12 C3
Longleat House 9 D3
Longny 19 D4
Longobucco 67 F2
Longós 82 A2
Long Preston 6 C1
Long Sutton 7 E3
Longtown 5 D3
Longué 23 E4
Longueville-sur-Scie 19 E2
Longuyon 20 C3
Longwy 20 C3
Lonigo 60 C1
Löningen 17 E2
Lonja 71 D3
Lonja *R* 71 D2
Lönsboda 109 D3
Lønsdal 97 E2
Lønset 100 B2
Lons-le-Saunier 26 C3
Looe 8 B4
Loop Head 12 A4
Loosdorf 57 E2
Lopar 70 B4
Lopare 72 B3
Lopcombe Corner 9 E3
Lopera 43 F2
Lopes, Mal i 76 C4
Loppa 94 C2
Loppi 107 E2
Lopud 75 F2
Lopud *I* 75 F2
Lora del Río 43 E2
Lorca 44 C2
Lorcé 51 D4
Lorch (Baden-Württemberg) 55 D2
Lorch (Hessen) 51 F4
Loreley 51 F4
Loreo 61 D1
Loreto 61 F4
Loreto Aprutino 64 A1
Lorgues 31 D4
Lorica 67 F3
Lorient 22 B4
Loriga 38 C2
Loriguilla, Emb de 41 D3
Loriol 30 B2
Lormes 26 B2
Lorn, Firth of 4 B1
Loro Ciuffenna 61 D4
Loroux-Bottereau, le 24 B2
Lorquin 21 E4
Lörrach 54 C4
Lorrez-le-Bocage 25 F1
Lorris 25 F1
Los 101 E3
Los Alcázares 45 D2
Losar 39 E2
Los Arcos 36 B2
Los Barreros 40 C4
Los Barrios 43 D4
Los Corrales de Buelna 35 F2
Los Cortijos 40 A4
Los Cristianos 42 B4
Los Dolores 45 D2
Losenstein 57 D3
Los Gallardos 44 C3
Losheim 54 B1
Los Hinojosos 40 B3
Lošinj 70 B4
Los Llanos de Aridane 42 A4
Los Lobos 44 C3
Los Navalmorales 39 F3
Los Navalucillos 39 F3
Los Palacios y Villafranca 43 D3
Los Santos 39 E2
Los Santos de Maimona 43 D1
Los Sauces 42 A4
Loßburg 54 C3
Lossiemouth 3 D3
Lossnen 101 D3
Lößnitz 53 D3
Lostwithiel 8 B4
Los Villares 44 A2
Los Yébenes 40 A3
Lot 29 E2
Lot (Dépt) 29 D3
Lote 100 A3
Løten 105 D2
Lot-et-Garonne 28 C3
Lothian 5 D2
Lötschbergtunnel 27 F3
Löttorp 109 E2
Loučná 53 E3
Loudéac 22 C3
Loudiás 79 F3
Loudiás *R* 79 F3
Loudun 25 D3
Loué 23 E3
Loue 26 C2
Loughborough 7 D3
Loughrea 12 B4
Louhans 26 C3
Louhisaari 107 D2
Louisburgh 12 B3
Loukinen 95 E4
Loukíssia 84 A4
Loulay 24 C4
Loulé 42 B3
Louny 53 E3
Loupe, la 19 E4
Loup, Gorge du (L) 21 D2
Loup, Gorges du (F) 31 E3
Lourdes 37 E1
Loures 38 A4
Lourical 38 B2
Lourinhã 38 A3
Loúros 82 B2
Loúros *R* 82 C2
Louroux, le 23 E4
Lousa 38 A4
Lousã 38 B2
Lousada 34 A4
Lousã, Sa da 38 B2
Louth 7 E2
Louth 13 D3
Loutrá Ardéas 79 E2
Loutrá Edipsoú 83 F3
Loutrá Eleftherón 80 C3
Loutrá Ipátis 83 E3
Loutrá Kaítsas 83 E2
Loutrá (Kikládes) 88 A2
Loutráki (Pelopónissos) 87 E1
Loutráki (Skópelos) 84 B2
Loutráki (Stereá Eláda) 82 C3
Loutrá Kilínis 86 B1
Loutrá Langadá 80 A3
Loutrá (Lésvos) 85 F3
Loutrá (Makedonía) 80 B4
Loutrá (Pelopónissos) 86 C2
Loutrá Smokóvou 83 D2
Loutrá Vólvis 80 A3
Loutró Elénis 87 E1
Loutropigí 83 D2
Loutrópirgos 87 E1
Loutrós 81 F2
Loútsa (Ípiros) 82 B2
Loútsa (Stereá Eláda) 88 A1
Louvain 50 C3
Louvain-la-Neuve 50 C4
Louvière, La 50 B4
Louviers 19 E3
Louvigné-du-Désert 18 B4
Lovag 76 B1
Lövånger 102 B1
Lövberga 101 F1
Lovćen 76 B3
Loveč 115 D2
Lovere 58 B4
Loviisa 107 F2
Lovisa 107 F2
Lovosice 53 F3
Lovran 70 B3
Lovrenc na Pohorju 70 B1
Lövstabruk 106 B2
Lövstabukten 106 B2
Lovund 97 D2
Löwenberg 49 D3
Lower L Erne 12 C2
Lowestoft 11 E1
Łowicz 112 B1
Low Street 7 F3
Lož 70 B2
Lozère 29 F2
Lozère, Mt 29 F3
Lozna 73 D4
Loznica 72 B3
Lozovac 75 D1
Lozovik 73 D3
Lozoyuela 40 B1
Luanco 35 D1
Luarca 35 D1

0°40
0°20
51°40
Aylesbury
Leeds, Birmingham
St Albans
Luton, Bedford
Grantham
High Wycombe
Oxford
Maidenhead, Reading
Bristol
Reading
Basingstoke
Southampton
Farnham, Southampton
Portsmouth
Worthing
Gatwick Airport
Crawley, Brighton
Chesham
Amersham
Watford
Potters Bar
Radlett
Borehamwood
Bushey
Rickmansworth
Chorleywood
Chalfont St. Giles
Chalfont St. Peter
Gerrards Cross
Beaconsfield
Edgware
BARNET
Mill Hill
Finchley
Hendon
Stanmore
Pinner
HARROW
Wembley
BRENT
Hampstead
Ruislip
Northwood
Denham
Uxbridge
HILLINGDON
Hayes
Southall
EALING
Acton
KENSINGTON
HAMMERSMITH
CHELSEA
FULHAM
Slough
Langley
Eton
Windsor
Datchet
Staines
Egham
Ashford
Feltham
HOUNSLOW
Richmond
RICHMOND UPON THAMES
Twickenham
Putney
WANDSWORTH
Wimbledon
MERTON
HEATHROW AIRPORT
Sunbury
Hampton Court
KINGSTON UPON THAMES
Chertsey
Weybridge
Walton-on-Thames
Esher
Ewell
SUTTON
Epsom
Ascot
Sunningdale
Virginia Water
Windsor Great Park
Woking
Cobham
Leatherhead
Banstead
Guildford
Dorking
Reigate
Box Hill
Great Bookham
East Horsley
Shere
Albury

London
1/200 000
0 1 2 3 4 5 6 km
0 1 2 3 4 miles
Cambridge
Norwich
Stansted Airport, Cambridge
Harlow
Ipswich
Southend-on-Sea
Southend-on-Sea
Ramsgate
Canterbury, Dover
Folkestone
Maidstone
Maidstone
Brighton
Eastbourne
Eastbourne
Hastings
0°
0°20
51°40
51°20
Cheshunt
Epping
Chipping Ongar
Ingatestone
Brentwood
Chigwell
Romford
Enfield
Tottenham
Walthamstow
Ilford
Barking
Dagenham
Upminster
Hornchurch
Woolwich
Greenwich
Lewisham
Croydon
Bromley
Orpington
Dartford
Grays Thurrock
Northfleet
Gravesend
Tilbury
Swanley
Sevenoaks
Caterham
Dartford Tunnel
Blackwall Tunnel
River Thames

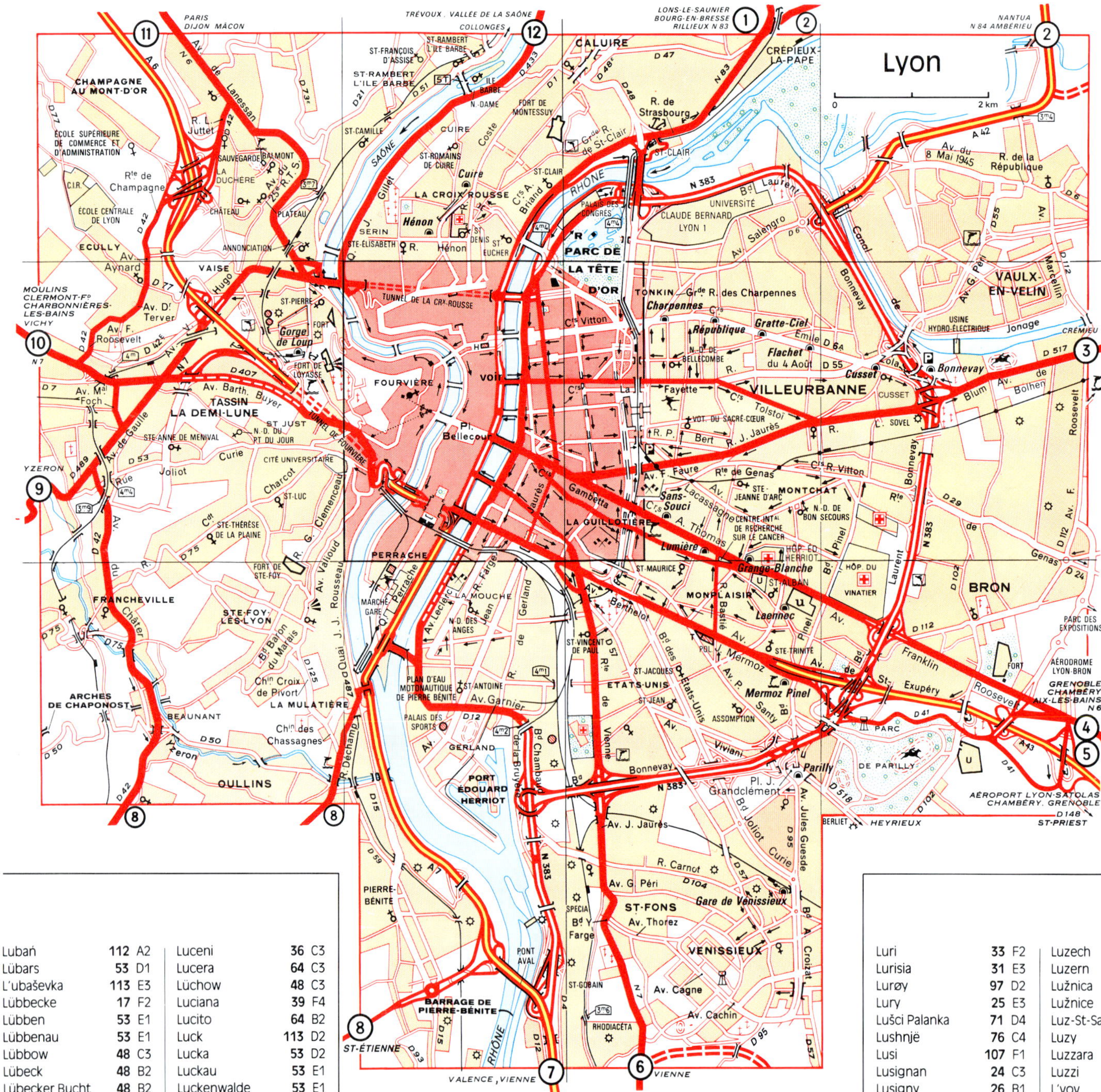
Lyon
0
2 km
PARIS
DIJON MÂCON
TRÉVOUX . VALLÉE DE LA SAÔNE
COLLONGES
LONS-LE-SAUNIER
BOURG-EN-BRESSE
RILLIEUX N 83
NANTUA
N 84 AMBÉRIEU
CHAMPAGNE AU MONT-D'OR
CALUIRE
CRÉPIEUX-LA-PAPE
LA CROIX ROUSSE
VAISE
ECULLY
PARC DE LA TÊTE D'OR
VILLEURBANNE
VAULX-EN-VELIN
FOURVIÈRE
TASSIN LA DEMI-LUNE
PERRACHE
LA GUILLOTIÈRE
MONTCHAT
MONPLAISIR
BRON
ETATS-UNIS
FRANCHEVILLE
STE-FOY-LÈS-LYON
LA MULATIÈRE
ARCHES DE CHAPONOST
OULLINS
GERLAND
PORT EDOUARD HERRIOT
PIERRE-BÉNITE
ST-FONS
VENISSIEUX
BARRAGE DE PIERRE-BÉNITE
RHÔNE
SAÔNE
ST-ÉTIENNE
VALENCE, VIENNE
VIENNE
HEYRIEUX
ST-PRIEST
AÉROPORT LYON-SATOLAS
CHAMBÉRY, GRENOBLE
GRENOBLE
CHAMBÉRY
AIX-LES-BAINS
AÉRODROME LYON-BRON
MOULINS
CLERMONT-Fᴰ
CHARBONNIÈRES-LES-BAINS
VICHY
YZERON

Lubań 112 A2
Lübars 53 D1
L'ubaševka 113 E3
Lübbecke 17 F2
Lübben 53 E1
Lübbenau 53 E1
Lübbow 48 C3
Lübeck 48 B2
Lübecker Bucht 48 B2
Lubenec 53 E4
Lubéron, Montagne du 30 C3
Lubersac 29 D1
Lubieszyn 49 E2
Lubin 112 A2
Lublin 112 C2
Lubliniec 112 B2
Lubmin 49 D1
Lubniewice 49 F4
Lubniewsko, Jez 49 F4
Lubny 113 F2
L'uboml' 112 C2
Lubrín 44 C3
Lubsko 53 F1
Lubsza 53 F1
Lübtheen 48 B3
Lübz 48 C3
Luc 18 C3
Lucainena de las Torres 44 C3
Lucan 13 D4
Lučani 73 D4
Lúcar 44 B3
Lucca 60 C3
Luče 70 B2
Luce B 4 B3
Lucena 43 F3
Lucena del Cid 41 E3
Lucenay-l'Evêque 26 B2
Luc-en-Diois 30 C2
Lučenec 112 B3
Luceni 36 C3
Lucera 64 C3
Lüchow 48 C3
Luciana 39 F4
Lucito 64 B2
Luck 113 D2
Lucka 53 D2
Luckau 53 E1
Luckenwalde 53 E1
Luc, le 31 D4
Lucomagno, Pso del 58 A3
Luçon 24 B3
Ludbreg 71 D1
Lude, le 23 F4
Lüdenscheid 17 E4
Ludiente 41 E3
Lüdinghausen 17 E3
L'udinovo 111 F3
Ludlow 9 D1
Ludvika 105 F3
Ludwigsburg 55 D2
Ludwigsfelde 49 D4
Ludwigshafen (Baden-Württemberg) 55 D4
Ludwigshafen (Rheinland-Pfalz) 54 C1
Ludwigslust 48 C3
Ludwigstadt 52 C3
Luère, Col de la 26 C4
Lug 75 E1
Lug R 73 D3
Luga 111 D1
Luga R 111 D1
Lugagnano Val d'Arda 60 B2
Lugano 58 A4
Lugau 53 D3
Lügde 52 A1
Lugnano in Teverina 63 E2
Lugnaquillia Mt 13 D4
Lugo 34 B2
Lugo 61 D2
Lugoj 114 C1
Lugones 35 D1
Luhačovice 112 A3
Luhalahti 102 C3
Luhanka 103 D3
Luhtapohja 103 F2
Luik 51 D4
Luimneach 14 B3
Luiña 35 D1
Luing 4 B1
Luino 58 A4
Luiro 95 F4
Luisenburg 53 D4
Luka (Bosna i Hercegovina) 75 F1
Luka (Hrvatska) 74 C1
Luka (Srbija) 73 E3
Lukavac 71 F3
Lukavica 71 F3
Lukovica 70 B2
Lukovit 115 D2
Lukovo (Makedonija) 77 D4
Lukovo (Srbija) 73 E4
Lukovo (Srbija) 77 D1
Lukovo Šugarje 70 C4
Luleå 98 C3
Luleälven 98 B3
Lüleburgaz 115 E3
Lumbarda 75 E2
Lumbier 36 C2
Lumbrales 31 D1
Lumbres 19 F1
Lumezzane 60 B1
Lumi i Tiranës 76 C4
Lumijoki 99 D4
Lumparland 106 C3
Lumparn 106 C3
Lumsås 108 c3
Lumsheden 105 F2
Lun 70 B4
Luna 37 D3
Luna, Emb Barrios de 35 D2
Luna, R 35 D2
Lunas 30 A4
Lund 108 C3
Lunde (Sogn og Fjordane) 100 A3
Lunde (Telemark) 104 C3
Lunden 47 F2
Lundy 8 B3
Lune 6 B1
Lüneburg 48 B3
Lunel 30 B4
Lünen 17 E3
Lünersee 58 B2
Lunéville 21 D4
Lungern 27 F3
Lungro 67 E2
Luninec 113 D1
Lunz 57 D3
Luodonselkä 99 D4
Luogosanto 66 B1
Luonteri 103 E3
Luopioinen 107 E1
Luosto 99 D1
Luoto 102 C1
Lupoglav 71 D2
Luque 43 F2
Lurbe-St-Christau 37 D1
Lurcy-Lévis 26 A3
Lure 27 D1
Lure, Mgne de 30 C3
Lurgan 13 E2
Luri 33 F2
Lurisia 31 E3
Lurøy 97 D2
Lury 25 E3
Lušci Palanka 71 D4
Lushnjë 76 C4
Lusi 107 F1
Lusignan 24 C3
Lusigny 26 B1
Lusk 13 E3
Luso 38 B2
Lussac 28 B2
Lussac-les-Châteaux 25 D4
Lussan 30 B3
Lustenau 58 B2
Luster 100 B3
Lustrafjorden 100 B3
Lütjenburg 48 B2
Luton 9 F2
Lutterberg 52 A2
Lutterworth 9 E1
Lutto 95 F3
Lutzelbourg 21 E4
Lützen 53 D2
Lutzerath 51 E4
Lutzmannsburg 57 F3
Lützow 48 B2
Luumäki 103 F4
Luupuvesi 103 D1
Luusua 99 E2
Luvia 107 D2
Luxembourg 21 D2
Luxembourg (Grand-Duché) 21 D2
Luxembourg (Prov) 20 C2
Luxeuil 27 D1
Luynes 25 D2
Lužani 71 E3
Luzarches 19 F3
Luzech 29 D3
Luzern 27 F2
Lužnica 77 E1
Lužnice 57 D1
Luz-St-Sauveur 37 E2
Luzy 26 B3
Luzzara 60 C2
Luzzi 67 E2
L'vov 112 C2
Lychen 49 D3
Lyckebyån 109 E3
Lycksele 98 A4
Lydd 11 D3
Lydney 9 D2
Lye 109 F4
Lygna 104 B4
Lyme B 9 D3
Lyme Regis 9 D3
Lymington 9 E3
Łyna 110 B4
Lyndhurst 9 E3
Lyness 3 D1
Lyngdal 104 B4
Lyngen 94 C2
Lyngseidet 94 C2
Lyngsnes 97 D4
Lynmouth 8 C3
Lynton 8 C3
Lyon 26 C4
Lyons-la-Forêt 19 E3
Lys 19 F1
Lysá 53 F3
Lysefjorden 104 A3
Lyseheiene 104 B3
Lysekil 108 C1
Lyss 27 E2
Lysvik 105 E3
Lytham St Anne's 6 B2

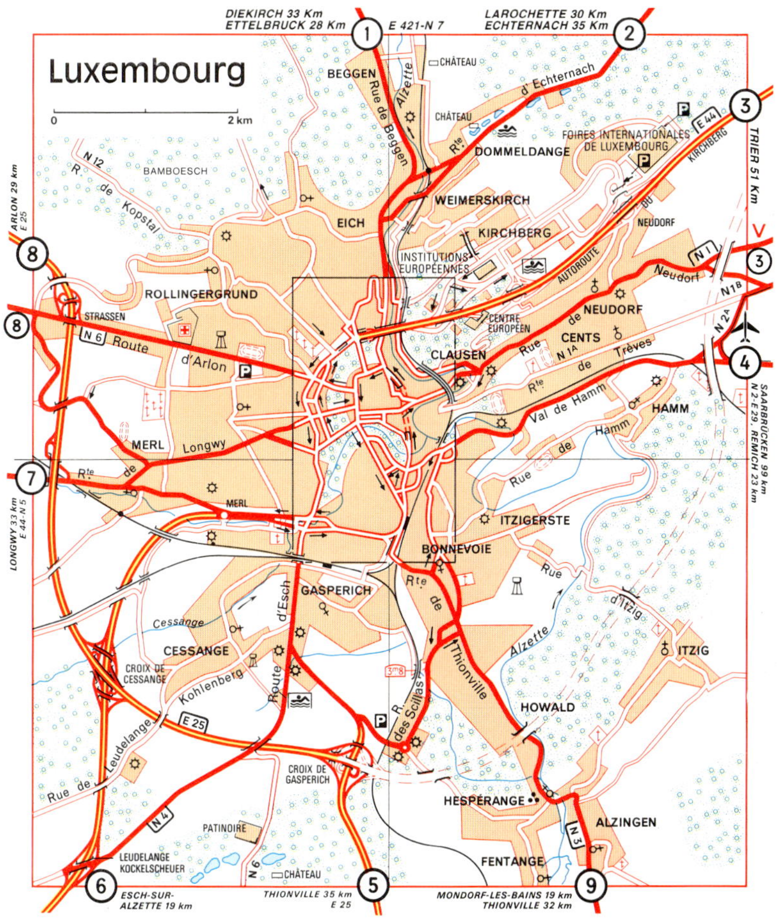
Luxembourg
0 2 km
DIEKIRCH 33 Km
ETTELBRUCK 28 Km
E 421-N 7
LAROCHETTE 30 Km
ECHTERNACH 35 Km
TRIER 51 Km
SAARBRÜCKEN 99 km
N 2-E 29 REMICH 23 km
MONDORF-LES-BAINS 19 km
THIONVILLE 32 km
THIONVILLE 35 km
E 25
ESCH-SUR-ALZETTE 19 km
LONGWY 33 km
E 44-N 5
ARLON 29 km
E 25
BEGGEN
DOMMELDANGE
WEIMERSKIRCH
EICH
KIRCHBERG
INSTITUTIONS EUROPÉENNES
FOIRES INTERNATIONALES DE LUXEMBOURG
BAMBOESCH
ROLLINGERGRUND
STRASSEN
NEUDORF
CENTRE EUROPÉEN
CENTS
CLAUSEN
HAMM
MERL
ITZIGERSTE
BONNEVOIE
GASPERICH
CESSANGE
CROIX DE CESSANGE
ITZIG
HOWALD
CROIX DE GASPERICH
HESPERANGE
ALZINGEN
PATINOIRE
LEUDELANGE KOCKELSCHEUER
FENTANGE
CHÂTEAU
Route d'Arlon
Rte de Longwy
Val de Hamm
Rue de Trèves
Rte de Thionville
Route d'Esch
Alzette
Kohlenberg
Rue de Leudelange
Rue de Kopstal
Rue de Beggen
Rte d'Echternach
Autoroute
Neudorf
Cessange
d'Itzig
R. des Scillas

M

Maakalla 102 C1
Maalanti 102 B2
Maam Cross 12 B3
Maaninka 103 E2
Maaninkavaara 99 E2
Maanselkä 103 E1
Maarestatunturit 95 E3
Maarianhamina 106 C3
Maarianvaara 103 E2
Maas 16 C3
Maaseik 51 D3
Maasmechelen 51 D3
Maassluis 16 B3
Maastricht 51 D3
Määttälänvaara 99 F2
Mablethorpe 7 E2
Macael 44 C3
Mação 38 B3
Macclesfield 6 C3
Macduff 3 E3
Maceda 34 B3
Macedo de Cavaleiros 34 C4
Macelj 70 C1
Macerata 61 F4
Macerata Feltria 61 E3
Macgillycuddy's Reeks 14 A4
Machault 20 B3
Machecoul 24 B3
Machero 39 F4
Machichaco, C 36 B1
Machine, la 26 A3
Máchovo jez 53 F3
Machrihanish 4 B3
Machynlleth 6 A3
Mackendorf 52 C1
Mackenrode 52 B2
Mačkovci 70 C1
Macocha 57 F1
Macomer 66 B2
Mâcon 26 C4
Macotera 39 F1
Macroom 14 B4
Macugnaga 27 F4
Mačvanska Mitrovica 72 C3
Mačvanski Pričinović 72 C3
Madara 115 E2
Maddalena, Arc della 66 B1
Maddalena, Colle della 31 E2
Maddalena, I 66 B1
Maddalena La 66 B1
Maddaloni 64 B3
Madeira, Arquipélago da 42 A3
Madeira, I da 42 A3
M'adel' 111 D3
Madeleine, Col de la 31 D1
Madero, Pto del 36 C3
Maderuelo 36 A3
Madesimo 58 B3
Madine, Lac de 20 C3
Madon 21 D4
Madona 110 C2
Madonie Nebrodi 68 C3
Madonna di Campiglio 58 C3
Madrid 40 A2
Madrid (Prov) 40 A2
Madridejos 40 B3
Madrigal de las Altas Torres 39 F1
Madrigal de la Vera 39 E2
Madrigalejo 39 E4
Madrona 40 A1
Madrona, Sa 44 A1
Madroñera 39 E3
Maël-Carhaix 22 B3
Maella 37 E4
Maesteg 8 C2
Mafra 38 A3
Magacela 39 E4
Magallón 36 C3
Magaña 36 B3
Magaz 35 F3
Magdalena, Pto de la 35 D2
Magdeburg 52 C1
Magenta 60 A1
Magerøya 95 E1
Maggia 58 A3
Maggiore, L 58 A4
Maghera 13 D1
Magherafelt 13 D2
Mágina 44 A2
Magione 61 E4
Maglaj 71 F3
Magliano di Marsi 63 F2
Magliano in Toscana 63 D2
Magliano Sabina 63 E2
Maglić 73 D4
Maglić *Mt* 76 A1
Maglie 65 F4
Magnac-Laval 25 E4
Magnissia 83 E2
Magnor 105 D3
Magny-en-Vexin 19 E3
Magoúla 86 B2
Magro, R 41 D4
Magura 77 D2
Maherádo 86 A1
Mahlu 103 D2
Mahón 45 F2
Mahora 41 D4
Mahovo 71 D2
Mähring 53 D4
Maia 34 A4
Maials 37 E4
Maîche 27 E2
Maida 67 F3
Maidenhead 9 F2
Maidstone 11 D3
Maiella, la 64 A2
Maienfeld 58 B2
Maignelay 19 F3
Maigue 14 B3
Maillezais 24 C4
Mailly-le-Camp 20 B4
Main 55 D1
Mainar 36 C4
Mainburg 55 F2
Maine-et-Loire 23 E4
Mainistir na Búille 12 C3
Mainland (Orkney) 3 D1
Mainland (Shetland) 3 F2
Maintenon 19 E4
Mainz 51 F4
Maira 31 E2
Mairena del Alcor 43 D2
Maisach 55 F3
Maison-Neuve 26 B1
Maisons-Blanches, les 25 D4
Maissau 57 E2
Maizières 21 D3
Maja 70 C3
Majales, Pto de los 40 A4
Majdanpek 73 E3
Majevica 72 B3
Majšperk 70 C1
Makarska 75 E2
Makce 73 E3
Makedonía 79 F2
Makedonija 77 E3
Makedonija 77 F3
Makedonski Brod 77 D3
Makljen 75 E1
Makó 114 B1
Makovo 77 E4
Makrakómi 83 E3
Mákri 81 E2
Makríamos 80 C3
Makrigialos 79 F3
Makrigialós 91 F4
Makrihóri (Makedonía) 80 C2
Makrihóri (Thessalía) 83 E1
Makrinítsa 83 F2
Makrinóros 82 C3
Makriplágio 80 C2
Makrirráhi 83 E3
Makrivrahos, Akr 81 E3
Makrohóri 79 E3
Makronissi 88 A2
Maksniemi 99 D3
Mala 14 B4
Malå 98 A4
Mala Bosna 72 B1
Malacky 57 F2
Maladeta 37 E2
Malaga 43 F4
Malagón 40 A4
Malahide 13 E4
Malaja Višera 111 E1
Malaja Viska 113 F2
Mala Kapela 70 C3
Mala Krsna 73 D3
Malalbergo 61 D2
Malámata 83 D4
Malandríno 83 E4
Malangen 94 B2
Mälaren 106 B3
Mala Subotica 71 D1
Malaucène 30 C3
Malax 102 B2
Malbork 110 B4
Malbuisson 27 D3
Malcata, Sa de 39 D2
Malcesine 58 C4
Malchin 49 D2
Malchiner See 49 D2
Malchow 49 D2
Maldegem 50 B3
Maldon 11 D2
Malé 58 C3
Maléas, Akr 87 E4
Máleme 90 B3
Malène, la 29 F3
Malente Gremsmühlen 48 B2
Male Pijace 72 C1
Máles 91 E4
Malesherbes 25 F1
Malessina 83 F3
Malestroit 22 C3
Malgomaj 97 F4
Malgrat de Mar 32 B4
Mália 91 E3
Malicorne 23 E4
Mali Haian 70 C4
Mali Iddos 72 B2
Mali kanal 72 B2
Mali Lošinj 70 B4
Malin 113 E2
Malines 50 B3
Malin Head 13 D1
Malinska 70 B3
Mali Požerevac 73 D3
Mališevo 77 D2
Maliskylä 103 D1
Malit, Maj'e 76 C3
Mali Zvornik 72 B4
Maljen 72 C4
Malko Târnovo 115 E2
Mallaig 2 B4
Mållejus 95 D2
Mallén 36 C3
Mallersdorf-Pfaffenberg 56 B2
Malles Venosta 58 C2
Mallnitz 59 E2
Mallorca 45 E2
Mallow 14 B4
Mallwyd 6 A3
Malm 101 D1
Malmberget 98 B2
Malmédy 51 D4
Malmesbury 9 E2
Malmköping 106 A4
Malmö 108 C3
Malmöhus Län 109 D3
Malmslätt 106 A4
Malo 59 D4
Maloja 58 B3
Malojaroslavec 111 F3
Malo Konjari 77 E4
Malo-les-Bains 19 F1
Malónas 93 F1
Malori 64 B4
Måløy 100 A3
Malpartida de Cáceres 39 D3
Malpartida de Plasencia 39 E2
Malpica (E) 34 A1
Malpica (P) 38 C3
Mals 58 C2
Målselv 94 B3
Målselva 94 B3
Målsnes 94 B3
Malsta 101 F3
Malta 59 F2
Malta / 68 B4
Maltby 7 D2
Maltiotunturi 95 F4
Malton 7 D1
Maluenda 36 C4
Malung 105 E2
Malungsfors 101 D4
Malveira 38 A4
Malvik 100 C2
Malzieu-Ville, le 29 F2
Mamaia 115 E1
Mamarrosa 38 B1
Mamers 23 F3
Mammola 67 F4
Mamonovo 110 B4
Mampodre 35 E2
Mamry, Jez 110 B4
Manacor 45 F3
Manacore 64 C2
Manamansalo 99 E4
Manasija 73 E3
Mancha Real 44 A2
Manche 18 B3
Manchester 6 C2
Manching 55 F2
Manciano 63 D2
Mandal 104 B4
Mandal selva 104 B4
Mandamádos 85 F2
Mandas 66 B3
Mandela 63 F2
Mandelieu 31 E4
Manderscheid 51 E4
Mandínia 87 D2
Mandoúdi 84 A3
Mandráki 89 F4
Mándra (Stereá Eláda) 87 F1
Mándra (Thráki) 81 F2
Mandre 70 B4
Mandrikó 93 E1
Mandrioli, Pso dei 61 D3
Manduria 65 E4
Måne 104 C3
Manerbio 60 B1
Manětín 53 E4
Manfredonia 64 C2
Manfredonia, G di 64 C2
Mangalia 115 E2
Mángana 81 D2
Manganári 88 C4
Manger 104 A2
Mangerton Mt 14 B4
Mangrt, Planica 59 F2
Mangualde 38 C1
Maniago 59 E3
Manilva 43 E4
Man, I of 6 A1
Máni (Pelopónissos) 87 D4
Máni (Thráki) 81 F1
Manisa 115 E4
Mánises 41 E4
Manjača 71 E4
Mank 57 E3
Månkarbo 106 B3
Manlleu 32 B3
Mannersdorf 57 F3
Mannheim 54 C1
Mannu 66 B4
Manojlovac slap 75 D1
Manojlovce 77 E1
Manoppello 64 A2
Manorhamilton 12 C2
Manosque 30 C3
Manresa 32 A4
Manschnow 49 F4
Mansfeld 52 C2
Mansfield 7 D3
Mansilla de las Mulas 35 E3
Mansilla, Emb de 36 B3
Mansle 25 D4
Manteigas 38 C2
Mantes 19 E4
Mantiel 40 C2
Mäntlahti 103 F4
Mantorp 109 E1
Mantova 60 C2
Mäntsälä 107 F2
Mänttä 103 D3
Mäntyharju 103 E3
Mäntyjärvi 99 E2
Mäntyluoto 102 B3
Manzanal, Pto del 35 D2
Manzanares 40 B4
Manzanares el Real 40 A2
Manzaneda 34 C3
Manzanera 41 E3
Manzat 26 A4
Manziana 63 E2
Maó 45 F2
Maqellarë 77 D3
Maqueda 40 A2
Maramureș 112 C3
Maranchón 40 C1
Maranchón, Pto de 40 C1
Maranello 60 C2
Maranhão, Bgem do 38 B4
Marano 59 F3
Marano di Napoli 64 B4
Marano, L di 59 F4
Marans 24 B4
Marão, Sa do 34 B4
Marássia 81 F1
Maratea 67 E2
Marateca 38 A4
Marathéa 83 D2
Marathiá, Akr 86 A2
Marathiás 83 D4
Marathókambos 89 E1
Marathónas 87 F1
Marathópoli 86 B3
Márathos 83 F2
Marbach 55 D2
Mårbacka 105 E3
Marbella 43 E4
Marburg 17 F4
Marby 101 E2
Marčana 70 A4
March (A) 57 F2
March (GB) 10 C1
Marchamalo 40 B2
Marchaux 27 D2
Marche 61 E4
Marche-en-Famenne 50 C4
Marchegg 57 F2
Marchena 43 E3
Marchenoir 25 E1
Marchiennes 20 A1
Marciac 28 C4
Marciana Marina 62 C1
Marcianise 64 B3
Marcigny 26 B4
Marcilla 36 C2
Marcillac-Vallon 29 E3
Marcillat-en-Combraille 25 F4
Marcilly-le-Hayer 20 B4
Marckolsheim 27 E1
Marco de Canaveses 34 A4
Marcoule 30 B3
Mære 101 D1
Maree, L 2 C3
Mare Ligure 60 A4
Marene 31 E2
Marennes 28 A1
Marentes 34 C2
Maréttimo, I- 68 A3
Mareuil (Dordogne) 28 C1
Mareuil (Vendée) 24 B3
Margarites 91 D3
Margaríti 82 B2
Margate 11 D2
Margherita di Savoia 65 D3
Marguerittes 30 B3
Maria 44 C2
Maria Cristina, Emb de 41 E3
Mariannelund 109 E1
Mariánské Lázně 53 E4
Maria Saal 70 A1
Maria Taferl 57 E2
Mariazell 57 E3
Maribo 108 B4
Maribor 70 C1
Mariborsko Pohorje 70 C1
Marica 115 D3
Mariefred 106 B4
Mariehamn 106 C3
Marienberg 53 E3
Marienborn 52 C1
Marienburg 51 E4
Marienstedt 48 B3
Mariestad 105 E4
Marignane 30 C4
Marigny 18 B3
Marigny-le-Châtel 20 B4
Marija Bistrica 70 C2
Marikirk 3 E4
Marin 34 A2
Marina 75 D2
Marina di Camerota 67 D2
Marina di Campo 62 C2
Marina di Carrara 60 B3

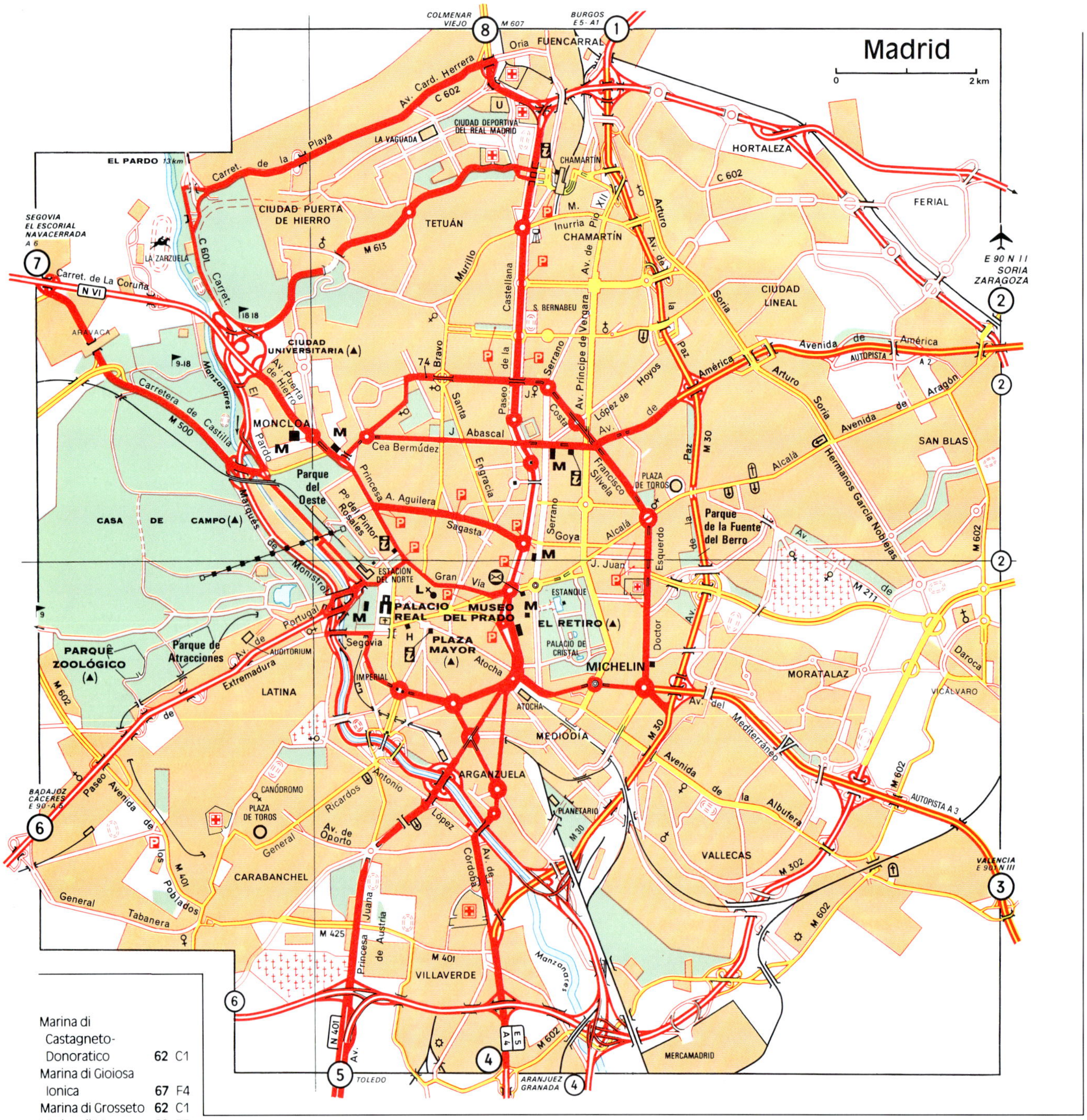
Madrid
0
2 km
COLMENAR VIEJO
M 607
BURGOS E5 - A1
FUENCARRAL
HORTALEZA
FERIAL
E 90 N II SORIA ZARAGOZA
CIUDAD LINEAL
SAN BLAS
CIUDAD PUERTA DE HIERRO
TETUÁN
CHAMARTÍN
EL PARDO 13 km
SEGOVIA EL ESCORIAL NAVACERRADA A 6
CIUDAD UNIVERSITARIA (▲)
MONCLOA
Parque del Oeste
CASA DE CAMPO (▲)
ESTACIÓN DEL NORTE
PALACIO REAL
MUSEO DEL PRADO
EL RETIRO (▲)
PLAZA MAYOR (▲)
MICHELIN
Parque de la Fuente del Berro
MORATALAZ
VICÁLVARO
PARQUE ZOOLÓGICO (▲)
Parque de Atracciones
LATINA
MEDIODÍA
ARGANZUELA
CARABANCHEL
VALLECAS
VILLAVERDE
MERCAMADRID
BADAJOZ CÁCERES E 90 - A 5
VALENCIA E 901 N III
TOLEDO
ARANJUEZ GRANADA

Marina di Castagneto-Donoratico 62 C1
Marina di Gioiosa Ionica 67 F4
Marina di Grosseto 62 C1
Marina di Massa 60 B3
Marina di Pietrasanta 60 B3
Marina di Pisa 60 C4
Marina di Ragusa 69 D4
Marina di Ravenna 61 D2
Marinella 68 B3
Marineo 68 B3
Marines 19 E3
Maringues 26 A4
Marinha Grande 38 A2
Marinkainen 102 C1
Marino 63 E3
Marismas, Pto de las 43 D2
Marjaniemi 99 D4
Marjina Gorka 111 D4
Markaryd 109 D3
Markdorf 55 D4
Marken 16 C2
Markermeer 16 C2
Market Drayton 6 C3
Market Harborough 9 F1
Markethill 13 D2
Market Rasen 7 D2
Market Weighton 7 D2
Markgröningen 55 D2
Markina 36 B1
Markisch Buchholz 53 E1
Markkleeberg 53 D2
Markneukirchen 53 D4
Markópoulo (Kefaloniá) 86 A1
Markópoulo (Atikí-Piréas) 84 B4
Markópoulo (Atikí-Piréas) 87 F1
Markovac (Srbija) 73 D3
Markovac (Vojvodina) 73 D2
Markov manastir 77 E3
Markranstädt 53 D2
Markstein, le 27 E1
Marktbreit 55 E1
Markt Erlbach 55 E1
Marktheidenfeld 55 D1
Markt Indersdorf 55 F3
Marktl 56 B3
Marktoberdorf 55 E4
Marktredwitz 53 D4
Markt St Florian 57 D3
Markušica 71 F2
Marl 17 E3
Marlborough 9 E2
Marle 20 B2
Marlow (D) 48 C2
Marlow (GB) 9 F2
Marmande 28 C3
Marmara Denizi 115 E3
Marmári 88 A1
Mármaro 85 F4
Marmolada, Mte 59 D3
Marmolejo 43 F2
Marmoutier 21 E4
Marnay 27 D2
Marne 47 F2
Marne (Dépt) 20 B4
Marne *R* 19 F4
Marne au Rhin, Canal de la 20 C4
Marnitz 48 C3
Marofa 39 D1
Marolles-les-Braults 23 F3
Marónia 81 E2
Maronias, Akr 81 E2
Maronne 29 E2
Maros 114 B1
Marostica 59 D4
Marotta 61 E3
Márpissa 88 C3
Marquartstein 56 B3
Marquion 19 F2
Marquise 19 E1
Marradi 61 D3
Marraskoski 99 D2
Marsaglia 60 A2
Marsala 68 A3
Marsberg 17 F3
Marsciano 63 E1
Marseillan 30 A4
Marseille 30 C4
Marseille-en-Beauvaisis 19 E3
Marsfjällen 97 E4
Marsico Nuovo 64 C4
Marske-by-the-Sea 5 F4
Mars-la-Tour 21 D3
Märsta 106 B3
Marstal 108 B4
Marstrand 108 C1
Marta 63 D2
Martano 65 F4
Martel 29 D2
Martelange 21 D2
Martes, Sa de 44 A2
Marthon 28 C1
Martignacco 59 F3
Martigné-Ferchaud 23 D4
Martigny 27 E4
Martigny-les-Bains 27 D1
Martigues 30 C4
Martim Longo 42 B2
Martin 112 B3
Martina 58 C2
Martina Franca 65 E3
Martin Brod 71 D4
Martinci Čepinski 71 F2
Martin de la Jara 43 E3
Martin de Yeltes 39 D1
Martinengo 60 B1
Martinet 32 A3
Martingança 38 A2
Martinniemi 99 D3
Martino 83 F4
Martin, R 41 E1
Martinšćica 70 B4
Martis 66 B2
Martjanci 70 C1
Martofte 108 B3
Martonvaara 103 F2
Martorell 32 A4
Martos 44 A2
Martti 95 F4
Marttila 107 D2
Marvão 38 C3
Marvejols 29 F2
Marxwalde 49 E4
Maryport 5 D4
Mary, Puy 29 E2
Marzagran 20 B3
Mas-Cabardès 32 B1
Mas-d'Agenais, le 28 C3
Mas-d'Azil, le 37 F1
Mas de Barberans 41 F2
Mas de las Matas 41 E2
Masegoso 40 C2
Masevaux 27 E1
Masi 95 D2
Maside 34 B2
Mask, L 12 B3
Masku 107 D2
Maslenica 74 C1
Maslinica 75 D2
Maslovare 71 E4
Måsøy 95 D1
Maspalomas 42 B4
Massa 60 B3
Massa Fiscaglia 61 D2
Massafra 65 E4
Massamagrell 41 E3
Massa Marittima 62 C1
Massa Martana 63 E1
Massarosa 60 C3
Massat 37 F2
Massegros, le 29 F3
Masseube 28 C4
Massiac 29 F1
Mastihári 89 F3
Mástiho, Akr 89 D1
Masueco 34 C4
Maszewo 49 F2
Mat 76 C3
Matachel, R 43 D1
Mátala 91 D4
Matalascañas 42 C3
Matalavilla, Emb de 35 D2
Matalebreras 36 C3
Matallana 35 D2
Matarànga 83 E2
Mataró 32 B4
Matarraña, R 41 F2
Mataruška Banja 73 D4
Matejče 77 E2
Matelica 61 E4
Matelles, les 30 A4
Matera 65 D4
Matese, Mti del 64 B3
Mateševo 76 B2
Mátészalka 112 C3
Mateus 34 B4
Matfors 101 F3
Matha 24 C4
Mathráki, N 78 A4
Máti 88 A1
Matignon 18 A4
Matka 77 D3
Matku 107 E2
Matlock 6 C3
Matosinhos 34 A4
Matour 26 B4
Mátra 112 B3
Matrei (Osttirol) 59 E2
Matrei (Tirol) 59 D2
Matterhorn 27 E4
Mattersburg 57 F3
Mattighofen 56 C3
Mattinata 64 C2
Mattsee 56 C3
Mattsmyra 101 E4
Matulji 70 B3
Matute 36 B3
Maubeuge 20 B1
Maubourguet 28 B4
Maubuisson 28 A2
Mauchline 4 C2
Mauerkirchen 56 C3
Mauguio 30 B4
Maula 99 D3
Maulbronn 54 C2
Maulde 29 D1
Mauléon 24 C3
Mauléon-Licharre 28 A4
Maumturk Mts. 12 B3
Maun 70 B4
Maure 23 D3
Maure, Col de 31 D3
Maures, Massif des 31 D4
Mauriac 29 E2
Mauria, Pso 59 E3
Mauron 22 C3
Maurs 29 E2
Mautern 57 D4
Mauterndorf 59 F1
Mauthausen 57 D2
Mauvezin 28 C4
Mauvoisin, Bge de 27 E4
Mauzé 24 C4
Mavrohóri 79 D3
Mavroklissio 81 F1
Mavroléfki 80 C2
Mavromáta 83 D3
Mavromáti 83 D2
Mavroúda 80 B3
Mavrovi Anovi 77 D3
Mavrovo 77 D3
Mavrovo, nac park 77 D3
Mavrovoúni (Makedonía) 79 E3
Mavrovoúni *Mt* 83 F1
Mavrovoúni (Thessalía) 83 E2
Mavrovsko ezero 77 D3
Maxhütte-Haidof 56 B1
Maxmo 102 B2
Maybole 4 C3
Mayen 51 E4
Mayenne 23 E3
Mayenne (Dépt) 23 E3
Mayenne *R* 23 E3
Mayerling 57 E3

1/200000
MANCHESTER
SALFORD
BOLTON
WIGAN
BURY
ROCHDALE
OLDHAM
STOCKPORT
WARRINGTON
Chorley
Heywood
Middleton
Prestwich
Radcliffe
Farnworth
Atherton
Tyldesley
Hindley
Leigh
Golborne
Swinton
Eccles
Worsley
Urmston
Stretford
Sale
Altrincham
Cheadle
Gatley
Wilmslow
Hyde
Denton
Ashton-under-Lyne
Stalybridge
Failsworth
Chadderton
Royton
Shaw
Milnrow
Littleborough
Horwich
Westhoughton
Lymm
Poynton
Marple
Romiley
Bredbury
Droylsden
Dukinfield
Mossley
MANCHESTER AIRPORT
Preston
Blackburn
Burnley
Leeds
Liverpool
Barnsley, Sheffield
Buxton, Chesterfield
Macclesfield
Stoke-on-Trent
Chester
Birmingham
Nantwich, Whitchurch
2°20
2°
53°20

Mayet 23 F4
Mayet-de-Montagne, le 26 B4
Maynooth 13 D4
Mayo 12 B2
Mayor, C 35 F1
Mayorga 35 E3
Mayrhofen 59 D2
Maza, Barrié Emb de la 34 A2
Mazagón 42 C3
Mazamet 32 B1
Mazara d. Vallo 68 A3
Mazarakiá 82 B2
Mazarete 40 C1
Mazarrón 45 D3
Mazarrón, G de 45 D3
Mažeikiai 110 B3
Mazères 32 A1
Mázi 78 C4
Mazières-en-Gâtine 24 C3
Mazorra, Pto de la 36 A2
Mazury 110 B4
Mazzarino 68 C4
Mazzarò 69 D3
Mealhada 38 B2
Meath 13 D3
Meaux 19 F4
Mechelen 50 B3
Meckenbeuren 55 D4
Mecklenburg-Vorpommern 49 D2
Mecklenburger B 48 C1
Meda 38 C1
Medda 73 D2
Medak 70 C4
Mede 60 A2
Medebach 17 F4
Meddedda 76 B1
Medelim 38 C2
Medellin 39 E4
Medel, Piz 58 A3
Medemblik 16 C2
Medena Selišta 71 E4
Mediano, Emb de 37 E2
Mediaş 113 D4
Medicina 61 D2
Medina Azahara 43 E2
Medinaceli 36 B4
Medina del Campo 35 E4
Medina de Pomar 36 A1
Medina de Rioseco 35 E4
Medina-Sidonia 43 D4
Médous, Grotte de 37 E1
Médoussa 81 D1
Medugorje 75 F2
Medulin 70 A4
Medđumajdan 71 D3
Meduna 59 E3
Meduno 59 E3
Medurečje 76 C1
Medvedda 77 D1
Medvednica 70 C2
Medveja 70 B3
Medvida 74 C1
Medvode 70 B2
Medyn' 111 F3
Medžitlija 77 E4
Meerane 53 D3
Meersburg 55 D4
Mées, les 31 D3
Mefjordbotn 94 B2
Mefjordvær 94 B2
Méga Dério 81 F2
Mega Horió (Stereá Eláda) 83 D3
Megalohóri 83 D1
Megalópoli 86 C2
Meganissi 82 B3
Megaplátanos 83 F3
Mégara 87 E1
Megárhi 83 D1
Méga Spileo 86 C1
Megève 27 E4
Megaló Horió (Agathonissi 89 F2
Megaló Horió (Tilos) 89 F4
Megisti 93 F2
Megisti, N 93 F2
Megístis Lávras 80 C4
Meg. Livádi 88 A3
Meg. Panagía 80 B3
Meg. Vólvi 80 B3
Mehamn 95 E1
Mehedeby 106 B2
Mehov Krš 76 C2
Mehun 25 F2
Meigle 5 D1
Meijel 17 D4
Meije, la 31 D2
Meilen 58 A2
Meillant 25 F3
Meimoa 38 C2
Meina 58 A4
Meinerzhagen 17 E4
Meiningen 52 B3
Meira 34 C1
Meira, Sa de 34 C1
Meiringen 27 F3
Meisenheim 54 B1
Meißen 53 E2
Meitingen 55 E3
Mel 59 E3
Melalahti 99 E4
Mélambes 91 D4
Melaniós 85 E4
Melánthio 78 C3
Melátes 82 C2
Melbeck 48 B3
Melbu 94 A3
Meldal 100 C2
Meldola 61 D3
Meldorf 47 F2
Melegnano 60 A1
Mêle, le 19 D4
Melenci 72 C2
Melendugno 65 F4
Melfi 64 C3
Melfjorden 97 E2
Melgaço 34 B3
Melgar de Abajo 35 E3
Melgar de Fernamental 35 F3
Melhus 100 C2
Melía 83 E2
Melide 34 B2
Melides 42 A1
Melidóni 91 D3
Meligalás 86 C3
Meliki 79 E3
Melilli 69 D4
Mélisey 27 D1
Mélissa 81 D2
Mélissa, Akr 82 B4
Melissáni 82 B4
Melíssi 87 D1
Melissohóri 84 A4
Melissópetra 78 C4
Melissourgós 80 B3
Meliti 279 D2
Melito di Porto Salvo 67 E4
Melivia (Thessalía) 83 F1

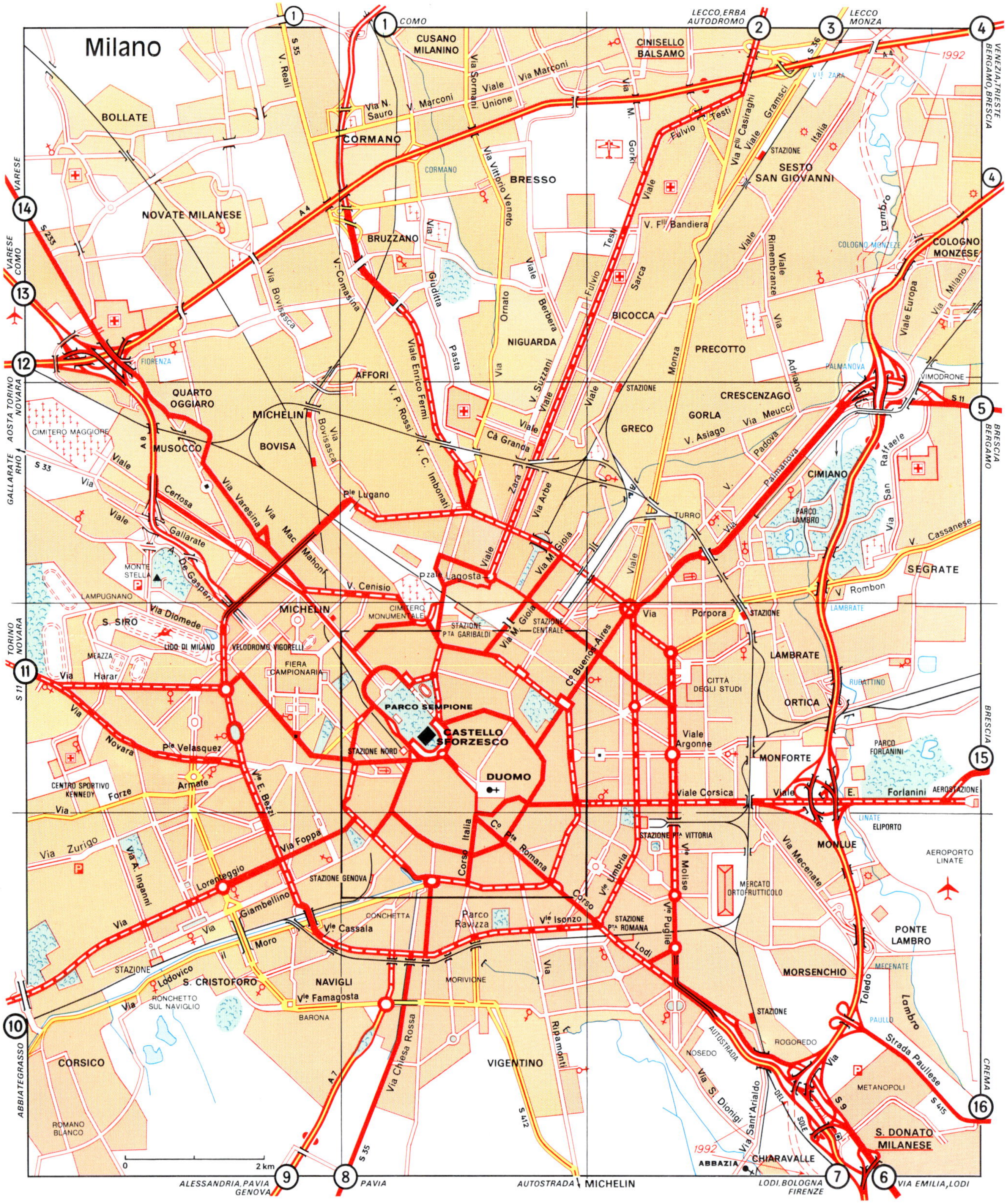
Milano
COMO
CUSANO MILANINO
LECCO, ERBA AUTODROMO
LECCO MONZA
CINISELLO BALSAMO
VENEZIA, TRIESTE BERGAMO, BRESCIA
BOLLATE
CORMANO
BRESSO
SESTO SAN GIOVANNI
NOVATE MILANESE
BRUZZANO
COLOGNO MONZESE
VARESE
VARESE COMO
BICOCCA
NIGUARDA
PRECOTTO
AFFORI
QUARTO OGGIARO
MICHELIN
CRESCENZAGO
GORLA
GRECO
AOSTA TORINO NOVARA
GALLARATE RHO
MUSOCCO
BOVISA
CIMIANO
BRESCIA BERGAMO
SEGRATE
LAMPUGNANO
S. SIRO
MICHELIN
LAMBRATE
TORINO NOVARA
FIERA CAMPIONARIA
CITTÀ DEGLI STUDI
ORTICA
PARCO SEMPIONE
CASTELLO SFORZESCO
DUOMO
MONFORTE
BRESCIA
PARCO FORLANINI
STAZIONE CENTRALE
STAZIONE NORD
STAZIONE GENOVA
AEROPORTO LINATE
MONLUE
PONTE LAMBRO
MORSENCHIO
S. CRISTOFORO
NAVIGLI
CORSICO
VIGENTINO
ROGOREDO
METANOPOLI
ABBIATEGRASSO
CREMA
ROMANO BLANCO
S. DONATO MILANESE
CHIARAVALLE
ABBAZIA
0
2 km
ALESSANDRIA, PAVIA GENOVA
PAVIA
AUTOSTRADA
MICHELIN
LODI, BOLOGNA FIRENZE
VIA EMILIA, LODI

Melivia (Thráki) 81 D1
Melk 57 E2
Melksham 9 E2
Mellan Fryken 105 E3
Mellansel 102 A2
Melle (D) 17 F2
Melle (F) 24 C4
Mellerstair 5 D2
Mellerud 105 D4
Mellieha 68 B4
Mellifont Abbey 13 D3
Mellilä 107 D2
Mellin 48 B4
Mellingen 52 C3
Mellrichstadt 52 B4
Mellum 47 F3
Melnica 73 E3
Melnice 70 B3
Mělnik 53 F3
Mělnik 53 F4
Melogno, Colle di 31 F3
Meløy 97 E2
Meløyfjorden 97 E2
Melpers 52 B3
Melrose 5 D2
Melsungen 52 A3
Meltaus 99 D2
Melton Mowbray 7 D3
Meltosjärvi 99 D2
Melun 19 F4
Melvich 3 D2
Melvin, L 12 C2
Membrilla 40 B4
Membrio 38 C3
Memmingen 55 E3
Mena 113 F1
Menaggio 58 B4
Menai Bridge 6 A2
Ménalo, Óros 86 C2
Menasalbas 40 A3
Menat 26 A4
Mencal 44 B3
Mendavia 36 B2
Mende 29 F3
Mendelpass 59 D3
Menden 17 E3
Mendenitsa 83 E3
Menderes, B 115 F4
Mendola, Pso della 59 D3
Mendrisio 58 A4
Menée, Col de 30 C2
Menen 50 A3
Menesjärvi 95 E3
Menetés 93 D3
Ménez-Hom 22 B3
Menfi 68 B3
Mengamuñoz 39 F2
Menga, Pto de 39 F2
Mengara 61 E4
Mengen 55 D3
Mengeš 70 B2
Mengibar 44 A2
Menídi 82 C2
Ménigoute 24 C3
Menikio, Óros 80 B2
Mennetou 25 E2
Menorca 45 F1
Menor, Mar 45 D2
Mens 30 C2
Mentana 63 E2
Menthon 27 D4
Menton 31 E3
Méntrida 40 A2
Menuires, les 31 D1
Meppel 17 D2
Meppen 17 E2
Mequinenza 37 E4
Mequinenza, Emb de 37 E4
Mer Adriatique 74 B2
Meråker 101 D2
Meran 59 D2
Merano 59 D2
Merate 60 A1
Mercadal 45 F1
Mercante, Pso di 67 E4
Mercantour, Parc Nat du 31 E3
Mercatale (Marche) 61 E3
Mercatale (Toscana) 61 D4
Mercatino Conca 61 E3
Mercator San Severino 64 B4
Mercato Saraceno 61 D3
Merćez 77 D1
Mercœur 29 D2
Mer de Crète 90 C2
Merdrignac 22 C3
Mer du Nord 16 A2
Mere 9 D3
Mer Égée 85 D4
Méréville 25 F1
Mergozzo 58 A4
Méribel 31 D1
Mérida 39 D4
Mérignac 28 B2
Mérihas 88 A2
Merijärvi 99 D4
Merikarvia 102 B3
Mering 55 F3
Merkendorf 55 E2
Merklingen 55 D3
Merlerault, le 19 D4
Mer Noir 115 F1
Merošina 77 D1
Merrenkurkku 102 B2
Merrick 4 C3
Mers 19 E2
Mersch 21 D2
Merseburg 53 D2
Merthyr Tydfil 8 C2
Mértola 42 B2
Méru 19 F3
Méry 20 B4
Merville (Calvados) 18 C3
Merville (Pas-de-Calais) 19 F1
Merzig 54 A2
Mesagne 65 F3
Mesão Frio 34 B4
Meschede 17 F3
Mescherin 49 E3
Meschers 28 A1
Mešeišta 77 D4
Mesići 76 A1
Mesihovina 75 E1
Meslay 23 E3
Mesocco 58 B3
Mesola 61 D2
Mesón do Vento 34 B1
Mesoraca 67 F3
Mespelbrunn 52 A4
Messanagrós 93 E2
Messarás, Órmos 91 D4
Messariá 88 B1
Meßdorf 48 C4
Messei 18 C4
Méssi 81 D2
Messiméri 79 F3
Messimvría 81 E2
Messina 69 D2
Messíni 86 C3
Messinia 86 C3
Messiniakós Kólpos 86 C4
Meßkirch 55 D3
Messlingen 101 D2
Messohóra 82 C2
Messohóri (Kárpathos) 93 D3
Messohóri (Thessalía) 83 E1
Messolóngi 82 C4
Messongí 82 A2
Messopótamo 82 B2
Messótopos 85 E2
Meßstetten 55 D3
Mestá 85 E4
Mesta 115 D3
Mestanza 44 A1
Mésti 81 E2
Mestlin 48 C2
Mestre 61 D1
Mesvres 26 B3
Metajna 70 C4
Meta, la 64 A2
Metalika 76 B1
Metalikó 79 F2
Metalio 83 E3
Metamórfossi (Halkidikí) 80 B4
Metamórfossi (Kilkís) 79 F2
Metangitsi 80 B4
Metanopoli 60 A1
Metauro 61 E3
Metaxádes 81 F1
Metéora 83 D1
Méthana 87 E2
Methil 5 D2
Methóni (Makedonía) 79 F3
Methóni (Pelopónissos) 86 C3

Metković 75 F2
Metlika 70 C2
Metnitz 57 D4
Metóhi (Ahaïa) 86 B1
Metóhi (Argolída) 87 E2
Metóhi (Évia) 84 B3
Metóhi (Thessalía) 83 F2
Metsäkylä 99 E3
Metsäkylä 103 F4
Metsämaa 107 E2
Métsovo 82 C1
Mettingen 17 E2
Mettlach 54 A1
Mettmann 17 E4
Metz 21 D3
Metzervisse 21 D3
Metzingen 55 D3
Meulan 19 E3
Meung 25 E2
Meursault 26 C3
Meurthe-et-Moselle 21 D4
Meuse 20 C3
Meuse (Dépt) 20 C3
Meuselwitz 53 D2
Mevagissey 8 B4
Meximieux 26 C4
Meyenburg 48 C3
Meymac 29 E1
Meyrand, Col de 30 B2
Meyrueis 29 F3
Meyzieu 26 C4
Mezas 39 D2
Mezdra 115 D2
Mèze 30 A4
Mézel 31 D3
Mézenc, Mt 30 B2
Mežgorje 112 C3
Mežica 70 B1
Mézidon 18 C3
Mézières 25 D4
Mezières-en-Brenne 25 E3
Mézin 28 C3
Mezőberény 112 C4
Mezőkövesd 112 B4
Mezőtúr 112 B4
Mezquita de Jarque 41 E2
Mezzano 59 D3
Mezzolombardo 58 C3
Mgarr 68 B4
Miajadas 39 E4
Miastko 110 A4
Michalovce 112 C3
Micheldorf 57 D3
Michelstadt 55 D1
Michendorf 49 D4
Mičurin 115 E2
Middelburg 16 B3
Middelfart 108 B3
Middelharnis 16 B3
Middelkerke-Bad 50 A3
Middlesbrough 5 F4
Middleton-in-Teesdale 5 E4
Middlewich 6 C3
Midhurst 9 F3
Midi, Canal du 32 B1
Midi de Bigorre, Pic du 37 E2
Midi d'Ossau, Pic du 37 D2
Midleton 14 C4
Midouze 28 B3
Midsund 100 B2
Mid Yell 3 F1
Miedes 36 C4
Miedwie, Jez 49 F3
Międzychód 112 A1
Międzylesie 112 A2
Międzyrzec Podlaski 112 C1
Międzyzdroje 49 E2
Miehikkälä 103 F4
Miekojärvi 98 C2
Miélan 28 C4
Mielec 112 B2
Mielno 49 F1
Mieluskylä 103 D1
Miera, *R* 35 F2
Miercurea-Ciuc 113 D4
Mieres 35 D2
Miesbach 56 B3
Mieszkowice 49 E3
Mietoinen 107 D2
Miettila 103 F3
Migennes 26 A1
Migliarino 61 D2
Miglionico 65 D4
Miguel Esteban 40 B3
Miguelturra 40 A4
Mihajlovac (Srbija) 73 D3
Mihajlovac (Srbija) 73 F3
Mihajlovgrad 115 D2
Mihas 86 C1
Mihói 86 B1
Mijas 43 E4
Mijoux 27 D3
Miki 81 D2
Mikínes 87 D2
Mikkeli 103 E3
Mikkelin Lääni 103 E3
Mikkelvik 94 B2
Mikleuš 71 E2
Míkonos 88 C2
Míkonos, N 88 C2
Mikrí Mandínia 86 C3
Mikrí Préspa, L 78 C3
Mikró Horió 83 D3
Mikrókambos 79 F2
Mikroklissoúra 80 B1
Mikrolímni 78 C3
Mikromiliá 80 C1
Mikrón Dério 81 F1
Mikron Eleftherohóri 79 E4
Mikrópoli 80 B2
Mikulov 57 F1
Milagro 36 C2
Milano 60 A1
Milano Marittimo 61 E3
Milatos 91 E3
Milazzo 69 D2
Mileševo (Srbija) 76 B1
Mileševo (Vojvodina) 72 C1
Milestone 14 C3
Miletići 70 C4
Mileto 67 E3
Miletto, Mte 64 B3
Milevsko 57 D1
Milford (GB) 9 F3
Milford (IRL) 13 D1
Milford Haven 8 B2
Milhão 34 C4
Mili 87 D2
Miliá (Makedonía) 79 D4
Miliá (Pelopónissos) 87 D2
Miliá (Thráki) 81 F1
Milići 72 B4
Miliés 83 F2
Milin 53 F4
Milína 83 F2
Milis 66 B3
Militello in Val di C. 69 D3
Miljevina 76 A1
Millas 32 B2
Millau 29 F3
Millesimo 31 F2
Millevaches, Plateau de 29 D1
Millom 6 B1
Millport 4 C2
Millstatt 59 F2
Millstreet 14 B4
Milltown Malbay 12 B4
Milly 19 F4
Milmarcos 36 C4
Milmersdorf 49 E3
Milna 75 D2
Miločer 76 B3
Milohnić 70 B3
Milopótamos 90 A1
Milos 88 A4
Miloševa Kula 73 E3
Milos, N 88 A4
Miltach 56 B1
Miltenberg 55 D1
Milton Keynes 9 F2
Milutinovac 73 F2
Mimizan 28 A3
Mimizan-Plage 28 A3
Mimoň 53 F3
Mina 87 D4
Mina de São Domingos 42 B2
Minas de Riotinto 42 C2
Minaya 40 C4
Minch, The 2 B2
Mincio 60 C1
Mindelheim 55 E3
Minden 17 F2
Mindin 24 A2
Minehead 8 C3
Minerbe 60 C1
Minerbio 61 D2
Minervino Murge 65 D3
Minglanilla 41 D3
Mingorria 39 F1
Minguez, Pto 41 D2
Mingulay 2 A4
Minho 34 A3
Minićevo 73 F4
Minilla, Emb de la 43 D2
Ministra, Sierra 36 B4
Minkiö 107 E2
Miño, R 34 B2
Minsk 111 D4
Mińsk Mazowiecki 112 B1
Minsterley 9 D1
Minthi, Óros 86 C2
Mintlaw 3 E3
Miokovićevo 71 E2
Mionica 72 C3
Mionnay 26 C4
Mira (E) 41 D3
Mira (I) 61 D1
Mira (P) 38 B1
Mirabella Imbaccari 68 C4
Mira de Aire 38 B3
Mirador de Coto Rondo 34 A2
Mirador del Fito 35 E1
Miraflores 35 F3
Miraflores de la Sierra 40 A1
Miramar (F) 31 E4
Miramar (P) 34 A4
Miramare 61 E3
Miramas 30 C4
Mirambeau 28 B1
Mirambélou, Kólpos 91 F3
Miramont-de-Guyenne 28 C2
Miranda de Ebro 36 B2
Miranda del Castañar 39 E2
Miranda do Corvo 38 B2
Miranda do Douro 34 C4
Mirande 28 C4
Mirandela 34 C4
Mirandola 60 C2
Mirano 61 D1
Mira, R 42 A2
Mirador de Llesba 35 E2
Miravalles 34 C2
Miravci 77 F3
Miravete, Pto de 39 E3
Mirditë 76 C3
Mirebeau (Côte-d'Or) 26 C2
Mirebeau (Vienne) 25 D3
Mirecourt 27 D1
Mirepoix 32 A2
Mires 91 D4
Mirgorod 113 F2
Miribel 26 C4
Mirina 85 D1
Mirna 70 B2
Mirna *R* 70 A3
Miroč 73 E3
Mironovka 113 E2
Miroševce 77 E1
Mirotice 56 C1
Mirovice 56 C1
Mirow 49 D3
Mirsini 87 D4
Mirtiés 89 E3
Mirtóo Pélagos 87 E3
Mirtos 91 E4
Mirtos, Akr 93 E2
Mirtou, Kólpos 82 B4
Mirueña 39 F1
Mišar 72 C3
Misi 99 D2
Misilmeri 68 B3
Miskolc 112 B3
Mislinja 70 B1
Mistelbach 57 F2
Misterbianco 69 D3
Mistrás 87 D3
Mistretta 68 C3
Místros 84 B4
Misurina 59 E2
Mitchelstown 14 C3
Mittelland-Kanal 17 F2
Míthimna 85 F2
Mítikas 82 C3
Mítikas *Mt* 79 E4
Mitilíni 85 F2
Mitilinii 89 E1
Mitrašinci 77 F3
Mitrópoli 83 D2
Mitsikéli, Óros 82 B1
Mittelberg (Tirol) 58 C2
Mittelberg (Vorarlberg) 58 B2
Mittenwald 55 F4
Mittenwalde 49 E4
Mittersill 59 E1
Mitterteich 53 D4
Mittweida 53 E2
Mizen Head 14 A4
Mjällån 101 F2
Mjällom 102 A2
Mjöbäck 108 C2
Mjölby 109 E1
Mjøndalen 104 C3
Mjøsa 105 D2
Mladá Boleslav 112 A2
Mladá Vožice 57 D1
Mladenovac 73 D3
Mlado Nagoričane 77 E2
Mladost, Ez 77 E3
Mlava 73 E3
Mława 112 B1
Mlini 76 A2
Mlinište 71 D4
Mljet 75 E2
Mljetski Kanal 75 F2
Mnichovo Hradiště 53 F3
Moälven 102 A2
Moaña 34 A3
Moate 12 C3
Mocejón 40 A3
Möckern 52 C1
Möckmühl 55 D2
Moclin 44 A3
Modane 31 D1
Modbury 8 C4
Modena 60 C2
Módi 83 E3
Modica 69 D4
Modigliana 61 D3
Mödling 57 F2
Modračko jez 71 F3
Modran 71 E3
Modřany 53 F4
Modrava 56 C1
Modriča 71 F3
Modrište 77 D3
Modugno 65 D3
Moëlan 22 B3
Moelv 105 D2
Moen 94 B3
Moena 59 D3
Moers 17 D3
Moesa 58 B3
Moffat 5 D3
Mogadouro 34 C4
Mogadouro, Sa do 34 C4
Mogente 45 D1
Mogila 77 E4
Mogil'ov 111 E4
Mogil'ov-Podol'skij 113 E3
Moglia 60 C2
Mogliano Veneto 59 E4
Mogón 44 B2
Mogorrit 41 D2
Moguer 42 C2
Mohács 114 B1
Moher, Cliffs of 12 B4
Mohill 12 C3
Möhkö 103 F2
Móhlos 91 F4
Möhne 17 F3
Moholm 105 E4
Moi 104 A4
Moià 32 A4
Moie 61 E4
Moimenta 34 C3
Moimenta da Beira 38 C1
Mo i Rana 97 E2
Moirans 30 C1
Moirans-en-Montagne 27 D3
Moisdon 23 D4
Moisiovaara 99 F4
Moisling 48 B2
Moissac 29 D3
Moita 38 A4
Mojácar 44 C3
Mojados 35 E4
Mojkovac 76 B2
Mojón Pardo, Pto de 36 B3
Mojstrana 70 A1
Mokra Gora 72 C4
Mokra Gora *Mts* 76 C2
Mokrin 72 C1
Mokronog 70 B2
Mokro Polje 75 D1
Mol (B) 50 C3
Mol (YU) 72 C1

Monaco
VENTIMIGLIA MENTON
MENTON A 8
A 8
MENTON
COUNTRY CLUB
A 8
D 2564
NICE
GDE CORNICHE
N 7
LA ROUSSA
ST-ROMAN
N 98
MONTE-CARLO BEACH
D 53
Guynemer
CORNICHE INFÉRIEURE
NICE LA TURBIE
Rte de la Turbie
MONT DES MULES
FAUSSIGNANA
PLAGE DU LARVOTTO
SPORTING CLUB
AUREILLA
BEAUSOLEIL
HALL DU CENTENAIRE
MONTE-CARLO
BORDINA
CORNICHE
Casino
MOYENNE
LES MONEGUETTI
PORT
LES RÉVOIRES
N 7
LA CONDAMINE
JARDIN EXOTIQUE
NICE EZE, A 8
MONACO
MUSÉE OCÉANOGRAPHIQUE
0 300 m
FONTVIEILLE
LES SALINES
ST-ANTOINE
HELIPORT
PORT DE CAP-D'AIL
N 98
PLAGE MARQUET
CAP-D'AIL VILLEFRANCHE-S-MER

Mola di Bari 65 E3
Molái 87 D4
Molat 74 B1
Molat *I* 74 B1
Molatón 41 D4
Mold 6 B3
Moldavija 113 E3
Molde 100 B2
Moldefjorden 100 B2
Moldova Nouă 114 C1
Moldoveanu 113 D4
Møldrup 108 B2
Moledo do Minho 34 A3
Molène 22 A2
Molfetta 65 D3
Molières 29 D3
Molina de Aragón 40 C2
Molina de Segura 45 D2
Molinella 61 D2
Molinicos 44 C1
Molins de Rei 32 A4
Molise 64 B2
Moliterno 65 D4
Molitg-les-Bains 32 B2
Mólivos, Akr 85 F2
Molkom 105 E3
Möllbrücke 59 F2
Mollerussa 37 F3
Molliens-Vidame 19 E2
Mollina 43 F3
Mölln 48 B2
Mollösund 108 C1
Mölnlycke 108 C1
Molodečno 111 D4
Mologa 111 F1
Mólos 83 E3
Molpe 102 B2
Mols 108 B3
Molsheim 21 E4
Molve 71 D1
Molveno 58 C3
Mombeltrán 39 F2
Mombuey 35 D3
Mommark 108 B4
Momo 60 A1
Møn 108 C4
Monach, Sd of 2 A3
Monadhliath Mts 2 C4
Monå fjärd 102 B2
Monaghan 13 D2
Monaghan (Co) 13 D2

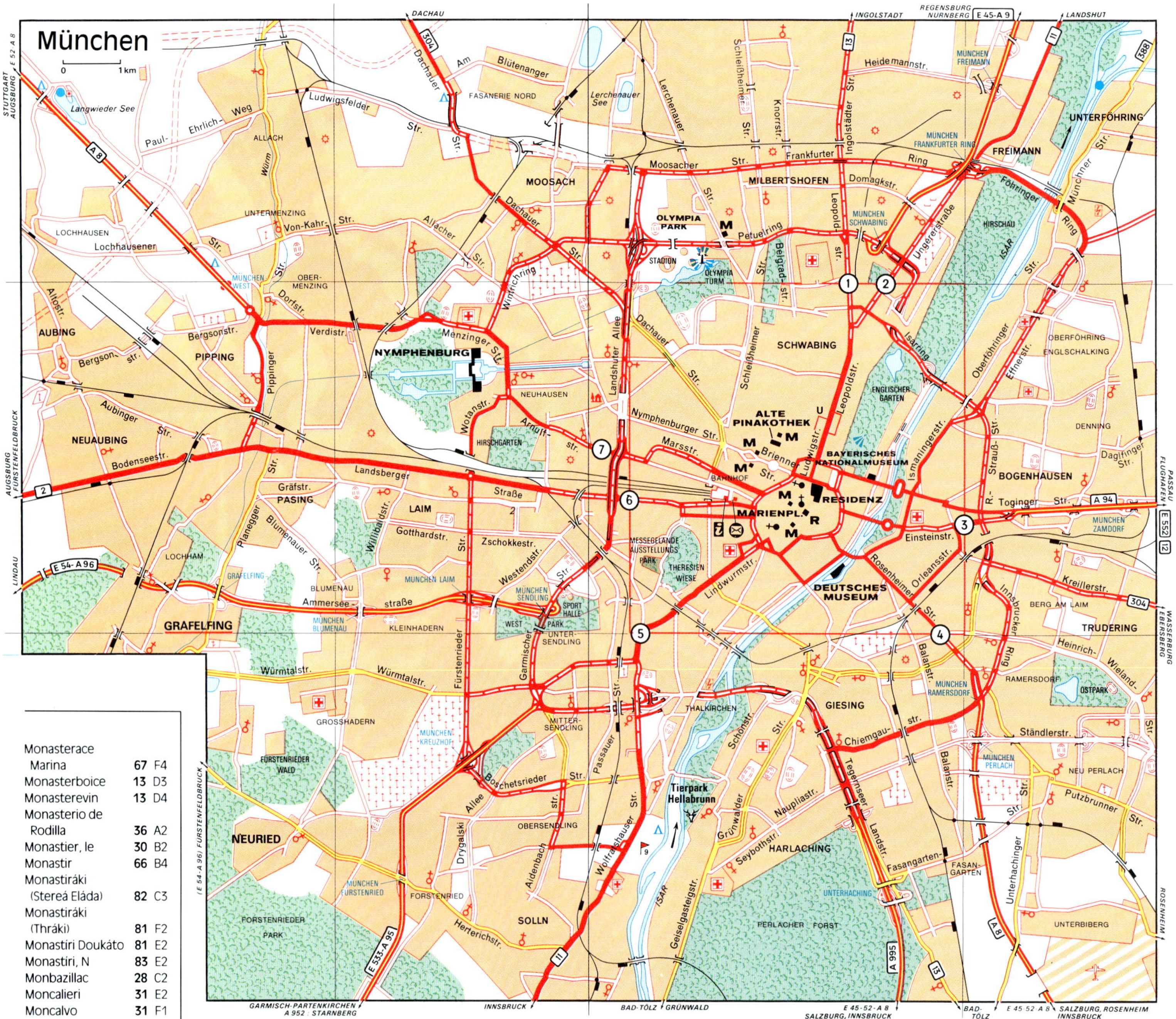
München
0 1 km
DACHAU
INGOLSTADT
REGENSBURG NÜRNBERG E 45-A 9
LANDSHUT
STUTTGART AUGSBURG E 52 A 8
Langwieder See
Paul-Ehrlich-Weg
ALLACH
Ludwigsfelder Str.
FASANERIE NORD
Lerchenauer See
Blütenanger
Heidemannstr.
MÜNCHEN FREIMANN
UNTERFÖHRING
FREIMANN
MOOSACH
Moosacher Str.
MILBERTSHOFEN
Frankfurter Ring
Domagkstr.
MÜNCHEN FRANKFURTER RING
UNTERMENZING
Von-Kahr-Str.
LOCHHAUSEN
Lochhausener Str.
OLYMPIA PARK
STADION
OLYMPIA TURM
Petuelring
MÜNCHEN SCHWABING
HIRSCHAU
ISAR
Föhringer Ring
MÜNCHEN WEST
OBER-MENZING
Dorfstr.
Verdistr.
Menzinger Str.
NYMPHENBURG
AUBING
Bergsonstr.
PIPPING
SCHWABING
OBERFÖHRING
ENGLSCHALKING
ENGLISCHER GARTEN
NEUHAUSEN
NEUAUBING
Bodenseestr.
Aubinger Str.
Wotanstr.
Arnulfstr.
HIRSCHGARTEN
Nymphenburger Str.
ALTE PINAKOTHEK
Marsstr.
Brienner Str.
BAYERISCHES NATIONALMUSEUM
Ismaningerstr.
DENNING
BOGENHAUSEN
Landsberger Straße
PASING
LAIM
Gotthardstr.
Zschokkestr.
RESIDENZ
MARIENPL.
Toginger Str.
MÜNCHEN ZAMDORF
PASSAU FLUGHAFEN
Einsteinstr.
LOCHHAM
LINDAU
E 54-A 96
MESSEGELÄNDE AUSSTELLUNGS PARK
THERESIEN WIESE
Lindwurmstr.
DEUTSCHES MUSEUM
Rosenheimer Str.
Orleansstr.
Kreillerstr.
BERG AM LAIM
TRUDERING
GRÄFELFING
Ammersee-straße
BLUMENAU
MÜNCHEN LAIM
Westendstr.
MÜNCHEN SENDLING
SPORT HALLE
WEST PARK
UNTER-SENDLING
KLEINHADERN
Innsbrucker Ring
WASSERBURG EBERSBERG
Würmtalstr.
GROSSHADERN
MITTER-SENDLING
THALKIRCHEN
GIESING
RAMERSDORF
OSTPARK
Chiemgau-str.
MÜNCHEN RAMERSDORF
Ständlerstr.
FÜRSTENRIEDER WALD
MÜNCHEN KREUZHOF
Boschetsrieder Str.
Tierpark Hellabrunn
MÜNCHEN PERLACH
NEU PERLACH
Putzbrunner Str.
NEURIED
OBERSENDLING
Naupliastr.
HARLACHING
Fasangarten-
FASAN-GARTEN
MÜNCHEN FÜRSTENRIED
FORSTENRIED
SOLLN
Herterichstr.
Wolfratshauser Str.
Geiselgasteigstr.
UNTERHACHING
PERLACHER FORST
Unterhachinger
UNTERBIBERG
ROSENHEIM
FORSTENRIEDER PARK
GARMISCH-PARTENKIRCHEN A 952 STARNBERG
INNSBRUCK
BAD-TÖLZ GRÜNWALD
E 45-52-A 8 SALZBURG, INNSBRUCK
BAD-TÖLZ
E 45 52 A 8 SALZBURG, ROSENHEIM INNSBRUCK

Monasterace Marina 67 F4
Monasterboice 13 D3
Monasterevin 13 D4
Monasterio de Rodilla 36 A2
Monastier, le 30 B2
Monastir 66 B4
Monastiráki (Stereá Eláda) 82 C3
Monastiráki (Thráki) 81 F2
Monastiri Doukáto 81 E2
Monastiri, N 83 E2
Monbazillac 28 C2
Moncalieri 31 E2
Moncalvo 31 F1
Monção 34 A3
Moncarapacho 42 B3
Moncayo, Sa de 36 C3
Mönchdorf 57 D2
Mönchengladbach 17 D4
Monchique 42 A2
Monchique, Sa de 42 A2
Monclar-de-Quercy 29 D3
Moncófar 41 E3
Moncontour (Côtes-d'Amor) 22 C3
Moncontour (Vienne) 24 C3
Moncoutant 24 C3
Monda 43 E4
Mondariz 34 A3
Mondavio 61 E3
Mondego, Cabo 38 A2
Mondego, R 38 B2
Mondéjar 40 B2
Mondello 68 B2
Mondim 34 B4
Mondolfo 61 E3
Mondoñedo 34 C1
Mondorf 21 D3
Mondoubleau 23 F3
Mondovi 31 F2
Mondragon 30 B3
Mondragone 64 A3
Mondsee 56 C3
Monein 28 B4
Monemvassía 87 E4
Monesi 31 E3
Monesterio 43 D1
Monestier-de-Clermont 30 C2
Monestiés 29 E3
Monêtier, le 31 D2
Moneygall 12 C4
Moneymore 13 D2
Monfalcone 59 F3
Monflanquin 28 C2
Monforte 38 C4
Monforte de Lemos 34 B2
Mongie, la 37 E2
Mongó 45 E1
Monguelfo 59 D2
Monheim 55 E2
Mönichkirchen 57 F3
Mon-Idée 20 B2
Monifieth 5 D1
Moni, N 87 E2
Monistrol 32 A4
Monistrol-d'Allier 29 F2
Monistrol-sur-Loire 30 B1
Mönkebude 49 E2
Monmouth 9 D2
Monnickendam 16 C2
Monodéndri 78 C4
Monódrio 84 B4
Monólithos 93 E2
Monopoli 65 E3
Monor 112 B4
Monóvar 45 D1
Monpazier 28 C2
Monreal 51 E4
Monreal del Campo 41 D2
Monreale 68 B3
Monrepós, Pto de 37 D2
Monroy 39 D3
Monroyo 41 E2
Mons 50 B4
Monsanto 38 C2
Monsaraz 42 C1
Monschau 51 D4
Monségur 28 C2
Monselice 61 D1
Monserrat 41 E4
Møns Klint 108 C4
Monsols 26 B4
Mönsterås 109 E2
Monsummano Terme 60 C3
Montabaur 51 F4
Montagnac 30 A4
Montagnana 61 D1
Montagne Noire 32 B1
Montagnes Noires 22 B3
Montagrier 28 C1
Montaigu 24 B3
Montaigu-de-Quercy 29 D3
Montaigut 26 A4
Montaione 60 C4
Montalbán 41 E2
Montalbo 40 C3
Montalcino 63 D1
Montalegre 34 B3
Montalieu 26 C4
Montalivet 28 A1
Montalto delle Marche 61 F4
Montalto di Castro 63 D2
Montalto Uffugo 67 E2
Montalvão 38 C3
Montamarta 35 D4
Montana 27 E3
Montañana 37 D3
Montánchez 39 D3
Montanejos 41 E3
Montargil 38 B3
Montargil, Bgem de 38 B4
Montargis 25 F1
Montastruc-la-Conseillère 29 D4
Montauban (Ille-et-Vilaine) 23 D3
Montauban (Tarn-et-Garonne) 29 D3
Montbard 26 B2
Montbazens 29 E3
Montbazon 25 D2
Montbéliard 27 E2
Montbenoit 27 D2
Mont Blanc 27 E4
Montblanc 37 F4
Mont Blanc, Tunnel du 27 E4
Montbozon 27 D2
Montbrió del Camp 37 F4
Montbrison 30 B1
Montbron 28 C1
Montceau-les-Mines 26 B3
Montcenis 26 B3
Mont Cenis, Col du 31 E1
Montchanin 26 B3
Montcornet 20 B2
Montcuq 29 D3
Mont-de-Marsan 28 B3
Montdidier 19 F3
Mont-Dore, le 29 E1
Monteagudo de las Vicarias 36 B4
Montealegre 35 E4
Montealegre del Castillo 45 D1
Montebello Ionico 67 E4
Montebello Vicentino 60 C1
Montebelluna 59 E4
Monte Bianco, Traforo di 27 E4
Montebourg 18 B3
Monte-Carlo-Monaco 31 E3
Montecarotto 61 E4
Montecatini-Terme 60 C3
Montecchio 61 E3
Montecchio Maggiore 60 C1
Montech 29 D3
Monte Citerna, Pso del 60 C3
Montecorvino Rovella 64 B4
Montecristo, I di 62 C2
Monte Croce Carnico, Pso di 59 E2
Monte Croce di Comelico, Pso 59 E2
Monte da Pedra 38 C3
Monte da Rocha, Bgem de 42 B2
Montedoro 68 C3
Montefalco 63 E1
Montefalcone di Val Fortore 64 B3
Montefalcone nel Sannio 64 B2
Montefeltro 61 D3
Montefiascone 63 E2
Montefiore dell' Aso 61 F4
Montefiorino 60 C3
Montefrio 43 F3
Montegallo 63 F1
Montegiorgio 61 F4
Monte Giovo, Pso di 59 D2
Montegranaro 61 F4
Montegrotto Terme 61 D1
Montehermoso 39 D2
Montejicar 44 A2
Montejo de Tiermes 36 A4
Montejunto, Sa de 38 A3
Monteleone di Spoleto 63 E1
Montélimar 30 B2
Montella 64 B4
Montellano 43 D3
Monteluco 63 E1

Montelupo Fiorentino 60 C4
Montemaggiore Belsito 68 C3
Montemagno 31 F1
Montemayor 43 F2
Montemayor de Pililla 35 E4
Montemor-o-Novo 38 B4
Motemor-o-Velho 38 B2
Montemuro, Sa do 38 C1
Montendre 28 B1
Montenegro de Cameros 36 B3
Montenero di Bisaccia 64 B2
Montenero Sabino 63 E2
Montepulciano 61 D4
Monte Real 38 B2
Montereale (Abruzzo) 63 F1
Montereale (Friuli-Venezia) 59 E3
Montereau 19 F4
Monte Redondo 38 B2
Monterenzio 61 D3
Monteriggioni 61 D4
Monteroni di Lecce 65 F4
Monte Rosa 27 F4
Monterosso al Mare 60 B3
Monterotondo 63 E2
Monterotondo Marittimo 62 C1
Monterroso 34 B2
Monterrubio de la Serena 43 E1
Monterubbiano 61 F4
Montesano sulla Marcellana 64 C4
Monte San Savino 61 D4
Monte Sant' Angelo 64 C2
Montesarchio 64 B3
Montescaglioso 65 D4
Montesilvano Marina 64 A1
Montesquieu-Volvestre 37 F1
Montesquiou 28 C4
Montet, le 26 A3
Montets, Col des 27 E4
Montevarchi 61 D4
Monteviejo, Pto de 35 E2
Montfaucon-en-Velay 30 B1
Montfaucon (Maine-et-Loire) 24 B2
Montfaucon (Meuse) 20 C3
Montfort 23 D3
Montfort-en-Chalosse 28 B4
Montfort-l'Amaury 19 E4
Montfort-sur-Risle 19 D3
Montgaillard 32 A2
Montgenèvre 31 D2
Montgenèvre, Col de 31 D2
Montgiscard 29 D4
Montgomery 9 D1
Montguyon 28 B1
Monthermé 20 C2
Monthey 27 E4
Monthois 20 C3
Monthureux 27 D1
Monti 66 B2
Montichiari 60 B1
Monticiano 61 D4
Montiel 44 B1
Montier-en-Der 20 C4
Montignac 29 D2
Montigny-le-Roi 26 C1
Montigny-sur-Aube 26 C1
Montijo (E) 39 D4
Montijo (P) 38 A4
Montilla 43 F2
Montioni 62 C1
Montivilliers 19 D3
Montjean 23 E4
Montlhéry 19 f4
Montlieu 28 B1
Montlouis 25 D2
Mont-Louis 32 A3
Montluçon 25 F4
Montluel 26 C4
Montmarault 26 A4
Montmartin 18 B3
Montmédy 20 C3
Montmélian 31 D1
Montmirail (Marne) 20 A4
Montmirail (Sarthe) 23 F3
Montmirey-le-Château 26 C2
Montmoreau 28 C1
Montmorency 19 F4
Montmorillon 25 D4
Montmort 20 B3
Montoggio 60 A3
Montoire 23 F4
Montoito 38 C4
Montone 61 D3
Montorio al Vomano 63 F1
Montoro 43 F2
Montòro, Emb de 43 F1
Montpellier 30 A4
Montpellier-le-Vieux, Chaos de 29 F3
Montpezat-de-Quercy 29 D3
Montpezat-sous-Bauzon 30 B2
Montpon-Ménestérol 28 C2
Montpont 26 C3
Montréal (Aude) 32 A2
Montréal (Gers) 28 C3
Montréal-la-Cluse 26 C4
Montredon-Labessonnie 32 B1
Montréjeau 37 E1
Montrésor 25 E2
Montresta 66 A2
Montreuil 19 E1
Montreuil-Bellay 24 C2
Montreux 27 E3
Montrevault 24 B2
Montrevel 26 C3
Montrichard 25 E2
Mont-roig del Camp 37 F4
Montrond-les-Bains 30 B1
Montrose 5 E1
Mont-St-Michel, le 18 B4
Mont-St-Vincent 26 B3
Montsalvy 29 E2
Montsant, Sa del 37 F4
Montsauche 26 B2
Montsec, Serra de 37 F3
Montseny 32 B4
Montseny, Sa de 32 B4
Montserrat 32 A4
Mont-sous-Vaudrey 26 C3
Monts-sur-Guesnes 25 D3
Montsûrs 23 E3
Montuenga 39 F1
Montuiri 45 F3
Monviso 31 E2
Monza 60 A1
Monzón 37 E3
Monzón de Campos 35 F3
Moordorf 47 E3
Moorfoot Hills 5 D2
Moosburg 56 B2
Mór 112 B4
Mora (E) 40 A3
Mora (P) 38 B4
Mora (S) 101 E4
Morača 76 B2
Morača *R* 76 B2
Morača klisura 76 B2
Móra d'Ebre 37 E4
Mora de Rubielos 41 E2
Moraira 45 E1
Moraira, Pta de 45 E1
Morais 34 C4
Moraïtika 82 A2
Morakovo, G. 76 B2
Móra la Nova 41 F1
Moral de Calatrava 40 A4
Moraleda de Zafayona 44 A3
Moraleja 39 D2
Moraleja de Sayago 39 E1
Morales de Rey 35 D3
Morales de Toro 35 E4
Morano Calabro 67 E2
Mora, Pto de la 44 A3
Morar, L 2 B4
Mörarp 108 C3
Morasverdes 39 D2
Morata de Jalón 36 C4
Morata de Tajuña 40 B2
Moratalla 44 C2
Morata, Pto de 36 C4
Morava 57 E1
Morava *R* 112 A3
Moravče 70 B2
Moravci 70 C1
Moravica 73 D4
Moravské Budějovice 57 E1
Moravske Toplice 70 C1
Moravský Krumlov 57 E1
Moray Firth 3 D3
Morbach 54 B1
Morbegno 58 B3
Morbihan 22 C3
Mörbisch 57 F3
Mörbylånga 109 E3
Morcenx 28 A3
Morciano di Romagna 61 E3
Morcone 64 B3
Morcote 58 A4
Morcuera, Pto de la 40 A1
Mordelles 23 D3
Morecambe 6 B1
Morecambe Bay 6 B1
Moreda 44 A3
Morée 25 E1
Moreleja del Vino 35 D4
Morella 41 E2
Møre og Romsdal 100 B2
Mores 66 B2
Morestel 30 C1
Moret 19 F4
Moreton 9 E2
Moretonhampstead 8 C3
Moreuil 19 F2
Morez 27 D3
Morfasso 60 B2
Mórfio 82 B2
Morgat 22 A3
Morges 27 D3
Morgex 27 E4
Morgins, Pas de 27 E4
Morhange 21 D3
Mori 58 C4
Morina 76 C2
Moritzburg 53 E2
Morjärv 98 C3
Morlaàs 37 E1
Morlaix 22 B2
Mormanno 67 E2
Mormant 19 F4
Mormoiron 30 C3
Mornant 30 B1
Mórnou, Teh L 83 E4
Morón de Almazán 36 B4
Morón de la Frontera 43 E3
Morosaglia 33 F3
Morović 72 B3
Morpeth 5 E3
Morrón 44 B3
Mörrum 109 D3
Mors 108 A2
Morsbach 17 E4
Mörsil 101 E2
Morsleben 52 C1
Mortagne 28 B1
Mortagne-au-Perche 19 D4
Mortagne-sur-Sèvre 24 C3
Mortágua 38 B2
Mortain 18 C4
Mortara 60 A2
Morteau 27 D2
Mortrée 19 D4
Morven 3 D2
Moryń 49 E3
Morzine 27 E4
Morzyczyn 49 F2
Mosbach 55 D2
Mosby 104 B4
Mošćenice 70 B3
Mošćenička Draga 70 B3
Moschendorf 57 F4
Mosel 51 E4
Moselle (Dépt) 21 D3
Moselle *R* 27 D4
Moshokariá 83 E3
Moshopótamos 79 E3
Mosjøen 97 E3
Moskenesøya 97 E1
Moskenstraumen 97 E1
Mosko 76 A2
Moskosel 98 B3
Moskva 111 F2
Moskva *R* 111 F2
Moslavačka gora 71 D2
Mosonmagyaróvár 112 A4
Mosor 75 E2
Mosqueruela 41 E2
Moss 105 D3
Mossala 107 D3
Mossat 3 D4
Mosses, Col des 27 E3
Mössingen 55 D3
Most (CS) 53 E3
Most (YU) 70 A2
Mosta 68 B4
Mostar 75 F2
Mosteiro 34 A2
Mosterhamn 104 A3
Mostiska 112 C2
Móstoles 40 A2
Mostonga 72 B2
Mostrim 12 C3
Mosty 110 C4
Møsvatn 104 B3
Mosvik 101 D1
Mota del Cuervo 40 B3
Mota del Marqués 35 E4
Motajica 71 E3
Motala 105 F4
Motala S 106 A4
Mothe-Achard, la 24 B3
Motherwell 4 C2
Mothe-St-Héray, la 24 C4
Motilla del Palancar 40 C3
Motovun 70 A3
Motril 44 A4
Motta di Livenza 59 E4
Motta S.A. 69 D3
Motta Visconti 60 A1
Motte-Chalancon, la 30 C2
Motte, la 31 D3
Mottola 65 E4
Mouchard 27 D3
Moudon 27 E3
Moúdros 85 D1
Mougins 31 E4
Mouhijärvi 107 D1
Mouilleron-en-Pareds 24 C3
Moulins 26 A3
Moulins-Engilbert 26 B3
Moulins-la-Marche 19 D4
Moult 18 C3
Moúnda, Akr 86 A1
Mountain Ash 8 C2
Mount Bellew 12 C3
Mountmellick 13 D4
Mountrath 12 C4
Mount's B 8 B4
Mountsoúna 88 C3
Moura 42 B1
Mourão 42 C1
Moúrdzeflos, Akr 85 D1
Mourenx 28 B4
Mouríki 84 A4
Mourmelon-le-Grand 20 B3
Mourne 13 D2
Mourne Mts 13 E3
Mourniés 90 B3
Mourujärvi 99 E2
Mouscron 50 A3
Moustiers-Ste-Marie 31 D3
Mouthe 27 D3
Mouthier 27 D2
Mouthoumet 32 B2
Moutier 27 E2
Moûtiers 31 D1
Moutiers-les-Mauxfaits 24 B3
Mouy 19 F3
Mouzakéi 82 C1
Mouzáki 83 D2
Mouzon 20 C2
Moville 13 D1
Moy 12 B2
Moyenneville 19 E2
Moyeuvre 21 D3
Moyuela 37 D4
Možajsk 111 F2
Mozirje 70 B1
Mozyr' 113 E1
Mrągowo 110 B4
Mrakovica 71 D3
Mramorak 73 D2
Mratinje 76 A1
Mrazovac 70 C3
Mrčajevci 73 D4
Mrežičko 77 E4
Mrkonjić Grad 71 E4
Mrkopalj 70 B3
Mrzeżyno 49 F1
Mšeno 53 F3
Msta 111 E1
Mstislavl' 111 E3
Mú 42 B2
Muć 75 D1
Muccia 61 E4
Much 17 E4
Mücheln 52 C2
Much Wenlock 9 D1
Mucientes 35 E4
Muck 2 B4
Muckle Roe 3 F1
Muckross House 14 B4
Mudanya 115 F3
Mudau 55 D1
Muddus 98 B2
Muel 37 D4
Muelas del Pan 35 D4
Muff 13 D1
Muge 38 B3
Mügeln 53 E2
Muggia 59 F4
Mugron 28 B4
Mugueimes 34 B3
Mühlbach 59 E1
Mühlberg 53 E2
Mühldorf 56 B3
Mühlen-Eichsen 48 B2
Mühlhausen 52 B2
Mühltroff 53 D3
Muhniemi 107 F2
Muhos 99 D4
Muhu 110 B2
Muineachán 13 D2
Muine Bheag 15 D3
Muirkirk 4 C3
Muir of Ord 2 C3
Mukačevo 112 C3
Mukos 77 E3
Mula 45 D2
Mülacker 54 C2
Mula, R 45 D2
Mulargia, L 66 B3
Mulhacén 44 A3
Mülheim 17 E3
Mulhouse 27 E1
Mull 4 B1
Müllheim 54 C4
Mullingar 13 D3
Mull of Galloway 4 B4
Mull of Kintyre 4 B3
Mull of Oa 4 A2
Müllrose 49 F4
Mull, Sd of 4 B1
Mullsjö 109 D1
Mulrany 12 B2
Multia 103 D3
Mumbles, The 8 C2
Muñana 39 F2
Münchberg 53 D4
Müncheberg 49 E4
München 56 A3
Münchhausen 17 F4
Münden 52 B2
Mundesley 7 F3
Mundford 11 D1
Mundo, R 44 C1
Munera 40 C4
Mungia 36 B1
Muñico 39 F2
Muniesa 37 D4
Munkebo 108 B3
Munkedal 105 D4
Munkfors 105 E3
Münnerstadt 52 B4
Muñogalindo 39 F2
Munsala 102 B2
Munsfjället 101 E1
Münsingen (CH) 27 E3
Münsingen (D) 55 D3
Munster (F) 27 E1
Münster (CH) 27 F3
Münster (Niedersachsen) 48 B3
Münster (Nordrhein-Westfalen) 17 E3
Münstertal 54 C4
Münzenberg 52 A4
Münzkirchen 56 C2
Muodoslompolo 95 D4
Muojärvi 99 F2
Muonio 95 D4
Muonioälven 95 D4
Muotkatonturit 95 E2
Mur 57 E4
Mura 70 C1
Muraglione, Pso del 61 D3
Murano 61 D1
Murat 29 E2
Murato 33 F3
Murat-sur-Vèbre 32 B1
Murau 57 D4
Muravera 66 C4
Murça 34 B4
Murchante 36 C3
Murcia 45 D2
Murcia (Reg) 44 C2
Mur-de-Barrez 29 E2
Mur-de-Bretagne 22 C3
Mureck 57 E4
Mure, la 30 C2
Mures 112 C4
Muret 29 D4
Murg 54 C2
Murguía 36 B1
Muri 27 F2
Murias de Paredes 35 D2
Murino 76 C2
Muriqan 76 B3
Müritz See 49 D3
Murjek 98 B2
Murnau 56 A4
Muro 33 F3
Muro de Alcoy 45 E1
Murol 29 E1
Murole 102 C3
Muro Lucano 64 C4
Muros 34 A2
Mürren 27 F3
Murrhardt 55 D2
Murska Sobota 70 C1
Mursko Središče 70 C1
Murten 27 E3
Murter 74 C1
Murter *I* 74 C1
Murtosa 38 B1
Murtovaara 99 F3
Murvica 74 C1
Murviel 30 A4
Mürz 57 E3
Mürzsteg 57 E3
Mürzzuschlag 57 E3
Musala 115 D3
Mussalo 103 F4
Musselburgh 5 D2
Musselkanaal 17 E1
Mussidan 28 C2
Mussomeli 68 C3
Mussy 26 B1
Mustair 58 C3
Mustasaari 102 B2
Muster 58 A3
Mustion as 107 E3
Mustvee 110 C1
Muta 70 B1
Mutala 102 C3
Mutterstadt 54 C1
Mutzschen 53 E2
Muurame 103 D3
Muurasjärvi 103 D1
Muuratjärvi 103 D3
Muurla 107 E2
Muurola 99 D2
Muuruvesi 103 E2
Muxía 34 A1
Muy, le 31 D4
Muzillac 22 C4
Muzzana del Turgnano 59 F3
Mweelrea Mts. 12 B3
Myckegensjö 101 F2
Mykines 96 A3
Myllykoski 107 F2
Myllykylä 102 C3
Myllymäki 102 C2
Mynämäki 107 D2
Mýrdalsjökull 96 B3
Myre 94 A3
Myrlandshaugen 94 B3
Myrskylä 107 F2
Myrviken 101 E2
Mysen 105 D3
Mysingen 106 B4
Myśla 49 F3
Myślibórskie, Jez 49 F3
Myślibórz 49 F3
Mývatn 96 B1
Mže 53 E4

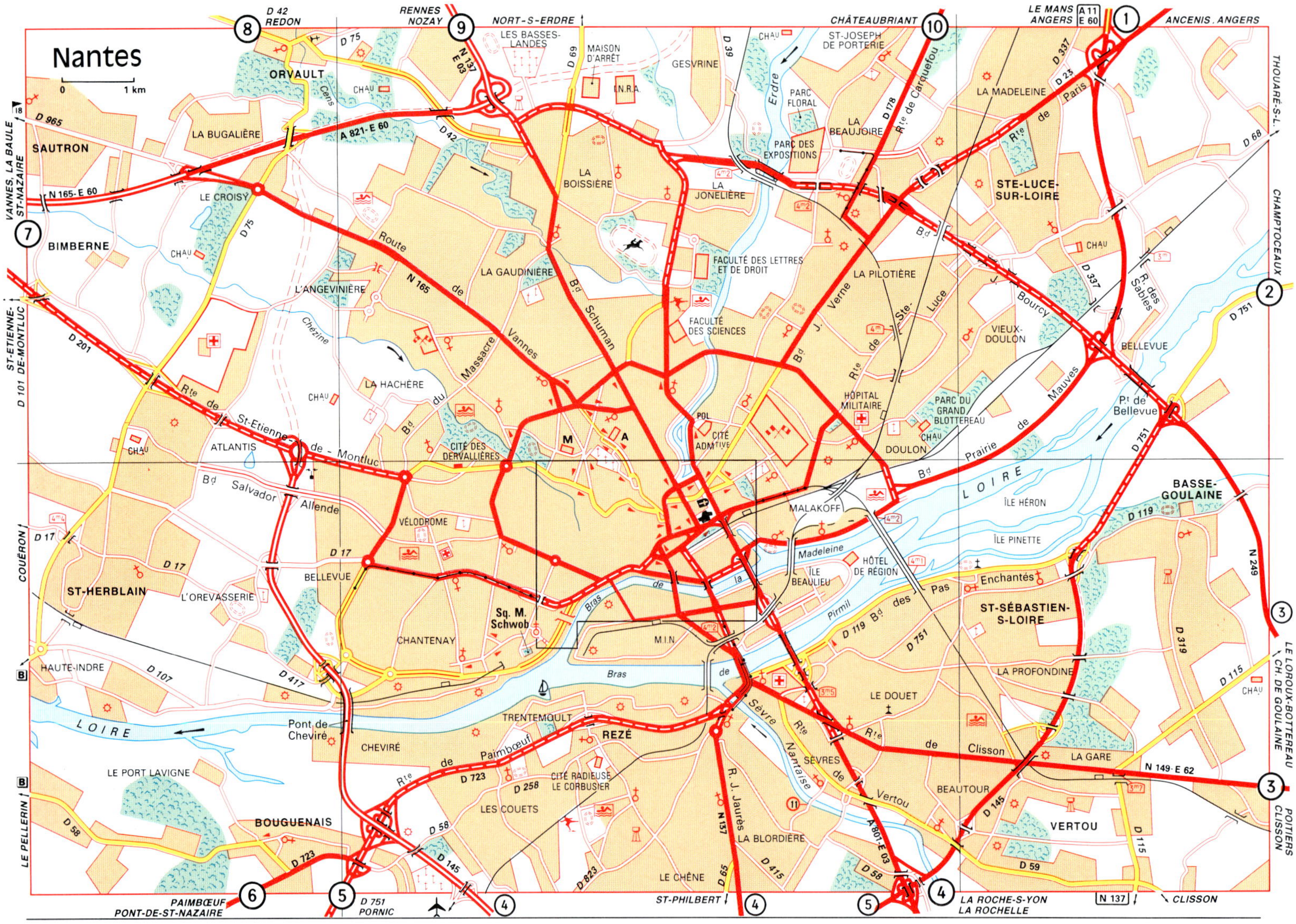
Nantes
0
1 km
ORVAULT
SAUTRON
LA BUGALIÈRE
BIMBERNE
LE CROISY
L'ANGEVINIÈRE
LA GAUDINIÈRE
LA BOISSIÈRE
LA JONELIÈRE
GESVRINE
LA MADELEINE
STE-LUCE-SUR-LOIRE
LA PILOTIÈRE
VIEUX-DOULON
BELLEVUE
DOULON
BASSE-GOULAINE
MALAKOFF
ATLANTIS
LA HACHÈRE
CITÉ DES DERVALLIÈRES
VÉLODROME
BELLEVUE
ST-HERBLAIN
L'OREVASSERIE
CHANTENAY
Sq. M. Schwob
HAUTE-INDRE
TRENTEMOULT
REZÉ
CHEVIRÉ
LE PORT LAVIGNE
BOUGUENAIS
LES COUETS
CITÉ RADIEUSE LE CORBUSIER
LA BLORDIÈRE
LE CHÊNE
SÈVRES
BEAUTOUR
VERTOU
LA GARE
LE DOUET
LA PROFONDINE
ST-SÉBASTIEN-S-LOIRE
HÔTEL DE RÉGION
ÎLE BEAULIEU
ÎLE HÉRON
ÎLE PINETTE
HÔPITAL MILITAIRE
FACULTÉ DES LETTRES ET DE DROIT
FACULTÉ DES SCIENCES
PARC DES EXPOSITIONS
PARC FLORAL
LA BEAUJOIRE
ST-JOSEPH DE PORTERIE
LES BASSES-LANDES
MAISON D'ARRÊT
I.N.R.A.
CITÉ ADM^TIVE
M.I.N.
LOIRE
D 42 REDON
RENNES NOZAY
NORT-S-ERDRE
CHÂTEAUBRIANT
LE MANS ANGERS
ANCENIS, ANGERS
THOUARÉ-S-L.
CHAMPTOCEAUX
LE LOROUX-BOTTEREAU CH. DE GOULAINE
POITIERS CLISSON
CLISSON
LA ROCHE-S-YON LA ROCHELLE
ST-PHILBERT
D 751 PORNIC
PAIMBOEUF PONT-DE-ST-NAZAIRE
LE PELLERIN
COUËRON
D 101 ST-ETIENNE-DE-MONTLUC
VANNES, LA BAULE ST-NAZAIRE
Route de Vannes
Bd Schuman
Rte de St-Etienne-de-Montluc
Bd Salvador Allende
Bd J. Verne
Rte de Ste-Luce
Rte de Carquefou
Rte de Paris
Bd de la Prairie de Mauves
Bd des Enchantés
Rte de Clisson
Rte de Vertou
R. J. Jaurès
Rte de Paimbœuf
Bras de Pirmil
Bras de la Madeleine
Sèvre Nantaise
Erdre
Chézine
A 821-E 60
N 165-E 60
N 149-E 62
N 137
N 249

N

Naab 55 F1
Naamijoki 98 C2
Naantali 107 D2
Naarajärvi 103 E3
Naarva 103 F2
Naas 13 D4
Näätämöjoki 95 F2
Nabburg 56 B1
Načeradec 57 D1
Náchod 112 A2
Naddvik 104 B1
Nadela 34 B2
Nădlac 114 C1
Nadur 68 B4
Nadvornaja 113 D3
Nafels 58 A2
Nafpaktías, Óri 83 D4
Náfpaktos 83 D4
Náfplio 87 D2
Naggen 101 F3
Nagold 54 C3
Nagu 107 D3
Nagyatád 114 A1
Nagykálló 112 C3
Nagykanizsa 114 A1
Nagykőrös 112 B4
Nahe 48 A2
Nahe *R* 54 B1
Naila 53 D4
Nailloux 32 A1
Nailsworth 9 D2
Nairn 3 D3
Najac 29 D3
Nájera 36 B2
Najerilla, R 36 B2
Nakkila 107 D1
Nakło 112 A1
Nakovo 72 C1
Nakskov 108 B4
Näljänkä 99 E3
Na Logu 70 A2
Nalón, R 35 E2
Naltijärvi 95 D3
Namdalseid 97 D4
Nämdöfjärden 106 B4
Náměšt 57 E1
Namsen 97 D4
Namsos 97 D4
Namsskogan 97 D4
Namur 50 C4
Namur (Prov) 50 C4
Nancy 21 D4
Nangis 19 F4
Nannestad 105 D2
Nant 29 F3
Nanterre 19 F4
Nantes 24 B2
Nantes, Canal de 22 C3
Nanteuil-le-Haudouin 19 F3
Nantiat 25 E4
Nantua 26 C4
Nantwich 6 C3
Nao, C de la 45 F1
Náoussa (Kikládes) 88 C3
Náoussa (Makedonía) 79 E3
Napapiiri 99 D2
Napoli 64 B4
Napoli, G di 64 A4
Napoule, la 31 E4
Narberth 8 B2
Nærbø 104 A4
Narbolia 66 B3
Narbonne 32 B1
Narbonne-Plage 30 A4
Narcao 66 B4
Narcea, R 35 D1
Nardò 65 F4
Narew 112 C1
Narila 103 E3
Narkaus 99 D2
Narni 63 E2
Naro 68 C4
Naro-Fominsk 111 F2
Nærøy 97 D4
Närpes 102 B3
Närpiö 102 B3
Narta 71 D2
Narthäki 83 E2
Narthäki, Óros 83 E2
Narva 111 D1
Narvik 94 B3
Nås 105 E2
Näsåker 101 F2
Năsăud 113 D4
Nasbinals 29 F2
Našice 71 E2
Näsijärvi 102 C3
Naso 69 D2
Nassau 51 F4
Nassereith 58 C2
Naßfeld-Paß 59 F2
Nässjö 109 D1
Nastola 107 F2
Næstved 108 C4
Natalinci 73 D3
Nattaset 95 F3
Nattavaara 98 B2
Nättraby 109 E3
Naucelle 29 E3
Nauders 58 C2
Nauen 49 D4
Naul 13 D3
Naumburg 52 C2
Naunhof 53 D2
Naussac, Bge de 29 F2
Naustdal 100 A3
Nauvo 107 D3
Nava 35 E1
Nava, Colle di 31 F3
Navacelles, Cirque de 29 F3
Navacepeda 39 E2
Navacerrada 40 A2
Navacerrada, Pto de 40 A1
Navachica 44 A3
Navaconcejo 39 E2
Nava de la Asunción 40 A1
Nava del Rey 35 E4
Navafria, Pto de 40 A1
Navahermosa 39 F3
Navalcán 39 F2
Navalcarnero 40 A2
Navaleno 36 B3
Navalmanzano 40 A1
Navalmoral de la Mata 39 E3
Navalperal de Pinares 40 A2
Navaluenga 39 F2
Navalvillar de Pela 39 E4
Navamorcuende 39 F2
Navan 13 D3
Navarra 36 C2
Navarredonda de la Sierra 39 F2
Navarrenx 28 B4
Navarrés 41 E4
Navarrete 36 B2
Navascués 37 D2
Navas del Madroño 39 D3
Navas de Oro 40 A1
Navas de San Juan 44 B2
Navasfrías 39 D2
Navatalgordo 39 F2
Nave 60 B1
Nävekvarn 106 A4
Navelli 63 F2
Naver, L 2 C2
Naveros 43 D4
Navia 34 C1
Navia de Suarna 34 C2
Navia, R 34 C1
Navl'a 111 F4
Náxos 88 C3
Náxos Dias 88 C3
Náxos, N 88 C3
Nay 37 E1
Nazaré 38 A3
Naze, The 11 D2
Nazilli 115 F4
Ndrejaj 76 C2
Ndroq 76 C4
Nea 101 D2
Néa Agathoúpoli 79 F3
Néa Alikarnassós 91 D3
Néa Anhíalos 83 F2
Néa Artáki 84 B4
Néa Éfessos 79 F4
Néa Epídavros 87 E2
Néa Fókeada 80 A4
Neagh, L 13 E2
Néa Hili 81 E2
Néa Iraklítsa 80 C2
Néa Kalikrátia 79 F4
Néa Kariá 81 D2
Néa Karváli 80 C2
Néa Kerassoús 82 C2
Néa Kíos 87 D2
Néa Koróni 86 C3
Néa Mákri 88 A1
Néa Messángala 83 F1
Néa Mihanióna 79 F3
Néa Moní 85 E4
Néa Moudaniá 80 A4
Néa Péla 79 F3
Néa Péramos (Stereá Eláda) 87 E1
Néa Péramos (Makedonía) 80 C2
Neápoli (Kríti) 91 E4
Neápoli (Makedonía) 79 D3
Neápoli (Pelopónissos) 87 E4
Néa Róda 80 B3
Néa Sánda (Makedonía) 79 F2
Néa Sánda (Thráki) 81 E2
Néa Sílata 80 A3
Néa Skióni 80 B4
Néa Stíra 84 B4
Néa Triglia 80 A4
Neath 8 C2
Néa Víssa 81 F1
Néa Zoí 79 E2
Néa Zíhni 80 B2
Nebel 47 F1
Nebelhorn 55 E4
Nebljusi 70 C4
Nebra 52 C2
Nechranická přehr nádrž 53 E3
Neckar 55 D1
Neckarelz 55 D2
Neckargemünd 54 C1
Neckarsteinach 54 C1
Neckarsulm 55 D2
Nečujam 75 D2
Neda 34 B1
Nédas 86 C2
Nedelišće 70 C1
Nedervetil 102 C1
Nedstrand 104 A3
Neede 17 D2
Needles, The 9 E3
Neermoor 47 E3
Nefyn 6 A3
Negoiu 113 D4
Negorci 77 F3
Negotin 73 F3
Negotino 77 E3
Negra de Urbión, L 36 B3
Negrar 60 C1
Negratin, Emb del 44 B2
Negreira 34 A2
Nègrepelisse 29 D3
Negru Vodă 115 E2
Neheim-Hüsten 17 F3
Neiden 95 F2
Neige, Crêt de la 27 D3
Neila 36 B3
Neiße 53 F1
Nejdek 53 E3
Nekromandío Efiras 82 B2
Neksø 109 D4
Nela, R 36 A1
Nelas 38 C1
Nelidovo 111 E2
Nellim 95 F3
Nelson 6 C2
Neman 110 B3
Neméa 87 D1
Nemirov 113 E3
Nemours 25 F1
Nemunas 110 C3
Nenagh 12 C4
Nene 10 C1
Nénita 85 F4
Nenzing 58 B2
Neohoráki 84 A4
Neohóri (Etolía-Akarnanía) 82 C4

Neohóri (Évia) 84 B4
Neohóri (Fthiótida) 83 E3
Neohóri (Ípiros) 82 C2
Neohóri (Karditsa) 83 D2
Neohóri (Magnissía) 84 A2
Neohóri (Pelopónissos) 86 C2
Neohóri (Thráki) 81 F1
Neohóri (Trikala) 83 D1
Néo Monastiri 83 E2
Néon Petrítsi 80 A2
Néos Marmarás 80 B4
Néos Skopós 80 B2
Néouvielle, Pic de 37 E2
Nephin 12 B2
Nephin Beg Range 12 B2
Nepomuk 56 C1
Nera 63 E1
Nérac 28 C3
Neráida (Amárandóos) 83 D2
Neráida (Neohóri) 83 D2
Neratovice 53 F3
Nerdvika 100 B1
Neresheim 55 E2
Nereto 63 F1
Neretva 76 A1
Neretva klisura 75 F1
Neretvanski kan 75 E2
Nestáni 87 D2
Nesterov 112 C2
Nestório 78 C3
Néstos 81 D2
Nesvik 104 A3
Nesviž 111 D4
Neto 67 F3
Netolice 56 C1
Netretić 70 C3
Nettetal 17 D4
Nettuno 63 E3
Neuastenberg 17 F4
Neubeckum 17 F3
Neubourg, le 19 D3
Neubrandenburg 49 D2
Neubukow 48 C2
Neuburg 55 F2
Neuchâtel 27 E2
Neu Darchau 48 B3
Neuenburg 47 E3
Neuenbürg 54 C2
Neuendorf 49 D1
Neuenhaus 17 E2
Neuenkirchen 48 A3
Neuenstadt 55 D2
Neuerburg 54 A1
Neufahrn 56 B2
Neuf-Brisach 27 E1
Neufchâteau 20 C2
Neufchâteau 20 C4
Neufchâtel 20 B3
Nerezi 77 D3
Nerezine 70 B4

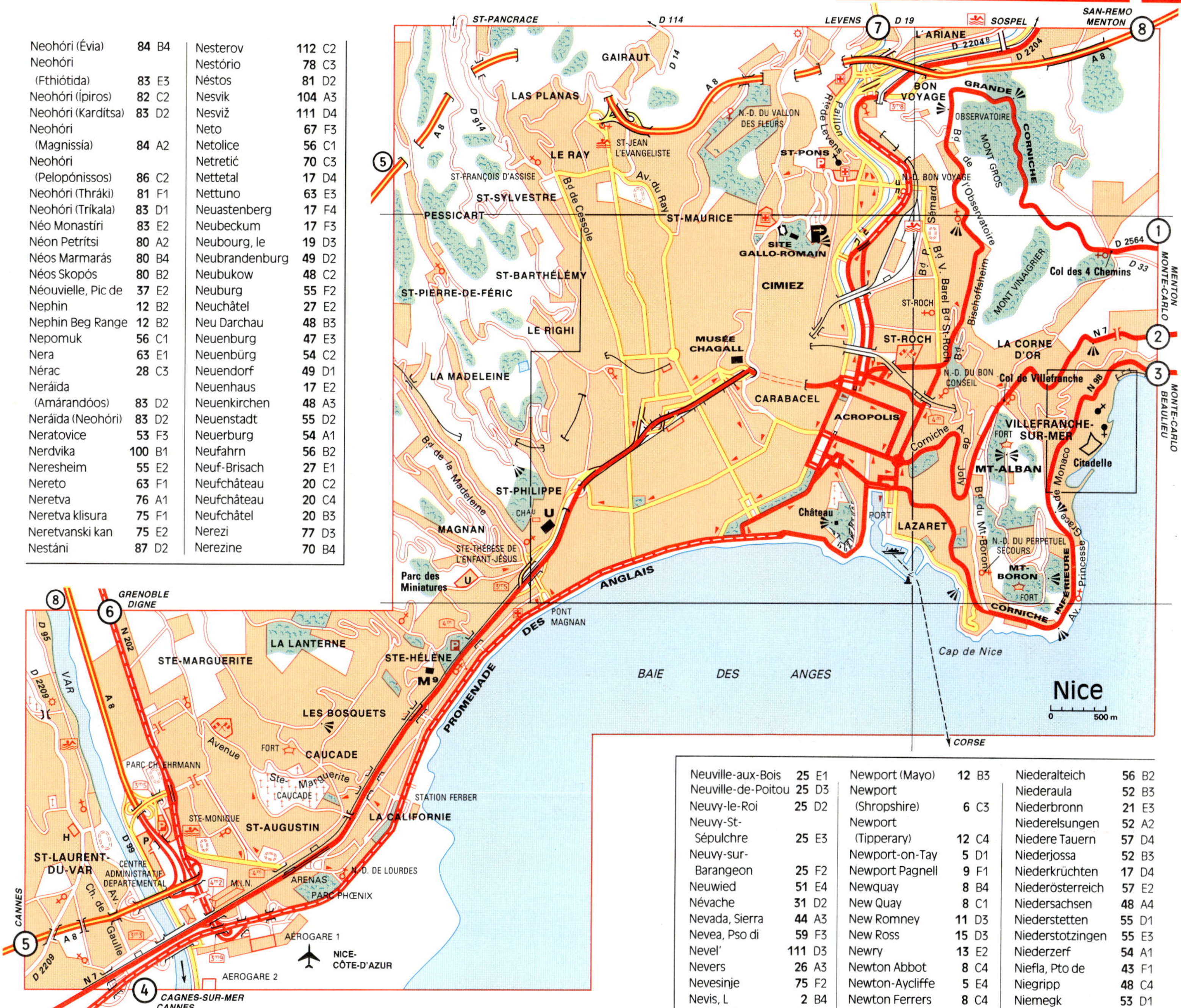

Nice
0 500 m
BAIE DES ANGES
PROMENADE DES ANGLAIS
Cap de Nice
CORSE
ST-PANCRACE
D 114
LEVENS
D 19
SOSPEL
SAN-REMO MENTON
L'ARIANE
GAIRAUT
LAS PLANAS
LE RAY
ST-SYLVESTRE
PESSICART
ST-MAURICE
ST-PONS
SITE GALLO-ROMAIN
CIMIEZ
ST-BARTHÉLÉMY
ST-PIERRE-DE-FÉRIC
LE RIGHI
MUSÉE CHAGALL
LA MADELEINE
CARABACEL
ACROPOLIS
ST-ROCH
BON VOYAGE
OBSERVATOIRE
MONT GROS
GRANDE CORNICHE
MONT VINAIGRIER
Col des 4 Chemins
MENTON MONTE-CARLO
LA CORNE D'OR
Col de Villefranche
MONTE-CARLO BEAULIEU
VILLEFRANCHE-SUR-MER
Citadelle
MT-ALBAN
LAZARET
Château
PORT
MT-BORON
CORNICHE INFÉRIEURE
ST-PHILIPPE
MAGNAN
Parc des Miniatures
PONT MAGNAN
GRENOBLE DIGNE
CANNES
LA LANTERNE
STE-MARGUERITE
STE-HÉLÈNE
LES BOSQUETS
CAUCADE
PARC CH. EHRMANN
STE-MONIQUE
ST-AUGUSTIN
STATION FERBER
LA CALIFORNIE
ST-LAURENT-DU-VAR
CENTRE ADMINISTRATIF DÉPARTEMENTAL
ARENAS
N.-D. DE LOURDES
PARC PHŒNIX
AÉROGARE 1
AÉROGARE 2
NICE-CÔTE-D'AZUR
CAGNES-SUR-MER CANNES

Nerežišca 75 D2
Neris 110 C3
Néris-les-Bains 25 F4
Nerja 44 A4
Néronde 26 B4
Nérondes 26 A3
Nerotrivía 84 A3
Nerpio 44 C2
Nerva 42 C2
Nervesa della Battaglia 59 E4
Nervi 60 A3
Nervión, R 36 B1
Nes (Akershus) 105 D3
Nes (Buskerud) 104 C2
Nes (NL) 16 C1
Nesbyen 104 C2
Nesebăr 115 E2
Nesjøen 101 D2
Neskaupstaður 96 C2
Nesle 19 F2
Nesoddtangen 105 D3
Nesseby 95 F1
Nesselwang 55 E4
Ness, L 2 C3
Neufchâtel-en-Bray 19 E2
Neufelden 56 C2
Neuffen 55 D3
Neugersdorf 53 F2
Neuhaus (D) 47 F2
Neuhaus (Mecklenburg-Vorpommern) 48 B3
Neuhaus (Niedersachsen) 47 F2
Neuhaus (Thüringen) 52 C3
Neuhausen 58 A1
Neuhaus-im-Solling 52 A2
Neuhofen an der Krems 57 D3
Neuillé-Pont-Pierre 25 D2
Neuilly-en-Thelle 19 F3
Neuilly-le-Réal 26 A3
Neuilly-l'Évêque 26 C1
Neuilly-St-Front 20 A3
Neu-Isenburg 52 A4
Neukalen 49 D2
Neukirch 53 F2
Neukirchen (A) 59 D1
Neukirchen (D) 47 F1
Neukloster 48 C2
Neulengbach 57 E2
Neu Lübbenau 53 E1
Neum 75 F2
Neumarkt (D) 55 F1
Neumarkt (Salzburg) 56 C3
Neumarkt (Steiermark) 57 D4
Neumarkt-St Veit 56 B3
Neumünster 48 A2
Neunagelberg 57 D2
Neunburg 56 B1
Neung 25 E2
Neunkirchen (A) 57 F3
Neunkirchen (D) 54 B2
Neuötting 56 B3
Neupölla 57 E2
Neuruppin 49 D3
Neusiedl 57 F3
Neusiedler See 57 F3
Neuss 17 D4
Neustadt (Baden-Württemberg) 54 C4
Neustadt (Brandenburg) 49 D3
Neustadt (Coburg) 52 C4
Neustadt (Hessen) 52 A3
Neustadt (Ingolstadt) 55 F2
Neustadt (Sachsen) 53 F2
Neustadt (Schleswig-Holstein) 48 B2
Neustadt (Thüringen) 53 D3
Neustadt am Rübenberge 48 A4
Neustadt an der Aisch 55 E1
Neustadt an der Waldnaab 53 D4
Neustadt an der Weinstraße 54 C2
Neustadt Glewe 48 C3
Neustift 59 D2
Neustrelitz 49 D3
Neu-Ulm 55 E3
Neuve-Lyre, la 19 D4
Neuves-Maisons 21 D4
Neuvic (Corrèze) 29 E1
Neuvic (Dordogne) 28 C2
Neuville 26 C4
Neuville-aux-Bois 25 E1
Neuville-de-Poitou 25 D3
Neuvy-le-Roi 25 D2
Neuvy-St-Sépulchre 25 E3
Neuvy-sur-Barangeon 25 F2
Neuwied 51 E4
Névache 31 D2
Nevada, Sierra 44 A3
Nevea, Pso di 59 F3
Nevel' 111 D3
Nevers 26 A3
Nevesinje 75 F2
Nevis, L 2 B4
Nevlunghavn 104 C4
New Abbey 4 C3
New Alresford 9 E3
Newark-on-Trent 7 D3
Newbiggin-by-the-Sea 5 E3
Newborough 6 A2
Newbridge 13 D4
Newburgh (Fife) 5 D1
Newburgh (Grampian) 3 E4
Newbury 9 E2
Newcastle 13 E2
Newcastle Emlyn 8 C1
Newcastle-under-Lyme 6 C3
Newcastle-upon-Tyne 5 E3
Newcastle West 14 B3
New Cumnock 4 C3
New Deer 3 E3
New Forest 9 E3
New Galloway 4 C3
Newgrange 13 D3
Newhaven 10 C3
Newmarket (GB) 11 D1
Newmarket (IRL) 14 B3
Newmarket on Fergus 12 B4
Newnham 9 D2
Newport (Dyfed) 8 B1
Newport (Gwent) 9 D2
Newport (I of Wight) 9 E3
Newport (Mayo) 12 B3
Newport (Shropshire) 6 C3
Newport (Tipperary) 12 C4
Newport-on-Tay 5 D1
Newport Pagnell 9 F1
Newquay 8 B4
New Quay 8 C1
New Romney 11 D3
New Ross 15 D3
Newry 13 E2
Newton Abbot 8 C4
Newton-Aycliffe 5 E4
Newton Ferrers 8 C4
Newtonmore 2 C4
Newton Stewart 4 C3
Newtownabbey 13 E2
Newtownards 13 E2
Newtownbutler 13 D2
Newtown (England) 9 D1
Newtown (Wales) 9 D1
Newtown-hamilton 13 D2
Newtown St Boswells 5 D3
Newtownstewart 13 D2
Nexon 29 D1
Neyland 8 B2
Nez de Jobourg 18 B2
Nežin 113 F1
Niáta 87 D3
Niaux, Grotte de 32 A2
Nibe 108 B2
Nicastro 67 E3
Nice 31 E4
Nickelsdorf 57 F3
Nicolosi 69 D3
Nicosia 68 C3
Nicotera 67 E4
Nidda 52 A4
Nidderau 52 A4
Nideggen 51 D3
Nidelva 104 B4
Nidri 82 B3
Niebla 42 C2
Niebüll 47 F1
Niechorze 49 F1
Nied 21 D3
Nieddu, M 66 C2
Niederalteich 56 B2
Niederaula 52 B3
Niederbronn 21 E3
Niederelsungen 52 A2
Niedere Tauern 57 D4
Niederjossa 52 B3
Niederkrüchten 17 D4
Niederösterreich 57 E2
Niedersachsen 48 A4
Niederstetten 55 D1
Niederstotzingen 55 E3
Niederzerf 54 A1
Niefla, Pto de 43 F1
Niegripp 48 C4
Niemegk 53 D1
Niemisel 98 C3
Nienburg (Niedersachsen) 48 A4
Nienburg (Sachsen-Anhalt) 52 C1
Nieras 94 B4
Nierstein 54 C1
Niesky 53 F2
Niesłysz, Jez 49 F4
Nieuweschans 47 E3
Nieuwpoort 50 A3
Nièvre 26 B2
Niforéka 86 B1
Nigrita 80 B2
Niinivesi 103 D2
Nijar 44 C3
Nijemci 72 B2
Nijkerk 16 C2
Nijmegen 17 D3
Nijverdal 17 D2
Nikea 83 E2
Nikí 79 D2
Nikiá 89 F4
Nikifóros 80 C2
Nikissiani 80 C2
Nikitas 80 B4
Nikkaluokta 94 C4
Nikolajev (L'vov) 112 C3
Nikolajev (Odessa) 113 F3
Nikoléika 86 C1
Nikopol 115 D2
Nikópoli 82 B3
Nikopólis, Órmos 82 B2

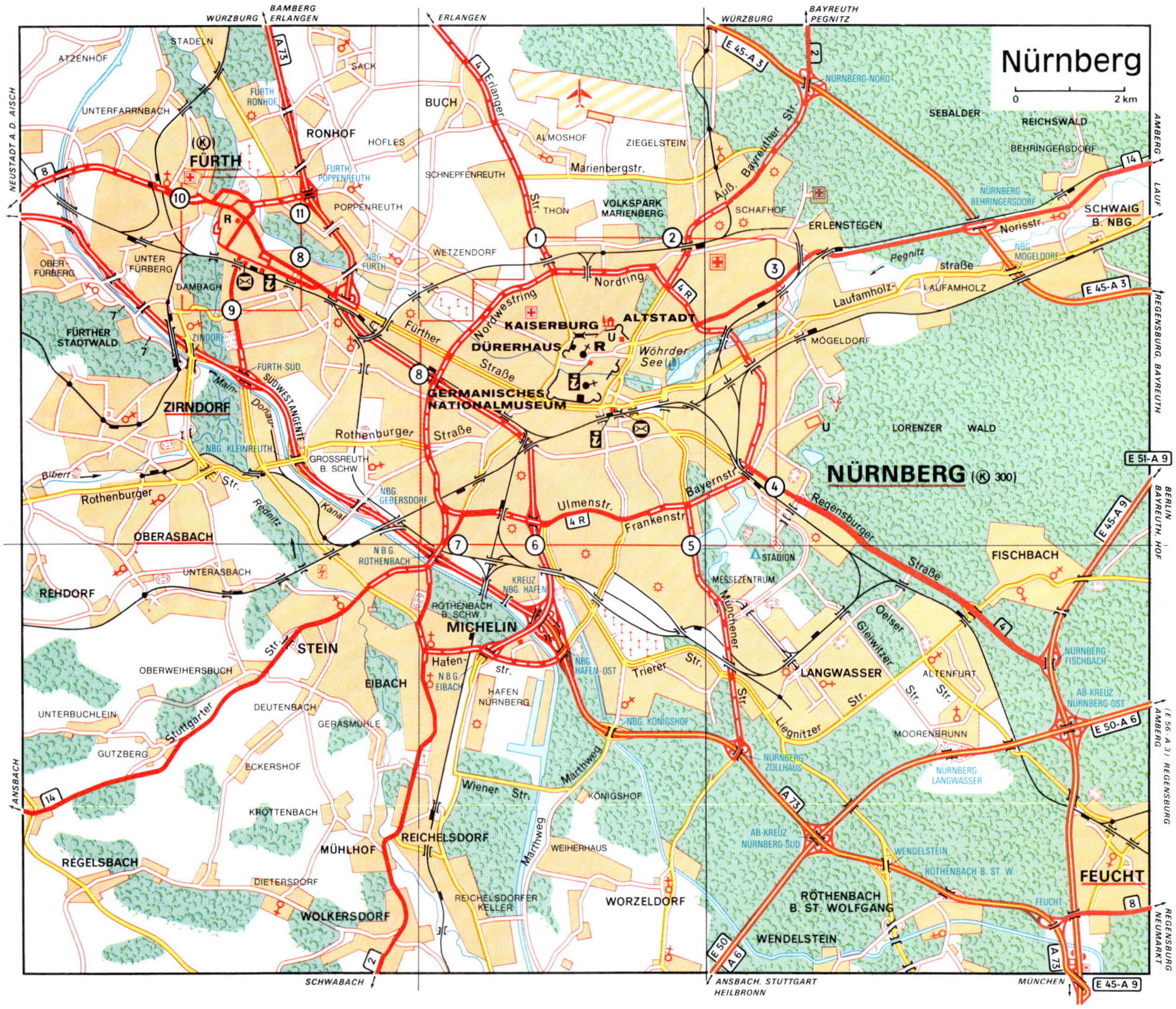
Nürnberg
0
2 km
NÜRNBERG
FÜRTH
ZIRNDORF
OBERASBACH
STEIN
FEUCHT
FISCHBACH
LANGWASSER
ALTSTADT
KAISERBURG
DÜRERHAUS
GERMANISCHES NATIONALMUSEUM
MICHELIN
REICHELSDORF
WORZELDORF
WENDELSTEIN
RÖTHENBACH B. ST. WOLFGANG
ERLENSTEGEN
LORENZER WALD
SEBALDER
REICHSWALD
BUCH
RONHOF
EIBACH
REHDORF
REGELSBACH
WOLKERSDORF
MÜHLHOF
FÜRTHER STADTWALD
WÜRZBURG
BAMBERG ERLANGEN
ERLANGEN
BAYREUTH PEGNITZ
SCHWABACH
ANSBACH, STUTTGART HEILBRONN
MÜNCHEN
ANSBACH
AMBERG
LAUF
REGENSBURG, BAYREUTH
BERLIN BAYREUTH, HOF
REGENSBURG NEUMARKT
NEUSTADT A.D. AISCH

Nikšić 76 B2
Nilakka 103 D2
Nilivaara 98 B2
Nilsiä 103 E2
Nîmes 30 B3
Nimféa 81 E2
Nimféo 79 D3
Nimos, N 93 E1
Nin 74 C1
Ninove 50 B3
Niort 24 C4
Nipfjället 101 D3
Nipsa 81 F2
Niš 77 E1
Nisa 38 C3
Nisa, Rib de 38 C3
Nišava 73 F4
Niscemi 68 C4
Niška Banja 77 E1
Nissáki 82 A1
Nissan 109 D2
Nisser 104 B3
Nissilä 103 D1
Nissiros, N 89 F4
Nissum Bredning 108 A2
Nissum Fjord 108 A2
Nith 4 C3
Niton 9 E4
Nitra 112 B3
Nitry 26 B2
Nittedal 105 D3
Nittenau 56 B1
Nittendorf 55 F2
Nivala 102 C1
Nive 28 A4
Nivelles 50 B4
Nivernais 26 B3
Nivolet, Colle del 31 E1
Niwica 53 F1
Nizke Beskydy 112 C3
Nizza Monferrato 31 F2
Njegoš 76 A2
Njivice 70 B3
Njunis 94 C3
Njupeskär 101 D3
Noailles 19 F3
Noáin 36 C2
Noarvaš 95 D3
Noblejas 40 B3
Nocera 64 B4
Nocera Tirinese 67 E3
Nocera Umbra 61 E4
Noceto 60 B2
Noci 65 E3
Nodeland 104 B4
Nogara 60 C1
Nogaro 28 B4
Nogent 26 C1
Nogent-le-Roi 19 E4
Nogent-le-Rotrou 23 F3
Nogent-sur-Seine 20 A4
Nogueira de Ramuin 34 B2
Nogueira, Sa de 34 C4
Noguera 41 D2
Noguera Pallaresa, R 37 F2
Noguera Ribagorçana, R 37 F3
Nohfelden 54 B1
Noia 34 A2
Noirétable 26 B4
Noirmoutier 24 A3
Noirmoutier, I de 24 A3
Noja 36 A1
Nokia 107 E1
Nola 64 B4
Nolay 26 B3
Noli 60 A3
Nomeny 21 D3
Nomexy 21 D4
Nómia 87 E4
Nonancourt 19 E4
Nonant-le-Pin 19 D4
Nonaspe 37 E4
None 31 E2
Nonio 58 A4
Nontron 28 C1
Nónza 33 F2
Noord-Brabant 16 C3
Noord-Holland 16 C2
Noord-Oost-Polder 16 C2
Noordwijk aan Zee 16 B2
Noordzee 46 B3
Noormarkku 102 B3
Nora 105 F3
Norberg 105 F3
Norcia 63 F1
Nord 20 A1
Nord Beveland 16 B3
Nordborg 108 A4
Nordby (Fanø) 108 A3
Nordby (Samsø) 108 B3
Norddeich 47 E3
Nordeide 100 A3
Norden 47 E3
Nordenau 17 F4
Nordenham 47 F3
Norderney 47 E3
Norderstedt 48 A2
Nordfjord 100 A3
Nordfjordeid 100 A3
Nordfold 97 E1
Nordfolda 97 E1
Nordfriesische Inseln 47 E1
Nordhalben 52 C3
Nordhausen 52 C2
Nordhorn 17 E2
Nordingrå 102 A2
Nordkapp 95 E1
Nordkinnhalvøya 95 E1
Nordkjosbotn 94 C3
Nordkvaløy 94 B2
Nordland 97 E2
Nord-Lenangen 94 C2
Nordli 97 E4
Nördlingen 55 E2
Nordmaling 102 A2
Nordmark 105 E3
Nord-Ostsee-Kanal 47 F2
Nordøyane 100 A2
Norðoyar 96 A3
Nordrana 97 E2
Nordreisa 94 C2
Nordrhein-Westfalen 17 E3
Nordsee 47 B2
Nordseter 105 D2
Nordstrand 47 F1
Nord Trøndelag 101 D1
Norðurfjörður 96 A1
Nore (IRL) 12 C4
Nore (N) 104 C2
Norefjell 104 C2
Nore, R 15 D3
Noresund 104 C2
Norfolk 7 F3
Norg 17 D1
Norheimsund 104 A2
Norra Bergnäs 98 A2
Norra Gloppet 102 B2
Norråker 101 F1
Norra Kvarken 102 B2
Norra Kvill 109 E1
Norra Råda 105 E3
Norra Storfjället 97 E3
Norrbottens Län 98 B1
Norrby 98 A4
Nørre Åby 108 B3
Nørre Alslev 108 C4
Nørre Nebel 108 A3
Norrent-Fontes 19 F1
Nørre Snede 108 A3
Nørre Vorupør 108 A2
Norrfjärden 101 F3
Norrköping 106 A4
Norrnäs 102 B3
Norrsunda 106 B3
Norrsundet 106 B2
Norrtälje 106 B3
Norrviken 108 C3
Norsjö 98 B4
Norsjø 104 C3
Norskehavet 96 B4
Nort 23 D4
Nörten-Hardenberg 52 B2
Northallerton 7 D1
Northam 8 C3
Northampton 9 F1
Northamptonshire 9 F1
North Berwick 5 D2
North Chan 13 E1
North Downs 10 C3
Northeim 52 B2
Northern Ireland 13 D2
North Esk 3 D4
North Foreland 11 D2
Northleach 9 E2
North Ronaldsay 3 E1
North Sound, The 3 E1
North Tyne 5 E3
North Uist 2 A3
Northumberland 5 E3
Northumberland Nat Pk 5 E3
North Walsham 7 F3
Northwich 6 C2
North York Moors Nat Pk 7 D1
North Yorkshire 6 C1
Norton 7 D1
Nortort 48 A2
Norwich 11 D1
Nosovka 113 E1
Nossebro 108 C1
Nossen 53 E2
Noss Head 3 D2
Noteć 112 A1
Nótia 79 E2
Nótia Pindos 82 C1
Nótios Evoikós Kólpos 84 B4
Nótio Stenó Kerkiras 82 B2
Noto 69 D4
Notodden 104 C3
Notre-Dame-de-Bellecombe 27 E4
Nottingham 7 D3
Nottinghamshire 7 D3
Nouan-le-Fuzelier 25 E2
Nousiainen 107 D2
Nouvion 19 E2
Nouvion-en-Thiérache, le 20 B2
Nœux 19 F1
Nouzonville 20 C2
Nova Breznica 77 D3
Nová Bystřice 57 D1
Novaci (Makedonija) 77 E4
Novaci (Srbija) 72 C3
Nova Crnja 72 C1
Novafeltria 61 E3
Nova Gorica (I) 59 F3
Nova Gorica (YU) 70 A2
Nova Gradiška 71 E3
Nova Kasaba 72 B4
Novales 37 D3
Nova Levante 59 D3
Novalja 70 B4
Nova Pazova 72 C2
Novara 60 A1
Novara di Sicilia 69 D2
Nova Siri 65 D4
Nova Topola 71 E3
Nova Vas 70 B2
Nova Vavos 76 B1
Nova Zagora 115 E2
Novelda 45 D1
Novellara 60 C2
Nove Město nad Váhom 112 A3
Noventa Vicentino 61 D1
Noves 30 C3
Nové Zámky 112 B4
Novgorod 111 D1
Novgorod-Severskij 111 F4
Novi Bečej 72 C2
Novi di Modena 60 C2
Novi Dojran 77 F3
Novigrad (Poreč) 70 A3
Novigrad (Zadar) 74 C1
Novi Grad 71 F3
Novigrad Podravski 71 D2
Novigradsko more 74 C1
Novi Karlovci 72 C2
Novi Kneževac 72 C1
Novi Ligure 60 A2
Novi Marof 70 C1
Novion-Porcien 20 B2
Novi Pazar 76 C1
Novi Pazar 115 E2
Novi Sad 72 C2
Novi Šeher 71 F4
Novi Senkovac 71 E2
Novi Slankamen 72 C2
Novi Travnik 71 E4
Novi Vinodolski 70 B3
Novo Brdo 77 D2
Novograd-Volynskij 113 D2
Novogrudok 111 D4
Novo Hopovo 72 C2
Novo Mesto 70 B2
Novo Miloševo 72 C1
Novomirgorod 113 F2
Novoržev 111 D2
Novoselica 113 D3
Novo Selo (Bosna i Hercegovina) 71 E3
Novo Selo (Makedonija) 77 F3
Novoukrainka 113 F3
Novovolynsk 112 C2
Novo Zvečevo 71 E2
Novozybkov 111 E4
Novska 71 D3
Nový Bor 53 F3
Novyj Bug 113 F3
Nový Jičín 112 B3
Nowa Sól 112 A2
Nowe Warpno 49 E2
Nowogard 49 F2
Nowy Sącz 112 B3
Nowy Targ 112 B3
Noyant 23 F4
Noyers 26 B1
Noyers-sur-Jabron 30 C3
Noyon 19 F3
Nozay 23 D4
Nuasjärvi 99 E4
Nueva 35 E1
Nueva Carteya 43 F2
Nuévalos Monasterio de Piedra 36 C4
Nuevo Baztán 40 B2
Nufenenpass 58 A3
Nuhppir 95 E2
Nuijamaa 103 F4
Nuits-St-Georges 26 C2
Nules 41 E3
Nulvi 66 B2
Numana 61 F4
Numancia 36 B3
Numedal 104 C2
Nummela 107 E2

Nummi 107 E2
Nuneaton 9 E1
Nunnanen 95 D3
Nuñomoral 39 D2
Nunspeet 17 D2
Nuorajärvi 103 F2
Nuorgam 95 E2
Nuoro 66 B2
Nurallao 66 B3
Nürburg 51 E4
Núria 32 B3
Nurmes 103 E1
Nurmijärvi (Pohjois-Karjalan Lääni) 103 F1
Nurmijärvi (Uudenmaan Lääni) 107 E2
Nurmo 102 C2
Nürnberg 55 F1
Nürtingen 55 D3
Nus 27 E4
Nusse 48 B2
Nuštar 71 F2
Nuthe 49 D4
Nuttlar 17 F3
Nuttupera 103 D1
Nuutajärvi 107 E2
Nuvvos-Ailigas 95 E2
Nyåker 102 A1
Nybergsund 105 E2
Nyborg 108 B4
Nybro 109 E2
Nyírbátor 112 C3
Nyíregyháza 112 C3
Nykarleby 102 B2
Nykøbing F (Storstrøm) 108 C4
Nykøbing M (Viborg) 108 A2
Nykøbing S (Vestsjælland) 108 C3
Nyköping 106 B4
Nykvarn 106 B4
Nynäshamn 106 B4
Nyon 27 D3
Nyons 30 C3
Nýřany 53 E4
Nýrdalur 96 B2
Nýrsko 56 B1
Nyrud 95 F2
Nysa 112 A2
Nysa Łużycka 53 F1
Nysäter 105 E3
Nyseter 100 B3
Nysted 108 C4
Nyvoll 95 D2

O

Oadby 9 F1
Oakham 9 F1
Oanes 104 A3
Óassi 87 D1
Oban 4 B1
O Barco 34 C3
Obbola 102 B1
Obdach 57 D4
Obdacher Sattel 57 D4
Obedska bara 72 C3
Obejo 43 F2
Oberalppass 58 A3
Oberammergau 55 F4
Oberau 56 A4
Oberaudorf 56 B4
Oberdrauburg 59 E2
Oberessfeld 52 C4
Obergeis 52 B3
Obergrafendorf 57 E2
Obergrünzburg 55 E4
Obergurgl 58 C2
Oberhaslach 21 E4
Oberhausen 17 E3
Oberhof 52 C3
Oberjoch-Paß 58 C1
Oberkirch 54 C3
Oberkirchen 17 F4
Oberkochen 55 E2
Obermarchtal 55 D3
Obernai 21 E4
Obernberg 56 C3
Obernburg 55 D1
Oberndorf (A) 56 C3
Oberndorf (D) 54 C3
Obernzell 56 C2
Oberölsbach 55 F1
Oberösterreich 56 C2
Oberprechtal 54 C3
Oberpullendorf 57 F3
Oberseebach 21 F3
Obersontheim 55 E2
Oberstaufen 55 E4
Oberstdorf 55 E4
Oberstein 54 B1
Obertauern 59 F1
Obertraun 59 F1
Oberursel 51 F4
Obervellach 59 E2
Oberviechtach 56 B1
Oberwart 57 F4
Oberwesel 51 E4
Oberwiesenthal 53 E3
Oberwölz 57 D4
Oberzeiring 57 D4
Óbidos 38 A3
Obilić 77 D2
Obing 56 B3
Obiou, l' 30 C2
Objat 29 D1
Obninsk 111 F3
O Bolo 34 C3
Obón 41 E1
Oborniki 112 A1
Obornjača 72 C1
Oborovo 70 C2
Obrenovac 72 C3
Obrež 72 C3
Obrov 70 A3
Obrovac (Split) 75 D1
Obrovac (Zadar) 74 C1
Obršani 77 E4
Obsteig 58 C2
Obudovac 71 F3
Obzor 115 E2
Obzova 70 B3
Očakov 113 F3
Oca, Mtes de 36 A2
Ocaña 40 B3
Oca, R 36 A2
Očauš 71 E4
Occhiobello 61 D2
Occhito, L di 64 B3
Očevlje 71 F4
Ochagavia 37 D2
Ochil Hills 5 D1
Ochsenfurt 55 E1
Ochsenhausen 55 E3
Ochtrup 17 E2
Ockelbo 106 A2
Öckerö 108 C1
Ocreza, R 38 C3
Ocrkavlje 76 A1
Ödåkra 108 C3
Odda 104 B2
Odden Færgehavn 108 B3
Odder 108 B3
Oddesund 108 A2
Odeceixe 42 A2
Odeleite 42 B2
Odelzhausen 55 F3
Odemira 42 A2
Ödemiş 115 F4
Odense 108 B3
Odenthal 17 E4
Oder 49 E3
Oderberg 49 E3
Oderbruch 49 E3
Oderbucht 49 E1
Oderhaff 49 E2
Oderzo 59 E4
Ödeshög 109 D1
Odessa 113 F4
Odet 22 B3
Odiel, R 42 C2
Odivelas 42 B1
Odivelas, Bgem de 42 B1
Odolo 60 B1
Odorheiu Secuiesc 113 D4
Odra 112 A2
Odžaci 72 B2
Odžak (Bosna i Hercegovina) 71 F3
Odžak (Crna Gora) 76 B1
Oebisfelde 48 B4
Oebro 105 F4
Oederan 53 E3
Oeiras 38 A4
Oelde 17 F3
Oelsnitz (Plauen) 53 D3
Oelsnitz (Zwickau) 53 D3
Oettingen 55 E2
Oetz 58 C2
Ofanto 64 C3
Ofenpass 58 C3
Offaly 12 C4
Offenbach 52 A4
Offenburg 54 C3
Offida 63 F1
Offranville 19 E2
Ofir 34 A4
Ofotfjorden 94 B3
Oggiono 60 A1
Ogliastro Cilento 67 D1
Oglio 58 C4
Ognon 27 D2
Ogošte 77 E2
Ogražden 77 F3
Ogre 110 C2
Ogulin 70 C3
Ohanes 44 B3
Óhi, Óros 88 A1
Ohiró 80 B1
Ohlstadt 56 A4
Ohorn 53 F2
Ohrdruf 52 C3
Ohre 48 B4
Ohře 53 E3
Ohrid 77 D4
Ohridsko Ez 77 D4
Ohringen 55 D2
Ohrit, Liq i 77 D4
Óhthia 82 C3
Ohthoniá 84 B4
Oijärvi 99 D3
Oijärvi L 99 D3
Oikarainen 99 D2
Oirschot 16 C3
Oise 20 B2
Oise (Dépt) 19 F3
Oisemont 19 E2
Oisterwijk 16 C3
Oitti 107 E2
Oituz 113 D4
Ojakylä 99 D4
Öje 101 E4
Öjebyn 98 B3
Ojén 43 E4
Ojos Negros 41 D2
Ojuelos Altos 43 E1
Öjung 101 E4
Okehampton 8 C3
Oker 48 B4
Oklaj 75 D1
Öknö 109 E2
Okol 76 C2
Oksbøl 108 A3
Oksby 108 A3
Øksfjord 95 D2
Øksfjorden 94 A3
Øksfjordjøkelen 94 C2
Øksnes 94 A3
Okstindan 97 E3
Okučani 71 E3
Okulovka 111 E1
Olafsfjörður 96 B1
Olafsvík 96 A2
Öland 109 E2
Olan, Pic d' 31 D2
Olargues 32 B1
Olazagutía 36 B2
Olbernhau 53 E3
Olbia 66 B1
Oldcastle 13 D3
Oldebroek 17 D2
Oldeide 100 A3
Olden 100 A3
Oldenburg (Niedersachsen) 47 F3
Oldenburg (Schleswig Holstein) 48 B1
Oldenzaal 17 E2
Olderdalen 94 C2
Oldervik 94 C2
Oldfjällen 101 E1
Oldham 6 C2
Old Head of Kinsale 14 B4
Oldmeldrum 3 E4
Oldsum 47 F1
Oleggio 60 A1
Oleiros 34 B1
Oleiros 38 C2
Ølen 104 A3
Oléron, Ile d' 24 B4
Olesa 32 A4
Oleśnica 112 A2
Oletta 33 F2
Olette 32 B2
Olevsk 113 D2
Ølgod 108 A3
Olhão 42 B3
Olhava 99 D3
Oliana 32 A3
Oliana, Emb d' 32 A3
Olib 70 B4
Olib I 70 B4
Oliena 66 B2
Oliete 37 D4
Olimbía 86 C2
Olimbiáda (Makedonía) 80 B3
Olimbiáda (Thessalía) 79 E4
Ólimbos 93 D2
Ólimbos, Óros (Évia) 84 B4
Ólimbos, Óros (Pieriá) 79 E4
Ólinthos 80 A4
Olite 36 C2
Oliva 45 E1
Oliva de la Frontera 42 C1
Oliva de Mérida 39 D4
Olivares 40 C3
Oliveira de Azeméis 38 B1
Oliveira de Frades 38 B1
Oliveira do Bairro 38 B1
Oliveira do Douro 34 B4
Oliveira do Hospital 38 C2
Olivenza 38 C4
Olivenza, R de 38 C4
Olivet 25 E1
Olivone 58 A3
Olleria, Pto de l' 41 E4
Ollerton 7 D3
Ollières, les 30 B2
Olliergues 29 F1
Ollioules 31 D4
Ollöla 103 F2
Olmedillo de Roa 35 F4
Olmedo (E) 35 E4
Olmedo (I) 66 A2
Olmeto 33 F4
Olocau del Rey 41 E2
Olofström 109 D3
Olombrada 35 F4
Olomouc 112 A3
Olonzac 32 B1
Oloron Ste Marie 37 D1
Olost 32 A3
Olot 32 B3
Olovo 71 F4
Olpe 17 F4
Olsberg 17 F3
Olshammar 105 F4
Olst 17 D2
Ølstykke 108 C3
Olsztyn 110 B4
Olszyna 53 F1
Olt 115 D2
Oltedal 104 A3
Olten 27 F2
Oltenia 115 D1
Oltenița 115 E1
Olula del Río 44 C3
Olvega 36 C3
Olvera 43 E3
Omagh 13 D2
Omalí 79 D4
Omalós 90 B3
Omarska 71 D3
Ombrone 63 D1
Omegna 58 A4
Omiš 75 E2
Omišalj 70 B3
Omme Å 108 A3
Ommen 17 D2
Omodeo, L 66 B3
Omoljica 73 D3
Omorfohóri 83 E1
Ömossa 102 B3
Oña 36 A2
Oñati 36 B1
Oncala, Pto de 36 B3
Onda 41 E3
Ondara 45 E1
Ondárroa 36 B1
Oneglia 31 F3
Onesse-et-Laharie 28 A3
Onich 2 C4
Onkamo (Lapin Lääni) 99 E2
Onkamo (Pohjois Karjalan Lääni) 103 F2
Onkivesi 103 E2
Ons, I de 34 A2
Ontaneda 35 F2
Ontiñena 37 E3
Ontinyent 45 E1
Ontojärvi 99 F4
Ontur 45 D1
Onzain 25 E2
Oostburg 16 B4
Oostelijk-Flevoland 16 C2
Oostende 50 A3
Oosterbeek 17 D3
Oosterend 16 C1
Oosterhout 16 C3
Oostkamp 50 A3
Oostmalle 50 C3
Oost-Vlaanderen 50 B3
Oost-Vlieland 16 C1
Ootmarsum 17 E2
Opatija 70 B3
Opatovac 72 B2
Opava 112 A3
Opladen 17 E4
Oplenac 73 D3
Opočka 111 D2
Opole 112 A2
Opovo 72 C2
Oppach 53 F2
Oppdal 100 C2
Oppenau 54 C3
Oppenheim 54 C1
Opphaug 100 C1
Oppido Lucano 64 C4
Oppido Mamertina 67 E4
Oppland 104 C1
Oputten 16 C2
Opuzen 75 F2
Ora 59 D3
Oradea 112 C4
Oradour-sur-Glane 25 D4
Oradour-sur-Vayres 28 C1
Orahova 71 D3
Orahovac 77 D2
Orahovica 71 E2
Oraison 31 D3
Orajärvi 98 C2
Orange 30 B3
Orani 66 B2
Oranienbaum 53 D1
Oranienburg 49 D3
Oranmore 12 B3
Orašac (Hrvatska) 75 F2
Orašac (Srbija) 73 D3
Orasi 76 B3
Orašje 71 F3
Orăștie 114 C1
Oravainen 102 B2
Oravais 102 B2
Oravikoski 103 E2
Oravița 114 C1
Orb 30 A4
Orba 45 E1
Ørbæk 108 B4
Orbassano 31 E2
Orbe 27 D3
Orbec 19 D3
Orbetello 63 D2
Orbey 27 E1
Orbigo, R 35 D2
Orce 44 B2
Orce, R 44 B2
Orcera 44 B1
Orchies 20 A1
Orcières 31 D2
Orcival 29 E1
Orco 31 E1
Ordes 34 A1
Ordesa, Parque Nac. de 37 E2
Ordino 32 A2
Ordizia 36 C1
Orduña 36 B1
Orduña, Pto de 36 B1
Ore 101 E4
Orea 41 D2
Öreälven 102 A1
Orebić 75 E2
Örebro Län 105 F3
Öregrund 106 B3
Öregrundsgrepen 106 B2
Orei 83 F3
Orellana de la Sierra 39 E4
Orellana, Emb de 39 E4
Orellana la Vieja 39 E4
Orense 34 B3
Oréo 81 D2
Oreókastro 79 F3
Orestiáda 81 F1
Oresund 108 C3
Orfós, Akr 89 F4
Orgáni 81 E2
Organyà 32 A3
Orgañyà 37 F3
Orgaz 40 A3
Orgejev 113 E3
Orgelet 26 C3
Orgères-en-Beauce 25 E1
Orgon 30 C3
Orgosolo 66 B2
Orhi, Pic d' 37 D1
Orhomenós 83 F4
Oria 44 C3
Oria 65 E4
Oria, R 36 C1
Origny-Sainte-Benoîte 20 A2
Orihuela 45 D2
Orihuela del Tremedal 41 D2
Orimattila 107 F2
Oriní 80 B2
Oriolo 65 D4
Oripää 187 D2
Orissaare 110 B2
Oristano 66 B3
Oristano, G di 66 A3
Orivesi 102 C3
Orivesi L 103 F2
Orjahovo 115 D2
Ørjavik 100 B2
Ørje 105 D3
Orjen 76 A2
Orjiva 44 A3
Orkanger 100 C2
Örkelljunga 109 D3
Orkla 100 C2
Orkney Is 3 E1
Ørlandet 100 C1
Orlando, C d' 69 D2
Orlane 77 D1
Orlate 77 D2
Orléans 25 E1
Orlická přehr nádrž 56 C1
Orlovat 72 C2
Orly 19 F4
Orménio 81 F1
Ormília 80 B4
Órmos 79 F3
Órmos Korthíou 88 B1
Órmos Panagías 80 B4
Órmos Prínou 80 C3
Ormož 70 C1
Ormsjö 97 F4
Ormsjön 101 F1
Ormskirk 6 B2
Ormtjernkampen 104 C1
Ornain 20 C4
Ornans 27 D2
Orne (Calvados) 18 C4
Orne (Dépt) 20 B3
Orne (Meuse) 21 D3
Ørnes 97 E2
Ornós 88 C2
Örnsköldsvik 102 A2
Or'ol 111 F4
Orolik 72 B2
Orom 72 B1
Oron-la-Ville 27 E3
Oropesa (Castilla la Mancha) 39 F3
Oropesa (Valencia) 41 F3
Orosei 66 C2
Orosei, G di 66 C2
Orosháza 112 B4
Orpierre 30 C3
Orpington 10 C2
Orra 100 C3
Orsa 101 E4
Orša 111 E3
Orsajön 101 E4
Orsay 19 F4
Orsières 27 E4
Orsogna 64 A2
Orșova 114 C1
Ørsta 100 A2
Örsundsbro 106 B3
Orta Nova 64 C3
Orta San Giulio 58 A4
Orte 63 E2
Ortegal, C 34 B1
Orth 57 F2
Orthez 28 B4
Ortigueira 34 B1
Ortisei 59 D3
Ortles 58 C3
Ortnevik 104 B1
Orton 5 D4
Ortona 64 A2
Ortrand 53 E2
Örträsk 102 A1
Orubica 71 E3
Orune 66 B2
Orusco 40 B2
Orvalho 38 C2
Orvieto 63 E1
Órvilos, Óros 80 B1
Orvinio 63 F2

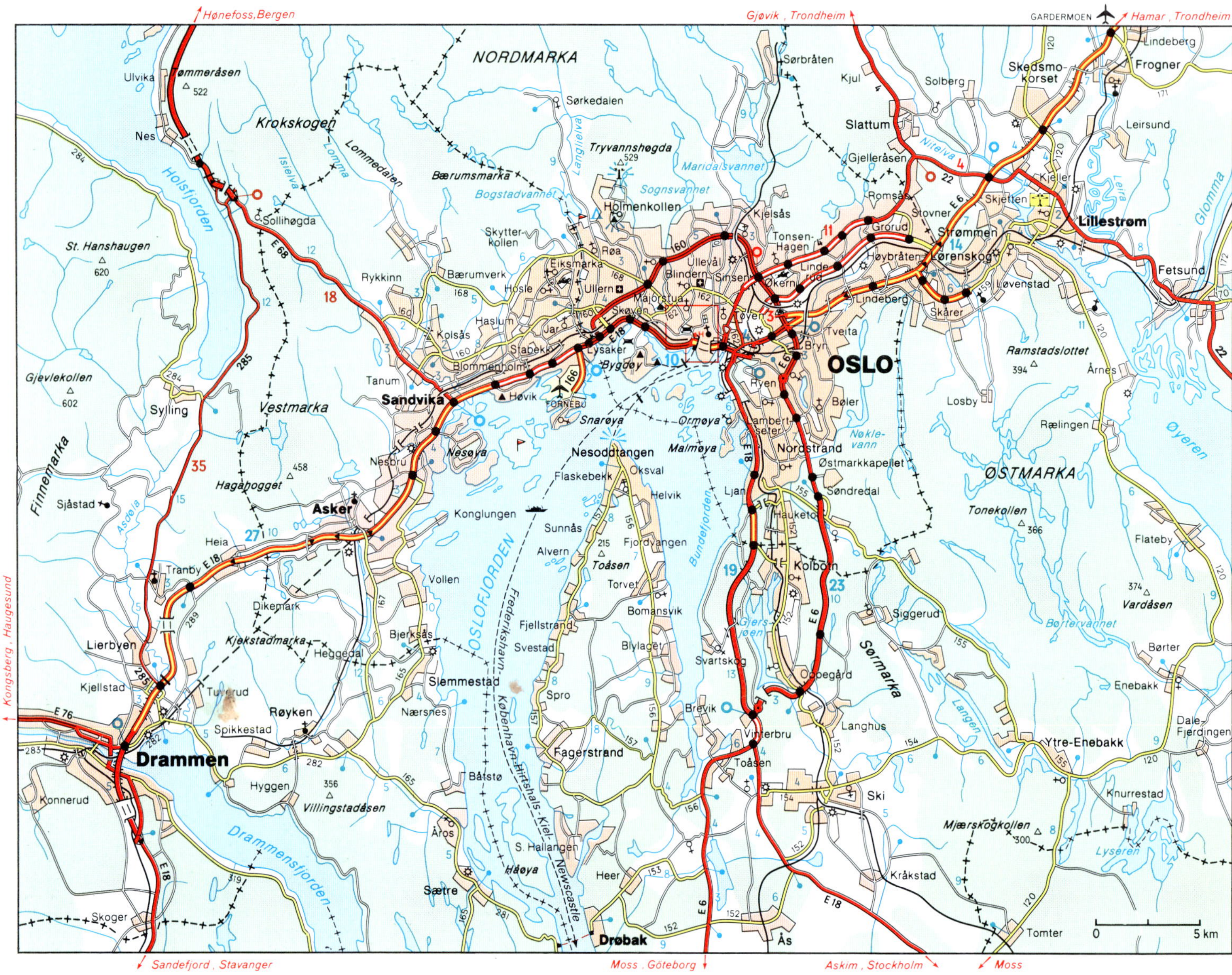
Hønefoss, Bergen
Gjøvik, Trondheim
GARDERMOEN
Hamar, Trondheim
NORDMARKA
Krokskogen
Sørkedalen
Tryvannshøgda
Maridalsvannet
Sognsvannet
Bogstadvannet
Bærumsmarka
Holmenkollen
Slattum
Sørbråten
Kjul
Solberg
Skedsmo-korset
Lindeberg
Frogner
Leirsund
Gjelleråsen
Lillestrøm
Strømmen
Lørenskog
Fetsund
Glomma
Kongsvinger
Bjørkelangen
Ulvika
Sommeråsen
Nes
Holsfjorden
Sollihøgda
St. Hanshaugen
Rykkinn
Bærumverk
Skytter-kollen
Eiksmarka
Røa
Ullevål
Blindern
Ullern
Majorstua
Skøyen
Hosle
Hasløm
Kolsås
Stabekk
Lysaker
Bygdøy
Blommenholm
Tveita
Bryn
OSLO
Lindeberg
Løvenstad
Skårer
Ramstadslottet
Årnes
Gjevlekollen
Sylling
Vestmarka
Tanum
Sandvika
Høvik
FORNEBU
Snarøya
Ormøya
Ryen
Bøler
Lambertseter
Nordstrand
Østmarkkapellet
Søndredal
Rælingen
Losby
Øyeren
ØSTMARKA
Askim
Finnemarka
Sjåstad
Hagahogget
Nesøya
Nesbru
Nesoddtangen
Malmøya
Oksval
Flaskebekk
Helvik
Ljan
Tonekollen
Flateby
Asker
Heia
Konglungen
Sunnås
Hauketo
Fjordvangen
Alvern
Tåsen
Torvet
Kolbotn
Vardåsen
Tranby
Vollen
Bunnefjorden
Bomansvik
Siggerud
Bøtervannet
Kongsberg, Haugesund
Dikemark
Lierbyen
Kjekstadmarka
Heggedal
Bjerkås
OSLOFJORDEN
Fjellstrand
Svestad
Blylaget
Svartskog
Sørmarka
Børter
Kjellstad
Tuverud
Slemmestad
Spro
Oppegård
Enebakk
Røyken
Spikkestad
Nærsnes
Brevik
Vinterbru
Langhus
Dale-Fjerdingen
Ytre-Enebakk
Drammen
Fagerstrand
Toåsen
Konnerud
Hyggen
Villingstadåsen
Båtstø
Ski
Knurrestad
Drammensfjorden
Åros
S. Hallangen
Mjærskogkollen
Lyseren
Håøya
Heer
Kråkstad
Sætre
Skoger
Drøbak
Ås
Tomter
Frederikshavn - København - Hirtshals - Kiel - Newcastle
0
5 km
Sandefjord, Stavanger
Moss, Göteborg
Askim, Stockholm
Moss

Orzinuovi 60 B1
Os 100 D3
Osa de la Vega 40 B3
Osâm 115 D2
Osby 109 D3
Oschatz 53 E2
Oschersleben 52 C1
Oschiri 66 B2
Osečina 72 C3
Oseja de Sajambre 35 E2
Osen 96 C4
Osera de Ebro 37 D4
Osijek 71 F2
Osilo 66 B2
Osimo 61 F4
Osinja 71 E3
Osipaonica 73 D3
Osipoviči 111 D4
Osječenica 71 D4
Oskarshamn 109 E2
Oskarström 108 C2
Oslava 57 E1
Oslo 105 D3
Oslo (Fylke) 105 D3
Oslofjorden 104 C3
Ösmo 106 B4
Osnabrück 17 F2
Ośno Lubuskie 49 F4
Osogovija 77 F2
Osogovske planine 77 E2
Osoppo 59 E3
Osor 70 B4
Osorno 35 F3
Osøyri 104 A2
Ospedaletti 31 E3
Ospitaletto 60 B1
Oss 16 C3
Óssa 80 A2
Ossa de Montiel 40 B4
Óssa, Óros 83 F1
Ossa, Sa de 38 C4
Ossiach 59 F2
Ossiacher See 59 F2
Óssios Loukás 83 F4
Ossun 37 E1
Ostaškov 111 E2
Østbirk 108 B3
Østby 105 E2
Oste 47 F3
Osted 108 C3
Osterburg 48 C4
Osterburken 55 D1
Østerby Havn 108 B2
Österbymo 109 E1
Österdalälven 101 D3
Østerdalen 100 C3
Österfärnebo 106 A3
Osterfeld 53 D2
Östergötlands Län 109 E1
Osterhofen 56 B2
Osterholz Scharmbeck 47 F3
Osteria del Gatto 61 E4
Osterode 52 B2
Osterøya 104 A2
Östersund 101 E2
Östersundom 107 F2
Östervåla 106 B3
Øster Vrå 108 B2
Osterwieck 52 B1
Østfold 105 D3
Ostfriesische Inseln 47 D3
Östhammar 106 B3
Ostheim 52 B4
Ostia Antica 63 E3
Ostiglia 60 C2
Östmark 105 E3
Ost'or 113 E1
Ostra 61 E3
Ostrach 55 D4
Östra Gloppet 102 B2
Östra Silen 105 D4
Ostrava 112 B3
Oštrelj 71 D4
Ostritz 53 F2
Ostróda 110 B4
Ostrog 113 D2
Ostrołęka 112 B1
Ostrov (CS) 53 E3
Ostrov (RO) 115 E1
Ostrov (SU) 111 D2
Ostrowiec Świętokrzyski 112 B2
Ostrów Mazowiecki 112 B1
Ostrów Wielkopolski 112 A2
Ostrožac (Bosna i Hercegovina) 70 C3
Ostrožac (Bosna i Hercegovina) 75 F1
Ostsee 48 C1
Osttirol 59 E2
Ostuni 65 E3
Osuna 43 E3
Oswestry 6 B3
Oświęcim 112 B2
Otanmäki 103 D1
Otava (CS) 56 C1
Otava (SF) 103 E3
Oteren 94 C3
Oteševo 77 D4
Othem 109 F4
Othery 9 D3
Othoní, N 78 A4
Óthris, Óros 83 E3
Otivar 44 A3
Otley 6 C2
Otnes 100 C3
Otočac 70 C4
Otočec 70 B2
Otok 72 B2
Otoka 71 D3
Otra 104 B4
Otranto 65 F4
Otsamo 95 E3
Otta 100 C3
Ottana 66 B2
Ottaviano 64 B4
Ottenschlag 57 E2
Ottensheim 57 D2
Otterburn 5 E3
Otter Ferry 4 B2
Otterlo 17 D3
Otterndorf 47 F2
Otterøy 97 D4
Ottersberg 47 F3
Otterup 108 B3
Ottery St Mary 9 D3
Ottmarsheim 27 E1
Ottnang 56 C3
Ottobeuren 55 E3
Ottobrunn 56 A3
Ottsjö 101 D2
Ottweiler 54 B2
Otwock 112 B1
Otziás 88 A2
Ötztal 58 C2
Ötztaleralpen 58 C2
Ouchy 27 D3
Oucques 25 E1
Oud Beijerland 16 B3
Ouddorp 16 B3
Oude Maas 16 B3
Oudenaarde 50 B3
Oudenbosch 16 C3
Oude-Pekela 47 E3
Ouessant, Ile d' 22 A2
Oughterard 12 B3
Ouistreham 18 C3
Oul 51 D4
Oulainen 99 D4
Oulanka 99 E2
Oulankajoki 99 E2
Oulchy-le-Château 20 A3
Oulu 99 D3
Oulujärvi 99 E4
Oulujoki 99 D4
Oulun Lääni 99 E4
Oulunsalo 99 D4
Oulx 31 D2
Ounasjoki 99 D2
Oundle 9 F1
Our 54 A1
Ouranópoli 80 B4
Ource 26 C1
Ourcq 20 A3
Ourense 34 B3
Ourique 42 B2
Ourol 34 B1
Ourthe 20 C1
Ourville 19 D2
Ouse, R 7 D2
Oust 37 F2
Outes, Sa de 34 A2
Outokumpu 103 E2
Outomuro 34 B3
Outwell 10 C1
Ouvèze 30 C3
Ouzouer 25 F2
Ouzouer-le-Marché 25 E1
Ovada 60 A2
Ovanåker 101 F4
Ovar 38 B1
Ovčar Banja 73 D4
Ovedskloster 109 D3
Overath 17 E4
Øverbygd 94 C3
Overflakkee 16 B3
Overhalla 97 D4
Överhörnäs 102 A2
Overijssel 17 D2
Overjise 50 C3
Överkalix 98 C2
Övermark 102 B2
Översjuktan 97 F3
Övertorneå 98 C2
Överum 109 E1
Överuman 97 E3
Oviedo 35 D1
Ovindoli 63 F2
Øvre Anarjokka 95 D3
Øvre Årdal 100 B3
Øvre Dividalen 94 C3
Övre Fryken 105 E3
Øvre Pasvik 95 F2
Övre Soppero 95 D4
Ovruč 113 E1
Owel, L 13 D3
Oxelösund 106 B4
Oxford 9 E2
Oxfordshire 9 E2
Oxiá, N 82 C4
Oxiá (Stereá Eláda) 83 D3
Oxiá (Thessalía) 83 D2
Oxie 108 C3
Oxílithos 84 B4
Ox Mts, The 12 B2
Oyarzun 36 C1
Oybin 53 F2
Øye 104 C1
Øyer 104 C1
Øyeren 105 D3
Oy-Mittelberg 55 E4
Oyntdartfjørdur 96 A3
Oyón 36 B2
Oyonnax 27 D4
Øystese 104 B2
Oyten 47 F3
Ozalj 70 C2
Ožbalt 70 B1
Ózd 112 B3
Ozeblin 70 C4
Ozieri 66 B2
Ozren 71 F3
Ozren Devica 73 E4

P

Paakkila **103** E2
Paalasmaa **103** E1
Páamo de Masa, Pto de **35** F3
Paar **55** F3
Paasselkä **103** F3
Paavola **99** D4
Pabianice **112** B2
Pacaudière, la **26** B4
Paceco **68** A3
Pachino **69** D4
Packsattel **57** E4
Paço de Sousa **34** A4
Paços de Ferreira **34** A4
Pacov **57** D1
Pacy **19** E4
Padasjoki **107** E1
Padej **72** C1
Padđene **75** D1
Paderborn **17** F3
Paderne **42** B2
Padiham **6** C2
Padina **72** C2
Padinska Skela **72** C2
Padirac, Gouffre de **29** D2
Padjelanta **97** F1
Padornelo **34** C3
Padova **61** D1
Padrela, Sa da **34** B4
Padrón **34** A2
Padru **66** B2
Padstow **8** B3
Padul **44** A3
Paesana **31** E2
Paestum **64** B4
Pag **70** C4
Pag *I* **70** B4
Paganico **63** D1
Pagassés, N **83** F2
Pagassitikós Kólpos **83** F2
Paglia **63** D1
Pagny **21** D3
Pagóndas (Évia) **84** A3
Pagóndas (Sámos) **89** E2
Pagoúria **81** D2
Paguera **45** E3
Páhi **87** E1
Pahiá Ámos **91** F4
Pahís, Akr **80** C3
Paide **110** C1
Paignton **8** C4
Päijänne **103** D3
Páiko, Óros **79** E2
Paimbœuf **23** D4
Paimio **107** D2
Paimpol **22** C2
Painswick **9** E2
Paisley **4** C2
Paistunturit **95** E2
País Vasco **36** B1
Paittasjärvi **94** C4
Paiva, R **38** B1
Pajala **98** C1
Pájara **42** C4
Pajares, Pto de **35** D2
Paklenica Nac Park **70** C4
Pakoštane **74** C1
Pakrac **71** E2
Pakračka Poljana **71** D2
Paks **112** B4
Palacios de la Sierra **36** A3
Palacios del Sil **34** C2
Palacios de Sanabria **34** C3
Palade, Pso del **58** C3
Paládio **81** D2
Paladru **30** C1
Palafrugell **32** C3
Palagía **81** E2
Palagiano **65** E4
Palagonia **69** D3
Palagruža **75** D3
Palaia **60** C4
Palaiseau **19** F4
Palais, le **22** C4
Palamás **83** E2
Palamós **32** C3
Palancia, R **41** E3
Palanga **110** B3
Pala, Pto del **34** C1
Palas de Rei **34** B2
Palata **64** B2
Palatitsía **79** E3
Palatna **77** D1
Palau **66** B1
Palavas **30** B4
Palazzo del Pero **61** D4
Palazzolo Acreide **69** D4
Palazzolo sull' Oglio **60** B1
Palazzo San Gervasio **64** C3
Palazzuolo sul Senio **61** D3
Paldiski **110** C1
Pale **76** A1
Paléa Epídavros **87** E2
Palékastro **91** F4
Palena **64** A2
Palencia **35** E3
Paleohóra (Égina) **87** F2
Paleohóra (Kríti) **90** B4
Paleohóri (Grevená) **79** D4
Paleohóri (Halkidikí) **80** B3
Paleohóri (Ípiros) **82** B2
Paleohóri (Lésvos) **85** F3
Paleohóri (Pelopónissos) **87** D3
Paleohóri (Thessalía) **83** D1
Paleokastrítsa **82** A1
Paleókastro (Halkidikí) **80** A3
Paleókastro (Kozáni) **79** D4
Paleókastro (Sámos) **89** F2
Paleókastro (Séres) **80** B2
Paleókastro (Stereá Eláda) **83** D3
Paleokómi **80** B2
Paleópirgos (Stereá Eláda) **83** D4
Paleópirgos (Thessalía) **83** F1
Paleópoli (Ándros) **88** B1
Paleópoli (Samothráki) **81** E3
Paleós Kavála **80** C2
Paleós Xánthis **81** D2
Palermo **68** B3
Páleros **82** C3
Palérou, Órm **82** B3
Palestrina **63** F2
Palež **72** B4
Páli **89** F4
Paliano **63** F3
Palić **72** B1
Palidoro **63** E2
Palinges **26** B3
Palinuro **67** D2
Palioúri **80** B4
Paliouriá **79** D4
Paliseul **20** C2
Pälkäne **107** E1
Pålkem **98** B2
Pallas Ounastunturi **95** D3
Pallastunturi **95** D4
Pallice, la **24** B4
Palluau **24** B3
Palma **45** E3
Palmaces, Emb de **36** B4
Palma del Río **43** E2
Palma di Montechiaro **68** C4
Palmadula **66** A2
Palmanova **59** F3
Palmela **38** A4
Palmi **67** E4
Palo del Colle **65** D3
Palojoensuu **95** D3
Palojoki **95** D3
Palokki **103** E2
Palomäki **103** E1
Palomares del Campo **40** C3
Palomas **39** D4
Palomas, Pto de las **44** B2
Palombara Sabina **63** E2
Palombera, Pto de **35** F2
Palomera **41** D2
Pálos, Akr **88** B2
Palos, C de **45** D3
Palos de la Frontera **42** C3
Pals **32** C3
Pålsboda **105** F4
Paltamo **99** E4
Paltaselkä **99** E4
Paluzza **59** E2
Pámfila **85** F2
Pamhagen **57** F3
Pamiers **32** A2
Pampilhosa **38** B2
Pampilhosa da Serra **38** C2
Pampliega **35** F3
Pamplona **36** C2
Pamporovo **115** D3
Pamukkale **115** F4
Panagía (Ípiros) **82** C2
Panagía (Límnos) **85** D1
Panagía (Makedonía) **79** D4
Panagía (Thássos) **81** D3
Panagía (Thessalía) **82** C1
Panagjurište **115** D2
Panahaikó, Óros **83** D4
Panarea, I **69** D2
Panaro **60** C3
Pancalieri **31** E2
Pančevo **73** D2
Pančićev vrh **77** D1
Pancorbo **36** A2
Pandánassa **87** E4
Pandeleimónas **79** F4
Pandino **60** B1
Pandokrátor **82** A1
Pandrup **108** B2
Panes **35** F2
Panetolikó, Óros **83** D3
Panetólio **82** C4
Panevėžys **110** C3
Pangbourne **9** E2
Pangéo, Óros **80** B2
Paniza, Pto de **36** C4
Pankajärvi **103** F1
Pankakoski **103** F1
Pankow **49** E4
Panórama (Dráma) **80** B2
Panórama (Thessaloníki) **80** A3
Panormítis **93** E1
Pánormos (Kikládes) **88** B2
Pánormos (Kríti) **91** D3
Päntäne **102** B3
Pantelleria **68** A4
Pantelleria, I di **68** A4
Paola **67** E2
Pápa **112** A4
Papádes **84** A3
Papádos **85** F3
Páparis **86** C2
Pápas, Akr **89** D2
Papasidero **67** E2
Papa Stour **3** F1
Papenburg **47** E3
Papikio **81** D2
Pápingo **78** C4
Pappenheim **55** F2
Papuk *Mt* **71** E2
Papuk (Reg) **71** E2
Parabita **65** F4
Paracin **73** E4
Paracuellos de Jiloca **36** C4
Parada de Cunhos **34** B4
Paradas **43** E3
Paradela **34** B3
Paradísia **86** C2
Parádissos **81** D2
Parainen **107** D3
Parajes **34** C1
Parakálamos **78** C4
Parákila **85** F2
Paralia (Ahaia) **86** C1
Paralía (Lakonía) **87** E3
Paralía (Makedonía) **79** F4
Paralía (Stereá Eláda) **83** F4
Paralía Akrátas **87** D1
Parália Ástros **87** D2
Paralía Kímis **84** B3
Paralía Kotsikiás **84** A3
Paralía Skotínas **79** F4
Paralía Tiroú **87** E3
Paralímni **84** A4
Paralovo **77** D2
Paramé **18** B4
Paramera, Pto de **39** F2
Paramithía **82** B2
Páramo del Sil **34** C2
Paranésti **80** C2
Parapanda **43** F3
Parapótamos **82** B1
Paraspóri, Akr **93** D2
Paray-le-Monial **26** B3
Parchim **48** C3
Pardubice **112** A3
Paredes **34** A4
Paredes de Coura **34** A3
Paredes de Nava **35** E3
Pareja **40** C2
Pareloup, Lac de **29** E3
Parentis-en-Born **28** A3
Párga **82** B2
Pargas **107** D3
Parikkala **103** F3
Parîngului, M **114** C1
Paris **19** F4
Parkalompolo **95** D4
Parkano **102** C3
Parla **40** A2
Parlavà **32** B3
Parma **60** B2
Parnassós, Óros **83** E4
Parndorf **57** F2
Párnitha, Óros **87** F1
Párnonas, Óros **87** D3
Pärnu **110** C2
Parola **107** E2
Páros **88** C3
Páros, N **88** B3
Parrett **9** D3
Parsberg **55** F2
Parsdorf **56** A3
Parseierspitze **58** C2
Parsęta **49** F1
Parsteiner See **49** E3
Partakko **95** F2
Partanna **68** B3
Partenen **58** B2
Partenkirchen **55** F4
Parthenay **24** C3
Parthéni **89** E3
Partille **108** C1
Partinico **68** B3
Partizani **73** D3
Partizanske Vode **72** C4
Partney **7** E3
Partry Mountains **12** B3
Pasaia-Pasajes **36** C1
Pas de Calais **11** E3
Pas-de-Calais (Dépt) **19** E1
Pas de la Case **32** A2
Pas-en-Artois **19** F2
Pasewalk **49** E2
Pashalítsa **83** E2
Pasikovci **71** E2
Pašman **74** C1
Pašman *I* **74** C1
Passais **18** C4
Passá-Limáni **85** E4
Passás, N **85** F4
Passau **56** C2
Passavás **87** D4
Passero, C **69** D4
Passignano sul Trasimeno **61** D4
Passwang **27** E2
Pastrana **40** B2
Paštrik **76** C3
Pásztó **112** B4
Patay **25** E1
Pateley Bridge **6** C1
Patéras, Óros **87** E1
Paterna del Campo **43** D2
Paterna de Rivera **43** D4
Paternion **59** F2
Paternò **69** D3
Paternopoli **64** B3
Patersdorf **56** B2
P'atichatki **113** F2
Patiópoulo **82** C2
Patitíri **84** B2
Pátmos **89** E2
Pátmos, N **89** E2
Pátra **83** D4
Patraïkós Kólpos **82** C4
Patreksfjörður **96** A1
Patrington **7** E2
Pattada **66** B2
Patterdale **5** D4
Patti **69** D2
Pattijoki **99** D4
Patvinsuo **103** F2
Pau **37** D1
Pauillac **28** B2
Paúl **38** C2
Paularo **59** F2
Paulhaguet **29** F2
Paullo **60** A1
Pavia (I) **60** A2
Pavia (P) **38** B4
Pavilly **19** D3
Pavino Polje **76** B1
Pávliani **83** E3
Pávlos **83** F4
Pavullo nel Frignano **60** C3
Paxí **82** A2
Paxí, N **82** A2
Payerne **27** E3
Paymogo **42** C2
Payrac **29** D2
Pazardžik **115** D3
Pazin **70** A3
Pčinja **77** E2
Péage-de-Roussillon, le **30** B1
Peak District Nat Pk **6** C2
Peal de Becerro **44** B2
Peanía **87** F1
Peares, Emb de los **34** B2
Peć **76** C2
Peča **70** B1
Peccioli **60** C4
Pečenjevce **77** E1
Pech-Merle, Grotte du **29** D3
Pećigrad **70** C3
Pećinci **72** C3
Pecka **72** C4
Peckelsheim **52** A2
Pécs **114** B1
Pećsa Banja **76** C2
Pečurice **76** B3
Pedaso **61** F4
Pedersker **109** D4
Pedersöre **102** C2
Pédi **93** E1
Pedrafita do Cebreiro **34** C2
Pedrafita do Cebreiro, Pto de **34** C2
Pedrajas de San Esteban **35** E4
Pedralba (Castilla-León) **34** C3
Pedralba (Valencia) **41** E3
Pedras Salgadas **34** B4
Pedraza de la Sierra **40** A1
Pedrera **43** E3
Pedrizas, Pto de las **43** F3
Pedro Abad **43** F2
Pedro Bernardo **39** F2
Pedrógão (Alentejo) **42** B1
Pedrógão (Estremadura) **38** A2
Pedrógão Grande **38** B2
Pedrola **36** C3
Pedro Muñoz **40** B4
Peebles **5** D2
Peel **6** A1
Peene **49** D2
Peenemünde **49** E1
Peer Gynt veien **100** C3
Pefkári **80** C3
Pefkí **83** F3
Péfkos **78** C3
Pega **38** C2
Pegalajar **44** A2
Pegau **53** D2
Pegli **60** A3
Pegnitz **55** F1
Pego **45** E1
Pego do Altar, Bgem de **38** B4
Pegognaga **60** C2
Pegolotte **61** D1
Pehčevo **77** F3
Peine **52** B1
Peio Terme **58** C3
Peira-Cava **31** E3
Peißenberg **56** A4
Peiting **56** A4
Peitz **53** F1
Pek **73** D3
Péla **79** E2
Péla (Nomos) **79** F3
Pelado **41** D3
Pelagie, Is **68** A4
Pelasgía **83** F3
Pelat, Mt **31** D3
Pełczyce **49** F3
Pelekános **79** D3
Pélekas **82** A1
Peletá **87** E3
Pelhřimov **57** D1
Pelinéo **85** E4
Pelister **77** E4
Pelješac **75** E2
Pelkosenniemi **99** E1
Pellegrino, M **68** B2
Pellegrino Parmense **60** B2
Pellegrue **28** C2
Pellerin, le **24** B2
Pellesmäki **103** E2
Pello **98** C2
Pellworm **47** F1
Pelopónissos **86** C2
Peloritani, M **69** D2
Peltosalmi **103** E1
Peltovuoma **95** D3
Pélussin **30** B1
Pelvoux, Mt **31** D2
Pembroke **8** B2
Pembroke Dock **8** B2
Pembrokeshire Coast Nat Pk **8** B1
Penacova **38** B2
Peña de Francia **39** D2
Peña de Francia, Sa de **39** D2
Peña de Oroel **37** D2
Penafiel **34** A4
Peñafiel **35** F4
Peñaflor **43** E2
Peñagolosa **41** E3
Peña Gorbea **36** B1
Peñalara **40** A1
Penalva do Castelo **38** C1
Penamacor **38** C2
Peña Mira **34** C3
Peña Nofre **34** B3
Peña Prieta **35** E2
Peñaranda de Bracamonte **39** F1
Peñaranda de Duero **36** A3
Peñarroya **41** E2
Peñarroya, Emb de **40** B4
Peñarroya-Pueblonuevo **43** E1
Penarth **9** D2
Peña, Sa de la **37** D2
Peña Sagra **35** F2
Peñas, C de **35** D1
Peñascosa **44** C1
Peñas de Cervera **36** A3
Peñas de San Pedro **44** C1
Peña Trevinca **34** C3
Peña Ubiña **35** D2
Peñausende **35** D4
Pendagii **83** D4
Pendálofo **82** C4
Pendálofos **78** C4
Pendéli **87** F1
Pendéli *Mt* **87** F1
Pendeória **83** E4
Pénde Vrisses **80** A2
Pendine **8** B2
Peneda-Gerês, Pque Nac da **34** A3
Peneda, Sa da **34** A3
Penedono **38** C1
Penela **38** B2
Pénestin **22** C4
Penha **34** A4
Penhas da Saude **38** C2
Penhas Juntas **34** C4
Penhir, Pte de **22** A3
Penice, Pso del **60** A2
Peniche **38** A3
Penicuik **5** D2
Penig **53** D3
Peñíscola **41** F2
Penkun **49** E3
Penmaenmawr **6** A2
Penmarch, Pte de **22** A3
Pennabilli **61** E3
Penne **63** F1
Penne-d'Agenais **28** C3
Pennes, Pso di **59** D2
Pennines, The **6** C1
Peñón de Ifach **45** E1
Penrhyndeudraeth **6** A3
Penrith **5** D4
Penryn **8** B4
Penserjoch **59** D2
Pentland Firth **3** D2
Pentland Hills **5** D2
Pentrefoelas **6** B3
Pen-y-bont **8** C2
Penzance **8** A4
Penzberg **56** A4
Penzlin **49** D2
Peqin **76** C4
Perahóra **87** E1
Peraleda de Zaucejo **43** E1
Peralejos de las Truchas **40** C2
Perales del Alfambra **41** D2
Perales del Puerto **39** D2
Perales de Tajuña **40** B2
Perales, Pto de **39** D2
Peralta **36** C2
Peralta de Alcofea **37** E3
Peralva **42** B2
Pérama (Ípiros) **82** C1
Pérama (Kérkira) **82** A1
Pérama (Kríti) **91** D3
Pérama (Lésvos) **85** F3
Pérama (Stereá Eláda) **87** F1
Peraméri **98** C3
Perä-Posio **99** E2
Peräseinäjoki **102** C2
Perast **76** B3
Peratáta **86** A1
Percy **18** B4
Perdido, M **37** E2
Pérdika (Égina) **87** F2
Pérdika (Ioánina) **82** C2
Pérdika (Thesprotía) **82** B2
Perdikáki **82** C3
Perdíkas **79** D3
Peréa (Péla) **79** E3
Peréa (Thessaloníki) **79** F3
Perejaslav-Chmel'nickij **113** F2
Pereruela **35** D4
Pereval Jablonickij **113** D3
Pereval Srednij Vereckij **112** C3
Pereval Užokskij **112** C3
Perg **57** D2
Pergine Valsugana **59** D3
Pergola **61** E4
Perho **102** C2
Perhonjoki **102** C1
Periana **43** F3
Périers **18** B3
Périgueux **28** C2
Períklia **79** E2
Perino **60** B2
Períssa **91** E1
Perísta **83** D3
Peristerá **80** A3
Peristéra, N **84** B2
Perithório **80** B1
Perívlepto **83** F2

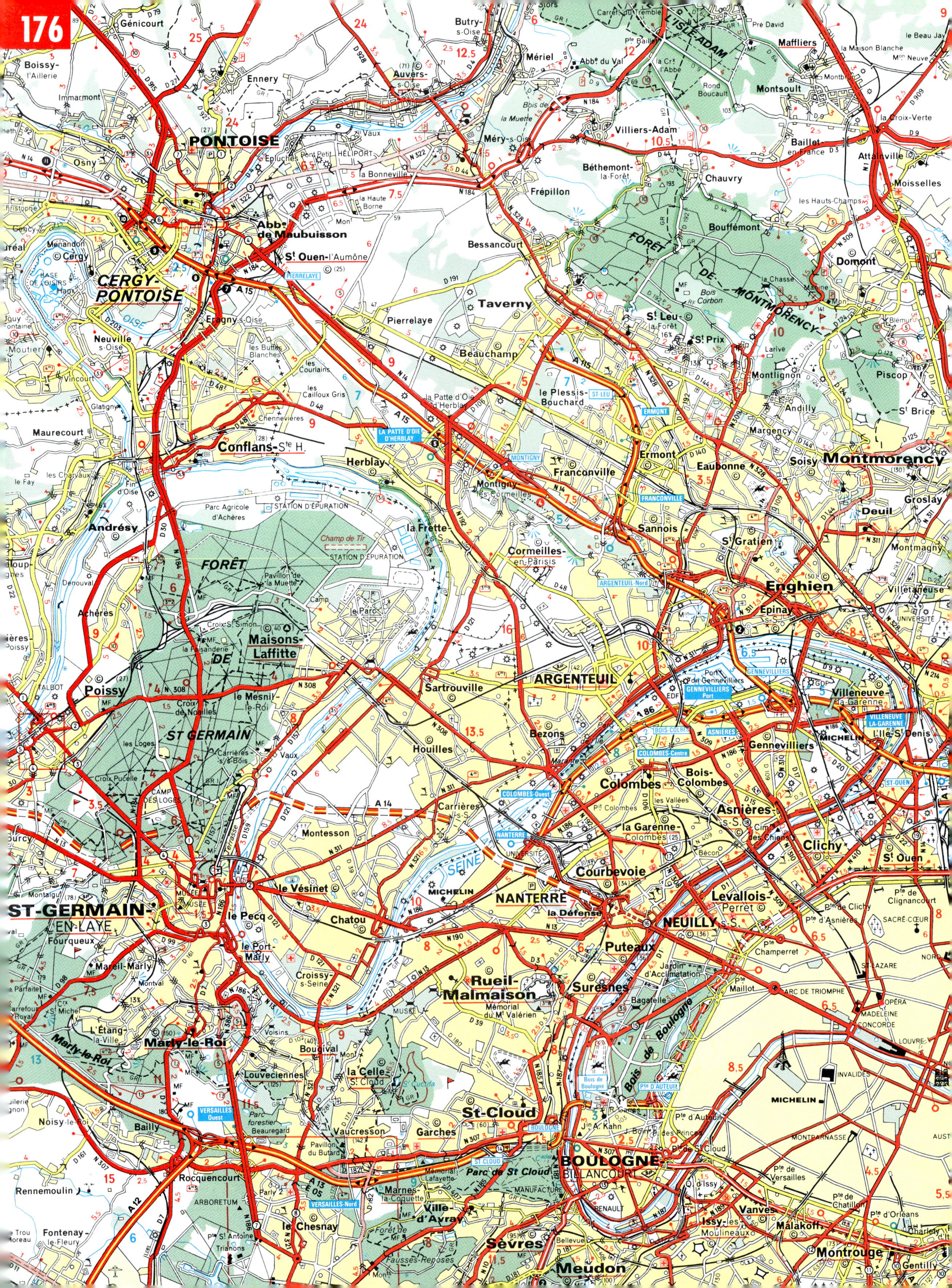
PONTOISE
CERGY-PONTOISE
Cergy
Osny
Génicourt
Boissy-l'Aillerie
Ennery
Auvers-s-Oise
Butry-s-Oise
Mériel
L'ISLE-ADAM
Maffliers
Montsoult
Villiers-Adam
Méry-s-Oise
Frépillon
Béthemont-la-Forêt
Chauvry
Baillet-en-France
Attainville
Moisselles
Abb.e de Maubuisson
St Ouen-l'Aumône
Bessancourt
Bouffémont
FORÊT DE MONTMORENCY
Domont
Taverny
Pierrelaye
Éragny-s-Oise
Neuville-s-Oise
St Leu-la-Forêt
St Prix
Piscop
Beauchamp
Montlignon
Le Plessis-Bouchard
Andilly
St Brice
Margency
Eaubonne
Soisy
Montmorency
Ermont
Franconville
Montigny-lès-Cormeilles
Herblay
Conflans-Ste H.
Maurecourt
Andrésy
Achères
La Frette-s-S.
Cormeilles-en-Parisis
Sannois
St Gratien
Deuil
Groslay
Montmagny
Enghien
Épinay
Villetaneuse
FORÊT DE ST GERMAIN
Maisons-Laffitte
Le Mesnil-le-Roi
Sartrouville
ARGENTEUIL
Poissy
Villeneuve-la-Garenne
L'Île-St Denis
Gennevilliers
Bezons
Houilles
Colombes
Bois-Colombes
Asnières-s-S.
Carrières-s-S.
Montesson
Clichy
St Ouen
La Garenne-Colombes
Courbevoie
Levallois-Perret
NEUILLY-S.-S.
NANTERRE
La Défense
Le Vésinet
Chatou
Le Pecq
ST-GERMAIN-EN-LAYE
Fourqueux
Le Port-Marly
Croissy-s-Seine
Rueil-Malmaison
Puteaux
Suresnes
Bois de Boulogne
Marly-le-Roi
L'Étang-la-Ville
Louveciennes
Bougival
La Celle-St Cloud
St-Cloud
Noisy-le-Roi
Bailly
Vaucresson
Garches
BOULOGNE-BILLANCOURT
Rocquencourt
Le Chesnay
Ville-d'Avray
Sèvres
Meudon
Issy-les-Moulineaux
Vanves
Malakoff
Montrouge
Gentilly
Rennemoulin
Fontenay-le-Fleury
Parc de St Cloud
MICHELIN
SEINE
OISE

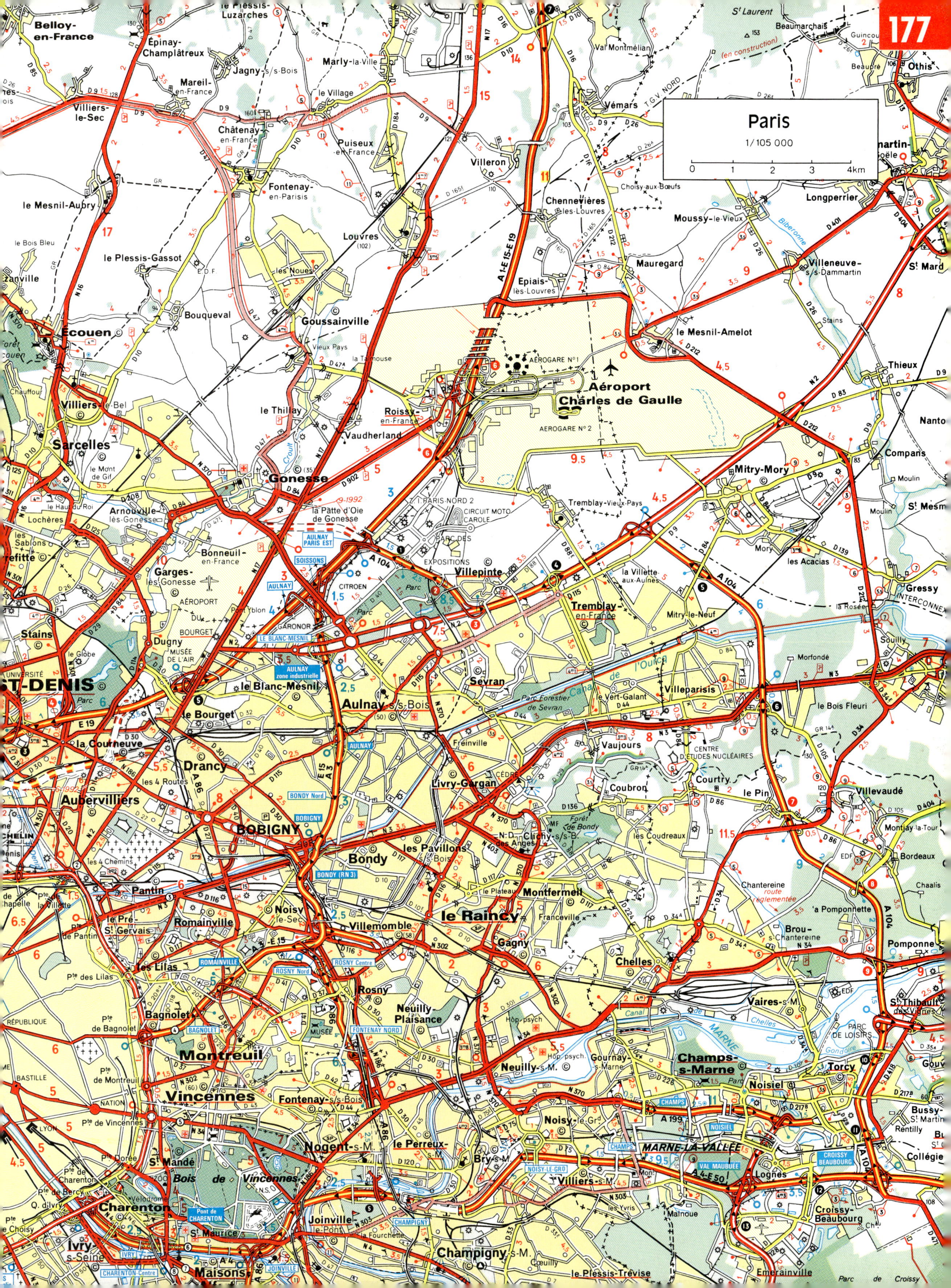
Paris
1/105 000
0 1 2 3 4km
Belloy-en-France
Épinay-Champlâtreux
Jagny-s/s-Bois
Marly-la-Ville
Villiers-le-Sec
Mareil-en-France
le Village
Châtenay-en-France
Puiseux-en-France
Vémars
Villeron
Fontenay-en-Parisis
le Mesnil-Aubry
Louvres
Chennevières-lès-Louvres
Moussy-le-Vieux
Longperrier
le Plessis-Gassot
Mauregard
Villeneuve-s/s-Dammartin
Epiais-lès-Louvres
Bouqueval
Goussainville
le Mesnil-Amelot
Ecouen
Aéroport Charles de Gaulle
AÉROGARE N°1
AÉROGARE N°2
Thieux
Villiers-le-Bel
le Thillay
Roissy-en-France
Vaudherland
Sarcelles
Gonesse
Compans
Mitry-Mory
Arnouville-lès-Gonesse
la Patte d'Oie de Gonesse
PARIS-NORD 2
CIRCUIT MOTO CAROLE
PARC DES EXPOSITIONS
Tremblay-Vieux-Pays
Bonneuil-en-France
Garges-lès-Gonesse
Villepinte
la Villette-aux-Aulnes
Mitry-le-Neuf
Gressy
AÉROPORT DU BOURGET
Tremblay-en-France
Stains
Dugny
le Blanc-Mesnil
Sevran
Villeparisis
ST-DENIS
le Bourget
Aulnay-s/s-Bois
Parc Forestier de Sevran
le Vert-Galant
le Bois Fleuri
la Courneuve
Drancy
Freinville
Vaujours
CENTRE D'ETUDES NUCLÉAIRES
Livry-Gargan
Coubron
Courtry
le Pin
Villevaudé
Aubervilliers
BOBIGNY
N.-D.-des-Anges
Clichy-s/s-B.
Forêt de Bondy
les Coudreaux
Bondy
les Pavillons-s/s-Bois
Montjay-la-Tour
Bordeaux
Pantin
le Plateau
Montfermeil
Chantereine
Noisy-le-Sec
le Raincy
Franceville
'a Pomponnette
Romainville
Villemomble
Brou-Chantereine
le Pré-St-Gervais
Gagny
Chelles
Pomponne
les Lilas
Rosny
Vaires-s-M.
St-Thibault-des-Vignes
Bagnolet
Neuilly-Plaisance
MARNE
PARC DE LOISIRS
Montreuil
Neuilly-s-M.
Gournay-s-Marne
Champs-s-Marne
Torcy
Noisiel
Vincennes
Fontenay-s/s-Bois
Noisy-le-Gd
Bussy-St-Martin
Rentilly
MARNE-LA-VALLÉE
Nogent-s-M.
le Perreux-s-M.
Bry-s-M.
Collégie
St-Mandé
Bois de Vincennes
Villiers-s-M.
Lognes
Charenton
Croissy-Beaubourg
Joinville-le-Pont
Malnoue
Ivry-s-Seine
St-Maurice
Champigny-s-M.
Maisons
le Plessis-Trévise
Emerainville
Parc de Croissy

Marly-le-Roi
Louveciennes
Bougival
la Celle St Cloud
Rueil-Malmaison
Mémorial du Mt Valérien
Puteaux
Suresnes
St-Cloud
Garches
Vaucresson
BOULOGNE BILLANCOURT
Bois de Boulogne
Parc de St Cloud
Ville-d'Avray
Sèvres
Meudon
Forêt de Meudon
Issy-les-Moulineaux
Vanves
Malakoff
Montrouge
Gentilly
Clamart
Châtillon
Bagneux
Arcueil
Cachan
Fontenay-aux-Roses
Bourg-la-Reine
L'Haÿ-les-Roses
le Plessis-Robinson
Châtenay-Malabry
Sceaux
Antony
Fresnes
Rungis
Wissous
Orly-Ouest
Aéroport
Chaville
Vélizy-Villacoublay
Viroflay
VERSAILLES
le Chesnay
Rocquencourt
Bailly
Noisy-le-Roi
St Cyr-l'École
Fontenay-le-Fleury
Rennemoulin
Buc
Jouy-en-Josas
Bièvres
Guyancourt
Montigny-le-Bretonneux
les Loges-en-Josas
Toussus-le-Noble
Châteaufort
Magny-les-Hameaux
Saclay
Vauhallan
Igny
Verrières-le-Buisson
Massy
Palaiseau
Villiers-le-Bâcle
St Aubin
Gif-s-Yvette
Orsay
Bures-s-Yvette
Champlan
Chilly-Mazarin
Morangis
Villebon-s-Yvette
Longjumeau
les Ulis
Courtabœuf
Saulx-les-Chartreux
Ballainvilliers
Villejust
Epinay-s-Orge
Savigny-sur-Orge
Villiers-s-Orge
Villemoisson-s-Orge
Ste Geneviève-des-Bois
Longpont-s-Orge
St Michel-s-Orge
Montlhéry
Marcoussis
Linas
Nozay
la Ville du Bois
Gometz-le-Châtel
Gometz-la-Ville
St Jean-de-Beauregard
Janvry
les Molières
Limours
Forges-les-Bains
Briis-s-Forges
Fontenay-les Briis
Bligny
St Rémy-lès-Chevreuse
Milon-la-Chapelle
Boullay-les-Troux
Leuville-s-Orge
le Plessis-Pâté
Forêt de la Roche-Turpin
CAMP DE LINAS-MONTLHÉRY
AUTODROME
ÉCOLE POLYTECHNIQUE
CENTRE D'ÉTUDES NUCLÉAIRES
MICHELIN

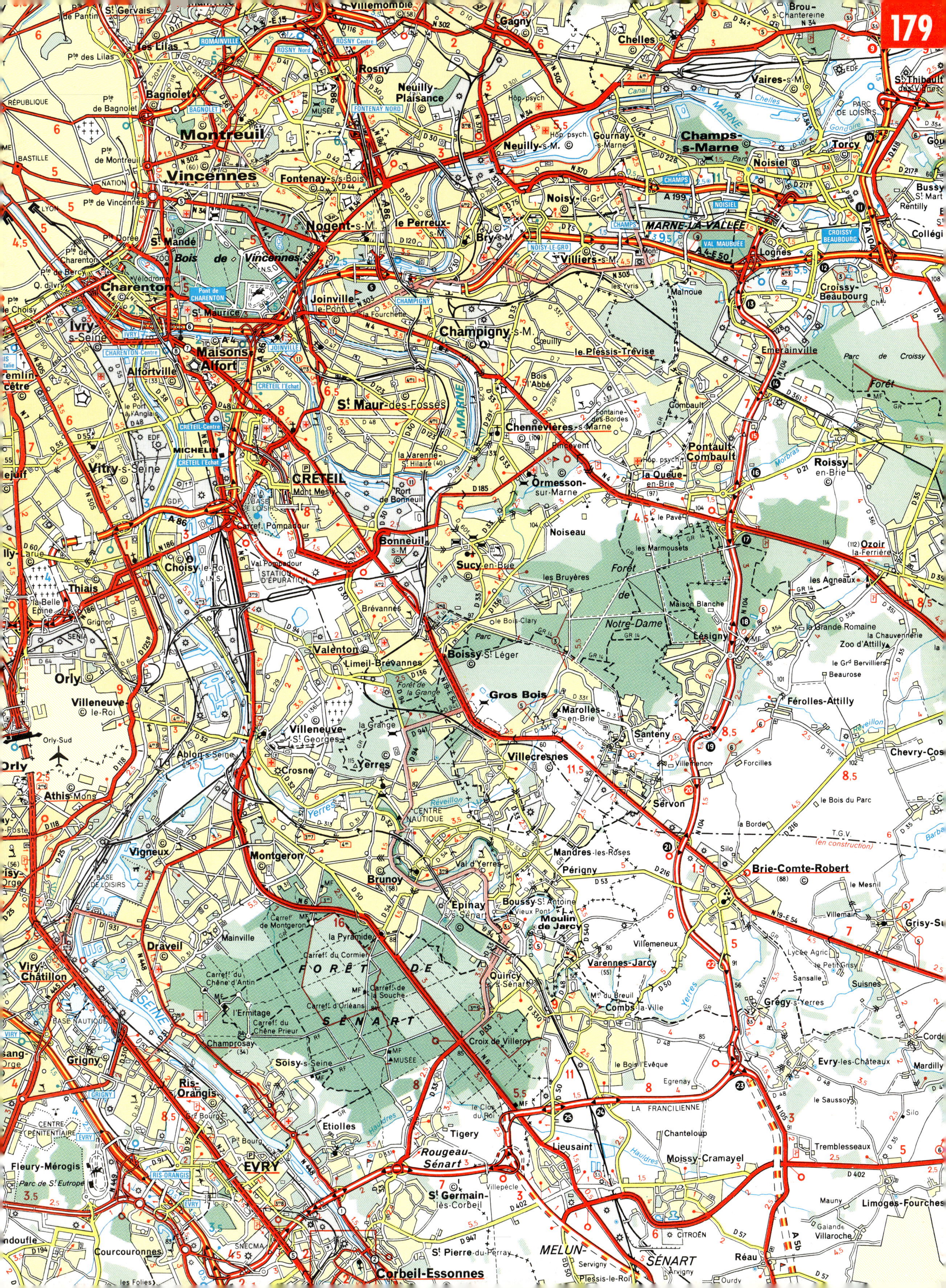

Montreuil
Vincennes
Bagnolet
les Lilas
Rosny
Neuilly-Plaisance
Chelles
Vaires-s-M.
Champs-s-Marne
Noisiel
Torcy
Fontenay-s/s-Bois
Nogent-s-M.
le Perreux-s-M.
Neuilly-s-M.
Noisy-le-Gd
Bry-s-M.
Villiers-s-M.
MARNE-LA-VALLÉE
Lognes
Croissy-Beaubourg
St Mandé
Bois de Vincennes
Charenton
Joinville-le-Pont
Champigny-s-M.
le Plessis-Trévise
Emerainville
Ivry-s-Seine
Maisons-Alfort
Alfortville
St Maur-des-Fossés
Chennevières-s-Marne
Pontault-Combault
Roissy-en-Brie
Vitry-s-Seine
CRÉTEIL
Ormesson-sur-Marne
la Queue-en-Brie
Noiseau
Ozoir-la-Ferrière
Choisy-le-Roi
Thiais
Bonneuil-s-M.
Sucy-en-Brie
Forêt de Notre-Dame
Lésigny
Orly
Villeneuve-le-Roi
Valenton
Limeil-Brévannes
Boissy-St Léger
Gros Bois
Marolles-en-Brie
Santeny
Férolles-Attilly
Chevry-Cossigny
Villeneuve-St Georges
Ablon-s-Seine
Crosne
Yerres
Villecresnes
Servon
Athis-Mons
Vigneux
Montgeron
Brunoy
Mandres-les-Roses
Périgny
Brie-Comte-Robert
Draveil
Epinay-s-Sénart
Boussy-St Antoine
Moulin de Jarcy
Varennes-Jarcy
Grisy-Suisnes
Viry-Châtillon
Forêt de Sénart
Quincy-s-Sénart
Combs-la-Ville
Grégy-s-Yerres
Grigny
Soisy-s-Seine
Ris-Orangis
Evry-les-Châteaux
Etiolles
Tigery
Lieusaint
Moissy-Cramayel
Fleury-Mérogis
EVRY
Rougeau-Sénart
St Germain-lès-Corbeil
Limoges-Fourches
Courcouronnes
St Pierre-du-Perray
MELUN-SÉNART
Réau
Corbeil-Essonnes

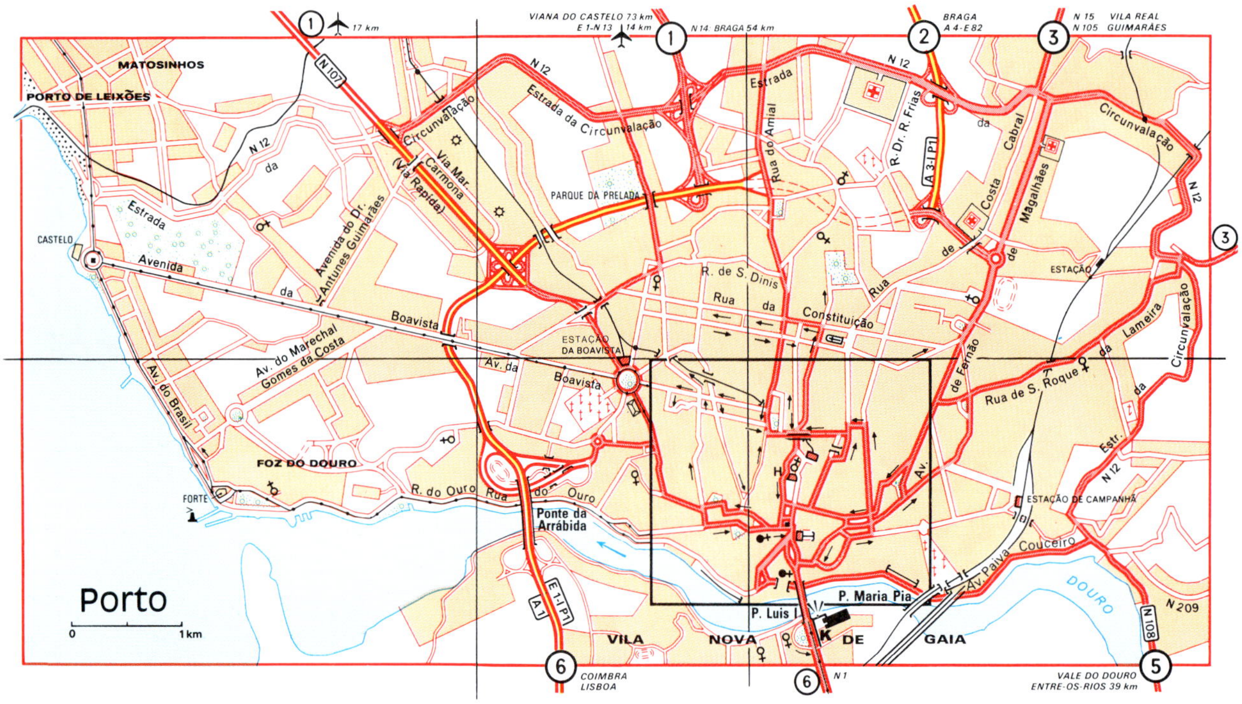

Porto
MATOSINHOS
PORTO DE LEIXÕES
CASTELO
FOZ DO DOURO
FORTE
Ponte da Arrábida
PARQUE DA PRELADA
ESTAÇÃO DA BOAVISTA
ESTAÇÃO DE CAMPANHÃ
P. Luis I
P. Maria Pia
VILA NOVA DE GAIA
DOURO
VIANA DO CASTELO 73 km
BRAGA A 4-E 82
N 15 N 105 VILA REAL GUIMARÃES
COIMBRA LISBOA
VALE DO DOURO ENTRE-OS-RIOS 39 km
1 km

Perivóli 78 C4
Perivóli, N. 83 E2
Perivólio 83 D3
Perjasica 70 C3
Perković 75 D1
Perleberg 48 C3
Perlez 72 C2
Permet 114 C4
Pernå 107 F2
Pernaja 107 F2
Pernarec 53 E4
Pernes 30 C3
Pernik 114 C2
Perniö 107 E3
Pernitz 57 E3
Pernštejn 57 E1
Péronne 19 F2
Perosa Argentina 31 E2
Pérouges 26 C4
Perpignan 32 B2
Perrero 31 E2
Perreux 26 B4
Perros-Guirec 22 B2
Persenbeug 57 D2
Pershore 9 E1
Perstorp 109 D3
Perth 5 D1
Perthus, le 32 B3
Pertisau 59 D1
Pertoča 70 C1
Pertoúli 83 D1
Pertteli 107 E2
Pertuis 30 C3
Pertunmaa 103 D3
Pertusa 37 E3
Perućac Vrelo 72 C4
Perućko jez 75 D1
Perugia 61 E4
Perušić 70 C4
Péruwelz 50 B4
Pervenchères 23 F3
Pervomajsk 113 F3
Pesaro 61 E3
Pescara 64 A1
Pescasseroli 64 A2
Peschici 64 C2
Peschiera del Garda 60 C1
Pescia 60 C3
Pescina 63 F2
Pescocostanzo 64 A2
Pescolanciano 64 A2
Pescopagano 64 C4
Pescorocchiano 63 F2
Peshkopi 77 D3
Pesiökylä 99 E3
Pesmes 26 C2
Pesočani 77 D4
Péso da Régua 34 B4
Pesoz 34 C1
Pessáni 81 F2
Peštani 77 D4
Pešter 76 C2
Pestovo 111 F1
Pešurići 72 B4
Petačinci 77 E1
Petajaskoski 99 D2
Petäjävesi 103 D3
Petalax 102 B2
Petalída, Akr 88 B3
Petalídi 86 C3
Petalii, Nissi 88 A1
Petalión, Kólpos 88 A1
Petaloúdes 93 F1
Pétange 21 D3
Pétas 82 C2
Petehovac 70 B3
Peterborough 9 F1
Peterhead 3 E3
Peterlee 5 E4
Petersfield 9 F3
Petershagen 17 F2
Pethelinós 80 B2
Petilia Policastro 67 F3
Petina 64 C4
Petite-Pierre, la 21 E3
Petit Morin 20 A4
Petit St-Bernard, Col du 27 E4
Petkula 95 E4
Petlovača 72 C3
Petoússio 82 B2
Petra (E) 45 F3
Pétra (Lésvos) 85 F2
Pétra (Makedonía) 79 E4
Petralia 68 C3
Petrálona 80 A3
Petraná 79 E4
Petrčane 74 C1
Petrel 45 D1
Petrella, Mte 64 A3
Pétres 79 D3
Petreto-Bicchisano 33 F4
Petrič 115 D3
Petrijevci 71 F2
Petrína 86 C3
Petrinja 71 D3
Petrodvorec 111 D1
Petrohóri 83 D4
Pétrola 45 D1
Petróna 82 C3
Petroșani 114 C1
Petrotá 81 F1
Petrothálassa 87 E2
Petroússa 80 B2
Petrovac (Bosna i Hercegovina) 70 C3
Petrovac (Crna Gora) 76 B3
Petrovac (Srbija) 73 E3
Petrovaradin 72 C2
Petrovčić 72 C3
Petrovec 77 E3
Petrovice 53 F4
Petrovići 72 B4
Pettenbach 56 C3
Pettigoe 12 C2
Petworth 9 F3
Peuerbach 56 C2
Peura 99 D2
Pewsey 9 E2
Peyrat-le-Château 29 D1
Peyrehorade 28 A4
Peyresourde, C de 37 E2
Peyriac-Minervois 32 B1
Peyrolles 30 C4
Peyrol, Pas de 29 E2
Peyruis 31 D3
Pézenas 30 A4
Pezinok 112 A3
Pezoúla 81 D2
Pfaffenhofen 55 F2
Pfäffikon 58 A2
Pfalzgrafenweiler 54 C3
Pfarrkirchen 56 B2
Pfeffenhausen 56 B2
Pforzheim 54 C2
Pfreimd 56 B1
Pfronten 55 E4
Pfullendorf 55 D4
Pfullingen 55 D3
Pfunds 58 C2
Pfungstadt 54 C1
Phalsbourg 21 E4
Philippeville 50 C4
Philippsreut 56 C2
Piacenza 60 B2
Piadena 60 B2
Piana 33 E3
Piana d. Albanesi 68 B3
Piancastagnaio 63 D1
Piancavallo 59 E3
Piandelagotti 60 C3
Pian delle Fugazze, Pso 59 D4
Pian del Voglio 60 C3
Pianella 64 A1
Pianello 61 E4
Pianoro 61 D3
Pianosa, I (Mare Adriatico) 64 C1
Pianosa, I (Mare Tirreno) 62 B2
Piansano 63 D2
Piapaxaro, P 34 C2
Pias 42 B1
Piatra-Neamt 113 D4
Piave 59 E4
Piazza al Serchio 60 B3
Piazza Armerina 68 C3
Piazza Brembana 58 B4
Piazzola sul Brenta 59 D4
Piber 57 E4
Pibeste, P de 37 E1
Pićan 70 A3
Picassent 41 E4
Piccolo San Bernardo, Colle del 27 E4
Picerno 64 C4
Pickering 7 D1
Pico 64 A3
Pico, Pto del 39 F2
Pico Ruivo 42 A3
Picos de Europa 35 E2
Picote, Bgem de 34 C4
Picquigny 19 F2
Pidna 79 F3
Piedicavallo 27 F4
Piedicroce 33 F3
Piediluco 63 E2
Piedimonte d'A. 64 B3
Piedrabuena 40 A4
Piedrafita 35 D2
Piedrahita 39 E2
Piedralaves 39 F2
Piedra, R 36 C4
Piedras Albas 39 D3
Piedra San Martin, Collado de la 37 D2
Piedras, Emb de 42 C2
Piedrasluengas, Pto de 35 F2
Piedratajada 37 D3
Pieksämäki 103 E3
Pielavesi 103 D2
Pielavesi L 103 D2
Pielinen 103 F1
Pieljekaise 97 F2
Piemonte 31 E2
Piennes 20 C3
Pienza 61 D4
Pieriá 79 E3
Piéria, Óri 79 E4
Pierowall 3 E1
Pierre-Buffière 29 D1
Pierre-de-Bresse 26 C3
Pierrefitte 20 C3
Pierrefitte-Nestalas 37 E2
Pierrefonds 19 F3
Pierrefontaine-les-Varans 27 D2
Pierrefort 29 E2
Pierrelatte 30 B3
Pieskehaure 97 F2
Piešt'any 112 A3
Pietersaaren mlk 102 C2
Pietersaari 102 C1
Pietra Ligure 31 F3
Pietralunga 61 E4
Pietraperzia 68 C3
Pietrasanta 60 B3
Pietra Spada, Pso di 67 F4
Pietrosu 113 D3
Pieux, les 18 B3
Pieve de' Burgondi del Cairo 60 A2
Pieve di Bono 58 C4
Pieve di Cadore 59 E3
Pieve di Soligo 59 E3
Pieve di Teco 31 F3
Pievepelago 60 C3
Pieve Santo Stefano 61 D4
Pigádi 83 F3
Pigés 82 C2
Pigí 83 D4
Pigna 31 E3
Pigón, L 82 C1
Pihlajaveden as 102 C3
Pihlajavesi 102 C3
Pihlajavesi L 103 F3
Pihlava 102 B3
Pihtipudas 103 D2
Piikkiö 107 D2
Piippola 103 D1
Piispajärvi 99 F3
Pikal'ovo 111 E1
Pikérmi 87 F1
Piła 112 A1
Pilat-Plage 28 A2
Pilas 43 D3
Pila, Sa de la 45 D2
Pilat, Mt 30 B1
Pilatus 27 F2
Piléa 81 F2
Piles 41 E4
Pilés 93 D3
Pili (Makedonía) 78 C2
Pili (Stereá Eláda) 87 F1
Pili (Thessalía) 83 D2
Pilica 112 B2
Pilio 84 A3
Pilio 89 F3
Pilio, Óros 83 F2
Pillon, Col du 27 E3
Pilorí 79 D4
Pilos 86 C3
Pilštanj 70 C2
Pina 37 D4
Piña de Campos 35 E3
Pinar 43 E3
Pineda de la Sierra 36 A2
Pineda de Mar 32 B4
Pinerolo 31 E2
Pineto 64 A1
Piney 20 B4
Pinhal de Leiria 38 A2
Pinhal Novo 38 A4
Pinhão 34 B4
Pinheiro 34 A4
Pinhel 39 D1
Piniós (Pelopónissos) 86 C1
Piniós (Thessalía) 83 E1
Pinkafeld 57 F3
Pinneberg 48 A3
Pino 33 F2
Pinofranqueado 39 D2
Pinols 29 F2
Pinoso 45 D1
Pinos Puente 44 A3
Pinsk 113 D1
Pintado, Emb de 43 D2
Pintamo 99 E3
Pinto 40 A2
Pinzano al Tagliamento 59 E3
Pinzolo 58 C3
Piobbico 61 E4
Piombino 62 C1
Pione 60 B2
Pionsat 26 A4
Piotrków Trybunalski 112 B2
Piove di Sacco 61 D1
Piovene Rocchette 59 D4
Pipéri, N 84 C2
Pipriac 23 D3
Piqueras, Pto de 36 B3
Piran 70 A3
Pir'atin 113 F2
Pireás 87 F1
Pirgadíkia 80 B3
Pirgetós 83 E1
Pirgi (Dráma) 80 B2
Pirgi (Híos) 85 E4
Pirgi (Kérkira) 82 A1
Pirgi (Kozáni) 79 E3
Pirgos (Íos) 88 C4
Pirgos (Kriti) 91 D4
Pirgos (Makedonía) 79 F3
Pirgos (Pelopónissos) 86 B2
Pirgos (Sámos) 89 E2
Pirgos (Stereá Eláda) 83 F4
Pirgos Diroú 87 D4
Piriac 22 C4
Pirin 115 D3
Pirkkala 107 E1
Pirmasens 54 B2
Pirna 53 F2
Pirok 77 D3
Pirot 77 E1
Pirovac 74 C1
Pirsógiani 78 C4
Pirttikoski 99 E2
Pisa 60 C4
Pisciotta 67 D1
Písek 56 C1
Piškorevci 71 F2
Pisogne 58 C4
Pisses 88 A2
Pissodéri 79 D3
Pissónas 84 B4
Pissos 28 B3
Pisticci 65 D4
Pistoia 60 C3
Pisuerga, R 35 E4
Piteå 98 B3
Piteälven 98 B3
Pitești 115 D1
Pithagório 89 E2
Píthio (Thessalía) 79 E4
Píthio (Thráki) 81 F1
Pithiviers 25 F1
Pitigliano 63 D2
Pitlochry 3 D4
Pitomača 71 D2
Pittenweem 5 D2
Pivka 70 A3
Pivnica 71 E2
Pivnice 72 B2
Pivsko jezero 76 A2
Pizarra 43 F3
Piz Buin 58 B2
Pizzighettone 60 B2
Pizzo 67 E3
Pizzoli 63 F2
Pjórsá 96 B2
Plabennec 22 A2
Plaćenska pl 77 D4
Plačkovica 77 F3
Plagiá (Makedonía) 79 F2
Plagiá (Thráki) 81 E2
Plagne, la 31 D1
Plaisance 28 B4
Pláka (Límnos) 85 D1
Pláka (Pelopónissos) 87 E3
Pláka (Thráki) 81 E2
Pláka, Akr 85 D1
Pláka Litohórou 79 F4
Plakiás 90 C4
Planá 53 E4
Plana 76 A2
Planches-en-Montagne, les 27 D3
Plancoët 22 C3
Plandište 73 D2
Planica Mangrt 70 A1
Plánice 56 C1
Planina (Celje) 70 C2
Planina (Jesenice) 70 A1
Planina (Postojna) 70 A2
Planinica 73 E4
Planitz 53 D3
Plános 86 A1
Plansee 58 C1
Plasencia 39 D2
Plaški 70 C3
Plasy 53 E4
Platamona Lido 66 A2
Platamónas (Kavalá) 80 C2
Platamónas (Piería) 79 F4
Platanákia 79 F2
Platanés 90 C3
Platani 68 B3
Plataniá (Makedonía) 80 C2
Platánia (Pelopónissos) 86 C2
Plataniá (Thessalía) 84 A2
Platanistós 88 A1
Platanítis 83 D4
Plátanos (Kriti) 90 B3
Plátanos (Pelopónissos) 87 D3
Plátanos (Thessalía) 83 F2
Platariá 82 B2
Plateau-d'Assy 27 E4

Plateés 87 E1
Pláti 81 F1
Platiána 86 C2
Platičevo 72 C3
Platikambos 83 E1
Platís Gialós (Kefaloniá) 86 A1
Platís Gialós (Mikonos) 88 C2
Platís Gialós (Sifnos) 88 B3
Platistomo 83 E3
Plattling 56 B2
Plau 48 C3
Plaue 49 D4
Plauen 53 D3
Plauer See (Brandenburg) 49 D4
Plauer See (Mecklenburg-Vorpommern) 48 C3
Plav 76 C2
Plavča 70 C3
Plavna 73 E3
Plavnica 76 B3
Plavnik *I* 70 B4
Plavnik *Mt* 70 B3
Playa Blanca 42 C4
Playa de Gandía 41 E4
Playa de San Juan 45 E1
Pleaux 29 E2
Pleine-Fougères 18 B4
Pleinfeld 55 F2
Pleiße 53 D2
Plélan-le-Grand 23 D3
Plélan-le-Petit 22 C3
Pléneuf 22 C2
Plentzia 36 B1
Plépi 87 E2
Plešin 76 C1
Plestin 22 B2
Pleternica 71 E2
Plettenberg 17 F4
Pletvar 77 E3
Pleumartin 25 D3
Pleumeur-Bodou 22 B2
Pleven 115 D2
Pleyben 22 B3
Pliego 44 C2
Plítra 87 D4
Plitvice 70 C3
Plitvička jezera 70 C3
Plitvički Ljeskovac 70 C4
Plješevica 70 C4
Pljevlja 76 B1
Ploaghe 66 B2
Ploče 75 E2
Plochingen 55 D2
Płock 112 B1
Plöckenpaß 59 E2
Plöckenstein 56 C2
Plоćno 75 E1
Ploërmel 22 C3
Ploiești 115 D1
Plomári 85 F3
Plomb du Cantal 29 E2
Plombières 27 D1
Plomin 70 B3
Plön 48 B2
Plonéour-Lanvern 22 A3
Płoń, Jez 49 F3
Płońsk 112 B1
Płoty 49 F2
Plouagat 22 C2
Plouaret 22 B2
Plouay 22 B3
Ploubalay 18 A4
Plœuc 22 C3
Ploudalmézeau 22 A2
Plouescat 22 B2
Plougasnou 22 B2
Plougastel-Daoulas 22 A3
Plougonven 22 B2
Plouguenast 22 C3
Plouha 22 C2
Plouigneau 22 B2
Ploumanach 22 B2
Plouzévédé 22 B2
Plovdiv 115 D3
Plumbridge 13 D2
Plungė 110 B3
Pl'ussa 111 D1
Pluvigner 22 C3
Plužine 76 A1
Plympton 8 C4
Plymstock 8 C4
Plzeň 53 E4
Po 60 C2
Poarta de Fier 114 C1
Pobierowo 49 F1
Poblet 37 F4
Pobrđe 76 C1
Počep 111 F4
Pöchlarn 57 E2
Počinok 111 E3
Počitelj 75 F2
Pocking 56 C2
Poćuta 72 C4
Podareš 77 F3
Podbořany 53 E3
Podčetrtek 70 C2
Podensac 28 B2
Podersdorf 57 F3
Podgajci Posavski 72 B3
Podgarič 71 D2
Podgora 75 E2
Podgorač (Hrvatska) 71 F2
Podgorac (Srbija) 73 E3
Podgrad 70 A3
Podhum 75 E1
Podjuchy 49 E2
Podkoren 70 A1
Podlugovi 71 F4
Podnovlje 71 F3
Podogorá 82 C3
Podohóri 80 B2
Podol'sk 111 F2
Podol'skaja Vozvyšennost' 113 D3
Podpec 70 B2
Podrašnica 71 E4
Podravska Slatina 71 E2
Podromanija 72 B4
Podsreda 70 C2
Podsused 70 C2
Podturen 71 D1
Podujevo 77 D1
Podunavci 73 D4
Poel 48 C2
Poganovo 77 E1
Poggibonsi 60 C4
Poggio Imperiale 64 C2
Poggio Mirteto 63 E2
Poggio Renatico 61 D2
Poggio Rusco 60 C2
Pöggstall 57 E2
Pogoniani 78 B4
Pogradec 77 D4
Pohja 107 E3
Pohja-Lankila 103 F3
Pohjaslahti (Keski-Suomen Lääni) 102 C3
Pohjaslahti (Lapin Lääni) 99 D2
Pohjois-Karjalan Lääni 103 F2
Pohořelice 57 F1
Pohorje 70 B1
Poiana Brașov 113 D4
Poio 34 A2
Poiré, le 24 B3
Poirino 31 F2
Poissons 20 C4
Poitiers 25 D3
Pöitsamaa 110 C2
Poix 19 E2
Poix-Terron 20 B2
Pojate 73 E4
Pojo 107 E3
Pokka 95 E3
Poklečani 75 E1
Pokljuka 70 A2
Pokupsko 70 C3
Polače 75 E2
Polacra, Pta de la 44 C4
Pola de Allande 34 C1
Pola de Gordón, la 35 D2
Pola de Laviana 35 E2
Pola de Lena 35 D2
Pola de Siero 35 D1
Polán 40 A3
Polcenigo 59 E3
Połczyn-Zdrój 110 A4
Polegate 10 C3
Poles 113 D1
Polesella 61 D2
Polessk 110 B4
Polhov Gradec 70 A2
Policastro 67 D1
Policastro, Golfo di 67 D2
Police 49 E2
Poličnik 74 C1
Policoro 65 D4
Polidéndri 84 B4
Polidrossos 83 E3
Poliégos, N 88 B4
Poliégou Folegándrou, Stenó 88 B4
Polígiros 80 A3
Polignano a Mare 65 E3
Poligny 27 D3
Polihnitos 85 F3
Polikárpi 79 E2
Polikástano 78 C3
Polikastro 79 F2
Polímilos 79 E3
Polinéri (Makedonía) 79 D4
Polinéri (Thessalía) 82 C2
Polióhni 85 D1
Polipótamo 79 D3
Polipótamos 84 C4
Poliraho 79 E4
Polirinía 90 B3
Polis, M 77 D4
Polissito 81 D2
Polistena 67 E4
Políthéa 82 C1
Politiká 84 A4
Poljana (Slovenija) 70 B1
Poljana (Srbija) 73 D3
Poljčane 70 C1
Polje 71 E3
Poljica 75 E2
Poljice 71 F4
Polla 64 C4
Pölläkkä 103 E2
Pöllau 57 E4
Polle 52 A1
Pollença 45 F2
Pollfoss 100 B3
Pollino, Mte 67 E2
Pollos 35 E4
Polmak 95 E2
Polock 111 D3
Polonnoje 113 D2
Polperro 8 B4
Poltava 113 F2
Polvijärvi 103 F2
Polzela 70 B2
Pomar 37 E3
Pomarance 60 C4
Pomarkku 102 B3
Pombal 38 B2
Pómbia 91 D4
Pomellen 49 E2
Pomezi 53 D4
Pomezia 63 E3
Pomigliano d'Arco 64 B4
Pommersfelden 55 E1
Pomokaira 95 E4
Pomorie 115 E2
Pomorze 110 A4
Pomovaara 95 E4
Pompei 64 B4
Pomposa 61 D2
Poncin 26 C4
Pondoiráklia 79 F2
Pondokómi 79 D3
Ponferrada 34 C2
Ponikovica 72 C4
Pons 28 B1
Ponsacco 60 C4
Pontacq 37 E1
Pontailler 26 C2
Pont-á-Marcq 19 F1
Pont-à-Mousson 21 D3
Pontão 38 B2
Pontardawe 8 C2
Pontarddulais 8 C2
Pontarion 25 E4
Pontarlier 27 D3
Pontassieve 61 D3
Pontaubault 18 B4
Pont-Audemer 19 D3
Pontaumur 26 A4
Pont-Aven 22 B3
Pont Canavese 31 E1
Pontcharra 31 D1
Pontchartrain 19 E4
Pontchâteau 23 D4
Pont-Croix 22 A3
Pont-d'Ain 26 C4
Pont-de-Beauvoisin, le 30 C1
Pont-de-Chéruy 26 C4
Pont-de-Claix, le 30 C2
Pont-de-Dore 26 A4
Pont-de-l'Arche 19 E3
Pont-de-Montvert, le 29 F3
Pont-de-Roide 27 E2
Pont-de-Salars 29 E3
Pont-d'Espagne 37 E2
Pont de Suert 37 F2
Pont-de-Vaux 26 C3
Pont-de-Veyle 26 C4
Pont-d'Oléron 28 A1
Pont-d'Ouilly 18 C4
Pont-du-Château 26 A4
Pont-du-Gard 30 B3
Ponte Arche 58 C3
Ponteareas 34 A3
Pontebba 59 F2
Pontecagnano 64 B4
Ponte Caldelas 34 A2
Ponteceno 60 B2
Ponte Ceso 34 A1
Pontecorvo 64 A3
Ponte da Barca 34 A3
Pontedecimo 60 A3
Ponte de Lima 34 A3
Pontedera 60 C4
Ponte de Sor 38 B3
Pontedeume 34 B1
Ponte di Legno 58 C3
Ponte di Piave 59 E4
Pontefract 7 D2
Pontelandolfo 64 B3
Ponte-Leccia 33 F3
Pontenelle Alpi 59 E3
Pont-en-Royans 30 C1
Ponte San Pietro 60 B1
Pontet, le 30 C3
Ponte Tresa 58 A4
Pontevico 60 B1
Pontfaverger-Moronvilliers 20 B3
Pontgibaud 29 E1
Pontigny 26 B1
Pontinia 63 F3
Pontinvrea 31 F2
Pontivy 22 C3
Pont-l'Abbé 22 A3
Pont-l'Evêque 19 D3
Pontlevoy 25 E2
Pontoise 19 E3
Pontones 44 B2
Pontón, Pto del 35 E2
Pontoon 12 B2
Pontorson 18 B4
Pontremoli 60 B3
Pontresina 58 B3
Pontrieux 22 C2
Pontrilas 9 D2
Ponts 37 F3
Pont-Ste-Maxence 19 F3
Pont-St-Esprit 30 B3
Pont St-Martin 31 E1
Pont-St-Vincent 21 D4
Pont-Scorff 22 B3
Ponts-de-Cé, les 23 E4
Pontsenni 8 C1
Pont-sur-Yonne 26 A1
Pontvallain 23 F4
Pontypool 9 D2
Pontypridd 8 C2
Ponza, I 63 F4
Ponziane, I 63 F4
Poole 9 E3
Poperinge 50 A3
Popinci 72 C3
Popoli 64 A2
Popovac 73 E4
Popovača 71 D2
Popova Šapka 77 D3
Popov Most 76 A1
Popovo 115 E2
Poppenhausen 52 B4
Poppi 61 D3
Poprad 112 B3
Porcari 60 C3
Porchov 111 D2
Porcuna 43 F2
Pordenone 59 E3
Poreč 70 A3
Pori 107 D1
Porjus 98 B2
Porkkalanselkä 107 E3
Porma, Emb del 35 E2
Porma, R 35 E2
Pornainen 107 F2
Pörnbach 55 F2
Pornic 24 A2
Pornichet 24 A2
Póros (Kefaloniá) 86 A1
Póros (Lefkáda) 82 B3
Póros (Póros) 87 F2
Póros, N 87 F2
Porozina 70 B3
Pórpi 81 D2
Porquerolles 31 D4
Porrentruy 27 E2
Porretta Terme 60 C3
Porriño 34 A3
Porsangen 95 E1
Porsangerhalvøya 95 D1
Porsgrunn 104 C3
Pórshöfn 96 C1
Portadown 13 D2
Portaferry 13 E2
Portaje, Emb de 39 D3
Porta, la 33 F3
Portalegre 38 C3
Portalé, Pto del 37 D2
Portalrubio 41 D2
Portariá 83 F2
Portarlington 13 D4
Port Askaig 4 B2
Portavogie 13 E2
Porta-Westfalica 51 F1
Port-Bacarès 32 B2
Portbail 18 B3
Portbou 32 C3
Port Charlotte 4 A2
Port, Col de 37 F2
Port-Cros 31 D4
Port-de-Bouc 30 C4
Porte, Col de 30 C1
Port-Einon 8 C2
Portella Femmina Morta 69 D3
Port Ellen 4 A2
Portelo 34 C3
Port-en-Bessin 18 C3
Port Erin 6 A1
Pórtes 87 F2
Portet-d'Aspet, Col de 37 F2
Portezuelo 39 D3
Port Glasgow 4 C2
Portglenone 13 E1
Porthcawl 8 C2
Porthmadog 6 A3
Porthmós Elafonissou 90 A1
Portici 64 B4
Portile de Fier 114 C1
Portilla de la Reina 35 E2
Portillo 35 E4
Portillo de la Canda 34 C3
Portillo de Padornelo 34 C3
Portillo, Pto del 39 E2
Portimão 42 A2
Portimo 99 D2
Portinatx, Cala de 45 D3
Portishead 9 D2
Port-Joinville 24 A3
Port Láirge 15 D4
Portland, Bill of 9 D4
Port-la-Nouvelle 32 B2
Portlaoise 13 D4
Port-Leucate 32 B2
Port-Louis 22 B4
Portman 45 D3
Port-Manech 22 B3
Portmarnock 13 E4
Portnacroish 4 B1
Portnaguran 2 B2
Portnahaven 4 A2
Port-Navalo 22 C4
Porto (F) 33 E3
Porto (P) 34 A4
Porto Azzurro 62 C1
Pórto Carrás 80 B4
Porto Ceresio 58 A4
Porto Cervo 66 B1
Porto Cesareo 65 F4
Porto Cristo 45 F3
Porto de Envalira 32 A2
Porto de Lagos 42 A2
Porto de Mós 38 A3
Portodemouros, Emb de 34 B2
Porto do Barqueiro 34 B1
Porto do Son 34 A2
Porto Empedocle 68 B4
Porto Ercole 63 D2
Portoferraio 62 C1
Portofino 60 A3
Port of Ness 2 B2
Porto Garibaldi 61 D2
Porto, G de 33 E3
Pórto Germenó 87 E1
Portogruaro 59 E4
Portohéli 87 E2
Pórto Kágio 87 D4
Pörtom 102 B2
Portomaggiore 61 D2
Portomarín 34 B2
Porto-Maurizio 31 F3
Porto Moniz 42 A3
Portomouro 34 A2
Portonovo 34 A2
Porto Petro 45 F3
Porto Pino 66 B4
Pórto Ráfti 88 A1
Porto Recanati 61 F4
Porto Rotondo 66 C1
Portorož 70 A3
Porto San Giorgio 61 F4
Porto Sant' Elpidio 61 F4
Porto Santo 42 A3
Porto Santo, I de 42 A3
Porto Santo Stefano 63 D2
Portoscuso 66 A4
Porto Tolle 61 D2
Porto Torres 66 A2
Porto-Vecchio 33 F4
Portovenere 60 B3
Portpatrick 4 B3
Portree 2 B3
Portrush 13 D1
Port-Ste-Marie 28 C3
Port-St-Louis 30 B4
Port St Mary 6 A1
Portsalon 13 D1
Pörtschach 70 A1
Portsmouth 9 F3
Portstewart 13 D1
Port-sur-Saône 27 D1
Port Talbot 8 C2
Porttipahdan tekojärvi 95 E4
Portugalete 36 B1
Portumna 12 C4
Port-Vendres 32 B2
Port William 4 C4
Porvoo 107 F2
Porvoonjoki 107 F2
Porzuna 40 A4
Posada 66 C2
Posadas 43 E2
Pöschenhöhe 56 C3
Pošechonje-Volodarsk 111 F1
Posedarje 74 C1
Posets, Pico 37 E2
Posio 99 E2
Positano 64 B4
Pößneck 52 C3
Possídi 80 A4
Possidonía 88 B2
Posta 63 F1
Postavy 111 D3
Postira 75 D2
Postojna 70 B2
Postojnska jama 70 A2
Poštorná 57 F1
Posušje 75 E1
Potamí 80 C1
Potamiá 87 D3
Potamiés 91 E4
Potamós (Andikíthira) 90 A2
Potamós (Kíthira) 90 A1
Potamoúla 82 C3
Potenza 64 C4
Potenza *R* 61 E4
Potenza Picenza 61 F4
Potes 35 E2
Potidea, N. 80 A4
Potigny 18 C3
Potoci 75 F1
Potok 71 D2
Potós 80 C3
Potpećko jez 76 B1
Potsdam 49 D4
Pottenstein 57 E3
Potters Bar 9 F2
Pöttmes 55 F2
Potton 9 F1
Pouancé 23 D4
Pougues-les-Eaux 26 A2
Pouilly (Nièvre) 26 A2
Pouilly (Rhône) 26 B4
Pouilly-en-Auxois 26 C2
Poulaphouca Reservoir 13 D4
Poúlari, Akr 92 C1
Pouldu, le 22 B3
Pouliguen, le 24 A2
Poúlithra 87 E3
Poúnda 88 C3
Poúnda, Akr 84 B4
Pournári 83 E2
Pournári, Teh L 82 C2
Pourniás, Kólpos 85 D1
Pourri, Mt 31 D1
Poussu 99 F3
Pouyastruc 37 E1
Pouzauges 24 C3
Pouzin, le 30 B2
Považská Bystrica 112 B3
Poveda 40 C2
Povlja 75 E2
Povljana 70 C4
Povljen 72 C4
Povoa de Lanhoso 34 A4
Póvoa de Varzim 34 A4
Powerscourt 13 D4
Powys 9 D1
Poysdorf 57 F2
Pöytyä 107 D2
Poza de la Sal 36 A2
Požarevac 73 D3
Požega 72 C4
Požeranje 77 D2
Poznań 112 A1
Pozo Alcón 44 B2
Pozoblanco 43 F1
Pozo Cañada 44 C1
Pozo de Guadalajara 40 B2
Pozo Higuera 44 C3
Pozohondo 44 C1
Pozondón 41 D2
Pozozal, Pto 35 F2
Pozuelo (Castilla-la-Mancha) 44 C1
Pozuelo (Extremadura) 39 D2
Pozuelo de Calatrava 40 A4
Pozzallo 69 D4
Pozzomaggiore 66 B2
Pozzuoli 64 A4
Pozzuolo 59 F3
Präbichl 57 D3
Prača 76 A1
Prachatice 56 C1
Prada, Emb de 34 C3
Pradairo 34 C2
Pradarena, Pso di 60 B3
Pradelles 29 F2
Prádena 36 A4
Prades (E) 37 F4
Prades (F) 32 B2
Prado del Rey 43 D3
Pradoluengo 36 A2
Prägraten 59 E2
Praha 53 F4
Prahecq 24 C4
Prahova 115 D1
Prahovo 73 F3
Praia a Mare 67 E2
Praia da Barra 38 B1
Praia da Rocha 42 A2
Praia da Vieira 38 A2
Praia de Mira 38 B1
Praia de Santa Cruz 38 A3

Praia de Tocha 38 B2
Prali 31 E2
Pralognan 31 D1
Pra-Loup 31 D2
Prámanda 82 C2
Pramollo, Pso di 59 F2
Prangio 81 F1
Pranjani 72 C4
Prapatnica 75 D1
Prassiá 83 D2
Prassiés 90 C3
Præstø 108 C4
Prat de Compte 41 F1
Pratella 64 A3
Prati di Tivo 63 F1
Prato (Toscana) 60 C3
Prato (Umbria) 63 E1
Pratola Peligna 64 A2
Pratomagno 61 D4
Prato-Sornico 58 A3
Prats-de-Mollo 32 B3
Pravdinsk 110 B4
Pravia 35 D1
Praz 27 E4
Prebold 70 B2
Précy-sous-Thil 26 B2
Predappio 61 D3
Predazzo 59 D3
Preddvor 70 B2
Predeal 113 D4
Predejane 77 E1
Predel 70 A2
Predela 115 D3
Predil, Pso di 59 F2
Predjama 70 A2
Predoi 59 D2
Predošćica 70 B3
Pré-en-Pail 23 E3
Preetz 48 B2
Pregarten 57 D2
Preiner Gscheid 57 E3
Prekaja 71 D4
Prekestolen 104 A3
Preko 74 C1
Preljina 73 D4
Prelog 71 D1
Prelošćica 71 D2
Premantura 70 A4
Prémery 26 A2
Premià de Mar 32 B4
Premilcuore 61 D3
Premnitz 49 D4
Premuda 74 B1
Premuda *I* 74 B1
Prenj 75 F1
Prenjas 77 D4
Prenzlau 49 E3
Prepolac 77 D1
Přerov 112 A3
Prerow 48 C1
Pré-St-Didier 27 E4
Preševo 77 E2
Presjeka 76 B2
Preslav 115 E2
Presolana, Pso della 58 B4
Prešov 112 B3
Prespansko Ez 77 D4
Pressath 53 D4
Pressbaum 57 E2
Prestatyn 6 B2
Presteigne 9 D1
Preste, la 32 B3
Prestfoss 104 C3
Přeštice 56 C1
Preston 6 B2
Prestonpans 5 D2
Prestwick 4 C2
Pretoro 64 A2
Prettau 59 D2
Prettin 53 D1
Pretzsch 53 D1
Preuilly 25 D3
Préveli 90 C4
Préveza 82 B3
Préveza (Nomos) 82 B2
Prevršac 71 D3
Prezid 70 B3
Pribini 71 E4
Priboj (Bosna i Hercegovina) 72 B3
Priboj (Srbija) 76 B1
Příbram 53 F4
Priego 40 C2
Priego de Córdoba 43 F3
Prien 56 B3
Prienai 110 C4
Prievidza 112 B3
Prigradica 75 E2
Prijeboj 70 C3
Prijedor 71 D3
Prijepolje 76 B1
Prilep 77 E3
Prilike 73 D4
Priluka 75 E1
Priluki 113 F1
Primaube, la 29 E3
Primel-Trégastel 22 B2
Primišlje 70 C3
Primolano 59 D3
Primorsk 111 D1
Primošten 75 D2
Primstal 54 B1
Princetown 8 C3
Prinés 90 C3
Prinos 80 C3
Prior, C 34 B1
Prip'at' 112 C1
Prisad 77 E3
Prislop 113 D3
Prisoje 75 E1
Priština 77 D2
Pritzerbe 49 D4
Pritzier 48 B3
Pritzwalk 48 C3
Privas 30 B2
Priverno 63 F3
Privlaka (Vincovci) 71 F2
Privlaka (Zadar) 70 C4
Prizren 77 D2
Prizzi 68 B3
Prnjavor (Bosna i Hercegovina) 71 E3
Prnjavor (Srbija) 72 B3
Proaza 35 D1
Probištip 77 E2
Probstzella 52 C3
Procida 64 A4
Pródromos 83 F4
Proenca-a-Nova 38 B3
Proevska Banja 77 E2
Profitis Ilias 93 E1
Profondeville 50 C4
Próhoma 79 F3
Prokletije 76 C2
Prokópi 84 A3
Prokuplje 77 D1
Prolom 77 D1
Prómahi 79 E2
Promahónas 80 A1
Promina, V. 75 D1
Promíri 84 A2
Pronsfeld 51 D4
Propriano 33 F4
Proskinás 83 F4
Prosna 112 A2
Prossedi 63 F3
Prossílio 81 D2
Prossotsáni 80 B2
Prostějov 112 A3
Próti 80 B2
Próti, N 86 B3
Protoklíssio 81 F1
Prötzel 49 E4
Proussós 83 D3
Provatónas 81 F2
Provence, Canal de 30 C4
Provenchères 21 E4
Provins 20 A4
Prozor 75 E1
Prudhoe 5 E3
Prukljansko jezero 75 D1
Prüm 51 D4
Pruna 43 E3
Prunetta 60 C3
Prut 113 D3
Prut 113 E4
Pružany 112 C1
Prvić 70 B4
Przasnysz 112 B1
Przełęcz Dukielska 112 C3
Przemyśl 112 C2
Przybiernów 49 F2
Psača 77 E2
Psahná 84 B4
Psáka 82 B2
Psális, Akr 88 A4
Psará 85 E4
Psarádes 78 C2
Psará, N 85 E4
Psári (Arkadía) 86 C2
Psári (Korinthía) 87 D1
Psári (Mt) 80 C3
Psáthi 88 B4
Psathópirgos 83 D4
Psathotópi 82 C2
Psérimos, N 89 F3
Psihikó 83 E2
Psihró 91 E4
Psínthos 93 F1
Pskov 111 D2
Pskovskoje Ozero 111 D2
Ps'ol 113 F2
Pšov 53 E3
Psunj 71 E2
Pteléa 80 C2
Ptéri 83 D2
Ptolemaïda 79 D3
Ptóo 84 A4
Ptuj 70 C1
Puchberg 57 E3
Pučišća 75 E2
Puckeridge 9 F2
Puçol 41 E3
Pudasjärvi 99 E3
Puebla de Alcocer 39 E4
Puebla de Almenara 40 B3
Puebla de Beleña 40 B1
Puebla de Benifasar 41 F2
Puebla de Don Fadrique 44 B2
Puebla de D. Rodrigo 39 F4
Puebla de Guzmán 42 C2
Puebla de la Calzada 39 D4
Puebla de la Reina 39 D4
Puebla del Caramiñal 34 A2
Puebla de Lillo 35 E2
Puebla de Obando 39 D3
Puebla de Sanabria 34 C3
Puebla de Trives 34 C3
Puebla Tornesa 41 F3
Pueblica de V. 35 D3
Puente de Domingo Flórez 34 C3
Puente de Génave 44 B1
Puente de los Fierros 35 D2
Puente Genil 43 F3
Puente la Reina 36 C2
Puente la Reina de Jaca 37 D2
Puentenansa 35 F2
Puente Nuevo, Emb de 43 E1
Puentes, Emb de 44 C2
Puentes Viejas, Emb de 40 B1
Puente Viesgo 35 F2
Puerto Castilla 39 E2
Puerto de Alcudia 45 F2
Puerto de Andratx 45 E3
Puerto de la Cruz 42 B4
Puerto de la Encina 43 E3
Puerto del Rosario 42 C4
Puerto de Mazarrón 45 D3
Puerto de Pollença 45 F2
Puerto de San Vicente 39 F3
Puerto de Sóller 45 E2
Puerto Lápice 40 B4
Puertollano 44 A1
Puerto Lumbreras 44 C3
Puerto Real 43 D4
Puerto Serrano 43 E3
Pugets-Théniers 31 E3
Puglia 65 D3
Puhos (Oulun Lääni) 99 E3
Puhos (Pohjois-Karjalan Lääni) 103 F3
Puhosjärvi 99 E3
Puhovac 271 F4
Puigcerda 32 A3
Puig Major 45 E2
Puignal 32 A2
Puig-reig 32 A3
Puigsacalm 32 B3
Puiseaux 25 F1
Puisserguier 30 A4
Pujols 28 B2
Pukë 76 C3
Pukiš 72 B3
Pukkila 107 F2
Pula (I) 66 B4
Pula (YU) 70 A4
Pulaj 76 B3
Puławy 112 C2
Pulborough 10 C3
Pulkau 57 E2
Pulkkila 99 D4
Pulpi 44 C3
Pulsnitz 53 E2
Pułtusk 112 B1
Punat 70 B3
Punkaharju 103 F3
Punkalaidun 107 E2
Punta Ala 62 C1
Punta di Penna 64 B2
Puntagorda 42 A4
Punta Križa 70 B4
Punta Raisi 68 B2
Punta Umbría 42 C3
Puokio 99 E4
Puolanka 99 E4
Purbach 57 F3
Purchena 44 B3
Purgstall 57 E3
Purkersdorf 57 E2
Purmerend 16 C2
Purnu 103 D3
Purullena 44 B3
Puruvesi 103 F3
Puškin 111 D1
Püspökladány 112 C4
Pustoška 111 D2
Pusula 107 E2
Puszcza 112 C1
Putanges 18 C4
Putbus 49 D1
Putgarten 49 D1
Putignano 65 E3
Putinci 72 C2
Putivl' 113 F1
Putlitz 48 C3
Puttelange 21 E3
Puttgarden 48 B1
Puula 103 D3
Puumala 103 E3
Puy de Dôme 29 E1
Puy-de-Dôme (Dépt) 29 E1
Puy de Sancy 29 E1
Puy-en-Velay, le 30 A2
Puy-Guillaume 26 A4
Puylaurens 29 D4
Puy-l'Evêque 29 D3
Puymirol 28 C3
Puymorens, Col de 32 A2
Pwllheli 6 A3
Pyhä-Häkki 103 D2
Pyhäjärvi (Hameen Lääni) 107 E1
Pyäjärvi (Oulun Lääni) 103 D1
Pyhäjärvi (Pohjois-Karjalan Lääni) 103 F3
Pyhäjärvi (Turun ja Porin Lääni) 107 D2
Pyhäjärvi *L* 103 D1
Pyhäjoki (Oulun Lääni) 99 D4
Pyhäjoki (Turun ja Porin Lääni) 107 D2
Pyhäjoki *R* 99 D4
Pyhälto 103 F4
Pyhäntä (Piipola) 103 D1
Pyhäntä (Ristijärvi) 99 E4
Pyhäranta 107 D2
Pyhäsalmi 103 D1
Pyhäselkä 103 F2
Pyhäselkä *L* 103 F2
Pyhätunturi 99 D2
Pyhatunturi 99 E2
Pyhävuori 102 C2
Pyhitysvaara 99 E3
Pyhrnpaß 57 D3
Pyhtää 107 F2
Pyla 28 A2
Pylkönmäki 103 D2
Pyrénées 37 E2
Pyrénées-Atlantiques 28 A4
Pyrénées-Orientales 32 B2
Pyrénées, Parc Nat des 37 E2
Pyrzyce 49 F3
Pyttis 107 F2

Q

Qaf'e Shllahut 76 C3
Qaf'e Shtamës 76 C4
Quakenbrück 17 E2
Quarré-les-Tombes 26 B2
Quarteira 42 B3
Quarto d'Altino 61 D1
Quartu San Elena 66 B4
Quatre Chemins 24 B3
Quatretonda 41 E4
Quedlinburg 52 C2
Queenborough 11 D2
Queen Elizabeth Forest Park 4 C2
Queensferry 6 B2
Quejigares, Pto de 40 A4
Queluz 38 A4
Queralbs 32 B3
Querfurt 52 C2
Quérigut 32 A2
Quero 40 B3
Quesada 44 B2
Quesnoy, le 20 A2
Questembert 22 C4
Quettehou 18 B3
Quiberon 22 C4
Quickborn 48 A2
Quiévrain 50 B4
Quigley's Point 13 D1
Quillan 32 B2
Quillane, Col de la 32 A2
Quillebeuf 19 D3
Quimper 22 B3
Quimperlé 22 B3
Quincinetto 31 E1
Quincoces de Yuso 36 A1
Quingey 27 D2
Quintana (Andalucía) 43 E2
Quintana (Extremadura) 39 E4
Quintana del Puente 35 F3
Quintana Martín Galíndez 36 A2
Quintanar de la Orden 40 B3
Quintanar de la Sierra 36 B3
Quintanar del Rey 40 C4
Quintana Redonda 36 B3
Quintanilha 34 C4
Quintanilla de Onésimo 35 F4
Quintin 22 C3
Quinto 37 D4
Quinzano d'Oglio 60 B1
Quipar, R 44 C2
Quiroga 34 C2
Quissac 30 B3
Qukës 77 D4
Quoich, L 2 C4

R

Raab 56 C2
Raab *R* 57 E4
Raabs 57 E1
Raahe 99 D4
Raajärvi 99 D2
Rääkkylä 103 F2
Raalte 17 D2
Raanujärvi 99 D2
Raasay 2 B3
Raasay, Sd of 2 B3
Raattama 95 D4
Rab 70 B4
Rab *I* 70 B4
Rába 112 A4
Rabac 70 B3
Rábade 34 B1
Rabastens 29 D4
Rabastens-de-Bigorre 37 E1
Rabat 68 B4
Rabe 72 C1
Rabka 112 B3
Rabrovo (Makedonija) 77 F3
Rabrovo (Srbija) 73 E3
Rača (Kragujevac) 73 D3
Rača (Radan) 77 D1
Racconigi 31 E2
Rače 70 C1
Rachov 112 C3
Racibórz 112 A2
Račinovci 72 B3
Račišće 75 E2
Radalj 72 B3
Radan 77 D1
Rădăuţi 113 D3
Radbuza 56 B1
Rade 48 A3
Råde 105 D3
Radeberg 53 E2
Radebeul 53 E2
Radeburg 53 E2
Radeče 70 B2
Radechov 112 C2
Radenci 70 C1
Radenthein 59 F2
Radevormwald 17 E4
Radici, Pso delle 60 C3
Radicondoli 60 C4
Radika 77 D3
Radimlje 75 F2
Radiovce 77 D3
Radlje 70 B1
Radljevo 72 C3
Radnice 53 E4
Radohinës, Maj'e 76 C2
Radojevo 73 D1
Radom 112 B2
Radomsko 112 B2
Radomyšl' 113 E2
Radotin 53 F4
Radovče 76 B2
Radoviči 76 B3
Radoviš 77 F3
Radovljica 70 A2
Radovnica 77 E2
Radøy 104 A2
Radstadt 59 F1
Radstädter Tauernpaß 59 F1
Radstock 9 D2
Raduša 75 E1
Radusa 77 D3
Radviliškis 110 C3
Radzyń Podlaski 112 C2

Raesfeld 17 E3
Raffadali 68 B4
Rafina 88 A1
Ragama 39 F1
Raglan 9 D2
Rago 97 F1
Ragua, Pto de la 44 B3
Raguhn 53 D1
Ragunda 101 F2
Ragusa 69 D4
Rahden 17 F2
Ráhes 83 F3
Rahlstedt 48 B3
Raia, Rib de 38 B4
Rain 55 F2
Räisälä 99 E2
Raisduoddarhal'di 94 C2
Raisio 107 D2
Raittijärvi 94 C3
Rajac 73 F3
Raja-Jooseppi 95 F3
Rajamäki 107 E2
Rajince 77 E2
Raka 70 C2
Rakalj 70 A4
Rakitna 70 B2
Rakitnica 71 D2
Rakkestad 105 D3
Rakova Bara 73 E3
Rakovac 71 E3
Rakovica 70 C3
Rakovnik 53 E4
Rakvere 110 C1
Ralja 73 D3
Ram 73 D2
Ramacca 69 D3
Ramales de la Victoria 36 A1
Ramallosa 34 A2
Ramberg 97 E1
Rambervillers 21 D4
Rambouillet 19 E4
Rambucourt 20 C4
Ramno 77 D2
Ramnoús 84 B4
Ramor, L 13 D3
Ramsau 56 B4
Ramsau 59 F1
Ramsele 101 F2
Ramsey (Cambridge) 9 F1
Ramsey (I of Man) 6 A1
Ramsgate 11 D3
Ramsjö 101 E3
Ramstein 54 B1
Ramsund 94 B3
Ramundberget 101 D2
Ramvik 101 F2
Rana 97 D3
Ranalt 59 D2
Rance 22 C3
Randaberg 104 A3
Randak 104 B3
Randalstown 13 E2
Randan 26 A4
Randanne 29 E1
Randazzo 69 D3
Randers 108 B2
Randijaure 98 A2
Randow 49 E2
Randsfjorden 105 D2
Råneå 98 C3
Råneälven 98 B2
Rangsdorf 49 E4
Rankweil 58 B2
Rannoch, L 4 C1
Ranovac 73 E3
Rantasalmi 103 E3
Rantsila 99 D4
Ranua 99 D3
Raon-l'Etape 21 E4
Rapallo 60 A3
Rapolano Terme 61 D4
Rapolla 64 C3
Rapperswil 58 A2
Rapsáni 83 E1
Raptópoulo 86 C3
Raša 70 A3
Räsälä 103 E2
Raša *R* 70 A3
Rasbo 106 B3
Rascafría 40 A1
Rasdorf 52 B3
Raseiniai 110 C3
Rasimbegov Most 77 E4
Rasina 73 E4
Raška 76 C1
Rasno 75 E2
Raso, C 38 A4
Rasquera 41 F1
Rastatt 54 C2
Rastede 47 F3
Rastegai'sa 95 E2
Rastenberg 52 C2
Rastenfeld 57 E2
Rasueros 39 F1
Rätan 101 E3
Rateče 70 A1
Ratekau 48 B2
Rates 34 A4
Rathdowney 12 C4
Rathdrum 13 D4
Rathenow 49 D4
Rathfriland 13 E2
Rathkeale 14 B3
Rathlin I 13 E1
Rath Luirc 14 B3
Rathmelton 13 D1
Rathmore 14 B4
Rathmullan 13 D1
Raticosa, Pso della 61 D3
Ratingen 17 E4
Ratkovac 76 C2
Ratkovo 72 B2
Ratten 57 E3
Rattenberg 59 D1
Rattersdorf 57 F3
Rattray 5 D1
Rattray Head 3 E3
Rättvik 101 E4
Ratzeburg 48 B2
Raubling 56 B3
Raucourt-et-Flaba 20 C2
Raudanjoki 99 D2
Raudaskylä 102 C1
Raufarhöfn 96 C1
Raufoss 105 D2
Rauha 103 E4
Rauhamäki 103 D3
Rauland 104 B3
Rauma (N) 100 B3
Rauma (SF) 107 D2
Rauris 59 E1
Rautalampi 103 D2
Rautas 94 C4
Rautavaara 103 E1
Rautio 102 C1
Rautjärvi 103 F3
Ravan 71 F4
Ravanica 73 E4
Ravanjska 70 C4
Ravanusa 68 C4
Ravello 64 B4
Raven 71 D2
Ravenna 61 D2
Ravensbrück 49 D3
Ravensburg 55 D4
Ravna Dubrava 77 E1
Ravna Gora 70 B3
Ravna Reka 73 E3
Ravne na Koroškem 70 B1
Ravnište 77 D1
Ravnje 72 B3
Ravno 75 F2
Ravno Bučje 73 F4
Ravno, G. 75 E1
Rawicz 112 A2
Rawtenstall 6 C2
Rayleigh 11 D2
Rayol 31 D4
Räyrinki 102 C2
Ražana 72 C4
Ražanac 70 C4
Razboj 71 E3
Razbojna 77 D1
Raždaginja 76 C1
Razelm 113 E4
Razgrad 115 E2
Razlog 115 D3
Razlovci 77 F2
Raz, Pte du 22 A3
Reading 9 F2
Reales 43 E4
Réalmont 32 B1
Rebais 20 A4
Rebbenesøy 94 B2
Rebordelo 34 C4
Reç 76 C3
Recanati 61 F4
Recco 60 A3
Recey 26 C1
Rechnitz 57 F4
Rečica (SU) 111 E4
Rečica (YU) 70 C3
Recke 17 E2
Recklinghausen 17 E3
Recknitz 48 C2
Recoaro Terme 59 D4
Recuerda 36 A4
Recz 49 F2
Redange 21 D2
Red B 13 E1
Redcar 5 F4
Redditch 9 E1
Redhill 10 C3
Redon 23 D4
Redondela 34 A3
Redondo 38 C4
Redruth 8 B4
Ree, L 12 C3
Rees 17 D3
Reeth 6 C1
Refsnes 94 A3
Reftele 109 D2
Rega 49 F2
Regalbuto 69 D3
Regen 56 B2
Regensburg 56 B2
Regenstauf 56 B2
Reggello 61 D4
Reggio di Calabria 67 E4
Reggiolo 60 C2
Reggio nell' Emilia 60 C2
Reghin 113 D4
Regnitz 55 E1
Reguengos de Monsaraz 42 B1
Rehau 53 D4
Rehburg-Loccum 48 A4
Rehden 17 F2
Rehna 48 B2
Reichenau (A) 57 E3
Reichenau (CH) 58 B2
Reichenbach (Dresden) 53 F2
Reichenbach (Karl-Marx-Stadt) 53 D3
Reichertshofen 55 F2
Reichshoffen 21 E3
Reigate 10 C3
Reignier 27 D4
Ré, Ile de 24 B4
Reillanne 30 C3
Reims 20 B3
Reinach 27 F2
Reinbek 48 B3
Reinberg 49 D1
Reine 97 E1
Reinfeld 48 B2
Reinheim 54 C1
Reinli 104 C2
Reinosa 35 F2
Reinøy 94 C2
Reisaelva 94 C2
Reischenhart 56 B3
Reisjärvi 103 D1
Reiss 3 D2
Reit im Winkl 56 B4
Reitzenhain 53 E3
Reka 70 A3
Rekovac 73 E4
Remagen 51 E4
Rémalard 23 F3
Remeskylä 103 D1
Remich 21 D2
Remiremont 27 D1
Remolinos 36 C3
Remouchamps 51 D4
Remoulins 30 B3
Rempstone 7 D3
Remscheid 17 E4
Rémuzat 30 C2
Rena 105 D2
Renaix 50 B3
Renazé 23 E4
Renchen 54 C3
Rende 67 E2
Rendína (Makedonía) 80 B3
Rendína (Thessalía) 83 D3
Rendsburg 48 A2
Renginio 83 F3
Rengsdorf 51 E4
Reni 113 E4
Renish Pt 2 A3
Renko 107 E2
Renkum 17 D3
Rennebu 100 C2
Rennerod 51 F3
Rennes 23 D3
Rennes-les-Bains 32 B2
Rennesøy 104 A3
Rennweg 59 F2
Reno 61 D2
Rensjön 94 C4
Renwez 20 B2
Réole, la 28 B2
Replot 102 B2
Replotfjärden 102 B2
Repojoki 95 E3
Reposaari 102 B3
République, Col de la 30 B1
Repvag 95 E1
Requena 41 D4
Réquista 29 E3
Rerik 48 C2
Resanovci 71 D4
Resavica 73 E3
Reschenpaß 58 C2
Resen (Makedonija) 77 D4
Resen (Srbija) 77 E2
Resende 34 B4
Resia, Pso di 58 C2
Reşiţa 114 C1
Resko 49 F2
Resmo 109 E3
Resna 76 B3
Resnik 73 D3
Ressons 19 F3
Restafjorden 94 C2
Restelica 77 D3
Resuttano 68 C3
Retezatului, M 114 C1
Rethel 20 B3
Rethem 48 A4
Rethen 52 B1
Réthimno 90 C3
Réthimno (Nomos) 90 C3
Retiers 23 D3
Retortillo, Emb de 43 E2
Retuerta 41 D1
Retuerta del Bullaque 39 F3
Retuerta, Emb de 36 A3
Retz 57 E2
Reuilly 25 E3
Reus 37 F4
Reusel 16 C4
Reuss 27 F2
Reuterstadt-Stavenhagen 49 D2
Reutlingen 55 D3
Reutte 58 C1
Revard, Mt 27 D4
Revel 29 D4
Revesbotn 95 D1
Revigny 20 C4
Revin 20 B2
Řevnikov 53 F3
Revolcadores 44 C2
Revonlahti 99 D4
Revsnes 104 B1
Rewal 49 F1
Reyðarfjörður 96 C2
Reykholt 96 A2
Reykjavík 96 A2
Rēzekne 111 D2
Rezzato 60 B1
Rezzoaglio 60 A3
Rgotina 73 F3
Rhaeadr 8 C1
Rhayader 8 C1
Rheda-Wiedenbrück 17 F3
Rhede 17 D3
Rhein 17 D3
Rheinbach 51 E4
Rheinberg 17 D3
Rheinböllen 54 B1
Rheine 17 E2
Rheinfelden (CH) 27 F2
Rheinfelden (D) 54 C4
Rheinhausen 17 D3
Rheinland-Pfalz 51 E4
Rheinsberg 49 D3
Rheinwaldhorn 58 B3
Rhêmes N.D. 31 E1
Rhenen 16 C3
Rheydt 17 D4
Rhinau 21 E4
Rhinow 49 D4
Rho 60 A1
Rhondda 8 C2
Rhône 26 C4
Rhône (Dépt) 26 B4
Rhône à Sète, Canal du 30 B3
Rhosneigr 6 A2
Rhossili 8 C2
Rhüden 52 B1
Rhum 2 B4
Rhum, Sd of 2 B4
Rhune, la 28 A4
Rhuthun 6 B3
Rhyl 6 B2
Rhynern 17 E3
Rhynie 3 E4
Riaillé 23 D4
Riákia 79 E3
Rial 34 A2
Riaño 35 E2
Riaño, Emb de 35 E2
Rians 30 C4
Riansares R 40 B3
Rianxo 34 A2
Riaza 36 A4
Ribadavia 34 B3
Ribadelago 34 C3
Ribadeo 34 C1
Riba de Saelices 40 C1
Riba de Santiuste 36 B4
Ribadesella 35 E1
Ribarci 77 E2
Ribariće 76 C1
Riba-roja, Emb de 37 E4
Ribarska Banja 73 E4
Ribas de Campos 35 E3
Ribas de Sil 34 B2
Ribatejo 38 B3
Ribble 6 C2
Ribe 108 A3
Ribeauvillé 27 E1
Ribécourt 19 F3
Ribeira de Pena 34 B4
Ribeira, Emb de la 34 B1
Ribemont 20 A2
Ribera 68 B3
Ribérac 28 C1
Ribera de Cardós 32 A2
Ribera del Fresno 43 D1
Ribes de Freser 32 B3
Ribiers 30 C3
Ribnica (Bosna i Hercegovina) 71 F4
Ribnica (Kočevje) 70 B2
Ribnica (Postojna) 70 A3
Ribnica na Pohorju 70 B1
Ribnik 70 C2
Ribnitz-Damgarten 48 C1
Ribolla 62 C1
Říčany 53 F4
Riccia 64 B3
Riccione 61 E3
Riceys, les 26 B1
Richelieu 25 D3
Richmond (London) 9 F2
Richmond (Yorks) 6 C1
Richtenberg 49 D1
Rickling 48 A2
Ricla 36 C4
Ricobayo, Emb de 35 D4
Riđica 72 B1
Riec 22 B3
Ried (Oberösterreich) 56 C3
Ried (Tirol) 58 C2
Riedenburg 55 F2
Riedlingen 55 D3
Riegel 54 C3
Riegersburg 57 F4
Riego de la Vega 35 D3
Riesa 53 E2
Riesi 68 C4
Riestedt 52 C2
Rietberg 17 F3
Rieti 63 E2
Rieumes 29 D4
Rieupeyroux 29 E3
Rieux 37 F1
Riez 31 D3
Riezlern 58 B2
Rīga 110 C2
Rigáni 83 D4
Rígeo 83 E2
Rigi 58 A2
Rignac 29 E3
Rignano Flaminio 63 E2
Rihéa 87 E3
Riihimäki 107 E2
Riisitunturi 99 E2
Riistavesi 103 E2
Riječa 72 B4
Rijeka 70 B3
Rijeka Crnojevića 76 B3
Rijssen 17 D2
Riksgränsen 94 B3
Rila 115 D3
Rila *Mts* 115 D3
Rillo 41 D2
Rillo de Gallo 40 C1
Rimavská-Sobota 112 B3
Rimbo 106 B3
Rimini 61 E3
Rîmnicu Sărat 113 E4
Rîmnicu Vîlcea 115 D1
Rímnio 79 E4
Rimske Toplice 70 B2
Rincón de la Victoria 43 F4
Rincón de Soto 36 C2
Rindal 100 C2
Ringaskiddy 14 C4
Ringe 108 B4
Ringebu 100 C3
Ringford 4 C3
Ringkøbing 108 A3
Ringkøbing Fjord 108 A3
Ring of Kerry 14 A4
Ringsaker 105 D2
Ringstad 104 A1
Ringsted 108 C3
Ringvassøy 94 B2
Ringwood 9 E3
Rínia, N 88 C2
Rinkaby 109 D3
Rinns Pt 4 A2
Rinteln 52 A1
Rinvyle Pt 12 A3
Río 83 D4
Riocavado de la Sierra 36 A3
Riogordo 43 F3
Riola Sardo 66 A3
Riolo Terme 61 D3
Riom 26 A4
Riomaggiore 60 B3
Rio Maior 38 A3
Rio Marina 62 C1
Riom-ès-Montagnes 29 E1
Rionero in Vulture 64 C3
Río, Punta del 44 B4
Rioseco de Tapia 35 D2
Rioz 27 D2
Ripač 70 C4
Ripanj 73 D3
Riparbella 60 C4
Ripatransone 61 F4
Ripley 7 D3
Ripoli 32 A3
Ripollet 32 A4
Ripon 6 C1
Riquewihr 27 E1
Risan 76 B2
Risbäck 97 E4
Risca 9 D2
Riscle 28 B4
Risle 19 D4
Risnes 104 B4
Risnjak 70 B3
Risør 104 C4
Risøyhamn 94 A3
Risøysundet 94 A3
Rissa 100 C1
Ristiina 103 E3
Ristijärvi 99 E4
Ristilampi 99 D2
Ristovac 77 E2
Risum-Lindholm 47 F1
Ritíni 79 E4
Ritoniemi 103 E2
Ritsóna 84 A4
Rittmannshausen 52 B3
Riudoms 37 F4
Riva 58 C4
Rivarolo Canavese 31 E1
Rive-de-Gier 30 B1
Rives 30 C1
Rivesaltes 32 B2
Rivière-Thibouville, la 19 D3
Rivio 82 C3
Rivisondoli 64 A2
Rivoli 31 E1
Rivolta d'Adda 60 B1
Ríza 83 D4
Rizário 79 E2
Rízia 81 F1
Rízoma 83 D1
Rizómilos 83 F2
Rizovoúni 83 D2
Rižskij Zaliv 110 B2
Rjånes 100 A2
Rjukan 104 C3
Roa 35 F4
Roadside 3 D2
Roan 96 C4
Roanne 26 B4
Roaringwater B 14 A4
Robbio 60 A1
Röbel 49 D3
Robertsfors 102 B1
Robertville 51 D4
Robič 70 A2
Roble 44 C1
Robledillo de Gata 39 D2
Robledo 44 C1
Robledo de Chavela 40 A2
Robres 37 D3
Roca, C da 38 A4
Rocamadour 29 D2
Rocca d'Aspide 64 C4
Rocca di Mezzo 63 F2
Rocca di Papa 63 E3
Roccalbegna 63 D1
Roccalumera 69 D2
Roccamonfina 64 A3
Roccapalumba 68 B3
Roccaraso 64 A2
Rocca San Casciano 61 D3
Rocca Sinibalda 63 F2
Roccastrada 63 D1
Roccella Ionica 67 F4
Rocchetta Sant' Antonio 64 C3
Roc de Fraussa 32 B3
Rochdale 6 C2
Roche-Bernard, la 22 C4
Rochebonne 30 B2
Roche-Canillac, la 29 D2
Roche-Chalais, la 28 B2
Rochechouart 28 C1
Roche-Derrien, la 22 C2
Roche-en-Ardenne, la 51 D4
Rochefort (B) 50 C4
Rochefort (F) 24 B4
Rochefort-en-Terre 22 C4
Rochefort-Montagne 29 E1
Rochefort-sur-Nenon 26 C2
Rochefoucauld, la 28 C1
Roche-Guyon, la 19 E3
Rochehaut 20 C2
Rochelle, La 24 B4
Rochemaure 30 B2
Roche-Posay, la 25 D3
Rochepot, le 26 C3
Roches, Col des 27 E2
Rocheservière 24 B3
Rochester 11 D2
Roche-sur-Foron, la 27 D4
Roche-sur-Yon, la 24 B3
Rochette, la 31 D1
Rochlitz 53 D2
Rociana del Condado 42 C3

Den Haag
Wateringen
Monster
Poeldijk
Kwintsheul
's-Gravenzande
Honselersdijk
Naaldwijk
Lange Watering
Zwethkanaal
Monsterwatering
52°
Kingston upon Hull
Harwich
Felixstowe
Hoekse Bosjes
Hoek van Holland
Heenweg
Nieuwe-Tuinen
Oostbuurt
De Lier
Lierwatering
Staelduinen
NIEUWE
WATERWEG
Westerlee
Maasdijk
(Werken in uitvoering)
(Travaux en cours)
8e Petroleumhaven
Europahaven
Maasvlakte
G.E.B.
E.C.T.
E.M.O
Mississippihaven
Hartelhaven
Hartelkanaal
Beerkanaal
EUROPOORT
6e Petroleumh.
B.P.
Dintelhaven
Beneluxhaven
4e Petroleumh.
SHELL
TEXACO
ESSO
5e Petroleumh.
KUWAIT PETROLEUM
Calandkanaal
Rijnpoorthaven
Poortershaven
Westwijk
Maassluis
Maasland
Westgaag
Middelvliet
Boonervliet
Suurhoffbrug
Dintelhavenbrug
Oostvoornse Meer
Brielse Meer
Stenenbaak
Kruiningergos
7e Petroleumh.
MOBIL
Zanddijk
Rozenburg
Calandbrug
Het Scheur
Mildenburgbos
Oostvoorne
Waranda
Heveringen
Helhoek
Strijpe
De Krabbeplaat
De Meeuw
Harmsenbrug
Brielle
Brielsebrug
Rugge
Brittanniëh.
I.C.I.
St. Laurensh.
Botlek
Gat van de Hawk
Brielse Gat
Voorne
Duinen van Voorne
Waterbos
Stuifakker
Tinte
VOORNE
Zwartewaal
Vierpolders
Sluiswetering
Seineh.
TEXACO
Chemieh.
De Pinguïn
De Waal
Rockanje
Rak van Scheelhoek
Heenvliet
Geervliet
A 15
Ronde Weibos
Quackjes water
Nieuwenhoorn
Abbenbroek
Voornsekanaal
Noord Pampus
De Quack
Nieuw-Helvoet
Haringvlietdam
Havenhoofd
Vlotbrug
Oudenhoorn
Hellevoetsluis
Zuidland
PUTTEN
HARINGVLIET
GOEREE
4°
Brouwersdam

Rockenhausen	54 B1	Rødberg	104 C2	Rødekro	108 A4
Rocroi	20 B2	Rødby	108 B4	Rodel	2 A3
Róda	82 A1	Rødbyhavn	108 B4	Rodellar	37 E3
Rodach	52 C4	Rødding (Ribe)	108 A3	Roden	47 D3
Rodacherbrunn	52 C3	Rødding (Viborg)	108 A2	Ródenas	41 D2
Roda de Isábena	37 E3	Rödeby	109 E3	Rödermark	52 A4
Rodavgí	82 C2	Rodeiro	34 B2	Rodewisch	53 D3

Rodez	29 E3	Rodohóri	79 E3	Rodopós	90 B3
Rodiezmo	35 D2	Rodolívos	80 B2	Ródos	93 F1
Rodi Garganico	64 C2	Rödön	101 E2	Ródos, N	93 F2
Roding	56 B1	Rodonit, Gjiri i	76 C4	Rodováni	90 B3
Roditis	81 E2	Rodópi (Nomos)	81 E2	Rodvattnet	102 A1
Rodnei, M	113 D3	Rodopi *Mts*	115 D3	Rødven	100 B2
Rododáfni	83 D4	Rodópoli	79 F2	Rødvig	108 C4

Roermond	17 D4
Roeselare	50 A3
Rogač	75 D2
Rogača	73 D3
Rogačica (Kosovo)	77 E2
Rogačica (Srbija)	72 C4
Rogačov	111 E4

Den Haag
Zoetermeer
Alphen a/d Rijn
A 12
DELFT
Pijnacker
Bleiswijk
Zevenhuizen
Den Hoorn
Delfgauw
Berkel en Rodenrijs
Bergschenhoek
Eendragtspolder
Buitenhof
Voorhof
Hodenpijl
Tanthof
Oostmeerpolder
Oude Leede
Rodenrijs
Schipluiden
Recreatiegebied Rottemeren
Rotte
Gouda
Negenhuizen
Hillegersberg
Ommoord
Nieuwerkerk a/d IJssel
ROTTERDAM ZESTIENHOVEN
Schiebroek
Zouteveen
Kerkbuurt
Overschie
Kralingsebos
Kralingen
Capelle a/d IJssel
Maaslandse vlietlanden
Broekpolder
Holy
Groenoord
Beatrixpark
Centraal Station
Blijdorp
Krimpen a/d IJssel
E 25
Vlaardingen
Vlaardingen Ambacht
Schiedam
ROTTERDAM
Willemsbrug
Kralingse Veer
Westwijk
Volkspark
Museum Park
Het Park
Delfshaven
Euromast
Brienenoordbrug
Maastunnel
Katendrecht
Beneluxtunnel
Heijplaat
Waalhaven
NIEUWE MAAS
IJsselmonde
Bolnes
Pernis
Charlois
Tuindorp-Vreewijk
Zuiderpark
Zuidwijk
Pendrecht
Lombardijen
Ridderkerk
Hoogvliet
Zuidhoek
De Punt
A 15
Barendrecht
Poortugaal
Rhoon
Smitshoek
Carnisse
Spijkenisse
Hekelingen
IJSSELMONDE
Delta Ziekenhuis
Heerjansdam
Beerenplaat
OUDE MAAS
Heinenoordtunnel
Heinenoord
Oud-Beijerland
Goidschalxoord
Blaaksedijk
Nieuw-Beijerland
Klaaswaal
Haringvlietbrug
s' Gravendeel
Dordrecht, Gorinchem
Schoonhoven
1/100 000

Rogaland 104 A3
Rogaška Slatina 70 C1
Rogatec 70 C2
Rogatica 76 A1
Rogatin 113 D3
Rogätz 48 C4
Rogen 101 D3
Rogen *L* 101 D3
Roggendorf 48 B2
Roggiano Gravina 67 E2
Roggosen 53 F1
Rogliano (F) 33 F2
Rogliano (I) 67 E3
Rognan 97 E2
Rogozna 76 C1
Rogoznica 75 D2
Rohan 22 C3
Rohr 52 B3
Rohrbach (A) 56 C2
Rohrbach (F) 21 E3
Rohrbrunn 52 A4
Rohrer Sattel 57 E3
Roignais 27 E4
Roine Mallasvesi 107 E1
Roisel 19 F2
Roissy 19 F4
Rojales 45 D2
Rök 109 D1
Rokiškis 110 C3
Røkland 97 F2
Rokovci 71 F2
Rokua 99 E4
Rokycany 53 E4
Røldal 104 B3
Rolfstorp 108 C2
Rolla 94 B3
Rollag 104 C3
Rolle 27 D3
Rolle, Pso di 59 D3
Rolvsøya 95 D1
Roma 63 E2
Romagnano Sesia 31 F1
Roman 113 D4
Romana 66 B2
Romanche 31 D1
Romangordo 39 E3
România 73 D1
Romanija 71 F4
Romans 30 C2

Romanshorn 58 B1
Romantische straße 55 E3
Rombas 21 D3
Rombo, Pso del 58 C2
Römhild 52 B4
Romilly 20 B4
Romny 113 F1
Rømø 108 A3
Romont 27 E3
Romorantin 25 E2
Romsdalen 100 B2
Romsdalsfjorden 100 B2
Romsey 9 E3
Rona 2 B3
Ronaldsway 6 A1
Roncade 59 E4
Roncal 37 D2
Ronce 28 A1
Roncegno 59 D3
Roncesvalles 36 C1
Ronchamp 27 D1
Ronchi 59 F3
Ronciglione 63 E2
Roncobilaccio 60 C3
Ronda 43 E3
Rondane 100 C3
Ronda, Serr de 43 E4
Rønde 108 B3
Rondeslottet 100 C3
Rondissone 31 F1
Rondvassbu 100 C3
Rönnäng 108 C1
Rønne 109 D4
Ronneburg 53 D3
Ronneby 109 E3
Ronnebyån 109 E3
Rønnede 108 C4
Rönnöfors 101 E1
Ronse 50 B3
Roosendaal 16 B3
Roperuelos del Páramo 35 D3
Ropi 94 C3
Ropinsalmi 94 C3
Ropotovo 77 E3
Roquebillière 31 E3
Roquebrun 30 A4
Roquebrune-Cap-Martin 31 E3
Roquebrussanne, la 31 D4
Roquecourbe 32 B1
Roquefort 28 B3
Roquefort-sur-Soulzon 29 F3
Roque-Gageac, la 29 D2
Roquemaure 30 B3
Roquesteron 31 E3
Roquetas de Mar 44 B4
Roquevaire 30 C4
Rora Head 3 D1
Rore 71 D4
Røros 101 D2
Rørøy 97 D3
Rorschach 58 B1
Rørvig 108 C3
Rørvik (Nord Trøndelag) 97 D4
Rørvik (Sør Trøndelag) 100 C1
Ros' 113 E2
Rosà 59 D4
Rosal de la Frontera 42 C1
Rosans 30 C2
Rosarito, Emb de 39 E2
Rosarno 67 E4
Roscoff 22 B2
Ros Comáin 12 C3
Roscommon 12 C3
Roscommon (Co) 12 C3
Roscrea 12 C4
Rose (I) 67 E2
Rose (YU) 76 A3
Rosegg 70 A1
Roselend, Cormet de 27 E4
Rosell 41 F2
Rosendal 104 A2
Rosenheim 56 B3
Rosenhof 56 B2
Rosenthal 53 F3
Roses 32 C3
Roses, Golfo de 32 C3
Roseto degli Abruzzi 64 A1
Rosheim 21 E4
Rosice 57 F1
Rosières 19 F2
Rosiers, les 24 C2
Rosignano Marittimo 60 C4
Roșiori de Vede 115 D2
Roskilde 108 C3
Roški slap 75 D1
Roslavl' 111 E3
Rosmaninhal 38 C3
Røsnæs 108 B3
Rosolina Mare 61 D1
Rosolini 69 D4
Rosoman 77 E3
Rosova dolina 115 D2
Rosporden 22 B3
Rossano 67 F2
Rossan Pt 12 C1
Rosscarbery 14 B4
Roßdorf 54 C1
Rosses Point 12 C2
Roßhaupten 55 E4
Rossija 111 E2
Rossio 38 B3
Rosskreppfjorden 104 B3
Rosslare 15 D4
Rosslare Harbour 15 D4
Roßlau 55 D1
Rosslea 13 D2
Rossön 101 F1
Ross-on-Wye 9 D2
Røssvatnet 97 E3
Roßwein 53 E2
Rosthwaite 5 D4
Røstlandet 97 D1
Rostock 48 C2
Rostrenen 22 B3
Rostrevor 13 E3
Rostujávri 94 C3
Røsvik 94 A4
Rosvik 98 C3
Rota 43 D3
Rotenburg (Hessen) 52 B3
Rotenburg (Niedersachsen) 48 A3
Roth 55 F1
Rötha 53 D2
Rothbury 5 E3
Röthenbach 55 F1
Rothenburg 53 F2
Rothenburg ob der Tauber 55 E1
Rothéneuf 18 B4
Rotherham 7 D2
Rothes 3 D3
Rothesay 4 B2
Rothwell 9 F1
Rotja, Pta 45 D4
Rotonda 67 E2
Rotondella 65 D4
Rotondo, M 33 F3
Rott (Bayern) 56 A3
Rott (Bayern) 56 B3
Rott *R* 56 B2
Rottach-Egern 56 A4
Rotten 27 F3
Rottenbach 52 C4
Rottenburg (Baden-Württemberg) 55 D3
Rottenburg (Bayern) 56 B2
Rottenmann 57 D4
Rottenmanner Tauern 57 D4
Rotterdam 16 B3
Rottne 109 D2
Rottneros 105 E3
Rottweil 54 C3
Rötz 56 B1
Roubaix 20 A1
Roudnice 53 F3
Rouen 19 E3
Rouffach 27 E1
Rougé 23 D4
Rougemont 27 D2
Rougemont-le-Château 27 E1
Rouillac 28 B1
Roujan 30 A4
Roulans 27 D2
Roulers 50 A3
Roundstone 12 A3
Rousay 3 E1
Roússa 81 E1
Rousses, les 27 D3
Rousset, Col de 30 C2
Rovaniemi 99 D2
Rovato 60 B1
Rovereto 59 D4
Roverud 105 D3
Roviés 83 F3
Rovigo 61 D2
Rovinj 70 A3
Rovišće 71 D2
Rovno 113 D2
Roxen 106 A4
Roxo, Bgem do 42 B1
Royal Canal 12 C3
Royal Leamington Spa 9 E1
Royal Tunbridge Wells 10 C3
Royan 28 A1
Royat 29 E1
Roybon 30 C1
Roye 19 F3
Royère-de-Vassivière 25 E4
Røyrvik 97 E4
Royston 9 F2
Röyttä 98 C3
Rožaje 76 C2
Rožanstvo 72 C4
Rozay-en-Brie 19 F4
Rozier, le 29 F3
Rožmberk 57 D1
Rožmitál 53 F4
Rožňava 112 B3
Rozoy 20 B2
Roztocze 112 C2
Roztoky 53 F3
Rozvadov 56 B1
Rrasë 76 C3
Rrëshen 76 C3
Rrogozhinë 76 C4
Rtanj 73 E4
Rtanj (Reg) 73 E4
Ruabon 6 B3
Rubbestadneset 104 A2
Rubena 35 F3
Rubeži 76 B2
Rubha a'Mhail 4 B2
Rubha Còigeach 2 C2
Rubha Réidh 2 B3
Rubí 32 A4
Rubiães 34 A3
Rubi de Bracamonte 39 F1
Rubielos de Mora 41 E3
Rubiera 60 C2
Rubio 35 F4
Rudare 77 D1
Rüdersdorf 49 E4
Rüdesheim 51 F4
Rudkøbing 108 B4
Rudn'a 111 E3
Rudna Glava 73 E3
Rudnica (Crna Gora) 76 B1
Rudnica (Srbija) 76 C1
Rudnik (Kosovo) 76 C2
Rudnik (Reg) 73 D4
Rudnik (Srbija) 73 D4
Rudo 76 B1
Rudolstadt 52 C3
Rue 19 E2
Ruecas, R 39 E4
Rueda 35 E4
Rueda de Jalón 36 C3
Ruelle 28 C1
Ruffec 25 D4
Ruffieux 27 D4
Rugby 9 E1
Rugeley 6 C3
Rügen 49 D1
Rugles 19 D4
Rugovska klisura 76 C2
Ruhla 52 B3
Ruhland 53 E2
Ruhner Berge 48 C3
Ruhpolding 56 B3
Ruhr 17 E3
Ruidera 40 B4
Rüiena 110 C2
Ruka 99 E2
Rukatunturi 99 E2
Ruma 72 C2
Rumblar, Emb del 44 A2
Rumboci 75 E1
Rumburk 53 F2
Rumengol 22 B3
Rumenka 72 C2
Rumigny 20 B2
Rumija 76 B3
Rumilly 27 D4
Runcorn 6 B2
Runde 100 A2
Rundvik 102 A2
Runn 105 F2
Runni 103 D1
Runtuna 106 B4
Ruohtir 95 E2
Ruokojärvi 103 F3
Ruokolahti 103 F3
Ruokovesi 103 E2
Ruokto 98 B1
Ruoms 30 B2
Ruotsinpyhtää 107 F2
Ruovesi 102 C3
Rupa 70 B3
Rupea 113 D4
Ruppiner See 49 D3
Rupt 27 D1
Rur 17 D4
Ruše 70 C1
Ruse 115 D2
Ruševo 71 E2
Rush 13 E3
Rushden 9 F1
Ruski Krstur 72 B2
Rusko 107 D2
Rusko Selo 72 C1
Rusksele 98 A4
Rüsselsheim 51 F4
Russenes 95 D1
Russey, le 27 E2
Russi 61 D3
Rust 57 F3
Rustefjelbma 95 E1
Ruswil 27 F2
Rute 43 F3
Rüthen 17 F3
Ruthin 6 B3
Rüti 58 A2
Rutigliano 65 E3
Rutledal 104 A1
Ruuhitunturi 99 E2
Ruukki 99 D4
Ruuponsaari 103 D2
Ruurlo 17 D3
Ruvo di Puglia 65 D3
Ruwer 54 A1
Ruynes-en-Margeride 29 F2
Ružomberok 112 B3
Ry 108 B3
Rybinsk 111 F1
Rybinskoje Vodochranilišče 111 F1
Rybnica 113 E3
Rybnik 112 B3
Rychnov nad Kněžnou 112 A3
Ryd 109 D3
Ryde 9 E3
Rye 11 D3
Ryfylke 104 A3
Rygge 105 D3
Rykene 104 B4
Ryl'sk 113 F1
Rymań 49 F1
Rymättylä 107 D2
Rypefjord 95 D1
Rysjedalsvika 104 A1
Ryttylä 107 E2
Rzepin 49 F4
Rzeszów 112 C2
Ržev 111 F2

S

Sääksjärvi 102 C2
Saal 55 F2
Saalach 59 E1
Saalbach 59 E1
Saale 52 C1
Saaler Bodden 48 C1
Saales 21 E4
Saalfeld 52 C3
Saalfelden 59 E1
Saane 27 E3
Saanen 27 E3
Saar 54 A1
Saarbrücken 54 B2
Saarburg 54 A1
Saaremaa 110 B2
Saarenkylä 99 D2
Saari 103 F3
Saariharju 99 E3
Saarijärvi 103 D2
Saarikoski 94 C3
Saariselkä 95 F3
Saariselkä (Reg) 95 F3
Saaristomeri 107 D3
Saarland 54 A2
Saarlouis 54 B2
Saas-Fee 27 F4
Šabac 72 C3
Sabadell 32 A4
Sabaudia 63 F3
Sabbioneta 60 C2
Sabero 35 E2
Sabiñánigo 37 D2
Sabini, Mti 63 E2
Sabiote 44 B2
Sablé 23 E4
Sables-d'Olonne, les 24 B3
Sables-d'Or 22 C2
Sæbo 100 A2
Sabóia 42 A2
Sabôr, R 34 C4
Sabres 28 B3
Sabrosa 34 B4
Sabugal 39 D2
Sæby 108 B2
Sa Calobra 45 E2
Sacavém 38 A4
Sacedon 40 C2
Saceruela 39 F4
Sachsen 53 F2
Sachsen-Anhault 48 C4
Sacile 59 E3
Sacra di San Michele 31 E1
Sacramenia 35 F4
Sacratif, C 44 A4
Sada 34 B1
Sádaba 36 C2
Sado, R 38 A4
Sadurniño 34 B1
Saelices 40 B3
Safara 42 C1
Säffle 105 E4
Saffron Walden 10 C2
Safonovo 111 E3
Sagard 49 D1
S'Agaró 32 B4
Sagéika 86 B1
Sagfjorden 94 A4
Sagiáda 82 B1
Sagra, Sa de la 44 B2
Sagres 42 A3
Sagres, Pta de 42 A3
Sagunto 41 E3
Sagvåg 104 A3
Sahagún 35 E3
Sahalahti 107 E1
Šahinovići 71 E3
Sahl 108 A2
Sahloinen 103 D3
Saidus 110 B3
Saignelégier 27 E2
Saija 95 F4
Saillagouse 32 A3
Saillans 30 C2
Saimaa 103 E3
Saimaanranta 103 E4
Sains-du-Nord 20 B2
Sains-Richaumont 20 B2
St Abb's Head 5 E2
St Aegyd 57 E3
St-Affrique 29 E3
St-Agnant 24 B4
St-Agrève 30 B2
St-Aignan 25 E2
St-Aignan-sur-Roë 23 E3
St Alban 29 F2
St Albans 9 F2
St Alban's Head 9 E4
St-Amand-en-Puisaye 26 A2
St-Amand-les-Eaux 20 A1
St-Amand-Longpré 25 D2
St-Amand-Montrond 25 F3
St-Amans-des-Cots 29 E2
St-Amans 29 F2
St-Amans-Soult 32 B1
St-Amant 29 F1
St-Amant-Roche-Savine 29 F1
St-Amarin 27 E1
St-Ambroix 30 B3
St-Amé 27 D1
St-Amour 26 C3
St Andrä 70 B1
St Andreasberg 52 B2
St-André-de-Cubzac 28 B2
St-André-de-l'Eure 19 E4
St-André-de-Vézines 29 F3
St-André-les-Alpes 31 D3
St Andrews 5 D1
St-Anthème 30 B1
St-Antonin-Noble-Val 29 D3
St Anton 58 C2
St-Arnoult 19 E4
St Asaph 6 B2
St-Astier 28 C2
St-Auban 31 D3
St-Aubin-d'Aubigné 23 D3
St-Aubin-du-Cormier 23 D3
St-Aubin 18 C3
St-Aulaye 28 C2
St Austell 8 B4
St-Avold 21 D3
St-Aygulf 31 D4
St-Beauzély 29 E3
St Bees Head 4 C4
St-Benoît-du-Sault 25 E3
St-Benoît 25 F2
St-Bertrand-de-Comminges 37 E1
St-Béat 37 F2
St-Bénin-d'Azy 26 A3
St Blasien 54 C4
St-Blin 26 C1
St-Bonnet 31 D2
St-Bonnet-de-Joux 26 B3
St-Bonnet-le-Château 30 B1
St-Brévin 24 A2
St-Briac 18 A4
St-Brice-en-Coglès 18 B4
St-Brides B 8 B2
St-Brieuc 22 C2
St-Calais 23 F3
St-Cast 18 A4
St Catherine's Pt 9 E4
St-Cergue 27 D3
St-Cernin 29 E2
St-Céré 29 D2
St-Chamas 30 C4
St-Chamond 30 B1
St-Chély-d'Apcher 29 F2
St-Chély-d'Aubrac 29 E2
St-Chinian 32 B1
St Christophen 57 E2
St-Ciers 28 B1
St-Cirq-Lapopie 29 D3
St-Clair-sur-l'Elle 18 C3
St-Clar 28 C3
St-Claud 25 D4
St-Claude 27 D3
St Clears 8 C2
St-Cyprien 29 D2
St-Cyprien-Plage 32 B2
St David's 8 B1
St David's Head 8 B1
St-Denis (Charente-Maritime) 24 B4
St-Denis-d'Orques 23 E3
St-Denis (Seine-St-Denis) 19 F4
St-Didier-en-Velay 30 B1
St-Dié 21 E4
St-Dier-d'Auvergne 29 F1
St-Dizier 20 C4
St-Donat-sur-l'Herbasse 30 C1
St-Eloy-les-Mines 26 A4
St-Emilion 28 B2
St-Etienne (Alpes-de-Haute-Provence) 30 C3
St-Etienne-Cantalès, Bge de 29 E2
St-Etienne-de-Baïgorry 28 A4
St-Etienne-de-Lugdarès 29 F2
St-Etienne-de-Montluc 24 B2
St-Etienne-de-St-Geoirs 30 C1
St-Etienne-de-Tinée 31 E3
St-Etienne-en-Dévoluy 31 D2
St-Etienne (Loire) 30 B1
St-Fargeau 26 A2
St-Félicien 30 B2
St Finan's B 14 A4

St-Firmin 31 D2
St-Florent (Cher) 25 F3
St-Florent (Corse) 33 F2
St-Florentin 26 B1
St-Flour 29 F2
St-François-Longchamp 31 D1
St-Fulgent 24 B3
St Gallen (A) 57 D3
St Gallen (CH) 58 B2
St Gallenkirch 58 B2
St-Galmier 30 B1
St-Gaudens 37 F1
St-Gaultier 25 E3
St-Genest-Malifaux 30 B1
St-Gengoux-le-National 26 C3
St-Geniez-d'Olt 29 E3
St-Genis-de-Stonge 28 B1
St-Genis-Laval 30 B1
St-Genix 30 C1
St-Geoire 30 C1
St Georgen (A) 56 C3
St Georgen am Langsee 70 B1
St Georgen (D) 54 C3
St-Georges 23 E4
St Georges Channel 8 A1
St-Georges-de-Didonne 28 A1
St-Georges-en-Couzan 29 F1
St-Germain-de-Calberte 29 F3
St-Germain-des-Fossés 26 A4
St-Germain-du-Bois 26 C3
St-Germain-du-Plain 26 C3
St-Germain-du-Teil 29 F3
St-Germain 19 F4
St-Germain-Laval 26 B4
St-Germain-Lembron 29 F1
St-Germain-les-Belles 29 D1
St-Germain-l'Herm 29 F1
St-Gertraud 58 C3
St-Gervais-d'Auvergne 26 A4
St-Gervais 27 E4
St-Gervais-sur-Mare 30 A4
St-Géry 29 D3
St-Gildas-de-Rhuys 22 C4
St-Gildas-des-Bois 23 D4
St-Gildas, Pte de 24 A2
St Gilgen 56 C3
St-Gilles-Croix-de-Vie 24 A3
St-Gilles 30 B4
St-Gingolph 27 E3
St-Girons 37 F2
St-Girons-Plage 28 A3
St Goar 51 E4
St Goarshausen 51 E4
St-Gobain 20 A3
St Govan's Head 8 B2
St-Guénolé 22 A3
St-Guilhem-le-Désert 29 F4
St-Haon-le-Châtel 26 B4
St Helens 6 B2
St-Hélier 18 B3
St-Hilaire-des-Loges 24 C3
St-Hilaire-de-Villefranche 28 B1
St-Hilaire-du-Harcouet 18 B4
St-Hilaire 32 B2
St-Hippolyte-du-Fort 29 F3
St-Hippolyte 27 E2
St-Honoré 26 B3
St-Hubert 20 C2
St-Imier 27 E2
St Ingbert 54 B2
St Ives (Cambs) 9 F1
St Ives (Cornwall) 8 A4
St-Jacques 23 D3
St-Jacut 18 A4
St Jakob 59 D2
St Jakob im Rosental 70 A1
St James 18 B4
St-Jean-Brévelay 22 C3
St-Jean-Cap-Ferrat 31 E3
St-Jean-d'Angély 24 C4
St-Jean-de-Bournay 30 C1
St-Jean-de-Daye 18 B3
St-Jean-de-Losne 26 C2
St-Jean-de-Luz 28 A4
St-Jean-de-Maurienne 31 D1
St-Jean-de-Monts 24 A3
St-Jean-du-Bruel 29 F3
St-Jean-du-Gard 30 A3
St-Jean-en-Royans 30 C2
St-Jean-Pied-de-Port 28 A4
St-Jeoire 27 D4
St Johann im Pongau 59 E1
St Johann in Tirol 59 E1
St John's Pt 13 E2
St-Jouin-de-Marnes 24 C3
St-Juéry 29 E3
St-Julien-Chapteuil 30 B2
St-Julien-de-Vouvantes 23 D4
St-Julien-du-Sault 26 A1
St-Julien-en-Genevois 27 D4
St-Julien 26 C3
St-Julien-l'Ars 25 D3
St-Junien 25 D4
St Just 8 A4
St-Just-en-Chaussée 19 F3
St-Just-en-Chevalet 26 B4
St-Justin 28 B3
St Keverne 8 B4
St Lambrecht 57 D4
St-Lary-Soulan 37 E2
St-Laurent (Calvados) 18 C3
St-Laurent-de-la-Salanque 32 B2
St-Laurent-du-Pont 30 C1
St-Laurent-en-Grandvaux 27 D3
St-Laurent-les-Bains 29 F2
St-Laurent-Médoc 28 B2
St-Laurent (Vendée) 24 C3
St-Laurent (Vienne) 28 C1
St-Léger 26 B3
St Leonhard (I) 59 D2
St Leonhard (Nieder österreich) 57 E3
St Leonhard (Tirol) 58 C2
St-Léonard-de-Noblat 25 E4
St Lorenzen 59 E2
St-Lô 18 C3
St-Louis 27 E2
St-Loup-Lamairé 24 C3
St-Loup-sur-Semouse 27 D1
St-Luc 27 F3
St-Lunaire 18 B4
St-Lys 29 D4
St-Macaire 28 B2
St Magnus B 3 F1
St-Maixent-l'Ecole 24 C3
St-Malo-de-la-Lande 18 B3
St-Malo 18 B4
St-Mamet-la-Salvetat 29 E2
St-Mandrier 31 D4
St-Marcellin 30 C1
St-Margarethen 48 A2
St Margaret's Hope 3 E1
St-Mars-la-Jaille 23 D4
St-Martin (Charente-Maritime) 24 B4
St-Martin-d'Auxigny 25 F2
St-Martin-de-Belleville 31 D1
St-Martin-de-Crau 30 B4
St-Martin-de-Londres 29 F4
St-Martin-de-Seignan 28 A4
St-Martin-de-Valamas 30 B2
St-Martin-en-Bresse 26 C3
St-Martin (Pyrénées-Orientales) 32 B2
St Martin's 8 A4
St-Martin-Vésubie 31 E3
St-Martory 37 F1
St Mary's 8 A4
St Märgen 54 C4
St-Mathieu 28 C1
St-Mathieu, Pte de 22 A3
St-Maurice 27 E4
St Mawes 8 B4
St-Maximin-la-Ste Baume 31 D4
St-Médard-en-Jalles 28 B2
St-Méen 22 C3
St Michaelisdonn 48 A2
St Michael (Salzburg) 59 F2
St Michael's Mount 8 A4
St Michael (Steiermark) 57 E4
St-Michel-de-Maurienne 31 D1
St-Michel-en-Grève 22 B2
St-Michel-en-l'Herm 24 B4
St-Michel 20 B2
St-Michel-Mont-Mercure 24 C3
St-Mihiel 20 C3
St Monance 5 D2
St-Moritz 58 B3
St-Nazaire 24 A2
St-Nectaire 29 E1
St Neots 9 F1
St-Nicolas-d'Aliermont 19 E2
St-Nicolas-de-la-Grave 28 C3
St-Nicolas-de-Port 21 D4
St-Nicolas-du-Pélem 22 C3
St-Niklaas 50 B3
St Niklaus 27 F4
St-Oedenrode 16 C3
St-Omer 19 F1
St Oswald 59 F2
St-Pair 18 B4
St-Palais (Charente-Maritime) 28 A1
St-Palais (Pyrénées-Atlantiques) 28 A4
St-Pardoux-la-Rivière 28 C1
St Paul (A) 70 B1
St-Paul (Alpes-de-Haute-Provence) 31 D2
St-Paul (Alpes-Maritimes) 31 E3
St-Paul-Cap-de-Joux 29 D4
St-Paul-de-Fenouillet 32 B2
St-Paulien 29 F2
St-Paul-Trois-Châteaux 30 B3
St-Père-en-Retz 24 A2
St-Pé-de-Bigorre 37 E1
St-Pée 28 A4
St-Péray 30 B2
St Peter in der Au 57 D3
St-Peter-Ording 47 F2
St Peter Port 18 A3
St-Philbert 24 B3
St-Pierre Charente-Maritime) 24 B4
St-Pierre-d'Albigny 31 D1
St-Pierre-de-Chartreuse 30 C1
St-Pierre-de-Chignac 28 C2
St-Pierre-Eglise 18 B2
St-Pierre-le-Moûtier 26 A3
St-Pierre (Morbihan) 22 C4
St-Pierre-sur-Dives 18 C3
St-Pois 18 C4
St-Pol-de-Léon 22 B2
St-Pol-sur-Ternoise 19 F2
St-Pons-de-Thomières 32 B1
St-Porchaire 28 B1
St Pölten 57 E2
St-Pourçain 26 A4
St-Privat 29 E2
St-Quay-Portrieux 22 C2
St-Quentin 20 A2
St-Rambert 30 B1
St-Rambert-d'Albon 30 B1
St-Rambert-en-Bugey 26 C4
St-Raphaël 31 E4
St-Renan 22 A2
St-Rémy-de-Provence 30 B3
St-Rémy-sur-Durolle 26 B4
St-Riquier 19 E2
St-Romain-de-Colbosc 19 D3
St-Rome-de-Tarn 29 E3
St-Saëns 19 E3
St-Satur 26 A2
St-Saulge 26 A2
St-Sauveur-en-Puisaye 26 A2
St-Sauveur-Lendelin 18 B3
St-Sauveur-le-Vicomte 18 B3
St-Sauveur-sur-Tinée 31 E3
St-Savin (Gironde) 28 B2
St-Savinien 24 C4
St-Savin (Vienne) 25 D3
St-Seine-l'Abbaye 26 C2
St-Sernin-sur-Rance 29 E3
St-Sever (Calvados) 18 C4
St-Sever (Landes) 28 B4
St-Sulpice-les-Feuilles 25 E4
St-Symphorien-de-Lay 26 B4
St-Symphorien-d'Ozon 30 B1
St-Symphorien 28 B3
St-Symphorien-sur-Coise 30 B1
St-Trivier-de-Courtes 26 C3
St-Trivier-sur-Moignans 26 C4
St-Trojan 28 A1
St-Tropez 31 D4
St-Truiden 50 C3
St Ulrich 59 D3
St-Vaast-la-Hougue 18 B3
St Valentin an der Haide 58 C2
St Valentin 57 D3
St-Valery 19 E2
St-Valery-en-Caux 19 D2
St-Valier 30 B1
St-Vallier-de-Thiey 31 D3
St-Varent 24 C3
St-Vaury 25 E4
St Veit 70 A1
St-Véran 31 E2
St-Vincent 27 F4
St-Vincent-de-Tyrosse 28 A4
St Vith 51 D4
St-Vivien-de-Médoc 28 A1
St-Wandrille 19 D3
St Wendel 54 B1
St Wolfgang 56 C3
St-Yorre 26 A4
St-Yrieix-la-Perche 29 D1
Ste-Adresse 19 D3
Ste-Anne-d'Auray 22 C4
Ste-Baume, la 31 D4
Ste-Croix-du-Mont 28 B2
Ste-Croix 27 D3
Ste-Croix, Lac de 31 D3
Ste-Croix-Volvestre 37 F1
Ste-Enimie 29 F3
Ste-Foy-la-Grande 28 C2
Ste-Foy-l'Argentière 30 B1
Ste-Geneviève-sur-Argence 29 E2
Ste-Hélène 28 B2
Ste-Hermine 24 B3
Ste-Livrade 28 C3
Ste-Lucie-de-Tallano 33 F4
Ste-Marie-aux-Mines 21 E4
Ste-Maure-de-Touraine 25 D2
Ste-Maxime 31 D4
Ste-Menehould 20 C3
Ste-Mère-Eglise 18 B3
Ste-Odile, Mt 21 E4
Ste-Sévère 25 F3
Ste-Suzanne 23 E3
Ste-Tulle 30 C3
Saintes 28 B1
Stes-Maries-de-la-Mer 30 B4
Saison *R* 37 D1
Saissac 32 B1
Šajkaš 72 C2
Sakarya 115 F3
Sakskøbing 108 B4
Sakule 72 C2
Säkylä 107 D2
Sala 106 A3
Salacgrīva 110 C2
Sala Consilina 64 C4
Salada 41 E3
Salakovac 73 D3
Salamajärvi 102 C2
Salamajärvi *L* 103 D2
Salamanca 39 E1
Salamína 87 F1
Salamína, N 87 E1
Salándi 87 E2
Salangen 94 B3
Salar 43 F3
Salardú 37 F2
Salas 35 D1
Salaš 73 F3
Salas de los Infantes 36 A3
Salazar, R 37 D2
Salbohed 105 F3
Salbris 25 E2
Salcombe 8 C4
Saldaña 35 E3
Sale 60 A2
Sålekinna 100 D3
Salem 55 D4
Salemi 68 A3
Sälen 101 D4
Salen (Highland) 2 B4
Salen (Mull) 4 B1
Salernes 31 D4
Salerno 64 B4
Salerno, Golfo di 64 B4
Salers 29 E2
Salève, Mt 27 D4
Salgótarján 112 B3
Salgueiro do Campo 38 C2
Sali 74 C1
Salice Terme 60 A2
Salies-de-Béarn 28 A4
Salies-du-Salat 37 F1
Salignac-Eyvigues 29 D2
Salihli 115 F4
Salime, Emb de 34 C1
Salina, I 69 D2
Salinas (Andalucía) 43 F3
Salinas (Asturias) 35 D1
Salinas, C 45 F3
Salindres 30 B3
Sälinkää 107 F2
Salins 27 D3
Salisbury 9 E3
Salla 99 E2
Sallanches 27 E4
Sallent 32 A4
Sallent-de-Gállego 37 D2
Salles 32 A1
Salles-Curan 29 E3
Salling 108 A2
Salling Sund 108 A2
Salmerón 40 C2
Salmoral 39 F1
Salò 60 B1
Salo 107 E2
Salobreña 44 A4
Salona 75 D1
Salon-de-Provence 30 C4
Salonta 112 C4
Salorino 38 C3
Salor, R 39 D3
Salou 37 F4
Salou, C de 37 F4
Salpausselkä 107 F2
Salsbruket 97 D4
Salses-le-Château 32 B2
Salso 68 C3
Salsomaggiore Terme 60 B2
Salsta 106 B3
Saltash 8 C4
Saltburn-by-the-Sea 5 F4
Saltcoats 4 C2
Saltee Is 15 D4
Saltfjellet 97 E2
Saltfjorden 97 E2
Salto 34 B4
Saltoluokta 94 B4
Saltvik 106 C3
Saluggia 31 F1
Saluzzo 31 E2
Salvacañete 41 D3
Salvagnac 29 D3
Salvan 27 E4
Salvaterra de Magos 38 A3
Salvatierra-Agurain 36 B2
Salvatierra de los Barros 42 C1
Salvattera de Miño 34 A3
Salvetat-Peyralès, la 29 E3
Salvetat-sur-Agout, la 32 B1
Salviac 29 D2
Sælvig 108 B3
Sálvora, I de 34 A2
Salza 57 E3
Salzach 56 B3
Salzburg 56 C3
Salzburg (Prov) 59 E1
Salzgitter-Bad 52 B1
Salzgitter-Lebenstedt 52 B1
Salzhausen 48 B3
Salzkammergut 56 C3
Salzkotten 17 F3
Salzwedel 48 C4
Šamac Slavonski 71 F3
Sama de Langreo 35 D1
Samarina 78 C4
Samatan 28 C4
Sambatiki 87 E3
Sambiase 67 E3
Samboal 40 A1
Sambor 112 C3
Sambre 50 B4
Sambuca di Sicilia 68 B3
Samedan 58 B3
Sameiro, Mte 34 A4
Samer 19 E1
Sámi 82 B4
Samikó 86 B2
Sammatti 107 E2
Sammichele 65 E3
Samnanger 104 A2
Samobor 70 C2
Samodreža 77 D2
Samoëns 27 E4
Samokov (BG) 115 D3
Samokov (YU) 77 D3
Samora Correia 38 A4
Samos 34 C2
Samoš 73 D2
Sámos 89 F1
Sámos, N 89 E1
Samothráki 81 E3
Samothráki, N 81 E3
Samper de Calanda 37 D4
Sampeyre 31 E2
Samsø 108 B3
Samsø Bælt 108 B3
Samtens 49 D1
Samugheo 66 B3
San 112 C2
San Adrián 36 C2
San Adrián, C de 34 A1
San Agata de Goti 64 B3
San Agata di Militello 69 D2
San Agustín 40 B2
San Amaro 34 B2
San Andrea Frius 66 B3
San Andrés del Rabanedo 35 D2
San Antioco, I di 66 A4
San Antioco 66 B4
San Antonio Abad 45 D3
San Antonio 66 B1
San Antonio, C de 45 F1
San Bartolomé de las Abiertas 39 F3
San Bartolomé de la Torre 42 C2
San Bartolomeo in Galdo 64 B3
San Benedetto del Tronto 61 F4
San Benedetto in Alpe 61 D3
San Benedetto Po 60 C2
San Bernardino 58 B3
San Bernardino, Psodel 58 B3
San Biagio Platani 68 B3
San Bonifacio 60 C1
San Candido 59 E2
San Carlos de la Ràpita 41 F2
San Carlos del Valle 40 B4
San Casciano in Val di Pesa 60 C4
San Cataldo (Puglia) 65 F4
San Cataldo (Sicilia) 68 C3
San Cipirello 68 B3
San Clemente, Emb de 44 B2
San Clemente 40 C4
San Colombano al Lambro 60 B2
San Cosme 34 C1
San Cristóbal 42 C1
San Cristóbal de Entreviñas 35 D3
San Cristóbal de la Polantera 35 D3
San Cristóbal de la Vega 39 F1
San Damiano d'Asti 31 F2
San Daniele del Friuli 59 E3
San Daniele Po 60 B2
San Demetrio Corone 67 E2
San Donaci 65 F4
San Donà di Piave 59 E4
San Emiliano 35 D2
San Esteban de Gormaz 36 A3
San Esteban del Molar 35 D3

SALZBURG
Braunau
Braunau
Linz, Wien
Linz
Bergheim
Maria Plain
Radeck
Kasern
Söllheim
Unteresch
Herrenau
Hagenau
Gaglham
Hallwang-Mayrwies
Daxlueg
47°50
E55-60
A1
Rott
Sam
Langwied
Heuberg
Glanbach
Alterbach
LIEFERING
ITZLING
Gruber
Esch
Kleßheim
Meierhof
Hauptbahnhof
GNIGL
Siezenheim
Taxham
Schallmoos
Kühlberg
Neuhaus
Hiesl
Kapuzinerberg
Parsch
München
E 52-60
Glanhofen
MAXGLAN
Mönchsberg
Kobenzl
AIGEN
Gaisberg
Hohensalzburg
Riedenburg
Salzach
Abfalter
Graz
Himmelreich
Loig
SALZBURG-MAXGLAN
Nonntal
Freisaal
Leopoldskroner Teich
Innsbruck
LEOPOLDSKRON
Kendler-siedlung
Kleingmain
Fellberg
Untermoos
Gneis
MORZG
Glas
Schwarzer-siedlung
Glansiedlung
Glasenbach
Klausbach
Morzg
Mittermoos
Eichethofsiedlung
E 55-A 10
Birkensiedlung
Hellbrunn
1/70 000
Obermoos
Elsbethen
13°
Klagenfurt
Grödig
Anif, Untersberg
A 10
Berchtesgaden
Hallein
Hallein

San Esteban del Valle 39 F2
San Esteban de Pravia 35 D1
San Fele 64 C4
San Felice a Cancello 64 B3
San Felice Circeo 63 F3
San Felices de Los Gallegos 39 D1
San Felice sul Panaro 60 C2
San Felipe 40 C2
San Feliu de Guíxols 32 B4
San Ferdinando di Puglia 64 C3
San Ferdinando di Puglia 64 C3
San Fernando 43 D4
San Francisco Javier 45 D4
San Fratello 69 D2
San Gavino Monreale 66 B3
San Gemini 63 E1
San Giacomo 59 D2
San Gimignano 60 C4
San Ginesio 61 F4
San Giorgio del Sannio 64 B3
San Giorgio di Nogaro 59 F3
San Giorgio Ionico 65 E4
San Giorgio 31 E1
San Giorgio Piacentino 60 B2
San Giovanni a Piro 67 D2
San Giovanni di Sinis 66 A3
San Giovanni in Fiore 67 F2
San Giovanni in Persiceto 60 C2
San Giovanni Lupatoto 60 C1
San Giovanni Rotondo 64 C2
San Giovanni Suergiu 66 B4
San Giovanni Valdarno 61 D4
San Giuliano Terme 60 C4
San Giustino 61 D4
San Glorio, Pto de 35 E2
San Gottardo, Pso del 58 A3
San Ildefonso o la Granja 40 A1
San Isidro 44 C3
San Isidro, Pto de 35 E2
San Javier 45 D2
San José (Andalucía) 44 C4
San José (Ibiza) 45 D4
San Juan Bautista 45 D3
San Juan de Alicante 45 E1
San Juan de Aznalfarache 43 D2
San Juan de la Peña 37 D2
San Juan del Olmo 39 F2
San Juan de los Terreros 44 C3
San Juan del Puerto 42 C2
San Juan, Emb de 40 A2
San Just Desvern 32 A4
San Just, Sa de 41 E2
San Lazzaro di Savena 61 D2
San Leo 61 E3
San Leonardo de Yagüe 36 A3
San Leonardo 59 D2
San Leonardo, Pso 64 A2
San Lorenzo 36 B2
San Lorenzo 63 D1
San Lorenzo de Calatrava 44 A1
San Lorenzo de la Parrilla 40 C3
San Lucido 67 E3
San Luis de Sabanillas 43 E4
San Luis 45 F2
San Marcello 61 F4
San Marcello Pistoiese 60 C3
San Marco Argentano 67 E2
San Marco dei Cavoti 64 B3
San Marco in Lamis 64 C2
San Marino 61 E3
San Martino di Castrozza 59 D3
San Martín de Castañeda 34 C3
San Martín de la Vega 40 B2
San Martín de Mondoñedo 34 C1
San Martín de Montalbán 39 F3
San Martín de Valdeiglesias 40 A2
San Mateo 41 F2
San Mateo de Gállego 37 D3
San Mauro Forte 65 D4
San Michele all' Adige 59 D3
San Miguel 45 D3
San Miguel de Escalada 35 E3
San Miguel del Arroyo 35 E4
San Miguel de Salinas 45 D2
San Millán 36 A2
San Millán de la Cogolla 36 B2
San Millán de Lara 36 A3
San Miniato 60 C4
San Nicolás del Puerto 43 E2
San Nicolás de Tolentino 42 B4
San Nicolò Ferrarese 61 D2
San Nicolò Gerrei 66 B3
San Ninfa 68 B3
San Pancrazio Salentino 65 F4
San Pedro 44 C1
San Pedro de Alcántara 43 E4
San Pedro del Arroyo 39 F1
San Pedro de Latarce 35 E4
San Pedro del Pinatar 45 D2
San Pedro de Mérida 39 D4
San Pedro Manrique 36 B3
San Pedro, Sa de 39 D3
San Pellegrino, Pso 59 D3
San Pellegrino Terme 58 B4
San Piero a Sieve 61 D3
San Pietro, I di 66 A4
San Pietro in Casale 60 C2
San Pietro Vernotico 65 F4
San Polo d'Enza 60 C2
San Quirico d'Orcia 63 D1
San Rafael de Navallana, Emb de 43 F2
San Rafael 40 A2
San Remo 31 F3
San Roque (Andalucía) 43 E4
San Roque (Galicia) 34 A1
San Rufo 64 C4
San Salvador de Cantamuda 35 F2
San Salvador 45 F3
San Salvo 64 B2
San Sebastiano Curone 60 A2
San Sebastián, Emb de 34 C3
San Sebastián 42 A4
San Severino Marche 61 F4
San Severo 64 C2
San Silvestre de Guzmán 42 C2
San Sperate 66 B4
San Stefano di Camastra 68 C3
San Stefano Quisquina 68 B3
San Telmo 42 C2
San Valentino alla Muta 58 C2
San Vicente de Alcántara 38 C3
San Vicente de la Barquera 35 F1
San Vicente de la Cabeza 35 D4
San Vicente del Raspeig 45 E1
San Vicenzo 62 C1
San Vigilio di Marebbe 59 D2
San Vigilio, Pso di 60 C1
San Vitero 34 C4
San Vito al Tagliamento 59 E3
San Vito Chietino 64 A2
San Vito dei Normanni 65 E3
San Vito di C. 59 E3
San Vito 66 C4
San Vito lo Capo 68 A3
San Vito sullo Ionio 67 F3
San Vittore del Lazio 64 A3
Sana 71 D4
Saná 80 A3
Sanabria, L de 34 C3
Sanary 30 C4
Sancergues 26 A2
Sancerre 26 A2
Sanchidrián 39 F1
Sancho, Emb de 42 C2
Sanclêr 8 C2
Sancoins 26 A3
Sancti Petri 43 D4
Sancti Spiritus 39 D1
Sand (Hedmark) 105 D2
Sand (Rogaland) 104 A3
Sandane 100 A3
Sandanski 115 D3
Sandarne 101 F4
Sandau 48 C4
Sanday 3 E1
Sandbach 6 C3
Sanddøla 97 D4
Sande (D) 47 E3
Sande (Møre og Romsdal) 100 A2
Sande (P) 34 A4
Sande (Vestfold) 104 C3
Sandefjord 104 C3
Sandeid 104 A3
Sandfjellet 95 E1
Sandgerði 96 A2
Sand in Taufers 59 D2
Sandnes 104 A3
Sandness 3 F1
Sandnessjøen 97 D3
Sando 39 E1
Sandoméri 86 B1
Sandomierz 112 C2
Sandown 9 E3
Sandoy 96 A4
Sandøy 100 A2
Sandrigo 59 D4
Sandringham House 7 E3
Sandstad 100 C1
Sandur 96 A4
Sandviken 106 B2
Sandvikvåg 104 A2
Sandwich 11 D3
Sandy 9 F1
Sånfjället 101 E3
Sangarcía 40 A1
Sangerhausen 52 C2
Sangis 98 C3
Sangonera, R 45 D2
Sangro 64 A2
Sangüesa 36 C2
Sanguinaires, Iles 33 E4
Sanguinet 28 A3
Sani 80 A4
Sanitz 48 C2
Sankt Olof 109 D3
Sanlúcar de Barrameda 43 D3
Sanlúcar de Guadiana 42 B2
Sanlúcar la Mayor 43 D2
Sanluri 66 B3
Sannainen 107 F2
Sannazzaro 60 A2
Sannicandro di Bari 65 D3
Sannicandro Garganico 64 C2
Sanok 112 C3
Sanquhar 4 C3
Sansepolcro 61 D4
Sanski Most 71 D3
Sant' Agata di Puglia 64 C3
Sant Agustí de Lluçanès 32 A3
Sant Andreu de Llavaneres 32 B4
Sant' Angelo de' Lombardi 64 C3
Sant' Angelo in Vado 61 E4
Sant' Angelo Lodigiano 60 A2
Sant Antoni de C. 32 B3
Sant Antoni, Emb de 37 F3
Sant' Apollinare in Classe 61 D3
Sant' Arcangelo di Romagna 61 E3
Sant Boi de Lluçanès 32 A3
Sant Celoni 32 B4
Sant Cugat 32 A4
Sant' Elia a Pianisi 64 B2
Sant' Elpidio a Mare 61 F4
Sant Esteve d'en Bas 32 B3
Sant'Eufemia, Golfodi 67 E3
Sant'Eufemia Lamezia 67 E3
Sant Gervàs 37 F3
Sant Hilari Sacalm 32 B3
Sant Hipòlit de Voltregà 32 A3
Sant Joan de les Abadesses 32 B3
Sant Julià de Lòria 32 A3
Sant Llorenc de Morunys 32 A3
Sant'Onofrio 67 E3
Sant Pau de Seguries 32 B3
Sant Pere de Roda 32 C3
Sant Pol de Mar 32 B4
Sant Ponc, Emb de 32 A3
Sant Quirze de Besora 32 B3
Sant Quirze Safaja 32 A4
Sant Ramon 37 F3
Sant Sadurni d'Anoia 32 A4
Santa Amalia 39 D4
Santa Ana 40 C4
Santa Anna, Emb de 37 E3
Santa Bàrbara (Catalunya) 41 F2
Santa Bàrbara (Andalucía) 42 C2
Santa Bàrbara *Mt* 44 B3
Santa Catarina 42 B3
Santa Caterina Pittinuri 66 A3
Santa Caterina Valfurva 58 C3
Santa Caterina Villarmosa 68 C3
Santa Cesarea Terme 65 F4
Santa Clara-a-Velha 42 A2
Santa Clara, Bgem de 42 A2
Santa Coloma de Farners 32 B3
Santa Coloma de Queralt 37 F4
Santa Colombo de Somoza 35 D3
Santa Comba Dão 38 B2
Santa Comba de Rossas 34 C4
Santa Comba 34 A1
Santa Cristina de Lena 35 D2
Santa Croce di Magliano 64 B2
Santa Cruz de Campezo 36 B2
Santa Cruz de la Palma 42 A4
Santa Cruz de la Sierra 39 E3
Santa Cruz de la Zarza 40 B3
Santa Cruz del Retamar 40 A2
Santa Cruz de Moya 41 D3
Santa Cruz de Mudela 44 A1
Santa Cruz de Tenerife 42 B4
Santa Cruz 36 C4
Santa Elena 44 A1
Santa Eufemia 43 E1
Santa Eugenia 34 A2
Santa Eulalia del Río 45 D3
Santa Eulalia de Oscos 34 C1
Santa Eulalia 41 D2
Santa Eulália 38 C4
Santa Fe 44 A3
Santa Fé 32 B4
Santa Fiora 63 D1
Santa Galdana, Cala 45 F2
Santa Gertrude 58 C3
Santa Giusta 66 B3
Santa Inés, Pto de 36 B3
Santa Liestra y San Quilez 37 E3
Santa Lucia d. Mela 69 D2
Santa Luz 34 C4
Santa Luzia 42 A2
Santa Magdalena de Pulpis 41 F2
Santa Margarida do Sádão 42 B1
Santa Margarida i Els Monjos 32 A4
Santa Margarita 45 F2
Santa Margherita 66 B4
Santa Margherita di Belice 68 B3
Santa Margherita Ligure 60 A3
Santa Maria Capua Vetere 64 B3
Santa Maria, C de 42 B3

Santa Maria da Feira 38 B1
Santa Maria d'Angeli 63 E1
Santa Maria del Campo Rus 40 C3
Santa Maria della Versa 60 A2
Santa Maria di Leuca,C 65 F4
Santa Maria la Real de Nieva 40 A1
Santa Maria la Real de Oseira 34 B2
Santa Maria Maggiore 58 A3
Santa Marina 35 E2
Santa Marina del Rey 35 D3
Santa Marinella 63 D2
Santa María de Huerta 36 B4
Santa María del Campo 35 F3
Santa María del Páramo 35 D3
Santa María de Nieva 44 C3
Santa María de Valverde 35 D3
Santa-Maria-Siché 33 F4
Santa Marta 39 D4
Santa Marta de Penaguião 34 B4
Santa Marta de Tormes 39 E1
Santa Olalla del Cala 43 D2
Santa Olalla 39 F3
Santa Pau 32 B3
Santa Pola 45 E2
Santa Ponsa 45 E3
Santa Sofia 61 D3
Santa Sofia d'Epiro 67 E2
Santa Susanna 32 B4
Santa Tecla 34 A3
Santa Teresa di Riva 69 D2
Santa Teresa, Emb de 39 E2
Santa Teresa Gallura 66 B1
Santaella 43 E2
Santana (Estremadura) 38 A4
Santana (Madeira) 42 A3
Santana de Serra 42 A2
Santander 35 F1
Santanyí 45 F3
Santarém 38 B3
Santas Martas 35 E3
Santeramo in Colle 65 D3
Santes Creus 37 F4
Santesteban 36 C1
Santhià 31 F1
Santiago de Alcántara 38 C3
Santiago de Compostela 34 A2
Santiago de la Espada 44 B2
Santiago de la Ribera 45 D2
Santiago do Cacém 42 A1
Santiago do Escoural 38 B4
Santibáñez de Béjar 39 E2
Santibáñez de la Peña 35 E2
Santibáñez de la Sierra 39 E2
Santibáñez de Vidriales 35 D3
Santillana del Mar 35 F1
Santiponce 43 D2
Säntis 58 B2
Santisteban del Puerto 44 B1
Santo Domingo de la Calzada 36 B2
Santo Domingo de Silos 36 A3
Santo Domingo, Ptode 43 D1
Santo Estêvão (Beira Baixa) 38 C2
Santo Estêvão (Estremadura) 38 A4
Santo Estêvão, Rib de 38 A4
Santo Pedro da Torre 34 A3
Santo Severa 63 D2
Santo Stefano di Cadore 59 E2
Santo Stefano d'Aveto 60 B2
Santo Stino di Livenza 59 E4
Santo Tirso 34 A4
Santo Tomé 44 B2
Santok 49 F3
Santolea, Emb de 41 E2
Santomera, Emb de 45 D2
Santoña 36 A1
Santo-Pietro-di-Tenda 33 F2
Santorini, N 91 E1
Santuario de San Ignacio de Loyola 36 B1
Santuario d'Oropa 27 F4
Santu Lussurgiu 66 B3
Santurtzi 36 B1
Sanxenxo 34 A2
Sanza 67 D1
São Bartolomeu de Messines 42 A2
São Brás de Alportel 42 B3
São Cristóvão 38 B4
São Domingos 42 A1
São Gregório 34 B3
São Jacinto 38 B1
São João da Pesqueira 34 B4
São João de Madeira 38 B1
São João de Tarouca 38 C1
São João dos Caldeireiros 42 B2
São José da Lamarosa 38 B3
São Leonardo 42 C1
São Mamede, Sa de 38 C3
São Manços 42 B1
São Marcos da Serra 42 A2
São Marcos do Campo 42 B1
São Martinho das Amoreiras 42 A2
São Martinho do Porto 38 A3
São Matias 42 B1
São Miguel de Machede 38 B4
São Pedro de Açor 38 C2
São Pedro de Moel 38 A2
São Pedro do Sul 38 C1
São Romão 38 C2
São Teotónio 42 A2
São Vicente, C de 42 A2
São Vicente da Beira 38 C2
Saône 26 C3
Saône-et-Loire 26 B3
Saorge 31 E3
Sapanca 115 F3
Sapataria 38 A3
Sápes 81 E2
Sapiéndza, N 86 C4
Sa Pobla 45 F2
Sappada 59 E2
Sappee 107 E2
Sapri 67 D1
Säräisniemi 99 E4
Sarajärvi 99 E3
Sarajevo 76 A1
Sarakiní 79 E2
Sarakiniko 84 B3
Saramon 28 C4
Sarandáporo 79 E4
Sarandáporos 78 C4
Sarandë 114 C4
Saraváli 86 C1
Saray 115 E3
Sarayköy 115 F4
Šarbanovac 73 E3
Sarbinowo (Gorzów Wlkp) 49 F3
Sarbinowo (Koszalin) 49 F1
Sárbogárd 112 B4
Sarca 58 C3
Sardara 66 B3
Sardegna 66 A2
Sardínia 82 C3
Sardoal 38 B3
Sardona, Piz 58 B2
Sarek 98 A1
Šarengrad 72 B2
Sarentino 59 D2
Särfjället 101 D2
Sargans 58 B2
Sariá, N 93 D2
Sari-d'Orcino 33 F3
Sarine 27 E3
Sariñena 37 E3
Sark 18 A3
Särkisalmi 103 F3
Särkisalo 107 D3
Sarlat-la-Canéda 29 D2
Sarmitunturi 95 F3
Särna 101 D3
Sarnano 61 F4
Sarnen 27 F2
Sarnico 60 B1
Sarno 64 B4
Sarnthein 59 D2
Sarny 113 D2
Sarö 108 C1
Sarón 35 F2
Sarone 59 E3
Saronida 87 F2
Saronikós Kólpos 87 F1
Saronno 60 A1
Sárospatak 112 C3
Sar Planina 77 D3
Sarpsborg 105 D3
Sarracín 35 F3
Sarral 37 F4
Sarralbe 21 E3
Sarrans, Bge de 29 E2
Sarre 21 E3
Sarrebourg 21 E4
Sarreguemines 21 E3
Sarre-Union 21 E3
Sarriá 34 B2
Sarrión 41 E3
Sarroch 66 B4
Sarsina 61 D3
Sars-Poteries 20 B2
Sarstedt 52 B1
Sarteano 63 D1
Sartène 33 F4
Sarthe 23 E4
Sarthe (Dépt) 23 F3
Sárti 80 B4
Sartilly 18 B4
Sarule 66 B2
Sárvár 112 A4
Sarvsjö 101 D2
Sarzana 60 B3
Sarzeau 22 C4
Sarzedas 38 C2
Sasa 77 F2
Sassari 66 A2
Sassello 60 A3
Sassenage 30 C1
Sassenberg 17 F3
Sassenheim 16 B2
Sassetta 62 C1
Saßnitz 49 D1
Sasso 63 E2
Sassoferrato 61 E4
Sassoleone 61 D3
Sasso Marconi 60 C3
Sassuolo 60 C2
Sástago 37 D4
Sasyk, Ozero 113 E4
Sátão 38 C1
Säter 105 F3
Satillieu 30 B1
Satolas 30 C1
Šator 75 D1
Sátoraljaújhely 112 C3
Šatorina 70 B4
Satov 57 E1
Satow 48 C2
Sátres 81 D2
Satrup 48 A1
Sattel 58 A2
Sattledt 57 D3
Satu Mare 112 C3
Saualpe 70 B1
Sauca 36 B4
Saucelle, Emb de 39 D1
Sauda 104 A3
Sauðárkrókur 96 B1
Sau, Emb de 32 B3
Sauerlach 56 A3
Sauerland 17 F4
Saugues 29 F2
Saujon 28 B1
Saukkovaara 99 E4
Sauland 104 C3
Sauldre 26 A2
Saulgau 55 D3
Saulieu 26 B2
Sault 30 C3
Saulx 27 D1
Saulxures 27 E1
Saumur 24 C2
Saundersfoot 8 B2
Sauris 59 E3
Saut du Doubs 27 E2
Sautet, Bge du 30 C2
Sautusjärvi 94 C4
Sauve 30 B3
Sauveterre-de-Béarn 28 A4
Sauveterre-de-Guyenne 28 B2
Sauveterre-de-Rouergue 29 E3
Sauvo 107 D2
Sauxillanges 29 F1
Sauze d'Oulx 31 E2
Sauze, le 31 D2
Sauze-Vaussais 24 C4
Sauzon 22 B4
Sava (I) 65 E4
Sava (YU) 71 E3
Savália 86 B1
Sävar 102 B1
Savelli 67 F2
Savenay 23 D4
Saverdun 32 A1
Saverne 21 E4
Savigliano 31 E2
Savignac-les-Eglises 28 C1
Savignano Irpino 64 C3
Savignano sul Rubicone 61 E3
Savigny-sur-Braye 23 F4
Saviñán 36 C4
Savine, Col de la 27 D3
Savines-le-Lac 31 D2
Savinja 70 B1
Savino Selo 72 B2
Savitaipale 103 E4
Sävja 106 B3
Šavnik 76 B2
Savognin 58 B3
Savona 60 A3
Savonlinna 103 E3
Savonranta 103 F3
Sævråsvåg 104 A2
Sävsjö 109 D2
Savudrija 70 A3
Savukoski 95 F4
Sawbridgeworth 10 C2
Sawel Mt 13 D1
Sax 45 D1
Saxmundham 11 E1
Saxnäs 97 E4
Sayatón 40 B2
Säynätsalo 103 D3
Säyneinen 103 E2
Sazadón, Pto de 35 D3
Sázava 112 A3
Scaër 22 B3
Scafa 64 A2
Scafati 64 B4
Scafell Pikes 5 D4
Scala di Santa Regina 33 F3
Scalasaig 4 B2
Scalby 7 D1
Scalea 67 E2
Scalloway 3 F2
Scalpay 2 B3
Scandiano 60 C2
Scanno 64 A2
Scansano 63 D1
Scanzano 65 D4
Scapa Flow 3 D1
Scarba 4 B1
Scarborough 7 D1
Scardovari 61 E2
Scarinish 2 A4
Scarpe 20 A1
Scarriff 12 B4
Šćedro 75 E2
Šćepan Polje 76 A1
Scey-sur-Saône 27 D2
Schaalsee 48 B2
Schachendorf 57 F4
Schafberg 56 C3
Schaffhausen 58 A1
Schafstädt 52 C2
Schagen 16 C2
Schaprode 49 D1
Scharbeutz 48 B2
Schärding 56 C2
Scharhörn 47 F2
Scharmützelsee 49 E4
Scharnitz 59 D1
Schauinsland Feldberg 54 C4
Scheeßel 48 A3
Scheggia 61 E4
Scheibbs 57 E3
Scheifling 57 D4
Scheinfeld 55 E1
Schelde 50 B3
Schenefeld (Hamburg) 48 A3
Schenefeld (Itzehoe) 48 A2
Scherfede 52 A2
Schermbeck 17 E3
Scheßlitz 52 C4
Scheveningen 16 B3
Schia 60 B3
Schiedam 16 B3
Schieder-Schwalenberg 52 A1
Schiehallion 4 C1
Schierling 56 B2
Schiermonnikoog 47 D3
Schiermonnikoog I 47 D3
Schiers 58 B2
Schifferstadt 54 C2
Schildau 53 D2
Schilpario 58 C4
Schiltach 54 C3
Schio 59 D4
Schirmeck 21 E4
Schirnding 53 D4
Schkeuditz 53 D2
Schkölen 53 D3
Schladming 59 F1
Schlagsdorf 48 B2
Schlanders 58 C3
Schlangenbad 51 F4
Schleching 56 B3
Schlei 48 A1
Schleiden 51 D4
Schleiz 53 D3
Schleswig 48 A1
Schleswig-Holstein 48 A1
Schleusingen 52 C3
Schlieben 53 E1
Schliersee 56 B4
Schlitz 52 B3
Schlotheim 52 B2
Schluchsee 54 C4
Schlucht, Col de la 27 E1
Schlüchtern 52 B4
Schluderbach 59 E2
Schluderns 58 C3
Schlüsselfeld 55 E1
Schlutup 48 B2
Schmalkalden 52 B3
Schmallenberg 17 F4
Schmidmühlen 55 F1
Schmilka 53 F2
Schmölln (Mecklenburg-Vorpommern) 49 E3
Schmölln (Thüringen) 53 D3
Schnackenburg 48 C3
Schnaittenbach 55 F1
Schneeberg (A) 57 E3
Schneeberg (Bayern) 53 D4
Schneeberg (Sachsen) 53 D3
Schneverdingen 48 A3
Schoberpaß 57 D4
Schöckl 57 E4
Schönau 54 C4
Schönberg (A) 59 D2
Schönberg (Bayern) 56 C2
Schönberg (Mecklenburg-Pommern) 48 B2
Schönberg (Sachsen) 53 D4
Schönberg (Schleswig-Holstein) 48 B1
Schönbrunn 57 F2
Schönebeck 52 C1
Schöneck 53 D3
Schönecken 51 D4
Schönefeld 49 E4
Schönewalde 53 E1
Schongau 55 F4
Schöningen 52 C1
Schönmünzach 54 C3
Schönsee 56 B1
Schönthal 56 B1
Schönwald 54 C3
Schönwalde 48 B2
Schoonhoven 16 C3
Schopfheim 54 C4
Schöppenstedt 52 B1
Schoppernau 58 B2
Schorndorf 55 D2
Schortens 47 E3
Schotten 52 A4
Schouwen Duiveland 16 B3
Schramberg 54 C3
Schrems 57 D2
Schrobenhausen 55 F2
Schröcken 58 B2
Schrozberg 55 E1
Schruns 58 B2
Schuls 58 C2
Schüttorf 17 E2
Schwaan 48 C2
Schwabach 55 E1
Schwäbisch Gmünd 55 D2
Schwäbisch Hall 55 D2
Schwabmünchen 55 E3
Schwaigern 55 D2
Schwalmstadt-Treysa 52 A3
Schwalmstadt-Ziegenhain 52 A3
Schwandorf 56 B1
Schwanebeck 52 C1
Schwanenstadt 56 C3
Schwanewede 47 F3
Schwarmstedt 48 A4
Schwarza (A) 57 E3
Schwarza (D) 52 C3
Schwarzach 59 E1
Schwarzach 59 E1
Schwarze Elster 53 E1
Schwarzenbach 53 D4
Schwarzenbek 48 B3
Schwarzenberg 53 E3
Schwarzenburg 27 E3
Schwarzenfeld 56 B1
Schwarzheide 53 E2
Schwarzsee 27 E3
Schwarzwald 54 C3
Schwaz 59 D1
Schwechat 57 F2
Schwedt 49 E3
Schweich 54 A1
Schweinfurt 52 B4
Schweinitz 53 E1
Schwelm 17 E4
Schwendi 55 E3
Schwenningen 54 C3
Schwerin 48 C2
Schweriner See 48 C2
Schwerte 17 E3
Schwetzingen 54 C1
Schwielochsee 53 F1
Schwyz 58 A2
Sciacca 68 B3
Scicli 69 D4
Scilla 67 E4
Scilly, Is of 8 A4
Scole 11 D1
Sconser 2 B3
Scopello 58 A4
Scordia 69 D3
Scorff 22 B3
Ščors 113 E1
Scorzè 59 E4
Scotch Corner 6 C1
Scotland 2 C4
Scourie 2 C2
Scrabster 3 D2
Scridain, L 4 B1
Scrivia 60 A2
Ščučin 110 C4
Scunthorpe 7 D2
Scuol 58 C2
Seaford 10 C3
Seaham 5 E4
Seaton 9 D3
Seaton Delaval 5 E3
Sebečevo 76 C1
Sebes 114 C1
Sebež 111 D3
Sebnitz 53 F2
Sečanj 73 D2
Secchia 60 C2
Seckau 57 D4
Seclin 19 F1
Secondigny 24 C3
Sedan 20 C2
Sedano 35 F2
Seda, Rib de 38 C3
Sedbergh 6 C1
Séderon 30 C3
Sedgefield 5 E4
Sedičany 53 F4
Sedico 59 E3
Sedilo 66 B2
Sedini 66 B2
Sedlare 77 D2
Sedlec-Prčice 53 F4
Sée 18 C4
Seebenau 48 B4
Seebergsattel 70 B1
Seeboden 59 F2
Seebruck 56 B3
Seefeld 58 C1
Seehaus 56 C3
Seehausen (Magdeburg) 52 C1
Seehausen (Stendal) 48 C3
Seeheim 54 C1
Seelisberg 58 A2
Seelow 49 E4
Sées 19 D4
Seesen 52 B1
Seevetal 48 A3
Seewalchen 56 C3
Seewiesen 57 E3
Sefkerin 72 C2
Segesta 68 A3
Segl 58 B3
Segni 63 F3
Segonzac 28 B1
Segorbe 41 E3
Segovia 40 A1
Segré 23 E4
Segre 37 E3
Segre, R 32 A3
Segura 38 C3
Segura de la Sierra 44 B1
Segura de León 43 D1
Segura de los Baños 41 D1
Segura, R 45 D2
Segura, Sa de 44 B2
Sehnde 52 B1
Seia 38 C2
Seiches 23 E4
Seifhennersdorf 53 F2
Seignelay 26 B1
Seil 4 B1
Seiland 95 D1
Seilandsjøkelen 95 D1
Seilhac 29 D1
Seille (Meurthe-et-Moselle) 21 D4
Seille (Saône-et-Loire) 26 C3
Seinäjoki 102 C2
Seine 19 E3
Seine-et-Marne 19 F4

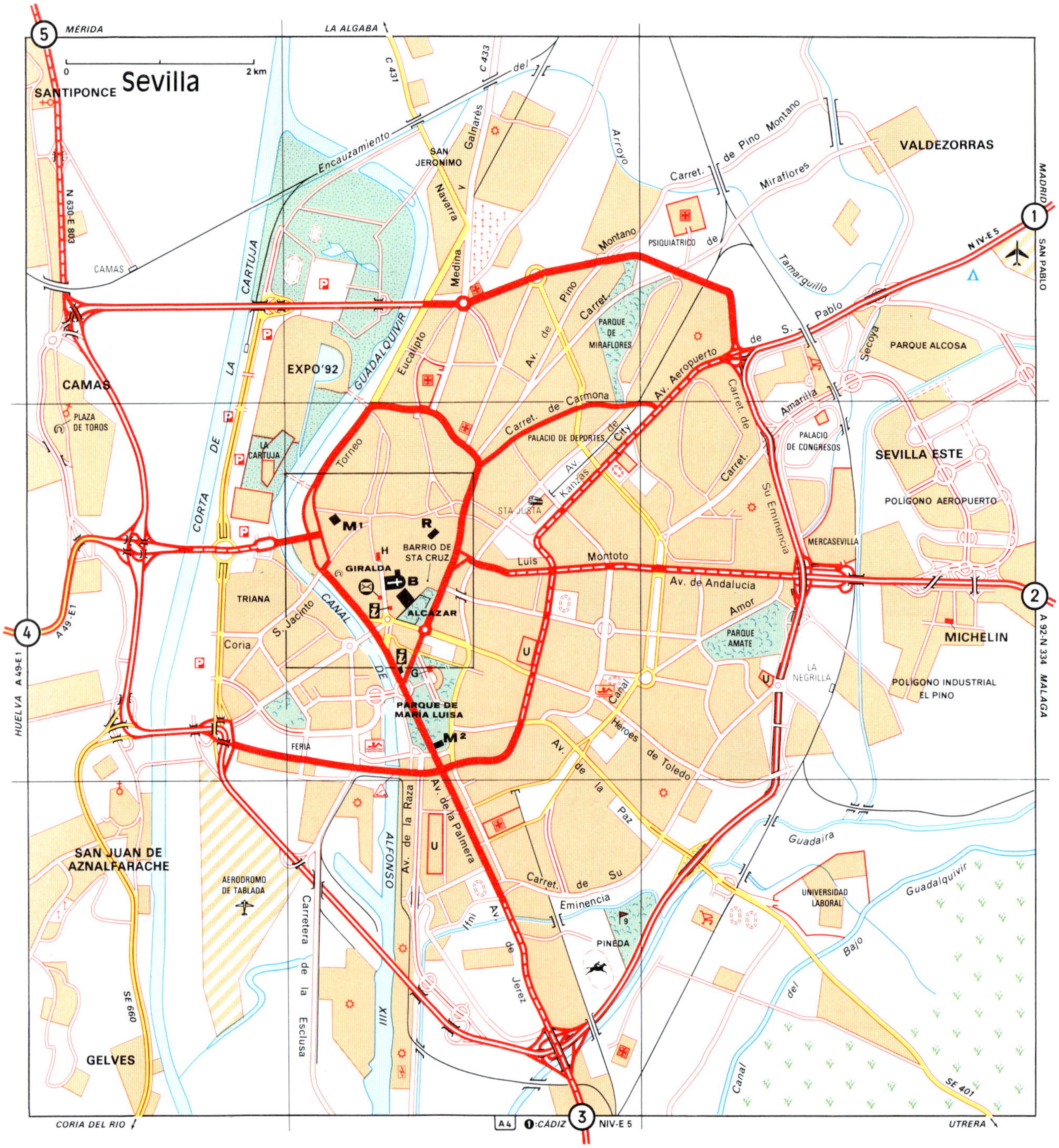
Sevilla
0
2 km
MÉRIDA
LA ALGABA
MADRID
SAN PABLO
N IV-E 5
MALAGA
A 92-N 334
HUELVA A 49-E 1
CORIA DEL RIO
CÁDIZ
NIV-E 5
UTRERA
SANTIPONCE
CAMAS
SAN JERÓNIMO
VALDEZORRAS
EXPO'92
LA CARTUJA
PLAZA DE TOROS
PARQUE DE MIRAFLORES
PSIQUIATRICO
PARQUE ALCOSA
PALACIO DE CONGRESOS
PALACIO DE DEPORTES
SEVILLA ESTE
POLÍGONO AEROPUERTO
MERCASEVILLA
BARRIO DE STA CRUZ
GIRALDA
ALCAZAR
TRIANA
Coria
PARQUE DE MARÍA LUISA
FERIA
PARQUE AMATE
LA NEGRILLA
MICHELIN
POLÍGONO INDUSTRIAL EL PINO
SAN JUAN DE AZNALFARACHE
AERODROMO DE TABLADA
UNIVERSIDAD LABORAL
PINEDA
GELVES
Guadaira
Guadalquivir
Carretera de la Esclusa
Av. de la Palmera
Av. de la Raza
Av. de Andalucia
Av. de la Paz
Heroes de Toledo
Carret. de Carmona
Av. Aeropuerto
Luis Montoto
Su Eminencia
Torneo
Eucaliptos
CANAL DE ALFONSO XIII
CORTA DE LA CARTUJA
Encauzamiento
SE 660
SE 401
N 630-E 803
C 431
C 433

Seine-Maritime 19 D3
Sein, I de 22 A3
Seitenstetten 57 D3
Seitsemisen 102 C3
Seixal 38 A4
Seixo 34 B3
Sejerø 108 B3
Sejerø Bugt 108 B3
Sejm 113 F1
Sékoulas 86 C2
Šekovići 72 B4
Selargius 66 B4
Selassia 87 D3
Selb 53 D4
Selbekken 100 C1
Selbu 101 D2
Selbusjøen 100 C2
Selby 7 D2
Selce 70 B3
Selçuk 115 E4
Sele 64 C4
Selečka pl 77 E4
Selenter See 48 B1
Sélero 81 D2
Sélestat 21 E4
Selevac 73 D3
Selfoss 96 A2
Séli 79 E3
Selia 90 C4
Selianítika 83 D4
Seligenstadt 52 A4
Selínia 87 F1
Selinunte 68 A3
Selishtë 76 C3
Selište 73 E3
Selje 100 A3
Seljord 104 C3
Selkämeri 102 B3
Selkirk 5 D3
Sellajoch 59 D3
Sella Nevea 59 F3
Sella, Pso di 59 D3
Selles 25 E2
Sellières 26 C3
Sellin 49 D1
Selm 17 E3
Selmsdorf 48 B2
Selna 71 F3
Selommes 25 E2
Selongey 26 C2
Seløy 97 D3
Selsey 9 F3
Selsey Bill 9 F3
Selters 52 A4
Seltz 21 F3
Sélune 18 C4
Selva 59 D3
Selvino 58 B4
Seman 114 B3
Semeljci 71 F2
Semič 70 B2
Seminara 67 E4
Semizovac 71 F4
Semmering 57 E3
Semmering -Paß 57 E3
Semois 20 C2
Semproniano 63 D1
Semur-en-Auxois 26 B2
Semur-en-Brionnais 26 B4
Sena 37 E3
Sénas 30 C3
Sendim 34 C4
Senez 31 D3
Senftenberg 53 E2
Sengsengeb 57 D3
Senigallia 61 F3
Senise 65 D4
Senj 70 B3
Senja Ånderdalen 94 B3
Senje 73 E4
Senlis 19 F3
Sennecey-le-Grand 26 C3
Sennen 8 A4
Sennestadt 17 F3
Sennori 66 A2
Senonches 19 E4
Senones 21 E4
Senorbi 66 B3
Senožeče 70 A2
Sens 26 A1
Senta 72 C1
Šentilj 70 C1
Šentjernej 70 C2
Šentjur 70 C2
Šentvid na Šlemenu 70 B1
Sépeaux 26 A1
Šepetovka 113 D2
Sepino 64 B3
Sepúlveda 36 A4
Sequeros 39 E2
Sequillo, R 35 E4
Seraing 50 C4
Seravezza 60 B3
Seregno 60 A1
Serein 26 B2
Serena, Emb de la 39 E4
Séres 80 B2
Séres (Nomos) 80 A2
Serfaus 58 C2
Serfopoúla, N 88 B3
Seriate 60 B1
Sérifos 88 A3
Sérifos, N 88 A3
Serifou, Stenó 88 A3
Sermaize-les-Bains 20 C4
Sermide 60 C2
Sermoneta 63 F3
Sernancelhe 38 C1
Serón 44 B3
Serón de Nágima 36 B4
Seròs 37 E4
Serpa 42 B1
Serpeddi, P 66 B4
Serpis, R 45 E1
Serra 41 E3
Serracapriola 64 B2
Serrada 35 E4
Serradifalco 68 C3
Serradilla 39 D3
Serramanna 66 B4
Serrana, Pto de la 39 E3
Serra San Bruno 67 F3
Serravalle Scrivia 60 A2
Serre Chevalier 31 D2
Serre-Poncon, Bge de 31 D2
Serres 30 C2
Serrières 30 B1
Serrota 39 F2
Sersale 67 F3
Sertã 38 B2
Servan 18 B4
Sérvia 79 E4
Servian 30 A4
Servigliano 61 F4
Servol, R 41 F2
Sesa 37 D3
Sesena 40 A2
Sesia 27 F4
Sesimbra 38 A4
Sesklio, N 93 E1
Sesma 36 C2
Sessa Aurunca 64 A3
Sesta Godano 60 B3
Šestanovac 75 E2
Sestino 61 E3
Sesto 59 E2
Sesto Calende 60 A1
Sesto Fiorentino 60 C3
Sesto San Giovanni 60 A1
Sestola 60 C3
Sestriere 31 E2
Sestri Levante 60 B3
Sestrunj 74 C1
Sestrunj I 74 C1
Sestu 66 B4
Sesvete 70 C2
Séta 84 B4
Setcases 32 B3
Sète 30 A4
Setenil 43 E3
Setermoen 94 B3
Setesdalen 104 B3
Setesdalsheiene 104 B3
Settebagni 63 E2
Settimo Torinese 31 E1
Settle 6 C1
Settons, les 26 B2
Setúbal 38 A4
Seudre 28 B1
Seui 66 B3
Seulo 66 B3
Seurre 26 C2
Sevastianá 79 E3
Sevenoaks 10 C3
Sévérac-le-Château 29 F3
Sever do Vouga 38 B1
Severn Bridge 9 D2
Severn, Mouth of the 9 D2
Severn, R 9 D2
Sever, R 38 C3
Seveso 60 A1
Sevettijärvi 95 F2
Sevilla 43 D2
Sevilleja de la Jara 39 F3
Sevlievo 115 D2
Sevnica 70 C2
Sevojno 72 C4
Sèvre Nantaise 24 C3
Sèvre Niortaise 24 C4
Sévrier 27 D4
Sevsk 111 F4
Sexten 59 E2
Seyches 28 C2
Seyda 53 D1
Seyðisfjörður 96 C2
Seyne 31 D3
Seyne, la 31 D4
Seyssel 27 D4
Sežana 70 A2
Sézanne 20 B4
Sezimovo-Ústí 57 D1
Sezze 63 F3
Sfáka 91 F4
Sfakiá 90 C4
Sfaktiria, N 86 C3
Sferracavallo 68 B2
Sfikiá, L 79 E3
Sfîntu Gheorghe 113 D4
Sforzacosta 61 F4
's Gravendeel 16 C3
's Gravenhage 16 B3
Sgùrr Mór 2 C3
Sgùrr na Ciche 2 B4
Shaftesbury 9 D3
Shanklin 9 E4
Shannon 12 B4
Shannon, Mouth of the 12 A4
Shannon, R 12 B4
Shap 5 D4
Shapinsay 3 E1
Shebenik, Mal i 77 D4
Sheelin, L 13 D3
Sheep Haven 12 C1
Sheep's Head 14 A4
's Heerenberg 17 D3
Sheerness 11 D2
Sheffield 6 C2
Shefford 9 F2
Shëmri (Shkodër) 76 C3
Shëmri (Tiranë) 76 C4
Shëngjin 76 C3
Sheppey, I of 11 D2
Shepshed 7 D3
Shepton Mallet 9 D3
Sherborne 9 D3
Shercock 13 D3
Sheringham 7 F3
's Hertogenbosch 16 C3
Shetland Is 3 E2
Shiel Bridge 2 C4
Shieldaig 2 B3
Shiel, L 2 B4
Shijak 76 C4
Shinás 79 E3
Shiniás 88 A1

Shin, L 2 C2
Shinos 83 D3
Shinoússa, N 88 C3
Shipston-on-Stour 9 E1
Shiza, N 86 C4
Shkodër 76 B3
Shkodrës, Liq i 76 B3
Shkumbin 76 C4
Sholári 80 A3
Shoreham 10 C3
Shpat, Mal i 77 D4
Shrewsbury 6 B3
Shrewton 9 E3
Shropshire 9 D1
Shupenzë 77 D4
Sía, Pto de la 36 A1
Siátista 79 D4
Šiauliai 110 C3
Sibari 67 E2
Sibbhult 109 D3
Sibbo 107 F2
Sibbofjärden 107 F2
Šibenik 75 D1
Šibenik *Mt* 75 E2
Sibinj 71 E3
Sibiu 113 D4
Sićevo 73 F4
Sichar, Emb de 41 E3
Sicié, Cap 31 D4
Sicignano degli Alburni 64 C4
Sicilia 68 B2
Sicó 38 B2
Šid 72 B2
Sidári 82 A1
Sideby 102 B3
Sidensjö 102 A2
Siderno 67 F4
Síderos, Akr 91 F3
Sidiró 81 F2
Sidirókastro 80 A2
Sidirónero 80 C1
Sidlaw Hills 5 D1
Sidmouth 9 D3
Siebenlehn 53 E2
Siedlce 112 C1
Sieg 51 E3
Siegburg 51 E3
Siegen 17 F4
Siegsdorf 56 B3
Siekierki 49 E3
Siena 61 D4
Sieppijärvi 98 C1
Sieradz 112 B2
Sierck 21 D3
Sierentz 27 E1
Sierninghofen 57 D3
Sierpc 112 B1
Sierra Boyera, Emb de 43 E1
Sierra de Fuentes 39 D3
Sierra de Yeguas 43 E3
Sierre 27 E3
Sievi 102 C1
Sievin as 102 C1
Sífnos, N 88 B3
Sífnou, Stenó 88 B3
Sigean 32 B2
Sigerfjord 94 A3
Siggjarvåg 104 A3
Sighetu Marmaţiei 112 C3
Sighişoara 113 D4
Siglufjörður 96 B1
Sigmaringen 55 D3
Signy-l'Abbaye 20 B2
Sigri 85 E2
Sigtuna 106 B3
Sigüenza 36 B4
Sigulda 110 C2
Siiddasjávri 94 B4
Siikainen 102 B3
Siikajoki 99 D4
Siikajoki *R* 99 D4
Siilinjärvi 103 E2
Sijarinska Banja 77 D1
Sikaminiá 85 F2
Sikås 101 E2
Sikí 84 A2
Sikiá (Makedonía) 80 B4
Sikiá (Pelopónissos) 87 E4
Síkinos 88 C4
Síkinos, N 88 C4
Sikióna 87 D1
Sikoráhi 81 E2
Sikoúrio 83 E1
Sikovuono 95 E3
Sila, La 67 F3
Silandro 58 C3
Silba 70 B4
Silba *I* 70 B4
Silbaš 72 B2
Sildegapet 100 A2
Şile 115 F3
Siles 44 B1
Siliqua 66 B4
Silistra 115 E1
Silivri 115 E3
Siljan (N) 104 C3
Siljan (S) 101 E4
Siljansnäs 101 E4
Silkeborg 108 A3
Silla 41 E4
Silleda 34 B2
Silleiro, C 34 A3
Sillé-le-Guillaume 23 E3
Sillian 59 E2
Silloth 5 D4
Šilo 70 B3
Silo 81 E2
Sil, R 34 C2
Sils 32 B4
Sils im Engadin 58 B3
Siltakylä 107 F2
Šilutė 110 B3
Silvalen 97 D3
Silvaplana 58 B3
Silvares 38 C2
Silves 42 A2
Silvi Marina 64 A1
Silvrettagruppe 58 B2
Silz 58 C2
Simancas 35 E4
Simandra 80 A3
Šimanovci 72 C3
Simav 115 F4
Simaxis 66 B3
Simbach (Inn) 56 B3
Simbach (Isar) 56 B2
Simbruini, Mti 63 F2
Simeto 69 D3
Simi 93 E1
Šimići 71 E3
Simi, N 93 E1
Simlångsdalen 108 C2
Simmerath 51 D4
Simmern 54 B1
Simo 99 D3
Simojärvi 99 E2
Simojoki 99 D3
Simola 103 F4
Simonos Pétras 80 C4
Simonsbath 8 C3
Simonswald 54 C3
Simópoulo 86 B1
Simplonpass 27 F3
Simrishamn 109 D3
Sinaia 113 D4
Sinalunga 61 D4
Sinarádes 82 A1
Sinarcas 41 D3
Sindelfingen 55 D2
Sindirgi 115 F4
Sindos 79 F3
Sines 42 A1
Sines, C de 42 A1
Sinettä 99 D2
Sineu 45 F3
Singen 55 D4
Singöfjärden 106 B3
Singra, Pto de 41 D2
Siniscola 66 C2
Sinj 75 D1
Sinjajevina 76 B2
Sinni 65 D4
Sinnicolau Mare 114 C1
Sinopoli 67 E4
Sinsheim 55 D2
Sintra 38 A4
Sinzig 51 E4
Siófok 112 B4
Sion 27 E3
Sioule 26 A4
Šipan 75 F2
Šipanska Luka 75 F2
Šipka 115 D2
Sipoo 107 F2
Sipoonselkä 107 F2
Šipovo 71 E4
Sippola 107 F2
Šiprage 71 E4
Sira 104 A4
Sira *R* 104 B4
Siracusa 69 D4
Sirdalen 104 B4
Sirdalvatn 104 A4
Siret 113 D3
Siret *R* 113 E4
Sirevåg 104 A4
Sirig 72 C2
Sirino, Mte 65 D4
Širitovci 75 D1
Sirkka 95 E4
Sirma 95 E2
Sirmione 60 C1
Sírna, N 92 C1
Široko Polje 71 F2
Sirolo 61 F4
Síros, N 88 B2
Siruela 39 F4
Sisak 71 D2
Šišan 70 A4
Sisante 40 C4
Šišljavić 70 C3
Sissa 60 B2
Sissach 27 F2
Sissonne 20 B3
Sisteron 31 D3
Sistiana 59 F3
Sistranda 100 C1
Sitges 32 A4
Sithonía 80 B4
Sitía 91 F4
Sitnica 77 D2
Sittard 17 D4
Sittensen 48 A3
Sittingbourne 11 D3
Siuntio 107 E3
Siuro 107 E1
Siurua 99 D3
Siuruanjoki 99 D3
Siusi 59 D3
Sivac 72 B2
Sivasli 115 F4
Síviri 80 A4
Sívota 82 B2
Sívros 82 B3
Siziano 60 A1
Sizun 22 B3
Sjælland 108 C3
Sjællands Odde 108 B3
Sjenica 76 C1
Sjeništa 76 A1
Sjøåsen 97 D4
Sjöbo 109 D3
Sjøholt 100 B2
Sjona 97 E2
Sjötorp 105 E4
Sjoutnäset 97 E4
Sjøvegan 94 B3
Sjulsmark 102 B1
Sjundea 107 E3
Sjusjøen 104 D2
Skåbu 100 C3
Skäckerfjällen 101 D1
Skadarsko jez 76 B3
Skadovsk 113 F4
Skafidiá 86 B2
Skaftá 96 B2
Skaftafell 96 C2
Skagafjörður 96 B1
Skage 97 D4
Skagen 108 B1
Skagern 105 E4
Skagerrak 108 A1
Skaill 3 E1
Skajálfandi 96 B1
Skála (Kefaloniá) 86 A1
Skála (Lésvos) 85 F2
Skála (Pátmos) 89 E2
Skála (Pelopónissos) 87 D3
Skála (Stereá Eláda) 83 F3
Skála Eressoú 85 E2
Skála Kalirráhis 80 C3
Skaland 94 B2
Skála Oropoú 84 B4
Skála Potamiás 81 D3
Skála Rahoníou 80 C3
Skalavik 96 A4
Skála Volissoú 85 E4
Skälderviken 108 C3
Skålevik 104 B4
Skálfandafljót 96 B2
Skalka 98 A2
Skalohóri (Lésvos) 85 E2
Skalohóri (Makedonía) 79 D3
Skalotí 80 C1
Skælskør 108 B4
Skamnéli 78 C4
Skandáli 85 D1
Skandári, Akr 89 F3
Skanderborg 108 B3
Skandzoúra, N 84 B3
Skåne 109 D3
Skånevik 104 A3
Skåningsbukt 94 C2
Skånland 94 B3
Skänninge 106 A4
Skanör Falsterbo 108 C4
Skara 109 D1
Skaraborgs Län 109 D1
Skaramangás 87 F1
Skærbæk 108 A4
Skarberget 94 B4
Škarda 74 B1
Skåre 105 E3
Skárfia 83 F3
Skärgårdshavet 107 D3
Skärhamn 108 C1
Skarnes 105 D3
Skarplinge 106 B2
Skarsvåg 95 E1
Skärvången 101 E1
Skarżysko-Kamienna 112 B2
Skattungbyn 101 E4
Skatval 100 C2
Skaulo 94 C4
Skaun 100 C2
Skee 105 D4
Skegness 7 E3
Skei (Møre og Romsdal) 100 B2
Skei (Sogn og Fjordane) 100 A3
Skeiðarársandur 96 B2
Skela 72 C3
Skellefteå 98 B4
Skellefteälven 98 B4
Skelleftehamn 98 B4
Skellig 14 A4
Skelmersdale 6 B2
Skenderbeut, M i 76 C4
Skender Vakuf 71 E4
Skepastó 80 B2
Skerries 13 E3
Ski 105 D3
Skiathos 84 A2
Skiáthos, N 84 A2
Skibbereen 14 B4
Skibby 108 C3
Skibotn 94 C2
Skiddaw 5 D4
Skídra 79 E3
Skien 104 C3
Skierniewice 112 B2
Skillingaryd 109 D2
Skiloundia 86 C2
Skinári, Akr 86 A1
Skiniás 91 E4
Skinnarbu 104 B3
Skinnskatteberg 105 F3
Skipagurra 95 F1
Skipton 6 C2
Skíros 84 C3
Skíros, N 84 C3
Skíti 83 F1
Skive 108 A2
Skivjane 76 C2
Skjeberg 105 D3
Skjern 108 A3
Skjersholmane 104 A3
Skjerstad 97 E2
Skjerstadfjorden 97 E2
Skjervøy 94 C2
Skjønhaug 105 D3
Sklavopoúla 90 B3
Sklithro 83 F1
Šklov 111 E3
Skočivir 77 E4
Škocjanske jame 70 A3
Skodje 100 B2
Škofja Loka 70 A2
Skofljica 70 B2
Skog (Gävleborgs Län) 101 F4
Skog (Västernorrlands Län) 102 A2
Skógafoss 96 B3
Skogerøya 95 F2
Skoghall 105 E3
Skogstorp 105 F4
Skokloster 106 B3
Skólis 86 B1
Skópelos (Lésvos) 85 F3
Skópelos (Skópelos) 84 B2
Skópelos, N 84 B3
Skopí 91 F4
Skopiá 83 E2
Skopje 77 E3
Skopós 79 D2
Skopun 96 A4
Skorenovac 73 D3
Skorovatn 97 E4
Skorped 101 F2
Skotína 79 F4
Skotterud 105 D3
Skoulikariá 82 C2
Skoúra 87 D3
Skoúrta 87 F1
Skoútari (Makedonía) 80 B2
Skoútari (Pelopónissos) 87 D4
Skoutáros 85 E2
Skövde 109 D1
Skrá 79 E2
Skrad 70 B3
Skradin 75 D1
Skradinski buk 75 D1
Skreia 105 D2
Skrim 104 C3
Skrolsvik 94 B3
Skrydstrup 108 A4
Skudeneshavn 104 A3
Skuleskogen 102 A2
Skull 14 A4
Skultuna 106 A3
Skuodas 110 B3
Skuov'gilraš'ša 95 D2
Skurup 109 D3
Skutskär 106 B2
Skutvik 94 A4
Skvira 113 E2
Skye 2 B3
Slagelse 108 B3
Slagnäs 98 A3
Slănčev Brjag 115 E2
Slancy 111 D1
Slane 13 D3
Slaney 15 D3
Slangerup 108 C3
Slano 75 F2
Slany 53 F3
Šlapanice 57 F1
Slapská přehr nádrž 53 F4
Slapy 53 F4
Śląsk 112 A2
Slatina (Bor) 73 E3
Slatina (Bosna i Hercegovina) 71 E3
Slatina (Kraljevo) 73 D4
Slatina (Makedonija) 77 D3
Slatina (RO) 115 D1
Slatine 75 D2
Slatinski Drenovac 71 E2
Slavgorod 111 E4
Slavinja 77 F1
Slavkovica 72 C4
Slavkov u Brna 57 F1
Slavnik 70 A3
Slavonice 57 E1
Slavonska Požega 71 E2
Slavonski Brod 71 E3
Slavonski Kobaš 71 E3
Slavuta 113 D2
Sławno 110 A4
Sławoborze 49 F2
Sleaford 7 D3
Slea Head 14 A3
Sleat, Sd of 2 B4
Slettfjellet 94 C2
Sliedrecht 16 C3
Sliema 68 B4
Slieve Bloom Mts 12 C4
Slieve Donard 13 E3
Slieve Mish Mts 14 A3
Slievenamon 14 C3
Slieve Snaght 13 D1
Sligachan 2 B3
Sligeach 12 C2
Sligo 12 C2
Sligo (Co) 12 B3
Sligo B 12 C2
Slišane 77 D1
Slite 109 F4
Sliven 115 E2
Sljeme 70 C2
Šljivovica 72 C4
Slobozia 115 E1
Slonim 112 C1
Sloten 16 C1
Slough 9 F2
Slovac 72 C3
Slovenska Bistrica 70 C1
Slovenija 70 A2
Slovenj Gradec 70 B1
Slovenske Konjice 70 C1
Slovenské Rudohorie 112 B3
Slovinci 71 D3
Słubice 49 F4
Sluck 111 D4
Sluderno 58 C3
Sluis 16 A4
Sluknov 53 F2
Slunj 70 C3
Słupsk 110 A4
Slyne Head 12 A3
Småland 109 D2
Smålandsfarvandet 108 B4
Smålands-stenar 109 D2
Šmarje 70 C2
Šmarješke Toplice 70 B2
Šmartin 70 B2
Smedby 109 E2
Smědeč 56 C2
Smederevo 73 D3
Smedjebacken 105 F3
Smederevska Palanka 73 D3
Smela 113 F2
Smigáda 81 E2
Smilčić 74 C1
Smilde 17 D1
Smiltene 110 C2
Smojmirovo 77 F3
Smokovec 70 B3
Smokovljan 75 F2
Smøla 100 B1
Smolensk 111 E3
Smolevići 111 D4
Smólikas, Óros 78 C4
Smoljan 115 D3
Smorgon 111 D4
Smørhamn 104 A1
Smygehamn 109 D4
Snaefell 6 A1
Snæfellsnes 96 A2
Snaith 7 D2
Snåsa 101 D1
Snasahögarna 101 D2
Snåsavatnet 101 D1
Sneek 16 C1
Sneem 14 A4
Snežnik 70 B3
Śniardwy, Jez 110 B4
Snigir'ovka 113 F3
Snillfjord 100 C2
Snizort, L 2 B3
Šnjegotina Velika 71 E3
Snøfjord 95 D1
Snøhefta 100 C3
Snøtinden 97 E2
Snowdon 6 A3
Snowdonia Forest and Nat Pk 6 A3
Soave 60 C1
Sobešlav 57 D1
Sobra 75 F2
Sobrado de los Monjes 34 B2
Sobral da Adiça 42 C1
Sobral de Monte Agraço 38 A3
Sobreira Formosa 38 C2
Sobrón, Emb de 36 B2
Søby 108 B4
Soča 70 A2
Soča *R* 70 A2
Sočanica 77 D1
Soccia 33 F3
Sochaczew 112 B1
Sochaux 27 E2
Socol 73 D2
Socovos 44 C1
Socuéllamos 40 B4
Sodankylä 95 E4
Söderåkra 109 E3
Söderbärke 105 F3
Söderfors 106 B3
Söderhamn 101 F4
Söderköping 106 A4
Södermanlands Län 106 A4
Söderskog 109 D3
Södertälje 106 B4
Sodražica 70 B2
Sodupe 36 B1
Soest (D) 17 F3
Soest (NL) 16 C2
Soestdijk 16 C2
Sofádes 83 E2
Sofia 115 D2
Sofiero 108 C3
Sofikó 87 E1
Sofó 83 E2
Sögel 17 E1
Sogliano al Rubicone 61 E3
Soglio 58 B3
Sogndal 100 B3
Søgne 104 B4
Sognefjell 100 B3
Sognefjorden 104 A1
Sognesjøen 104 A1
Sogn og Fjordane 100 A3
Soham 11 D1
Sohós 80 A2
Soignies 50 B4
Soini 102 C2
Soinlahti 103 D1
Soissons 20 A3
Söke 115 E4
Sokna 104 C2
Soko Banja 73 E4
Sokolac 72 B4
Sokolov 53 D4
Sokołow Podlaski 112 C1
Sokosti 95 F3
Sola (Rogaland) 104 A3
Sola (Sogn og Fjordane) 104 A1
Solana de los Barros 39 D4
Solana del Pino 43 F1
Solares 35 F2
Solberg 101 F1
Solbergfjorden 94 B3
Solčava 70 B1
Sol'cy 111 D2
Solda 58 C3
Sölden 58 C2
Soldeu 32 A2
Solent, The 9 E3
Solenzara 33 F4
Solesmes (Nord) 20 A2
Solesmes (Sarthe) 23 E3
Solevåg 100 A2
Solf 102 B2
Solferino 60 C1
Solholmen 100 B2
Solignac (Haute-Loire) 29 F2
Solignac (Haute-Vienne) 29 D1
Soligorsk 111 D4
Solihull 9 E1
Solin 75 D1
Soline 74 B1
Solingen 17 E4
Sölkerpaß 57 D4
Söll 59 D1
Sollana 41 E4
Sollefteå 101 F2
Sollenau 57 F3
Sollentuna 106 B3
Söller 45 E2
Sollerön 101 E4
Søllested 108 B4
Solliès-Pont 31 D4
Solnečnogorsk 111 F2

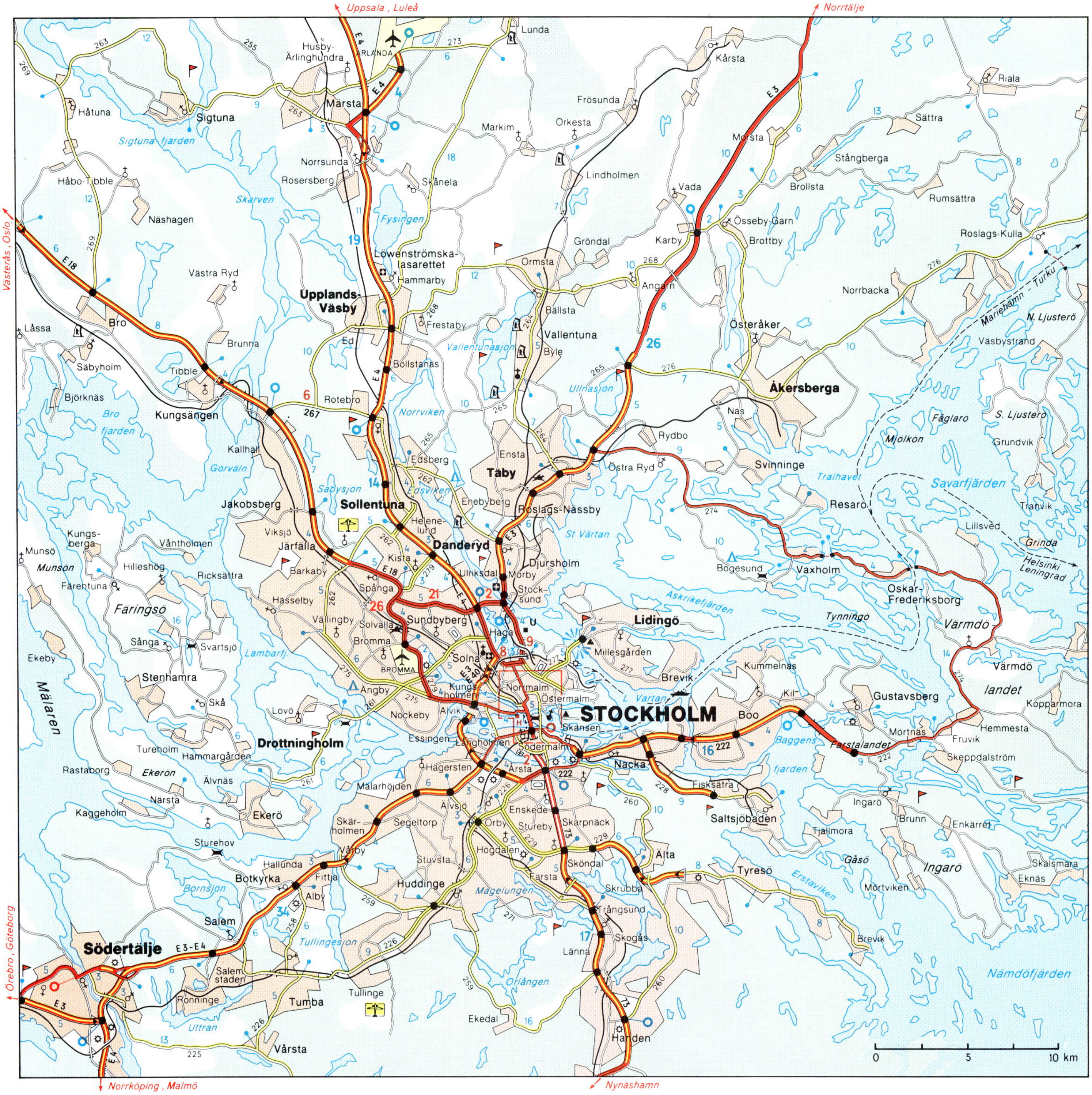

Uppsala, Luleå
Norrtälje
Västerås, Oslo
Örebro, Göteborg
Norrköping, Malmö
Nynäshamn
STOCKHOLM
Södertälje
Sigtuna
Märsta
Arlanda
Upplands-Väsby
Sollentuna
Danderyd
Täby
Lidingö
Åkersberga
Österåker
Vallentuna
Järfälla
Jakobsberg
Kungsängen
Bro
Sundbyberg
Solna
Bromma
Drottningholm
Huddinge
Botkyrka
Tumba
Salem
Nacka
Saltsjöbaden
Tyresö
Haninge
Handen
Värmdö
Gustavsberg
Boo
Vaxholm
Ekerö
Mälaren
Nämdöfjärden
0 5 10 km

Solofra 64 B4
Solosancho 39 F2
Solothurn 27 E2
Solre-le-Château 20 B2
Solrød 108 C3
Solsona 32 A3
Šolta 75 D2
Soltau 48 A3
Solunska Glava 77 E3
Solunto 68 B3
Solvay 60 C4
Sölvesborg 109 D3
Solvorn 100 B3
Solway Firth 4 C4
Solynieve 44 A3
Soma 115 E4
Sombernon 26 C2
Sombor 72 B2
Someren 17 D4
Somero 107 E2
Somerset 9 D3
Somes 112 C4
Somiedo, Pto de 35 D2
Sommarøy 94 B2
Sommatino 68 C4
Somme 19 E2
Somme (Dépt) 19 F2
Sommen 109 E1
Sömmerda 52 C2
Sommesous 20 B4
Sommières 30 B3
Sømna 97 D3
Somolinos 36 A4
Somosierra, Pto de 36 A4
Sompio 95 F3
Somport, Pto de 37 D2
Šomrda 73 E3
Soncillo 35 F2
Soncino 60 B1
Søndeled 104 C4
Sønderborg 108 B4
Sønderby 108 B4
Sønder Felding 108 A3
Sondershausen 52 C2
Søndersø 108 B3
Sondrio 58 B3
Songeons 19 E3
Sonkajärvi 103 E1
Sonnblick 59 E2
Sonneberg 52 C4
Sonnewalde 53 E1
Sonogno 58 A3
Sonsbeck 17 D3
Sonseca 40 A3
Son Servera 45 F3
Sonta 72 B2
Sonthofen 55 E4
Sontra 52 B3
Sopeira 37 F3
Sopilja 76 A1
Sopište 77 D3
Sopoćani 76 C1
Sopot (PL) 110 A4
Sopot (YU) 73 D3
Sopotnica 77 D4
Sopron 112 A4
Sora 64 A3
Soragna 60 B2
Söråker 101 F3
Sørarnøy 97 E2
Sorbas 44 C3
Sorbe, R 40 B1
Sore 28 B3
Soresina 60 B1
Sørfjorden 104 B2
Sør-Flatanger 96 C4
Sørfolda 94 A4
Sörfors 102 A1
Sorga 52 B3
Sorgono 66 B3
Sorgues 30 B3
Sørgutvik 97 D4
Soria 36 B3
Soriano nel Cimino 63 E2
Sørkjosen 94 C2
Sorø 108 B3
Soroki 113 E3
Soro, M 69 D3
Soroni 93 E1
Sørøya 95 D1
Sørøysundet 95 D1
Sorraia, R 38 A4
Sørreisa 94 B3
Sorrento 64 B4
Sor, Rib de 38 B3
Sørrollnes 94 B3
Sorsakoski 103 E2
Sorsele 98 A3
Sorso 66 A2
Sort 37 F2
Sortino 69 D4
Sortland 94 A3
Sortlandsundet 94 A3
Sør Trøndelag 100 C2
Sorunda 106 B4
Sørvågen 97 E1
Sørvágur 96 A4
Sørvær 94 C1
Sørværøy 97 E1
Sörvattnet 101 D3
Sos del Rey Católico 37 D2
Soses 37 E4
Sosnovyj Bor 111 D1
Sosnowiec 112 B2
Sospel 31 E3
Šoštanj 70 B1
Sóstis 81 D2
Šostka 111 F4
Sotaseter 100 B3
Sotillo de la Adrada 39 F2
Sotin 72 B2
Sotíra 79 E2
Sotkamo 99 E4
Soto del Barco 35 D1
Soto de los Infantes 35 D1
Soto de Luiña 35 D1
Soto de Sajambre 35 E2
Sotogrande 43 E4
Sotopalacios 35 F3
Sottomarina 61 D1
Sottunga 106 C3
Sotuélamos 40 C4
Soúda 90 C3
Souesmes 25 F2
Soufflenheim 21 F3
Souflí 81 F2
Soúgia 90 B4
Souillac 29 D2
Souilly 20 C3
Soulac 28 A1
Soulaines-Dhuys 20 C4
Soulinári 86 C3
Souliou, Óri 82 B2
Soulópoulo 82 B1

Soultz (Bas-Rhin) 21 E3
Soultz (Haut-Rhin) 27 E1
Soúnio 88 A2
Soúnio, Akr 88 A2
Souppes 25 F1
Source de la Loue 27 D2
Source du Lison 27 D3
Sourdeval 18 C4
Soure 38 B2
Sournia 32 B2
Sourotí 80 A3
Soúrpi 83 F2
Sousceyrac 29 D2
Sousel 38 C4
Soustons 28 A4
Soutelo 34 B2
Souterraine, la 25 E4
Southam 9 E1
Southampton 9 E3
Southborough 10 C3
South Downs 9 F3
Southend 4 B3
Southend-on-Sea 11 D2
Southern Uplands 4 C3
South Esk 3 D4
South Foreland 11 D3
South Molten 8 C3
Southport 6 B2
South Queensferry 5 D2
South Ronaldsay 3 E1
Southsea 9 F3
South Shields 5 E3
South Tyne 5 D3
South Uist 2 A3
Southwell 7 D3
Southwold 11 E1
Souvála 87 F2
Souvigny 26 A3
Sovata 113 D4
Sövdeborg 109 D3
Soverato 67 F3
Soveria Mannelli 67 F3
Sovetsk 110 B3
Søvik 100 A2
Sož 111 E4
Sozopol 115 E2
Spa 51 D4
Spaichingen 55 D3
Spakenburg 16 C2
Spalding 7 E3
Spánda, Akr 90 B3
Spandau 49 D4
Spangenberg 52 B3
Spanish Pt 12 B4
Sparlösa 108 C1
Spárta 87 E1
Spárti 87 D3
Spartivento, C (Calabria) 67 E4
Spartivento, C (Sardegna) 66 B4
Spárto 82 C3
Spas-Demensk 111 F3
Spáta 87 F1
Spatharéi 89 E2
Spathí, Akr (Kíthira) 90 A1
Spathí, Akr (Pelopónissos) 87 F2
Spodnjii Brnik 70 B2
Spean Bridge 2 C4
Speikkogel 57 E4
Spello 63 E1
Spennymoor 5 E4
Sperhiáda 83 E3
Sperhiós 83 E3
Sperillen 104 C2
Sperlonga 63 F3
Sperrin Mts 13 D1
Spétses 87 E3
Spétses, N 87 E3
Spetsopoúla, N 87 E3
Speyer 54 C2
Spey, R 3 D3
Spezzano Albanese 67 E2
Spezzano della Sila 67 E2
Spiddle 12 B3
Spiekeroog 47 E2
Spielfeld 70 C1
Spiez 27 F3
Spijkenisse 16 B3
Spilea Dirou 87 D4
Spíli 90 C4
Spiliá 83 E1
Spilimbergo 59 E3
Spilsby 7 E3
Spinalónga 91 E3
Spinazzola 65 D3
Spincourt 20 C3
Špionica Donja 71 F3
Špišić Bukovica 71 E2
Spišská-Nová Ves 112 B3
Spital 57 D3
Spittal 59 F2
Spitz 57 E2
Spjelkavik 100 A2
Split 75 D2
Spluga, Pso dello 58 B3
Splügen 58 B3
Splügenpass 58 B3
Spodsbjerg 108 B4
Špola 113 F2
Spoleto 63 E1
Spornitz 48 C3
Spotorno 60 A3
Spreča 71 F3
Spree 49 E4
Spreewald 53 E1
Spremberg 53 F1
Spresiano 59 E4
Springe 52 A1
Sprogø 108 B4
Spurn Head 7 E2
Spuž 76 B2
Squillace, Golfo di 67 F3
Squinzano 65 F4
Srb 71 D4
Srbac 71 E3
Srbica 77 D2
Srbija 73 D4
Srbobran 72 C2
Srđevići 75 E1
Srebrenica 72 C4
Središče 70 C1
Sredna Gora 115 D2
Srednje 71 F4
Srednji kanal 74 C1
Srednogorie 115 D2
Sredska 77 D3
Sremska Kamenica 72 C2
Sremska Mitrovica 72 C3
Sremska Rača 72 B3
Sremski Karlovci 72 C2
Srnetica 71 D4
Srnice Donje 71 F3
Środa Wielkopolska 112 A1
Srpska Crnja 72 C1
Srpske Moravice 70 B3
Srpski Itebej 73 D1
Srpski Miletić 72 B2
Stabbursdalen 95 D2
Stade 48 A3
Stádio 87 D2
Stadskanaal 17 E1
Stadthagen 52 A1
Stadtilm 52 C3
Stadtkyll 51 D4
Stadtlohn 17 E3
Stadtoldendorf 52 A2
Stadtroda 52 C3
Stadtsteinach 52 C4
Stadt Wehlen 53 F2
Staffa 4 A1
Staffanstorp 108 C3
Staffelsee 56 A4
Staffelstein 52 C4
Staffin 2 B3
Stafford 6 C3
Staffordshire 6 C3
Stágira 80 B3
Stahle 52 A2
Stahovica 70 B2
Staines 9 F2
Stainz 57 E4
Stajovce 77 E2
Stalać 73 E4
Štalcerji 70 B3
Stalída 91 E3
Stall 59 E2
Stalle, Pso di 59 E2
Stallersattel 59 E2
Stalowa Wola 112 C2
Stamford 9 F1
Stamnes 104 A2
Stams 58 C2
Stamsund 94 A4
Stange 105 D2
Stanišić 72 B1
Stanišinci 73 D4
Štanjel 70 A2
Stanke Dimitrov 115 D3
Staňkov 56 B1
Stankovci 74 C1
Stanley 5 E4
Stanós 80 B3
Stános 82 C3
Stans 27 F2
Stansstad 27 F2
Stansted 10 C2
Stapar 72 B2
Starachowice 112 B2
Stara Gradina 71 E2
Staraja Russa 111 E2
Stara Moravica 72 B1
Stara Novalja 70 B4
Stara Pazova 72 C2
Stara Pl (BG) 115 D2
Stara Pl (YU) 73 F4
Stará Role 53 E4
Staravina 77 E4
Stara Vrata 70 C4
Stara Zagora 115 D2
Staretina 75 D1
Stargard Szczeciński 49 F2
Stårheim 100 A3
Stari 77 F3
Stari Bar 76 B3
Stari Begej 72 C2
Starica 111 F2
Starigrad (Hvar) 75 D2
Starigrad (Velebit) 70 B4
Stari Gradac 71 E2
Starigrad Paklenica 70 C4
Stari Jankovci 72 B2
Stari Log 70 B2
Stari Majdan 71 D3
Stari Mikanovci 71 F2
Starnberg 56 A3
Starnberger See 56 A3
Starodub 111 F4
Starogard Gdański 110 A4
Starokonstantinov 113 D2
Staro Nagoričane 77 E2
Staro Petrovo Selo 71 E3
Staro Slano 76 A2
Start Pt 8 C4
Starý Smokovec 112 B3
Staßfurt 52 C1
Statland 97 D4
Staußfurt 52 C2
Stavanger 104 A3
Staveley 7 D3
Stavelot 51 D4
Stavenisse 16 B3
Staveren 16 C1
Stavern 104 C4
Stavri, Akr 88 C3
Stavrodrómi 86 C1
Stavrohóri 91 F4
Stavrós (Évia) 84 B3
Stavrós (Imathía) 79 E3
Stavrós (Itháki) 82 B4
Stavrós (Kríti) 90 C3
Stavrós (Thessalía) 83 E2
Stavrós (Thessaloníki) 80 B3
Stavrós, Akr (Kríti) 91 D3
Stavrós, Akr (Thássos) 81 D3
Stavroúpoli 80 C2
Steblevë 77 D4
Štěchovice 53 F4
Steckborn 58 A1
Steeg 58 C2
Steenbergen 16 B3
Steenvoorde 19 F1
Steenwijk 17 D2
Stefáni (Ípiros) 82 B2
Stefáni (Stereá Eláda) 87 F1
Stefaniná 80 B3
Stefanovikio 83 F2
Stege 108 C4
Stegersbach 57 F4
Steibis 55 E4
Steiermark 57 D4
Steigen 97 E1
Stein (A) 57 E2
Stein (N) 105 D2
Steinach (A) 59 D2
Steinach (D) 52 C3
Steinau 52 A4
Steinbach-Hallenberg 52 B3
Stein (Baden-Württemberg) 55 D4
Stein (Bayern) 55 E1
Steine 104 A1
Steinestø 104 A2
Steinfeld 17 F2
Steinfeld 59 F2
Steinfurt 17 E2
Steingaden 55 F4
Steinhaus 59 D2
Steinhausen 55 D3
Steinheim (Baden-Württemberg) 55 E2
Steinheim (Bayern) 55 E3
Steinheim (Nordrhein-Westfalen) 52 A2
Steinkjer 101 D1
Steinnuder Meer 48 A4
Steinpaß 59 E1
Steinshamn 100 A2
Steinsland 104 A2
Stekene 50 B3
Stelvio, Parco Naz della 58 C3
Stelvio, Pso dello 58 C3
Stená Klissoúras 79 D3
Stenay 20 C3
Stendal 48 C4
Steni 84 B4
Stenlille 108 B3
Stenløse 108 C3
Stenness 3 D1
Stenó 87 D2
Stenó, Akr 88 B2
Stenó Ithákis 82 B4
Sténoma 83 D3
Stenudden 98 A2
Stenungsund 108 C1
Stepanci 77 E3
Stepnica 49 E2
Stepojevac 72 C3
Stereá Eláda 83 D3
Sterkrade 17 E3
Stérna (Makedonía) 80 C2
Stérna (Pelopónissos) 87 D2
Stérna (Thráki) 81 F1
Sternberg 48 C2
Stérnes 90 C3
Sterup 48 A1
Sterza, la 60 C4
Sterzing 59 D2
Stevenage 9 F2
Stevns 108 C4
Stevns Klint 108 C4
Stewarton 4 C2
Steyr 57 D3
Steyrermühl 56 C3
Stia 61 D3
Stigliano 65 D4
Stigtomta 106 A4
Stilfserjoch 58 C3
Stilida 83 E3
Stilo 67 F4
Stimánga 87 D1
Stimfalia, L 87 D1
Štimlje 77 D2
Stintino 66 A1
Štip 77 E3
Stipsi 85 F2
Stira 84 C4
Stirling 4 C2
Štirovača 70 C4
Štitar 72 C3
Štivan 70 B4
Stjärnhov 106 B4
Stjärnsund 105 F4
Stjernøya 95 D2
Stjernsund 95 D2
Stjørdal 100 C2
Stjørdalselva 101 D2
Stjørnfjorden 100 C1
Stobi 77 E3
Stockach 55 D4
Stockbridge 9 E3
Stockelsdorf 48 B2
Stockerau 57 F2
Stockholm 106 B4
Stockholms Län 106 B3
Stockport 6 C2
Stocksbridge 6 C2
Stockton-on-Tees 5 E4
Stod 53 E4
Stöde 101 F3
Stogovo 77 D4
Stoke-on-Trent 6 C3
Stokke 104 C3
Stokmarknes 94 A3
Stol 73 E3
Stolac 75 F2
Stolac *Mt* 72 C4

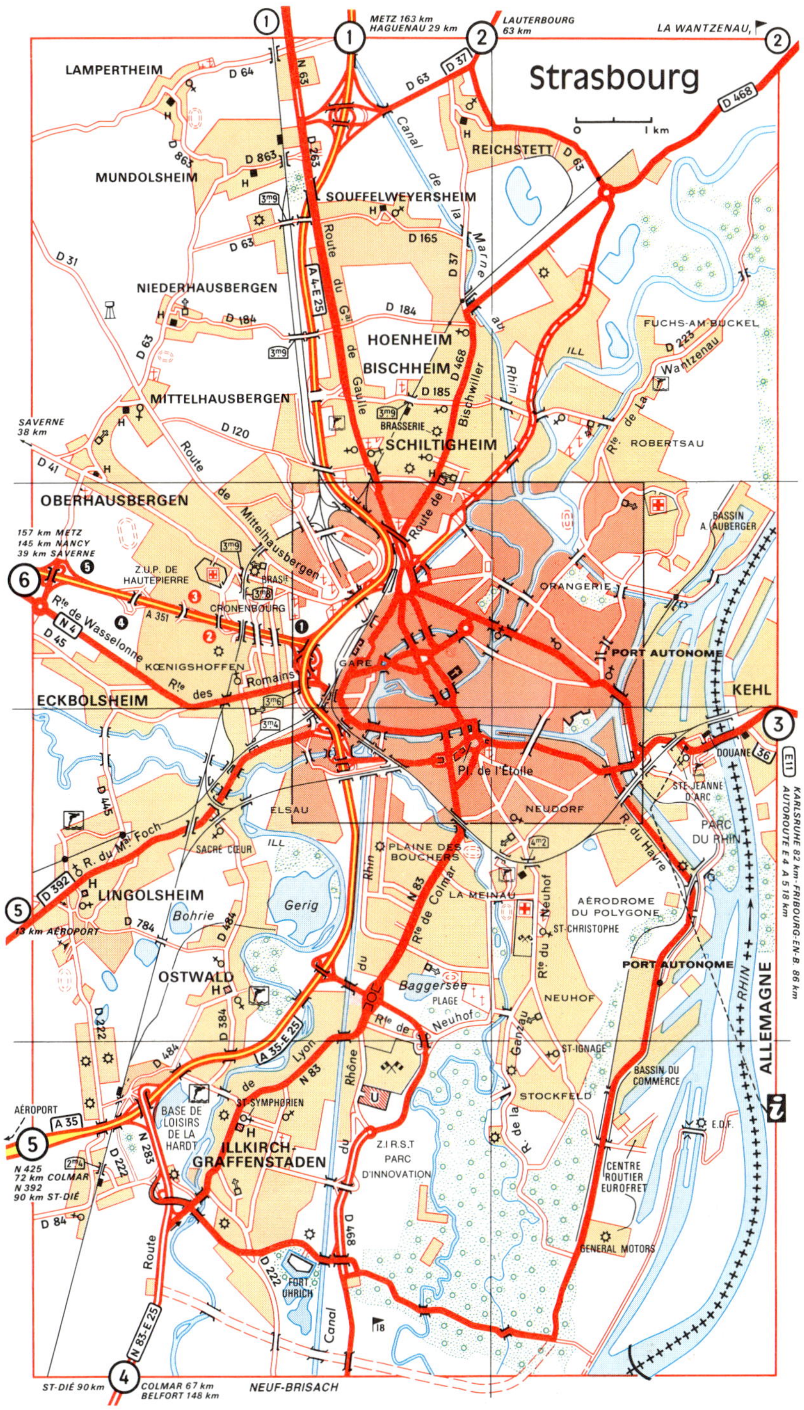
Strasbourg
1 km
METZ 163 km
HAGUENAU 29 km
LAUTERBOURG 63 km
LA WANTZENAU
LAMPERTHEIM
MUNDOLSHEIM
REICHSTETT
SOUFFELWEYERSHEIM
NIEDERHAUSBERGEN
HOENHEIM
BISCHHEIM
FUCHS-AM-BUCKEL
MITTELHAUSBERGEN
SCHILTIGHEIM
ROBERTSAU
SAVERNE 38 km
OBERHAUSBERGEN
157 km METZ
145 km NANCY
39 km SAVERNE
Z.U.P. DE HAUTEPIERRE
CRONENBOURG
ORANGERIE
PORT AUTONOME
KŒNIGSHOFFEN
GARE
ECKBOLSHEIM
KEHL
DOUANE
Pl. de l'Étoile
ELSAU
NEUDORF
PARC DU RHIN
KARLSRUHE 82 km - FRIBOURG-EN-B. 86 km
AUTOROUTE E 4 A 5 18 km
SACRÉ CŒUR
PLAINE DES BOUCHERS
LINGOLSHEIM
Gerig
LA MEINAU
AÉRODROME DU POLYGONE
ST-CHRISTOPHE
13 km AÉROPORT
OSTWALD
PORT AUTONOME
Baggersee
NEUHOF
ALLEMAGNE
RHIN
BASSIN DU COMMERCE
STOCKFELD
AÉROPORT
ILLKIRCH-GRAFFENSTADEN
Z.I.R.S.T PARC D'INNOVATION
CENTRE ROUTIER EUROFRET
N 425 72 km COLMAR
N 392 90 km ST-DIÉ
GENERAL MOTORS
FORT UHRICH
ST-DIÉ 90 km
COLMAR 67 km
BELFORT 148 km
NEUF-BRISACH

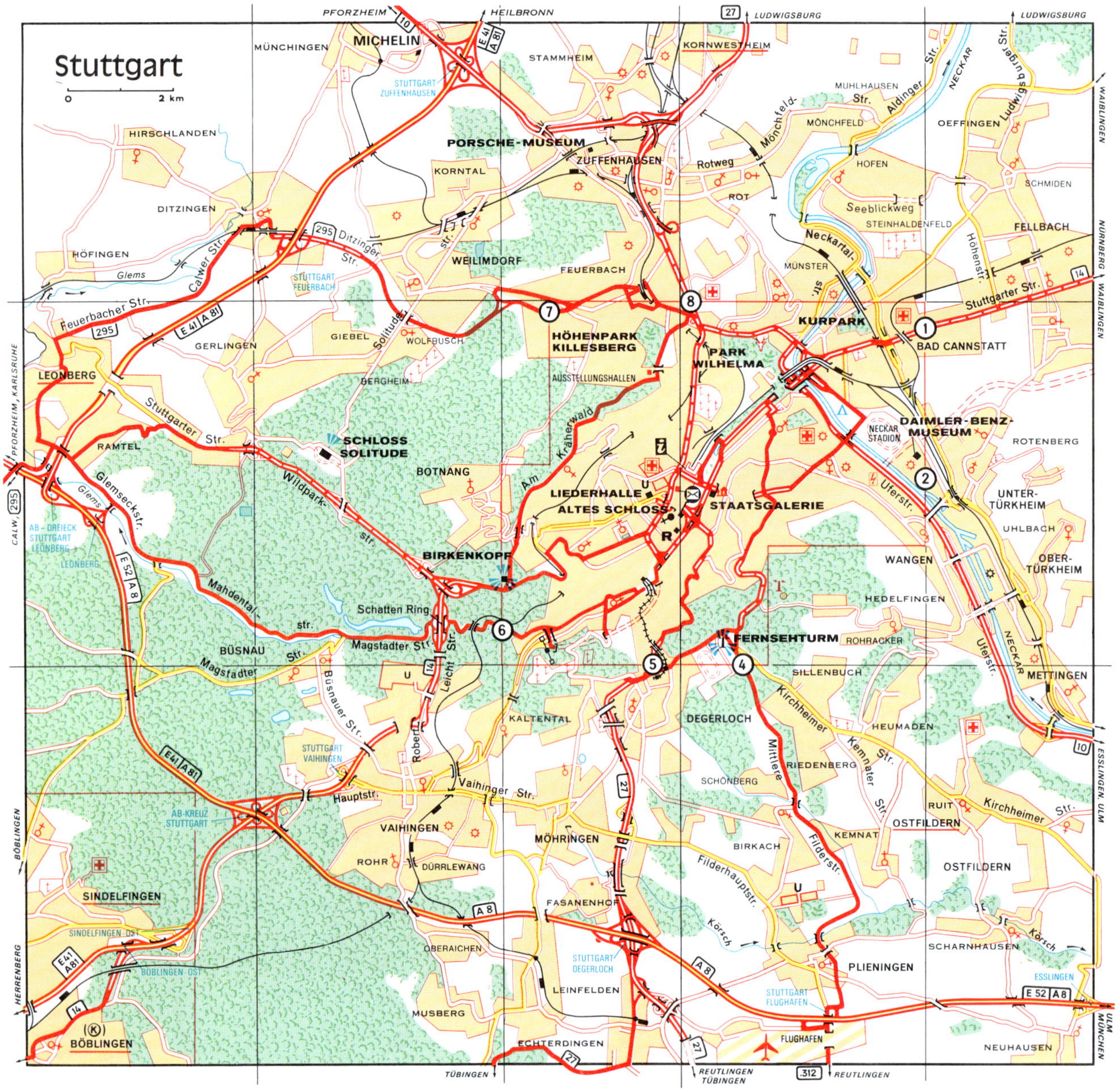
Stuttgart
0 2 km
PFORZHEIM
HEILBRONN
LUDWIGSBURG
MÜNCHINGEN
MICHELIN
STAMMHEIM
KORNWESTHEIM
HIRSCHLANDEN
PORSCHE-MUSEUM
ZUFFENHAUSEN
KORNTAL
MÜHLHAUSEN
MÖNCHFELD
OEFFINGEN
HOFEN
SCHMIDEN
DITZINGEN
WEILIMDORF
FEUERBACH
ROT
FELLBACH
HÖFINGEN
MÜNSTER
KURPARK
BAD CANNSTATT
GERLINGEN
GIEBEL
WOLFBUSCH
HÖHENPARK KILLESBERG
PARK WILHELMA
LEONBERG
BERGHEIM
AUSSTELLUNGSHALLEN
DAIMLER-BENZ-MUSEUM
NECKAR STADION
ROTENBERG
RAMTEL
SCHLOSS SOLITUDE
BOTNANG
LIEDERHALLE
ALTES SCHLOSS
STAATSGALERIE
UNTER-TÜRKHEIM
UHLBACH
OBER-TÜRKHEIM
BIRKENKOPF
WANGEN
HEDELFINGEN
FERNSEHTURM
ROHRACKER
BÜSNAU
SILLENBUCH
METTINGEN
KALTENTAL
DEGERLOCH
HEUMADEN
RIEDENBERG
SCHÖNBERG
VAIHINGEN
MÖHRINGEN
KEMNAT
OSTFILDERN
RUIT
BIRKACH
ROHR
DÜRRLEWANG
SINDELFINGEN
FASANENHOF
OBERAICHEN
LEINFELDEN
PLIENINGEN
SCHARNHAUSEN
ESSLINGEN
MUSBERG
ECHTERDINGEN
FLUGHAFEN
NEUHAUSEN
BÖBLINGEN
TÜBINGEN
REUTLINGEN
ULM MÜNCHEN
WAIBLINGEN
NÜRNBERG
ESSLINGEN, ULM
HERRENBERG
CALW
PFORZHEIM, KARLSRUHE

Stolbcy 111 D4
Stolberg (Nordrhein-Westfalen) 51 D3
Stolberg (Sachsen-Anhalt) 52 C2
Stolice 72 B3
Stolice *Mt* 73 E4
Stolin 113 D1
Stollberg 53 E3
Stöllet 105 E2
Stolpen 53 F2
Stølsheimen 104 B2
Stolzenau 48 A4
Stómio 83 F1
Ston 75 F2
Stone 6 C3
Stonehaven 3 E4
Stonehenge 9 E3
Stonglandet 94 B3
Stopanja 73 E4
Stör 48 A2
Storå 105 F3
Stora Alvaret 109 E3
Stora Blåsjön 97 E4
Stora Lulevatten 98 A2
Stora Sjöfallet 94 B4
Stora Sjöfallet (National park) 94 B4
Stora Skedvi 105 F2
Stora Sundby 105 F4
Storavan 98 A3
Storby 106 C3
Stord 104 A2
Stordal 100 B2
Store Bælt 108 B3
Storebø 104 A2
Storebro 109 E2
Store Heddinge 108 C4
Store Molvik 95 F1
Store Mosse 109 D2
Støren 100 C2
Storfjellet 97 F2
Storfjorden 100 B2
Storfors 105 E3
Storforsen 98 B3
Storforshei 97 E2
Storglomvatnet 97 E2
Storkow 49 E4
Storlien 101 D2
Stormi 107 D2
Stornoway 2 B2
Storo 58 C4
Storožinec 113 D3
Storr, The 2 B3
Storsjö 101 D2
Storsjøen 105 D1
Storsjön (Gävleborgs Län) 106 B2
Storsjön (Ljungdalen) 101 D2
Storsjön (Östersund) 101 E2
Storsjouten 97 E4
Storskarven 101 D2
Storslett 94 C2
Storsteinnes 94 C3
Storstrømmen 108 C4
Storuman 97 F4
Storuman *L* 97 F3
Storvik (N) 95 D2
Storvik (S) 106 A2
Storvindeln 97 F3
Stotel 47 F3
Stoúpa 86 C3
Stour 11 D2
Stourbridge 9 E1
Stournaréika 83 D2
Stourport 9 D1
Støvring 108 B2
Stowmarket 11 D1
Stow-on-the-Wold 9 E2
Strà 61 E1
Strabane 13 D1
Stracin 77 E2
Stradella 60 A2
Stradsett 11 D1
Straelen 17 D3
Stragari 73 D4
Strakonice 56 C1
Stralsund 49 D1
Stranda 100 B2
Strandebarm 104 A2
Strandhill 12 C2
Strangford 13 E2
Strangford *L* 13 E2
Strängnäs 106 B3
Stranice 70 B1
Stranorlar 12 C1
Stranraer 4 B3
Strasbourg 21 E4
Strasburg 49 E2
Straßburg 70 A1
Straßwalchen 56 C3
Stratford-upon-Avon 9 E1
Strathaven 4 C2
Strathclyde 4 C2
Strathy Pt 3 D2
Stratóni 80 B3
Stratoníki 80 B3
Strátos 82 C3
Stratton 8 B3
Straubing 56 B2
Straumen (Bodø) 97 E2
Straumen (Fauske) 97 F1
Straumen (Nord Trøndelag) 101 D1
Straumsjøen 94 A3
Straumsnes (Nordland) 97 E1
Straumsnes (Troms) 94 B2
Straupitz 53 E1
Strausberg 49 E4
Straža (Srbija) 73 E4
Straža (Vojvodina) 73 D2
Straža, G. 70 B2
Stražbenica 76 B1
Strážný 56 C2
Streatley 9 E2
Street 9 D3
Strehaia 114 C1
Strehla 53 E2
Streitberg 52 C4
Strengberg 57 D3
Stresa 58 A4
Streymoy 96 A3
Strezimirovci 77 E1
Strezovce 77 D2
Stříbro 53 E4
Strimónas 80 B2
Strimonikó 80 A2
Strimonikós Kólpos 80 B3
Strmac 71 E2
Strmica 75 D1
Strobl 56 C3
Strofádes, N 86 A3
Strofiliá 84 A3
Strojkovce 77 E1
Strokestown 12 C3
Stromberg 54 B1
Stromboli, I 69 D1
Stromeferry 2 B3
Strömfors 107 F2
Stromness 3 D1
Strömsbruk 101 F3
Strömsnäsbruk 109 D2
Strömstad 105 D4
Strömsund 101 F1
Ströms vattudal 101 E1
Strongoli 67 F2
Stronsay 3 E1
Stronsay Firth 3 E1
Strontian 2 B4
Stroud 9 D2
Strovlés 90 B3
Strub, Paß 59 E1
Struer 108 A2
Struga 77 D4
Struge 70 B2
Struma 115 D3
Strumble Head 8 B1
Strumica 77 F3
Strumica *R* 77 F3
Stryj 112 C3
Stryn 100 A3
Strzelce Krajeńskie 49 F3
Stubalpe 57 D4
Stubbekøbing 108 C4
Stubbenkammer 49 D1
Štubej 73 E3
Štubik 73 F3
Stubličke Toplice 70 C2
Stubline 72 C3
Stučka 110 C3
Stuckenborstel 48 A3
Studena 77 E1
Studenci 75 E1
Studenica 76 C1
Stugun 101 F2
Stühlingen 54 C4
Stuhr-Brinkum 17 F1
Stupnik 70 C2
Stura di Demonte 31 E3
Sturehov 106 B4
Sturminster Newton 9 D3
Sturup 108 C3
Stuttgart 55 D2
Stykkishólmur 96 A2
Styr' 113 D1
Suances 35 F1
Subbiano 61 D4
Subiaco 63 F2
Subijana 36 B2
Subotica 72 B1
Subotište 72 C3
Suc-au-May 29 D1
Suceava 113 D3
Sučevici 71 D4
Suceviţa 113 D3
Suchań 49 F2
Suchiniči 111 F3
Süchteln 17 D4
Sucina 45 D2
Suck 12 C3
Sućuraj 75 E2
Sudbury (Derbys) 6 C3
Sudbury (Suffolk) 11 D2
Suddesjaur 98 A3
Sude 48 B3
Süderbrarup 48 A1
Suðuroy 96 A4
Suðuroyarfjørdur 96 A4
Sueca 41 E4
Sueros 35 D2
Suffolk 11 D1
Suhl 52 C3
Suhopolje 71 E2
Suho Polje 72 B3
Šuica 75 E1
Suinula 102 C3
Suippes 20 B3
Suir, R 14 C3
Sukeva 103 E1
Sukobin 76 B3
Sukošan 74 C1
Sukovo 77 E1
Sukth 76 C4
Sula 113 F2
Suldal 104 B3
Suldalsvatn 104 B3
Sulden 58 C3
Sulęcin 49 F4
Sulina 113 F4
Sulingen 17 F2
Sulitjelma 97 F2
Sulitjelma *Mt* 97 F2
Sulkava 103 E3
Sully 25 F2
Sulmona 64 A2
Sultanhisar 115 F4
Sulz 54 C3
Sulzbach (Baden-Württemberg) 55 D2
Sulzbach (Saarland) 54 B2
Sulzbach-Rosenberg 55 F1
Sulzemoos 55 F3
Sunmartin 75 E2
Sumba 96 A4
Sumburgh 3 F2
Sumburgh Head 3 F2
Sümeg 112 A4
Šumen 115 E2
Sumiainen 103 D2
Sumiswald 27 F2
Šumperk 112 A3
Sumy 113 F1
Sunart, L 2 B4
Sund 106 C3
Sunde (Hordaland) 104 A2
Sunde (Sør Trøndelag) 100 C1
Sunderland 5 E4
Sundern 17 F4
Sundini 96 A3
Sundom 102 B2
Sundsvall 101 F3
Sundsvallsbukten 101 F3
Suni 66 B2
Sunja 71 D3
Sunnansjö 105 F3
Sunndalen 100 C2
Sunndalsøra 100 B2
Sunne (Jämtlands Län) 101 E2
Sunne (Värmlands Län) 105 E3
Sunnemo 105 E3

Sunnylvsfjorden 100 B3
Suodenniemi 107 D1
Suolahti 103 D2
Suolijärvet 99 E2
Suolijoki 99 D2
Suomenlinna 107 E3
Suomenniemi 103 E3
Suomusjärvi 107 E2
Suomussalmi 99 F3
Suomutunturi 99 E2
Suonenjoki 103 E2
Suontee 103 D3
Suopelto (Kuopion Lääni) 103 D2
Suopelto (Mikkelin Lääni) 103 D3
Super-Besse 29 E1
Super-Molina 32 A3
Supetar 75 D2
Supetarska Draga 70 B4
Supino 63 F3
Šuplja-Stijena 76 B1
Surahammar 105 F3
Suraž 111 E4
Surbo 65 F4
Surčin 72 C3
Surduc 114 C1
Surdulica 77 E1
Surdup 76 B2
Sûre 21 D2
Surgères 24 C4
Súria 32 A3
Surnadalsøra 100 C2
Surrey 10 C3
Sursee 27 F2
Survilliers 19 F3
Susa 31 E1
Suså 108 C4
Sušac 75 E3
Susak 70 B4
Susak *I* 70 B4
Susch 58 B2
Susek 72 B2
Sušice 56 C1
Suspiro del Moro, Ptodel 44 A3
Susqueda, Emb de 32 B3
Süßen 55 D2
Sustenpass 58 A3
Susurluk 115 F3
Sutinjske Toplice 70 C2
Sutivan 75 D2
Sutjeska 73 D2
Sutjeska nac park 76 A1
Sutomore 76 B3
Sutri 63 E2
Sutterton 7 E3
Sutton 9 F2
Sutton Coldfield 9 E1
Sutton-in-Ashfield 7 D3
Sutton-on-Sea 7 E3
Suva gora 77 D3
Suva pl 77 E1
Suva Reka 77 D2
Suvasvesi 103 E2
Suvereto 62 C1
Suvobor 72 C4
Suvodol 77 E3
Suwałki 110 C4
Suze, la 23 F4
Suzzara 60 C2
Sval'ava 112 C3
Svalöv 108 C3
Svaneke 109 D4
Svanstein 98 C2
Svanvik 95 F2
Svappavaara 94 C4
Svärdsjö 105 F2
Svarstad 104 C3
Svarta 105 E4
Svartevatn 104 B3
Svartevatn *L* 104 B3
Svartisen 97 E2
Sværvolthalvøya 95 E1
Svattälven 105 F3
Svedala 108 C3
Sveg 101 E3
Svelgen 100 A3
Svelvik 104 C3
Svendborg 108 B4
Svenljunga 108 C2
Svensby 94 C2
Svenstavik 101 E2
Švermov 53 F3
Svetac 75 D2
Sveti Andrija 77 D3
Sveti Ilija 75 E2
Sveti Janez 70 A2
Sveti Jovan Bigorski 77 D3
Sveti Naum 77 D4
Sveti Nikita 77 D2
Sveti Nikola 76 B3
Sveti Nikole 77 E3
Sveti Pantelejmon 77 D3
Sveti Rok 70 C4
Sveti Stefan 76 B3
Svetlogorsk (Belorussija) 111 E4
Svetlogorsk (Rossija) 110 B4
Svetlovodsk 113 F2
Svetozarevo 73 D4
Svetozar Miletić 72 B1
Svidnik 112 C3
Švihov 56 B1
Svilaja 75 D1
Svilajnac 73 E3
Svilengrad 115 E3
Svingvoll 104 C1
Svinjar 71 E3
Svinoy 96 A3
Svištov 115 D2
Svitavy 112 A3
Svodđe 77 E1
Svolvær 94 A4
Svor 53 F3
Svorkmo 100 C2
Svoronáta 86 A1
Svorónos 79 F4
Svrljig 73 F4
Swadlincote 6 C3
Swaffham 11 D1
Swale 6 C1
Swalmen 17 D4
Swanage 9 E4
Swanley 10 C2
Swanlinbar 12 C2
Swansea 8 C2
Świdnica 112 A2
Świdwin 49 F2
Świebodzin 112 A2
Świecie 112 A1
Świecko 49 F4
Świerzno 49 F1
Swilly, L 13 D1
Swindon 9 E2
Swinford 12 B3
Świnoujście 49 E2
Swords 13 D3
Sybil Head 14 A3
Syčovka 111 F2
Sykäräinen 102 C1
Syke 17 F1
Sykkylven 100 A2
Sylene 101 D2
Sylling 104 C3
Sylt 47 F1
Sylt Ost 47 F1
Sylvenstein-Stausee 56 A4
Synod Inn 8 C1
Syötekylä 99 E3
Syre 3 D2
Sysmä 103 D3
Sysslebäck 101 D4
Syväjärvi 99 D1
Syväri 103 E2
Syvde 100 A3
Syvdsnes 100 A2
Syyspohja 103 E3
Szarvas 112 B4
Szczecin 49 E2
Szczecinek 110 A4
Szczeciński, Zalew 49 E2
Szczytno 110 B4
Szécsény 112 B3
Szeged 114 B1
Székesfehérvár 112 B4
Szekszárd 114 B1
Szentendre 112 B4
Szentes 112 B4
Szigetvár 114 B1
Szolnok 112 B4
Szombathely 112 A4

T

Tabanovce 77 E2
Tábara 35 D4
Tabarca, I de 45 E2
Taberg 109 D1
Tabernas 44 B3
Tabernes de Valldigna 41 E4
Taboada 34 B2
Tábor 57 D1
Tábua 38 B2
Tabuaço 34 B4
Tabuenca 36 C3
Täby 106 B3
Tachov 53 E4
Tadcaster 7 D2
Tafalla 36 C2
Tafjord 100 B3
Taganheira 42 A1
Taggia 31 F3
Tagliacozzo 63 F2
Tagliamento 59 E3
Taglio di Po 61 D2
Tahal 44 C3
Tahkvuori 103 E2
Taibilla, Sa de 44 C2
Taïgetos, Óros 87 D3
Tain 3 D3
Tain-l'Hermitage 30 B2
Taipadas 38 A4
Taipalsaari 103 E4
Taivalkoski 99 E3
Taivassalo 107 D2
Tajera, Emb de la 40 C1
Tajo, R 40 B2
Tajuña, R 40 B2
Takovo 73 D4
Taktikoúpoli 87 E2
Tálanda 87 E4
Talarrubias 39 E4
Talaván 39 D3
Talave, Emb de 44 C1
Talavera de la Reina 39 F3
Talavera la Real 39 D4
Talayuela 39 E2
Talayuelas 41 D3
Taldom 111 F2
Talgarth 9 D1
Talkkunapää 95 F3
Talla 61 D4
Tallante 45 D3
Tallard 31 D2
Tällberg 101 E4
Tallinn 110 C1
Talloires 27 D4
Tallow 14 C4
Talluskylä 103 D2
Talmont 24 B3
Tal'noje 113 E2
Talsi 110 B2
Talvik 95 D2
Tamames 39 E1
Tamar 8 B3
Támara 35 F3
Tamarite de Litera 37 E3
Tamási 112 B4
Tambre, R 34 A2
Tâmega, R 34 A4
Tamélos, Akr 88 A2
Tamiš 72 C2
Tammela 107 E2
Tammisaari 107 E3
Tamnava 72 C3
Tampere 107 E1
Tamsweg 56 C4
Tamworth 9 E1
Tana 95 E1
Tana *R* 95 E1
Tanafjorden 95 E1
Tanágra 84 A4
Tanagro 64 C4
Tanamea, Pso di 59 F3
Tanaro 31 F2
Tancarville, Pont de 19 D3
Tandådalen 101 D4
Tandragee 13 D2
Tandsbyn 101 E2
Tandsjöborg 101 E3
Tangerhütte 48 C4
Tangermünde 48 C4
Tanhua 95 F4
Taninges 27 E4
Tanlay 26 B1
Tann 52 B3
Tännäs 101 D3
Tanndalen 101 D3
Tannheim 58 C1
Tannila 99 D3
Tanumshede 105 D4
Taormina 69 D3
Tapa 110 C1
Tapia de Casariego 34 C1
Tar 70 A3
Tara 72 C4
Tara *R* 76 B1
Taracena 40 B2
Tara klisura 76 B2
Tarancón 40 B3
Taranto 65 E4
Taranto, Golfo di 65 E4
Tarare 26 B4
Taraš 72 C2
Tarašča 113 E2
Tarascon (Ariège) 32 A2
Tarascon (Vaucluse) 30 B3
Taravo 33 F3
Tarayuela 41 E2
Tarazona 36 C3
Tarazona de la Mancha 40 C4
Tarbat Ness 3 D3
Tarbert (IRL) 14 B3
Tarbert (Strathclyde) 4 B2
Tarbert (Western Is) 2 B2
Tarbes 37 E1
Tarbet 4 C1
Tarcento 59 F3
Tarčin 75 F1
Tardets-Sorholus 37 D1
Tardienta 37 D3
Tärendo 98 C2
Tärendöälven 98 C1
Targon 28 B2
Târgovište 115 E2
Tarifa 43 D4
Tarm 108 A3
Tarmstedt 47 F3
Tarn 29 D3
Tarn (Dépt) 29 E3
Tärnaby 97 E3
Tarna, Pto de 35 E2
Tärnäsjön 97 E3
Tarn-et-Garonne 29 D3
Tarn, Gges du 29 F3
Tarnobrzeg 112 C2
Tarnos 28 A4
Tarnów 112 B2
Taro 60 B2
Tarouca 38 C1
Tarp 48 A1
Tarporley 6 B3
Tarquinia 63 D2
Tarragona 37 F4
Tarrasa 32 A4
Tàrrega 37 F4
Tarrekaise 98 A2
Tårs 108 B4
Tarsia 67 E2
Tartas 28 B3
Tartu 110 C2
Tarvasjoki 107 D2
Tarvisio 59 F2
Täsch 27 F4
Tåsinge 108 B4
Tåsjo 101 F1
Tåsjön 101 F1
Tassin 26 C4
Tåstrup 108 C3
Tata 112 B4
Tatabánya 112 B4
Tatarbunary 113 E4
Tatry 112 B3
Tau 104 A3
Tauber 55 D1
Tauberbischofsheim 55 D1
Taucha 53 D2
Tauerntal 59 E2
Tauerntunnel 59 E2
Taufers i. M. 58 C3
Taufkirchen 56 B3
Taulé 22 B2
Taunton 9 D3
Taunus 51 F4
Taunusstein 51 F4
Tauplitz 57 D4
Tauragė 110 B3
Taurianova 67 E4
Taurion 25 E4
Tauste 36 C3
Tauves 29 E1
Tavankut 72 B1
Tavannes 27 E2
Tavarnelle Val di Pesa 60 C4
Tavastila 103 F4
Tavaux 26 C2
Taverna 67 F3
Tavernelle 63 E1
Tavernes 31 D4
Tavignano 33 F3
Tavira 42 B3
Tavistock 8 C3
Tavolara, I 66 C1
Tavropós 83 D2
Tavropoú, Teh L 83 D2
Tavşanli 115 F3
Taw 8 C3
Taxenbach 59 E1
Taxiárhis 80 B3
Tay 5 D1
Tayinloan 4 B2
Tay, L 4 C1
Taynuilt 4 B1
Tayport 5 D1
Tayside 3 D4
Tazones 35 E1
Tczew 110 A4
Teano 64 A3
Teba 43 E3
Tebay 5 D4
Tech 32 B3
Techendorf 59 F2
Tecklenburg 17 E2
Tecuci 113 E4
Tees 5 E4
Teesside 5 E4
Teféli 91 D4
Tegéa 87 D2
Tegel 49 E4
Tegelen 17 D4
Tegernsee 56 A4
Teggiano 64 C4
Teguise 42 C3
Teide 42 B4
Teide *Mt* 42 A4
Teide, Pque Nac del 42 B4
Teignmouth 8 C4
Teijo 107 D3
Teil, le 30 B2
Teilleul, le 18 C4
Teisendorf 56 B3
Teisko 102 C3
Teixeiro 34 B1
Teixoso 38 C2
Tejeda, Sa de 43 F3
Tejo, R 38 A3
Tekeriš 72 C3
Tekija 73 E2
Tekirdağ 115 E3
Telč 57 E1
Telde 42 B4
Telemark 104 C3
Télendos, N 89 E3
Teleno 34 C3
Telese 64 B3
Telford 6 C3
Telfs 58 C2
Telgte 17 E3
Tellingstedt 48 A2
Telti 66 B1
Teltow 49 D4
Témbi 83 E1
Tembleque 40 B3
Temerin 72 C2
Temmes 99 D4
Tempelhof 49 E4
Tempio Pausania 66 B1
Templemore 12 C4
Templin 49 D3
Temse 50 B3
Temska 73 F4
Tenala 107 E3
Ténaro, Akr 87 D4
Tenbury Wells 9 D1
Tenby 8 B2
Tence 30 B2
Tende 31 E3
Tende, Col de 31 E3
Tende, Colle di 31 E3
Tendilla 40 B2
Tenerife 42 A4
Tenhola 107 E3
Tenja 71 F2
Tennes 94 B3
Tenniöjoki 95 F4
Teno 95 E2
Tensta 106 B3
Tenterden 11 D3
Tentudia 43 D1
Teolo 61 D1
Teovo 77 E3
Tepelenë 114 C4
Teplá 53 E4
Teplice 53 E3
Tepsa 95 E4
Teramo 63 F1
Ter Apel 17 E1
Tera, R 35 D3
Terebovl'a 113 D3
Terena 38 C4
Terespol 112 C1
Terezino Polje 71 E2
Terges, Rib de 42 B2
Tergnier 20 A2
Terjärv 102 C2
Terlizzi 65 D3
Termas de Monfortinho 39 D2
Terme Luigiane 67 E2
Termini Imerese 68 B3
Terminillo 63 F2
Terminillo, Mte 63 F2
Termoli 64 B2
Terneuzen 16 B4
Terni 63 E2
Ternitz 57 E3
Ternopol' 113 D2
Térovo 82 C2
Térpilos 80 A2
Terpní 80 B2
Terpsithéa 83 D4
Ter, R 32 B3
Terracina 63 F3
Terra de Basto 34 B4
Terradets, Emb dels 37 F3
Terråk 97 D4
Terralba 66 B3
Terranova di Pollino 67 E2
Terranuova Braccio lini 61 D4
Terras de Bouro 34 A3
Terrassa 32 A4
Terrasson-la-Villedieu 29 D2
Terrenoire 30 B1
Terriente 41 D2
Terschelling 16 C1
Teruel 41 D2
Tervakoski 107 E2
Tervo 103 D2
Tervola 99 D2
Tervuren 50 C3
Terzaga 40 C2
Tešanj 71 F3
Teslić 71 E3
Tessin 48 C2
Tessy 18 C3
Teste, la 28 A2
Tetbury 9 E2
Teterev 113 E2
Teterow 49 D2
Tetica 44 B3
Tetijev 113 E2
Tetovo 77 D3
Tetrákomo 82 C2
Tettnang 55 D4
Teuchern 53 D2
Teufen 58 B2
Teulada 66 B4
Teupitz 53 E1
Teuva 102 B3
Tevere 63 E2
Teviot 5 D3
Tewkesbury 9 E2
Texel 16 C1
Thabor, Mt 31 D1
Thale 52 C2
Thalfang 54 B1
Thalgau 56 C3
Thalheim 53 E3
Thalmässing 55 F2
Thalwil 58 A2
Thame 9 F2
Thames, R 11 D2
Thanes, K e 76 C4
Thann 27 E1
Thannhausen 55 E3
Thaon 27 D1
Tharandt 53 E2
Tharsis 42 C2
Thássos 80 C3
Thássos, N 81 D3
Thatë, Mal i 77 D4
Thau, Bessin de 30 A4
Thaya 57 F1
Thégonnec 22 B2
Theil, le 23 F3
Themar 52 C3
Thenon 29 D2
Theológos (Stereá Eláda) 83 F3
Theológos (Thássos) 80 C3
Théoule 31 E4
Thérain 19 F3
Thérma (Ikaría) 89 D2

Torino

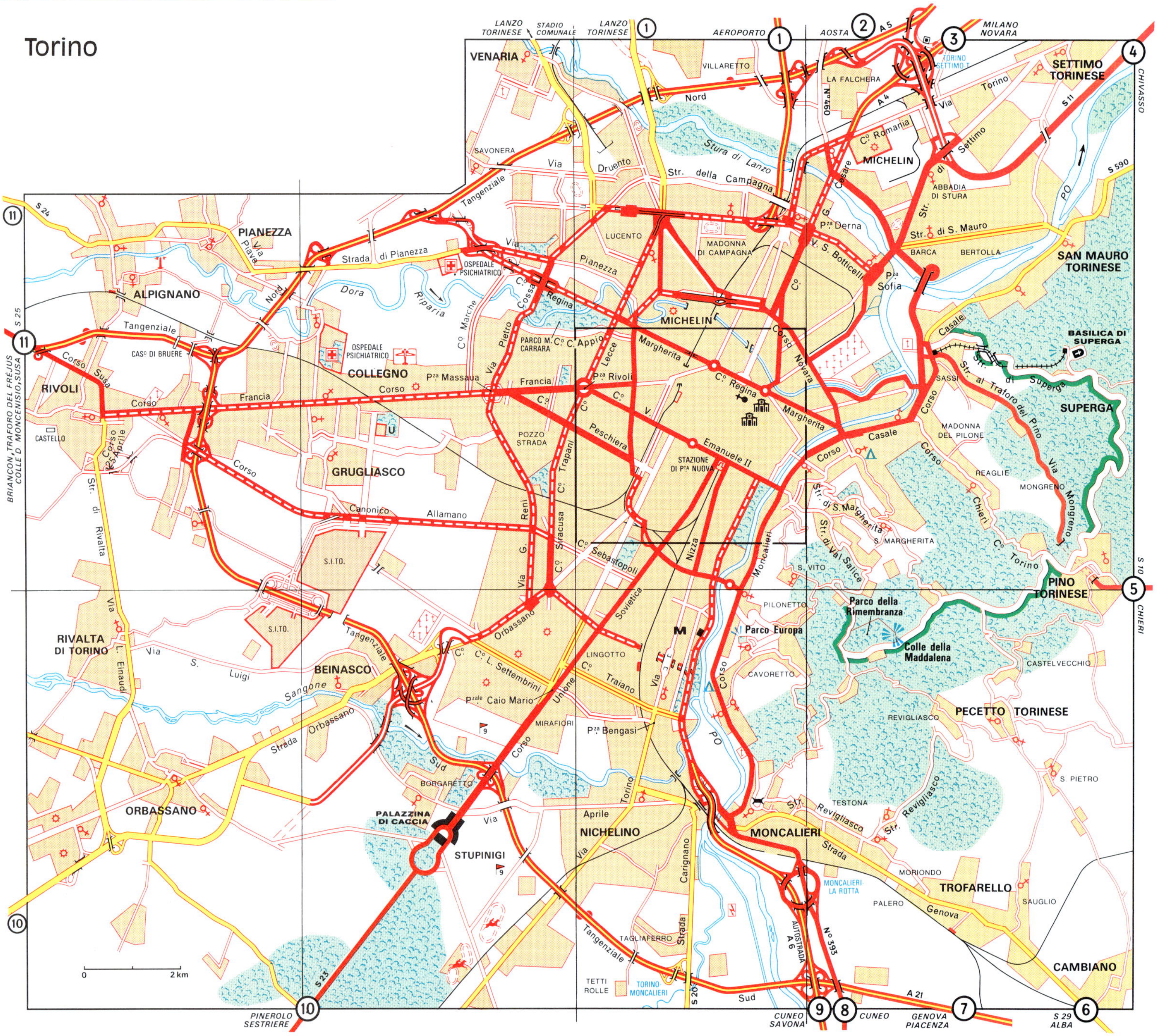
VENARIA
SETTIMO TORINESE
PIANEZZA
ALPIGNANO
SAN MAURO TORINESE
RIVOLI
COLLEGNO
GRUGLIASCO
SUPERGA
BASILICA DI SUPERGA
PINO TORINESE
RIVALTA DI TORINO
BEINASCO
PECETTO TORINESE
ORBASSANO
NICHELINO
MONCALIERI
TROFARELLO
STUPINIGI
PALAZZINA DI CACCIA
CAMBIANO
MICHELIN
LUCENTO
MADONNA DI CAMPAGNA
STAZIONE DI Pta NUOVA
LINGOTTO
MIRAFIORI
CAVORETTO
Parco della Rimembranza
Colle della Maddalena
Parco Europa
Stura di Lanzo
Dora Riparia
PO
Sangone
Tangenziale
AEROPORTO
LANZO TORINESE
STADIO COMUNALE
AOSTA
MILANO NOVARA
CHIVASSO
CHIERI
ALBA
GENOVA PIACENZA
CUNEO SAVONA
CUNEO
PINEROLO SESTRIERE
BRIANCON, TRAFORO DEL FRÉJUS COLLE D. MONCENISIO, SUSA
2 km

Thermá (Makedonía) 80 B2
Thérma (Samothráki) 81 E3
Thermaïkós Kólpos 80 A4
Thérma Lefkádas 89 D2
Thérmi 79 F3
Thermí 85 F2
Thermissia 87 E2
Thérmo 83 D4
Thermopiles 83 E3
Thérouanne 19 F1
Thespiés 83 F4
Thesprotía 82 B2
Thesprotikó 82 B2
Thessalía 83 E2
Thessaloníki 79 F3
Thessaloníki (Nomos) 80 A3
Thetford 11 D1
Theux 51 D4
Thèze 28 B4
Thézenay 24 C3
Thíamis 82 B1
Thiaucourt 21 D3
Thiberville 19 D3
Thiéblemont-Farémont 20 C4
Thiendorf 53 E2
Thiene 59 D4
Thiers 26 B4
Thiesi 66 B2
Thiessow 49 D1
Thillot, le 27 E1
Thimariá 81 F2
Thímena 89 E2
Thímena, N 89 E2
Thiní, Akr 87 E2
Thionville 21 D3
Thira 91 E1
Thira, N 91 E1
Thirassia, N 91 E1
Thirsk 7 D1
Thisted 108 A2
Thiva 84 A4
Thiviers 28 C1
Thizy 26 B4
Thoissey 26 C4
Tholen 16 B3
Tholey 54 B1
Thollon 27 E3
Tholó 86 C2
Tholopotámi 85 E4
Thólos 80 B2
Thomastown 15 D3
Thônes 27 D4
Thonon 27 D3
Thorens-Glières 27 D4
Thorikó 88 A2
Thorne 7 D2
Thornhill 4 C3
Thouarcé 24 C2
Thouars 24 C3
Thouet 24 C2
Thouría 86 C3
Thoúrio 81 F1
Thráki 81 E2
Thrakikó Pélagos 81 D3
Thrapston 9 F1
Threshfield 6 C1
Thueyts 30 B2
Thuile, la 27 E4
Thuin 50 B4
Thuir 32 B2
Thum 53 E3
Thun 27 E3
Thur 58 A1
Thüringen 58 B2
Thüringen (Land) 52 C3
Thüringer Wald 52 B3
Thurles 14 C3
Thurn, Paß 59 E1
Thursby 5 D4
Thurso 3 D2
Thury-Harcourt 18 C3
Thusis 58 B3
Thy 108 A2
Thyborøn 108 A2
Tibro 109 D1
Tichvin 111 E1
Ticino 60 A1
Ticino *R* 58 A3
Tidaholm 109 D1
Tidö 106 A3
Tiefenbronn 54 C2
Tiefencastel 58 B3
Tiefensee 49 E4
Tiel 16 C3
Tielt 50 A3
Tienen 50 C3
Tiengen 54 C4
Tierbmesvarri 94 C3
Tiercé 23 E4
Tierga 36 C3
Tierp 106 B3
Tiétar, R 39 E2
Tigharry 2 A3
Tighnabruaich 4 B2
Tignes 31 D1
Tignes, Bge de 31 E1
Tiheró 81 F2
Tihio 79 D3
Tihuța 113 D4
Tiilikkajärvi 103 E1
Tiistenjoki 102 C2
Tijesno 74 C1
Tijola 44 B3
Tikkakoski 103 D3
Tikkala 103 F2
Tikveš, Ez 77 E3
Tilburg 16 C3
Tilbury 10 C2
Tilissos 91 D3
Tillberga 106 A3
Tillières 19 E4
Tilly-sur-Seulles 18 C3
Tílos, N 89 F4
Timanfaya, Parque Nac. de 42 C3
Timbáki 91 D4
Timbano 81 D2
Timfi, Óros 78 C4
Timfristós 83 D3
Timfristós *Mt* 83 D3
Timiș 114 C1
Timișoara 114 C1
Timmelsjoch 58 C2
Timmendorfer Strand 48 B2
Timok 73 F3
Timoleague 14 B4
Timrå 101 F3
Timv. Peristéria 86 C3
Tinahely 13 D4
Tinchebray 18 C4
Tindari 69 D2
Tinée 31 E3
Tineo 35 D1
Tingáki 89 F3
Tinglev 108 A4
Tingsryd 109 E2
Tingvoll 100 B2
Tingvollfjorden 100 B2
Tinja 71 F3
Tinn 104 C3
Tinnsjø 104 C3
Tínos 88 C2
Tiñosillos 39 F1
Tínos, N 88 C2
Tiñoso, C 45 D3
Tintagel 8 B3
Tinténiac 23 D3
Tinto, R 42 C2
Tiobraid Árann 14 C3
Tione di Trento 58 C3
Tipasoja 103 E1
Tipperary 14 C3
Tipperary (Co) 12 C4
Tiranë 76 C4
Tirano 58 C3
Tiraspol' 113 E3
Tire 115 F4
Tiree 2 A4
Tirgo-Neamt 113 D4
Tirgoviște 115 D1
Tirgu Frumos 113 E3
Tirgu Jiu 114 C1
Tirgu Mureș 113 D4
Tirgu Secuiesc 113 D4
Tirig 41 F2
Tírintha 87 D2
Tiriolo 67 F3
Tírnavos 83 E1
Tirol 58 C2
Tirós 87 D3
Tirrenia 60 C4
Tirreno, Mare 68 B2
Tirschenreuth 53 D4
Tirso 66 B2
Tirstrup 108 B3
Tirteafuera, R 39 F4
Tisa 72 C2
Tiscar, Pto de 44 B2
Tisnaren 105 F4
Tišnov 57 E1

Tisvildeleje 108 C3
Tisza 112 B4
Tiszafüred 112 B4
Tiszavasvári 112 C3
Titaguas 41 D3
Titaríssios 83 E1
Titel 72 C2
Titisee 54 C4
Titlis 58 A3
Tito 64 C4
Titograd 76 B3
Titova Korenica 70 C4
Titova Mitrovica 77 D1
Titov Drvar 71 D4
Titovo Užce 72 C4
Titov Veles 77 E3
Titov vrh 77 D3
Titran 100 B1
Tittmoning 56 B3
Tiumpan Head 2 B2
Tivat 76 B3
Tiveden 105 E4
Tivenys 41 F2
Tiverton 8 C3
Tivissa 41 F1
Tivoli 63 E2
Tjaktjajaure 98 A2
Tjällmo 105 F4
Tjeggelvas 98 A2
Tjeldøya 94 B3
Tjeldstø 104 A2
Tjentište 76 A1
Tjøme 104 C4
Tjong 97 E2
Tjørnuvik 96 A3
Tjøtta 97 D3
Tkon 74 C1
Tobarra 44 C1
Tobercurry 12 B2
Tobermore 13 D2
Tobermory 2 B4
Toberonochy 4 B1
Toblach 59 E2
Toce 58 A3
Tocha 38 B2
Tocina 43 D2
Todi 63 E1
Todmorden 6 C2
Todorići 71 E4
Todtmoos 54 C4
Todtnau 54 C4
Toe Head (GB) 2 A2
Toe Head (IRL) 14 B4
Töfsingdalen 101 D3
Toft 3 F1
Tofte 104 C3
Toftir 96 A4
Toftlund 108 A4
Tohmajärvi 103 F2
Toholampi 102 C1
Toijala 107 E2
Toivakka 103 D3
Toivala 103 E2
Tojšici 72 B3
Tok 53 F4
Tokaj 112 C3
Tolbuhin 115 E2
Toledo 40 A3
Toledo, Mts de 40 A3
Tolentino 61 F4
Tolfa 63 D2
Tolga 100 C3
Tollarp 109 D3
Tollense 49 D2
Tølløse 108 C3
Tolmezzo 59 E3
Tolmin 70 A2
Toló 87 D2
Tolosa (E) 36 C1
Tolosa (P) 38 C3
Tolox 43 E4
Tolva 99 E2
Tolve 65 D4
Tomar 38 B3
Tomaševac 73 D2
Tomaševo 76 B2
Tomašica 71 D3
Tomaszów Lubelski 112 C2
Tomaszów Mazowiecki 112 B2
Tombebœuf 28 C3
Tomelilla 109 D3
Tomelloso 40 B4
Tomiño 34 A3
Tomintoul 3 D4
Tomma 97 D2
Tømmervøg 100 B2
Tomra 100 B2
Tomtabacken 109 D2
Tona 32 B3
Tonale, Pso del 58 C3
Tonara 66 B3
Tonbridge 10 C3
Tondela 38 B1
Tønder 108 A4
Tongeren 50 C3
Tongue 2 C2
Tonnay-Boutonne 24 C4
Tonnay-Charente 24 C4
Tonneins 28 C3
Tonnerre 26 B1
Tönning 47 F2
Tønsberg 104 C3
Tonstad 104 B4
Töpen 53 D3
Topeno 107 E2
Topla 70 B1
Toplica 77 D1
Topli Do 73 F4
Toplita 113 D4
Toploú 91 F4
Topola 73 D3
Topolčani 77 E4
Topol'čany 112 B3
Topólia 90 B3
Topolovnik 73 E3
Topusko 70 C3
Torà de Riubregòs 32 A3
Torano Castello 67 E2
Torbay 8 C4
Torbole 58 C4
Torcello 61 D1
Torchiarolo 65 F3
Tordera 32 B4
Tordesillas 35 E4
Tordesilos 41 D2
Tore 2 C3
Töre 98 C3
Töreboda 105 E4
Torella d. Sannio 64 B3
Toreno 34 C2
Torgau 53 E2
Torgelow 49 E2
Torhout 50 A3
Torigni 18 C3
Torija 40 B2
Torino 31 E1
Torio, R 35 D2
Torla 37 E2
Törmänen 95 F3
Törmänmäki 99 E4
Tormes, R 39 E1
Tormos 37 D3
Tornavacas 39 E2
Tornavacas, Pto de 39 E2
Torneälven 94 C4
Torneträsk 94 C3
Tornik 76 B1
Tornio 98 C3
Tornionjoki 98 C2
Tornjoš 72 C1
Toro 35 D4
Törökszentmiklós 112 B4
Toro, Monte 45 F1
Toróni 80 B4
Toropec 111 E2
Torpo 104 C2
Torpoint 8 C4
Torpshammar 101 F3
Torquay 8 C4
Torquemada 35 F3
Torralba de Calatrava 40 A4
Torrão 42 B1
Torre 38 C2
Torre Annunziata 64 B4
Torre Baja 41 D3
Torre Beretti 60 A2
Torreblanca 41 F3
Torrecaballeros 40 A1
Torrecampo 43 F1
Torre Canne 65 E3
Torrecilla 43 E4
Torrecilla en Cameros 36 B2
Torrecillas de la Tiesa 39 E3
Torre de Abraham, Emb de 40 A3
Torre de D. Chama 34 C4
Torre de Embesora 41 E2
Torre de Juan Abad 44 B1
Torre del Aguila, Emb de 43 D3
Torre de la Higuera 42 C3
Torre del Bierzo 35 D2
Torre del Campo 44 A2
Torre del Greco 64 B4
Torre del Mar 43 F4
Torredembarra 37 F4
Torre de Moncorvo 34 C4
Torre de Passeri 64 A2
Torre d. Impiso 68 A3
Torredonjimeno 43 F2
Torre Faro 69 E2
Torre Grande 66 A3
Torregrossa 37 F4
Torreira 38 B1
Torrejoncillo 39 D2
Torrejoncillo del Rey 40 C3
Torrejón de Ardoz 40 B2
Torrejón de la Calzada 40 A2
Torrejón el Rubio 39 E3
Torrejón-Tajo, Emb de 39 E3
Torre la Carcel 41 D2
Torrelaguna 40 B1
Torrelapaja 36 C3
Torrelavega 35 F2
Torrellano 45 E2
Torrelobatón 35 E4
Torrelodones 40 A2
Torremaggiore 64 B2
Torremegia 39 D4
Torre Mileto 64 C2
Torre Miró, Pto de 41 E2
Torremocha 39 D3
Torremolinos 43 F4
Torrent 41 E4
Torrente de Cinca 37 E4
Torrenueva 44 B1
Torre Orsáia 67 D1
Torre-Pacheco 45 D2
Torre Pellice 31 E2
Torreperogil 44 B2
Torres del Rio 36 B2
Torres Novas 38 B3
Torres Vedras 38 A3
Torrevieja 45 D2
Torrico de San Pedro 38 C3
Torri del Benaco 60 C1
Torridon 2 B3
Torridon, L 2 B3
Torriglia 60 A3
Torrijas 41 D3
Torrijo 36 C4
Torrijos 40 A3
Tørring 108 A3
Torrita di Siena 61 D4
Torroella de Montgrí 32 C3
Torröjen 101 D1
Torrox 43 F4
Torsås 109 E3
Torsby 105 E3
Torshälla 106 A3
Tórshavn 96 A4
Torsken 94 B2
Torsminde 108 A2
Tórtoles de Esgueva 35 F4
Tortoli 66 C3
Tortona 60 A2
Tortorici 69 D2
Tortosa 41 F2
Tortosendo 38 C2
Toruń 112 B1
Torup 108 C2
Tørvikbygd 104 B2
Tory I 12 C1
Toržok 111 F2
Torzym 49 F4
Toscana 60 C4
Toscolano Maderno 60 C1
Tosenfjorden 97 D3
Toses, Collada de 32 A3
Tosno 111 D1
Tossa 32 B4
Tostedt 48 A3
Totak 104 B3
Totana 44 C2
Tôtes 19 E3
Totes Gebirge 56 C3
Tøtlandsvik 104 A3
Totnes 8 C4
Toucy 26 A1
Toul 21 D4
Toulon (Saône-et-Loire) 26 B3
Toulon (Var) 31 D4
Toulouse 29 D4
Toumbítsi 86 C2
Touques 19 D3
Touquet-Paris-Plage, le 19 E1
Tourcoing 19 F1
Tour-d'Auvergne, la 29 E1
Tour-du-Pin, la 30 C1
Tour-Fondue, la 31 D4
Touriñan, C 34 A1
Tourlída 82 C4
Tourmalet, Col du 37 E2
Tournai 50 A4
Tournan 19 F4
Tournay 37 E1
Tournoël 26 A4
Tournon-d'Agenais 28 C3
Tournon-St-Martin 25 D3
Tournon-sur-Rhône 30 B2
Tournus 26 C3
Tourouvre 19 D4
Tours 25 D2
Toury 25 E1
Toussuire, la 31 D1
Toutes Aures, Col de 31 D3
Touvet, le 30 C1
Toužim 53 E4
Tovariševo 72 B2
Tovarnik 72 B2
Tovdal selva 104 B4
Tovel, L di 58 C3
Tøvik 100 B2
Towcester 9 F1
Töysä 102 C2
Trabanca 34 C4
Trabancos, R 39 F1
Trabazos 34 C4
Traben-Trarbach 54 B1
Trabla 68 B3
Trabotivište 77 F2
Tracino 68 A4
Trafalgar, C de 43 D4
Trafaria 38 A4
Trafoi 58 C3
Tragacete 41 D2
Trahiá 87 E2
Trahili 84 B4
Tráhilos, Akr 83 F4
Tráhilos, Akr (Dodekánissa) 89 F4
Tráhilos, Akr (Stereá Eláda) 83 E4
Traiguera 41 F2
Traisen 57 E3
Traisen R 57 E3
Traiskirchen 57 F3
Traismauer 57 E2
Trajanova Tabla 73 E2
Trakai 110 C4
Trakošćan 70 C1
Tralee 14 A3

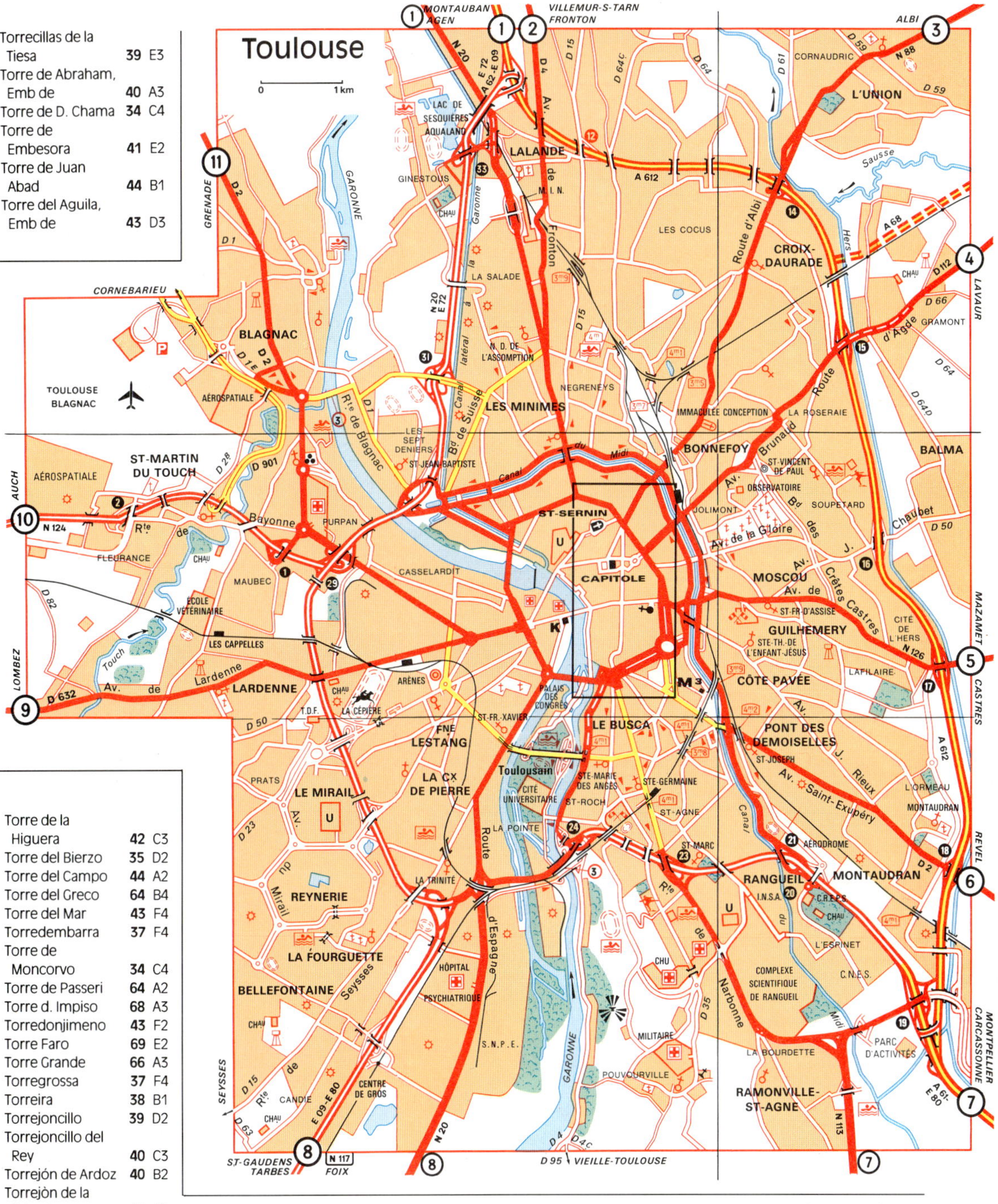

Toulouse
0 1 km
MONTAUBAN AGEN
VILLEMUR-S-TARN FRONTON
ALBI
LAVAUR
MAZAMET CASTRES
REVEL
MONTPELLIER CARCASSONNE
VIEILLE-TOULOUSE
ST-GAUDENS TARBES
FOIX
SEYSSES
LOMBEZ
AUCH
GRENADE
CORNEBARIEU
TOULOUSE BLAGNAC
BLAGNAC
AÉROSPATIALE
ST-MARTIN DU TOUCH
LALANDE
GINESTOUS
LES COCUS
CROIX-DAURADE
L'UNION
CORNAUDRIC
BALMA
LES MINIMES
NEGRENEYS
LA SALADE
BONNEFOY
ST-SERNIN
CAPITOLE
CASSELARDIT
MAUBEC
PURPAN
FLEURANCE
LES CAPPELLES
LARDENNE
MOSCOU
GUILHEMERY
CÔTE PAVÉE
PONT DES DEMOISELLES
LE BUSCA
FNE LESTANG
LA CX DE PIERRE
LE MIRAIL
PRATS
REYNERIE
LA FOURGUETTE
BELLEFONTAINE
RANGUEIL
MONTAUDRAN
L'ORMEAU
POUVOURVILLE
RAMONVILLE-ST-AGNE
CANDIE
CENTRE DE GROS
COMPLEXE SCIENTIFIQUE DE RANGUEIL
PARC D'ACTIVITÉS
LA BOURDETTE
L'ESPINET
C.N.E.S.
GARONNE
Canal du Midi
Toulousain

Tralee B 14 A3
Trá Lí 14 A3
Tramagal 38 B3
Tramariglio 66 A2
Tramatza 66 B3
Tramonti di Sopra 59 E3
Tramore 15 D4
Tranås 109 D1
Tranche, la 24 B4
Tranco, Emb del 44 B2
Trancoso 38 C1
Trandrandsfjällen 101 D4
Tranebjerg 108 B3
Tranemo 109 D2
Tranent 5 D2
Trænfjorden 97 D2
Trani 65 D3
Tranóvalto 79 E4
Tranøy 94 B3
Tranquera, Emb de la 36 C4
Transilvania 113 D4
Transtrand 101 D4
Trapani 68 A3
Trápeza 86 C1
Trappstadt 52 C4
Trasacco 63 F2
Trasimeno, L 61 D4
Trás os Montes 34 B4
Trassem 54 A1
Trasvase Tajo Segura, Canal de 40 C4
Traun 57 D3
Traun *R* 56 C3
Traunkirchen 56 C3
Traunreut 56 B3
Traunsee 56 C3
Traunstein 56 B3
Travemünde 48 B2
Travnik 71 E4
Trayas, le 31 E4
Trbovlje 70 B2
Trbuk 71 F3
Trbušani 73 D4
Trdinov Vrh 70 C2
Trebbia 60 B2
Trebbin 49 D4
Trébeurden 22 B2
Trebević nac park 76 A1
Třebíč 57 E1
Trebinje 76 A2
Trebisacce 67 F2
Trebišnjica 75 F2
Trebišov 112 C3
Trebnje 70 B2
Třeboň 57 D1
Tréboul 22 A3
Trebsen 53 D2
Trebujena 43 D3
Trecastagni 69 D3
Trecate 60 A1
Tre Croci, Pso 59 D2
Tredegar 9 D2
Tredozio 61 D3
Treene 48 A1
Treffort 26 C4
Treffurt 52 B3
Trefynwy 9 D2
Tregaron 8 C1
Trégastel 22 B2
Tregnago 60 C1
Tregony 8 B4
Tréguier 22 C2
Trehörningsjö 102 A1
Treia (D) 47 F1
Treia (I) 61 F4
Treignac 29 D1
Trelleborg (S) 108 C4
Trelleborg (SF) 108 B3
Trélon 20 B2
Tremblade, la 28 A1
Tremestieri 69 D2
Tremezzo 58 B4
Tremiti, I 64 C2
Tremp 37 F3
Trenčin 112 B3
Trendelburg 52 A2
Trentino-Alto Adige 58 C3
Trento 59 D3
Trent, R 7 D2
Trepča (Crna Gora) 76 C2
Trepča (Kosovo) 77 D1
Tréport, le 19 E2
Trepuzzi 65 F4
Tresco 8 A4
Trescore Balneario 60 B1
Tresenda 58 B3
Tresfjord 100 B2
Tresjuncos 40 B3
Treska 77 D3
Treskavica 75 F1
Tres Mares, Pico de 35 F2
Trešnjevica 73 E4
Trešnjevik 76 B2
Trespaderne 36 A2
Třešť 57 E1
Trets 30 C4
Tretten 104 C1
Treuchtlingen 55 E2
Treuen 53 D3
Treuenbrietzen 53 D1
Treungen 104 B4
Trevélez 44 A3
Trèves 29 F3
Trevi 63 E1
Trévières 18 C3
Treviglio 60 B1
Trevignano Romano 63 E2
Treviño 36 B2
Treviso 59 E4
Trévoux 26 C4
Trezzo sull' Adda 60 A1
Trgovište 77 E2
Trhové Sviny 57 D2
Triánda 93 F1
Tría Nissiá 92 C1
Triaucourt 20 C3
Tribanj Krušćica 70 C4
Triberg 54 C3
Tribsees 49 D2
Tricarico 65 D4
Tricase 65 F4
Tricesimo 59 F3
Trichiana 59 E3
Trie 37 E1
Trieben 57 D4
Trier 54 A1
Trieste 59 F4
Trieste, G di 59 F4
Trifels 54 C2
Trifili 81 F2
Triglav 70 A2
Trigóna 82 C1
Trigueros 42 C2
Trihonída, L 83 D4
Trijueque 40 B2
Tríkala (Makedonía) 79 F3
Tríkala (Nomos) 82 C1
Tríkala (Pelopónissos) 87 D1
Trikala (Thessalía) 83 D1
Trikeri 83 F2
Trilj 75 E1
Trillevallen 101 D2
Trillo 40 C2
Trilofo 83 E3
Trim 13 D3
Trimouille, la 25 D3
Trindade 34 C4
Třinec 112 B3
Tring 9 F2
Tringia 82 C1
Trinità d'Agultu e V. 66 B1
Trinitapoli 64 C3
Trinité, la 22 C4
Trinité-Porhoët, la 22 C3
Trino 31 F1
Triora 31 F3
Tripi 87 D3
Tripití 80 B3
Tripití, Akr 85 D2
Trípoli 87 D2
Triponzo 63 E1
Tripótama 86 C1
Triptis 53 D3
Trisanna 58 C2
Trischen 47 F2
Trittau 48 B3
Trittenheim 54 B1
Trivento 64 B2
Trizina 87 E2
Trlica 76 B1
Trnava 112 A3
Trnovo (Bosna i Hercegovina) 75 F1
Trnovo (Slovenija) 70 A2
Trnova Poljana 75 D1
Troarn 18 C3
Trofa 34 A4
Trofaiach 57 E4
Trofors 97 E3
Trogir 75 D2
Troglav, V. 75 D1
Tróhalos 83 E1
Troia 64 C3
Tróia, Pen de 38 A4
Troina 68 C3
Troisdorf 51 E3
Trois Epis, les 27 E1
Trois-Moutiers, les 24 C3
Trois-Ponts 51 D4
Trojan 115 D2
Trojane 70 B2
Trollhättan 108 C1
Trollheimen 100 C2
Troms 94 C3
Tromsdalen 94 B2
Tromsø 94 B2
Trondheim 100 C2
Trondheimsfjorden 100 C1
Trondsheimsleia 100 B1
Tronö 101 F4
Tronto 63 F1
Troo 23 F4
Troon 4 C2
Tropea 67 E3
Trópea 86 C2
Tropojë 76 C2
Trosa 106 B4
Trossachs, The 4 C1
Trostan 13 E1
Trostberg 56 B3
Trouville 19 D3
Trowbridge 9 D2
Troyes 26 B1
Trpanj 75 E2
Trpezi 76 C2
Trpinja 71 F2
Trsa 76 B2
Tršić 72 B3
Trstenik (Kosovo) 77 D2
Trstenik (Pelješac) 75 E2
Trstenik (Srbija) 73 D4
Trsteno 75 F2
Trubčevsk 111 F4
Trubia 35 D1
Trubia, R 35 D1
Trubjela 76 B2
Truchas 34 C3
Truchtersheim 21 E4
Trujillo 39 E3
Trun 19 D4
Truro 8 B4
Trutnov 112 A2
Truyère, Gorges de la 29 E2
Tryde 109 D3
Trysilelva 100 D3
Tržac 70 C3
Trzcińsko-Zdrój 49 E3
Trzebiatów 49 F1
Trzebież 49 E2
Tržič Golnik 70 A2
Tsamandás 82 B1
Tsambíka 93 F1
Tsangaráda 83 F2
Tsangário 82 B2
Tsaritsani 83 E1
Tsarkassiános 82 B4
Tsotíli 79 D4
Tsoukaládes 82 B3
Tuaim 12 B3
Tuam 12 B3
Tua, R 34 B4
Tuath, L 4 B1
Tubilla del Agua 35 F2
Tübingen 55 D3
Tubre 58 C3
Tučepi 75 E2
Tuchan 32 B2
Tudela 36 C3
Tudela de Duero 35 E4
Tuella, R 34 C3
Tuerto, R 35 D2
Tuffé 23 F3
Tuheljske Toplice 70 C2
Tuhkakylä 103 E1
Tui 34 A3
Tuineje 42 C4
Tukums 110 B2
Tulach Mhór 12 C4
Tulare 77 D1
Tulcea 113 E4
Tul'čin 113 E3
Tulla 12 B4
Tullamore 12 C4
Tulle 29 D1
Tullgarn 106 B4
Tullins 30 C1
Tulln 57 E2
Tullow 13 D4
Tulppio 95 F4
Tulsk 12 C3
Tumba 106 B4
Tunbridge Wells, Royal 10 C3
Tundža 115 E3
Tunnhovdfjorden 104 C2
Tunnsjøen 97 E4
Tuohikotti 107 F2
Tuoro sul Trasimeno 61 D4
Tupalaki 95 E3
Turalići 72 B4
Turballe, la 22 C4
Turbe 71 E4
Turbie, la 31 E3
Turckheim 27 E1
Turda 112 C4
Turégano 40 A1
Turenki 107 E2
Turgutlu 115 F4
Turi 65 E3
Türi 110 C1
Túria, R 41 E3
Turija (Bosna i Hercegovina) 71 F3
Turija (Srbija) 73 E3
Turija (Vojvodina) 72 C2
Turinge 106 B4
Turis 41 E4
Turjak 70 B2
Türkheim 55 E3
Turku 107 D2
Turmiel 40 C1
Turnberry 4 C3
Turnhout 50 C3
Türnitz 57 E3
Turnov 112 A2
Turnu Măgurele 115 D2
Turnu Roșu 113 D4
Turracherhöhe 59 F2
Turre 44 C3
Turriff 3 E3
Tursi 65 D4
Turtola 98 C2
Tuscania 63 D2
Tuse 108 C3
Tušilović 70 C3
Tustna 100 B2
Tutin 76 C1
Tutrakan 115 E2
Tuttlingen 55 D3
Turun ja Porin Lääni 107 D2
Tuturano 65 F3
Tutzing 56 A3
Tuulos 107 E2
Tuupovaara 103 F2
Tuusniemi 103 E2
Tuusula 107 E2
Tuxford 7 D3
Tuzi 76 B3
Tuzla 71 F3
Tvedestrand 104 C4
Tverrfjellet 100 B3
Tvøroyri 96 A4
Tweed, R 5 E2
Twelve Pins, The 12 A3
Twimberg 70 B1
Twist 17 E2
Twistringen 17 F1
Tydal 101 D2
Tyin 104 C1
Tyin *L* 100 B3
Týn 57 D1
Tyndrum 4 C1
Tynemouth 5 E3
Tynkä 102 C1
Tynset 100 C3
Tyräjärvi 99 E3
Tyresö 106 B4
Tyrifjorden 104 C3
Tyringe 109 D3
Tyristrand 104 C3
Tyrnävä 99 D4
Tyrone 13 D2
Tysfjorden 97 F1
Tysnesøy 104 A2
Tysse 104 A2
Tyssebotn 104 A2
Tyssedal 104 B2
Tysvær 104 A3
Tywi 8 C2
Tywyn 6 A3

U

Ub 72 C3
Ubaye 31 D2
Úbeda 44 A2
Überlingen 55 D4
Ubľa 112 C3
Ubli (Crna Gora) 76 B2
Ubli (Lastovo) 75 E3
Ubrique 43 E4
Uchte 17 F2
Učka 70 B3
Uckange 21 D3
Uckfield 10 C3
Uclés 40 B3
Udbina 70 C4
Udbyhøj 108 B2
Uddevalla 108 C1
Uddheden 105 E3
Uddjaure 98 A3
Uden 16 C3
Udine 59 F3
Udovo 77 F3
Udvar 72 A1
Uebigau 53 E2
Uecker 49 E2
Ueckermünde 49 E2
Uelzen 48 B3
Uetersen 48 A2
Uetze 48 B4
Uffenheim 55 E1
Ugao 76 C1
Ugento 65 F4
Ugijar 44 B3
Ugine 27 D4
Uglič 111 F1
Ugljan 74 C1
Ugljan *I* 74 C1
Ugljane 75 E1
Ugljevik 72 B3
Ugra 111 F3
Ugrinovci 73 D3
Uherské Hradiště 112 A3
Uhingen 55 D2
Úhlava 56 C1
Uhrsleben 52 C1
Uig 2 B3
Uimaharju 103 F2
Uithoorn 16 C2
Uithuizen 47 D3
Ukkola 103 F2
Ukmergė 110 C3
Ukonselkä 95 E3
Ukraina 113 E2
Ukrina 71 E3
Ulcinj 76 B3
Uleåborg 99 D3
Ulefoss 104 C3
Uleila del Campo 44 C3
Ulëzë 76 C3
Ulfborg 108 A2
Uljanik 71 D2
Uljanovka 113 E3
Uljma 73 D2
Ullånger 102 A2
Ullapool 2 C3
Ulla, R 34 B2
Ullared 108 C2
Ullava 102 C1
Ulldecona 41 F2
Ullsfjorden 94 C2
Ullswater 5 D4
Ulm 55 E3
Ulmen 51 E4
Ulog 75 F1
Ulricehamn 109 D1
Ulrichsberg 56 C2
Ulsberg 100 C2
Ulsta 3 F1
Ulsteinvik 100 A2
Uludağ 115 F3
Ul'ugai'sa 95 E2
Ulva 4 B1
Ulverston 6 B1
Ulvik 104 B2
Ulvila 107 D1
Ulvsjö 101 E3
Ulzës, Liq i 76 C3
Umag 70 A3
Uman' 113 E3
Umbertide 61 E4
Umbrail, Pass 58 C3
Umbria 63 E1
Umbukta 97 E3
Umčari 73 D3
Umeå 102 B1
Umeälven 98 A4
Umhausen 58 C2
Umin Dol 77 E2
Umka 72 C3
Umljanović 75 D1
Una 71 D3
Unac 71 D4
Unari 99 D1
Unari *L* 99 D1
Uncastillo 37 D2
Unden 105 E4
Undersåker 101 D2
Undredal 104 B2
Uneča 111 F4
Unešić 75 D1
Úněšov 53 E4
Ungeny 113 E3
Ungilde 34 C3
Unhais da Serra 38 C2
Unhošt 53 F4
Unije 70 B4
Universales, Mts 41 D2
Unna 17 E3
Unnaryd 109 D2
Unnukka 103 E2
Unquera 35 F1
Unst 3 F1
Unstrut 52 C2
Unterach 56 C3
Unterhaching 56 A3
Unter-Schleissheim 55 F3
Unterwalden 27 F3
Unterwasser 58 B2
Unterweißenbach 57 D2
Upavon 9 E3
Upinniemi 107 E3
Upper L Erne 13 D2
Uppingham 9 F1
Upplands-Väsby 106 B3
Uppsala 106 B3
Uppsala Län 106 B3
Upton 9 E1
Uras 66 B3
Urbania 61 E3
Urbasa, Pto de 36 C2
Urbasa, Sa de 36 C2
Urbe 60 A3
Urbino 61 E3
Urbión, Sa de 36 B3
Urdos 37 D2
Ure 6 C1
Uredakke 97 E4
Urepel 36 C1
Urfahr 57 D2
Urfeld 56 A4
Urho Kekkonens kansallispuisto 95 F3
Uri (CH) 58 A3
Uri (I) 66 A2
Uriage 30 C1
Urjala 107 E2
Urk 16 C2
Urla 115 E4
Urlingford 14 C3
Urnäsch 58 B2
Urnes 100 B3
Uroševac 77 D2
Urovica 73 F3
Urquiola, Pto 36 B1
Urshult 109 D3
Ursprungpaß 59 D1

Urtivaara 95 D3
Ururi 64 B2
Ury 25 F1
Urziceni 115 E1
Usagre 43 D1
Uşak 115 F4
Ušće 73 D4
Usedom 49 E2
Usedom *I* 49 E1
Useras 41 E3
Usingen 51 F4
Usk 9 D2
Usk *R* 9 D2
Uskoplie 76 A2
Üsküdar 115 F3
Uslar 52 B2
Ussat-les-Bains 32 A2
Ussé 25 D2
Usseglio 31 E1
Ussel 29 E1
Usseln 17 F4
Ustaoset 104 B2
Ustaritz 28 A4
Uster 58 A2
Ustevatn 104 B2
Ustibar 76 B1
Ustica, I di 68 B2
Ustikolina 76 A1
Ústi nad Labem 53 F3
Ustiprača 76 B1
Ustka 110 A4
Ustronie Morskie 49 F1
Ust'užna 111 F1
Utajärvi 99 D4
Utåker 104 A3
Utbjoa 104 A3
Utebo 37 D3
Utelle 31 E3
Utena 110 C3
Utiel 41 D3
Utne 104 B2
Utrecht 16 C3
Utrecht (Prov) 16 C2
Utrera 43 D3
Utrillas 41 E2
Utsjoki 95 E2
Utsjoki *R* 95 E2
Uttendorf (Oberösterreich) 56 C3
Uttendorf (Salzburg) 59 E1
Utting 56 A3
Uttoxeter 6 C3
Uudenmaan Lääni 107 F2
Uukuniemi 103 F3
Uurainen 103 D2
Uusikaarlepyy 102 B2
Uusikaupunki 107 D2
Uvac 76 B1
Uvac *R* 76 B1
Uvdal 104 C2
Uzdin 72 C2
Uzel 22 C3
Uzerche 29 D1
Uzès 30 B3
Užgorod 112 C3
Uzin 113 E2
Uzunköprü 115 E3

V

Vä 109 D3
Vaajakoski 103 D3
Vääkiö 99 E3
Vaala 99 E4
Vaalajärvi 95 E4
Vaalimaa 103 F4
Vaals 51 D3
Vaaraslahti 103 D2
Vaasa 102 B2
Vaasan Lääni 102 C2
Vaassen 17 D2
Vabre 32 B1
Vác 112 B4
Vaccarès, Etang de 30 B4
Vacha 52 B3
Väddö 106 B3
Vadehavet 108 A4
Vadheim 100 A3
Vado Ligure 60 A3
Vadsø 95 F1
Vadstena 109 D1
Vaduz 58 B2
Vadvetjåkka 94 B3
Vaféika 81 D2
Vafiohóri 79 F2
Vågaholmen 97 E2
Vågåmo 100 B3
Vågan 97 E1
Vaganj 75 E1
Vaganski vrh 70 C4
Vágar 96 A3
Våge 104 A2
Vægerløse 108 C4
Vaggeryd 109 D2
Vágia 83 F4
Vagioniá 91 D4
Vagnhärad 106 B4
Vagos 38 B1
Vågsfjorden 94 B3
Vågsøy 100 A3
Vágur 96 A4
Váh 112 B3
Vähäkyrö 102 B2
Vahto 107 D2
Vái 91 F3
Vaiano 60 C3
Vaiges 23 E3
Vaihingen 55 D2
Vailly (Aisne) 20 A3
Vailly (Cher) 26 A2
Vainikkala 103 F4
Vaisaluokta 94 B4
Vaison-la-Romaine 30 C3
Vaksdal 104 A2
Vålådalen 101 D2
Valadares 34 A4
Valais 27 E4
Valalta 70 A3
Valamen 103 E2
Valandovo 77 F3
Val-André, le 22 C2
Valareña 36 C3
Valašské Meziříčí 112 B3
Valax 107 F2
Valberg 31 E3
Vålberg 105 E3
Valbiska 70 B3
Valbo 106 B2
Valbondione 58 B3
Valbonë 76 C2
Valbonnais 31 D2
Val Camonica 58 C4
Valcarlos 36 C1
Valdagno 59 D4
Valdahon 27 D2
Valdaj 111 E1
Val-d'Ajol, le 27 D1
Valdajskaja Vozvyšennost' 111 E2
Valdavia, R 35 E3
Valdeazogues, R 43 F1
Valdecaballeros 39 E4
Valdecabras 40 C3
Valdecañas, Emb de 39 E3
Valdecarros 39 E1
Valdecebollas 35 F2
Valdediós 35 E1
Valdeganga 41 D4
Valdeinfierno, Emb de 44 C2
Valdelacasa de Tajo 39 E3
Valdelinares 41 E2
Valdemarsvik 109 E1
Valdemeca 41 D2
Valdemorillo 40 A2
Valdemoro 40 A2
Valdenoceda 36 A2
Valdeobispo, Emb de 39 D2
Valdepeñas 44 A1
Valdepeñas da Jaén 44 A2
Valderaduey, R 35 D4
Valderas 35 E3
Val de Reuil 19 E3
Valderiès 29 E3
Valderøy 100 A2
Valderrepisa, Pto de 43 F1
Valderrobres 41 F2
Valdestillas 35 E4
Valdeverdeja 39 E3
Valdevimbre 35 D3
Valdezcaray 36 B2
Valdieri 31 E3
Valdihuela 39 F2
Val-d'Isère 31 D1
Valdobbiadene 59 D3
Valdosa 36 A3
Valdres 104 C2
Valdres Flya 100 B3
Vale de Açor 42 B2
Vale de Cambra 38 B1
Vale de Estrela 38 C2
Vale de Prazeres 38 c2
Vale, Emb de 37 F2
Valeggio sul Mincio 60 C1
Valença do Minho 34 A3
Valençay 25 E2
Valence-d'Albigeois 29 E3
Valence (Drôme) 30 C2
Valence (Gers) 28 C3
Valencia 41 E4
Valencia (Prov) 41 D4
Valencia de Alcántara 38 C3
Valencia de Don Juan 35 D3
Valencia de las Torres 43 D1
Valencia del Ventoso 43 D1
Valencia I 14 A4
Valenciennes 20 A1
Valensole 31 D3
Valentano 63 D2
Valentigney 27 E2
Valenza 60 A2
Våler (Hedmark) 105 D2
Våler (Østfold) 105 D3
Valeria 40 C3
Valevåg 104 A3
Valfabbrica 61 E4
Valga 110 C2
Val Gardena 59 D3
Valgorge 30 B2
Valgrisenche 31 E1
Valguarnera Caropepe 68 C3
Valhelhas 38 C2
Valico della Forchetta 64 A2
Valimitika 83 E4
Valíra 86 C3
Valjevo 72 C3
Valjok 95 E2
Valjunguera 41 F1
Valkeakoski 107 E2
Valkeala 107 F2
Valkenburg 51 D3
Valkenswaard 16 C4
Valko 107 F2
Valladolid 35 E4
Vallata 64 C3
Vallbo 101 D2
Valldal 100 B2
Vall d'Alba 41 E3
Valldemossa 45 E2
Vall de Uxó 41 E3
Valle 104 B3
Valleberga 109 D4
Valle Castellana 63 F1
Valle d'Aosta 27 E4
Valle de Abdalajís 43 E3
Valle de la Serena 39 E4
Valle de los Caidos 40 A2
Valle de Matamoros 42 C1
Vallehermoso 42 A4
Vallejera, Pto de 39 E2
Valle-Mosso 31 F1
Vallentuna 106 B3
Valleraugue 29 F3
Vallet 24 B2
Valletta 68 B4
Vallgrund 102 B2
Valli di Comacchio 61 D2
Vallø 108 C3
Vallo della Lucania 67 D1
Valloire 31 D1
Vallombrosa 61 D3
Vallon-en-Sully 25 F3
Vallon-Pont-d'arc 30 B3
Vallorbe 27 D3
Vallorcine 27 E4
Valls 37 F4
Vallsta 101 F4
Valmiera 110 C2
Valmojado 40 A2
Valmont 19 D2
Valmontone 63 F3
Valogne 18 B3
Valongo 34 A4
Valoria la Buena 35 E4
Valpaços 34 b4
Valpalmas 37 D3

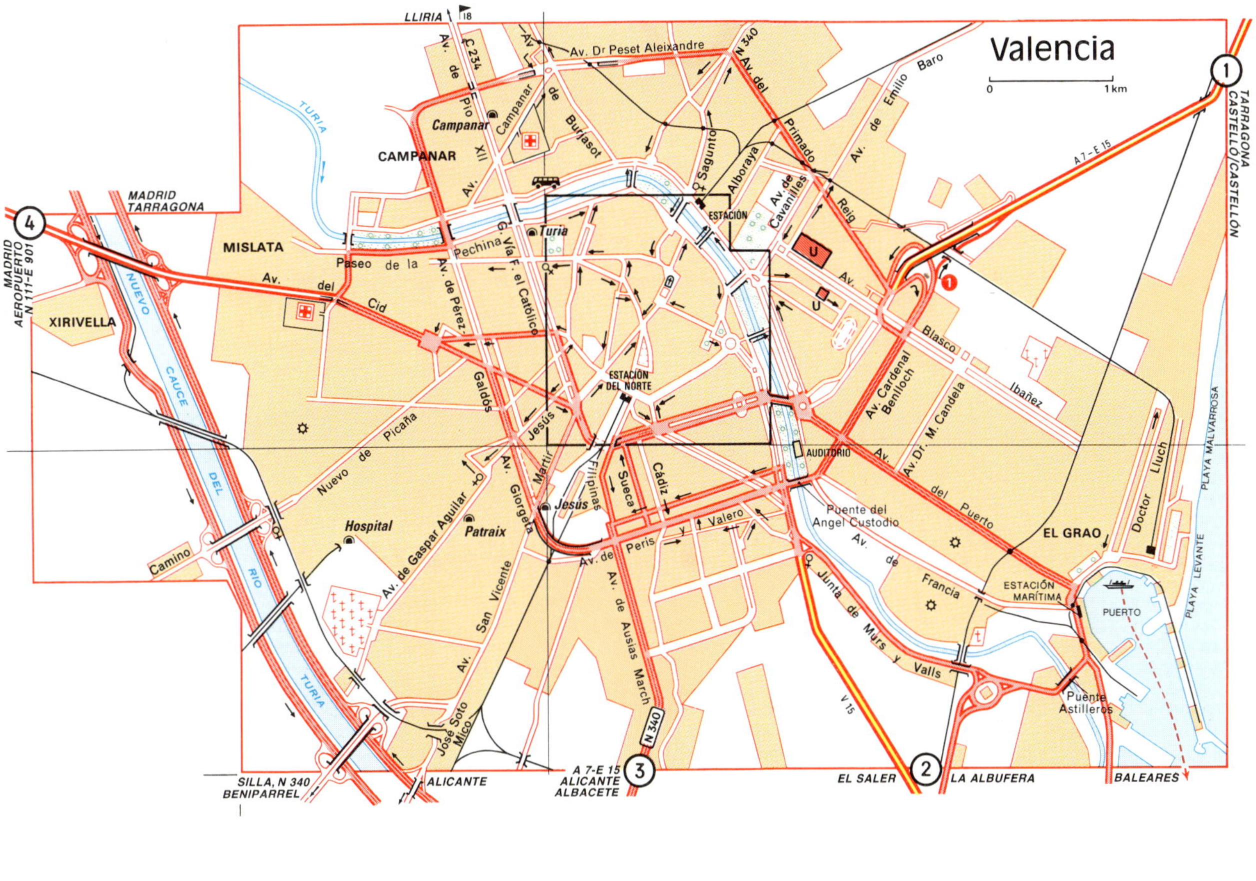

Valencia
0
1 km
LLIRIA
TARRAGONA
CASTELLÓ/CASTELLÓN
MADRID
TARRAGONA
MADRID
AEROPUERTO
N 111-E 901
CAMPANAR
Campanar
MISLATA
XIRIVELLA
Av. Dr Peset Aleixandre
Av. del Cid
Paseo de la Pechina
Turia
ESTACIÓN
ESTACIÓN DEL NORTE
AUDITORIO
Av. Blasco Ibañez
Av. del Puerto
EL GRAO
Doctor Lluch
ESTACIÓN MARÍTIMA
PUERTO
PLAYA MALVARROSA
PLAYA LEVANTE
Puente del Angel Custodio
Av. de Francia
Junta de Murs y Valls
Puente Astilleros
Hospital
Patraix
Av. Nuevo de Picaña
Av. de Gaspar Aguilar
Av. San Vicente
José Soto Mico
Av. de Ausias March
Av. Peris y Valero
Cádiz
Sueca
Filipinas
Jesús
Av. Giorgeta
Av. Pérez Galdós
Gran Vía F. el Católico
Camino
NUEVO CAUCE DEL RIO TURIA
SILLA, N 340
BENIPARREL
ALICANTE
A 7-E 15
ALICANTE
ALBACETE
N 340
EL SALER
LA ALBUFERA
BALEARES

Venezia
300 m
Vaporetti Canal Grande
Linea circolare
LAGUNA
ISOLA S. MICHELE
FONDAMENTE NUOVE
CANAL GRANDE
TORCELLO BURANO
ISOLA S. MICHELE MURANO
VIGNOLE, S. ERASMO
MESTRE TRONCHETTO
TRONCHETTO
CANALE D. GIUDECCA
FUSINA STAZIONE MARITTIMA
CANAL GRANDE
S. ELENA, LIDO
LIDO
CHIOGGIA
Chiesa del Redentore
Campo Ghetto Nuovo
Ghetto
Rio Terrà S. Leonardo
Campo S. Geremia
Pal. Labia
Anconeta
Rio Terrà Maddalena
Lista di Spagna
CANAL GRANDE
Lista Vecchia dei Bari
CA' D' ORO
PAL. PESARO
Campo S. Giac. dall' Orio
Campo Naz. Sauro
Campo dei Gesuiti
Fondamente Nuove
Strada Nova
Campo S.S. Apostoli
S. Mª DEI MIRACOLI
Scuola di S. Marco
S. ZANIPOLO
RIO DEI MENDICANTI
Piazzale Roma
Corte Canal
Fondamenta S. Simeon Piccolo
Calle Lunga
Calle della Laca
Calle del Botter
Calle del Paradiso
S. Mª GLORIOSA DEI FRARI
SCUOLA D. S. ROCCO
Campo dei Frari
Campo S. Rocco
Campo S. Polo
PTE DI RIALTO
Riva del Carbon
Campo S. Mª Formosa
Salizzada S. Lio
PAL. QUERINI STAMPALIA
S. Francesco della Vigna
Campo S. Francesco
Campo S. Lorenzo
SCUOLA DI S. GIORGIO DEGLI SCHIAVONI
Rio Terrà dei Pensieri
S. Pantaleone
Rio Nuovo
SCUOLA DEI CARMINI
Campo S. Margherita
Fondamenta d'Arzere
PAL. REZZONICO
Campo Manin
C. dei Fabbri
Marzarie
Calle Lion
BASILICA
S. ZACCARIA
PTE DEI SOSPIRI
Prigioni
PZA S. MARCO
PROCURATIE
PAL. DUCALE
Pte d. Paglia
Riva d. Schiavoni
Arsenal
Campo della Tana
Via Garibaldi
Riva Cà di Dio
Riva S. Biagio
Riva dei 7 Martiri
Campo S. Anzolo
Campo Morosini
S. Stefano
Campo S. Samuel
Campo S. Maurizio
Campo S. Mª del Giglio
C. Larga 22 Marzo
Calle Lunga S. Barnaba
Traghetto
Angelo Raffaele
S. Sebastiano
STAZIONE MARITTIMA
GALLERIE DELL' ACCADEMIA
S. MARIA DELLA SALUTE
Campo S. Gregorio
Dogana di Mare
Piscina d. Forner
Rio Terrà M. Foscarini
Zattere al Ponte Lungo
Zattere ai Gesuati
Zattere allo Spirito Santo
Zattere ai Saloni
CANALE DELLA GIUDECCA
CANAL DI SAN MARCO
S. GIORGIO MAGGIORE
ISOLA DI S. GIORGIO
TEATRO VERDE
ISOLA SACCA FISOLA
Isola della Giudecca
Fondam. S. Giacomo

Valparaiso, Emb de 35 D3
Val Passiria 59 D2
Valpovo 71 F2
Valprato Soana 31 E1
Valras-Plage 30 A4
Valréas 30 C3
Valsamónero 91 D4
Valsavarenche 31 E1
Valserine 27 D4
Valset 100 C1
Valsjöbyn 101 E1
Vals-les-Bains 30 B2
Valtellina 58 B3
Valtessiniko 86 C2
Val-Thorens 31 D1
Valtierra 36 C3
Valtimo 103 E1
Váltos 81 F1
Valtotópi 80 B2
Váltou, Óri 82 C2
Valtournenche 27 F4
Valun 70 B4
Valvasone 59 E3
Valverde (Is Canarias) 42 A4
Valverde (La Rioja) 36 C3
Valverde del Camino 42 C2
Valverde de Leganés 38 C4
Valverde del Fresno 39 D2
Valverde del Júcar 40 C3
Valøya 97 D4
Våmb 109 D1
Våmhus 101 E4
Vamlingbo 109 F4
Vammala 107 D1
Vampula 107 D2
Vamvakás, Akr 85 F4
Vamvakoú (Pelopónissos) 87 D3
Vamvakoú (Thessalía) 83 E2
Vanajavesi 107 E2
Vanån 101 D4
Vanda 107 E2
Vandellòs 41 F1
Vänern 105 E4
Vänersborg 108 C1
Vangshylla 101 D1
Vangsnes 104 B1
Vangsvik 94 B3
Vanha Vaasa 102 B2
Vanna 94 C2
Vännäs 102 A1
Vannavålen 94 C2
Vannes 22 C4
Vannsjø 105 D3
Vannsundet 94 C2
Vanoise, Massif de la 31 D1
Vanoise, Parc Nat de la 31 D1
Vansbro 105 E2
Vans, les 30 B3
Vantaa 107 E2
Vanttauskoski 99 D2
Vaour 29 D3
Vaqueira 37 F2
Var 31 D4
Vara 108 C1
Varades 23 E4
Varallo 58 A4
Varangerbotn 95 F1
Varangerfjorden 95 F1
Varangerhalvøya 95 F1
Varano de' Melegari 60 B2
Varano, L di 64 C2
Varaždin 70 C1
Varaždinske Toplice 71 D1
Varazze 60 A3
Varberg 108 C2
Vârbica 115 E2
Varda 72 C4
Várda 86 B1
Vardar 77 E3
Varde 108 A3
Vardenik 77 E2
Vardø 95 F1
Vårdö 106 C3
Vardoússia, Óri 83 D3
Varel 47 F3
Vareleíi 84 C4
Varengeville 19 D2
Varenna 58 B4
Varennes-en-Argonne 20 C3
Varennes-sur-Allier 26 A4
Varennes-sur-Amance 26 C1
Vareš 71 F4
Varese 58 A4
Varese Ligure 60 B3
Vårgårda 108 C1
Vargas 35 F2
Vargsund 95 D1
Varhaug 104 A4
Vári (Kikládes) 88 B2
Vári (Stereá Eláda) 87 F1
Varilhes 32 A2
Varimbómbi 87 F1
Váris 79 D4
Varkaus 103 E3
Várkiza 87 F2
Varmahlíð 96 B1
Värmlands Län 105 E3
Varmo 59 E3
Varna (BG) 115 E2
Varna (YU) 72 C3
Värnamo 109 D2
Varnhem 109 D1
Varnsdorf 53 F2
Värö 108 C2
Varoš Selo 77 D2
Varpaisjärvi 103 E1
Várpalota 112 B4
Värriötunturit 95 F4
Vars 31 D2
Vars, Col de 31 D2
Vartdalsfjorden 100 A2
Vartholomió 86 B1
Vartius 99 F4
Värtsilä 103 F2
Varvára 80 B3
Varvarin 73 E4
Varzi 60 A2
Varzy 26 A2
Vasa 102 B2
Vasarapera 99 E2
Vásárosnamény 112 C3
Vascão, Rib do 42 B2
Vasikkaselkä 95 F2
Vasil'kov 113 E2
Vaskijärvi 107 D2
Vaskio 107 E2
Vaskivesi 102 C3
Vaslui 113 E4
Vassarás 87 D3
Vassés 86 C2
Vassieux 30 C2
Vassiliká (Évia) 84 A3
Vassiliká (Lésvos) 85 F2
Vassiliká (Makedonía) 80 A3
Vassilikí (Lefkáda) 82 B3
Vassilikí (Thessalía) 83 D1
Vassilikó 84 B4
Vassilikós 86 A2
Vassilis 83 E2
Vassilítsa 78 C4
Vassy 18 C4
Västanbäck 101 F2
Västanfjärd 107 D3
Vastenjaure 97 F1
Västerås 106 A3
Västerbottens Län 98 A4
Västerdalälven 101 D4
Väster Haninge 106 B4
Västernorrlands Län 101 F2
Västervik 109 E1
Västmanlands Län 105 F3
Vasto 64 B2
Vatan 25 E3
Väte 109 F4
Vaterá 85 F3
Vateró 79 D4
Váthia 87 D4
Vathí (Dodekánissa) 84 B4
Váthi (Lefkáda) 79 F2
Vathí (Makedonía) 92 C1
Vathí (Stereá Eláda) 82 B3
Vathilakos (Dráma) 80 C2
Vathilakos (Kozáni) 79 E4
Vathilakos (Thessaloníki) 79 F3
Vathípetro 91 D4
Vathis 89 F3
Vatin 73 D2
Vatnajökull 96 B2
Vatne 100 B2
Vatólakos 79 D4
Vatopedíou 80 C4
Vatra Dornei 113 D4
Vättern 109 D1
Vattholma 106 B3
Vaucluse 30 C3
Vaucouleurs 20 C4
Vaud 27 D3
Vau i Dejës 76 C3
Vaut të Dejës, Liq i 76 C3
Vauvert 30 B4
Vauvillers 27 D1
Vaux-le-Vicomte 19 F4
Vávdos 80 A3
Växjö 109 D2
Våxtorp 108 C3
Vayrac 29 D2
V'az'ma 111 F3
Veberöd 109 D3
Vecht 17 D2
Vechta 17 F1
Vechte 17 E2
Vecinos 39 E1
Vedelago 59 E4
Vedrá, I 45 D4
Vedungfjället 101 D3
Veendam 47 D3
Veenendaal 16 C3
Veere 16 B3
Vefsna 97 E3
Vefsnfjorden 97 D3
Vega 97 D3
Vega de Espinareda 34 C2
Vegadeo 34 C1
Vega de Valcarce 34 C2
Vegafjorden 97 D3
Vegarienza 35 D2
Vegårshei 104 C4
Vegas 35 E2
Vegas del Condado 35 E2
Vegesack 47 F3
Veghel 16 C3
Vegoritida, L 79 E3
Vehkalahti 103 F4
Vehmaa 101 D2

Vehmersalmi 103 E2
Veidnesklubben 95 E1
Veikkola 107 E2
Veines 95 F1
Veinge 108 C2
Veiros 38 C4
Vejen 108 A3
Vejer de la Frontera 43 D4
Vejle 108 A3
Velada 39 F3
Velagići 71 D4
Vela Luka 75 E2
Velanidia 87 E4
Velate, Pto de 36 C1
Velayos 39 F1
Velbert 17 E4
Velburg 55 F1
Velde 101 D1
Velden (A) 70 A1
Velden (Nüberg) 55 F1
Velden (München) 56 B3
Veldhoven 16 C4
Velebit 70 C4
Velebitski kanal 70 B4
Velenje 70 B1
Velešta 77 D4
Velestino 83 F2
Veleta, Pico 44 A3
Velež 75 F2
Vélez Blanco 44 C2
Vélez de Benaudalla 44 A3
Vélez-Málaga 43 F3
Vélez Rubio 44 C2
Velfjorden 97 D3
Veličani 75 F2
Veliés 87 E4
Velika 71 E2
Velika Drenova 73 E4
Velika Gorica 70 C2
Velikaja 111 D2
Velika Jablanica 76 C2
Velika Jamnička 70 C2
Velika Kapela 70 B3
Velika Kladuša 70 C3
Velika Kopanica 71 F3
Velika Kruša 77 D2
Velika Morava 73 D3
Velika Mučna 71 D1
Velika Plana (Morava) 73 D3
Velika Plana (Prokuplje) 77 D1
Velika Tresta 73 E3
Veliki Alan 70 B4
Veliki Bastaji 71 E2
Veliki Gaj 73 D2
Veliki Grdđevac 71 D2
Veliki Izvor 73 F3
Veliki Jastrebac 77 D1
Velikije Luki 111 E2
Veliki kanal 72 B2
Veliki Krš 73 E3
Veliki Popović 73 E3
Veliki Prolog 75 E2
Veliki Radinci 72 C2
Veliki Trnovac 77 E2
Veliki Vitao 76 A2
Veliki Zdenci 71 D2
Veliko Gradište 73 D2
Veliko Lašče 70 B2
Veliko Orašje 73 D3
Veliko Târnovo 115 D2
Velilla del R Carrion 35 E2
Veli Lošinj 70 B4
Velimlje 76 A2
Vélines 28 C2
Velingrad 115 D3
Velino 63 F2
Velino, Mte 63 F2
Veliž 111 E3
Veljun 70 C3
Velká Biteš 57 E1
Velké Meziříčí 57 E1
Velkua 107 D2
Vellahn 48 B3
Velletri 63 E3
Vellinge 108 C3
Velopoúla 87 F3
Vélos 84 B4
Velpke 48 B4
Velten 49 D4
Velvendós 79 E4
Vemdalen 101 E3
Vemdalsskalet 101 E3
Vemhån 101 E3
Véna 81 E2
Venaco 33 F3
Venafro 64 A3
Venarey-les-Laumes 26 B2
Venaria 31 E1
Venčani 73 D3
Vence 31 E3
Venda Nova 34 B4
Vendas Novas 38 B4
Vendée 24 B3
Vendel 106 B3
Vendeuvre 26 B1
Vendôme 25 E2
Vendsyssel 108 B2
Veneheitto 99 D4
Veneta, Laguna 61 D1
Veneto 61 D1
Venezia 61 D1
Vengjaneset 104 A2
Venialbo 35 D4
Venjan 101 E4
Venjansjön 101 E4
Venlo 17 D4
Vennesla 104 B4
Vennesund 97 D3
Venosa 64 C3
Venosta 58 C3
Venray 17 D3
Venta 110 B3
Venta de Cruce 43 D3
Venta de Don Quijote 40 B3
Ventana, Pto de 35 D2
Venta Nueva 34 C2
Ventas de Huelma 44 A3
Ventimiglia 31 E3
Ventnor 9 E4
Ventotene, I 63 F4
Ventoux, Mt 30 C3
Ventspils 110 B2
Venturina 62 C1
Vera (E) 44 C3
Vera (N) 101 D1
Vera de Bidasoa 36 C1
Verbania-Pallanza 58 A4
Verberie 19 F3
Verbicaro 67 E2
Verbier 27 E4
Vercelli 31 F1
Vercel-Villedieu 27 D2
Verchnedvinsk 111 D3
Verdalsøra 101 D1
Verde, Col de 33 F3
Verden 48 A4
Verdikoússa 83 D1
Verdon 31 D3
Verdon, le 28 A1
Verdun (Meuse) 20 C3
Verdun (Saône-et-Loire) 26 C3
Verdun (Tarn-et-Garonne) 29 D3
Verfeil 29 D4
Vergato 60 C3
Vérgi 80 A2
Vergiate 60 A1
Vergina 79 E3
Vergio, Col de 33 F3
Vergt 28 C2
Véria 79 E3
Verin 34 B3
Verl 17 F3
Vermand 20 A2
Vermenton 26 B2
Vérmio, Óros 79 E3
Verna, Pzo di 69 D2
Vernet-les-Bains 32 B2
Verneuil 19 D4
Vernon 19 E3
Vérno, Óros 79 D3
Vernoux-en-Vivarais 30 B2
Verny 21 D3
Veroli 63 F3
Verona 60 C1
Verpillière 30 C1
Verran 101 D1
Verrès 27 F4
Versailles 19 F4
Versmold 17 F2
Verteillac 28 C1
Vertiskos, Óros 80 A2
Vertus 20 B4
Verucchio 61 E3
Veruela 36 C3
Verviers 51 D4
Vervins 20 B2
Verzuolo 31 E2
Verzy 20 B3
Vesanto 103 D2
Vescovato 33 F3
Veselí 57 D1
Vesijärvi 107 F2
Vesilahti 107 E1
Vesivehmaa 107 F2
Vesjegonsk 111 F1
Veskoniemi 95 F3
Vesle 20 B3
Vesoul 27 D2
Véssa 85 E4
Vest-Agder 104 B4
Vestby 105 D3
Vestbygda 104 A4
Vesterålen 94 A3
Vesterø Havn 108 B2
Vestertana 95 E1
Vestfjorden 97 E1
Vestfold 104 C3
Vestmanna 96 A3
Vestmannaeyjar 96 B3
Vestnes 100 B2
Vestone 58 C4
Vestre Jakobselv 95 F1
Vestvågøy 94 A4
Vésubie, Gorges de la 31 E3
Vesuvio 64 B4
Veszprém 112 B4
Veteli 102 C2
Veternica 77 E1
Vetlanda 109 E2
Vetralla 63 E2
Vetriolo Terme 59 D3
Vetschau 53 E1
Vettore, M 63 F1
Veules-les-Roses 19 D2
Veulettes 19 D2
Veurne 50 A3
Vevey 27 E3
Vévi 79 D3
Veynes 30 C2
Veyre 29 F1
Veyrier 27 D4
Vezdemarbán 35 D4
Vézelay 26 B2
Vézelise 21 D4
Vézénobres 30 B3
Vézère 29 D2
Vézins-de-Lévézou 29 E3
Vezzani 33 F3
Vezzano 58 C3
Via Appia 63 F3
Via Aurelia 60 C4
Via Casilina 63 E2
Via Cassia 63 D1
Viadana 60 C2
Via Emilia 61 D3
Via Flaminia 61 E3
Viana 36 B2
Viana do Bolo 34 C3
Viana do Castelo 34 A3
Vianden 21 D2
Viano do Alentejo 42 B1
Viareggio 60 B3
Viar, R 43 D2
Vias 30 A4
Via Salaria 63 E2
Via Tiburtina Valeria 63 F2
Viaur 29 E3
Viborg 108 A2
Vibo Valentia 67 E3
Vibraye 23 F3
Vič 70 B1
Vic (E) 32 A3
Vic (F) 19 F3
Vicálvaro 40 B2
Vicdessos 37 F2
Vic-en-Bigorre 28 B4
Vicenza 59 D4
Vic-Fézensac 28 C4
Vich 32 A3
Vichy 26 A4
Vic-le-Comte 29 F1
Vico 33 E3
Vico del Gargano 64 C2
Vico Equense 64 B4
Vico, Lago di 63 E2
Vic-sur-Cère 29 E2
Victoria 68 B4
Vidå 108 A4
Vidago 34 B4
Viðareidi 96 A3
Vidauban 31 D4
Viddal 100 A3
Videbæk 108 A3
Vidiáki 86 C1
Vidigueira 42 B1
Vidin 114 C2
Vidio, C 35 D1
Viðoy 96 A3
Vidreres 32 B4
Vidrovan 76 B2
Vidsel 98 B3
Viduša 76 A2
Viechtach 56 B2
Viechtwang 56 C3
Vieira 38 A2
Vieira do Minho 34 B4
Viejo, Pto 39 D2
Viekinjärvi 103 F1
Vielha 37 F2
Vielle-Aure 37 E2
Vielmur 32 A1
Vielsalm 51 D4
Vienenburg 52 B1
Vienne 30 B1
Vienne (Dépt) 25 D3
Vienne *R* 25 D4
Vierema 103 D1
Viernheim 54 C1
Vierraden 49 E3
Viersen 17 D4
Vierumäki 107 F2
Vierzehnheiligen 52 C4
Vierzon 25 F2
Vieste 64 C2
Vietas 94 B4
Vietri di Potenza 64 C4
Vietri sul Mare 64 B4
Vieux-Boucau 28 A3
Vieux Chaillol 31 D2
Vif 30 C2
Vig 108 C3
Vigan, le 29 F3
Vigeland 104 B4
Vigeois 29 D1
Vigevano 60 A1
Viggiano 65 D4
Vígla 82 C2
Vígla, Akr 91 D1
Vignale 31 F1
Vignanello 63 E2
Vignemale 37 E2
Vignes, les 29 F3
Vigneulles 20 C3
Vignola 60 C2
Vignole Borbera 60 A2
Vignory 26 C1
Vigo 34 A3
Vigo di Fassa 59 D3
Vigone 31 E2
Vigonza 61 D1
Vigrestad 104 A4
Vihanti 99 D4
Vihiers 24 C2
Vihtavuori 103 D3
Vihteljärvi 102 C3
Vihti 107 E2
Viiala 107 E2
Viinijärvi 103 F2
Viipustunturit 95 E3
Viitasaari 103 D2
Vik (Aust-Agder) 104 B4
Vík (IS) 96 B3
Vik (Nordland) 97 D3
Vik (Sogn og Fjordane) 104 B1
Vika 105 F2
Vikajärvi 99 D2
Vikanes 104 A2
Vikebukt 100 B2
Vikedal 104 A3
Vikersund 104 C3
Vikeså 104 A4
Vikevåg 104 A3
Vikingstad 106 A4
Vikna 97 D4
Vikoč 76 A1
Vikran 94 B2
Viksdalen 100 A3
Viksjö 101 F2
Viksjøfjell 95 F2
Viksta 106 B3
Vila Boim 38 C4
Vilada 32 A3
Viladamat 32 B3
Vila de Cruces 34 B2
Vila de Rei 38 B3
Vila do Bispo 42 A2
Vila do Conde 34 A4
Viladrau 32 B3
Vila Fernando 38 C4
Vila Flor 34 C4
Vila Franca das Naves 38 C1
Vilafranca del Penedès 32 A4
Vila Franca de Xira 38 A4
Vila Fresca de Azeitão 38 A4
Vilagarcia de Arosa 34 A2
Vilaine 22 C4
Vilaller 37 F2
Vilán, C 34 A1
Vilanova 34 C1
Vila Nova da Barquinha 38 B3
Vilanova de Arousa 34 A2
Vila Nova de Cerveira 34 A3
Vila Nova de Famalicão 34 A4
Vila Nova de Foz Côa 39 D1
Vila Nova de Gaia 34 A4
Vila Nova de Milfontes 42 A2
Vila Nova de Ourém 38 B3
Vila Nova de Paiva 38 C1
Vila Nova de Poiares 38 B2
Vilanova de Sau 32 B3
Vilanova i la Geltrú 32 A4
Vila Pouca de Aguiar 34 B4
Vila Praia de Âncora 34 A3
Vilar de Barrio 34 B3
Vila Real 34 B4
Vila-real 41 E3
Vila Real de Santo António 42 B3
Vila-rodona 37 F4
Vila-seca 37 F4
Vila Velha de Ródão 38 C3
Vila Verde 34 A3
Vila Verde de Ficalho 42 C1
Vila Verde de Raia 34 B3
Vila Viçosa 38 C4
Vilches 44 A2
Vilejka 111 D4
Vilhelmina 97 F4
Vilia 87 E1
Viljakkala 102 C3
Viljandi 110 C2
Vilkaviškis 110 C4
Vilkovo 113 E4
Villa Adriana 63 E2
Villa Bartolomea 60 C1
Villablanca 42 C2
Villablino 35 D2
Villabona 36 C1
Villabrágima 35 E4
Villabuena del Puente 35 D4
Villacãas 40 B3
Villacarriedo 35 F2
Villacarrillo 44 B2
Villacastín 40 A1
Villach 59 F2
Villacidro 66 B4
Villada 35 E3
Villa del Prado 40 A2
Villa del Rio 43 F2
Villadiego 35 F3
Villadossola 27 F4
Villaescusa de Haro 40 C3
Villafáfila 35 D4
Villafamés 41 E3
Villaflores 39 F1
Villafranca 36 C2
Villafranca del Bierzo 34 C2
Villafranca del Cid 41 E2
Villafranca de los Barros 43 D1
Villafranca de los Caballeros 40 B3
Villafranca di Verona 60 C1
Villafranca in Lunigiana 60 B3
Villafranca-Montes de Oca 36 A2
Villafranca Piemonte 31 E2
Villafranca Tirrena 69 D2
Villafranco del Guadalquivir 43 D3
Villafrati 68 B3
Villafrechos 35 E4
Villafruela 35 F4
Villafuerte 35 F4
Villagarcía del Llano 40 C4
Villager 35 D2
Villaggio Mancuso 67 F3
Villagonzalo 39 D4
Villaharta 43 E1
Villahermosa 44 B1
Villahoz 35 F3
Villaines-la-Juhel 23 E3
Villajoyosa 45 E1
Villa, la 59 D2
Villala 103 F3
Villalba 34 B1
Villalba de Guardo 35 E2
Villalba de la Sierra 40 C2
Villalba de los Barros 43 D1
Villalba del Rey 40 C2
Villalcampo, Emb de 35 D4
Villalcázar de Sirga 35 E3
Villalenga 36 C4
Villa Literno 64 A4
Villalón de Campos 35 E3
Villalonga 45 E1
Villalpando 35 E4
Villalpardo 41 D4
Villamañán 35 D3
Villamanrique 44 B1
Villamarchante 41 E3
Villamartín (Andalucía) 43 D3
Villamartín (Castilla-León) 35 E3
Villamassargia 66 B4
Villamayor 37 D3
Villamayor de Campos 35 E3
Villamayor de Santiago 40 B3
Villameca, Emb de 35 D2
Villa Minozzo 60 C3
Villandraut 28 B3
Villandry 25 D2
Villanova Monteleone 66 A2
Villanubla 35 E4
Villanueva de Alcardete 40 B3
Villanueva de Alcolea 41 F3
Villanueva de Alcorón 40 C2
Villanueva de Algaidas 43 F3
Villanueva de Argaño 35 F3
Villanueva de Arzobispo 44 B2
Villanueva de Bogas 40 A3
Villanueva de Cameros 36 B3
Villanueva de Córdoba 43 F1
Villanueva de Franco 40 B4
Villanueva de Gállego 37 D3
Villanueva de la Concepción 43 F3
Villanueva de la Fuente 44 B1
Villanueva de la Jara 40 C4
Villanueva de la Reina 44 A2
Villanueva de la Serena 39 E4
Villanueva de la Sierra 39 D2
Villanueva de las Torres 44 B2
Villanueva de la Vera 39 E2
Villanueva del Campo 35 D3
Villanueva del Duque 43 E1
Villanueva del Fresno 42 C1
Villanueva del Huerva 37 D4
Villanueva de los Castillejos 42 C2
Villanueva de los Infantes 44 B1
Villanueva del Rey 43 E1
Villanueva del Río y Minas 43 D2
Villanueva del Trabuco 43 F3
Villanueva de San Carlos 44 A1
Villa Opicina 59 F3
Villa Potenza 61 F4
Villaquejida 35 D3
Villaquilambre 35 D2
Villarcayo 36 A1
Villard-de-Lans 30 C2
Villar de Cañas 40 C3
Villardecievos 35 D3
Villar de Domingo García 40 C2
Villardefrades 35 E4
Villar del Arzobispo 41 E3
Villar del Rey 39 D4
Villar de Peralonso 39 E1
Villarejo de Fuentes 40 C3
Villarejo de Orbigo 35 D3
Villarejo de Salvanés 40 B2
Villarente 35 E3
Villares de la Reina 39 E1
Villares del Saz 40 C3
Villargordo de Cabriel 41 D4
Villaricos 44 C3
Villarin de Campos 35 D4
Villarino 34 C4
Villarquemado 41 D2
Villarramiel 35 E3
Villarrobledo 40 C4
Villarroya 36 C3
Villarroya de la Sierra 36 C4
Villarroya de los Pinares 41 E2
Villarroya, Pto de 41 E2
Villarrubia de Santiago 40 B3
Villars 27 E3
Villars-les-Dombes 26 C4
Villarta de San Juan 40 B4
Villarubia de los Ojos 40 A4
Villasalto 66 C3
Villasana de Mena 36 A1
Villasandino 35 F3
Villa San Giovanni 67 E4
Villa Santa Maria 64 A2
Villasante 36 A1
Villa Santina 59 E3
Villasarracino 35 E3

Villasayas, Pto de 36 B4
Villaseco de los Reyes 39 E1
Villasequilla de Yepes 40 A3
Villasimius 66 C4
Villasor 66 B4
Villatobas 40 B3
Villatoro, Pto de 39 F2
Villatoya 41 D4
Villava 36 C2
Villavaara 95 F2
Villaverde del Río 43 D2
Villaviciosa 35 E1
Villaviciosa de Córdoba 43 E2
Villaviciosa de Odón 40 A2
Villavieja de Yeltes 39 D1
Villa Vomano 63 F1
Villé 21 E4
Villebois-Lavalette 28 C1
Villedieu, la 25 D3
Villedieu-les-Poêles 18 B4
Ville-en-Tardenois 20 B3
Villefagnan 24 C4
Villefort 29 F3
Villefranche-d'Albigeois 29 E3
Villefranche-de-Lauragais 29 D4
Villefranche-de-Lonchat 28 C2
Villefranche-de-Rouergue 29 E3
Villefranche-du-Périgord 29 D2
Villefranche-sur-Cher 25 E2
Villefranche-sur-Mer 31 E3
Villefranche-sur-Saône 26 C4
Villel 41 D2
Villemur 29 D3
Villena 45 D1
Villenauxe-la-Grande 20 A4
Villeneuve 30 B3
Villeneuve-de-Berg 30 B2
Villeneuve-de-Marsan 28 B3
Villeneuve-l'Archevêque 26 A1
Villeneuve-sur-Lot 28 C3
Villeneuve-sur-Yonne 26 A1
Villeréal 28 C2
Villers 19 D3
Villers-Bocage (Calvados) 18 C3
Villers-Bocage (Somme) 19 F2
Villers-Bretonneux 19 F2
Villers-Cotterêts 19 F3
Villers-devant-Orval 20 C2
Villersexel 27 D2
Villers-Farlay 27 D2
Villers la Ville 50 C4
Villers-le-Lac 27 E2
Villerupt 21 D3
Villerville 19 D3
Ville-sur-Tourbe 20 C3
Villeta Barrea 64 A2
Villiers-St-Georges 20 A4
Villingen-Schwenningen 54 C3
Villoldo 35 E3
Villoria 39 E1
Villotta 59 E3
Villuercas 39 E3
Vilnius 110 C3
Vilppula 102 C3
Vils (Bayern) 55 F1
Vils (Bayern) 56 B2
Vilsbiburg 56 B2
Vilseck 55 F1
Vilshofen 56 C2
Vilusi 76 A2
Vilvoorde 50 B3
Vimercate 60 A1
Vimianzo 34 A1
Vimieiro 38 B4
Vimioso 34 C4
Vimmerby 109 E1
Vimoutiers 19 D4
Vimpeli 102 C2
Vimperk 56 C1
Vinac 71 E4
Vinadio 31 E3
Vinaixa 37 F4
Vinalapó, *R* 45 D2
Vinaròs 41 F2
Vinay 30 C1
Vinça 32 B2
Vinča 73 D3
Vinchiaturo 64 B3
Vinci 60 C3
Vindafjorden 104 A3
Vindelälven 102 A1
Vindelfjällens N.R. 97 E3
Vindeln 102 A1
Vinderup 108 A2
Vindsvik 104 A3
Vingåker 105 F4
Vingelen 100 C3
Vingeveien 100 C3
Vinhais 34 C3
Vinica (Makedonija) 77 F3
Vinica (Slovenija) 70 C3
Viničani 77 E3
Vinje 104 B3
Vinkovci 71 F2
Vinnica 113 E2
Vinsternes 100 B2
Vinstra 100 C3
Vinstri 104 C1
Vintilänkaira 95 F4
Viñuelas 40 B2
Vinuesa 36 B3
Viotia 83 F4
Vipava 70 A2
Vipava *R* 70 A2
Vipiteno 59 D2
Vir (Bosna i Hercegovina) 75 E1
Vir (Hrvatska) 70 C4
Vir *I* 70 C4
Vira 75 D2
Vire 18 C4
Virgen 59 E2
Virgen de la Cabeza 43 F2
Virginia 13 D3
Virieu 30 C1
Virieu-le-Grand 27 D4
Virihaure 97 F1
Virkby 107 E3
Virkkala 107 E3
Virkkula 99 E2
Virksund 108 A2
Virmasvesi 103 D2
Virmutjoki 103 F3
Virolahti 103 F4
Virónia 80 A2
Virovitica 71 E2
Virpazar 76 B3
Virrat 102 C3
Virsbo 105 F3
Virserum 109 E2
Virsko more 70 C4
Virtasalmi 103 E3
Virton 20 C3
Virtsu 110 B2
Vis 75 D2
Vis *I* 75 D2
Visaurin 37 D2
Visby 109 F4
Visé 51 D3
Višegrad 72 C4
Višegradska Banja 72 C4
Viserba 61 E3
Viseu 38 C1
Viševica 70 B3
Viskan 108 C2
Viški kan 75 D2
Višnja Gora 70 B2
Višnjica 73 D3
Visočica 75 F1
Visočica *R* 73 F4
Viso del Marqués 44 A1
Visoki Dečani 76 C2
Visoko 71 F4
Visovac 75 D1
Visp 27 F3
Vissani 78 B4
Visselhövede 48 A3
Vissenbjerg 108 B3
Vissiniá 79 D3
Visso 63 F1
Vistabella del Maestrazgo 41 E2
Vistasväggi 94 B4
Vistheden 98 B3
Vistonída, L 81 D2
Visuvesi 102 C3
Vitaby 109 D3
Vítala 84 B4
Vitanovac 73 D4
Vitebsk 111 E3
Viterbo 63 E2
Vitez 71 E4
Vitigudino 39 D1
Vitina 86 C2
Vitina (Bosna i Hercegovina) 75 E2
Vitina (Kosovo) 77 D2
Vitlycke 105 D4
Vito d'Asio 59 E3
Vitoli 83 D3
Vitolište 77 E4
Vitomirica 76 C2
Vitoria-Gasteiz 36 B2
Vitorog 71 E4
Vitoša 115 D2
Vitovlje 71 E4
Vitré 23 D3
Vitrey 27 D1
Vitry-en-Artois 19 F2
Vitry-le-François 20 B4
Vitsa 78 C4
Vitsand 105 E2
Vittangi 94 C4
Vittangiälven 94 C4
Vitteaux 26 B2
Vittel 27 D1
Vittoria 69 D4
Vittoriosa 68 B4
Vittorio Veneto 59 E3
Vittsjö 109 D3
Vitznau 58 A2
Viù 31 E1
Vivaro 59 E3
Vivel del R Martín 41 E2
Viver 41 E3
Viverio 34 B1
Viverols 29 F1
Viveros 44 B1
Vivier, le 18 B4
Viviers 30 B2
Vivonne 25 D4
Vizille 30 C2
Vižinada 70 A3
Vizitsa 83 F2
Vižnica 113 D3
Vizzavona 33 F3
Vizzavona, Col de 33 F3
Vizzini 69 D4
Vjosë 114 B4
Vlaardingen 16 B3
Vladičin Han 77 E1
Vladievci 77 F3
Vladimirci 72 C3
Vladimirovac 73 D2
Vladimirovo 77 F3
Vladimir-Volynskij 112 C2
Vlagtwedde 17 E1
Vlaháva 83 D1
Vlahérna (Ípiros) 82 C2
Vlahérna (Pelopónissos) 86 C2
Vlahiótis 87 D3
Vlahokerassiá 87 D2
Vlahomándra 83 D4
Vlahópoulo 86 C3
Vlanen 16 C3
Vlasenica 72 B4
Vlašić (Bosna i Hercegovina) 71 E4
Vlašić (Srbija) 72 C3
Vlasina Okruglica 77 E1
Vlasinsko jez 77 E1
Vlasotince 77 E1
Vlássio 83 D2
Vlásti 79 D3
Vlieland 16 C1
Vlihó 82 B3
Vlissingen 16 B4
Vlorë 114 B4
Vlotho 17 F2
Vltava 53 F3
Vobbia 60 A2
Voćin 71 E2
Vöcklabruck 56 C3
Vodice (Rijeka) 70 A3
Vodice (Šibenik) 74 C1
Vodna 73 E3
Vodňany 56 C1
Vodnjan 70 A4
Voe 3 F1
Vogatsikó 79 D3
Vogel 70 A2
Vogelsberg 52 A4
Vogelsdorf 49 E4
Voghera 60 A2
Vogošća 72 B4
Vohenstrauß 56 B1
Vöhringen 55 E3
Void 20 C4
Voikoski 107 F1
Vóio, Óros 78 C3
Voiron 30 C1
Voiteur 26 C3
Voitsberg 57 E4
Vojens 108 A3
Vojka 72 C3
Vojmsjön 97 F4
Vojnić 70 C3
Vojnik 70 B1
Vojska 73 D3
Vojtanov 53 D4
Vojvodina 72 C2
Vólakas 80 B1
Volary 56 C2
Volchov 111 E1
Volchov *R* 111 E1
Volda 100 A3
Voldafjorden 100 A2
Volders 59 D2
Volendam 16 C2
Volga 111 F1
Volimes 86 A1
Volissós 85 E4
Volkach 52 B4
Völkermarkt 70 B1
Völklingen 54 B2
Volkmarsen 52 A2
Volkovija 77 D3
Volkovysk 110 C4
Volmunster 21 E3
Voločisk 113 D2
Volokolamsk 111 F2
Volonne 31 D3
Vólos 83 F2
Vološin 111 D4
Volpiano 31 E1
Volta 60 C1
Volterra 60 C4
Voltri 60 A3
Volturara Appula 64 B3
Volturino, Mte 64 C4
Volturno 64 A3
Volvic 26 A4
Vólvi, L 80 B3
Volyn' 113 D2
Volyně 56 C1
Vónitsa 82 C3
Vonnas 26 C4
Voors 17 D2
Voorschoten 16 B3
Voorthuizen 16 C2
Vopnafjörður 96 C1
Vörå 102 B2
Vorarlberg 58 B2
Vóras, Óros 79 E2
Vorau 57 E3
Vorchdorf 56 C3
Vordernberg 57 E4
Vorderrhein 58 A3
Vorderriß 56 A4
Vordingborg 108 C4
Vorë 76 C4
Voreppe 30 C1
Vorey 30 A1
Vóri 91 D4
Vória Pindos 78 C4
Vóries Sporádes 84 C2
Vøringfossen 104 B2
Vórios Evoïkós Kólpos 83 F3
Vório Stenó Kerkiras 82 A1
Vorma 105 D3
Vormsi 110 B1
Vorna 99 D4
Voronet 113 D3
Vorsfelde 48 B4
Vorskla 113 F2
Võrtsjärv 110 C2
Võru 110 C2
Vosges (Dépt) 27 D1
Voss 104 B2
Votice 53 F4
Votonóssi 82 C1
Voúdia 88 B4
Vouga, R 38 C1
Vouglans, Lac de 27 D3
Vouhorina 79 D4
Vouillé 25 D3
Voukoliés 90 B3
Voúla 87 F1
Voulgára 83 D2
Vouliagméni 87 F1
Voulkariá, L 82 B3
Voúlpi 83 D3
Voulte, la 30 B2
Vouná Goúras 83 E2
Vouraïkós 86 C1
Voúrinos, Óros 79 D4
Vourkári 88 A2
Vourliótes 89 E1
Voúrvoura 87 D2
Vourvouroú 80 B4
Voutás 83 F3
Vouvant 24 C3
Vouvray 25 D2
Voúxa, Akr 90 B3
Vouzela 38 B1
Vouziers 20 B3
Voves 25 E1
Vovoússa 78 C4
Voxnan 101 E4
Vöyri 102 B2
Voz 70 B3
Vozarci 77 E3
Voznesensk 113 F3
Vrå 108 B2
Vraca 115 D2
Vraca pl 77 D3
Vračev Gaj 73 D2
Vračevšnica 73 D4
Vrådal 104 B3
Vraháti 87 D1
Vrahiónas, Óros 86 A2
Vrahnéika 86 C1
Vrams-Gunnarstorp 108 C3
Vrana 70 B4
Vrancei, M 113 D4
Vranduk 71 F4
Vranica 71 E4
Vranja 70 A3
Vranjak 75 F2
Vranje 77 E2
Vranjska Banja 77 E2
Vranovská přehr nádrž 57 E1
Vran pl 75 E1
Vransko 70 B2
Vransko jezero 74 C1
Vrástama 80 B3
Vratarnica 73 F4
Vratnica 77 D2
Vratnik 70 B3
Vratno 70 C1
Vravróna 88 A1
Vražogrnac 73 F3
Vrbanja 72 B3
Vrbanja *R* 71 E3
Vrbas 72 B2
Vrbas *R* 71 E3
Vrbaška 71 E3
Vrbas klisura 71 E4
Vrbljani 71 D4
Vrbnica 77 D3
Vrbnik 70 B3
Vrboska 75 E2
Vrbovec 71 D2
Vrbovsko 70 B3
Vrčin 73 D3
Vrdnik 72 C2
Vreden 17 E3
Vrela 76 C2
Vrelo (Hrvatska) 70 C4
Vrelo (Srbija) 73 E4
Vreoci 72 C3
Vresse 20 C2
Vrésthena 87 D3
Vreta Kloster 106 A4
Vrginmost 70 C3
Vrgorac 75 E2
Vrh Kapele 70 C3
Vrhnika 70 A2
Vrhpolje 71 D4
Vria 79 E4
Vrinena 83 F3
Vrissa 85 F3
Vrisses 90 C3
Vrissiá 83 E2
Vrissoúla 82 B2
Vrlika 75 D1
Vrnjačka Banja 73 D4
Vrnograč 70 C3
Vrondádos 85 F4
Vrondamás 87 D3
Vronderó 78 C3
Vrondissí 91 D4
Vrondoú 79 E4
Vrondoús, Óri 80 B2
Vrossína 82 B1
Vrouhás 91 E3
Vrpolje (Osijek) 71 F2
Vrpolje (Šibenik) 75 D1
Vršac 73 D2
Vršani 72 B3
Vrsar 70 A3
Vrsi 70 C4
Vrška Čuka 73 F4
Vrtac 76 B2
Vrtoče 71 D4
Vrutok 77 D3
Vučitrn 77 D2
Vučjak 77 F3
Vučje 77 E1
Vučkovica 73 D4
Vue des Alpes 27 E2
Vuka 71 F2
Vukovar 72 B2
Vulcano, I 69 D2
Vulture, Mte 64 C3
Vuohijärvi 107 F2
Vuohijärvi *L* 107 F1
Vuokatti 99 E4
Vuokkijärvi 99 F3
Vuokojaure 94 C3
Vuoksenniska 103 F3
Vuolijoki 99 E4
Vuollerim 98 B2
Vuolvojaure 98 A2
Vuonislahti 103 F2
Vuorji 95 D2
Vuosjärvi 103 D2
Vuoskuvarri 95 D3
Vuostimo 99 E2
Vuotso 95 E3
Vyškov 57 F1
Vyšnij Voločok 111 E2

W

Waal 16 C3
Waalwijk 16 C3
Waasmunster 50 B3
Wabern 52 A3
Wachau 57 E2
Wachow 49 D4
Wächtersbach 52 A4
Waddeneilanden 16 C1
Wadebridge 8 B3
Wädenswil 58 A2
Wagenfeld 17 F2
Wageningen 17 D3
Waging 56 B3
Wagrain 59 E1
Wągrowiec 112 A1
Wahlstedt 48 A2
Waiblingen 55 D2
Waidhaus 56 B1
Waidhofen (Ybbs) 57 D3
Waidhofen (Thaya) 57 E2
Waidring 59 E1
Waischenfeld 52 C4
Waizenkirchen 56 C2
Wakefield 7 D2
Wałbrzych 112 A2
Walchensee 56 A4
Walcheren 16 B3
Walchsee 59 D1
Wałcz 112 A1
Wald 58 A2
Waldbröl 17 E4
Waldeck 52 A2
Waldenbuch 55 D3
Waldenburg 53 D3
Waldfischbach-Burgalben 54 B2
Waldheim 53 E2
Waldkappel 52 B3
Waldkirch 54 C3
Waldkirchen 56 C2
Waldkraiburg 56 B3
Wald-Michelbach 54 C1
Waldmünchen 56 B1
Waldsassen 53 D4
Waldshut 54 C4
Walensee 58 B2
Walenstadt 58 B2
Wales 8 C1
Wallasey 6 B2
Walldorf 54 C2
Walldürn 55 D1
Wallenfels 52 C4
Wallersdorf 56 B2
Wallerstein 55 E2
Wallingford 9 E2
Walls 3 F2
Walsall 9 E1
Walsrode 48 A4
Walsum 17 D3
Waltershausen 52 B3
Walton-on-the-Naze 11 D2
Waltrop 17 E3
Wanderup 48 A1
Wandlitz 49 E3
Wanfried 52 B2
Wangen 55 E4
Wangenbourg 21 E4
Wangerland-Hooksiel 47 E3
Wangerooge 47 E2
Wängi 58 A1
Wanna 47 F2
Wanne-Eickel 17 E3
Wantage 9 E2

Klosterneuburg
16°20
Tulln
Praha
Praha
Brno
Seyring
WIEN
FLORIDSDORF
DONAUSTADT
DÖBLING
WÄHRING
HERNALS
OTTAKRING
PENZING
HIETZING
LIESING
FAVORITEN
SIMMERING
LEOPOLDSTADT
BRIGITTENAU
ALSERGRUND
JOSEFSTADT
NEUBAU
MARIAHILF
MARGARETEN
WIEDEN
LANDSTRASSE
RUDOLFSHEIM
FÜNFHAUS
MEIDLING
Donau
Neue Donau
Alte Donau
Donaukanal
Prater
Stephansdom
Hofburg
Schönbrunn
Leopoldsberg
Kahlenberg
Hermannskogel
Lainzer Tiergarten
Lobau
Schwechat
Vösendorf
Perchtoldsdorf
Kaltenleutgeben
Strebersdorf
Kagran
Aspern
Stadlau
Breitenlee
Süßenbrunn
Gerasdorf-Oberlisse
Neusüßenbrunn
Zentralfriedhof
Kaiser-Ebersdorf
Albern
Rannersdorf
Kledering
Zwölfaxing
Lanzendorf
Leopoldsdorf
Hennersdorf
Rustenfeld
Rothneusiedl
Oberlaa
Unterlaa
Laaerberg
Inzersdorf
Siebenhirten
Atzgersdorf
Mauer
Kalksburg
Rodaun
Speising
Hetzendorf
Altmannsdorf
Hütteldorf
Hadersdorf
Weidlingbach
Weidling
Haselbach
Hohenau
Gsängerh.
Windischh.
Sophienalpe
Exelberg
Rotes Kreuz
Hochbruckenberg
Jägerwaldsiedlung
Neuwaldegg
Dornbach
Grinzing
Heiligenstadt
Nußdorf
Jedlesee
Kaisermühlen
UNO-City
Donauturm
Reichsbrücke
Praterbrücke
Stadion
Wulzendorf
Hirschstetten
Neukagran
Leopoldau
Großjedlersdorf
Großfeldsiedlung
Nordrandsiedlung
Napoleons Hauptquartier
Gr. Biberhaufen
Angern a.d. March
Raasdorf
Hainburg a.d. Donau
Flughafen Bratislava
Bruck, Budapest
Himberg
Mödling
Eisenstadt Jugoslavija
Laxenburg
Graz
Wiener Neustadt
Salzburg, Linz
Hint. Föhrenberg
Teufelstein
1/100000

Wantzenau, la 21 F4
Wanzleben 52 C1
Warburg 52 A2
Wardenburg 47 F3
Ware 9 F2
Waregem 50 B3
Wareham 9 D3
Waremme 50 C3
Waren 49 D2
Warendorf 17 F3
Warin 48 C2
Warkworth 5 E3
Warmensteinach 53 D4
Warminster 9 E3
Warnemunde 48 C2
Warnow 48 C2
Warrenpoint 13 E3
Warrington 6 B2
Warstein 17 F3
Warszawa 112 B1
Warszów 49 E2
Warta 49 F3
Warth 58 B2
Wartha 52 B3
Warwick 9 E1
Washington 5 E4
Wash, The 7 E3
Wasselonne 21 E4
Wassen 58 A3
Wassenaar 16 B3
Wassenberg 17 D4
Wasseralfingen 55 E2
Wasserbillig 21 D2
Wasserburg 56 B3
Wasser-Kuppe 52 B3
Wassertrüdingen 55 E2
Wassigny 20 A2
Wassy 20 C4
Wasungen 52 B3
Watchet 8 C3
Waterfoot 13 E1
Waterford 15 D4
Waterford (Co) 14 C4
Waterford Harbour 15 D4
Waterloo 50 B3
Waternish Pt 2 B3
Waterville 14 A4
Watford 9 F2
Wattens 59 D2
Watton 11 D1
Wattwil 58 A2
Watzmann 56 C4
Waulsort 50 C4
Waveney 11 D1
Wavre 50 C3
Waxweiler 51 D4
Wear 5 E4
Wechsel 57 E3
Wedel 48 A3
Wedemark-Mellendorf 48 A4
Weener 47 E3
Weert 17 D4
Weferlingen 48 C4
Wegberg 17 D4
Wegeleben 52 C1
Weggis 27 F2
Węgorzewo 110 B4
Węgorzyno 49 F2
Wegscheid 56 C2
Wehr 54 C4
Weibersbrunn 52 A4
Weichshofen 56 B2
Weida 53 D3
Weiden 56 A1
Weikersheim 55 D1
Weilburg 51 F4
Weil der Stadt 55 D2
Weilheim (Baden-Württemberg) 55 D3
Weilheim (Bayern) 56 A3
Weimar 52 C3
Weinfelden 58 A1
Weingarten 55 D4
Weinheim 54 C1
Weinsberg 55 D2
Weismain 52 C4
Weißbriach 59 F2
Weiße Elster 53 D3
Weißenbach 58 C1
Weißenberg 53 F2
Weißenburg 55 F2
Weißenfels 53 D2
Weißenhorn 55 E3
Weissenstadt 53 D4
Weissenstein 27 E2
Weissfluhgipfel 58 B2
Weißenkirchen 57 E2
Weißensee 52 C2
Weißensee (L) 59 F2
Weißkirchen 57 D4
Weißkugel 58 C2
Weißwasser 53 F1
Weitra 57 D2
Weiz 57 E4
Wejherowo 110 A4
Weldon 9 F1
Welgetschlag 57 D2
Welland 9 F1
Wellin 20 C2
Wellingborough 9 F1
Wellington 9 D3
Wellington Bridge 15 D4
Wells 9 D3
Wells-next-the-Sea 7 E3
Wels 56 C3
Welsberg 59 D2
Welschnofen 59 D3
Welshpool 9 D1
Weltenburg 55 F2
Welwyn Garden City 9 F2
Welzheim 55 D2
Wem 6 B3
Wemding 55 E2
Wemyss Bay 4 C2
Wendelstein 56 B4
Wenden 52 B1
Wengen 27 F3
Wenns 58 C2
Werbellinsee 49 E3
Werben 48 C3
Werdau 53 D3
Werder 49 D4
Werdohl 17 E4
Werfen 59 E1
Werl 17 F3
Werlte 17 E1
Wermelskirchen 17 E4
Wermsdorf 53 E2
Wernberg 56 B1
Werne 17 E3
Werneck 52 B4
Werneuchen 49 E4
Wernigerode 52 C1
Werra 52 B3
Wertach 55 E4
Wertach (R) 55 E3
Wertheim 55 D1
Werther 17 F2
Wertingen 55 E3
Wervik 50 A3
Wesel 17 D3
Wesenbeerg 49 D3
Wesendorf 48 B4
Weser 47 F3
Weser-Elbe-Kanal 48 C4
Wesselburen 47 F2
Wessobrunn 56 A3
West Auckland 5 E4
West Bridgford 7 D3
Westbury 9 D3
Westendorf 59 D1
Westenholz 48 A4
Westerburg 51 F4
Westerholt 47 E3
Westerland 47 F1
Westerlo 50 C3
Westernbödefeld 17 F4
Western Isles 2 B2
Wester Ross 2 C3
Westerstede 47 E3
Westerwald 51 E3
Westhofen 54 C1
West Kilbride 4 C2
West Linton 5 D2
West Loch Tarbert 2 A2
Westmeath 12 C3
West Mersea 11 D2
Weston-Super-Mare 9 D2
Westport 12 B3
Westray 3 E1
Westray Firth 3 E1
West Sussex 9 F3
West-Terschelling 16 C1
West-Vlaanderen 50 A3
Wetherby 7 D2
Wetter 17 E3
Wetteren 50 B3
Wettin 52 C2
Wettringen 17 E2
Wetwang 7 D1
Wetzikon 58 A2
Wetzlar 51 F3
Wexford 15 D3
Wexford (Co) 15 D3
Weyer-Markt 57 D3
Weyhausen 48 B4
Weyhill 9 E3
Weymouth 9 D3
Weyregg 56 C3
Whaley Bridge 6 C2
Whalsay 3 F1
Wharfe 6 C1
Whernside 6 C1
Whitburn 5 D2
Whitby 5 F4
Whitchurch 6 B3
White Bridge 2 C4
Whitehaven 5 D4
Whitehead 13 E2
Whiteness 3 F2
Whiten Head 2 C2
Whithorn 4 C4
Whitland 8 B2
Whitley Bay 5 E3
Whitstable 11 D3
Whittlesey 9 F1
Wick 3 D2
Wickford 11 D2
Wicklow 13 E4
Wicklow (Co) 13 D4
Wicklow Head 13 E4
Wicklow Mts 13 D4
Widnes 6 B2
Wiehe 52 C2
Wiek 49 D1
Wieliczka 112 B3
Wieluń 112 B2
Wien 57 F2
Wiener-Neudorf 57 F2
Wiener Neustadt 57 F3
Wienerwald 57 E3
Wies (A) 70 B1
Wies (D) 56 A4
Wiesau 53 D4
Wiesbaden 51 F4
Wieselburg 57 E3
Wiesenburg 53 D1
Wiesensteig 55 D3
Wiesentheid 55 E1
Wiesenttal 52 C4
Wiesing 59 D1
Wiesloch 54 C2
Wiesmath 57 F3
Wiesmoor 47 E3
Wigan 6 C2
Wight, I of 9 E4
Wigton 5 D4
Wigtown 4 C3
Wigtown B 4 C4
Wijhe 17 D2
Wil 58 A2
Wildalpen 57 D3
Wildbad 54 C2
Wildeck 52 B3
Wildeshausen 17 F1
Wildon 57 E4
Wildspitze 58 C2
Wildstrubel 27 E3
Wilfersdorf 57 F2
Wilhelmina kan 16 C3
Wilhelm Pieck-Stadt 53 F1
Wilhelmsburg (A) 57 E3
Wilhelmsburg (D) 48 A3
Wilhelmshaven 47 F3
Wilhering 57 D2
Wilkau-Haßlau 53 D3
Willebroek 50 B3
Willemstad 16 B3
Willingen 17 F4
Williton 8 C3
Wilmslow 6 C2
Wilnsdorf 17 F4
Wilsdruff 53 E2
Wilseder Berg 48 A3
Wilster 48 A2
Wilton 9 E3
Wiltshire 9 E3
Wiltz 21 D2
Wimborne Minster 9 E3
Wimereux 19 E1
Wincanton 9 D3
Winchcombe 9 E2
Winchelsea 11 D3
Winchester 9 E3
Windeck 51 E3
Windermere 5 D4
Windischeschenbach 53 D4
Windischgarsten 57 D3
Windsbach 55 E1
Windsor 9 F2
Winkleigh 8 C3
Winklern 59 E2
Winnenden 55 D2
Winnigstedt 52 B1
Winnweiler 54 B1
Winschoten 47 E3
Winsen (Celle) 48 A4
Winsen (Lüneburg) 48 B3
Winsford 6 C3
Winsum 47 D3
Winterberg 17 F4
Winterswijk 17 D3
Winterthur 58 A2
Wintzenheim 27 E1
Wipper 52 C2
Wipperfürth 17 E4
Wisbech 10 C1
Wischhafen 48 A2
Wisełka 49 E2
Wishaw 4 C2
Wisła 110 B4
Wismar 48 C2
Wissant 19 E1
Wissembourg 21 F3
Wissen 51 E3
Witham 7 D3
Witham 11 D2
Withernsea 7 E2
Witney 9 E2
Witnica 49 F3
Wittdün 47 F1
Witte 49 D1
Witten 17 E3
Wittenberg 53 D1
Wittenberge 48 C3
Wittenburg 48 B3
Wittichenau 53 F2
Wittingen 48 B4
Wittlich 51 E4
Wittmund 47 E3
Wittow 49 D1
Wittstock 49 D3
Witzenhausen 52 B2
Władysławowo 110 A4
Włocławek 112 B1
Włodawa 112 C2
Wöbbelin 48 C3
Woburn 9 F2
Woburn Abbey 9 F2
Woensdrecht 16 B4
Woerden 16 C3
Wohlen 27 F2
Woippy 21 D3
Woking 9 F3
Wokingham 9 F2
Wołczenica 49 F2
Woldegk 49 E2
Wolfach 54 C3
Wolfegg 55 E4
Wolfen 53 D2
Wolfenbüttel 52 B1
Wolfhagen 52 A2
Wolfratshausen 56 A3
Wolfsberg 70 B1
Wolfsburg 48 B4
Wolgast 49 E2
Wolin 49 E2
Wolin (Reg) 49 E2
Woliński Park Narodowy 49 E2
Wolkenstein 59 D3
Wolkersdorf 57 F2
Wöllersdorf 57 F3
Wollersheim 51 D3
Wollin 49 D4
Wolmirstedt 48 C4
Wolsingham 5 E4
Wolsztyn 112 A2
Wolvega 17 D1
Wolverhampton 9 E1
Wolverton 9 F1
Wolznach 55 F2
Woodbridge 11 D1
Woodhall Spa 7 E3
Woodstock 9 E2
Wooler 5 E3
Worb 27 E2
Worbis 52 B2
Worcester 9 D1
Wörgl 59 D1
Workington 5 D4
Worksop 7 D2
Workum 16 C1
Wörlitz 53 D1
Wormerveer 16 C2
Wormhout 19 F1
Worms 54 C1
Worms Head 8 C2
Wörnitz 55 E2
Wörrstadt 54 C1
Wœrth 21 E3
Wörth (Donau) 56 B2
Wörth (Main) 55 D1
Wörth (Rheinland-Pfalz) 54 C2
Worther See 70 A1
Worthing 10 C3
Woświn, Jez 49 F2
Wragby 7 D3
Wrath, Cape 2 C2
Wrecsam 6 B3
Wrexham 6 B3
Wriezen 49 E3
Wrocław 112 A2
Wroughton 9 E2
Września 112 A1
Wulfen 17 E3
Wullowitz 57 D2
Wümme 48 A3
Wümme *R* 48 A3
Wünnenberg 17 F3
Wünsdorf 49 E4
Wunsiedel 53 D4
Wunstorf 48 A4
Wuppertal 17 E4
Würzburg 55 D1
Wurzen 53 D2
Wurzen-Paß 59 F2
Wusterhausen 49 D3
Wustrow (Rostock) 48 C1
Wustrow (Wismar) 48 C2
Wuustwezel 50 C2
Wye, R 9 D2
Wyk 47 F1
Wymondham 11 D1

X

Xallas, R 34 A2
Xanten 17 D3
Xánthi 81 D2
Xánthi (Nomos) 81 D2
Xarrama, R 42 B1
Xàtiva 41 E4
Xeresa 41 E4
Xerovoúni 82 C2
Xerta 41 F2
Xertigny 27 D1
Xesta, Pto de la 34 C1
Xifianí 79 E2
Xilagani 81 E2
Xilikí 83 E3
Xilis, Akr 87 D4
Xilókastro 87 D1
Xilopáriko 83 D2
Xilópoli 80 A2
Xilóskalo 90 B3
Xiniáda 83 E3
Xinó Neró 79 D3
Xinzo de Limia 34 B3
Xiró 83 F3
Xirokámbi 87 D3
Xirókambos 89 E3
Xirolímni 79 D3
Xistral 34 B1
Xódoto, Akr 89 D3
Xubia 34 B1
Xunqueira de Ambia 34 B3

Y

Yaiza 42 C4
Yalova 115 F3
Yanguas 36 B3
Yare 7 F4
Yarmouth 9 E3
Yarmouth, Great 7 F4
Ybbs 57 D2
Ybbs *R* 57 D3
Yebra 40 B2
Yecla 45 D1
Yeguas, Emb de 43 F2
Yeguas, R de las 43 F1
Yell 3 F1
Yell Sd 3 F1
Yelmo 44 B2
Yeltes, R 39 D1
Yenne 27 D4
Yeovil 9 D3
Yepes 40 B3
Yerville 19 D3
Yesa 36 C2
Yesa, Emb de 37 D2
Yeşilova 115 F4
Yeste 44 C1
Yeu, I d' 24 A3
Yèvre 26 A2
Y-Fenni 9 D2
Yildiz Dağlari 115 E3
Ylämaa 103 F4
Ylämylly 103 F2
Yläne 107 D2
Ylihärmä 102 C2
Yli-Kärppä 99 D3
Ylikiiminki 99 D3
Yli-Kitka 99 E2
Yli-li 99 D3
Yli-Muonio 95 D4
Yli-Nampa 99 D2
Yli-Olhava 99 D3
Ylistaro 102 B2
Ylitornio 98 C2
Ylivieska 102 C1
Ylläs 95 D4
Ylläsjärvi 95 D4
Ylöjärvi 102 C3
Yngaren 106 A4
Yonne 20 A4
Yonne (Dépt) 26 A1
York 7 D2
Yorkshire Dales Nat Pk 6 C1
Youghal 14 C4
Youghal B 14 C4
Yoxford 11 E1
Ypäjä 107 E2
Yport 19 D2
Yppäri 99 D4
Ypres 50 A3
Yr Wyddgrug 6 B3
Yser 19 F1
Yssingeaux 30 B1
Ystad 109 D4
Y Trallwng 9 D1
Ytterhogdal 101 E3
Yttermalung 105 E2
Yuncos 40 A2
Yunquera 43 E4
Yunquera de Henares 40 B2
Yuste 39 E2
Yverdon 27 E3
Yvetot 19 D3
Yvoir 50 C4
Yvoire 27 D3

Z

Zaandam 16 C2
Žabali 72 C2
Žabari 73 D3
Zablaće 75 D1
Žabljak (Durmitor) 76 B1
Žabljak (Titograd) 76 B3
Žabno 71 D2
Zabok 70 C2
Zabrdđe 72 B3
Zadar 74 C1
Zadarski kanal 70 B4
Zadvarje 75 E2
Zafarraya 43 F3
Zafóra, Ni 92 C2
Zafra 43 D1
Žaga 70 A2
Żagań 112 A2
Zaglavak 72 C4
Zagorá 83 F2
Zagória 82 C1
Zagorje 70 B2
Zagreb 70 C2
Žagubica 73 E3
Zagvozd 75 E2
Zahara de los Atunes 43 D4
Zahara, Emb de 43 E3
Zaháro 86 B2
Zahinos 42 C1
Zahna 53 D1
Záhony 112 C3
Zaidin 37 E4
Zajas 77 D3
Zaječar 73 F3
Zákinthos 86 A1
Zákinthos, N 86 A1
Zakopane 112 B3
Zákros 91 F4
Zala 112 A4
Zalaegerszeg 112 A4
Zalamea de la Serena 43 E1
Zalamea la Real 42 C2
Zalău 112 C4
Žalec 70 B2
Zaleščiki 113 D3
Zalew Wiślany 110 B4
Zalla 36 A1
Zálongo 82 B2
Zaltbommel 16 C3
Zalužnica 70 C4
Zambrana 36 B2
Zamora 35 D4
Zamość 112 C2
Záncara, R 40 B4
Zandvoort 16 B2
Zángano, Pto del 39 D4
Zanglivéri 80 A3
Zannone, I 63 F4
Zaorejas 40 C2
Zaostrog 75 E2
Zaovine Vežanja 72 C4
Zapadnaja Dvina 111 E2
Zapadnaja Dvina *R* 111 E2
Zapadna Morava 73 D4
Zapardiel, R 39 F1
Zapatón, R 39 D3
Zápio 83 E2
Zapponeta 64 C3
Zaprešić 70 C2
Zaragoza 37 D3
Zárakes 84 B4
Zaratán 35 E4
Zarautz 36 C1
Zarcilla de Ramos 44 C2
Zárkos 83 E1
Zarós 91 D4
Zaroúhla 87 D1
Zarrentin 48 B3
Žary 112 A2
Zarza la Mayor 39 D2
Zasieki 53 F1
Žaškov 113 E2
Žatec 53 E3
Zatoka Gdańska 110 B4
Zaton 75 F2
Zavala 75 F2
Zavattarello 60 A2
Zavidovići 71 F4
Zavlaka 72 C3
Zavratnica 70 B4
Zawiercie 112 B2
Žažina 71 D2
Zbaraž 113 D2
Zbraslav 53 F4
Žďár nad Sázavou 112 A3
Zdenac 70 C3
Zdice 53 F4
Ždrelac 74 C1
Ždrelo 73 E3
Zdunje 77 D3
Zduńska Wola 112 B2
Zebë, Maj'e 76 C3
Zebreira 38 C2
Žednik 72 B1
Zeebrugge 50 A3
Zeeland 16 B3
Zefiría 88 A4
Žegovac 77 D2
Žegra 77 D2
Žegulja 75 F2
Zehdenick 49 D3
Zeist 16 C3
Zeitz 53 D2
Zejtun 68 B4
Žekovec 70 B1
Zele 50 B3
Zelengora 76 A1
Zelengora (Reg) 76 A1
Zelenika 76 A3
Zelenogorsk 111 D1
Železná Ruda 56 C1
Železnik 72 C3
Železniki 70 A2
Železnogorsk 111 F4
Zelina 70 C2
Zélio 83 F3
Željezno Polje 71 F4
Željin 73 D4
Zell (D) 54 B1
Zell (Oberösterreich) 56 C2
Zell (Tirol) 59 D2
Zella-Mehlis 52 C3
Zell am See 59 E1
Zellerrain 57 E3
Zeltweg 57 D4
Zelzate 50 B3
Zemun 72 C3
Zenica 71 F4
Zen'kov 113 F2
Žep 72 B4
Žepče 71 F4
Zerbst 53 D1
Zeri 60 B3
Zermatt 27 F4
Zernez 58 B3
Zergan 77 D4
Zestoa 36 B1
Zeta 76 B2
Zetel 47 E3
Zeulenroda 53 D3
Zeven 48 A3
Zevenaar 17 D3
Zevgaráki 82 C4
Zevgolatio 86 C3
Zevio 60 C1
Zêzere, R 38 C2
Žiča 73 D4
Zicavo 33 F4
Židlochovice 57 F1
Ziefsdorf 57 E2
Ziegenrück 52 C3
Zielona Góra 112 A2
Zierikzee 16 B3
Zierzow 48 C3
Ziesar 49 D4
Zi, Guri i 77 D4
Zijemlje 75 F1
Žilina 112 B3
Žilindar 76 C1
Ziller 59 D2
Zillertal 59 D1
Zimnicea 115 D2
Zinal 27 F4
Zingst 49 D1
Zinnowitz 49 E1
Zinnwald 53 E3
Zirbitzkogel 57 D4
Zirchow 49 E2
Žiri 70 A2
Žirje 74 C1
Zirl 58 C2
Zirndorf 55 D4
Zirndorf 55 E1
Zíros 91 F4
Zistersdorf 57 F2
Žitište 72 C2
Žitkovac 73 E4
Žitkoviči 113 D1
Žitomir 113 E2
Žitomislići 75 F2
Žitoradđa 77 D1
Zittau 53 F2
Živinice 71 F3
Živogošće 75 E2
Žizdra 111 F3
Zjum 77 D2
Zlarin 75 D1
Zlarin I 75 D1
Zlata 77 D1
Zlatar 76 B1
Zlatar Bistrica 70 C2
Zlatarevo 77 F3
Zlatari 77 D1
Zlatarsko jez 76 B1
Zlatibor 72 C4
Zlatica 72 C4
Zlatni Pjasăci 115 E2
Zlatokop 77 E2
Zletovo 77 E2
Žljebovi 72 B4
Žlobin 111 E4
Zlot 73 E3
Žlutice 53 E4
Zmajevo 72 C2
Žman 74 C1
Žmerinka 113 E3
Žminj 70 A3
Znamenka 113 F2
Znojmo 57 E1
Zöblitz 53 E3
Zoetermeer 16 B3
Zogaj 76 C2
Zollikofen 27 E2
Zoločev 113 D2
Zolotonoša 113 F2
Žoltyje Vody 113 F2
Zonári, Akr 93 F1

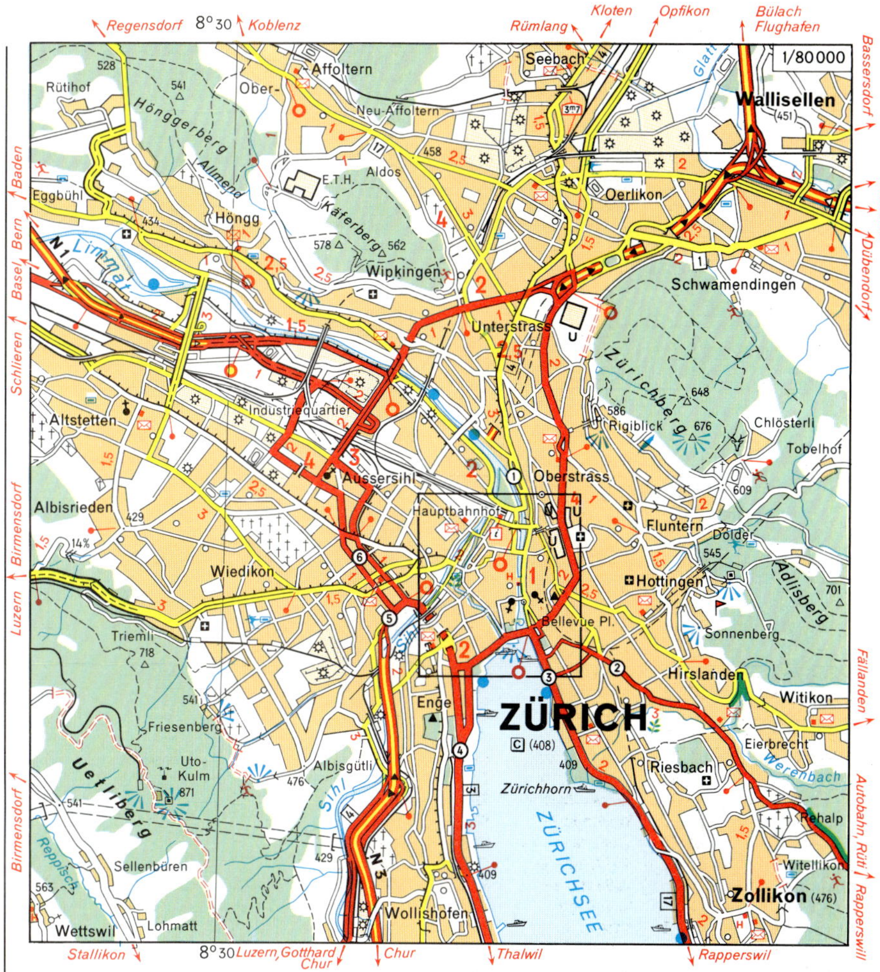

Regensdorf
8°30
Koblenz
Rümlang
Kloten
Opfikon
Bülach Flughafen
1/80 000
Affoltern
Seebach
Wallisellen
Rütihof
Ober-
Neu-Affoltern
Hönggerberg
Allmend
E.T.H.
Aldos
Oerlikon
Eggbühl
Höngg
Käferberg
Wipkingen
Schwamendingen
Limmat
N1
Unterstrass
Zürichberg
Industriequartier
Rigiblick
Chlösterli
Altstetten
Tobelhof
Aussersihl
Oberstrass
Albisrieden
Hauptbahnhof
Fluntern
Dolder
Wiedikon
Hottingen
Adlisberg
Triemli
Bellevue Pl.
Sonnenberg
Hirslanden
Witikon
Friesenberg
Enge
ZÜRICH
Eierbrecht
Uto-Kulm
Albisgütli
Riesbach
Zürichhorn
Uetliberg
Sihl
ZÜRICHSEE
Rehalp
Witellikon
Sellenbüren
N3
Zollikon
Wettswil
Lohmatt
Wollishofen
Stallikon
Luzern, Gotthard Chur
Chur
Thalwil
Rapperswil
Bassersdorf
Schaffhausen Winterthur
Dübendorf
Fällanden
Autobahn, Rüti
Rapperswil
Baden
Bern
Basel
Schlieren
Birmensdorf
Luzern
Birmensdorf

Zóni 81 F1
Zonianá 91 D3
Zonza 33 F4
Zoodóhos Pigí (Makedonía) 79 E3
Zoodóhos Pigí (Pelopónissos) 87 F2
Zörbig 53 D2
Zorita 39 E3
Zossen 49 E4
Zoúrvas, Akr 87 F2
Zoutkamp 47 D3
Zoutleeuw 50 C3
Zoúzouli 78 C4
Zrenjanin 72 C2
Zrin 71 D3
Zrinska gora 71 D3
Zrmanja *R* 74 C1
Zrmanja 75 D1
Žrnovnica 75 D2
Zrze 77 D2
Zschopau 53 E3
Zschopau *R* 53 E3
Zubcov 111 F2
Zubin Potoku 76 C2
Žuč 77 D1
Zucaina 41 E3
Zuckerhütl 58 C2
Zudar 49 D1
Zuera 37 D3
Zufre 43 D2
Zufre, Emb de 43 D2
Zug 58 A2
Zugspitze 55 F4
Zuid Beveland 16 B4
Zuidelijk-Flevoland 16 C2
Zuid Holland 16 B3
Zuidlaren 17 D1
Zújar 44 B3
Zújar, Emb del 39 E4
Zújar, R 43 E1
Žukovka 111 F3
Zuljana 75 E2
Zülpich 51 D3
Zumaia 36 B1
Zumárraga 36 B1
Zundert 16 C3
Zuoz 58 B3
Županja 71 F3
Žur 77 D3
Zürich 58 A2
Zurrieq 68 B4
Zürs 58 B2
Zurzach 58 A1
Zusmarshausen 55 E3
Žut 74 C1
Žuta Lokva 70 C3
Zutphen 17 D2
Žužemberk 70 B2
Zvečan 77 D1
Zvenigorodka 113 E2
Zvijezda nac park 72 C4
Zvikovec 53 E4
Zvolen 112 B3
Zvonce 77 E1
Zvorničko jez 72 B4
Zvornik 72 B4
Zweibrücken 54 B2
Zweisimmen 27 E3
Zwenkau 53 D2
Zwettl (Niederösterreich) 57 D2
Zwettl (Oberösterreich) 57 D2
Zwickau 53 D3
Zwickauer Mulde 53 D3
Zwiefalten 55 D3
Zwiesel 56 C2
Zwijndrecht 16 C3
Zwolle 17 D2
Żyrardów 112 B1
Żywiec 112 B3

Þ

Þingeyri 96 A1
Þingvallavatn 96 A2
Þingvellir 96 A2
Þistilfjörður 96 C1
Þjórsá 96 B2
Þorlákshöfn 96 A2
Þórshöfn 96 C1
Þórsmörk 96 B3

Notes

EXPLORING VENUS

By Emily Kington

CONTENTS

Where is Venus? 4
Planet Facts 6
The Hottest Planet? 8
Can We Visit Venus? 10
Space Probe Discoveries 12
Fact File 14
What Can We See? 16
Discoveries Under the Clouds 18
Why We Study Venus 20
What's Next? 22
Glossary 24

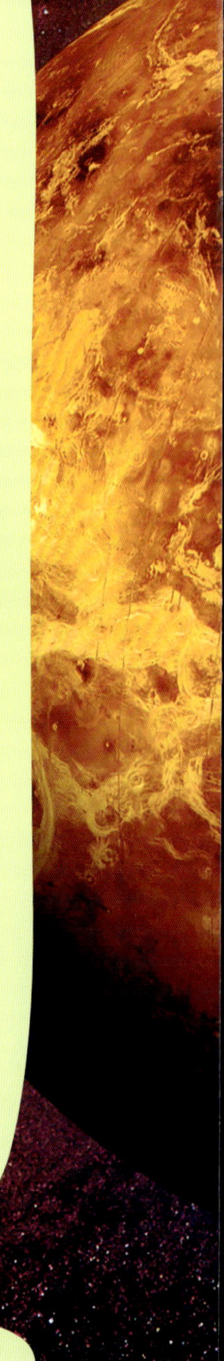

First published in 2026 by Hungry Tomato Ltd
F15, Old Bakery Studios, Blewetts Wharf, Malpas Road, Truro, Cornwall, TR1 1QH, UK.

A CIP catalogue record for this book is available from the British Library.

ISBN 9781835697085

Printed in China

Discover more at
www.hungrytomato.com

Front cover image is an edited image of Venus and the Veritas spacecraft.
Title page image is an edited image of Venus.
Contents page image is an edited image of Venus.

Words in **BOLD** can be found in the glossary.

WHERE IS VENUS?

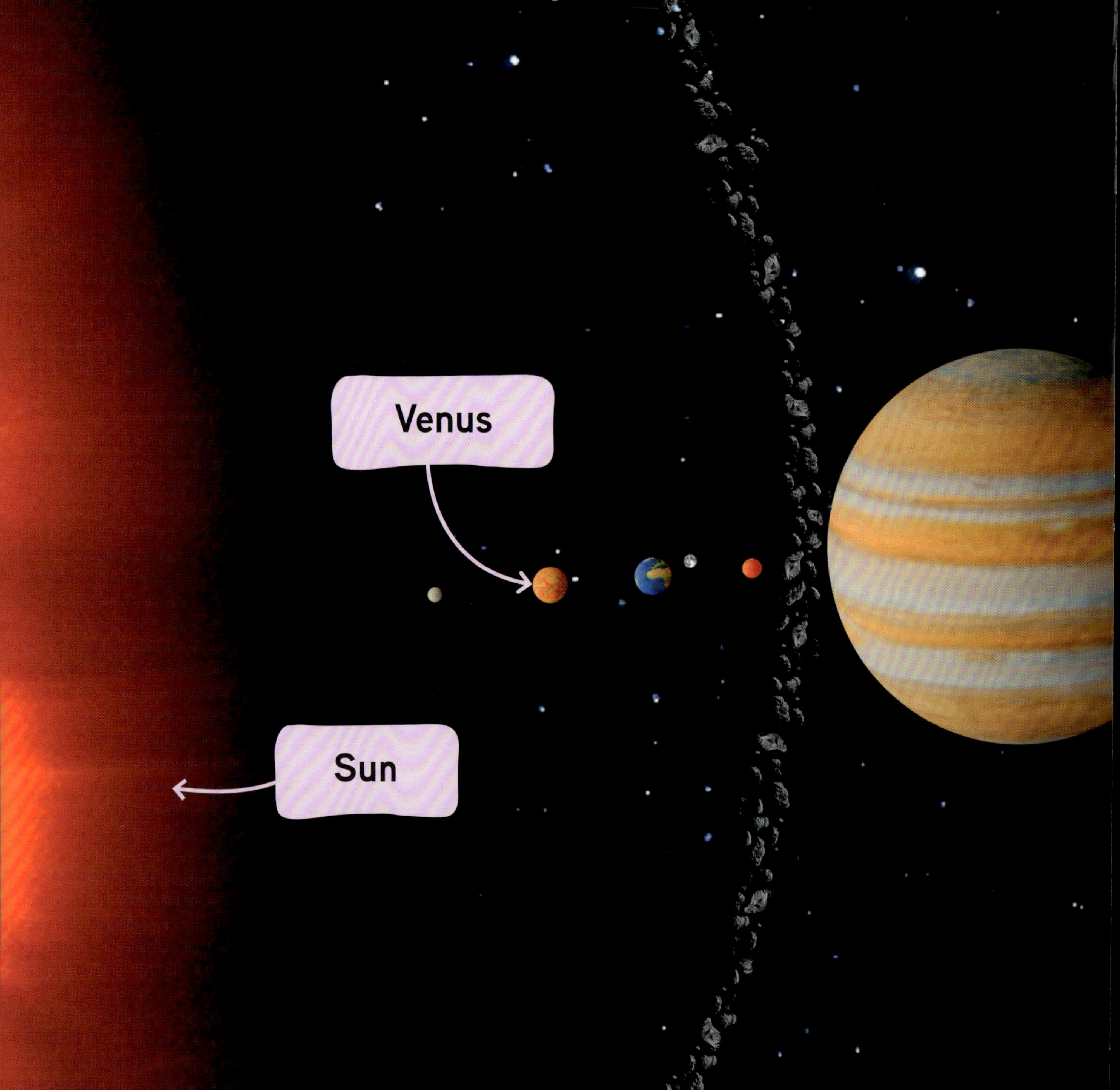

There are eight planets in our **solar system**. All of them travel around the Sun. Venus is the second closest planet to the Sun.

The time it takes a planet to travel around the Sun once is called a year. Venus travels around the Sun once every 225 **Earth days**. This journey is called Venus's **orbit**.

PLANET FACTS

Planets are always spinning. A day is the time it takes a planet to spin around once. Venus is the slowest-spinning planet – a day lasts the same as 243 Earth days!

Venus is one of two planets in our solar system that doesn't have a moon.

Whilst orbiting the Sun, Venus spins clockwise on its **axis**. This means that on Venus, the Sun rises in the west and sets in the east! The only other planet to do this is Uranus.

Uranus

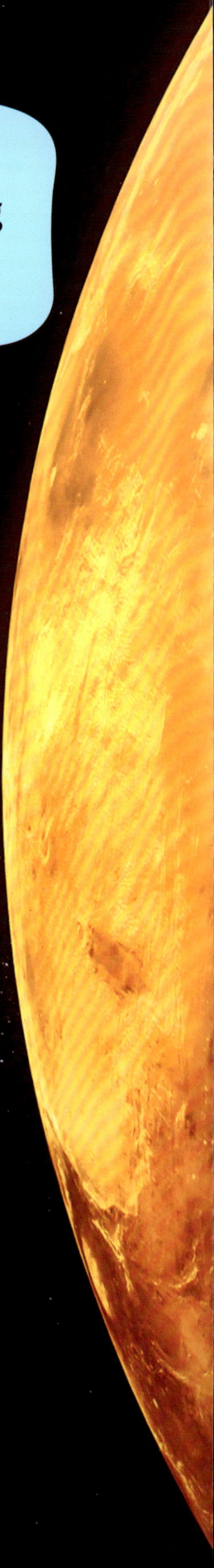

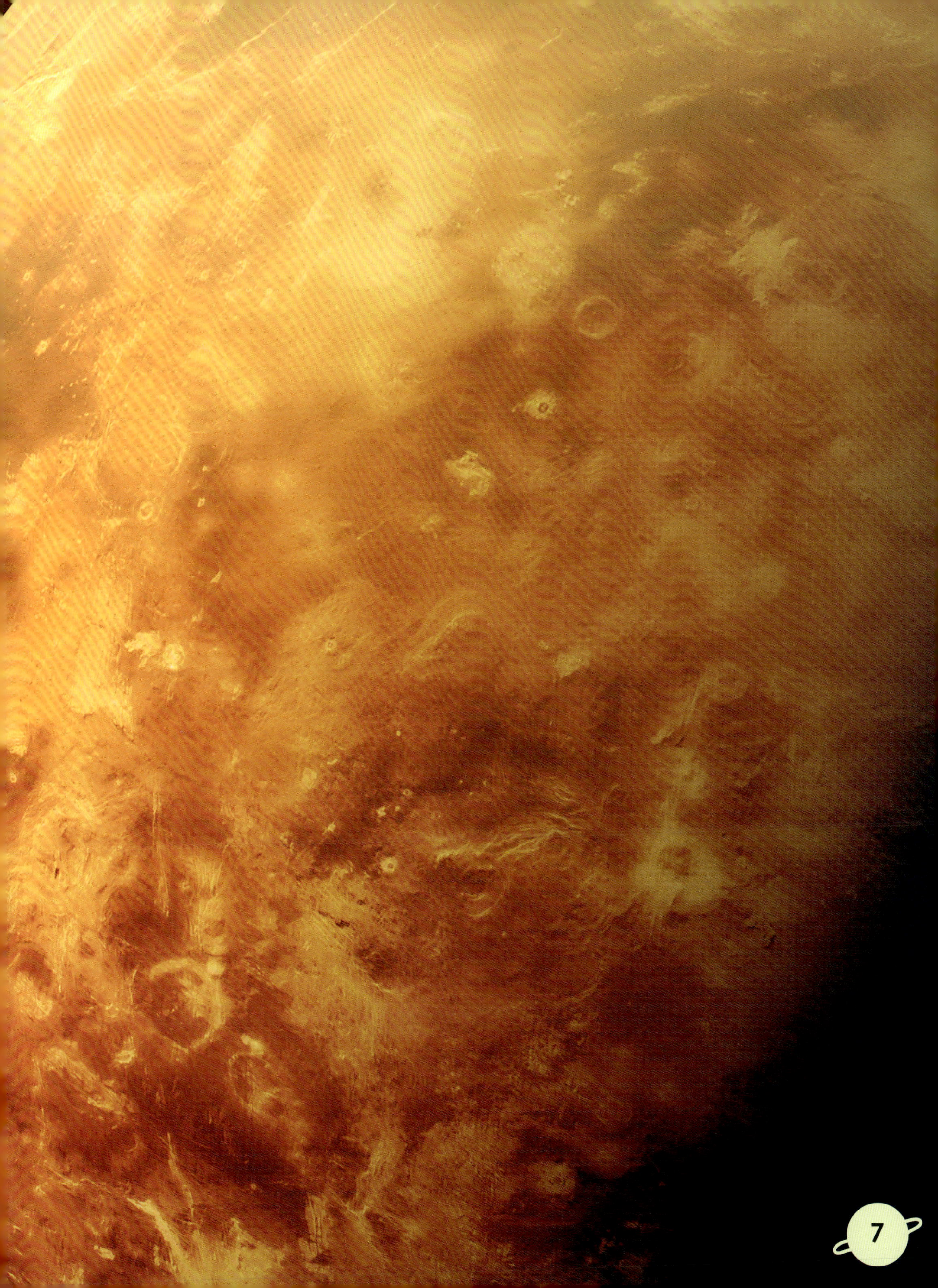

THE HOTTEST PLANET

Venus is covered in very thick layers of **atmosphere**, which traps in heat from the Sun like a blanket.

Even though it is not the closest planet to the Sun, Venus is the hottest planet in our solar system!

Its very thick clouds make it impossible to see its surface through a **telescope**!

The highest temperature on Mercury is about 430 °C (806 °F).

The top temperature on Venus is about 480 °C (896 °F)!

The highest temperature measured on Earth is 58 °C (136 °F).

CAN WE VISIT VENUS?

The thick atmosphere means Venus will never cool down enough for humans to ever visit.

There is a lot of pressure on its surface – Venus would crush humans immediately!

Space **probes** have taken pictures of the surface and spacecraft have landed, but not survived for much more than two hours.

Venera 12 is one of only a few spacecraft to have ever landed on Venus.

Venera 12

The Messenger space probe has flown past Venus and collected important information about its atmosphere.

NASA's Messenger space probe

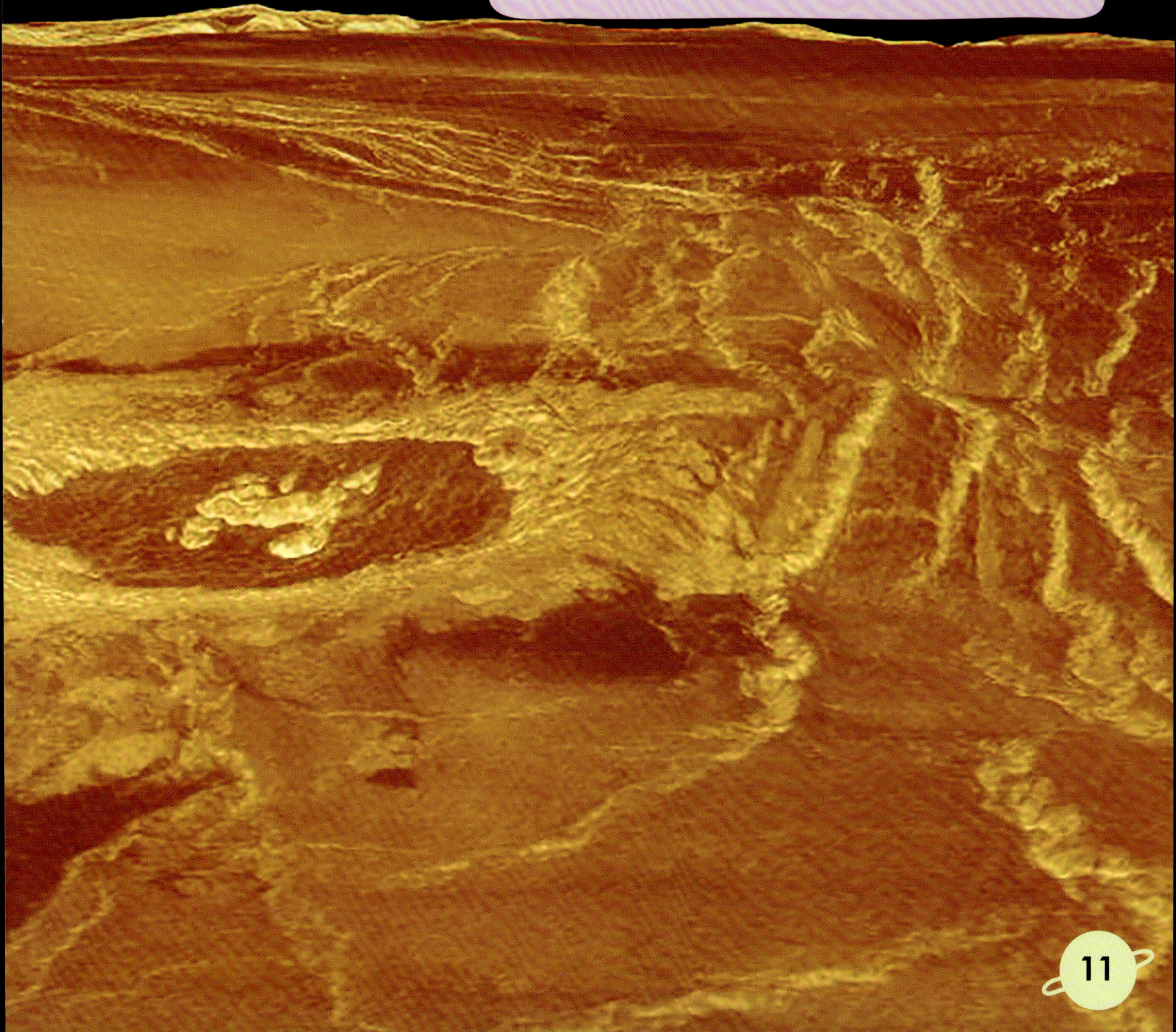

SPACE PROBE DISCOVERIES

Space probes and **landers** that have visited Venus are remotely controlled – scientists control them all the way from Earth!

These high-tech spacecraft have allowed us to discover what the surface of Venus looks like under its clouds.

Venus has valleys, **mountains** and thousands of volcanoes. The highest mountain, Skadi Mons, is almost 11 kilometres (7 miles) tall. That makes it taller than any mountain here on Earth.

Maat Mons volcano is almost as tall as Earth's Mount Everest!

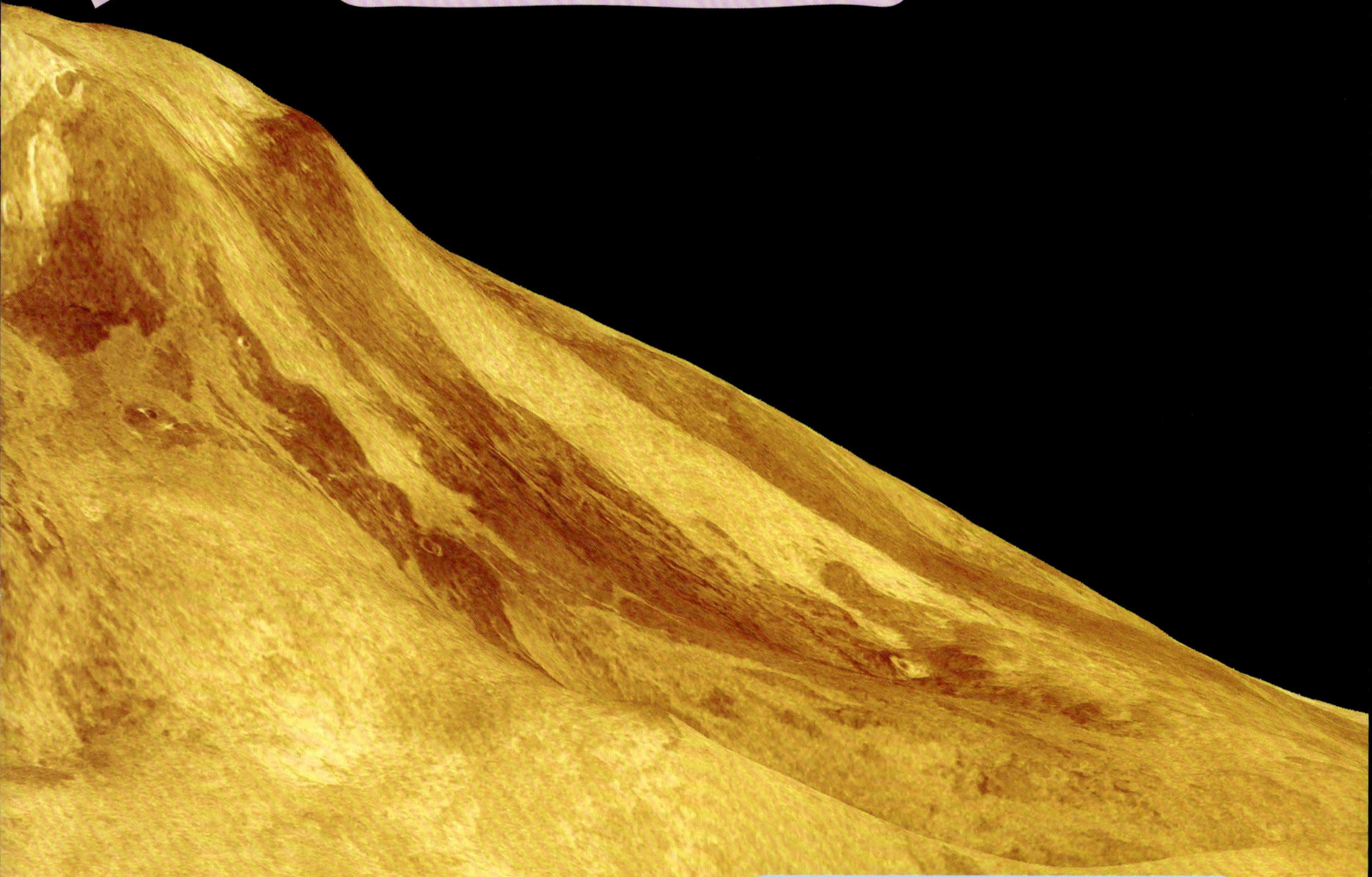

The Magellan spacecraft has helped scientists make lots of discoveries about Venus.

Magellan spacecraft

FACT FILE

Venus is the brightest of all planets in our solar system.

Venus was named after the Roman goddess of love and beauty, because it was the most beautiful sight, shining in the morning and evening sky.

Venus shining bright

Because of this, people have always been curious about Venus, even before telescopes were invented.

Venus is almost the same size as Earth. That's why it is often called Earth's twin! But the planet is deadly – there's no way humans could live there.

WHAT CAN WE SEE?

Venus is the third brightest natural object in the night sky after the Sun and Moon.

Clouds of **sulphuric acid** circle Venus and prevent us seeing its surface. The clouds **reflect** most of the sunlight that reaches it back into space...

Underneath Venus's clouds is a thick layer of carbon dioxide.

... making it look so bright and shiny it can sometimes be seen on a clear day!

Venus may look bright from Earth, but when it passes the Sun, it looks black!

DISCOVERIES UNDER THE CLOUDS

In 1975, the Russian Venera 9 was the first lander to capture pictures of Venus's surface. After less than two hours, it was destroyed by the heat!

What it found was a rocky, **barren** surface and scorching temperatures, unable to support life.

In 1982, data and photographs collected from Venera 13 and 14 probes had scientists agreeing that liquid water does not exist on Venus. But maybe it could have once...

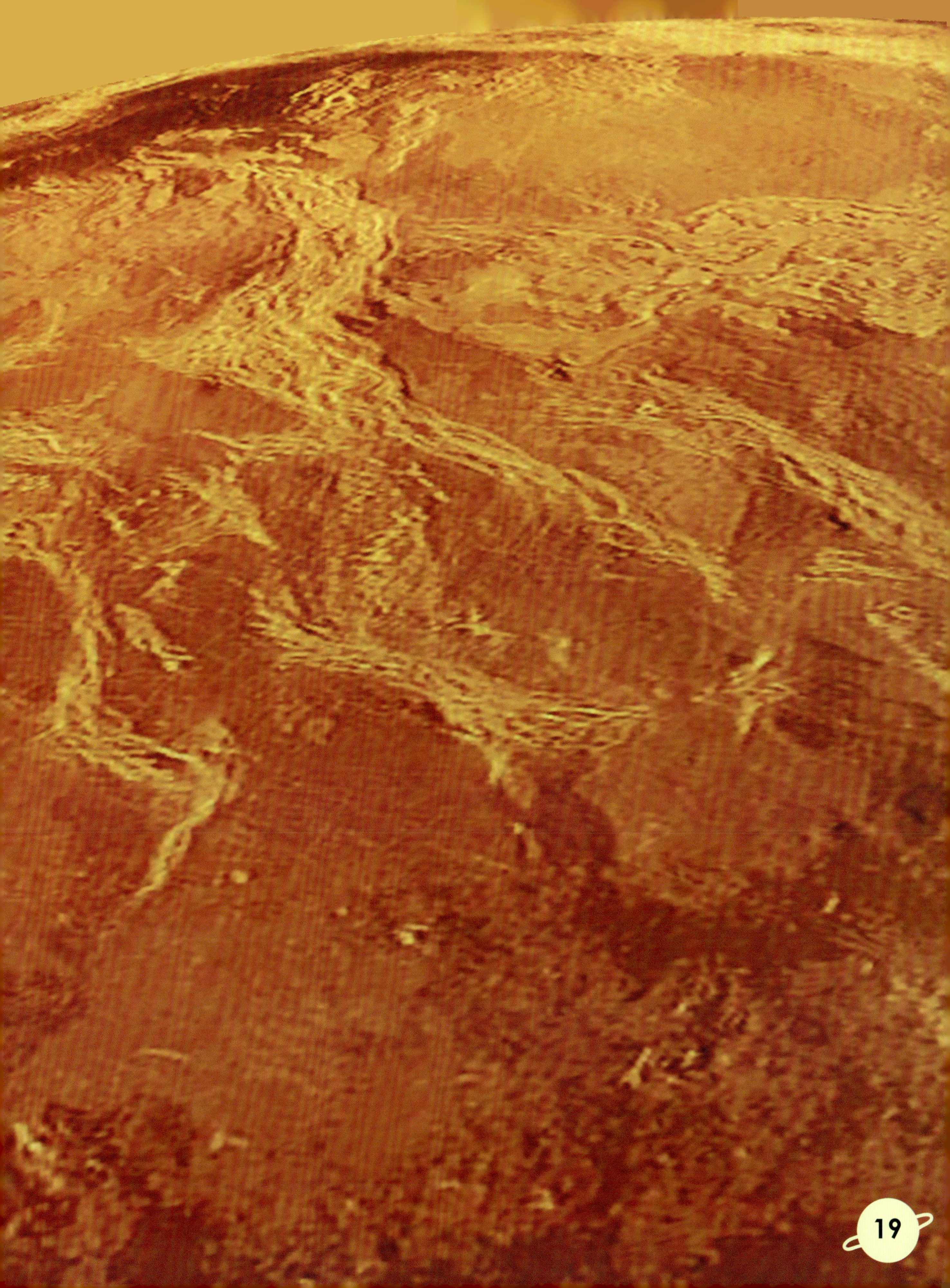

WHY DO WE STUDY VENUS?

Scientists that study other planets are like space detectives. Their work helps us understand more about our own planet.

Venus, like Earth, is actively changing. Knowing more about these changes can help us understand what is happening to our own climate.

Could Venus hold the secret to saving Earth?

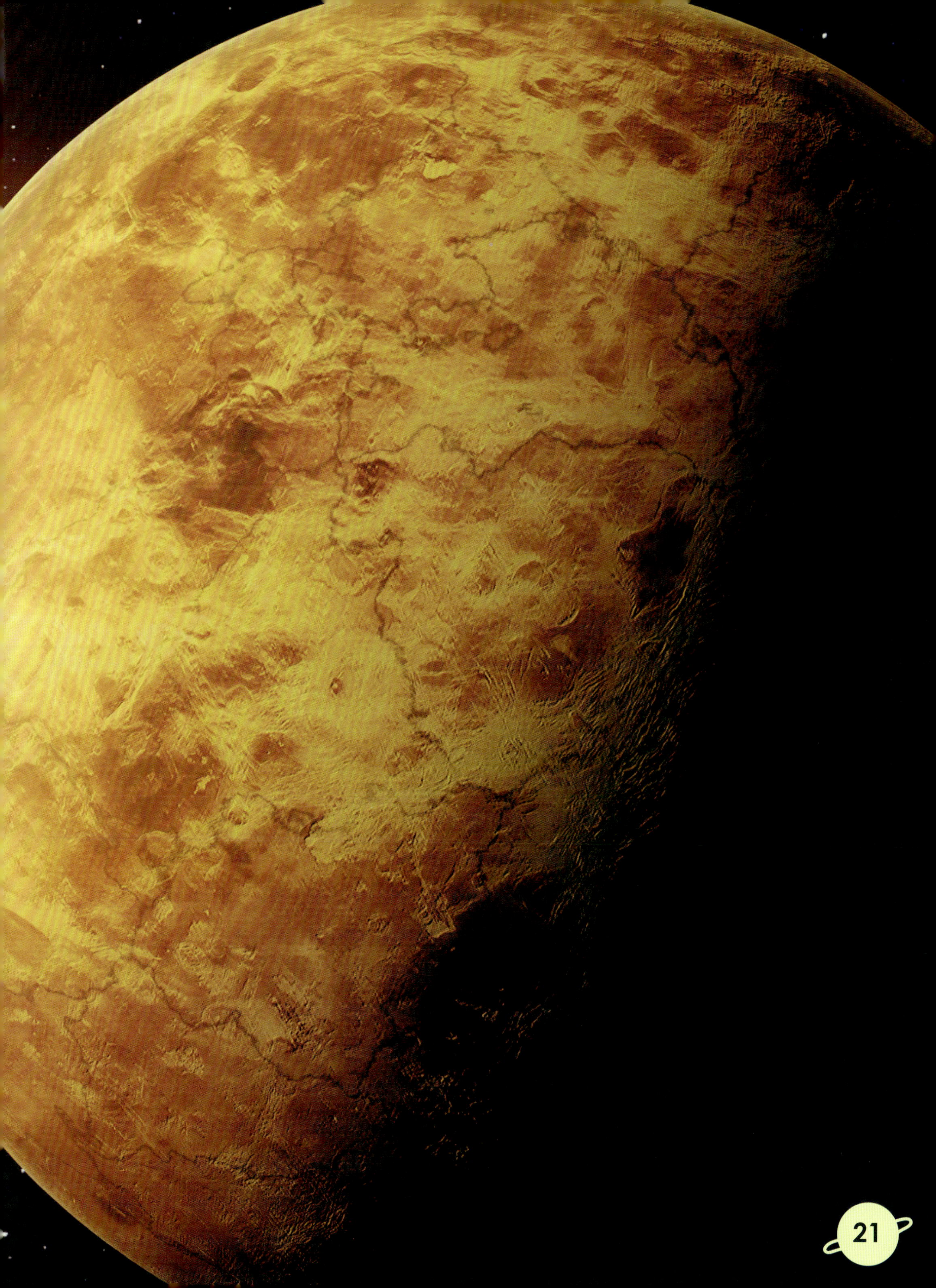

WHAT'S NEXT?

Missions to study space are planned by **space agencies** from all over the world. They build rockets and robots and sometimes send **astronauts** into space!

They will have to build tougher machines to withstand the heat and pressure on Venus, that can melt and break them in a very short time!

NASA and the **European Space Agency** are planning some exciting missions to learn more about why Venus is so different to Earth.

GLOSSARY

Astronauts – people trained to travel into outer space.

Atmosphere – the gases that surround a planet or star.

Axis – an invisible line that something spins around.

Barren – a place that is empty, where nothing grows.

Carbon dioxide – an invisible gas in the air.

Climate – long-term temperatures and weather conditions.

Earth days – the amount of time that a day lasts for on Earth (24 hours).

European Space Agency – a space agency run by a group of countries in Europe that studies outer space.

Landers – Spacecraft designed to land on the surface of other planets.

Mountains – rocky landforms that rise high above their surroundings.

NASA – the National Aeronautics and Space Administration is an agency that deals with space exploration.

Orbit – the path taken by one object circling around another object in space.

Pressure – a force that pushes on something.

Probes – uncrewed spacecraft sent to explore outer space.

Reflect – to shine back.

Solar system – the Sun and everything that moves around it.

Space agencies – organisations that design and launch missions to explore space.

Sulphuric acid – a very strong and dangerous liquid.

Telescope – an instrument that makes faraway objects appear bigger.

Picture credits:
(t=top; b=bottom; m=middle; l=left; r=right):

Wikipedia: By Don S. Montgomery, U.S. Navy (Ret.) - http://www.defenseimagery.mil; VIRIN: DN-SC-86-01099, Public Domain 10bm; By Kevin M. Gill - https://www.flickr.com/photos/53460575@N03/50513674188/, CC BY 2.0 16bl; By Magellan Team (NASA - Jet Propulsion Laboratory) - This image or video was catalogued by Jet Propulsion Laboratory of the United States National Aeronautics and Space Administration (NASA) under Photo ID: PIA00233., Public Domain 10-11bg; By NASA - [[:File:Venus,_Earth_size_comparison.jpghttps://astrogeology.usgs.gov/search/map/Venus/Magellan/Colorized/Venus_Magellan_C3-MDIR_Colorized_Global_Mosaic_4641mhttps://commons.wikimedia.org/wiki/File:The_Blue_Marble_(remastered).jpg]], Public Domain 15ml; By NASA/JPL-Caltech - https://www.jpl.nasa.gov/news/nasa-selects-investigations-for-future-key-planetary-mission; original archived at https://web.archive.org/web/20190202192152/https://www.jpl.nasa.gov/news/news.php?feature=4727 (image link), Public Domain 22-23bg. NASA: Images-assets.nasa.gov/image/GSFC_20171208_Archive_e001737/GSFC_20171208_Archive_e001737~orig.jpg 17bl; images-assets.nasa.gov/image/PIA18145/PIA18145~orig.jpg 11tr; images-assets.nasa.gov/image/s30-71-052/s30-71-052~orig.jpg 13br; images-assets.nasa.gov/image/PIA00254/PIA00254~orig.jpg 12-13bg.
Shutterstock: 19 STUDIO 20bl; Anna Marin N 20-21bg; Artsiom P 8-9bg; AstroStar 16-17bg; Buradaki 6br, 9tr; CSSF 360 11tr (background); FastMotion 18-19bg; Feng Cheng 14mr; Gidenilson 4-5bg; Janez Volmajer 24bg; NASA Images 1bg, 2-3bg; Steven_mol 6-7bg; Vovan 14-15bg.

EXPLORING MERCURY

By Emily Kington

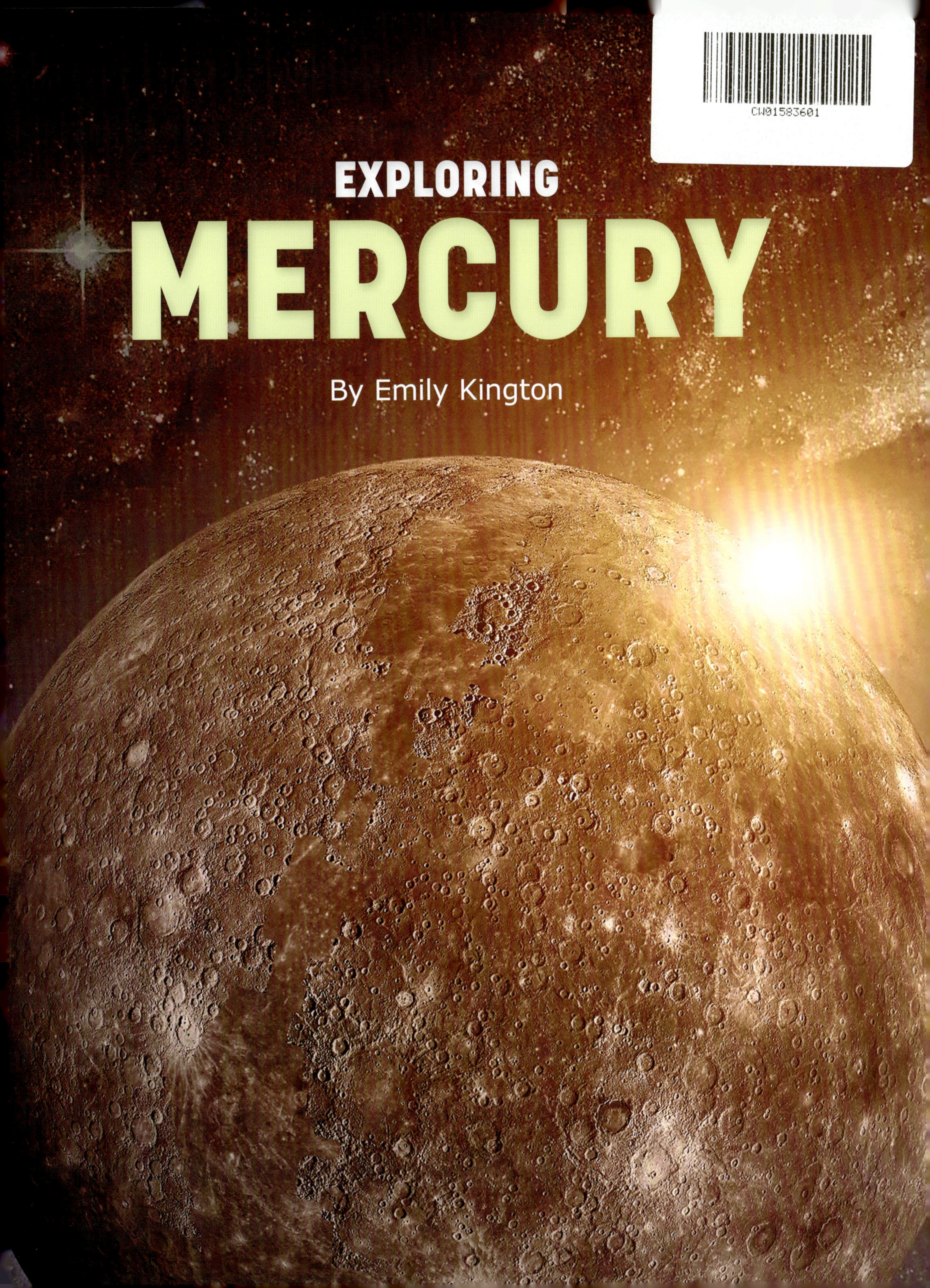

CONTENTS

Where is Mercury?	4
Planet Facts	6
Why is Mercury So Heavy?	8
Could We Live on Mercury?	10
An Amazing Discovery	12
What Can We See?	14
Mercury's Surface	16
Why Do We Study Other Planets	18
Fact File	20
What's Next?	22
Glossary	24

MIX
Paper | Supporting responsible forestry
FSC® C158492

First published in 2026 by Hungry Tomato Ltd
F15, Old Bakery Studios, Blewetts Wharf, Malpas Road,
Truro, Cornwall, TR1 1QH, UK.

A CIP catalogue record for this book is available from the British Library.

ISBN 9781835697078

Printed in China

Discover more at
www.hungrytomato.com

Front cover image is an artist's impression of Mercury and the Messenger spacecraft. Mercury is shown in false-colour. Title page image is an edited image of Mercury. Contents page image is an edited image of Mercury.

Words in **BOLD** can be found in the glossary.

WHERE IS MERCURY?

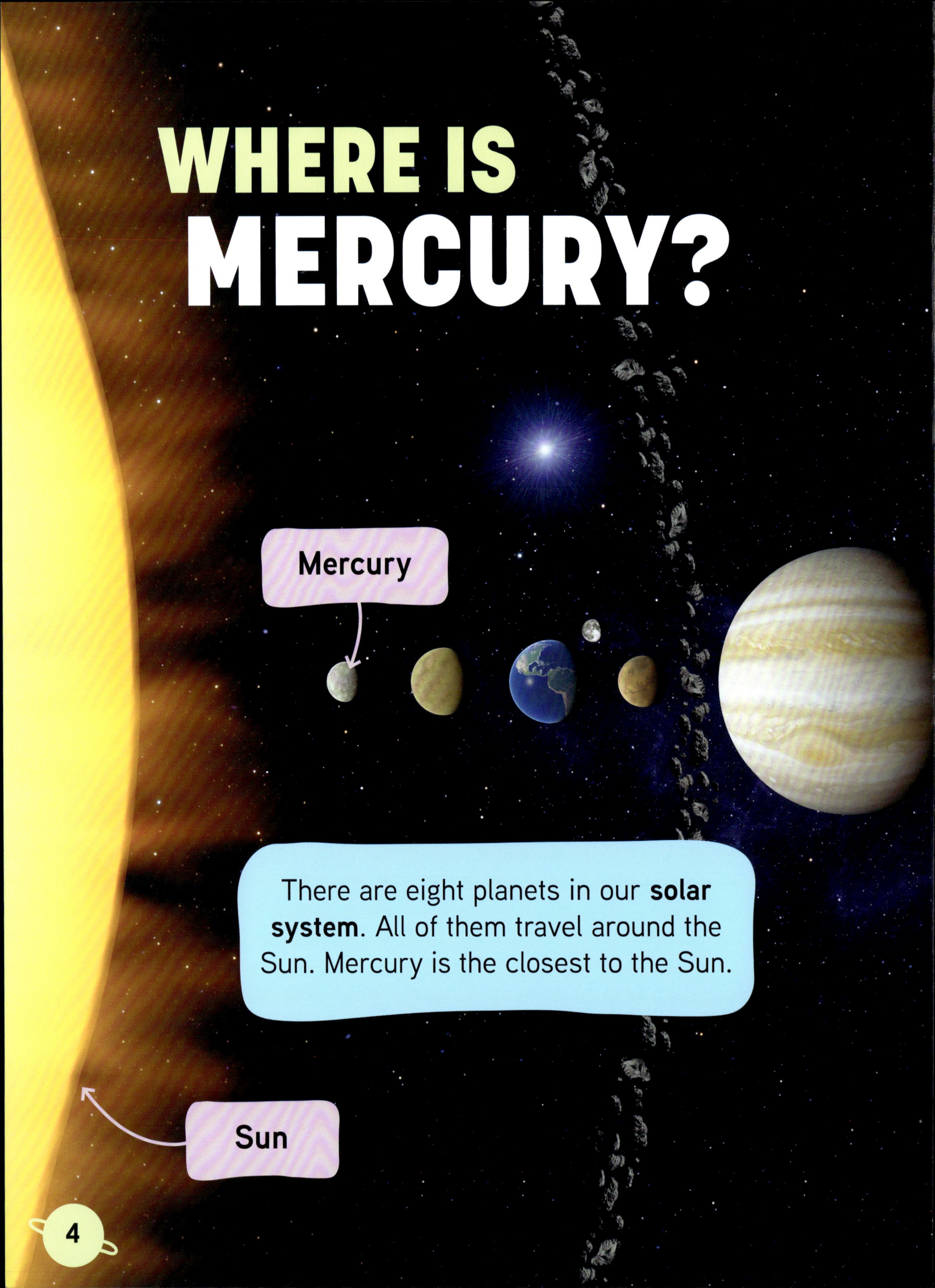

There are eight planets in our **solar system**. All of them travel around the Sun. Mercury is the closest to the Sun.

The time it takes for a planet to travel around the Sun once is called a year. Mercury travels around the Sun once every 88 **Earth days**. This journey is called its **orbit**.

Mercury's orbit around the Sun is shaped like an egg!

PLANET FACTS

Planets are always spinning. A day is the time it takes a planet to spin around once.

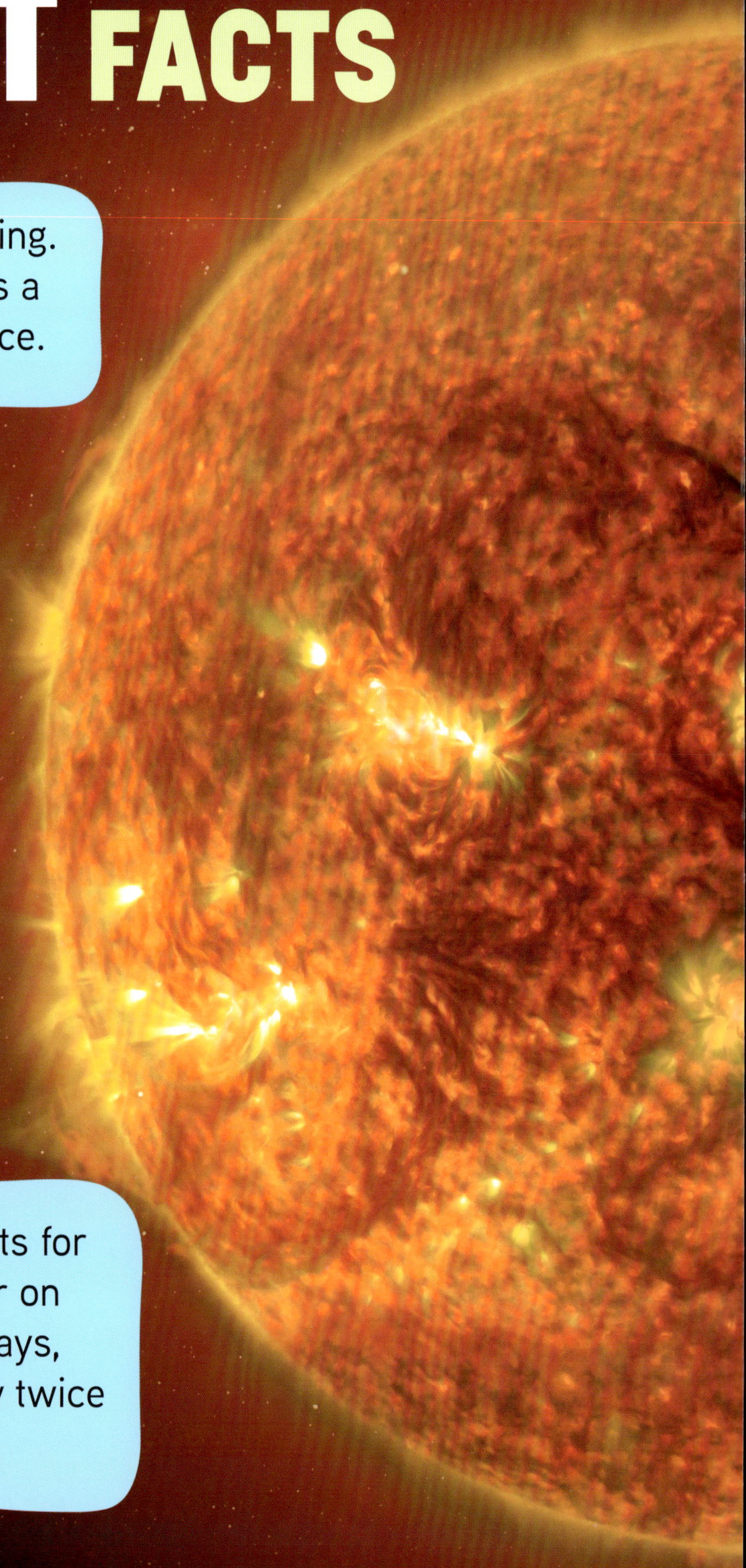

One day on Mercury lasts for 176 Earth days. A year on Mercury is 88 Earth days, making a day on Mercury twice as long as a year!

Mercury orbits the Sun faster than any other planet in our solar system at 104,400 miles per hour (169,200 kilometres per hour)!

WHY IS MERCURY SO HEAVY?

Mercury is a rocky planet. It is also the smallest planet in the solar system.

If Mercury were the size of a golf ball, Earth would be the size of a grapefruit!

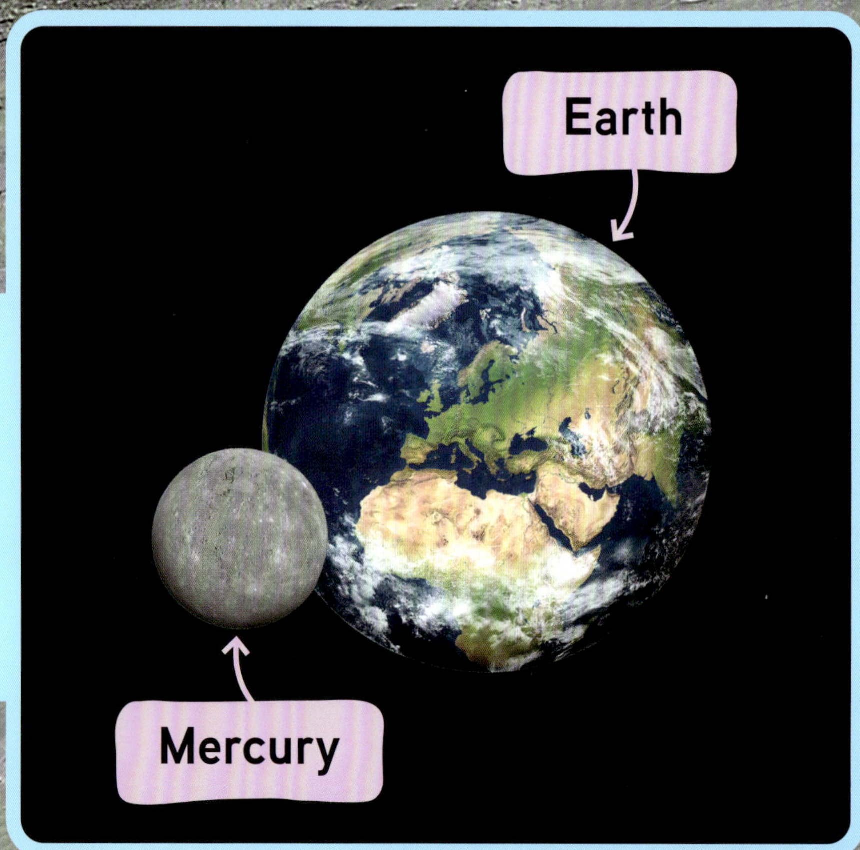

Even though it is the smallest planet, Mercury is heavy for its size. Scientists think its iron-rich **core** makes up most of the planet's total size.

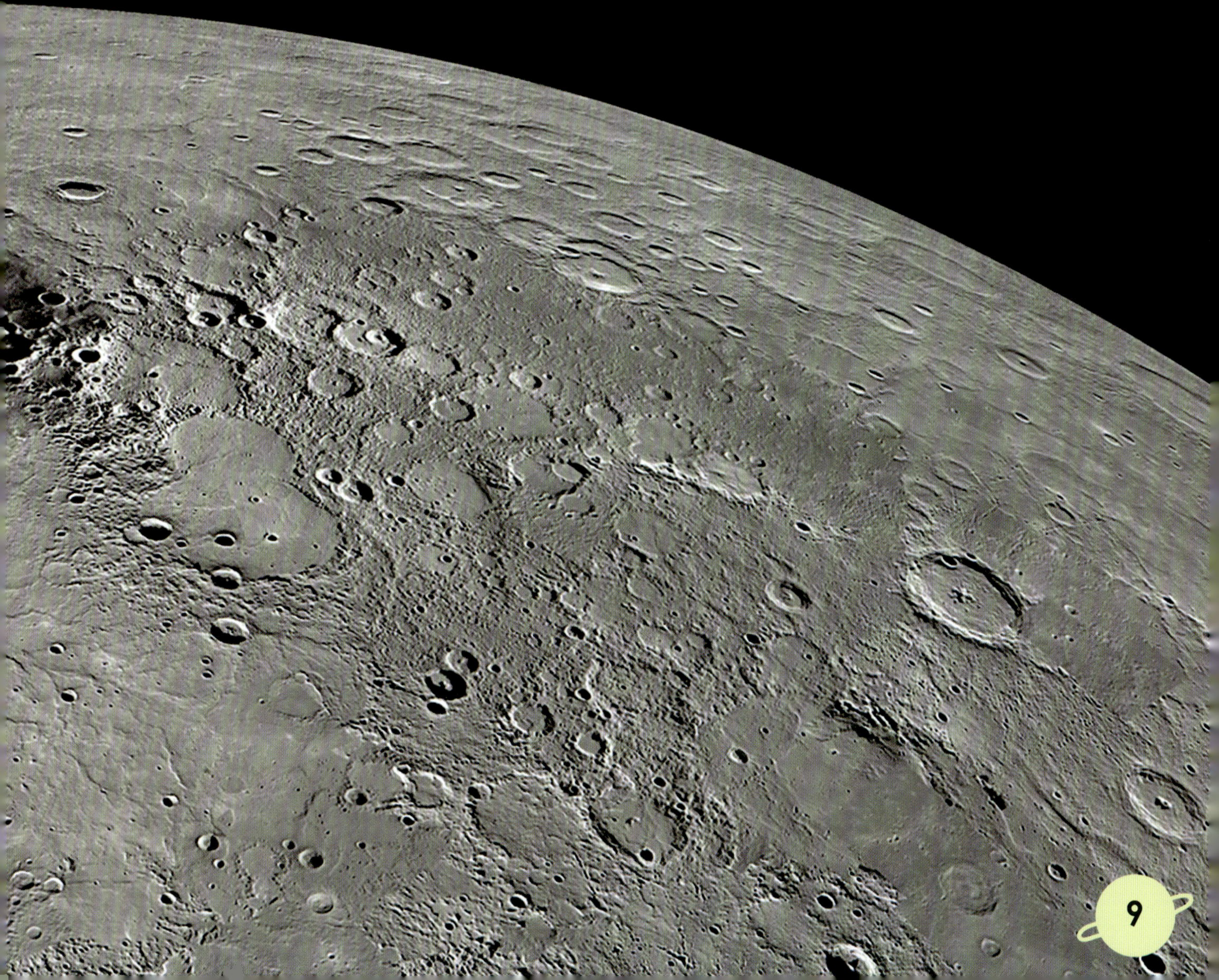

COULD WE LIVE ON MERCURY?

Living on Mercury would be very difficult. There is no air to breathe, and it gets very hot during the day on the side of the planet that faces the Sun.

Earth's **atmosphere** holds in heat like a blanket. But on Mercury there is no atmosphere, so it gets extremely cold on the side that doesn't face the Sun.

Mercury is also hit with a lot of **solar radiation** that is very harmful to humans and machines.

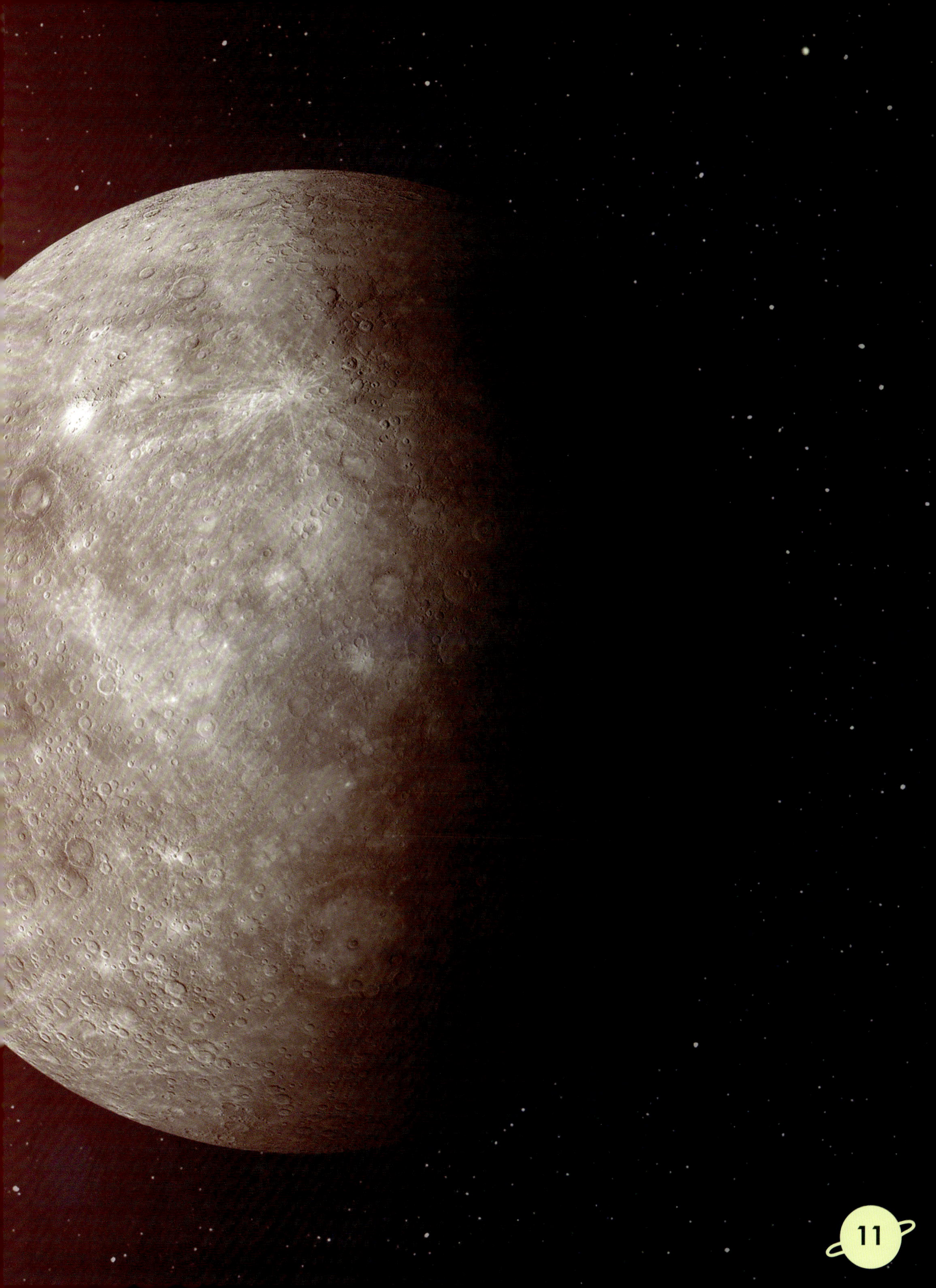

AN AMAZING DISCOVERY

Mercury is one of the most difficult planets to study because of where it is – right next to the Sun! Only three missions have ever been sent towards Mercury.

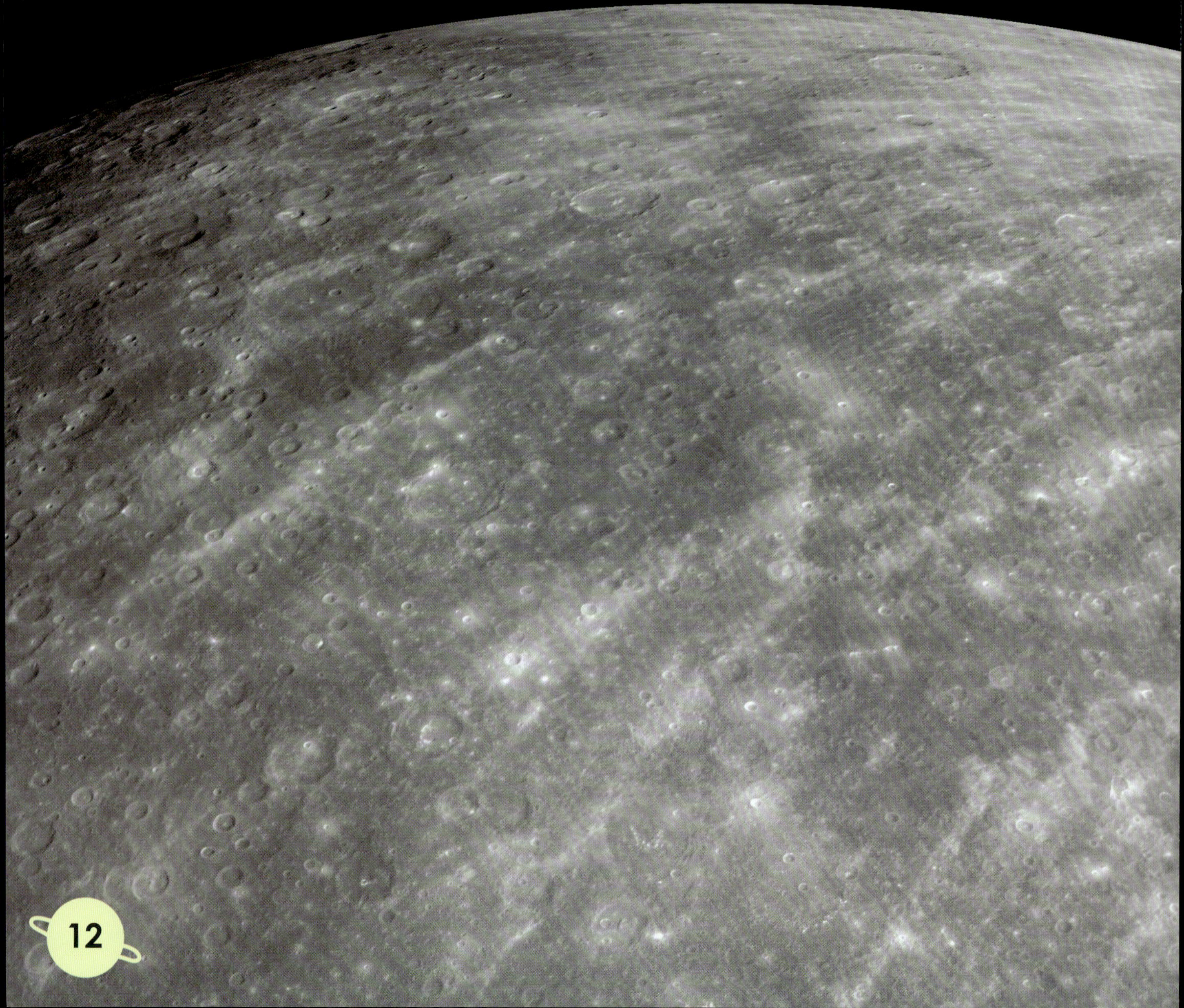

Messenger is one of the spacecraft that has been to Mercury. It found that there is ice in deep **craters** at Mercury's north **pole**! This ice never melts because sunlight doesn't reach it.

Messenger

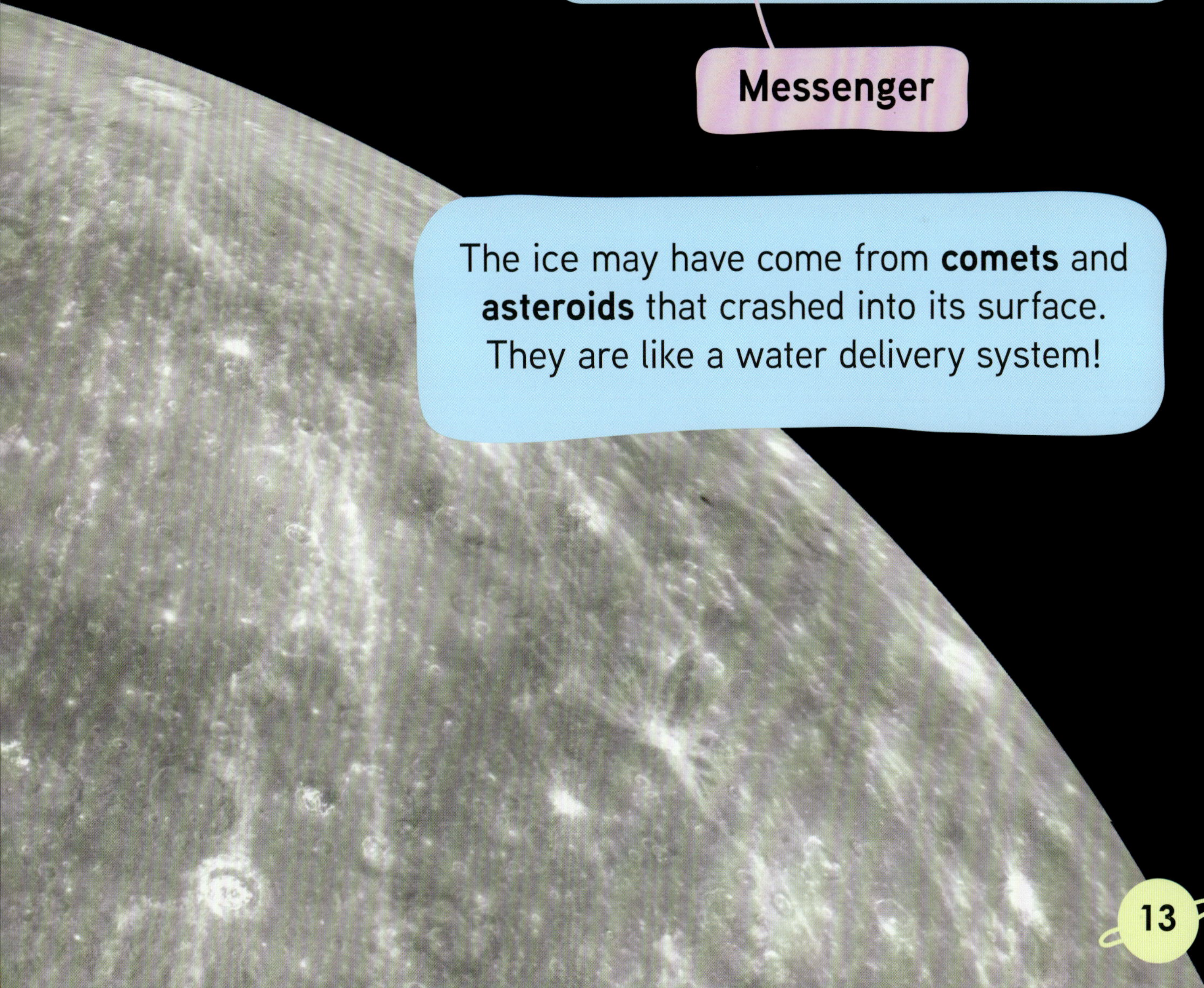

The ice may have come from **comets** and **asteroids** that crashed into its surface. They are like a water delivery system!

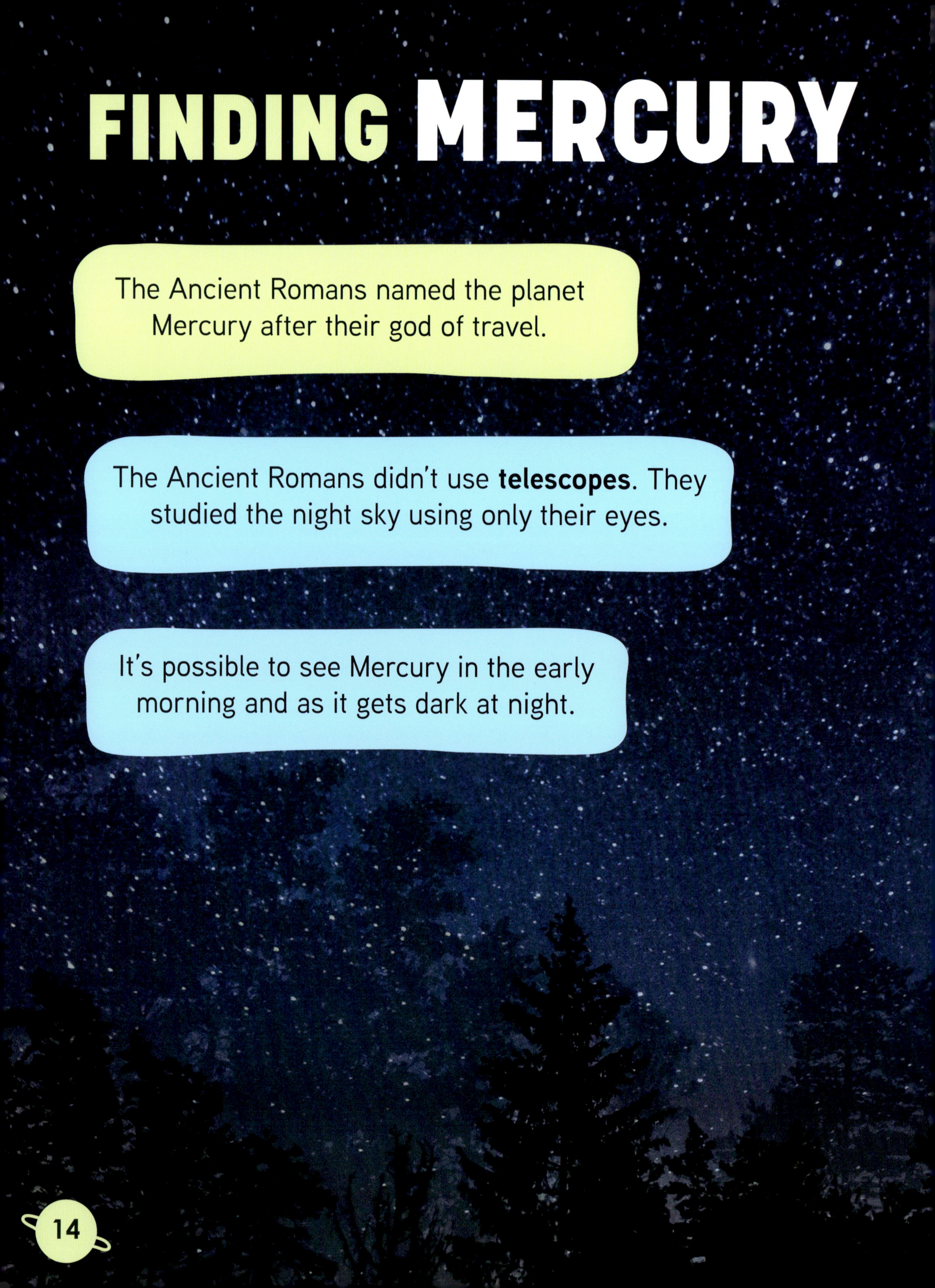

FINDING MERCURY

The Ancient Romans named the planet Mercury after their god of travel.

The Ancient Romans didn't use **telescopes**. They studied the night sky using only their eyes.

It's possible to see Mercury in the early morning and as it gets dark at night.

But it can be tricky. To see Mercury from Earth, we have to look towards the Sun, which is very dangerous! Looking directly at the Sun damages our eyes.

MERCURY'S SURFACE

Mercury is a rocky planet. Its surface looks a lot like the Moon.

It's covered in craters that were created by comets and asteroids crashing into it over billions of years.

The Caloris Basin is the largest crater on the planet. It's 2,500 kilometres (1,550 miles) wide! A giant rock hit Mercury so hard that it made the crater and cracked the surface on the other side!

The camera on **NASA**'s Messenger spacecraft that took this photo made the colours of the planet much brighter than they actually are!

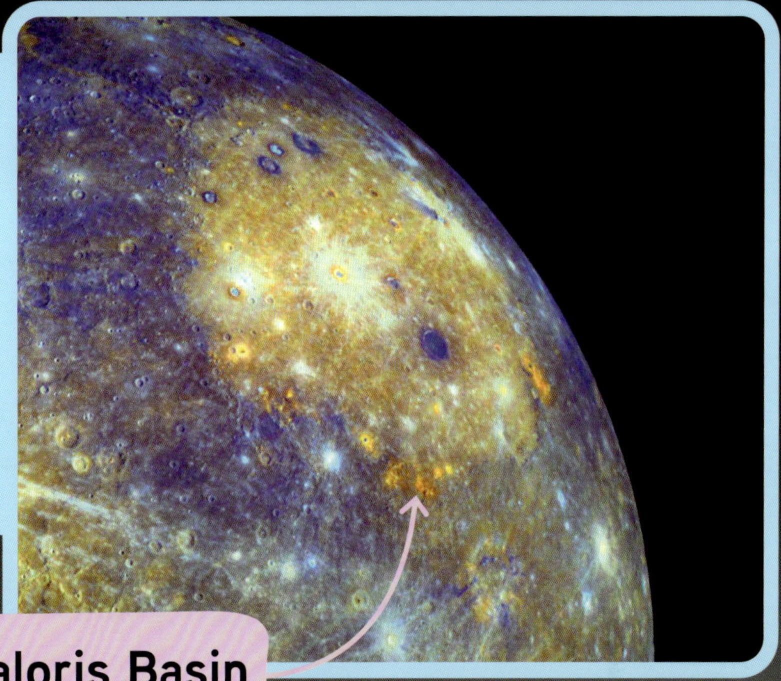

The Caloris Basin

WHY DO WE STUDY PLANETS?

Scientists who study other planets are like space detectives. Their work helps us understand more about our own planet!

They are also looking for valuable materials like rare **minerals** that can be used on Earth for things like energy.

They are also searching to see if there is another planet just like Earth!

FACT FILE

Scientists have several ways that they can study Mercury – but they also have to be careful!

The **Hubble Space Telescope** is forbidden from viewing Mercury because light from the Sun would cause it too much damage.

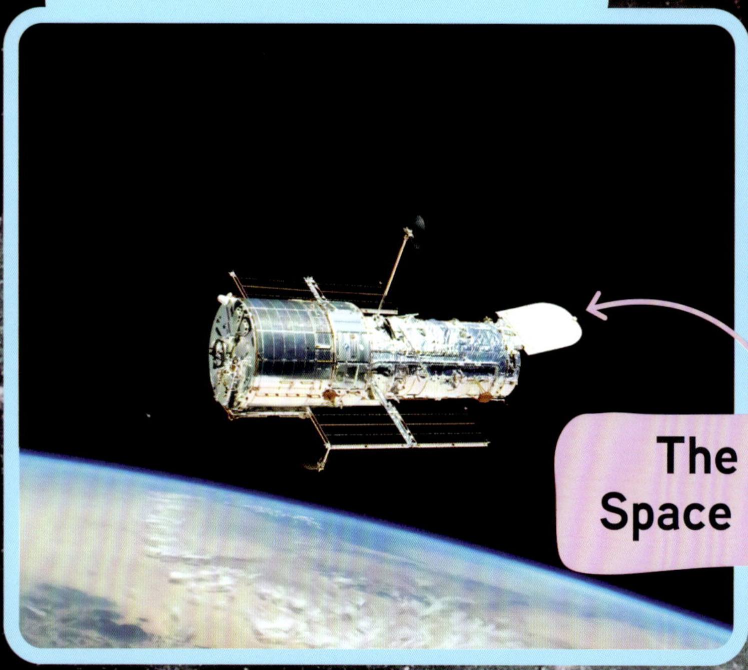

The Hubble Space Telescope

Scientists used **fissures** in Iceland to learn about Mercury's ice. Ice hidden beneath the surface doesn't melt because sunlight can't reach it!

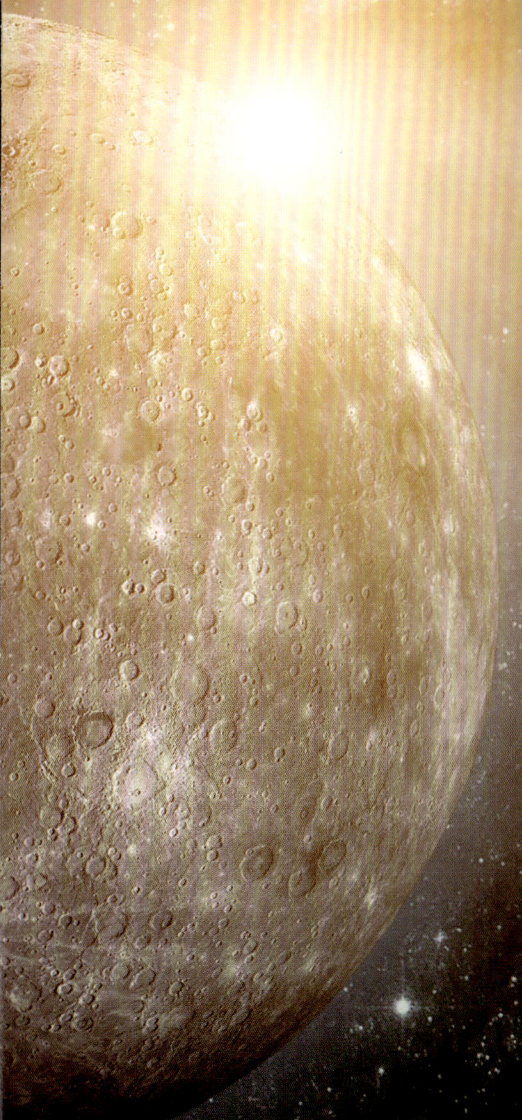

WHAT'S NEXT?

Most missions to study space are planned by **space agencies** from all over the world. They build rockets and **robots** and sometimes send **astronauts** into space!

Japan Aerospace and the **European Space Agency** launched a joint mission to Mercury in 2018. BepiColombo has completed multiple **flybys**, collecting data and photographs for scientists.

BepiColombo's mission is to take a closer look and learn more about Mercury's surface!

BepiColombo's rocket

GLOSSARY

Asteroids – small space rocks that orbit the Sun.

Astronauts – people trained to travel into outer space.

Atmosphere – the gases that surround a planet.

Comets – objects made of dust and ice that orbit the Sun.

Core – the middle of a planet.

Craters – large holes that have been created by something hitting the ground.

Earth day – the amount of time that a day lasts for on Earth (24 hours).

European Space Agency – an agency run by a group of countries in Europe that studies outer space.

Fissures – a split or crack in the ground.

Flybys – the closest approaches of a spacecraft to a planet or moon.

Hubble Space Telescope – a telescope in orbit around Earth.

Japan Aerospace Exploration Agency – an agency in Japan that studies outer space.

Minerals – substances that are found in things like rocks, sand, and soil.

NASA – the National Aeronautics and Space Administration is an agency that deals with space exploration.

Orbit – the path taken by one object circling around another object in space.

Pole – the point furthest north or south on a planet.

Robots - machines controlled by a computer that can do tasks on their own without a human.

Solar radiation – a type of energy created by the Sun.

Solar system – the Sun and everything that moves around it.

Space agencies – organisations that design and launch missions to explore space.

Telescopes – instruments that make faraway objects appear bigger.

Picture credits:
(t=top; b=bottom; m=middle; l=left; r=right):

NASA: images-assets.nasa.gov/image/PIA10359/PIA10359~orig.jpg 17tr; images-assets.nasa.gov/image/PIA16549/PIA16549~orig.jpg 8-9bg; images-assets.nasa.gov/image/PIA13508/PIA13508~orig.jpg 12-13bg. Unknown 9tl. Shutterstock: 3D Sculptor 13tr; Alexandra Lande 23tl; Alones 22-23bg; Artsiom P 20bl; Buradaki 6-7bg, 10-11bg; Davido Caridl 2-3bg; Istiana wati 14-15bg; Iva Foto 4-5bg; Jurik Peter 16-17bg; Max Dallocca 8br; Muratart 15mr; NASA Images 1bg, 8br, 20-21bg; Procy 24bg; Shivam Chy 18-19bg; T.Schneider 21mr; Waniga Ashan 2-3bg.